VEG FOR ALL SEASONS

Linda Evans

Linda and her Husband Prof Francis Evans were very kind to me. When I asked Linda to tell me how to make white sauce or cheese sauce. She said "its all in my book".

This is a wonderful book but apart from white sauce (for Christmas pudding) I don't think I need it. But I seized the chance and bought it as a token of my appreciation of two lovely people. Sadly Francis died suddenly in 2005. How Linda found the time to write such a Tome is beyond me.

R Louise Jennings

Published in 2012 by FeedARead.com Publishing – Arts Council funded

CONTENTS

Introduction

Welcome to my book

This is a book of seasonal vegetarian dishes centred on British vegetables. It's aimed at people who cook day in, day out, and want to widen their repertoire, move towards less or no meat, and eat more locally. These are the preoccupations of a growing number of adults, for reasons connected with climate change, world ecology, anti-globalisation, avoidance of air miles and a wish to be more connected with the local and the natural.

Lots of people like this have started growing vegetables. Others take a vegetable box, shop in farmer's markets, buy local and organic. These used to be signs of the crank; now they mean that the person is ahead of the trend, because this is how it will, increasingly, have to be. However, we have all become accustomed to lively, interesting food, and don't want to give this up. Reconciling these two divergent trends is what this book is about.

Eating locally and seasonally demands a change of attitude. When I was a young married, I'd decide what to eat for the next few days, and go and buy the necessary. While I would swap around if a bargain presented itself, my cooking was menu-driven. As a seasonal eater, my cooking became ingredient-driven; see what's available first, and devise menus and dishes to use it. It's a more fundamental change than you would expect.

All the dishes in here are vegetarian, but I'd be disappointed if these recipes were only cooked by vegetarians. Many, if not all, the main dishes have been eaten by omnivores and vegetarians, and no-one has complained about the lack of meat. As why should they? A good dish is good if people enjoy it, and only the terminally prejudiced will refuse to enjoy on the basis of an absence. I'm not a vegetarian myself, but my cooking was moving away from meat even before I started the book.

Vegetarianism is no longer the mark of the crank and the health-food nut, but a mainstream lifestyle choice. And even meat-eaters are starting to move towards eating less and better meat, with one or two or more vegetarian days a week. What I hope to show is that local vegetables, cooked with a variety of flavourings, can be as delicious and satisfying as any other style of eating.

I am a domestic cook, not a chef, and my food is home-style. I think that the objectives of the home cook are different from those of the chef. At home, there are four criteria, and over a period – a week, say – one wants to balance taste, cost, nutrition, and time. None of these is more important than the others, though it's always worth remembering that food your eaters don't like and don't eat won't nourish them, will be wasted, and will be a waste of the cook's time. And, as a cook, I've always like to vary what I'm doing, to keep my interest engaged, so I've cooked a very wide range of dishes.

The objectives of the chef are different. He/she doesn't need to be concerned with long-term nutrition, since most customers are eating just one meal. Timing constraints are much tighter, because a course has to be ready in a reasonable time after being ordered. And display and presentation are much more important in a restaurant. Restaurants have been responsible for the introduction and popularisation of many new foods, for which the home cook can be grateful. They have also led to a perception that home cooking, especially when entertaining, should be like restaurant food, and that being a chef should be the ambition of a good home cook. I strongly disagree with both these last two points.

One of the delightful things about a vegetarian meal is the way it frees up putting a meal together. You can have a one-dish meal, with or without salad. You can have a conventional main dish with accompanying vegetables. You can have a collection of small dishes, either as a full meal or as a starter, followed by a main dish if you like. You can have soup and cheese; soup and salad; soup and dessert. It's true that you can do all these with meat, but convention has a much stronger hold on the meat-centred meal. This flexibility is why I haven't given number-of-servings for a recipe; a dish may serve 8 as part of a spread, or 2 (or even 1 greedy teenager) if it's the complete meal. Experience with your own "family" will guide you about how much to prepare.

Thoughts on nutritional theory; it's something I'm sceptical about. When I started being interested in food, protein content in the diet was the most important aspect, and not having enough protein was to be guarded against. Then we had the problem perceived as too much carbohydrate, too much sugar, leading to the first version of the Hays diet. For the last twenty years or so, fat has been the bugbear, especially saturated fat Nutritionists have urged people away from butter and on to margarine. Because they didn't know about trans fats, this advice has probably led to a large number of earlier deaths. Now a recent study in the US indicates that saturated fat in the diet is no worse than any of the versions of unsaturated fat for heart health and longevity; what gets you is not the details, but the total amount. This hasn't yet penetrated dietary advice in newspapers, and probably the manufacturers of low-fat products will behave like cigarette manufacturers in denying the evidence.   Nonetheless, I think you should prepare for another of the periodic overturns in theory, though without expecting anyone to say they were mistaken.

I think that Michael Pollan sums up commonsense advice admirably, when he says: "Eat food; not too much; mainly plants". The food bit is meant to cut out all sorts of over-processed, supplemented, tweaked items, and include more fresh and unmodified foods. For myself, I'd say watch your eaters, and yourself. If they/you are healthy, and their weight is pretty constant when grown, then you have to believe you've got it right. Just learn to ignore the latest fads and wonder foods, and keep up the variety of real foods you eat.

I'd recommend using organic vegetables wherever possible, but it does partly depend on taste. I find the taste of organic potatoes so much better that I wouldn't use anything else. Others fall for organic carrots or lettuce or apples. Make your choice at least partly on taste grounds. Remember, also, that organic certification is expensive, and many a small grower can be organic or nearly without having the label. And freshness is important, so locally-grown non-organic veg. may taste much better than imported organics from South America, and be better for the environment generally. I think, on the whole, buying fresh and local is slightly more important than buying organic, but it would be

8

ideal if you could have both. And the balance does vary from vegetable to vegetable.

At the time of writing, organic produce is more expensive than "conventional". This is partly because organics are more labour-intensive, but the major reason is that many of the true costs of conventional farming aren't included in the price. Conventional farming uses so much oil in many forms – fertiliser and pesticide both depend on cheap energy – that it's one of the top 6 contributors to global warming. And this cost to all of us isn't included in the price. Organic farming has become so much better over the past fifty years or so – yields are comparable with those from conventional farming, energy inputs are smaller, and it's much more scientifically based than the old "muck-and-mystery" idea. But as peak oil passes, energy becomes more expensive and labour comparatively cheaper, conventional farming will have to move back in the organic direction. Probably not totally, but much closer than it is today.

As for GM produce, I avoid it as far as possible. I simply don't want to be part of a gigantic human experiment. And there really is no need for it. Yields are slightly less than non-GM crops, over a period; farmers don't use less weedkiller but more, on average, and the crops are less resilient in poor weather conditions – which we are going to have more of. GM crops are good for the balance sheets of the large companies, but they don't seem to offer anything but costs and disadvantages to the rest of us.

None of the recipes in this book uses Quorn, TVP, or other industrialised foods. I have aesthetic objections, because I personally don't want to eat food made in a factory. This is an objection with no moral force behind it, it's simply my taste. Vegetarians using these foods will easily see how to fit them into the recipes, or use as dishes alongside some of the recipes.

All my cooking life, I've had to be conscious of costs. This hasn't meant avoiding treats and celebrations, but balancing them out with really cheap meals before and after. I think it's a mistake to try to keep expenditure even throughout a week; people are much happier with some treats, and some cheap and simple homely dishes. But the great thing about being cost-conscious is that you avoid buying ready-prepared and processed foods. Cooking from scratch gives you much more control over content and cost of a meal. Vegetarian food gives you scope for more treats; without expensive meat, you can, if you like, have more asparagus in season, more exotic mushrooms, more fancy cheeses . . . whatever. But equally, let's not go overboard about saving money. Good food is important for all sorts of reasons, connected with daily pleasure, good health, and family solidarity. We, collectively, spend a historically very low proportion of our income on food, and economising on other areas of expenditure often has less impact on the quality of life. Good food isn't necessarily expensive, but it isn't dirt cheap either. "If you pay factory prices, you get factory food". It all starts with clever shopping.

I must put in a good word for supermarkets here. I grumble about them like everyone else -- their dominance, the way they drive out small businesses, the way they treat suppliers, their attempt to blind us to food seasonality. It's all true. Still, before the supermarkets, shops were open 9 a.m. to 5.30 p.m., closed at lunch-time on Saturdays and one day during the week, and often showed no interest in supplying what the customer wanted. Supermarkets have made life much easier for working shoppers, who are still mostly women. And they have introduced us all to new and delicious fruits and vegetables. The availability of celeriac, for example, is supermarket-driven. They are not cheaper than an old-fashioned market – in fact, for seasonal fruit they are considerably more expensive – but the ability to buy when it's convenient for you rather than the shopkeeper is worth quite a lot. Sometimes.

• •

There are a lot of recipes in this book – about 1200. My idea was that there would be a selection of ways to use any of the local vegetables, cooked as side-dishes, as salads, used in soup, and as the basis of main dishes. In almost every case, the chapter starts with a "default"; this is the recipe to use for a vegetable side dish, when time and other ingredients are short.

The numbers of recipes in each chapter vary. There are most recipes for using cabbage – 59 of them. I've concentrated on the cheap, readily available vegetables, which are practically ignored in other books. So there are more ways of using Brussels sprouts than there are recipes for aubergines; more ways of using swedes than using sweet corn. This is partly as a reaction to other books, which have tended to use vegetables with more status, which are often more generally liked as well. Various media cooks and chefs have said that we can't be expected to stop using imported veg. in winter, as a diet of cabbages and roots is so dull. They are wrong in at least two ways – first, we have many more local vegetables available now than – say – fifty years ago, and secondly, dullness is a property of the cook not the vegetable.

Perhaps I should say here that I do actually enjoy cooking. If preparing meals is seen as a chore, done for others, there isn't much pleasure or interest in it. If cooking becomes one of one's hobbies, with preparation of meals in the same category as potting or painting, then it's full of pleasure, interest, and satisfaction. And the switch from chore to hobby is, to a large extent, a personal choice. Having said that, I have to admit that there are times when 3 meals a day can daunt even a hobbyist, and there's a lot to be said for getting someone else to cook occasionally, or having some meals – breakfasts, lunches, which are self-assembly jobs. This is impossible with very small children, of course; but in this case, I found that the "hobby" aspect helped to keep me sane and remind me that I had some interest outside the needs of three under-fives. So my cooking has always been experimental and as varied as I could make it.

The recipes in this book are mostly not original -- how could they be? A few are my own inventions, and I've signposted these. On the other hand, where a recipe of someone else's seems unimprovable, I've either got permission to reproduce it, or, if this is refused, pointed to the book where it can be found. The majority of the recipes is neither original or a direct copy; I've tested all these recipes, and changed them so they are more to my taste. It will be evident that I like strong, robust flavours, mostly; and sometimes rich and subtle dishes.

In any event, every cook interprets a recipe differently. When a friend and I were doing outside catering, we would use the same recipe, and the results would be considerably different. I preferred mine; he preferred his; and the customers liked both. So, while all my recipes produce results I like, they are not rigid prescriptions. If you like more sweetness, more chili, less butter, less salt, or whatever, then do it.

11

Connected with this idea, I have used metric measurements throughout. But precision, in most savoury dishes, is not important. If you use 15g butter where I have said 20g, it won't matter. It's a case for your judgement. In real life, when I'm not trying out a recipe, 15g butter is a small lump, 30g butter is larger, and 50-60g butter is a mean quarter of a packet. And the same is true of other seasonings, and indeed the quantity of the main ingredient. This isn't true for baking and cake-making, but even there there is some leeway. Otherwise, how could Americans with cup measurements ever produce a repeatable cake?

I've also defined the seasons in an unusual order. For a gardener, there is spring, harvest (summer and early autumn), and winter (including late autumn). Spring is the traditional "hungry gap" for growers and farmers. This slides into summer and early autumn, with many and delicious crops maturing. Somewhere about the end of October, the last home-grown tomatoes, peppers, beans, peas, can be picked, and then winter has green vegetables above ground and roots below. Long-standing, long-keeping, but not running to fruit and seed quickly and urgently. So this is the way I've split my groups of chapters. A month is too short – most vegetables are at their best for two, even three, months – but the conventional seasons don't fit well with the rhythm of growing and harvest. Modern growers in polytunnels can extend the season of almost any sufficiently desirable vegetable – though not, it seems, asparagus so far. But if you are growing your own veg, or getting a veg box or buying at farmer's markets, this is the pattern to expect.

Cooking, I've suggested above, is a craft, and it's like any other craft in that mastery of techniques takes time and practice. You can turn an acceptable pot quite soon when working with clay, but expertise takes a lot longer. So it is with cooking. Many opportunities to practise, even the failures don't hang around to haunt you, and a continuing source of pleasure and satisfaction. You come to develop an original style and confidence, and an ever-increasing repertoire whatever happens to food supplies. So have at it, and enjoy yourself.

Cooking Methods and Techniques

There are some dishes which call for one specific vegetable, and nothing else will do. There aren't many of these; usually, the many ways of preparing one vegetable can be applied to many – or even most – others. If you have a vegetable and want to do something with it, consider:

1. Plain boiled or steamed, buttered or oiled, with or without suitable herb, spice, flavouring
2. Cooked by the reduction method, when all the cooking liquid has evaporated as the vegetable is done
3. Butter- or oil-sweating, and braising.
4. Roast
5. Mashed or pureed. Can be a single vegetable or a mix, and can be flavoured with herbs, spices, sauces.
6. Stir-Fried
7. Chips and Crisps
8. Fritters
9. Croquettes
10. Barbecued
11. Salad
12. Soup
13. Vegetable stews
14. Curries
15. Omelettes and Frittatas
16. Soufflés and Sformatos
17. With pasta
18. Risotto
19. On pizza or other flatbread
20. Tarts, pies, flans, crumbles, quiches
21. Gratins
22. Savoury bread-and-butter puddings, e.g. leek and Caerphilly soufflé
23. Pancake filling (calling them cannelloni if you feel Italian)
24. Sandwiches
25. Stuffed
26. Stuffings; without what they are stuffed into usually. I've called these Liberated Stuffings.
27. Made into a dip

28.   Preserved, for long or short term
29.   Used in unexpected ways like cake – courgettes, carrots, beetroot are all well-known here.

This chapter goes through these options in turn, with an outline general recipe where appropriate.

A note on gravy There are a few vegetarian dishes which can be dry when eaten alone, such as nut or vegetable loaves, and these respond to a liquid accompaniment. You can call it sauce or gravy, but it's pourable, liquid, well-flavoured and complements the dish. For vegetarian purposes, gravy is thickened stock. The stock (see Basics) should be good, possibly enriched with dried mushrooms and some form of tomato flavour, and thickened at the last minute using arrowroot or cornflour. For this, mix **1 tsp. arrowroot or cornflour** with a little cold water in a cup, and pour into about **300 ml. boiling stock**. Bring back to the boil, stirring, and boil till thickened, then serve. You can also flavour with walnut or mushroom ketchup, soy sauce, miso, or Marmite; just taste till you think it's good.

1. Boiling and Steaming.

You might think there's not much to say about this, and you'd be right, compared with other methods. It is the first technique to come to the minds of British cooks, for everything except salad vegetables like cucumber, lettuce and other greens, watercress. Apparently when the first potatoes arrived in England in Elizabeth's reign, the cook to whom they were handed boiled the greens and threw away those nasty dirty roots. They were not appreciated. And my grandfather insisted on eating his (own, allotment-greenhouse-grown) tomatoes boiled, with sugar.

Just because it's so simple, it means that any shortcomings are amplified. Boiling green beans means hovering over the pan, tasting one frequently, until they reach the point you like them at. Soggy boiled potatoes or Brussels sprouts, overdone asparagus have nothing to hide their defects. In fact, I'd say it's a general rule that the simpler the technique you use, the more care you need to take with it. And care is not something you can give a recipe for, it's down to the character of the cook.

There are two schools of thought about whether the prepared vegetable should go into boiling water or be started from cold. My view is that short-cooked vegetables – green beans, sweetcorn, broccoli, for example, -- need a lot of boiling water. That way it reboils again quickly and the boiled vegetable can be tasted and drained quickly. I know nutritionists say that this way vitamins are lost; in my view, the short cooking time, and the more appetising nature of the result, more than make up for this. Long-cooking vegetables – 20 mins or more – can easily be started in cold water. Or, as I tend to, put on the pan to boil and put in the vegetable – potatoes in particular – as it's peeled and cut up. NEVER leave any vegetable to soak once it's been prepared. Modern potatoes, peeled and cut-up, can sit, dry, in a covered pan for a couple of hours without discolouring, if you want to have the preparation done in advance. I recently tried some heritage potatoes, where this didn't work, and the potatoes browned while waiting.

To peel or not to peel? The fashion with potatoes is not to peel, but this surely depends on taste. I prefer my spuds peeled. New potatoes, with earth still on them, seem to me nicer scraped, and the water with scrapings goes on the garden. If you buy baby potatoes from the supermarket, ready washed, it's tempting just to chuck them in; and some varieties, like Anya, would be impossible to peel. With old boiled potatoes, the great thing about peeling is that you can see if there are any bits which should be cut off or out, and find how deep they go. Other roots for boiling, like salsify, parsnip and swede, should certainly be peeled. Beetroot, far from being peeled, needs its top and tail left on, or the juice will bleed and the taste with it. Jerusalem artichokes are a hassle to peel or to scrub, with all their knobs and re-entrant bits, but I don't like them so much unpeeled. I've tried boiling first, peeling afterwards, but usually they fall apart and it's worse than peeling raw. So far as possible, the vegetable should be cut into pieces of about the same size.

Some veg I never boil – carrots, turnips, cauliflower. I think there are better ways, no more trouble, and nicer. Greens need varied treatment according to their tenderness and strength of flavour. For spinach, you just stuff quantities of the washed (and stemmed, if mature) leaves into a pan, clamp on the lid, and let it cook in the water clinging to it. Turn over from time to time in the 5 mins or so that it takes. Drain very well. At the other green extreme, Cretans boil their wild assorted greens in 2 or 3 changes of water, cooking fairly briefly each time, to reduce the bitterness and tenderise the fibre. Kale is usually fairly tough, and takes 15 mins or more boiling, if mature. But I have a friend who steams her (garden, young) shredded kale for just 4 mins, and loves it like that. And Brussels sprouts are almost always boiled, even if briefly before treating them further. Incidentally, the habit of cutting a cross in the bottom isn't needed if your sprouts are small and tight. If they are big and floppy enough for the cross to make a difference, they are probably too old to be good plain, and should be treated another way.

Draining very well is important with all the boiled vegetables I can think of. This means a colander, not the apparent saver of pouring off the water through the lid with a crack at the low side. Think of asparagus or artichokes with a small pool of water around them, or greens oozing water. Not at all attractive. You may want to preserve the cooking water to use later, as for example with mashed potatoes, but the potatoes themselves should be dry.

Basic boiled vegetables, whether posh like asparagus and globe artichokes, or everyday like potatoes or sprouts, need butter or oil for serving. Asparagus and artichokes have their melted butter, or oil or other dressing, on the side. Sweetcorn on the cob needs cold butter to spread on it. Others have little pieces of butter distributed over them, like runner beans, potatoes, broad beans, broccoli. Sometimes chopped herbs as well. Or the butter/oil can be flavoured with a herb, or spice, or horseradish, or Worcester sauce, or even Tabasco. It depends how much you like the vegetable on its own. You can have a sauce, white or cheese or herb or tomato; this often happens to leeks, because the line between undercooked and overcooked is so fine. I think other ways of cooking leeks are better. Boiled marrow is so dull, and even worse in white sauce, that you should do something else with it.

Generally, boiling and steaming are interchangeable. I often choose to boil, since then there's only one thing to wash up. Some shredded greens, like the young kale mentioned above, respond very well to steaming. Old floury potatoes often fall apart when boiled, so steaming

16

these keeps them together. Steaming tends to take a little longer than boiling – old potatoes I reckon 30 mins steamed, 20 boiled. If you have a modern electric steamer, then obviously it will get used for many vegetables. Preservation of vitamins; just remember that you only get the vitamins in what you eat, and eating much more of a more appetising dish will be better for you than eating less of a vitamin-preserved but not-so-nice one.

2. Reduction cooking.

The idea with this is that the prepared vegetable is put in a pan with a little butter or oil, salt, and often sugar, and a little water, and cooked so that the vegetable is done just as the last of the water evaporates. You can go further, and let the now-dry vegetable toast a little bit on the pan bottom. Much nicer taste, much harder to wash up. Cauliflower is brilliant like this; just cauliflower florets, butter, salt, and 3-4 tbsp. water; a lid on the pan; about 10-15 mins. This really should catch just a little, so there's some brown bits in among the tender vegetable. (Incidentally, I just cannot see the point of cooking cauliflower whole; it's bound to be unevenly cooked, with some bits soggy and overdone. Too high a price to pay for prettiness.)

Carrots done this way, with a little sugar added, turn into an approximation of carrots Vichy. Real Vichy carrots are cooked in Vichy water, and I don't think it makes enough difference to notice. It's a method for old carrots, which should be peeled and sliced into discs. Then water to cover, a piece of butter, salt, a tsp. white sugar. Boil hard, without a lid, for this, so all the water evaporates, and the carrots get a light-brown toasted coating. I hardly ever use another way. Young turnips are delicious this way, but they take a little longer so the lid should be left on the pan for 5 mins or so before taking it off to boil away the liquid. So are baby onions and shallots, which are then called glazed and are a favourite French garnish.

I often do potatoes this way, peeled and cut into fairly thick slices, and cooked with a little water, and butter and salt. These are known to my younger son as "favourite potatoes", and I have hardly ever made enough. Just as well, because the leftovers aren't so much use as those from plain boiled potatoes. This is for old potatoes only; new or waxy ones can take a treatment without water.

17

The same treatment produces brilliant cabbage or other greens. Shredded leaves, 2-3 tbsp. water, salt, and a herb or spicy seed, cooked with a lid on for 5 mins or so, makes some of the nicest cabbage you'll ever taste.

3. Sweating, and braising.

The difference between these two is in the length of the cooking time. A sweated vegetable is prepared, and cooked, covered and on a low heat, with butter or oil, and seasoning. This is one of my favourite ways with new potatoes, giving a soft but browned outside and a delicious concentrated potato flavour. When braised, the vegetable is initially fried gently, then a little flavoursome liquid is added, the pan covered, and cooked on a low heat for a longer time than you'd expect. This gives a deep-tasting blend of flavours and a soft texture. Broccoli can be braised (p.198), and red cabbage almost always is.

4. Roasting vegetables

For some reason, this is a new technique, except for potatoes. I can't find any references more than about 20 years old. However, it produces delicious and more-ish results, is very easy to do, and is also fashionable.

What you do is take mixed prepared veggies – peeled, chunked, seeded, whatever is needed, and put them in a roasting tray. Pour over olive oil, salt, maybe garlic and/or herbs, mix all with your hands, and put into a medium hot oven for 45 mins to an hour. There should be quite a lot of browned edges. It's best, I find, with a mix of 4 or 5 vegetables. Onions are almost always one of them. Others can be potatoes, winter roots, peppers, aubergine, courgettes, squashes, -- anything, really, that isn't green. I can hardly speak too highly of this method.

You can cook some individual vegetables this way. Old potatoes baked. Blanched parsnips roast with butter. See the individual vegetables for ideas.

5 Mashed vegetables.

In outline, the prepared vegetables is boiled or steamed, and then reduced to a puree with flavourings and enrichments. This can either be eaten as it is, or used as a starting point for other preparations – soufflés, croquettes, sformati.

Mashed potatoes are the example that leaps to mind, and there are differences here between potatoes and almost everything else that is pureed. In most cases, the trusty food processor will puree the vegetable with no effort. IT WON'T DO FOR SPUDS. They become gluey and resistant to the addition of liquid, and unpleasant to eat. The best thing for potatoes is a mouli-legumes, with a disc with large perforations. I've had one for forty years, and it is old and tired and the edges on the holes are almost worn away. I've just got a new one, made by Oxo Good Grips, and this seems to be a successful replacement.   There are potato mashers; there is the traditional method with a fork and a lot of wrist action; there are potato ricers. They can all be OK, but for the best mash you need a mouli-legumes. (They are notoriously hard to wash. When you've finished pushing your potatoes, or whatever, through, instantly run under cold water, taking it apart while you do so. This makes washing it a comparative doddle.) Having pureed your potatoes, season, beat in butter and warm liquid – milk if English, potato water if French, olive oil instead of butter if modern, and beat the mash well with a fork. My mother used to add a little baking powder to lighten the mash with less beating; I don't recommend this. Heston Blumenthal has very labour-intensive mashed potatoes, which are amazing once in a while, but aren't going to be part of my daily repertoire.

Other purees, and the uses of the purees, can be found under the individual vegetables.

6 Stir-frying.

Modern English stir-fries are adapted from the Chinese, and can be used for practically any vegetable. Quick to do – once the preparation is out of the way – with good and varied textures and lively seasoning, it's no wonder stir-frying is popular. There's usually more than one vegetable, ranging from a little onion to start with, to the Feast of the Buddhist Saints, which has eight, mostly dried, and is superlative. (No recipe here, because of the dried exotic vegetables; try a Chinese vegetarian book) Again, in principle, the process is simple. Heat a little oil in wok or large frying pan till VERY hot, and add the prepared vegetables in order of the time they will take. Stir round so they keep moving and any water extruded can evaporate. Depending on the vegetable, you may need to blanch it beforehand, and/or add a little liquid and let it cook covered for a few mins. When nearly done, add a little seasoning liquid, (soy sauce, wine, maybe some thickener) and toss till the seasoning is evaporated or thickened, for a short sauce. The thickener in England can be either arrowroot, preferable, or cornflour, more readily available.

It's not restricted to Chinese vegetables, though it would be the method of choice for bok choy, for example. I repeat here the recipe for stir-fried bok choy, as a typical stir-fry.

Stir-fried Bok Choy . Allow **300g bok choy** for 4 people. Separate the leaves from the bok choy stems, which take longer to cook. Cut the stems crosswise in pieces about 3-cm; slice the leaves across to roughly the same size. Heat **1 tbsp. oil** in wok or large frying pan, add the stems and stir and toss for 1-2 mins. Add the leaves, and stir till the leaves wilt. Add a little **water or stock –2-4 tbsp**, depending on pan size – and a **splash of soy sauce** or a little salt, turn again, cover, and cook on moderate heat for 1-5 mins., depending on the age of the vegetable. The stems should be crisp and tender when done. Eat IMMEDIATELY.

Other recipes for stir-fried vegetables include carrots, Chinese leaves, and spinach, and there are other mixed dishes, e.g. with Jerusalem artichokes. This is really such a good fast useful technique that it's worth practicing till you are happy with it.

7.   Chips and Crisps.

These are both deep-fried pieces of a vegetable, without coating. It's usually a root vegetable with high starch content, leading to surface browning. Chips are stick shaped, crisps are very thin slices. Home deep-frying has gone very much out of fashion, but I don't know how much less deep-fried food is eaten. Which means it's mostly bought outside or ready-prepared, at much higher cost. We must recognise that people like deep-fried food, a lot, so it's highly likely they will eat it one way or the other. It's true that too much deep-fried food is bad for you, but if it's seen as an occasional treat, cooked well at home, it will at least help to develop discrimination about the quality of what you buy. Myself, I can't bring myself to eat the average chip-shop chips, which are undercooked and soggy and very oily. (The French, Dutch, Belgians do much better) There are certainly safety concerns about home deep-frying, but I think they are exaggerated, and care to keep any handles turned in, cooking at the back of the stove, and never going away while deep-frying keep any risks minimal. I've never had a chip-pan fire, but if one does happen, DON'T try to use water to put it out. Get it off the heat, and cover. From this point of view, there's a lot to be said for a stand-alone electric deep-fryer. I've never had one; by the time I felt it was affordable, the children had grown up and left home, and I didn't need it for 1 or 2 people.

English tradition always uses a chip-basket, which I think is almost always unnecessary.

Potatoes, obviously, are the vegetable most often deep-fried. Peel potatoes, and cut into lengthwise slices and then into sticks. The larger your chips the less oil they absorb, but the harder it is to cook them through properly. Make sure they are dry. You need at least 5-cm depth of oil, but it shouldn't come more than half-way up the pan, and a bit less is better. Heat the oil in a deep pan (may be called chip-pan, but need not be) until a small piece of bread dropped in bubbles and browns in about 20 sec. Add a handful of chips – don't add too many, or the oil will bubble up and try to overflow. Move pan off heat if this overflow threatens. Keep the pan on high heat, and the chips will lose water from the outside, and the bubbles will subside. Keep moving them round with a metal skimmer, as they gradually brown. When browned to your liking, scoop them out on to newspaper. Add the next lot of chips, and while these are starting to cook, shake the chips on the newspaper round to lose as much oil as possible. Transfer them to a dish lined with kitchen paper to absorb more, and salt lightly. Keep these warm till you've done enough.

This is the simple domestic method. Restaurants may cook twice, once at a lower heat to cook through and then a final fry at high heat to brown. This is obviously convenient for the way they operate. Heston Blumenthal cooks his chips 3 times. These MAY give marginally nicer chips, but I think domestically the once-through method is easier, more convenient, and does very well indeed.

If you can deep-fry chips, you can deep-fry anything else. Potato crisps, very thin slices cut on slicing blade of box grater, food processor, mandolin. But it's very hard to get them thin enough by hand. Beetroot crisps. Parsnip crisps. Sweet-potato crisps or chips. Swede chips, parsnip chips. The whole collection of croquettes, fritters, tempura and things covered with batter. And poppadums. Deep-frying is such a good way of combining the texture of crispness and the flavour of "browned" that it's not surprising that it's universally liked.

If you use a pan of deep-frying oil once, it's pretty wasteful not to use it again. If it's got bits in it, pour the oil through a paper towel lining a sieve to clean the oil, and take advantage of the empty pan to wash it. But after several fryings – the number depends on your heat control – the oil will be tired, smell stale, and will give off the horrid smell of too many commercial fryers when heated. If it seems to be getting to that stage, THROW IT AWAY. Not down the sink, obviously. A good compost heap will be enriched. Otherwise, a non-recyclable closed jar or bottle is the best compromise at the present stage of waste disposal.

8. Fritters.

Anything deep-fried with a batter coating. There are 3 frying batters in the Basics section. Fritters are made from single vegetables in small pieces, raw or previously cooked lightly. Cauliflower, raw or cooked. Mushrooms, sliced in hammer shapes. Courgettes. Aubergine. Fennel. Celery. Onion. Jerusalem artichokes. You can also make fritters from vegetables mixed into the batter, which may be modified for the occasion, like onion bhajias. Peas work well here, too. Radish probably would. You can have just a few fritters as a garnish or small side-dish or part of spread, or you can make a whole meal from freshly-cooked vegetable fritters with lemons to squeeze on. Don't even try and keep fritters hot for more than a few minutes; they really are best straight from the pan, drained, and eaten almost hot enough to burn the mouth.

When I was a child, my mother used to make potato fritters called "specials" towards the end of some weeks. Thin slices of potato in batter; it takes skill to cook the potato through without overcooking the batter. My brother and I loved and looked forward to a meal of chips and specials. Nutritionally questionable, but English cooking of the poor, which is said not to exist but is simply not recorded.

All the cautions about deep-frying chips also apply to frying fritters. Prepare all the vegetables you are going to use in advance, and keep them by the stove. Likewise the batter. Heat the oil, dip slices in the batter and lift out with your fingers, and drop in the pan. Not too many at once. Move about with the skimmer, turn over to make sure both sides brown, lift out when done, drain well, and eat. DON'T GO AWAY. If doing vegetables mixed with the batter, use a tablespoon to drop in quantities. Large bhajias almost always absorb too much oil.

9.   Croquettes.

Egg-and-breadcrumbed cork-shaped portions of a mashed vegetable, deep-fried. Lovely crisp outside, and an amazing way to use leftover purees. The puree must be fairly stiff, so mashed potatoes without milk are better than with milk. Other possible vegetables include parsnip and swede, both stiffened with potato. You can also make a croquette mixture with a very thick white or cheese sauce with a cooked vegetable added, or chopped hard-boiled eggs. (For meat-eaters, it's a great thing to do with scraps of leftover meat when there's very little of it; mince and mix into potato or white sauce)

Have ready 3 shallow bowls, one with flour, one with a beaten egg, and one with breadcrumbs (Japanese panko crumbs are good here, or your own dried crumbs. There are several new brands of dried toasted breadcrumbs which are very good. Commercial orange breadcrumbs are looked down on, but they are cheap and convenient and I have no objection to them.) Scoop out about a rounded tbsp of mixture, roll in your hands to a cork shape, then pass through flour, rolling to coat; then beaten egg, ditto, then crumbs, heaping them over the croquette and shaking off excess. There is no denying this is messy, and you'll need to wash your hands a couple of times in the process. Chill the crumbed croquettes. When nearly ready to eat, heat oil for deep frying; when really hot, drop in the croquettes, a few at a time. Fry till well-browned, scoop out, and drain on newspaper then kitchen paper; continue till all are done. Serve straightaway. The frying is quite brief, because the inside is already cooked and just needs to be heated.

You wouldn't do all this just for 1 person, and even 2 is a bit doubtful. I find frozen potato croquettes, reheated in the oven, pretty good, and I wish they'd do frozen croquettes with other vegetables.

10. Barbecued Vegetables.

This isn't really here as a recipe, just a reminder that lots of vegetables, particularly Mediterranean ones like peppers, courgettes, aubergines, fennel, and others like mushrooms and onions, can be roasted on a barbecue. It's easiest if the barbecue has a heated plate, Australian style, rather than bars over the coals. In this case you can cook vegetables and slices of halloumi, and have a complete fast meal. Tofu does well on a barbecue plate, as well. Vegetables can be plain or marinated. And it's always worth using residual heat to toast some red peppers, and then skin them.

11. Salad.

Very hard to define what is a salad. It can be as simple as lettuce with dressing, or as complex as a composed salad of several vegetables. It is usually cold, but can be warm – though warm salads usually have some sort of dressing. I don't think there is a vegetable here which can't be used as a salad, though some, like stinging nettles, need cooking first. The main hurdle to get over in increasing your salad intake is the idea that they are restricted to warm weather, and cold weather demands heavier, warming foods. This used to be so when people lived in cold houses in winter. Nowadays, our winter quarters are usually at least comfortable, and we don't need extra food in winter to generate more body heat. How long do you spend outside in winter, in the cold? In the US, buildings are often cooler in summer than in winter, because of the air conditioning – a ridiculous state of affairs, but it illustrates the point I'm making. So, eat more winter salads, grow winter salad leaves on the windowsill, and eat cooked veg. cold with dressing. It can only do you good nutritionally and taste-wise.

The best thing you can do for your salads is make your own dressings, and avoid bought ones, full of emulsifiers, preservatives, and unwanted flavourings. All you need for a salad dressing is **3 tbsp. oil, 1 tbsp good vinegar or lemon juice, salt and pepper**, and this can be

24

stirred together in a cup, or shaken in a clean lidded jar, in no time. Extra-virgin olive oil is my favourite, but sunflower oil makes a perfectly OK dressing and is much cheaper.

12. Soup.

Every vegetable can go into a soup, alone or with others. And soups can vary from thin, light, almost transparent mixtures to thick, nourishing affairs which make a whole meal with just a bit of bread alongside. A thick soup can slide into being a vegetable stew The most generalised soup recipe goes: sweat chopped onion in oil or butter, add prepared, cut-up vegetable or vegetables, maybe with cubes of potato, sweat a bit more, add stock and cook till veg are done. Maybe puree. Reheat and serve with additions or garnishes or alone. There are specific recipes in 43 of the vegetable chapters, sometimes more than one, and the vegetables which don't have soup recipes are often too good alone, like purple sprouting broccoli, or too rare, like salsify and tomatillos, to be used in soup. They can still go into mixed vegetable soups or be used alone as the above general recipe if you have a lot. In fact, there is a nearly infinite number of soup variations, and what is good is to find the favourites and use those, *and* keep experimenting. I don't see why one meal every week, maybe two, shouldn't be a soup meal.

13. Vegetable Stews

Mixed vegetables cooked gently together in a pot, with some liquid. Ratatouille is a summer stew. This **Ten-Vegetable Couscous** can be for any season, but will probably be cooked in autumn or winter.
Peel, halve, thinly slice **2 red onions**, and fry in **3 tbsp. olive oil**. When softened, add **4 peeled carrots** in chunks, **2 small turnips** peeled and chunked, **½ butternut squash** peeled seeded and chunked, **2 green chilis** seeded and chopped, and **1 aubergine** chunked. Stir and sweat 5-10 mins (depends on base size of pan) with cover. Add **1 tsp. salt, 2 heaped tsp. ras el hanout and 4 or more chunked cloves garlic.** Stir again. Add **1 tin peeled tomatoes**, with juice, **1 chunked fennel, 1 tin chickpeas drained and rinsed, 1 seeded and chunked red pepper, 4 oz dried apricots** soaked briefly and halved. Add about **300 ml water, good tsp salt.** Cook 20 mins. Add **250g courgettes chunked**, cook 10 mins more. Sprinkle with **1 packet**

chopped green coriander, juice of 1 lemon. Serve with harissa and couscous with lots of chopped parsley. You can also use sweet potatoes, celeriac, etc, or miss some out. I think 7 veg is minimum for the complex taste. Doesn't taste of individual veg, but a melange, and slightly sweet. So the hot contrast from the harissa is important. You need quite a lot of juice to moisten couscous and mix with the harissa. I usually use Belazu rose harissa; it's easily available and not too hot.

You get the principle. Another illustration is this **Winter Vegetable Goulash.** Sweat **2 chopped onions** in **2 tbsp. sunflower oil** for 10 mins, without browning. Add **florets from a small cauliflower, 3 sliced carrots and 3 chopped cloves garlic**, and sweat 5 mins more. Add **200g cut-up butternut squash and ½ swede**, peeled and diced, and stir in. Add **1 tsp. caraway seeds**, if you like them. (I do in goulash but not in cake) Take the pan off the heat, and add **2 tsp. Hungarian paprika**, the best you can find. (You can use Spanish smoked paprika if you can't get Hungarian, but it's not as good in a goulash) Then add **300 ml. stock, 1 tbsp. tomato puree, 2 tsp salt**, and simmer for 30 mins or till the vegetables are cooked.

Both these illustrate another point about vegetable stews; they can be reheated next day, so it's worth making a large amount. (Both the above will do for 6-8 people) You can also add more liquid and cook dumplings in them, or put pie crust, or crumble, or scone mix on top. I could go on with specific recipes, but really it depends on what you have and what you want.

14. Curries.

What distinguishes a curry from other vegetable stews is the presence of curry spices; simple as that. The 10-vegetables couscous has Moroccan spices, the goulash Hungarian, and either could become a curry by varying the spicing. The simplest vegetable curry I do – and do most often – has onions, potatoes, tinned tomatoes, and peas, because I always have these around. Chop **1 large onion** and fry on moderate heat till softened. Add a **couple of cloves of garlic**, chopped, and **2-3 diced raw peeled potatoes**. Stir round a few minutes, then add **½ tsp. turmeric, ½ tsp. salt, 1 tsp. garam masala, ¼ tsp. cayenne (or less)**. Add the contents of a **tin of tomatoes**, whole or chopped. Cook, covered, until the potatoes are done. This takes longer than usual, because of the flavoured liquid. Just before serving, add a **couple of handfuls frozen peas**, and eat when they have warmed through. Chopped fresh green coriander if you have some; plain yoghurt on the side; plain boiled rice. This is deliberately a vague recipe, simply because quantities and proportions don't matter that much. It is always good.

15. Omelettes and Frittatas

These are both eggs plus filling, but very different from each other. In an omelette, the main element is the egg wrapping, cooked very fast, and the filling is a small but flavourful addition. In a frittata, there is more filling than egg element, and it's cooked as slowly as possible. Neither, however, is anything like scrambled egg. The omelette is the ideal fast food - in hurried times, I have made and eaten a cheese omelette in 7 minutes, and been satisfied until the next meal. A frittata makes a meal from not-very-much of anything, and can be eaten hot, cold, warm, or in a sandwich. Omelettes must be eaten straightaway.

For a plain omelette with herbs, for 1, break **3 eggs** into a bowl. **Salt, pepper, chopped herbs.** Beat just enough to mix, not enough to make the whole thing uniform – 8-10 turns with a fork is about right. Heat the omelette pan on high heat; for this size omelette, the pan base should be 7-8", or 17-20 cm. Drop a **small nut of butter** in the pan, and swirl it round. It will melt and start to bubble, then the bubbles subside and the butter starts to brown. You seize the moment between bubbles subsiding and butter browning, and empty the eggs into the pan. Swirl to make sure the bottom is quite covered, then start to lift the mixture with the flat of a fork, to let liquid egg run underneath. Vary the part of the pan where you are lifting, and keep the liquid parts moving. When it is all nearly set, and in layers from letting liquid egg run under cooked egg, it's ready to turn out. Have a hot plate waiting, and fold one-third of the omelette over the top. Then tilt the pan so the whole thing slides out, meanwhile assisting the top folded two-thirds to fold over the other empty third. Folded omelette on plate. If it's for someone else who is sitting waiting, take it to them, and do another for yourself. Don't make an omelette for anyone else until they are sitting waiting; the whole cooking process takes less than a minute. The centre should be not cooked, not uncooked - in the same in-between state as the yolk of a soft-boiled egg.

The pan is obviously crucial to a good omelette; a non-stick pan won't do, because of the scraping, stirring action of the fork; but a pan which sticks is also disastrous. A well-seasoned pan is what you need, and it should hardly ever need washing or be washed. Just wipe with a piece of kitchen paper after cooking the omelette. A seasoned surface builds up gradually, with cooking omelettes and pancakes, and can be destroyed by washing and abrasion. Also by cooking salty things in it; it doesn't apply to vegetarians, but cooking bacon in an omelette pan will make the omelette stick.

Fillings go in just as the top surface of the omelette is cooked, and immediately before rolling. Grated cheese, about 25g. Sorrel, see recipe. Thick tomato/garlic puree, see recipe. A few crisp croutons. There are many many more possibilities, (I have a book with 100 omelette recipes) but I think it's best to keep this simple and fresh.

There is also the **soufflé omelette**, much liked by my husband. For this you need **2 eggs per person**. Separate the eggs, and beat the yolks with salt and pepper. Beat the whites separately, then fold into the yolks. Heat the omelette pan over a moderate heat, and preheat the grill. Add a **nut of butter** to the pan, swirl till melted, then add the egg mixture. Cook on moderate heat till the bottom is golden-brown (lift an edge to peek). Sprinkle any filling – grated cheese is the most likely – on top, then put the pan under the preheated grill until the top is cooked. Serve unfolded. A savoury soufflé omelette is very good, but it finds its natural home as a sweet. For this, forget the salt and pepper, and just cook the mix of 2 egg yolks and 2 beaten whites in a little butter. Heat 1-2 tbsp. jam. When the top of the omelette has been cooked under the grill, put the jam on it, a little off-centre, and fold the omelette in two. This lends itself to lily-gilding, when you pour over a couple of tbsp. of a suitable alcohol and light it as you serve it up. Eau-de-vie de Framboise for raspberry jam; eau-de-vie de Prunes for plum jam, kirsch for strawberry or apricot or cherry jam, and so on. If you have a few slices of fried apple, you can use those instead of the jam, and flame with Calvados. Myself, I think burning these delicious alcohols is sadly wasteful, and I'd sooner have a small glass of them with the unburnt omelette. But you may feel differently. But without any alcohol at all, this is a dessert of simplicity, elegance, succulence, deliciousness -- and without the alcohol it's cheap, too.

Frittatas, as I've said, have much more filling per egg, and are always cooked and served flat. Frittata is the Italian term, but the same process makes tortillas in Spain and kuku in Iran, with different names in in-between areas. It's simpler to get this right than to get an omelette right, because the cooking is slower. It's always cooked on oil, not butter, which means it can be eaten cold, and almost always has garlic to enliven its vegetables.

Courgette frittata is a model for all these. Heat **1 tbsp. olive oil** in a frying pan with a lid, add **2 cloves garlic** very finely chopped. When this starts to cook, add **4-5 young courgettes**, trimmed and sliced thinly. Stir round, **salt and pepper,** then turn the heat very low, put a lid on the pan, and leave 20 mins. or so. Stir from time to time. If there is any liquid, turn up the heat and let it boil away. Beat **4 eggs** with **salt and pepper**, pour over the courgettes, and cook slowly till done. Ideally it should be turned over as a unit, to gild the second side, but I usually break it into convenient chunks to turn over individually, and let them meld together again while the second side cooks. You can modify this by adding onion at the start, or by adding cubes of cooked potato with the courgettes, or using other Mediterranean vegetables like red pepper. Spinach and other greens make good frittatas, and so does asparagus. You can also preheat the grill; when the first side is cooked, sprinkle with a little grated cheese – Cheddar, Parmesan, goat, blue, what-you-will – and grill the top so that the egg cooks and the cheese melts.

16. Soufflés and Sformatos.

Both these have a base of thick white sauce plus vegetable and eggs, and both are cooked in the oven. The difference, as I understand it, is that soufflés have separated egg whites beaten in to the mix with egg yolks, and sformati use whole eggs. But sometimes sformatos also have beaten egg whites, in which case they are really soufflés. I hope that's not confusing! Here are the two recipes from the Courgette chapter for sformato and soufflé; they illustrate the method, and the differences, between the two dishes.

Sformato of Courgettes Cut **700g. courgettes into quarters**, then into ½-cm slices. Cook these quite quickly in **20g. butter**, with a sprinkle of **salt**, till they are slightly browned and barely tender. You may need to do this in more than 1 batch, depending on the size of your pan; in this case you may need more butter.

In a separate pan, melt **40g. butter**, add **30g flour**, and cook gently 2 mins. Add **300 ml milk**, and bring to boil, stirring. **Salt, pepper, nutmeg**, and **60g strong Cheddar**, grated. Off the heat, beat in **2 eggs**, then add the courgettes and fold together gently. Butter a 22-cm. round baking dish, and sprinkle with **fresh bread crumbs**. Pour in the courgette mix, sprinkle with **30g. more grated cheese**, and bake at 170 for 30 mins, or until a knife inserted in the mix comes out clean. Serve warm.

Courgette Soufflé. The ingredients are very much the same as those for the sformato. Make the white sauce with seasoning and cheese, and cook the courgettes as above. Whizz the two together in a food processor, and add the **yolks of 3 eggs** and whizz again. Beat the **whites of the 3 eggs**, with a **pinch of salt**, till stiff, and fold into the courgette mixture. The best way is to take a dollop of the stiff egg whites and beat into the puree, to lighten it a little, and then tip this on top of the remainder of the beaten whites and fold in gently. Pour into a buttered straight-sided dish, no crumbs. Sprinkle the top with cheese, and run a finger through the mixture close to the edge of the dish. This bit of magic helps it to stick to the dish and rise high in the middle. Bake at 180 for 30 mins or so.

Soufflés do have an intimidating reputation, but this is based on the difficulty of making a soufflé when the oven was coal-fired and didn't have a thermostat. With a modern oven it's a doddle. Still, you can take advantage of the reputation to enhance your own.

17.   With Pasta.

All the vegetables here can go into a pasta sauce, and there are explicit recipes for most of them. It's simply a standard way of using any vegetables, and currently, no more exotic than boiling. There are two types of pasta + vegetable dishes; the Italian kind, where the dish is expected to be a first course, and is lighter than the English/American kind, where we expect it to be a full meal. Don't restrict yourself to one of the other. The two recipes for cauliflower pasta illustrate this well; the first has cauliflower cooked with garlic and chili, mixed with pasta, and eaten. The second adds beaten eggs, and is a main dish, where only a salad needs to be added.

Lasagne is another pasta dish which has been enthusiastically adopted in England as the main event for a party. The courgette lasagne fits this case well, but there is also asparagus lasagne for a celebration, which is much classier (and more expensive). Once you have the principle of lasagne sheets layered with white sauce, a vegetables, tomato sauce, and cheese, it's very easy to make your own signature version.

I haven't included any instructions for making ravioli, cappelletti, or any other of the Italian stuffed pastas. I think the work/reward ratio is far too high. Maybe if I'd grown up with an Italian cook, I'd feel much more comfortable with the process, but as it is, I'm not. And even in Italy home-made stuffed pasta is for holidays and celebrations, not an everyday dish. And I'd sooner do stuffed pancakes than cannelloni any time. But don't judge stuffed pasta on the supermarket offerings, because the real thing is very, very much better. If you know a shop that makes its own stuffed pasta, try that and see if you want to compete.

18. Risotto

Successful risottos need more technique than many of the other ways of turning a vegetable into a meal, but it's simple to acquire. Two crucial points: the proper Italian risotto rice, and the quality of the stock you use. I'll give a basic risotto here, and there are specialised ones dotted throughout. For 4 people, you need **250g rice**. Arborio is commonest, and very satisfactory. I've tried Vialone, at much higher cost, but my palate wasn't sensitive enough to detect much difference. DON'T WASH IT. You need about **1½ litres of stock**, and ideally it should be flavoured with some of the vegetable you are using. So, for asparagus risotto, cook the asparagus trimmings in existing stock, or make a normal stock adding the trimmings. I really don't think packet stock is good enough for a risotto. **Salt** the stock lightly, about 1 tsp. for this amount. You also need a wide pan, deeper than the average frying pan, though you can use a frying pan if necessary. Heat the stock on a burner next to the risotto pan, and keep it nearly simmering while you cook. Start by melting **a chopped onion, or 2-3 chopped shallots** (better) in **50g butter**. (Northern Italians historically use butter not oil in their cooking) Add the rice, stir round, and let it cook gently 3-5 mins. The rice's appearance changes. Add a **glass of dry white wine** (not always; see individual recipes) and let it cook over moderate heat, stirring now and then, until it's nearly dry. Add a soup ladle, or half a cup, of the stock. Stir, let it evaporate and be absorbed. Add another ladle, and keep going, so the rice never has too much liquid but never dries out. Stir as often as you can. After 20-25 mins the rice will be cooked and the pan nearly dry. Taste for salt; add

pepper. Add **30g more butter** and **30g grated Parmesan**, and beat these in. Eat. Depending on the vegetable, this can be added with the rice at the beginning, or mixed in at the end, but even a plain risotto is very good indeed. Some of my family like risotto with dried and fresh mushrooms so much they request it for birthdays.

Don't be tempted by recipes which say you can add all the liquid at once, and cook in the oven. The results they produce are OK, but not as good as the real thing. If you do the all-in-one method, avoid disappointing people by calling it something else.

19. Pizza

See Basics for the principles of pizza making, and specific recipes for uses. There are pizzas with chicory, courgettes, fennel (p.226), peppers and tomatillos (p.312), as well as basics with tomato and mushroom. Other flatbreads can be used with pizza-like toppings, and toasted. Or you can sandwich 2 wheat tortillas with refried beans, cheese, and a vegetable (lettuce shreds, peppers, fennel, or any other that you have/appeals to you, and fry gently so the cheese just melts and the outside crisps; these are quesadillas. Perhaps these should be part of sandwiches, below.

20. Tarts, Pies, Flans and Crumbles

Generally, a tart has a bottom pastry crust with a filling, a pie has a top crust and maybe a bottom crust, a flan may be like a tart or may be just filling, with no pastry at all, and a crumble has a pastry mix without any liquid added. But names can get confused, so sometimes these rules don't hold. This means you can call a pastry dish what you like. A quiche has a bottom crust and a filling with eggs and cream, which puffs when bakes. Instructions for pastry are in the Basics chapter.

A new French idea (I think) is to make up some ready-cooked crumble, either savoury or sweet, which can then be sprinkled over a cooked fruit or vegetable with juices or a sauce, with no further cooking. The savoury version uses **50g plain flour** (white, brown, spelt, whatever) mixed with **50g rolled oats** (not instant). Rub in **50g butter**, **½ tsp. salt,** and spread out on an oven tray. Cook at 180 till browned and delicious, and store in a closed jar in the fridge. The **sweet version** omits salt and adds **50g sugar** (dark brown, light brown, Demerara, white) to the mix. But I find that Granola in its various forms is a good version of a sweet crumble topping, especially with ice cream and sauce.

21. Gratins

A gratin has a crisp, browned topping over a mix to be baked. The topping can be as simple as breadcrumbs with dots of butter, but is most usually grated cheese. Some gratins, like Dauphinoise potatoes, don't need any additions to make a topping; they have milk or cream, which browns on top of the dish. See the individual recipes for specifics, for potatoes (p.505), parsnip (p.466) and cauliflower (p. 109) The thing about gratins is that most people like them a lot; it's partly the contrast of texture between body of dish and top, and partly the "browned" flavour which is so appetising.

22. Savoury Bread-and-Butter Puddings.

They can also be known as "strata" or layers, which is the American name which makes them sound more exotic, less domestic. Whatever you call them, they are a thoroughly domestic dish, and usually much liked. Essentially, you make sandwiches with bread and the vegetable or vegetable-and-cheese filling, arrange in baking dish, pour over a mixture of eggs and milk, well-seasoned, and let them stand an hour or so so the bread absorbs the milk-egg mixture. Then bake in a moderate oven until the savoury custard is set and the top browned. See Leek Strata (p.460) for an example. None of these are classic dishes, so they are open to improvisation and creativity. I like a tomato-and-mushroom version with tomato juice instead of milk.

23. Pancake Fillings.

This is not here to give instructions, just to remind you that many vegetable mixtures can be wrapped in pancakes and either served straightaway or reheated. See, specially, spinach (p.150) and Swiss chard (pp. 172, 175).

24. Sandwiches.

A reminder. All sorts of pates, dips, pastes can be a filling, or part of a filling. Bread can be standard, sourdough, flatbread, French bread, . . .

I think that whatever it is should be good of its kind, though I know there are writers who love tomato sandwiches, for example, on soggy white sliced. I can't join them.

25. Stuffed Vegetables.

Anything that has a hollow, and some that don't, has been stuffed. Aubergines, courgettes, peppers, potatoes, mushrooms, cabbages (leaves rolled round stuffing), all spring to mind easily. I have in my collection a recipe for stuffed Brussels sprouts, which I think is going to extremes. In fact, I think many, but not all, stuffed veg. originated as a way of eking out small amounts of meat, often leftover, and I won't have any truck with this sort of recipe adapted to be meatless. Peppers and cabbage, though, are real stars in the stuffed-vegetable field, and worth the fiddle of making them. They can be made ahead and cooked/heated just before a meal, which is in their favour.

26. Liberated Stuffings.

Stuffings used to go inside fowl or meat to be roasted. Recently, people have noticed how much better both components turn out if the stuffing is baked separately, and the stuffing is often nicer than the meat it's supposed to complement. So all I have done is recommend serving some of these stuffings as a dish alone. Stuffings based on carrots, chestnuts, . . . are good enough to be a centrepiece alone. They do tend to need a gravy or a liquid sauce, or another vegetable with a liquid sauce. Breadcrumbs or rice, vegetable component, sometimes nuts, herbs, egg to bind -- don't feel restricted to my ideas on the subject.

27. Dips

I love having a dip with raw vegetables and tortilla chips as a first course, and so do my eaters. It's definitely informal, but it's easy and friendly to eat. You can buy a restricted selection of dips in supermarkets, but they are expensive and nowhere near as good as the ones you make fresh. Salsas fit in here as well. I don't know any dips using root veg or greens, but apart from these the whole range is open to make or improvise a small bowl of something strongly-flavoured and healthy.

28. Preserved Vegetables.

You can preserve vegetables for two reasons, because you have a glut from the garden, or because the end result is delicious. Ideally the result should taste good even in case 1, but that hasn't always been the case. The spread of domestic freezers has removed us from the runner beans preserved in salt of my childhood, and I'm glad of it. Now we can get our preserved vegetables frozen, dried, tinned, in jars, and there really isn't a life-preserving need for home preservation in most cases. People still make chutney because they love it. Some pickles from the Far East are simply brilliant and compulsive eating, but I haven't given these because they are occasionals for me, not something I feel expert at. I recommend bread-and-butter pickle (p.218), under Cucumber, because it is so good and you can't buy anything like it. Green tomato chutney is good, but green tomato mincemeat is better. So my advice here is to make only those preserves that you love. If you have a glut of something that you don't like preserved, eat what you can and give the rest away. You'll come to dislike the jars sitting for years on your shelves, because they aren't eaten and represent wasted effort. Bread on the waters will come back to you later.

29. Unexpected Ways.
Carrot cake (p.395). Courgette muffins (p. 213). Beetroot and chocolate cake. Potato bread. All of these use a vegetable in a baked context, and they can all be very good. Potato bread (p.515), in particular, is really worth knowing. These dishes don't really have much in common, and perhaps have more impact because of the shock value. I think you'd like carrot cake if you didn't know it had carrots in, but I'm not sure about beetroot-and-chocolate cake.

Ingredients

I have put these in alphabetical order, and you can also use the index to find any particular ingredient.

Bread.

If you have good bread, then you're at least 50% of the way to having a happy, healthy family, on the kitchen front. If you don't have good bread, then many of your efforts will fall short of the mark. And good bread, alas, is not always easy to come by.

DO find some good bread, almost certainly unsliced. It may well be local, if you're lucky. It may be brown, white, in-between, rye, seedy, or a host of other things. Home-made bread can be just the way(s) you like it, but there are times when it just isn't practical. And I do resent the fact that I can't buy good bread without a special car journey!

Bread can be good in many different ways, but let me say what it isn't. It doesn't stick to your teeth and palate. If you squeeze it, it doesn't squash, it rebounds. Softness is not a desirable quality, generally, in spite of the adverts; your bread needs texture, resistance to the bite, and crust. Technically, it is not made by the Chorleywood process, which was invented in the 1950's and has been the ruination of English bread. This process works by condensing the fermentation of bread into 5 mins or less, so the dough has no time to develop flavour. If this dough is then undercooked and wrapped in plastic, you get the typical sliced loaf. At least 90% of English commercial bread uses this method. And this is without allowing for the pernicious effects of bleaches, dough improvers, and other unnecessary additives. I believe, without being able to prove, that Chorleywood-process bread is responsible for a lot of the spread of gluten allergies and coeliac disease.

I do understand why the local baker has largely disappeared. My parents had a bread/cake shop in the 1950's, and it was a very hard way of life. Up at 4 am every weekday morning, except Saturdays when it was 2 am. They lasted 5 years before they had to give up because of health problems. But at that time bread prices were controlled, so no-one had the option of paying more for a better product. Now we have the option, but in many cases the supply just isn't there. There is a demand for good bread. At one stage, Tesco were selling loaves imported from California, at very high prices. It was good, but I couldn't bring myself to buy it, with all those air miles. Now it's made under licence in the UK, and isn't the same at all.

Let me urge you to try making your own bread. Start off by making a standard tin loaf. The recipe is in Basics. Bread machines seem to me to be a halfway house; they are convenient, but the bread isn't as good as it can be. (At least, I've tried bread made in their machines by 4 or 5 friends, and their bread is acceptable but no more.) They do have the advantage that you become familiar with the process. But a bread machine makes 1 loaf at a time. My method makes 3 large loaves, for a total of approximately 10 mins. work. There isn't a lot of time saved with the machine, therefore. What is easier with a machine is the fact that you put in the ingredients and take out a loaf, and don't have to do anything in between.

Cheese.

Most vegetarians I know eat any cheese, and don't restrict themselves to vegetarian cheese. Maybe I know an odd group. However, I have suggested cheese varieties throughout without worrying about their vegetarian (or not) nature. If you eat only vegetarian cheese, the type mentioned in a recipe is a guide to the sort to use. You will know best what is available from your suppliers.

I have no time for "reduced-fat" cheeses. I'd rather use a bit less of a tastier traditional variety, or eat something else altogether. But this too is up to you; if the reduced-fat cheese produces a result to your taste, why wouldn't you use it?

Chilis

I use quite a lot of chilis, even though I don't like very hot food. There is a lot of machismo involved in eating hotter food, if you aren't brought up with it. (If you were, you probably find food without chilis dull and bland) But chilis can have an effect in the finished dish ranging from a mild warmth to as-hot-as-you-can take, and always enliven the rest of the ingredients. You need chilis for Indian, Thai, Mexican food, and they add punch to a lot of other foods as well. There are an enormous number of varieties, and we in the UK don't see many of them.

Chilis come fresh and dried. I almost always have some fresh chilis in the fridge, along with garlic and ginger. I don't buy the really hot birds'-eye chilis for Thai food, or the Scotch bonnet or habanero types for Caribbean and Mexican food. The medium-size, conical chilis about 5-cm long are my staple, and I don't mind if they are red or green. These look like jalapenos, which are now seen on every hot pizza, but they aren't as hot. There are really mild chilis available in the US; poblano chilis are about the size of a red or green pepper. I'd love to see them here. The hottest part of any fresh chili is the seeds, so I always scrape them out and discard them after cutting off the top of the chili. Many people say that the veins inside the pod are hotter than the seeds; I don't find it so, and never remove veins. In US books you'll often find instructions to wear rubber gloves when preparing chilis. I think this is going too far. However, if you are preparing chilis DON'T touch any part of your face or body before washing your hands; the results on sensitive areas like eyes can be very painful.

The dried chilis we most often find are in Indian shops, and they are pretty hot. I tend to use these whole, dropping them into a pan of lentils or other pulses while they boil, then fishing them out before anyone bites into one. Larger forms of dried chili are Mexican, of which the most desirable is the ancho chili. Flattened, ruddy black in colour, roughly square and 5-7 cm a side, they give a beautiful fruity chili flavour without more than a pervasive warmth. Availability of these is increasing; Tesco has them, and they are easy to buy on the Net. When using these chilis, tear them into pieces, discarding the cap. There are a lot of seeds; you can discard these, or keep them to toast and use as a seasoning. When you have pieces of the pepper body, they need soaking. Pour a little boiling water to cover over them in a bowl, and let them sit at least 10 mins. Usually, water and chili pieces are then whizzed in a blender, before being cooked with other ingredients.

Another noteworthy dried Mexican chili is the chipotle. This is a dried smoked jalapeno, and adds considerable heat and a fruity, smoky flavour to anything it's used in. You can buy them dried, but the most common form is "chipotles en adobo", where the chilis are cooked in a sauce. Chipotles are also turning up in bottled sauces. One of the strange properties of chipotles in adobo is that the dish they are used in becomes significantly hotter with time. I notice this most with chipotle mayonnaise (make in blender as usual, adding cautious ½-1 tsp. chipotles-in-adobo per egg halfway through adding the oil), which is warm and pleasant the first day, and blow-your-head-off by the second.

Dried powdered chilis . The most common of these are Cayenne pepper, and (Indian) chili powder. These are pure dried ground hot chilis, and are very hot. ¼- ½ tsp is enough for a vegetable curry for 4, I find. You will also come across something labelled "chili powder" which is the American-style blend for making chili beans, chili con carne, and so on. This has a list of ingredients, and you need to be careful not to use one when you intended the other. Making chili sin carne with 2 tbsp. Indian chili powder, which I once did, is a pure waste of the ingredients. (I had heard about cooking potatoes in something to reduce heat; I did this about 5 times over 2 days, and the dish was still inedibly hot)

If you ever come across Kashmiri chili powder, snap up a supply. Less hot than Indian chili powder, with much more flavour. Madhur Jaffrey imitates this with a mix of paprika and Indian chili powder, but the real thing is nicer, though hard to find. Bart's made it at one stage, but I haven't seen it for some years. In Indian stores it would be "Kashmiri degi mirch".

Hungarian paprika, and Spanish smoked pimenton, are fairly mild but flavourful dried powdered chilis. Hungarian paprika is by far the best thing to use in goulash-type dishes, as you'd expect. It's been hard to find recently, whereas the Spanish smoked pimenton has become popular and easily available. Small jars from big manufacturers, labelled "paprika", are in my experience intended only for sprinkling on as a garnish. They just don't give you the effect you want when you cook with them.

If you like the effects of chili in food, then it's always worth snapping up a new kind when you see it, or when travelling. National tastes are partly formed by the sort of chili used in the cooking, and won't taste as they should without it.

Most bottled chili sauces come under the bottled sauce heading, but I think Tabasco belongs here for its pure heat and chili flavour. Tabasco seems to me to be a kitchen essential, one of the things one should never run out of. It gets used to improve almost anything savoury that tastes a little dull, as well as being essential for Bloody Marys and various sauces.

I've recently discovered the "Very Lazy" chopped chili, as well as other versions with slightly altered names. They are useful and good, but if you use them all the time then everything will start to taste the same. Worth keeping in stock.

There are also various chili products used as relishes or as part of a little-dish table. Pickled jalapeno slices in the Mexican section, Peppadew plain or stuffed small chili peppers, lots more. If you like them, uses will occur to you.

Chinese Things.

Under this heading go all kinds of tinned and dried vegetables which we can't buy fresh, as well as the characteristic Chinese seasonings – soy sauce, sesame oil, hoisin sauce. These certainly don't come under any sort of "local" heading, but they come by sea not air, and seem to me acceptable on that basis. And the punch they carry makes a lot of fairly bland material taste better, to me.

Soy sauce. All I want to say here is that you should go for either "made in China" soy sauce, which is cheap, or expensive "shoyu" or "tamari" from a natural-foods shop. Do a comparative tasting to see which you prefer. My family tasting came up with a split verdict.

Sesame oil. Chinese sesame oil is toasted, and very strong in flavour. About ½ tsp., added to a stir-fry at the end, will perfume enough for 4. If you see, as you do sometimes, a recipe that tells you to fry in this, DON'T. The really strong flavour overwhelms everything else, and the oil burns at a low temperature, as well. The recipe probably has not been tried. But, used properly and in small amounts, toasted sesame oil is marvellous.

Hoisin Sauce. This can be found in tins, jars, bottles, packets. Its sweet stickiness and depth of savoury flavour obviously appeal to lots of people, and that includes me. But it does have restricted uses, and isn't universal in the way that soy sauce is, for example.

Dried Black Beans. Small, black, available cheaply in large bags from Chinese groceries. Incredibly good keeper. I think they are a variety of soybean. For use in stir-fries, they are soaked by having boiling water poured over them, drained, and smeared to a paste. A characteristic and delicious flavour. Black bean sauces bought in small jars are not the same at all. Note that these are not the same as the large dried black beans, which are used as a major ingredient, not a seasoning, and originate in the Americas.

Tofu, or Bean curd. This has cut loose from its Chinese/Japanese roots, and is now a vegetarian staple. High protein, low fat, cheap. People complain that its flavour is dull and bland – well, it would be if you ate it alone, but there is no reason not to add lots of flavour with seasonings, sauces, vegetables, when it becomes delicious. I like it a lot. Chinese Buddhists have a whole vegetarian cuisine where various soy products are elaborated to make very convincing imitations of meat – like pork belly or kidneys – but this is probably for the very devoted home cook. I haven't included any recipes in this book. There are other Chinese dried soy products from a Chinese store, like bean curd sticks, which I haven't included, and transparent noodles, which occur in a couple of dishes using bok choy and Chinese leaves.

Chinese tinned vegetables – water chestnuts, bamboo shoots, Szechwan vegetable. Tins of these in the larder are a good thing to have. I am particularly keen on Szechwan vegetable, which is a salt-and-chili pickled swollen stem base from a local brassica. A terrific source of heat and flavour for many dishes. Supermarkets do water chestnuts and bamboo shoots, but you need a Chinese shop or the Net for Szechwan vegetable.

Dried Chinese mushrooms (shiitake). Again, a Chinese shop is the best source for these, in large bags at quite a reasonable price. You need to

41

soak them by pouring over boiling water, and leaving to stand 20-30 mins. The stems are always cut off, as they are tough. Then slice up larger caps before they go into a dish of mixed stir-fried veg., a soup, a rice or noodle dish. . and so on. They taste different to fresh shiitake, which you can now buy in supermarkets, and I think they are much nicer. The soaking water is hardly ever used in Chinese recipes I've seen; since the Chinese are famously not wasteful, there must be a reason, but I don't know it.

Alcohol in Chinese dishes. In China they would use rice wine. None of the rice wine I have bought and tried here has been very nice, but I expect that it's different on home ground. The substitute usually suggested is dry sherry, and this is indeed good. If you keep sherry in stock, then this isn't a problem. If you are doing a lot of Chinese food over the next few weeks, it's worth buying a bottle of cheapish dry sherry. But if neither of these applies, simply use white wine as the alcoholic contributor to sauces.

Miso is Japanese rather than Chinese, but falls conveniently here. It comes in several colours, with flavour increasing as colour darkens. It's a product of a particular type of soy fermentation, and is deeply rich and savoury. It usually comes as a paste in a squeezy bag, and you need no more than a couple of tbsp. to flavour a dish for 4. It usually needs thinning out with a little liquid before stirring into soups, vegetable stews, pie fillings, and so on. You can think of miso as Japanese Marmite, with more texture.

Coconut Milk.

Coconut water is the thin and delicious liquid that sloshes about inside a bought coconut. Coconut milk is NOT this. Coconut milk is extracted from the white meat inside the coconut. If you want to make it yourself, first you break the coconut open, having poured the water out by piercing at least 2 of the 3 eyes at one end. Then, the easiest way to open the coconut is to put it, whole, in a hot oven for 20-30 mins, then hit with a hammer until it breaks into pieces. Then lever out the meat – a screwdriver is good – and peel off the brown skin still sticking to it. Chop this finely, and pour over an equal volume of boiling water. Stir, sieve over a bowl and you have the "first" coconut milk, which is rich and will give coconut cream, which floats to the top on standing. You then repeat the extraction with boiling water to give "second" milk, most often used in long-cooked dishes. Actually, this is not the easiest way; the easiest way is to get someone else to do it. Domestically, this means someone who enjoys using tools. Commercially, you can see why most coconut milk used in the UK is bought ready-prepared. In coconut-growing countries, there are all sorts of handy gadgets to make meat extraction easier, and the coconuts are fresher and easier to break open. But we aren't there.

Tins of coconut milk are now in every supermarket. If you want a thicker, creamier liquid, blocks of "coconut cream" comes in 250g packets; with these you grate as much as you need, and just cover with boiling water. The gratings dissolve almost instantly. This is the liquid you need for the cucumber/coconut salad on p. 154. With these two products on hand, you're equipped for anything using liquid coconut. There are more, and doubtless even more will be marketed soon.

Desiccated coconut is a product which has been around for many years, and is mostly used in cakes and sweetmeats, in England. It can also be toasted and go into the spice mixture for curries; I find it's worth having some in stock just for this.

Curry Powder.

You can buy curry powder, but please don't. Almost any mixture you make up will smell swooningly delicious as it comes out of the grinder, and it can vary with your mood and your dish. This really is one of the details which makes the difference between excellence and run-of-the mill, and it's easy to do. You need an electric coffee grinder; I used to have one with two heads, one for coffee and one for spices. But if you only have one, use it for spices and buy ground coffee; the difference is greater.

Indian curries use different spice mixtures for different sorts of curry, always freshly made. They may be home-made or bought, but fresh blends for each kind of curry are really necessary if you are cooking Indian. However, the mixed spicy flavour has also been taken over in other countries; even French food has dishes lightly flavoured with curry powder. For this sort of generalised blend, toast lightly **1 tbsp. each of coriander seeds and cumin seeds**. Grind these with ½ **tsp.**

fenugreek seeds, 2-cm cinnamon stick, and **the seeds from 2 brown cardamom pods**. Mix in **1 tsp turmeric** and **½ tsp cayenne pepper**, and keep the mixture in a sealed jar in the fridge.

If you really haven't time on a particular occasion, use 1 tsp. garam masala with 1 tsp turmeric and ½ tsp cayenne.

Dried Mushrooms.

The king of these is the dried porcini, or cepe, which reliably adds deliciousness and savouriness and umami flavour to anything it's added to. There are only two problems; one is the cost, which is always high, and the other is restraining yourself from adding dried porcini to everything. Cost does check the second tendency to some extent! You want to buy packets as large as you can afford, which work out a lot cheaper per unit weight, and also means that you can see recognisable slices of mushroom in the packet. You don't need many for a dish; I'd suspect any recipe that used more than 30g. for 4-6 people.

Half-an-hour before you want to use the mushrooms, put them in a bowl and pour over boiling water to cover. Let it cool. Then lift out the pieces and cut up if they are large. KEEP THE SOAKING WATER, as a lot of the flavour is in here. Generally, this water is added to the dish you're making. If for some strange reason it isn't, the soaking water can go into a stock or indeed be a stock on its own.

Fresh porcini, or cepes, or Boletus edulis, are found throughout Europe including the British Isles. They are most valued in France, Italy, and Poland, where early-morning forays to hunt mushrooms are a regular part of country life. Most English porcini, reputedly penny-bun mushrooms, are left to rot, or kicked apart by people who do this to all fungi. I haven't gathered them myself, as I haven't enough confidence in identification.

Morels are another European mushroom which is rich and savoury and expensive dried. I believe these are found as far away as North India, where they are dried and exported to the US. I originally bought some in Switzerland, where they are a bargain in Swiss terms. I don't find them as flexible in use as porcini, but they are remarkably good.

44

Sometimes you find packets of mixed dried wild mushrooms, nowhere near as expensive as porcini or morels. They aren't as good, either, but still well worth having and using.

Dried Chinese mushrooms are discussed under Chinese Things.

Dried Peas, Beans, and Lentils.

An indispensable part of a vegetarian diet. They come in many varieties; when I was running cookery classes, I collected 20 different sorts, and there are more. Lentils don't need soaking, so are more convenient if you need something in a hurry. But with a stock of dried chickpeas, dried haricots or cannellini, dried red beans, dried split peas, channa dal, masoor dhal, and moong dhal in the larder, you can feel confident that you have a store of future meals in reserve. And there are so many ways to use them – Indian, Mexican, Caribbean, Italian, French, Middle Eastern, East European; your bean dishes can take all these ethnic flavours and taste completely different from each other. Regions have one or two favourite pulses, like chick peas in the Middle East and North Africa, and red beans in the Caribbean.

The only English pulse available at the moment is dried peas, whole or split, and these get used in soup or mushy peas. A few years back, there was a brief vogue for English "field beans", which are small dried broad beans, and very ancient in this country. Alas, they didn't taste very nice, and have now disappeared again.

I cover soaking, and quick-soaking, in Basics. When you're in a hurry, though, it almost has to be tins. They have their slight drawbacks, because you can't flavour the liquid while they are cooking, and the liquid in the tin is not usable. Always rinse dried tinned beans well. Tinned lentils should be good, but I haven't found a variety I like, and lentils don't take long to cook – orange lentils, or dhal masoor, cook in 15-20 mins. Tins are more expensive, but not much more.

Rather than try to cover all the varieties, I will just note my favourites.

Chick peas. Dried or tinned. For hummus, vegetable stews, patties, soups. Respond well to spices. Dried split chick peas are channa dhal, one of the commonest varieties used for an Indian dhal. Channa dhal looks remarkably like English yellow split peas, but don't be misled; the split peas take about twice as long to cook, 1 hr. instead of 20-30 mins for channa dhal. This is a good place to put my basic recipe for **Channa Dhal.** Cover **250g channa dhal** with cold water, after picking over for small stones and washing. Bring to the boil, adding **a slice of lemon, 2 whole small dried chilis**, and **1 tsp. turmeric**. When boiling, turn down the heat, and simmer until the dhal is soft and breaks up when stirred. There should be just enough water to give a puree, but it can be thick or thin or in-between. **Salt** to taste. When ready to eat, heat **2 tbsp. oil** in a frying pan, add **1 tsp. cumin seeds** and 1 tsp. mustard seeds. When the mustard seeds are popping well, tip the whole contents of the pan into the dhal, with a great aromatic sizzle. Stir quickly and eat as soon as reasonably possible. If you can see the chilis and the lemon, take them out. If not, warn people not to eat them. You can also use masoor dhal, or orange lentils, or split moong beans.

Red Beans. Dried or tinned. For chili sin carne (or con carne, if not vege.) Caribbean rice and peas. Curried whole. Salads.

White beans, which can be cannelloni or haricots. Dried or tinned. French and Italian, in salads, stews, soups.

French Flageolet beans. Dried or tinned; in this case they are easier to find in the tinned version. I think these have the best flavour of any of the dried beans, so I tend to keep the other flavours I'm using mild to get the benefit of the flageolets. Soup, salad, vegetable dish, with mushrooms, or tomatoes.

Butter Beans. A very large and meaty sort of dried beans. They are used in Spain, and you find very expensive jars of "judias". Greek "gigantes" are these beans, and used as a meze salad with tomato dressing. Dishes using butter beans won't taste the same if anything else is used instead.

Whole Lentils. To my mind, nothing beats French lentilles du Puy, which are so prized in France they have an appellation to specify the product and how it's grown. They can also come from Canada, which are very good but not quite the same. And there are other posh versions of lentils, like "Beluga" and Italian Castelluccio and Pardina. Good, but I'll stick with the Puy lentils.

Split Lentils. Masoor dhal. Moong dhal. Tarka dhal. Urd dhal. All Indian, and split pulses. Some are not strictly lentils, like moongs. They all make good dhals, with many possible variations.

Peanuts. Strictly speaking they are a dried legume, and raw peanuts can be cooked, made into soup, ground for hummus-like purees and dips, and used like any other pulse. Normally they are classified with nuts, and toasted, salted, eaten as a snack or used in salads.

I could write a whole book on cooking with dried pulses, but this isn't it.

Eggs

All the recipes in this book using eggs are for large organic hen's eggs. As I write, they cost 30-35p each. Why would you use anything else?

The only other thing to say about eggs is that fresher is better. Soft-boiled eggs, poached eggs need to be fresh for best effect. A stale egg, poached, will have drifting clouds of white which don't cling to the yolk. When you fry a fresh egg, the white stays compact and doesn't spread all over the pan. The only occasion where less than very fresh eggs is fine is hard-boiled; very fresh hard-boiled eggs are difficult to peel cleanly. But they taste better. If you can get fresh eggs from a backyard or hobby producer, a day-old egg of this type will taste better than a week-old certified organic egg. But this choice doesn't often come along.

French Goodies.

By this I mean tins or jars you can buy in French supermarkets when on holiday and carry home to enliven future meals. Tins of salsify. Tins of celery. I've seen tins of cardoons, but only in the Alpine regions. Local, unusual cheeses. Dried lentilles du Puy. Dried cepes and other mushrooms. Jars of baby gherkins, or cornichons. Unusual herbs and spices, fresh or dried. Fresh vegetables and fruits from markets.—depending on when you are there, it may be wood strawberries, mirabelle plums, beautiful greengages, medlars. Things have got much better in the UK over the past twenty years; for example, I no longer need to buy a year's worth of Dijon mustard in France, because I can buy it locally. With your last few euros, buy some packets of sea salt, which are incredibly cheap by English standards and keep indefinitely. A discriminating poke round market and supermarket will find lots of things worth buying. I'm sure the same is true of Italy and Spain and Portugal, but you tend to fly there and thus can't carry a lot home.

Garlic.

I cover this with onions, in the all-year-round section. Can't do without it.

Ginger.

Fresh ginger is wonderful. The shape. The scent when you cut a slice. The effect it has in Indian, Chinese, Thai dishes. I hope it comes by sea rather than air, but in this case I don't really care. You don't need very much at a time, so buy as small a piece as possible. It will keep a couple of weeks in the fridge, but it does start to dry up and lose its juices. It's always peeled and chopped finely or pounded, as most people don't like to taste chunks in their food. The Very Lazy ginger is a useful standby, as are various frozen, chopped versions. Both of these save waste, but don't taste quite as good.

Dried ginger is something I hardly ever use. Some cakes need it; some curries use it, in small amounts. It's traditional English to use it with melon; some people like it. But ginger powder doesn't have the freshness or the scent; you can't use it instead of fresh ginger. Ginger also comes preserved in heavy sugar syrup, or crystallised, or even chocolate covered. Nice occasional sweet treats if you like ginger.

Herbs.

What I mean by herbs is aromatic and strong-tasting green leaves, often used to finish a dish. There are some recipes using quantities of a particular herb, but mostly they are used in fairly small quantities. Fresher is always better, and these are ideal things to grow in pots on windowsill or balcony or by the back door if you don't have a garden.

48

You will use more if they are easily available. I do buy little supermarket packets sometimes, especially in winter, but try as I might to use them up I often end up with half a packet gone brown and smelly. Some of the growing herbs sold by supermarkets can be repotted and grown on; some come in strange little pots to stop you doing this, and can't even be watered properly. Experiment to find out which is which.

I have found, though, that the herbs which grow well and easily for me are not the ones I most want. I used to have lovage, an enormous plant 2m tall and broad with it. Lovage is a very strong herb, tasting like a cross between celery and Marmite, and you only want a few leaflets at a time. So I have given this up. I could use lots of basil and tarragon, but they only work in the garden in good summers, and tarragon seems to die off every winter in the open garden. I keep trying with these because I love the flavour so much.

There are lots of books about cooking with herbs, and these always seem to me to be trying too hard. Herbs make marvellous auxiliary flavours, but there are very few cases where a herb is the main flavour in a dish, and the herb being used can't be changed. Some recipes for herb-heavy dishes are below, but in general the use of herbs is for experiment and the inspiration of the moment.

Parsley. Chopped parsley can go with almost anything, and you can use a lot. Some people have success growing it, and have rows of healthy parsley; I haven't had much luck. But it's probably the easiest herb to buy. There are several dishes which use parsley in large quantities, almost as a vegetable. I think the most useful of these is **Tabbouleh**, which should be a parsley salad with some burghul in it, rather than a grain salad with a bit of parsley. Start with **250g parsley**, and chop finely with the **leaves from 4-6 sprigs mint**. A food processor is ideal for this. Soak **100g burghul** (also called bulgur wheat) in water to cover for about 30 mins. Drain, and squeeze out as much water as you can, the spread out on a clean teatowel for at least 10 mins. Chop **4-6 trimmed spring onions**, and mix into the dried burghul. **Salt and pepper. 4 tbsp. extra-virgin olive oil, juice of 2 lemons.** The parsley and mint. Mix well, and taste for salt, pepper, lemon. I tend to eat this with a spoon, though in its home, it's served with lettuce leaves for scooping. A dish of black olives is almost

49

essential next to the tabbouleh. I've used couscous instead of the burghul, but the texture isn't as good.

A simple potato/onion soup with a large bunch of parsley, chopped, added is delicious and unexpected.

Fresh green coriander. The garnish of choice for dishes from tropical countries round the world – Chinese, Indian, Mexican, Caribbean. It's almost always chopped and sprinkled over a dish at the last minute. Almost any salsa will benefit from a sprinkle – I was amazed when I put some in a pineapple salsa how well the flavours go. Fresh coriander has only become really available here over the past 20 years, and more and more people have taken to it. Previous to this, when it was rare, it was often disliked – the phrase was "smells of bedbugs". I always wondered how these people knew what bedbugs smell like. It's always worth buying fresh coriander from an Indian shop if possible, as it's so much cheaper there. If you have more than you need, make the rest into a **Green Coriander Chutney.** This doesn't keep for more than a couple of days, but it's so more-ish that it will almost certainly be eaten. Put the **leaves from a large bunch of coriander and a small bunch of mint** into the food processor. **Add 1-2 fresh chilis, coarsely chopped, ½ small onion, coarsely chopped, and 1 tsp. salt.** Whizz till all is finely chopped, then add the **juice of 1-2 lemons or limes** to taste. You can use all coriander, but the version with some mint is preferable. You can also mix the chopped herbs, etc, into yoghurt, for a milder-tasting chutney.

Basil. Probably the most fashionable herb at the moment. It's a pity that home-grown doesn't start till July and is practically over by October, because I'd like to use it year-round. Goes with tomatoes in almost every context. Also essential for **Pesto,** for which you need quite a lot. Pesto means pounded, and it should therefore be made in a mortar. I don't; a food processor does very well, and is quicker and easier. Try making it by pounding as well as processor if you want to see whether the difference is worth it to you. Start with **100g basil leaves, 2 cloves garlic, roughly cut up, 25g pine nuts, 1 tsp. salt, and 100 ml. extra-virgin olive oil, preferably Italian.** Whizz all these. Add **60g grated Parmesan,** and whizz again. This can now be frozen. Some Italians like to replace some of the Parmesan with pecorino Romano; this is good, but I wouldn't go hunting for the pecorino just for this.

50

Mint. This is the quintessential English herb, and the scent of mint boiling with new potatoes is a sure sign of summer. Others like it too; mint tea in Morocco, in Indian food. It's only the French who are stroppy and sneer at English mint sauce. There are many many varieties of mint; I like apple mint, and grow only this. In a pot. Mints have a habit of running underground, popping up some distance away, and taking over the patch, so confining them is a good idea.

Chives The most delicate of the onion tastes, in long, thin leaves. Only add them at the end of cooking, as otherwise the flavour is wasted. You can eat the flowers, too.

Thyme Comes as ordinary thyme and lemon thyme, from a cook's point of view. Gardeners will know of many other varieties. Woody stems, tiny leaves, can take long cooking. So thyme goes into stocks, soups, long-cooked stews, as well as being used as leaves stripped from the stem and sprinkled at the last moment. Thyme flowers, when around, are also good as last-moment additions.

Bay Leaves. These are unusual as a herb, as they normally come dried, and traditionally they always go in at an early stage of cooking in liquid. They are not eaten, just used for the flavour they give. If you have some, break one and sniff. If you can't smell anything, throw them away. A fresh, or recently dried, bay leaf, has a wonderful smell, unlike anything else, and it can transfer this to other foods. If you skewer vegetables for barbecueing, put a bay leaf between some of the vegetable pieces. You will be amazed how much flavour is transferred. Likewise in milk puddings.

Tarragon Tarragon is predominantly a French herb, and finds its natural home in rich buttery sauces. I wouldn't like to be without it, but I don't use a lot.

Oregano and Marjoram Supposedly, these are varieties of the same plant, but the flavours are quite different. Marjoram is sweet and gentle. Oregano is much stronger in taste, grows in baking Mediterranean heat, and is one of the few herbs that dries well. Oregano is predominantly the pizza herb, but will add oomph and pizzazz to all sorts of Mediterranean stews.

Rosemary Tough by nature, tough in texture. I have a bush in the garden, and it's very pretty, especially in flower. It's very easy to over-use it. If you put in a branch in a stew, then most of the needles will fall off, and get stuck in people's teeth. If you're going to eat the needle-like leaves, they really should be chopped. It's a herb that really goes with roast food – potatoes, onions, squash – where the flavour is absorbed by the roasting fat and passed to the food.

Dill and Fennel Both have a slightly aniseed-y flavour, and I tend to use them interchangeably. Dill adds a Scandinavian flavour to most things; fennel, for some reason, less so. You shouldn't grow them both in the garden, I am told, as they will cross to give progeny not as good as either parent. So I have fennel in the garden, repeating every year, and dill in pots in the porch.

Chervil A real little darling of a lacy-leaved herb, which must be grown at home. It's very perishable, wilting almost as soon as picked, but really nice for sauces, garnishes, and general finishing. Do try it.

Lemon Balm Once you grow this, you have it for good, as it will pop up all over the place. It has a lovely scent, rather like lemon soap, which is just like the scent of lemon grass. I see no reason why this vigorous native leaf shouldn't be substituted for lemon grass in Thai dishes.

Bouquet Garni What this should be is parsley stems, sprigs of thyme, and a bay leaf all tied together with string, often in a little cheesecloth bag, for flavouring stocks and cooking liquids and stews. I really can't be bothered; I just drop the herbs in whatever-it-is, and mostly fish them out before serving. Even if I don't, people know enough not to eat bay leaves.

Dried Herbs The best dried herb is oregano, and it's worth having a small quantity in winter dishes. Dried Herbes de Provence fill the same role, with a bit more complication of flavour (I like the versions with a little lavender in) Bay, as I've remarked, always comes dried. Apart from these, I think that if you haven't got the fresh herb, you are better missing it out than using the dried version.

Horseradish

Probably the strongest native British flavour, and scandalously underused. It grows as a weed on roadsides, even by motorways; it's so vigorous that it will threaten to take over your garden unless confined. Mine pushes up through paving next to its bed. When did you last see any for sale? So grow it, in a tub if that's all you can use, and use it as a condiment with stews, baked dishes covered with mash, dumplings, pastry, and other dishes that will occur to you once you get almost addicted to this pungent, almost hot root. Don't make the mistake of putting it into things – heat destroys the pungency. You can serve it as a simple grated heap of white shreds, or make horseradish sauce by adding the grated root to whipped cream, to taste. Salt, too. I've tried it in crème fraiche, where it's also very good. The English Provender Co. do a jar of grated horseradish, which is the next best thing to the real item. But horseradish sauces in jars are just a token, a symbol of the real thing. Don't bother with them.

Nuts and Seeds

Almonds, Brazil nuts, cashews, chestnuts, hazelnuts, macadamias, pecans, pistachios, walnuts. They are all good, and almost always interchangeable to give different effects. Except chestnuts. Chestnuts cover the whole spectrum of dishes from soup to dessert (chestnut soup, liberated stuffing, mash, chestnut chocolate log are all among my regulars) and many of these exploit their ability to give a rich mealy puree, which other nuts largely don't. Otherwise, nuts can be used as they are, roasted (carefully), chopped, ground. I use them a lot. You can get organic and fairtrade nuts for the imported varieties, and walnuts, hazelnuts, chestnuts all grow in this country. In Sheffield the chestnuts which can be picked up in autumn seldom grow very large, so I'd hate to be peeling them, but for roast chestnuts they are fine. If you have a walnut tree, or know a local one where you can get permission, you can pick green walnuts in June/July and make your own pickled walnuts. A truly original and English traditional condiment. You used to be able to get "wet" walnuts, fresh, undried, and nicer than the standard kiln-dried nuts-in-shell, which mostly come from China. What a strange world we live in, where our local crop is ignored in favour of a product from the other side of the world. Wet walnuts have a fairly short season, usually October; ask for them, create a demand. We are seeing more fresh hazelnuts/filberts in autumn, with the little green ruff surrounding the nut In France, in August, you can buy green almonds, where the outer husk has not yet dried and hardened. Worth looking for in the South of England.

Peanuts are not really a nut, but taste- and use-wise they fit into the nut category. Especially roast salted peanuts, where a handful can really improve a salad. Peanut butter is the inspiration for other nut butters, made from almonds, cashews, hazelnuts, ground very fine so they liberate their own oil which binds them together.

Seeds I always have in stock are sunflower, pumpkin, sesame. They're good as they are – sunflower seeds are usually husked when bought– but almost always nicer toasted. I use an enamel plate under the grill, for moderate quantities. The smell helps you keep track of the stage they're at, and avoid burning them.

Nuts and seeds are all chock-full of various trace nutrients, though not the same ones. Brazil nuts are said to have lots of selenium; sunflower seeds have a lot of the B-vitamin, pantothenic acid, and so on. If you use a varied selection, and use them often, this can only be a good thing.

Tahina, ground-up sesame seeds, fits well here. From being rare, it's now easily available. You need it for home-made hummus, for tahina salad, for all sorts of Eastern-Mediterranean vegetable purees for the meze, or starter, table. I always have some. If left to stand, it settles out to become a thick paste at the bottom and oil on top, and these need dedicated stirring to remix. Try keeping the jar upside-down, on a plate to catch any leakage, as this gives a good start on the remixing process. You can also buy Chinese sesame paste, made from toasted seeds, which is good but has many fewer uses than the standard.

Home-Made Hummus with Tahina. Drain and rinse the **chick peas from 1 tin**. Put in the food processor with **2-3 tbsp. water**, and whizz for quite a long time, scraping down at least once. (If you are devoted to smoothness, the chickpeas should be skinned. A long job. I don't do it). Add **3-4 chopped cloves garlic, about ¼ jar tahina, ½ tsp. salt.** Whizz briefly, then add the **juice of 3-4 lemons.** I like my hummus really lemony. Keep tasting. If the mix is too thick when you've added

54

enough lemon juice, thin down with more water. Commercial versions – which are not bad at all – use less tahina, and oil. Mine has no oil in it.

Oils and Butter

These as supporting ingredients help food to taste good, and a minimum amount is necessary for health. At the same time, it's easy to eat too much of them, as they have twice the calories of protein and carbohydrate. Latest nutritional theory says that we have been mistaken for the last thirty years in thinking that saturated fats (butter) are much worse for you than unsaturated fats (all oils except coconut). What is bad for you is processed carbohydrate, as in fast food, and eating too much altogether. I find this reassuring, as I have gone on using butter to cook with all these years, in spite of the clucks of friends, and now find I was right all along.

<u>Butter</u> There really is nothing like it for flavour and improving the simplest of vegetable preparations. What sort you use – salted, unsalted, butter from sweet cream (English) or matured cream (French, Danish, Continental generally), butter from grass-fed cows (New Zealand) – is up to you. I tend to use a variety, partly depending on what's on offer when I'm buying, and partly butters made on a smaller scale when I see them. I find goat's cheese butter has too strong a flavour for general use, but it has its virtues from time to time. Unsalted butter used in a savoury dish, or savoury pastry, often needs a little more salt in the mix to bring out the flavours, but I think it's nicer as a spread. The posh French butters with sea-salt crystals added seem to me to go too far, yet I'm very fond of salty Welsh butter with bread. Choice of butter is another of the decisions you make which has an almost subliminal effect on the food you make, but makes your cooking different from your neighbour's. You might not want to taste butter neat, in very small pieces, but that's the way to find out what you like.

<u>Ghee</u> is Indian clarified butter. You don't ever HAVE to use it; most Indians have gone over to cheaper oils for their cooking. In the process of making ghee, salt and the protein component are removed from the butter, which means it is a purer and less tasty fat. It can be heated to higher temperatures without burning, and it keeps, out of a

fridge, for a long time. So there are tradeoffs. To make ghee, as I do it, you need at least 2 packets (total 500g) of cheap butter. Heat gently until it melts, then go on cooking over a low heat. There will be bubbles on top, and a sedimentary layer of solids at the bottom. Cook till the solids look slightly golden. Skim off the bubble layer; keep it. Turn off the heat and let the hot mixture settle, then pour off the top layer of ghee, leaving sediment and liquid behind. Let the ghee solidify, and keep. Put the bubbles with the sedimentary layer, and use this within a few days. I like vegetables dressed with this salty, tasty, not-very-fatty mixture, and sometimes it goes into bread. You can buy ghee, expensively, in tins in most supermarkets.

Olive Oil. I wouldn't like you to think that I use only butter; I use olive oil at least as often. Most of all for salads, but also roasting, frying, with hot vegetables, and much more. Availability of different sorts of olive oil has changed enormously, and is still changing. When extra-virgin olive oil first appeared – and it's no more than 30 years ago – there were many many different kinds, small brands as well as large, and there was a hefty premium over straight "olive oil". Now it seems that the moderately-priced market is the preserve of big brands, cheap "extra-virgin" is cheaper than straight "olive oil", and small brands have priced themselves out of my reach. So now I keep a cheap extra-virgin for cooking and a moderate-price extra-virgin for using straight. I like the taste of Cretan oil, and of the sort of Italian oil that comes in bottles with clip-on caps. I tend to alternate between these and any promising newcomers. Again, tasting 2 or 3 from a teaspoon is the way to decide what you like.

Sunflower Oil. For many kinds of cooking you need a neutral-tasting oil which doesn't burn easily. Chinese food needs this, but so do lots of other things. I wouldn't, for example, fry eggs in anything else. Sunflower is the one I've used for years. I'm thinking of changing to rapeseed oil, which is more local and has the right properties, but it's still a bit expensive for everyday use. This will change.

Walnut Oil, Hazelnut Oil. Beautiful tasty oils for special uses, and not really expensive any more. It would be wasteful to cook with these, but in salads with nuts, or sauces, these oils really add to the effect. They are not long-keeping, even unopened, and once they are opened they must be kept in the fridge. Sniff before you use, even so; the smell of turned walnut oil is horrid, and you wouldn't want to use it for anything.

<u>Toasted Sesame Oil</u> See "Chinese Things" above.

<u>Cheap Mixed Oils, Margarine, Non-Dairy Spreads.</u> DON'T use them. You want these basics of your kitchen to be identifiable, and not coming with a long list of ingredients. A "Light Olive" spread, for example, has at least 16 ingredients, some of which you wouldn't recognise as related to food if you met them alone. If butter and good oil have too many calories for you, miss them out altogether rather than using chemicalised substitutes.

Pasta

Pasta is becoming a new staple, pushing out potatoes and bread. It's so flexible, so variable, cheap, non-seasonal, long-keeping . . . and goes with almost everything. I think, though, that all the shapes pasta comes in are too many for regular use. I don't, myself, find spaghetti very easy to eat, and I can't respond to the subtle differences Italians find between the shapes. I just use fusilli for almost everything. And this way you don't get a little of several different sorts left at the bottom of a packet, all needing different cooking times. I do find that pasta made with bronze dies may be a bit more expensive than the standard, but it's also nicer to eat and holds the sauce better. See what you think.

Another sort I like, and often have in stock, is orecchiete, little hard-wheat ears from Southern Italy, quite expensive, but distinctive in its cooked texture and feel in the mouth. Not one for clinging sauces, but as a complement to, e.g, sprouting broccoli, with oil and strong tastes of chili and garlic. It's nice to have orzo, the pasta which looks like grains of rice. And small soup pasta, often alphabet shaped. You see how easy it is to get a cupboard full of different types of pasta.

I'm not a devotee of wholemeal pasta. It seems to me that people use it for reasons other than its taste, like the extra fibre. Surely if you are eating a lot of vegetables and fruit, you don't need more fibre? It's different if you actually prefer the taste.

As well as the multitudinous forms of Italian hard-wheat pasta, there are all the Oriental forms. Egg (wheat) noodles, rice noodles, "transparent" noodles; they are all good and easy and liked by almost everyone. I don't see how you can go wrong.

Bottled Sauces, Ketchups, Condiments.

The trinity I wouldn't be without is tomato ketchup, HP sauce, and Tabasco. I think that if HP sauce were recently launched on a world which didn't know it, it would be an enormous hit, with the combination of sweet from sugar and molasses, sour from vinegar and tamarind, and the spicy notes. Other brown sauces just aren't the same.

Lea and Perrins' Worcester sauce is another that I rely on, but not for vegetarians. The vegetarian version isn't bad at all, though missing a little piquancy.. If substituting, I use mushroom ketchup, which nearly vanished at one time, but has made a limited comeback. It doesn't, and isn't meant to, taste like Worcester sauce, but the dark mushroom/soy flavour is very good in itself.

Apart from these, there is a dizzying range of bottled sauces in every supermarket, coming and going. Marinades, dressings, sauces; you could probably buy a different one every month, and with the rate of introductions, never have to repeat yourself in your lifetime. Most of them are OK but unnecessary, and there aren't many you'd try to buy again. A sweet chili sauce is a good thing to have, but preferred brands change rapidly.

Mustard is such an English dressing/relish/tracklement. (I like the word tracklement, meaning the strong-tasting things that go with a main course. Mustard and horseradish are the main ones, but mint sauce counts; so does apple sauce.) I almost always use Dijon mustard, both on the side of the plate and to go into creamy sauces, and I could cope with just this if necessary. Seedy mustards are a nice change of pace, and there are some good English ones (and some not-so-good; taste and decide what you like. I like English Tracklements' black mustard) English powdered mustard, made up with a little water 10 mins before eating, is clean and strong and excellent and wasteful, because there is always some left and it's nowhere near as good the second day. I don't think the jars of English mustard have the proper kick. Prepared mustard, like horseradish, loses its bite and even its identity when heated for a long time. In fact, jars of made-up mustard, whether Dijon or other, lose punch with time even when kept in the fridge. I find that after 2-3 weeks, with a small jar, I need to use nearly twice as much to get the same effect. So buy small jars.

Pomegranate molasses doesn't quite fit in here, but doesn't fit anywhere else either. Sweet-sour and thick, if you have it you will find savoury and sweet uses for it. In the same Middle-Eastern vein, there are jars of pickled lemons. I love these, and add them to salads and stews as a finishing touch. Books assure you they are easy to make; I haven't been successful with any of their formulae. On the other hand, the olive stall on French markets sells them loose, and these are nicer than the jars.

Rice.

Checking stocks, I have Patna rice, Basmati rice, brown rice, risotto rice, pudding rice, rice flour, wild rice, and a wild rice/brown rice mix. I don't have jasmine rice, glutinous rice, Camargue red rice, Spanish rice for paella. The ones I have are all staples, so that I buy some more just before I run out. I have this many because I do quite a lot of Indian food, Chinese food, Italian risotti, and American/modern British with the wild rice. You need to have the right kind of rice for the nationality you're cooking. So you may want jasmine rice for Thai food as part of your stores, but not wild rice.

I have recently found the best way to cook Basmati rice, so that you can appreciate its special virtues and scent. Start with a **mug of Basmati**, not quite full. Wash and drain it, then put in a basin with a **mugful of cold water**, using the same mug (A mug for 2 people is about 200g, but do this by volume) Soak the rice for 30 mins, then drain through a sieve, KEEPING THE SOAKING WATER. Heat **20g butter** in a pan with a tight lid, tip in the rice, and shake now and then for 2-3 mins. Add the soaking water and ½ **tsp. salt**. Bring to a boil, cover, and cook on very low heat for about 15 mins. There will be no visible water. Put a clean folded teatowel between pan and lid, turn off the heat, and let it sit 10 mins. The nicest plain rice ever.

Plain boiled rice is faster and simpler. Large pan of boiling water, with salt. Pour in the long-grain rice with the pan on high heat, to return to the boil as quickly as possible. Boil, uncovered and quite hard, for 11-12 mins. Pour the lot through a colander. Put a little cold water into the pan (from the tap), swirl round to dislodge any grains that have stuck, and pour through the draining rice. Shake, put in serving dish. Some people claim this is difficult, but it really isn't.

Pepper

The most essential spice, which everyone has, is pepper. It comes as black peppercorns, white peppercorns (which are de-husked black peppercorns), green peppercorns (fresh black peppercorns), dried or preserved in brine, and also in ready-ground versions to be avoided. If you don't already have a pepper mill, get one as soon as possible; there is little that's so cheap which will make such a consistent difference to the niceness of your food. And use it with black peppercorns if you only have one.

I've realised, while writing this book, that I often use black peppercorns as a true spice, rather than a grind as part of "salt-n-pepper". Quite often, I will grind ½-1 tsp peppercorns (sometimes more) in the spice grinder as part of the spicing for a dish. Terrific! And also I have started to be careful about the automatic addition of fresh-ground pepper; sometimes it just isn't appropriate. Dishes with chilis in often don't need any more pepper, for example. I suppose I'm saying that pepper deserves attention rather than the automatic response.

People recommend using freshly-ground white pepper for sauces to avoid spoiling the colour with little black flecks. Well, I prefer my sauces with black flecks and pepper taste, and I don't think the appearance is spoiled. My husband used to like freshly ground white pepper with boiled eggs, and that's essentially all it's used for in my house.

Spices

I've already talked about peppercorns, ginger, and various forms of chili. The rest can be divided into 3 categories:

<u>European cooking:</u>   Essential: nutmeg

Nice to have: mace, juniper berries, caraway, 5-peppercorn mix, ground cinnamon, black and/or white poppy seeds

<u>Indian Cooking:</u>   Essential: cumin, coriander, ground turmeric, black mustard seed, cinnamon sticks, cloves, green cardamoms, garam masala

Nice to have: hing (asafoetida), black cumin, fennel seeds, tamarind paste or block, brown cardamoms, black poppy seeds, anardana (dried pomegranate seeds), ajowan, kalonji (onion seeds), nigella, amchoor

<u>Other Tropical, especially Chinese.</u>

Nice to have: star anise, anise seeds, Szechwan pepper, annatto, allspice, sumac

This is, obviously, my choices and my ratings; other people might well think differently However, I think the kit of 9 spices I've called "essential" isn't difficult to assemble, and will see you through most spice-using recipes. I always buy whole spices, and strongly recommend that you do the same. They are so much better when freshly ground, more aromatic, more flavourful. I use the coffee-grinding head of a blender for spices. I think fresh-grinding makes more difference to spices than to coffee.

Bought garam masala is always a powder. I think making your own, once a month or so if you do a lot of Indian food, is well worth the effort, which really isn't much. Mix in a coffee grinder **1 tbsp. green cardamom seeds, 1 tsp each of whole cloves, black peppercorns, black cumin seeds, 5-cm cinnamon stick, and a large-ish piece of mace**. Grind finely. Grate in **1/3 of a whole nutmeg**, and mix in. Store in a tightly closed jar, ideally in the fridge.

Vinegar

The minimum, to my mind, is good red wine vinegar. It should not be too cheap. Modern versions often have the name of the grape variety used; in France, the phrase "futs de chene", or oak barrels in which the vinegar is matured, will appear somewhere on the label. It can go in dishes of any nationality without making them taste "French".

Next is probably cider vinegar, English and organic. To me it does add a local flavour, which you may or may not want, but it is a superior vinegar. And better for pickles than wine vinegar.

Sherry vinegar adds a rich and distinctive flavour to salads, and also when you deglaze a pan with a little. I like to have it, but a bottle lasts a year or so.

White wine vinegar is essential for the sort of sauce where shallots and (usually) tarragon are boiled down with the vinegar, and the strained essence used to flavour Bearnaise sauce and white butter sauce. Everywhere else red wine vinegar does at least as well.

Balsamic vinegar has been very fashionable, and is now declining somewhat in popularity. There was a stage when a supermarket shelf would have 20-30 different sorts of balsamic, and barely 1 of other sorts. If balsamic vinegar is traditionally made, it should be very expensive indeed. Who knows what compromises have been made to produce the many versions, affordable to very cheap, which are so easy to buy? If I liked it, this probably wouldn't worry me, but it's a condiment I'm simply not keen on. I find it too sweet, and too insistent in flavour, for almost everything I've tried. You probably don't agree with me.

Malt vinegar is my least favourite ingredient. I think its insistent acidity spoils almost everything it's used for. Even in malt vinegar, though, there are gradations, from a vinegar which is actually made from the malt used for beer, to something which is almost entirely a chemical and factory product. Malt vinegar is necessary for many characteristically English tastes – chip-shop chips, pickled onions, pickled red cabbage – and if you want these, try to get a good naturally-brewed malt vinegar.

In my recipe for bortsch, in the beetroot chapter, I have mentioned alegar, which is home-made beer which has gone sour. This is delightful stuff, full of flavour and not very acid. It is, however, a rare product, and cannot be bought.

The Family Tasting.

Where there are several versions of an ingredient, like soy sauce, butter, Worcester-sauce substitutes, it's very interesting to get the family to taste various versions side-by-side and decide which they prefer. You have to arrange for the tasting to be blind, with, e.g different saucers or cups for each sample. And afterwards, you have to stick to the collective verdict! My family really enjoyed these sessions, and they felt their tastes were respected and they were involved in making the decision.

Basics

Stock

Whenever I refer to stock, I mean vegetarian stock – how could I not? So I haven't said vegetarian stock every time; I assume that you know what I mean, which is the flavoured liquid from the boiling of vegetables and trimmings. I always leave stock unsalted till the point of use, as it gives more flexibility.

Vegetable stock is different from meat or poultry stocks in 2 main ways:

Its flavour is not strengthened by boiling down, but it is changed, and not for the better. The way to get a more tasty vegetable stock is to use more vegetables.

Vegetable stock doesn't jelly when cold, and this is potentially a weak point. It means it doesn't have the mouth-filling, sticky qualities of a meat stock when hot, and I think these are desirable. The answer to this textural problem – and it is texture, not taste, we are talking here – is seaweed. Agar-agar adds jellying texture without extra flavours. Laverbread and nori add different flavours. Laverbread is Welsh and hence preferable in my terms of local produce. Nori is (but needn't be) imported, but as a light dry product it can be shipped rather than flown.

Three ways of making vegetable stock, ranging from the simple and mild to the stronger-flavoured and more time-consuming. The ingredients are the same in every case – onion, carrot, celery, leek, garlic, herbs. Plus any vegetables or trimmings which will add good flavours. Only miss out any cabbage-type leaves; given their tendency to produce overboiled cabbage smells when long-cooked with a lot of water, you DO NOT want them. Starchy veg. can cloud the stock – which doesn't much matter – and make it go sour more quickly, which may matter. But the scrubbed peel of celery root, the bases of asparagus stems, fennel, celery leaves, red or orange peppers surplus to requirements, tomato skins, or whole tomatoes if you have a surplus, mushroom trimmings . . . all add flavour and make today's stock a bit different from yesterday's. I keep Parmesan rinds in a bag in the freezer, and adding a Parmesan rind to a stock deepens and improves the flavour.

Stock 1. Simple. **2 medium onions**, not peeled but quartered**, 2-3 chunked carrots**, scrubbed but not peeled, **2-3 stalks celery, 1 leek**, tops and all, washed, **1-2 cloves garlic, a bay leaf, sprigs of thyme and parsley stalks**. Any other ingredients, like seaweed, Parmesan rind, other vegetable flavourings go in now, too. Put all these into a large pan, cover with water, bring to the boil and simmer 30 mins or so. Drain, keeping the stock and putting the veg remains on the compost heap. It keeps, in the fridge, 2-3 days.

Stock 2. Medium. Cut the basic veg, onion, carrot, celery, leek in small pieces and sweat in 25g butter until they are golden and well flavoured. Add water and other ingredients, simmer half an hour.

Stock 3. Darker and stronger. Put the basic veg in a roasting tin, with any suitable additions – fennel, whole tomatoes, for example – and add a splash of olive oil. Rub this over the veg, then roast at 200 for 30 mins. Tip these roasted vegetables into your large pan, add herbs, any other veg trimmings, Parmesan rind if using, seaweed if using, cover with water. Pour a little water into the roasting tin, and bring to the boil, scraping the bottom with a spoon to detach any flavoursome patches. Pour this water into the stock pan., and add more water to cover. Now simmer all this for 30 mins or so, strain, and keep in the fridge.

At least some of the time, you will probably be using instant, Marigold, vegetable stock. But home-made stock does make a difference – the simpler the dish you're making, the more difference home-made stock makes. Do make it; don't make a fetish or a burden of it.

Dried Beans

There is no doubt that tins of these are convenient. They are also comparatively expensive, always the same flavour, and you need to rinse them so you don't get any stock for other uses. Further, there are more kinds of beans, peas, lentils, and other pulses out there than will ever appear in tins, and they are all worth experimenting with.

Lentils and dhals (split pulses of many kinds) don't need soaking. You simply put the required amount in a pan, add whatever flavourings you want – but NO SALT – cover with water, and simmer till done. Most lentils and dhals take about half an hour, and pink (actually, orange) lentils, also known as masoor dhal, take 15-20 mins. Given a 500g packet of these in the cupboard, and some rice, you can feed up to 12 surprise visitors in less than half an hour without going out of the house, and you have enough time while they are cooking to have a drink with your friends. Unbeatable!

Whole peas, beans, chickpeas need soaking before they are cooked. There are two ways of doing this; one is soaking overnight, and the other is quick-soaking. Overnight is so simple if you know you will need the beans (or whatever) tomorrow; tip dried beans, etc., into bowl, cover with cold water before you go to bed. And in the morning they will be swollen and ready to drain and cook at some time during the day. If you haven't thought of it the night before, what you do is tip the beans into a pan, cover well with cold water, bring to the boil and boil 5 mins. Turn off the heat, put on the lid, and leave for an hour. Drain, and they are ready to go. The soaking water is no use for anything in the kitchen, but can be used to water plants in the garden.

Cooking whole beans from scratch means you can add flavourings appropriate to what you are doing with them. Onion and celery for European; onion, garlic, and 1 or 2 dried chilis for Eastern beans; just the chili and garlic for Mexican. DO NOT ADD SALT till they are cooked; it really slows the process down. It's almost always a good idea to cook 2 or 3 times the amount of beans you need on one occasion. They freeze very well, and there they are ready for another use.

This water that beans are cooked in can be very useful. It's good as the base liquid for stock, and it can be used as the liquid in bread-making. Bean soups and refried beans depend on it. Incidentally, I had great trouble with refried beans following recipes; they implied the beans should be drained and mashed into a puree in a frying pan with oil. Very solid mash which took more and more oil to make it a smooth

66

damp puree. What you need is beans + cooking liquid; heat sunflower or other neutral oil in frying pan, and add ladles of beans with some liquid. Then mash away and you'll get the right sort of puree, liquid enough to spread. My favourite refried beans have chipotle chilis in them; 1 or 2 dried chipotles cooked with 500g beans give the right heat to my taste.

Polenta

It's a personal lack of taste; I don't really like polenta – or any other corn meal mush, come to that. So while I've read about the proper North-Italian way to produce it, stirring the spitting pot for an hour at a time and stopping it burning all that time, I feel no urge to do it like that. There is instant polenta; there is ready-made polenta in plastic bags in the supermarket. So though I use these occasionally -- the solid bags are really pretty good for slicing and grilling or frying polenta – it wouldn't be a deep disappointment if I couldn't get these and therefore gave polenta up for life. If you really like the instant polenta and want to see how much of an improvement the real thing is, I will admire you and not emulate. Everything in this book which uses polenta – particularly in the cabbage section – has been tested using the instant variety and following the packet instructions.

Blanching Almonds

Supermarkets sell almonds in their brown skins, ready-blanched almonds, flaked almonds, nibbed almonds, ground almonds, roast salted almonds, and probably more I haven't seen. So you may feel that you don't need to know how to blanch almonds. In an absolute sense, you're right; you don't NEED to. But freshly-blanched almonds are juicier and more flavourful; the ready-blanched versions have dried out and lost some of the volatile flavour compounds. So I do blanch my own almonds for special dishes. Not if they need flaking, but for eating whole or ground. It's easy enough to do; pour boiling water over brown-skinned almonds and leave to cool enough that you can handle the almonds. Drain in a sieve, and then shear the almond between finger and thumb. In a few cases you may need to nick the skin, but normally the clean cream shiny almond comes popping out. It's quite like skinning broad beans.

Egg-Yolk and Cream Thickening for Soups.

Makes a thin vegetable soup rich and luscious and satisfying. Don't use it if you have creamy dishes elsewhere in the meal, but for meals of soup/salad or sandwich/fruit it can add substance and balance. You need **2-3 egg yolks** and **100 ml. cream** for a soup for 4 people. Beat the egg yolks in a bowl, beat in the cream. Take a ladle of the very hot/boiling soup, pour into the egg yolk mix, and stir quickly and well. Make sure the soup on the stove is not boiling, and tip the mix in, stirring. Don't let it boil again. Sometimes it will thicken a little straight away; sometimes you have to heat gently to persuade the egg yolks to thicken. But, again, it MUST NOT BOIL, or the eggs will scramble and the soup is spoilt. When it's thickened – and it doesn't ever get very thick – take off the stove, taste for salt and seasoning, and serve. Using this thickening method means the soup can't be reheated. Used in celery soup.

Hollandaise Sauce.

Mentioned for use with Brussels sprouts, but delectable with almost anything. Think of it as mayonnaise with butter not oil. It is much easier to make in a blender than any other way. Put **2 egg yolks** into the blender jar, **salt, pepper, lemon juice**. Start whizzing, and pour **125 g melted butter** (half a packet) slowly through the hole in the lid. It will thicken. That's it. You might like it to be a little more strongly flavoured, in which case add 1 tsp. French mustard to the egg yolks at the beginning. **Sauce Maltaise** is a classic for asparagus, where the juice of a blood orange is added to the egg yolks at the start. This should end up a delicate orange. Unfortunately, blood oranges and asparagus seldom overlap in the UK -- though you could freeze a couple of blood oranges just for this. It would really be worth the (minimal) effort.

Mayonnaise in the Blender.

Extremely quick and easy. All my kids learnt how to make it at 8 or 9, and I never had to do it again myself till they all left home. Put **a whole egg** in the blender jar. Add **salt, mustard, vinegar, pepper**. (I remember this order because of the old skipping rhyme) Mustard is French, a mean tsp.; vinegar is wine vinegar, a small slurp, about 1 tbsp. Start running the blender, and pour in, gradually, through the hole in the lid, **180 ml. sunflower oil** from the measuring jug. It thickens; turn off, and pour and scrape out. It's not worth making even a 1-egg quantity if you only need 2 tbsp., and in this case the trusty Hellmann's comes into play. But the real thing is so much nicer. Ask yourself whether you are tempted to dip a crust in real mayo standing in the kitchen. I am, but I wouldn't dream of doing this with Hellmann's.

Mayonnaise lends itself to lots of other flavours. Green, with herbs and lightly-blanched spinach whizzed in at the end. Garlic; pound 3 cloves garlic per person in a mortar with a little salt, and stir in the blender mayonnaise a little at a time (I don't think there's much point in having gentle garlic mayo with delicate amounts of garlic). Chipotle; half-way through the oil addition, stop, add 1 or 2 chipotle chilis in adobo (jar), and then finish adding the oil. This gets much hotter if it stands overnight.

If you ever volunteer to do something involving mayonnaise for 30-40 people, the old-fashioned, handmade route is actually easiest. Egg yolks, mustard, salt and pepper in large bowl. Beat, and start adding sunflower oil in tablespoon quantities. As it starts to thicken, you can up the amounts, so that by halfway through the process you are pouring straight from the bottle. Add wine vinegar to taste at the end. Mayonnaise for 30 would mean **10 egg yolks, 1 tbsp. French mustard**, and **1½ litres oil** or a little more. If you are doing this for a buffet, you will almost certainly be able to use up the egg whites for meringue cakes. Everyone loves these; no-one realises why they are there.

Frying Batter.

Two Western kinds, and a very simple tempura-style batter.

First Western Frying Batter. This needs to rest for an hour, and needs egg whites. Put **250g plain white flour** into a bowl; add ¼ **tsp. salt, 6 tbsp. olive oil**, and beat to a cream with **300 ml. warm water**

(not hot). Leave an hour. Beat **2 egg whites** stiff, mix into the flour mix, and use straight away.

Second Western Frying Batter   250g self-raising flour, 150 ml. light beer, 300 ml. cold water. Beat smooth and use straightaway.

The second is the batter of choice when you have beer; the first when you have time. Both make good crisp coatings for anything deep-fried.

Very Simple Tempura Batter. 120g plain flour, 1 tsp. bicarbonate of soda, 300 ml. iced water. Mix quickly with a fork, and use immediately while still lumpy. This one is best for delicate things like courgette flowers.

Cheese Sauce, White Sauce. Cheese sauce is white sauce with grated cheese added, so one recipe covers both. Butter is melted, flour added and cooked a little, liquid is added and brought to the boil, and there, a sauce!. To make a sauce of medium thickness, use **25g butter, 20g plain flour** to **300 ml. milk, flavoured milk, or stock**. Melt the butter but don't let it brown, add the flour, stir in, and cook over a low heat for 2-3 mins. The usual term is "honeycombed"; the mixture has lots of little bubbles. This mixture, called a roux, must be soft enough to spread over the pan bottom. If it's too tight, too paste-like, the sauce will be lumpy. Anyhow, pour all the liquid in one go into the roux, stirring well with the other hand; turn up the heat a little, and keep stirring intermittently but often till the sauce thickens. Season while this is happening or at the end. Most books will tell you to heat the liquid, or add in dribs and drabs and thicken each time; but cooks doing these get more lumps than I do. If you are having a plain white sauce, it's a good idea to flavour the milk by heating it with a sliced onion, a bay leaf, some thyme – at least. Bring the milk to a boil with these things, then put the lid on the pan and let it sit till you're ready to use it. At this point pour the milk through a sieve; use the milk, discard the rest. Don't bother to put peppercorns in the milk, as often advised; unless they are broken up they have very little to give. If you are making a cheese sauce, I wouldn't bother to flavour the milk; just make the plain sauce, season with salt, pepper, freshly ground nutmeg. Off the heat, add **30-60g grated cheese**

I've mentioned the use of stock above in making this very basic sauce. Two possible reasons; using stock mixed with milk makes the sauce less nourishing. Alternatively, using stock introduces good flavours into the sauce, which can then be richened by adding cream. The second, not surprisingly, is much nicer. You can get the best of both worlds by adding 1 tsp. Marigold stock granules to the milk you use.

Pastry, 4 kinds.

I've used 4 kinds of pastry in this book: shortcrust, used by far the most often; puff pastry, for luxury and celebrations; brioche pastry, for kulebiaka in the Cabbage chapter; and German pastry for sweet spinach tart. Too much pastry, too many pastry dishes, are certainly bad for you, but an occasional dish using pastry seems to me just fine. The device I use to avoid eating too much is to insist on home-made pastry, as then time and energy constraints mean it doesn't happen too often. The availability of ready-made (even ready-rolled) puff pastry in the supermarkets makes it so much easier and convenient to use it that it becomes less of a treat, and downgrades it. It's good, but not as good as homemade. Anyhow, that's my device for limiting pastry, but I don't expect people to agree with me.

Shortcrust Pastry. A two-minute affair in the food processor. Put **250g plain white flour** in the processor bowl, and add **150g butter**, cut in chunks. Break **1 egg** into a cup, and add **1 tbsp. cold water**. Whizz, and pour in egg+water through the funnel while processing. Continue until the pastry forms a lump. Tip out onto greaseproof paper, consolidate into a ball, wrap, and chill at least 30 mins.

Baking Blind means cooking an empty tart case, which is then filled with something that needs further cooking, or doesn't. The point is that the case is cooked at a heat that suits it, so a filling can be cooked at the temperature that suits *it* Take the pastry ball out of the fridge. You will use most of it for a 22-25 cm case, (9-10") and half for a 18-cm case (7") Put the pastry, or half if using that, on a smooth floured surface. Marble is best, no question, but the supply of ancient washstands whose marble tops can be adapted has dried up. If you are a keen pastry person, a monumental mason is the place to find a suitable slab. If it's only occasional, a clean dry worktop of any material will do. Flatten it into a disc with your hand, and start to roll. You don't actually need a rolling pin if you don't make pastry often; I used an empty claret bottle for 15 years. But if you do get a rolling pan, a plain wooden cylinder is best – no handles, as these stop you getting tactile feedback from the rolling process. And forget anything filled with cold water, etc; a commercial gimmick. No professional would touch one. Flour the top of the pastry and the pin lightly, and don't roll too much in any one direction. You are flattening, not stretching. Roll to about 3 times the initial size in one direction, then lift it and turn a quarter circle. Probably add a scattering more flour under the pastry as you turn, and a little more on top. The flour is there to stop sticking, not to be blended into the pastry. Keep rolling and turning till the pastry disc is about 5 cm larger all round than the pie pan base. You would like it to be a circle, but it won't be a very good one. The pastry disc will not be stuck to the surface. Lift the far end over the rolling pin, and bring the pin towards you rolling pastry over it, so you finish with the pastry hanging down each side of the pin. Drape over the pie tin. Then push it onto the base of the tin, without stretching, and use the forefinger knuckle to press into the angle at the edge. You will have pastry draping over the sides; cut off any large protrusions, and then form the rest into an upright edge, ideally taller than the side of the tin. Put the lined tin into the fridge for 30 mins or so. Take it out; prick the base with a fork, line the pastry case with aluminium foil, fitting it closely. Tip some dried beans into the foil case, to hold the base flat. Put the case into a preheated 200 oven – even if you have a fan oven, which usually doesn't need preheating. Cook for 7-8 mins, look, and lift out the foil lining. Return to the oven for 5 mins or a bit more, until the base is light gold. It does often happen that one of the sides will collapse a little, which is why you made them taller in the first place. I've made this sound a right performance, but this is because I've tried to cover the process in detail. In real life it takes less than 5 mins to roll and shape the pastry, and 2-3 to get it ready for baking.

The beans can be used again, and again, essentially for ever. Have a labelled jar to keep them in.

Puff Pastry.

Wonderful stuff, and success is all in the technique. And the technique itself is simple but repetitive. The best description I know of puff-making is in Mastering the Art of French Cookery, vol. 2. My instructions are a cut-down version of the instructions there. If you want more detail, you can't do better than look at the original. Don't start your pastry endeavours by trying puff.

You need 2 pastes, butter paste and flour paste, which must be as close to the same consistency as possible, and not too cold. This sounds odd, because we're normally told to keep pastry-making cool. But if your butter is too cold to spread, it won't spread out in puff as it must. So a temperature around 18-20 C in the kitchen. (You can't get by using spreadable butter, which has added water; it just won't work!) Make the flour component with **400g white bread flour**, and rub in **80g best butter**. (Rub in: lift small pieces of butter with flour, press out between fingertips into smaller pieces, repeat until mix is sandy in consistency) If unsalted, which is a bit better, add **2 flat tsp. salt**; if salted, add **1 tsp. salt**. Make into a paste with **180-200 ml. cold water**; add 180 ml first and a little more if needed to make a soft, coherent, non-sticky dough. Wrap and put in fridge for 1 hr. For the butter component, smear **350g of the same butter** into small flat mass, and work in **60g white bread flour**. Use your hands; messy but best. Scrape up butter/flour mix and make into a square about 15 cm a side. Put to the side of your marble or other surface, and roll the chilled flour paste into a circle about 30-cm diameter. Put the butter in the middle, fold over sides then top and bottom, to make a parcel. Squash with the rolling pin to seal. Now roll this parcel to a strip, twice as long as wide. Here is where the value of mixes of the same consistency is evident; cold butter will poke through the surface. Fold this lengthwise strip into 3; turn bottom third over middle, fold over top third. They should match at the edges! Rotate this parcel a quarter turn, and roll out again to strip of same dimensions. Fold in 3 again. That is 2 turns. Now wrap up this parcel, and put somewhere cool for about an hour.

The remaining steps are easy. Unwrap, bash with rolling pin to start rolling process, roll into strip, fold, turn parcel a quarter turn, roll, fold, wrap and keep cool about 1 hr. Turns 3 and 4. Repeat, making turns 5 and 6. It's now ready to roll out and use, with 729 layers of flour interspersed with layers of butter.

There will be leftover trimmings, whatever you make with your puff pastry. Don't gather them together at random, but lie them on top of each other keeping the layer structure vertical.

I can't resist telling you my favourite thing to do with trimmings when there isn't enough for another use. Clear your pastry surface of flour, and instead sprinkle well with caster sugar. Roll trimmings into a rectangle, width two-thirds length, approximately. Sprinkle the top with sugar. Fold sides to middle of dough, sprinkle with sugar again, then fold in middle. Cut this folded object into 1-cm slices, and arrange the slices on a baking tray, quite far apart. Sprinkle them with sugar once more, and bake at 200 for about 10 mins. The sugar will caramelise slightly, but keep an eye on it, as it's very easy to let it burn. Use a flat spatula to lift onto cooling rack. These are palmiers, and are lovely biscuits by themselves or with fruit desserts or ice cream. They used to be sandwiched, two at a time, with whipped cream, but that's just too much for me now.

German Pastry.

This is THE best sweet pastry, for tarts, pies, mince pies – anything sweet you do with pastry. My mother learnt it in the 30's from a Swiss patissier, when her employers sent her on a "masterclass" course. She was always cross with me for passing on a trade secret. This is not made like any other pastry. I always make it by hand, though I expect it could be done in a processor. Warm, but don't melt, **300g butter**, and blend in **180g caster sugar**. It isn't to be creamed, just amalgamated. Add **a whole egg**, and mix in. Add **500g plain flour**, and bring the whole together. Wrap in greaseproof paper, and chill. Bring back to (English) room temperature before using. Even now, it is very difficult to roll out without tearing. So what you do is take the amount you are going to roll out, and work with your hands till it feels like Plasticine. It will now roll out well and easily and thinly. While not relevant to this book, this makes the very best mince pies. Here, I've only used it for the sweet spinach tart.

Brioche Pastry

Brioche is normally slow to rise and therefore to make; this recipe uses a lot of yeast to get it to rise more quickly. It's also made in the food processor, which is a little faster than by hand and considerably less messy.

Melt **120g butter** and let it cool. Put **250g white bread flour** in the processor with **2 packets instant dried yeast** (as sold in all supermarkets), **1 tbsp. sugar, 1 tsp salt, 3 eggs, 50 ml. milk**, and the cooled melted butter. Whizz for 10 secs, stop, scrape down the sides, and whizz again till well mixed. Turn and scrape into a bowl, and start to knead, adding a little more flour as needed. The dough should be rather elastic and quite soft. It will stick to your hands a little, but not too much. Let it rise in the bowl in a warm place; covered, until it has doubled in size. Punch it down; it's ready to use. In this book it's used for cabbage koulebiaka. You can also bake it as is, or make little brioches, or wrap vegetable pates in it. A good one to have in the repertoire, but not a dough to start on.

Homemade Bread.

If you serve people fresh, warm, home-made bread, they will be so impressed that any deficiencies in the rest of the meal will slide past unnoticed. And once you are used to making bread, it takes so little effort. I reckon a batch of 3 large (900g) loaves takes me less than 15 mins working time. It's true it takes 3-4 hours start to finish, but it's not your working time. I make all my own bread, and have done for years. I started when I had 3 small children, and found it easier to make bread than get them all ready and take them out to buy it. The only trouble is that once you are used to good bread, it becomes harder to pay over money for something which is so much inferior to yours, and/or much more expensive. I rather resent the fact that it's so hard to buy good bread with texture, crust, and flavour locally, but having partly grown up in an old-fashioned bakery, I understand the pressures on artisan bakers.

Brown or white bread? Mostly I prefer white myself, but many home bakers prefer wholemeal or half-and-half. The important thing is the quality of the flour. Must be bread flour, almost certainly should be organic.

Tip a **1.5 kg bag of bread flour** into a large bowl. Add **3 tsp. salt, 1 tsp sugar, and 2 packets instant dried yeast.** Shake the bowl to mix. Pour in **950 ml lukewarm water** – 1 part boiling water and 2 parts tap water. Add **4 tbsp. sunflower oil**. Now cup your hand, with fingers apart, and start raking through the bowl to mix flour and liquid. Go right down to the bottom and turn over. By the time you've finished this mixing process, all the flour will be wetted and you will almost have a dough. Now start to knead, still in the bowl. You are only using one hand in this process, so you can if need be use the other to answer the door or phone, or whatever else. Stretch and turn the dough until it is smooth, uniform, and feels "right" – the closest I can come is like a breast. Also, it would rather stick to itself than to your fingers. Cover the bowl with a teatowel and let the dough rise to about double. It will go quicker in a warm place –1½ to 2 hours – than it will if cool, but the dough will rise in the fridge if you want it to take a long time, like overnight. Quick rising is tempting, but the flavours of flour develop with a longer rise, so there are advantages both sides. I normally put mine on the central-heating boiler, so bread started around 8 am is ready for lunch. (Then I walk the dog and do the shopping, and it's nearly ready when I get back) Dough risen, you now punch it down – literally, make a fist, and knock the air out. Knead a little more, divide into 3 roughly, and put in lightly oiled bread tins for large loaves. Let it rise again, till slightly domed, and bake at 200 for 30-35 mins. Tip one loaf (that closest to the front) from its tin, and tap the bottom with your knuckles. It should sound hollow, not a doughy thud. If not done, put back without the tin for 5-10 mins more, and try again. If done, take the other tins from the oven, tip out the loaves, and cool in free air, either standing crosswise on the tin or on a cooling tray. Letting loaves cool in the tin makes them harder to remove, and makes the crust soggy. Let it cool at least 20 mins – 40 better – before eating.

I freeze 1 or 2 of these loaves, depending on demand, and defrost over the next couple of days as needed.

After you have shaped the dough and put it in its tins, fill the bowl in which you made the dough with cold water, and let it soak at least an hour. This makes it very easy to wash up; the dough softens and can be brushed off. Let leftover traces of dough harden, and they are difficult to remove.

DO try this. I don't think anything improves your pleasure and satisfaction in the kitchen more than the competent feeling you have and the unstinted admiration from your eaters when you have made bread.

You will note that what I make is a traditional English tin loaf, as needed for sandwiches and toast. However, once you are happy making this bread, you can make ANY other bread that takes your fancy. French sticks, ciabatta, rolls, freeform peasant breads, granary, seedy bread, milk bread, potato bread .. .the technique is the same and only the ingredients vary.

Pizza Dough.

Pizzas (or pizze, if you want to be Italian and correct) are made with bread dough. A dough made with 250g flour will make 1 pizza 30-cm across, or 2 20-cm pizze. So for this dough you need **250g bread**

flour, ½ tsp. salt, ½ packet instant dried yeast (But it's OK to use one packet; the dough will rise faster), **150 ml warm water, 1 tbsp. olive oil.** Mix and rise as above; punch down. Let it rest 5-10 mins, then roll or stretch to the size you want. Put on the topping, and bake in a hot oven till risen and cooked. Commercial pizza ovens are much hotter than domestic ones, and cook the dough in under 5 mins; this isn't long enough to damage the more fragile components of a topping. Domestic ovens take 15-20 mins. Toppings, as you already know, are very various, but it's hard to beat the basic oil—cooked tomato—cheese—herbs of the simplest pizza.

Pancakes.

You could see pancakes as a form of English flatbread, or wrap. My family has a great weakness for pancakes plain and stuffed, and eat vast quantities when allowed. (My younger son claims his record is 23 pancakes-with-sugar-and-lemon) The basic mix is **120g flour, ½ tsp salt, beaten with 1 egg, 1 tbsp. sunflower oil, 150 ml. each milk and water.** Put the egg and oil into a well in the flour, and start beating, adding milk gradually and blending in all the flour. When the milk is used, add the water, and when it's all mixed, beat well for 1 min with an electric beater or a couple of minutes by hand. You can make this in a blender – liquids first, but I don't like to. Let the mix stand for an hour or so. It does make a difference, though no-one knows why.
Heat a 17-18 cm (7") frying pan, and add 1 tsp. sunflower oil. Let it get really hot, then pour away what you can. Add enough pancake mix to make a thin coating, rolling it round the pan to cover the whole base. Let it sit on the heat till the top is no longer liquid, then slide a frying slice or spatula under the edges, then to the middle and flip over. Don't be tempted to toss; they are too thin and fragile. Less time on this second side, slide the pancake out, repeat till the mixture is gone. The first pancake won't be a disaster if the pan is hot enough to start with. You don't have to keep oiling the pan, as the oil in the batter will be enough to stop sticking. This amount of mixture makes 8-9 pancakes, enough for 2 adult appetites, or 3 if the pancakes are to be stuffed. Just multiply up the quantities for the number of pancakes you want/are willing to make. Again a guideline; one batch takes about 10 mins to cook, 40 pancakes, or 4 batches, takes 40 mins.

Equipment

I have assumed throughout this book that you are already cooking, with a kitchen. This means you have pans and implements that you are pretty happy with, and used to. I like reading other people's lists of what you need to set up a kitchen, but mostly I am amazed by some of the choices and wonder why they have missed out some things I think of as essential. What I'm doing here is offering a few thoughts on some of my essentials, should you want to change/upgrade/declutter.

Knives. Everyone will say that you need good sharp knives, and of course you do. And if they are good you don't need many. Keep sharpening day to day with a steel; take them to be sharpened now and then. Sharp knives – and again this is generally agreed – are actually safer than blunt ones, because they do what you want them to instead of slipping. And keep them in some form of rack or block, not in a drawer with other tools, or you will blunt the knives and stand a good chance of cutting yourself. My favourite knife goes camping with me, goes on self-catering holidays, and even when I'm cooking in other people's kitchens.

Cooker. I have a dual-fuel cooker, with gas top and electric grill and fan oven. Electric oven makes it much more likely there will be a timer, which is useful. Gas burners respond much faster. But I have friends with all-gas, all-electric, and even Aga cookers, and they are all satisfied because they are used to coping with the vagaries of what they have. I'd love a range cooker, with two ovens or more and more burners, but I simply don't have room. What you do need, whichever type you have, is an **OVEN THERMOMETER**, free-standing. They are cheap and available everywhere, and it's nice to know how your oven temperature relates to what you want. My own fan oven, through some quirk of manufacture, is about 50C hotter than the thermostat says. All oven temperatures in the book have been adjusted to actual, desired, thermometer-measured temperatures.

Electric Kettle. I think almost everyone in England has one. I bought a book on "Green Cooking" in Canada, and that said that using an electric kettle as opposed to boiling water on the stovetop is one of the greenest things Canadians can do in the kitchen. So you're ahead already.

Heavy, non-stick, lidded frying pan, like those made by SKK in Sweden. These are expensive but a joy to use. The non-stick coating is so tough that you can (but probably shouldn't) chop onions in the base of the pan. And in this pan you can do stews, cook 2 kg onions to caramelising point, make hashes and frittatas, as well as fry. Worth saving up for.

Large thin deep pan for deep-frying, if you plan to deep-fry. You don't need a basket, but it's good to have a thin light pan for fast response to changes of heat. Mine is 25 cm diameter, about 20cm deep, and was bought for about £3 in France. If you're not using a basket, you do need a proper scoop of some sort with which to remove the food.

Food Processor. Makes heavy, time-consuming chores feel easy and pleasurable, and makes possible things you otherwise wouldn't dream of making – hummus, for example. I use mine a lot, even though I always work out whether washing it up is preferable to doing whatever-it-is by hand. It almost always is.

Blender with extra coffee-grinding head. The coffee grinding head is for spices. The blender bit is for soups, smoothies, mayonnaise, and various similar wet mixes that food processors aren't good at. Nowadays blenders come without a coffee-grinding head, on the whole. There are many separate coffee grinders, but hardly any are suitable for spices. Dedicated electric spice grinders do exist, and are very much worth their (apparently excessive) cost.

Mouli-legumes, which I normally just call a mouli. Mine is old and tired and mostly used for mashed potatoes nowadays; it makes really really good mash. Also useful for baby food, and holding back inedible bits – for example, if you are pureeing gooseberries for a fool or ice cream, you don't have to top and tail if you put them through the mouli. I know a Frenchwoman who makes redcurrant jelly by cooking redcurrants, on their stalks, with an equal weight of sugar for 5-10 mins, and then putting the lot through a mouli. The liquid can simply be potted, and sets. It isn't as clear as a jelly made with jelly-bag, etc, but it's a lot easier. A mouli-legumes is supposed to be hard to wash up, but if you run cold water through it when you've finished using it, and keep it wet until you wash up, it isn't difficult at all.

Two other little French gadgets, of the same style as the mouli-legumes, and originally made by the same people. One is for chopping small quantities of herbs, a **Parsmint**, where you turn a handle and get the herb chopped for garnish. The other is a **Parmesan grater**. Modern Parmesan is easier to grate on a standard grater than it was, but still the mouli-gadget produces fine, airy, Parmesan of just the right consistency to go on pasta and risottos.

Pestle and Mortar. You really do need one. Crushing a few spices; making a paste of garlic and salt before making aioli, tahina, pesto. Furthermore, I find that using a pestle and mortar makes me feel like a competent and old-fashioned cook.

Kitchen Scales. When I got married, one of the first things we bought was a set of brass, sweet-shop-style scales, with a set of weights. That's 45 years ago, and they are still both use and ornament. Going metric just means buying a different set of weights. I think everybody needs scales, whether up-to-date electronic, old-fashioned like mine, or one of the many varieties in between.

Cheesecloth. I'm not suggesting you make cheese, though some cheesecloth is useful if you want to drain yoghurt. Most commonly, I cut off little squares and use them to cover mayonnaise jars when sprouting seeds. Water goes through these tops; seeds don't. Amazon sells it, so do John Lewis stores. The smallest quantity you can buy will last for ages, but it is really nice to have it on hand.

Baking tins, tartlet tins, muffin pans, etc. Let me recommend vintage versions of these. I have my mother's and my grandmother's bread tins and tartlet tins, with a comfortable coating from years of use that makes them truly non-stick. If you can't get something like this, then of course you want non-stick, but remember you then shouldn't use a knife to cut pies or remove cake or bread.

Electric Gadgets. Microwave, electric steamer, breadmaker, electric deep-fryer, slow cooker, electric knife sharpener, and doubtless more. If you have them you either love them, or, more likely, put them away in a cupboard and forget about them. Truly, none of these is essential, though they may be nice.

A **dishwasher**, on the other hand, may not be absolutely essential but is very very useful. I'm delighted that the modern dishwasher uses less water than washing-up by hand, though it's hard to believe. What it does give you is TIME. When there were 6 of us at home, the introduction of a dishwasher gave me 1-2 hrs extra per day – and no rows while one tried vainly to get the children to do it. Wonderful gadget!

Spring

Asparagus

Nettles

Samphire

Swiss Chard

Asparagus
Broad Beans
Cauliflower
Nettles
New Carrots
New Potatoes
New Turnips
Purple Sprouting Broccoli
Radish
Rocket
Samphire
Sorrel
Spinach
Spring Greens
Spring Onions
Swiss Chard
Watercress
Wild Garlic

New Turnips

Purple Sprouting
Broccoli

Sorrel

Asparagus

The prize of spring, and a treat to be looked forward to year-round. I don't think there has been a time when asparagus was not respected and loved, even when only scrawny wild asparagus was available in the Mediterranean lands. Romans loved it. We in England are accustomed to asparagus being expensive; it's part of the way we recognise its status. This isn't true elsewhere, as France and Germany both have asparagus seasons where the vegetable is made much of, with festivals, special asparagus menus in restaurants, and market stalls full of it. In the States, asparagus became a common vegetable, little more expensive than cabbage.

The English season runs from late April to mid June, and more is being grown to satisfy an increasing wish to eat it fresh. English asparagus is always green, and stalks range in thickness from about 1 cm down. I used to buy "grass" on Cambridge market, cheap, with stalks no thicker than a pencil. Most of the American asparagus I've seen is green, too. Continentals, on the other hand, like their asparagus white, which means it is earthed up and grows completely underground till cut. It's also much thicker than English asparagus. I much prefer the flavour of the green, which is fortunate, because I live in England and that's what I can get.

I did try to grow asparagus, but with very little success. The plants hung on for 10 years, but when you are getting less asparagus every year you eventually lose heart and give up. It's worth a try, though, because no asparagus is as delicious as the stalks cut just before cooking. In fact, whether grown or bought, freshness is key. This is the major reason I reject air-freighted imports, though there are other, social, reasons. (The moral difficulty with air-freighted crops comes when they taste *better* than local ones and are out-of-season here. I find Argentinian cherries in November hard to resist, but strawberries and asparagus flown in aren't good enough to tempt.)

When I was thinking about this section, I intended to be purist, saying fresh asparagus can be dealt with by boiling/steaming, or by roasting, and eaten hot or cold, and that's all you should do with it. Then I thought about my celebration dishes with asparagus, for birthdays in the magic season; they couldn't be left out.   There is soup, using more of the stalks than other methods. There is the fact that sometimes you want not just an asparagus course, but a one-dish meal using it – pasta, risotto, with eggs . . . So the section has grown.

Asparagus Preparation. Most asparagus on sale has a fibrous base to the stalk, which isn't eaten by most people. There are two ways of coping with this: (a) peeling. Peel the stems quite thickly at the bottom, tailing off about halfway up; (b) snapping. Hold the asparagus stalk about halfway along in your left hand, thumb underneath. Put your right hand near the base in the same pose, and exert increasing pressure downwards. The time will come when the stalk snaps, and the bottom part is saved for stock or soup. This is hard to explain in words, but easy when you get your hands on a stalk. You are feeling for the point where it snaps. When you've done one or two, it's very easy. Much faster than peeling, and gives you more useful soup-making material. Snapping is my chosen method. It does mean that most sessions of eating asparagus are followed by asparagus soup, but I don't see this as a problem.

Default.   The traditional English method of boiling. There is a traditional utensil, the asparagus cooker, where the stems stand upright. Water boils in the bottom, cooking the lower stalks, and just steaming the more tender tip. I don't own one of these, and I don't think they are necessary. (They also have to be stored somewhere for 10 months of the year) Simply boil about 5 cm. salted water in a large pan, and drop in the snapped, shortened asparagus stems. Put on a lid, and cook for 5-7 mins. Fish the asparagus out with tongs or a scoop, and drain in a sieve or colander. I think you need at least a dozen stalks per head, and more is better. (This leaves the cooking water, lightly flavoured with asparagus, to start the stock or soup made with the fibrous bottom ends) Put them on a hot plate to serve. Melted butter is traditional and delicious. I find it's easier to melt individual helpings of butter in small bowls in the microwave; that way, there isn't waste butter swilling round plates, and people can control for themselves how much butter they have. EAT WITH YOUR FINGERS. Pick up a stalk, dip in the butter, and eat. Butter-hounds will take 2-3 dips per stalk; most people just have one. Cloth napkins are much better than paper ones here, and adds to the sense of occasion. In English

84

tradition, asparagus is always a separate course, usually at the start of the meal.

If you want to eat the asparagus cold, drain as before, dress with oil and lemon, salt and pepper, and let cool. Or you can have little bowls of dressing, and still have the fun of eating with your fingers.

Roast Asparagus. Prepare the stalks as usual, and put into a baking dish which has been oiled with olive oil. As close to one layer as possible, but it's better to have a few extra to one layer than leave empty spaces where the juices can burn. Pour over a little more oil, sprinkle with coarse sea salt if you have it, and use your hands to make sure all the spears are coated with oil. Roast at 200 for 15 mins, or until the asparagus stalks are a bit wizened and a bit brown. This is a successful and delicious way, but for me won't replace the default.

Celebration Dish 1: Asparagus Lasagne. For 4-6 people start with **1 kg asparagus**. Snap the bottoms from the stalks, and boil the main part of the stalks in salted water for 5 mins. Scoop out the asparagus, add the bases to the pan, and boil 15 mins. Strain. You need 700-750 ml. asparagus stock. Melt **50g butter**, add **40g flour**, and cook the roux, stirring, for 2-3 mins. Add the asparagus stock, bring to the boil, stirring, and simmer for 5 mins. Off the heat, add **200g** grateable, but not too strong, **goat's cheese**, grated, and stir until melted. Add the **zest of a lemon**, grated, and taste for **salt. Pepper.** Grate **80g Parmesan**. Cut the asparagus in 3-cm lengths. You now need **6-8 sheets no-cook lasagne**. Spread a thin coating of the sauce in a large buttered baking dish, and put in a layer of lasagne sheets. Layer sauce, asparagus pieces, good sprinkle Parmesan, and repeat, finishing with a sheet of pasta and the rest of the sauce. Beat **250 ml double cream** with a pinch of salt till it thickens, and spread on top. Sprinkle with the rest of the Parmesan. Bake at 200 for 30 mins, or till the top is golden and bubbling. Let it rest 10 mins. before eating.
If you are making your own lasagne sheets and boiling them before making up the lasagne, you only need about half the quantity of sauce. No-cook lasagne absorbs a lot of liquid.

Celebration Dish 2: Feuillete of Asparagus. This consists of fresh, hot puff pastry rectangles, halved horizontally and filled with asparagus, and served with a sauce with herbs. It is rich, nutritionally excessive, and tricky to get everything ready exactly together, which is what it needs – but it's an absolutely show-stopping first course. Follow it with a simple main course and a fruit dessert – pineapple with kirsch? Home-made sorbet? Elderflower water ice is in season, and can only be home-made. Anyhow, for 4 people you need about **300g weight of made puff pastry**. (See Basics) It really should be homemade. Roll it out to a rectangle 20 x 30 cm, and cut this in 4. Put these on a wetted baking sheet, and keep in the fridge till ready to bake. Trim 500g **asparagus**. The sauce is simply **double cream**, reduced, seasoned, with chopped herbs added – **chervil** would be best, or a mix of **parsley and tarragon**. Reduce the cream and have the sauce ready to reheat. Preheat the oven to 220. Brush the tops of the rectangles with **egg-wash** (1 beaten egg, 1 tbsp. water), making sure it doesn't run down the sides, and put the baking sheet in the oven. The water on the baking sheet is there to turn into steam and help the rise (at least I think so. My mother, a professional baker/confectioner, always did it, but it may be a bit of professional's ritual) Bake for 10-15 mins, till well risen and browned. Meanwhile, boil the asparagus, timing it to be drained 2 mins after the pastry comes out. Reheat the sauce, and finish with a squirt of **lemon juice**, to taste. Halve the rectangles horizontally, on their own hot plates, and distribute the asparagus over the bottom. Put on the lid over the asparagus. Pour the sauce ROUND, not on, the pastry. You can't eat this with your fingers.

Asparagus Soup. A real contrast to the celebration dishes, as it uses the ends snapped off when preparing asparagus. Save these ends for up to a couple of days. You also need **a bunch of asparagus** for 4 people. Snap the ends from this as well, and make a stock by simmering the ends with **leek greens**, a little **carrot**, a little **celery**, **bay** and **parsley** for about 30 mins. Strain and keep the stock; you need just over a litre. Cut off the tips of the asparagus, and keep them. Cut up the stems roughly. Cook the white parts of **3 medium leeks** in **40g butter** till softening, then add the asparagus stem pieces, **parsley**, and the stock. Salt as required. Simmer 10 mins. Then let the pot cool a bit, and blend the contents well. What you MUST do now is put the soup through a food mill, or sieve it, otherwise the fibres will stick in your teeth and spoil the whole thing. Reheat the soup, taste for **salt**, add **pepper**, and a squeeze of **lemon juice**. Add the tips, and cook 2-3 mins. You can add a little **cream** – **4-5 tbsp** – but I prefer it without. The soup is thin but tasty; if you would like it a bit thicker, add a couple of potatoes after the leek has sweated. Make sure everyone has their share of tips.

Asparagus with Parmesan. Trim and boil **1 kg. asparagus,** lift it from the pan, and drain well. Smear the bottom of a rectangular baking dish with part of **50g butter**, and arrange the asparagus in the dish, making sure all the tips are exposed. By this I mean staggered rows, with one row reaching to the shoulders of the lower row. Sprinkle with **salt** and **60g grated Parmesan**, and dot with the rest of the butter. Bake at 200 for 10-15 mins, till the cheese has melted and formed a gold crust.

Asparagus with Eggs. Trim and boil **asparagus** for the number of people you are feeding, drain, and arrange on individual plates. Sprinkle with melted **butter** – more for poached eggs than fried – and put **1 or 2 freshly cooked eggs per person** on top of the stems. The eggs can be either fried or poached. Sprinkle the whole with grated **Parmesan. Pepper** on the table, to be added to taste. In Italy, this is a first course; I find it makes a hearty lunch, and don't want another dish.

Asparagus Frittata For 4 people use **6 eggs** and **500g asparagus**. Snap the ends from the asparagus, boil, and drain. When cool, cut into 1-cm lengths. Beat the eggs lightly, add **salt and pepper** (it gets mixed in better if added now), then the asparagus pieces and **50g grated Parmesan**. Melt **40g butter** in a large heavy frying pan, tip in the mixture, and cook on a very low heat until nearly set throughout, with a little runniness on the top. This should take 10-15 mins. Put the pan under a preheated grill to set the top. Or you can turn it over at a slightly earlier stage, letting it break as you turn over pieces as large as possible. They will re-cohere as cooking goes on. Eat in wedges, hot, warm, or cold, but not chilled; eat with a salad, in sandwiches, alone . .

Pasta with Asparagus and Peas. Snap the ends from **500g asparagus**, and cut into 1-cm lengths. Defrost **500g frozen peas**. Boil a large pan of water, with salt, and cook the asparagus pieces in this for 3 mins. Scoop them out, and add **300g. pasta**. While this is cooking, soften **2 chopped shallots** in **20g butter**, and add **300 ml double cream**. Let it reduce a little, **salt**, and add the drained asparagus pieces and the peas. Drain the pasta when done, and add to the sauce and toss. **Pepper**, and the **juice of ½ lemon**. Serve on hot plates with grated **Parmesan**.

Asparagus Risotto Snap the ends from **500g asparagus**, and cut the tender parts into 2-cm lengths. Keep the tips separate, and add to the risotto only at the end. Cook the middle portion of the asparagus in boiling salted water till half-done, about 2 mins. Scoop them out. The remaining water is to be turned into stock for making the risotto; either strengthen the liquid with Marigold stock powder and cook the hard stem bases in this; or use the bases with other components of vegetable stock – onion, carrot, leek, celery, bay, thyme, a little salt, other veg as available but not fennel or tomato – to make a fresh stock. The better the stock the better the risotto. You need **about 1¼ litres of stock** for **400g Arborio or other risotto rice**, for a risotto for 6 as a starter or 4 as a main course. Keep the stock nearly simmering on the stove. Soften **3 chopped shallots** in **50g butter** in a large frying pan; add the cut-up partially cooked asparagus, and stir gently. Add the rice, stir gently again until the rice is well-coated, and let cook a couple of minutes. Add the first ladle of hot stock, stir, and simmer gently until almost dry, when you add the next ladle of stock. Keep going until the rice is cooked, stirring often. If you run out of stock, continue using nearly-boiling water. But you may have some stock left; it depends on the balance between evaporation and absorption. Add the asparagus tips when the rice is nearly cooked – you want 2-3 mins cooking time for the tips. When the rice is done, turn off the heat. Add **pepper** to taste, **salt** if needed, and **30g butter** and **30g grated Parmesan**. Stir these in well, and eat immediately. **More grated Parmesan** on the table. This is not only a terrific dish in its own right, but stretches 500g asparagus to feed 6.

Asparagus and Swiss Chard with Parmesan. A dish with many virtues, as well as good taste. It uses Swiss chard stalks, which can be problematic, and it stretches 500g asparagus to feed 4 amply. And it can be prepared early in the day, and just finished in the oven for 15 mins. before eating. And it's unusual in England, though much commoner in Italy. Trim **800g Swiss chard** of all the leaves, leaving only the stalks. Save the leaves for another use. Cut the stalks into lengths and widths that match your asparagus, and boil them in UNSALTED water till tender, 5-10 mins depending on age. Scoop out the stalks, drain well. Add **2 tsp. salt** to the cooking water, and add

500g asparagus, prepared. Cook till just tender. Scoop out and drain. (The remaining water, cooked with the asparagus bases, is a good start on a stock). Smear **20g butter** over the bottom of a baking dish, and layer the two veg, starting with chard. Sprinkle the top with **60g grated Parmesan**, dot with **50g butter**. Bake at 200 for 15 mins or so, until the cheese has formed a pale crust. Let it stand a few mins before eating.

Spring Vegetables Vinaigrette. A platter with just-cooked spring vegetables. Asparagus, broad beans, young carrots, new potatoes, peas, and anything else your garden supplies, arranged in areas of each vegetable, and sprinkled with vinaigrette. Good bread, white wine, eating outside in the evening – simple bliss.

Asparagus Rolls. This antiquated dish is still found at unsmart weddings, usually made with tinned asparagus and commercial sliced bread. Sometimes it's been frozen, so the bread is soggy. It's quite popular, too. If I wanted to do asparagus with bread, I'd go for pea-sized pieces of cooked fresh asparagus in a sauce of reduced cream with chervil or parsley, served in hollowed-out and heated crisp bread rolls. Much harder to prepare for a buffet, and much harder to eat – just nicer.

You can also make asparagus quiche – mostly it appears with a few stalks cartwheeled on top of an ordinary quiche, and is there as a token; custard, crumble, and so on. I can't recommend them. Keep it so that you taste the vegetable, and its freshness, and try not to degrade asparagus by using small quantities for ornaments. It is, after all, our most esteemed common vegetable.

Broad Beans

Broad beans are a very old, very European vegetable. All the other forms of beans we use fresh come from the Americas; broad beans are ours from prehistory. And in that case, it is sad that what we can buy are just pods, usually mature at least, and sometimes downright elderly. The broad bean has so many delights to offer growers. There are tops. There are young pods which can be cooked whole. There are delicate young beans, fingernail-size, which can be eaten raw. Larger beans, still fresh, before the seam at the top has gone black. And if you let the crop get away – by going on holiday, for example – there are still things you can do with elderly beans. Broad beans aren't a heavy-yielding crop, so it's good to use every possible bit. If you have a vegetable garden, put broad beans high on the list.

Start with the **Broad Bean Tops.** Any gardening manual will tell you to pinch out the growing tops after the plant has flowered, to deter blackfly. It does do this, but, more importantly, the tops are delicious. The tops are washed and boiled in plenty of salted water for about 5 mins, drained, and roughly chopped. Butter, more salt if needed, pepper. You only get enough for one meal from a 10m row, but they are exceptionally delicious. One son says they are his favourite vegetable. Anyone who tries them once will line up next year for the treat. If you find an excess in farmer's markets or vegetable boxes, you could put some in soup, but it would be a shame.

Baby Pods Cooked Whole.
For this the pods should be about 10 cm long, not much more, and they are cooked Turkish-style to melting tenderness. Trim and string **500g of broad bean pods**, and mix them with **½ tsp. salt** and the **juice of a lemon.** Let them sit and absorb these tastes, while you slice **4 large spring onions** and chop a **handful of fennel lea**ves and the **leaves from 3-4 sprigs mint** Put half the beans in a pan with a lid, and add the spring onions, half the fennel, the mint, **¼ tsp sugar**, and a ground spice mix of **½ tsp black pepper, 2 cm piece cinnamon,** and **a few blades of mace**. Add the other half of the beans, **4 tbsp. olive oil**, and **300 ml. water**. Simmer very gently, covered, for 1½ hours, making sure the pan doesn't boil dry. Eat them warm or cold, with yoghurt and the rest of the fennel. While these are delicious, it really cuts down on

the crop, so is unlikely to be used often. However, if you're going away and the tiny pods will be overblown by the time you get back, this is the recipe to use.

Raw Baby Broad Beans.
The beans, when shelled, should be smaller than your fingernail. Taste one or two; if you don't like them raw, or find them bitter, change your plans and cook them (below). Many years ago, I read an Elizabeth David description of a Sardinian starter with raw broad bean pods, pecorino cheese, salami and chunks of bread. I find that with this as a starter you don't need more meal, just some fruit to finish. Obviously the salami is out; try substituting hard-boiled eggs or quail's eggs with salt, or some smoked or pickled tofu. Maybe add some baby tomatoes? Whatever, this is a meal which can easily be a picnic, or, eaten indoors on a dank summer day, makes you feel as if you're picnicking in the sun!

If you have more than you can eat this way, (how lucky you must be) try using them in the green salad with feta or the Chinese leaves and broad bean salad below. Alternatively, if there are some small ones among the standard broad beans you are podding, keep them aside, and add the raw baby beans to the final cooked dish.

Standard Broad Beans. These are the sort you will come across if you are buying your beans. I've had some deliciously fresh and small from a veg. box, but what I see in supermarkets has me turning away disappointed. If supermarket beans are all you can access, I think you are better off with frozen broad beans; they are fairly small, quickly frozen after harvest, and available year-round. They are not as good as the best, but better than most you can buy.

With shelled broad beans comes the problem of to peel or not to peel the cooked beans As the beans mature inside the pod, they develop a coat which becomes progressively less pleasant. If they are quite large, it's worth peeling; blanch the beans till almost cooked, drain, and dump into cold water to stop the cooking. Drain again, and pop the bright-green inside bean out of its shell. If using frozen beans, defrost, then peel. It's easy to do, once you've got the knack with the first 5 or 6. It is undeniably time-consuming – if you are cooking for more than 4 on a domestic basis, I'd guess it won't happen. But peeled broad beans are so delicious and so pretty, and so much nicer to eat without the outer coat. As a guideline, I'd say definitely peel if they are large, or a garnish, or a few with something where you want the colour effect. In other cases it's up to the balance between time and perfectionism.

This all applies to beans which don't have a black line where they are attached to the pod. If they do have a black line, they are really too old, and even the peeled bean is mealy rather than tender. If you need to use these for some reason, think of the various purees and soups, and PEEL.

There are so many ways of using standard beans that I've had to leave a lot out and just pick favourites. They are roughly arranged as beans as a side dish, in salads, main dishes, and soups and oddments like dips. The first 3 categories blend into each other, particularly in summer.

Default. Plain boiled, with butter. Pod the beans, and plunge into boiling salted water. Cook for a time depending on size and taste – 3-10 mins. Drain, add a knob of butter, and eat.

Italian Broad Beans.
This really brings out the difference in philosophy between English and Italian methods; this is a dish rather than an accompaniment. Less pure in taste, instead there are complementary flavours to set off the taste of the beans. Shell **1½ kg bean pods (yielding about 500g)** Put in a pan with **2 tbsp. extra-virgin olive oil, 4 or 5 sage leaves**, and **water to cover by 2 cm.** Cover, and cook on low heat for 30 mins. Add **salt** and freshly ground black **pepper**, stir. Just before serving, swirl in another **2 tbsp. extra-virgin olive oil**. Serve with the juices and good bread. I am not keen on sage, so I would use another herb instead – savoury if you have it (it is the classic herb for beans), marjoram, or thyme.

Broad Beans with Cream.
Shell **2 kg. broad bean pods**, and boil the beans for 5-7 mins till almost tender. Drain. Put back in the pan, and add **20g butter**, stirring to coat the beans. Add **200 ml double cream**, and add **salt, pepper, a grating of nutmeg**. Cook gently till the cream has thickened slightly,

sprinkle with **chopped herbs** (parsley and chives, or marjoram, or chervil if you have it), and serve. Not for every day, but so delectable.

Broad Beans with Almonds.
Cook the beans from **1½ kg. pods**. Saute **4 chopped spring onions** and **2 chopped cloves garlic** in **3 tbsp. olive oil**, add a **handful of parsley**, chopped, and mix with the beans. Add **toasted flaked almonds, about 50g**, but don't mix in. Serve.

Polish Broad Beans.
Heat **200 ml. plain yoghurt** with **1 dsp. Dijon mustard, 1 dsp. runny honey**, and **salt** to taste. Add **cooked broad beans, from about 1 kg. pods**. Warm everything well, **pepper** to taste, and eat.

Broad Beans with Egg and Lemon.
Boil **500g shelled beans** as usual. When draining, keep **a cupful of the water they have cooked in**. Beat **2 egg yolks** with the **juice of a lemon**, mix the reserved water in this, and heat very gently, beating all the time until the mixture has thickened slightly. **Salt** to taste. Pour it over the beans. Eat hot or cold. Getting the sauce to thicken is tricky, and it's all too easy to let the egg start to scramble. It's easier to use a double boiler, or beat in 1 tsp. cornflour with the egg yolks. Other vegetables can be added to the beans; cooked baby new potatoes; chunks of courgette, lightly steamed; sliced raw radish; very thinly sliced raw celery sticks. Only one at a time. Whatever it is, it shouldn't have so much taste that the bean/lemon flavour is swamped. Incidentally, if you use the juice of 2 limes instead of lemon, and add a little grated lime rind, the difference – and the effect – is amazing.

Normandy Style Broad Beans.
Shell and cook the **beans from 2 kg. pods**. Drain, reserving **a cupful of the cooking water**. Meanwhile, chop the bulbs of **a bunch of spring onions, about 12**, and sweat them in **50g butter**. Beat **2 egg yolks** with the reserved bean water, and add beans and eggy liquid to the onions in the pan. Warm VERY gently, stirring, and lifting the pan off the heat if necessary, until the liquid thickens slightly. Taste for **salt**, add **pepper**. Stir in **4 tbsp. cream**, sprinkle with chopped herbs – **parsley** is probably best, but a little chervil would be good. Eat, with good bread.

Chinese Broad Bean and Mushroom Stir Fry.

Shell **2 kg pods.** Slice **200g small mushrooms** thinly – either closed-cup or small chestnut mushrooms. Mix **1 flat tsp. cornflour** with **3 tbsp. water, 1 tbsp. sherry or white wine (or rice wine, if you keep it)** Heat **1 tbsp. oil** in wok or frying pan, add the mushrooms, and stir-fry for 1 min or so, until they have seized in the oil but aren't thoroughly cooked. Tip out onto a plate. Heat **another tbsp. oil**, add the beans, and stirfry 1 min. Add **120 ml stock or water**, with **salt** if needed, and **1 tsp. sugar**. Cook, stirring, over high heat for 2 mins. Put back the mushrooms. There should not be much liquid left. Stir the cornflour mixture again, tip into the pan, and stir till it thickens. You can drizzle over **½ tsp. toasted sesame oil** if you have it, OR sprinkle with **chopped green coriander**. Not both.

Simple Broad Bean Salad.

Boil about **400g shelled beans**, and drain. Peel if necessary. Make a dressing from   **½ tsp French mustard, 1 tbsp. white wine vinegar, 4 tbsp. extra-virgin olive oil, salt** and **pepper**, and **chopped herbs – parsley, chives, marjoram if you have it.** Pour the dressing over the hot beans and let it cool. You can substitute mint for the parsley, which tastes quite different but equally good.

Garlicky Salad.

Cook **400g broad beans**, shelled, and drain. Make a dressing from **1-2 cloves garlic**, pounded or mashed with **½ tsp. salt, the juice of a lemon, 4 tbsp. extra-virgin olive oil,** and **some chopped fresh basil**. Pour over the beans and let them cool. Add **2 medium tomatoes**, chopped into bean-sized pieces, and **2-3 chopped spring onions**.

Broad Bean Salad with Herbed Yoghurt Sauce.

This is essentially tzatziki with broad beans and herbs added, and a truly delicious and rather filling salad. Ideal for lunch on a hot day. Cook **250g broad beans**, and drain. Grate **half a cucumber, salt** for half an hour or so, rinse, drain, and squeeze in a teatowel. Mix the cucumber into **250g Greek (or Greek-style) yoghurt**, and add **4 tbsp. extra-virgin olive oil, the juice of 1 lemon, 1 finely chopped clove garlic, 3-4 sprigs of mint, leaves chopped, salt to taste,** and **pepper.** Add the beans and leave for about an hour. This makes enough for 6. It keeps overnight in the fridge.

Chinese Leaf and Broad Bean Salad.

Very simple, very good. About **half a head of Chinese leaves**, sliced thinly, and **200g broad beans, cooked.** Mix. For the dressing, mix **2 tbsp. soy sauce, 2 tsp. caster sugar,** and **the juice of ½ lemon**, and stir till the sugar has dissolved. Add **1 tbsp. sunflower oil**, and **a little very finely chopped fresh ginger** to taste. Pour over the salad and toss.

Green Salad with Broad Beans and Cheese.

This is a very free-form recipe, in fact more of a suggestion. The greens can be simply lettuce – cos, butterhead, loose-leaf – or can be mixed with other greens, like baby spinach or watercress. I think you want them green not pale. Broad beans can be raw, if young, or cooked, and probably peeled. About 100g for 4 people. Cheese should be crumbly and have a distinct taste; try chevre, feta, Lancashire, white Stilton. The dressing can have balsamic vinegar if you like it, otherwise standard vinaigrette with a little mustard.

Broad Bean Salad with Pickled Lemon.

Cook and drain **enough broad beans for your eaters**; the broad beans are the main component here, with small amounts of strong flavour. Let the beans cool in an **oil-and-lemon dressing**, and then add, to taste, **shredded pickled lemon**, and **a few black olives**. If you like raw onion this is a good place for **very thinly sliced red onion rings.**

Broad Bean Salad with Raw Mushrooms and Cheese.

For 4 people, cook **500g broad beans**, drain, and add to 4. tbsp. vinaigrette to cool. (Make up the vinaigrette with **5 tbsp. extra-virgin olive oil, 1½ tbsp. wine vinegar, salt and pepper**) Slice **250g small white mushrooms**, mix with about 2 tbsp. vinaigrette, and add to the beans when they are cool. Cut into cubes **200g English hard cheese**. Cheddar, Cheshire, Caerphilly all add a different note, and Sage Derby, when you can find it, is very good. If you like some of the modern cheeses with additions – apricots or cranberries or the like – you might try some of these here. You can scale this up for buffets for large numbers, and it always vanishes. With the cheese, it's more of a meal salad than a light side dish.

Broad Bean and New Potato Salad.

Equal quantities (say 400g of each) of **cooked broad beans** and **new potatoes**, cooked and cut into bean-sized pieces. You can use a vinaigrette here, but I prefer the mustard/mayo/yoghurt mix, with **1 tbsp. Hellmann's, 1 tbsp. Greek yoghurt, and 1 tsp Dijon mustard**. Sprinkle the top with quite a lot of chopped **fennel leaves or dill**, and garnish with **a few capers or baby gherkins**.

Broad Bean Salad with Rice.

Cooked, cooled rice. Cooked broad beans. Roasted red or yellow pepper, sliced, not too much. **Chopped spring onion or red onion rings. Vinaigrette dressing. Capers or olives** on top. Almost any mix here will be delicious, so adjust quantities to your taste and your eaters.

Broad Beans with Eggs and Croutons.

Cube **2-3 slices bread, decrusted**, and fry the cubes until brown in **2-3 tbsp. olive oil, or 50g butter**. Add **250g podded beans**, cooked if fresh and thawed if frozen (and peeled if they need it/you have time), and stir gently together for a minute or two. **Salt** and **pepper**, and the **juice of ½ lemon**. Meanwhile, scramble **6-8 eggs** with **butter or olive oil**, whichever you used for the croutons, and add the bean/crouton mix just before the eggs are done. Goes best with some form of potato; plain boiled new if in season.

Broad Bean Omelette.

For each person, cook **50-60g broad beans**, and PEEL. Beat **3 eggs** lightly with **salt** and **pepper**, mix in the beans, and cook the omelette in **butter** as usual (see Techniques) Just before it's ready, add a sprinkling of **cheese**, grated (Cheddar or hard goat cheese), crumbled (Lancashire) or cut in tiny cubes (Gruyere, Gouda) Roll the omelette and serve immediately, to someone who should be sitting waiting. This is an ideal use for a few leftover cooked beans.

Broad Beans Basquaise.

Sweat **1 large chopped onion** in **2 tbsp. olive oil**. When soft and starting to become gold, add **2 green peppers**, seeded and thinly sliced, and **2 chopped cloves garlic**. Cover the pan, and cook for about 10 mins. Off the heat, stir in **½ –1 tsp. smoked Spanish paprika**, Add **a tin of tomatoes, salt, pepper**, and simmer 5 mins more. Now add **500g or more of raw broad beans**, cover again, and cook on low heat 20 mins or more, until the broad beans are well-cooked. This is nice with something crisp, like toast or even fried bread.

Hot and Sour Broad Beans with Baby Onions.

The Indian spices here, and the souring from the tamarind, make this thoroughly Indian in taste. Certainly goes with a rice dish (or couscous). I wouldn't do a dhal, because the broad beans are already a pulse, but a curried green vegetable (see spinach) would be super. Shell the **beans from 1 kg. pods**. Peel **250g baby onions**, and brown them all over (as far as possible) in **2 tbsp. sunflower oil** (or other, neutral-tasting oil) in a large flat pan with a lid. Take out the small onions, add **another tbsp. oil** to the pan, and add **1 tsp. each of black mustard seeds, cumin seeds and fennel seeds**. When the mustard seeds have popped, add **1 medium chopped onion**, stir, and let it soften. Then add **3 cloves garlic**, chopped, the small onions, the broad beans, and **a chopped fresh chili**. Stir and leave a couple of mins. Add **3 tsp. tamarind puree**, from a jar, and **about 200 ml. water**. Add **2 tsp. dark brown sugar, ½ tsp. salt.** Simmer, covered, until the veg are done, about 30 mins. If there is too much liquid left, take off the lid and turn up the heat to evaporate the excess.

Chinese Bean Fritters with Sweet-Sour Sauce.

Shell, boil, drain, peel **300g broad beans**. Make a batter with **100g white flour, pinch of salt, about the same amount of black pepper (more than usual), 4 tbsp. water, 1 tbsp. oil,** and **1 egg white stirred in (unbeaten)**. Put the beans in this. Deep-fry the mixture in tablespoonfuls, and lift out when golden brown. Drain on absorbent paper, like newspaper. Heat **2 tbsp. oil** in a separate frying pan, and add **5 cloves chopped garlic**. Add **3 tbsp. tomato ketchup, 4 tbsp. water, 1 tbsp. sugar, 1 tbsp. wine vinegar,** and ½ tsp salt. Bring to boil, and add fritters. Stir round to coat with the sauce, and serve immediately.

Broad Bean Soup.

Really a minestrone of spring vegetables, so the ingredients can be varied according to what you have. This is a really good version, though, so try it first. Shell **3 kg broad bean pods**. Sweat, covered, **2 chopped onions, 4 young carrots, peeled and finely cubed, 4 finely** sliced celery stalks, and 2 small leeks, finely sliced, in 3 tbsp. olive oil. When soft, add 2-4 cloves garlic, chopped fine, 2 sprigs thyme, and 3 new potatoes, scraped and finely cubed. After 2 mins, add the broad beans, stir, and let it all sit, cooking gently, for a few mins. Add 600 ml. stock or water, salt if needed, and simmer covered about 30 mins. Take out the thyme. If you have a hand-held blender, use this to chop some of the veg. more finely. If not, don't! You cut the veg in small pieces earlier, so there's nothing awkward to spoon up. Taste for salt; pepper. Dribble with extra-virgin olive oil, and serve with lots of grated Parmesan. Or miss out the oil and cheese, and have pesto (p.50) for people to add their own.

North African Broad Bean Dip.

Shell 1 kg. broad bean pods, and boil and drain the beans, keeping the cooking water. Peel the beans, and put in a food processor with 2 chopped cloves garlic, 2 sprigs oregano or marjoram, chopped, 1 tsp. ground cumin, sprinkle chili flakes, and 150 ml. extra-virgin olive oil. Salt and pepper. Add 8 tbsp. cooking water, and whizz. If it's too thick, then add more cooking water. Taste and adjust; it may benefit from lemon juice. Transfer to bowl, and use as dip, spread, or in sandwiches. It's also good on toast with a poached egg on top. If a dip, then dilute a tsp. rose harissa (from a jar) with olive oil, and dribble over the top.

Broad Bean Pate.

This, like the dip above, is a use for any broad beans which have got large, old, and mealy. When the beans are pureed, the mealy texture vanishes, leaving only flavour, and peeling the beans get rid of tough skins. You don't want bits of skin in your puree. Cook 300g broad beans, drain, peel, and put in food processor. Add 100g. cottage cheese, the juice of a lemon, and 2 tbsp. cream. Salt and pepper. Whizz and taste. It may need more cream, depending on the maturity of the beans. Sometimes I like to add a little grated horseradish.

As well as all these, broad beans appear in Fritedda, succotash, and new carrot and broad bean pilau,

Edamame, or Green Soy Beans.

These are a new vegetable, following intense efforts to breed a soybean which can be grown in this country. You might find them sold in the pod, and then you can boil the small pods and suck out the beans when they are done. Not elegant but fun. Or you can find packets of frozen edamame beans in most supermarkets. In this case, I'd say treat them like broad beans, and any of the above bean recipes can be used. Or you could try using the recipes for shell beans; the Tuscan recipe goes particularly well.

Cauliflower

Beautiful unmistakable cauliflower. I love it. Others complain about strong flavours and cooking smells. Strong and distinctive flavour is good, in my book, and I think you only get cooking smells when there is a lot of water and the cauliflower is overcooked. English cauliflowers can turn up at any time of the year, but mostly in spring and autumn. I've put it in spring because that's when there are fewer other vegetables around.

There is, likewise, a lot of discussion on whether the cauliflower should stay whole or be cut up. I'm definitely on the cutting-up side. A whole cauliflower is bound to cook unevenly, and needs to be cooked for longer. It's true it can look more spectacular on the table, but I wouldn't ever trade looks for taste and goodness. So all my recipes use cauliflower broken or cut up into florets, seldom more than 3 cm. across the top. This way, too, it's easier to find any pests which also want their share. And you would rather have the possibility of pests than something so sprayed that you can be sure there are none – wouldn't you? You can use the small pale leaves inside the cauli, and the base sliced thinly and cooked with it. I once knew someone who thought the cauliflower stalk, shaved thin and eaten raw, was the cook's perk.

It is often tempting to try a mixture of cauliflower and its close relative broccoli. The colours are complementary, and it seems like a witty thing to do. I've never made a success of it; the flavours seem to clash. Perhaps the incompatibility is best shown with cheese sauce; cauli loves it, broccoli, to my taste, doesn't go with cheese sauce at all.

Default. This is a recipe which my mother picked up from Philip Harben on the telly, about the early 50's, and I've never found a better basic way. Cut the **cauli** into florets, including some of the inner leaves if you like, and slicing the thick stem thinly. Put in a pan with a good lid, and add **3 tbsp. water, a chunk of butter about 30g, and ½ tsp. salt.** You want the florets not to be too deep in the pan, so an average cauli will need a large saucepan. Put on the lid, bring to a boil, and cook 5-10 mins. on a moderate heat. When it's done, the water will have evaporated – no draining needed – and the cauli will be tender. By accident or design, you can let it cook a little longer, so the bits in contact with the pan toast. This is delightful for the eaters but not so good for the washer-up!

If you find you'd like variations on this, add chopped herbs, or nuts – roasted peanuts, walnuts, almonds, whatever – or chopped olives. There are many recipes where the cauli. is boiled first, then tossed in butter and garnishes like these added. My way is simpler, nicer, and makes less washing up.

Roast Spiced Cauliflower.

This closely follows Nigella Lawson in How to Eat, where she thinks of it as diet food. I think it's good enough to be just food. Break a **cauli** into florets, sprinkle with **salt** and ground **cumin**, and roast at 180 for about 20 mins. It has the wonderful toasted flavour, supported by the spice. It's even good cold.

Cauliflower with Garlic, Ginger and Chili.

For a **medium cauliflower** use **2-6 cloves garlic, a knob of ginger**, and **2 fresh chilis**, deseeded. Chop all finely. Cook the cauli., cut into florets, by steaming or cooking in a covered pan in a little water. Heat **2 tbsp. olive oil**, add the garlic/ginger/chili mix and stir, then add the cauli. If it's hot, just fry together a little, stirring, and adding **salt**. If the cauli is cold, add to the pan, **salt**, mix well, and then cover and cook on low heat until all is hot. Take off the lid, turn up the heat, and fry 2-3 mins more. You can do this with just chili, with garlic and chili, or with all three; they are all very good indeed.

Cauliflower with Tomato Sauce.

Steam or boil in little water the florets from a **medium cauliflower**. Drain. Cook **3 chopped cloves garlic** in **6 tbsp. olive oil**, till starting to change colour. Add a small bunch of **parsley,** chopped finely, and stir. Then add the contents of a **tin of whole tomatoes**, drained well, and cut up. Stir round, and cook fairly quickly for about 10 mins, till the sauce is slightly thickened. Add the cauli florets, **salt** and **pepper**, and cook 5 mins more, stirring. Taste and serve. It's fine alone, as an accompaniment, or with pasta.

Cauliflower with Tomatoes and Green Olives.

Cook florets from a **medium cauliflower** by steaming or boiling, covered, with a little water. Cook **a small onion**, finely chopped, in **3**

101

tbsp. extra-virgin olive oil till pale gold, then add the florets, a handful of pitted and cut-up green olives and a little salt (because the olives are salty). Cook quite quickly for 2-3 mins, stirring, till everything is warm and blended, and then add 250g peeled diced tomatoes, the best you can find. Keep stirring from time to time, and cook 5 mins. more. Pepper, quite a lot. Serve straightaway. This makes quite a lot, and I find that any leftovers with a little more oil and a little vinegar make a good salad next day.

Cauliflower with Sultanas and Pine Nuts.

A Southern Italian dish, hence the pine nuts. But if you have no pine nuts, hazelnuts or almonds are fine. Cook a medium cauliflower, cut into florets, by steaming or boiling in a little water. Then you need a frying pan, with a lid, so that the florets pack in as close to one layer as possible. In it, cook 4 cloves garlic, chopped finely, in 6 tbsp. olive oil. When the garlic starts to change colour, add cauli, 30g. each sultanas and pine nuts, salt, and about twice the pepper you'd normally use. Cover the pan, and cook for 10 mins on low heat, stirring from time to time.

Cauliflower with Almonds and Broad Beans, Chinese-style.

As with all Chinese stir-fries, get everything ready first and then the cooking goes smoothly and fast. Cook 200g broad beans, if fresh, or defrost, if frozen. Cut ½ a medium cauli into small florets. Mix 1½ tsp cornflour with 1 tbsp. dry sherry, 1 tsp. sugar, and 2 tbsp. water in a cup. Toast 50g whole almonds under the grill. Chop 2 cloves garlic, and bash with a pestle 2 thin peeled slices fresh ginger (These are not to be eaten). You can now start. Heat 2 tbsp. oil in wok or large frying pan, add garlic and ginger, and stir for about 10 secs. Add the cauli, broad beans, and ½ tsp. salt. Stir and fry for 2 mins, then add 2 tbsp. water and cover. Cook another 2-5 mins, and taste to see if cauli is done to your liking. Take off cover, stir the contents of the cup and add to the pan, and stir till the sauce has thickened. Add the almonds, dribble in 1 tsp. dark sesame oil, and serve immediately. You can take out the ginger if you can see it; otherwise just warn your eaters not to eat it.

Cauliflower with Cream.

Not something to eat every day, but so rich and delicious as an occasional treat. Cook the cauliflower florets as usual, and put in a serving dish. Meanwhile, cook **2 shallots** in **50g butter** till soft. Add **4 tbsp. wine vinegar** and boil down till 1 tbsp. is left. (Alternatively, if you have access to shallot wine vinegar, reduce 4 tbsp. of this in the same way) Stir in **250 ml. double cream**, and cook till the sauce is thick. **Salt** and **pepper**. Pour over the cauli. You could use parsley, but I think this should be a virginal creamy foodscape.

Green Cauliflower for Spring.

I have to admit that this dish, where a pea puree is poured over cooked cauliflower, would look much prettier with a whole cauli. But I don't care; florets are just fine. Anyhow, cook florets from a **medium cauli**, by steaming or boiling in a little water. Cook **3 prepared chopped spring onions** in **25 g. butter** till soft. Add **300g best frozen peas**, thawed. Cook 5 mins, add **150 ml. double cream, salt, pepper** and **nutmeg,** and bubble briefly. Whizz in food processor or blender. Reheat if needed, and pour over the dish of cauliflower.

Cauliflower and Turnip Puree.

A simple cauliflower puree is easy enough (cook and puree in food processor with butter, herbs, seasonings) but it isn't particularly exciting. This mixture, which perhaps should be given a different name, is really interesting, and it's quite a puzzle to work out the ingredients if you don't know. Cook florets from **a small cauliflower**. Peel and chop **250g new turnips**, and sweat, covered, in **25g butter** with **2 tbsp. water, a bay leaf** and **a slice of lemon** till done. This will take 20 mins or so if the turnips are small, up to an hour if they're older. So do it in advance. Take out lemon and bay. Puree cauliflower and turnips and put the puree in the top of a double boiler. Add **4 tbsp. double cream, salt** and **pepper** and ground **nutmeg**. Add a dash or two of **Tabasco**, stir, and taste and adjust. Reheat/keep hot over simmering water – a good vegetable to avoid a last minute flurry. Just before serving, add **25g butter**, and beat in.

Cauliflower and Watercress Puree.

I'm not sure if this is a side or a main dish; it's here because it is a puree. It needs plain things to go with it – bread, salad, maybe bean burgers without buns. Nothing with oil, butter or cheese, anyhow. Cut a **medium head of cauliflower** into florets, and drop into boiling salted water. After 5 mins, add the **leaves from a bunch (or a packet) of watercress**, and cook another 4-5 mins. Drain. Puree this mixture, and add **400 ml. bechamel sauce** (Basics; **50g butter, 40g flour, 400 ml milk, salt and pepper**). Gradually add **up to 150 ml. cream** – the puree should not be too thin. Add **60g grated cheese, salt** and **pepper** to taste. Put in a buttered baking dish, sprinkle the top with grated **cheese** and **breadcrumbs**. You can stop at this stage till 20 mins. before eating; at that point, put into a 180 oven and cook till brown on top.

Cauliflower Parmesan Fritters.

The batter for these is almost like a tempura batter, but includes Parmesan. They are simply wonderful. Start by cooking the **cauliflower florets** lightly, so they still have some firmness. (Boiling/steaming in a little water; 7 mins) Put **8 tbsp. lukewarm water** in a bowl, and beat in **40g plain flour**. Add **30g grated Parmesan**, and a pinch of **salt**. Add **1 egg**, beaten separately, and beat together well. Heat **oil for deep-frying**. When a cube of bread dropped into the oil sizzles, and browns in 20-30 sec, the oil is ready. Dip a few florets in the batter, let them drain over the batter bowl, and drop into the hot oil. Cook till golden. Scoop them out and add the next batch. As they are removed from the oil, drain on a rack or on kitchen paper, then transfer to a serving dish. Serve as soon as you can. (Ideally, you'd have people in the kitchen snatching as soon as they are cool, but this isn't suitable for such a civilised dish. It should be sat down to)

Cauliflower Fritters with Chili Mayonnaise.

In this case, dip the cooked florets in a standard frying batter (Basics), deep-fry, and serve with chili mayonnaise or chili dipping sauce. Chili mayonnaise is best if blender made, with 2 chilis-en-adobo added to a 1-egg mayonnaise. This is really only for the young and reckless, or physically active – alas.

Cauliflower Salads. Here is a question which only you can decide. Some people really like their salads made with raw cauliflower, crunchy and healthy and taking all sorts of complementary flavours. Others, like me, like a little bit of a salad with raw cauli, but will eat much more, and enjoy it much more, if the cauli is cooked. All my salads here use cooked cauliflower, but in many of them you can use raw cauli, and have a different taste which you may prefer. All salads using cooked cauliflower (or any other cooked vegetable, come to that) taste better if dressed while they are still warm. So if you are using leftovers, as we all do from time to time, be a bit more positive with seasoning and additions, and use a bit less oil and vinegar, because it's not absorbed so well. Most of these you can, but need not, serve on green salad leaves. I tend to have the green salad separately, as once dressed it wilts quickly, whereas vegetable salads can last overnight easily.

Pure Cauliflower Salad is simply cooked cauliflower florets with a vinaigrette dressing. Chopped herbs to improve. You can add other vegetables you have around, so getting **Cauliflower Salad with Broad Beans** (garlic in the dressing), **Cauliflower Salad with Green Beans** (with Chinese dressing of soy sauce, vinegar, little sugar, LITTLE toasted sesame oil), **Cauliflower Salad with Radish and Spring Onions** (very fresh and spring-like)

Sicilian Christmas Cauliflower Salad.
I assume this is the season for cauliflowers in Sicily. Add to the **cooked cauliflower florets 1 roasted red pepper**, cut in strips; **black olives**, halved and stoned; **capers**; sliced **baby pickled gherkins** (cornichons, if you buy them in France). **Extra-virgin olive oil** and **wine vinegar dressing**, with **salt** and **pepper.** What makes it so suitable for Christmas is that you can add more of the garnish next day (and the days after, if it doesn't get too strong).

Horseradish Cauliflower Salad
Mix **½ a small tub of sour cream** with **horseradish** –fresh grated, or from a jar of horseradish – to taste. (Have no truck with jars of creamed horseradish, horseradish sauce, etc, unless you actually don't like the taste of horseradish and want a symbol of it) **lemon juice, salt** and **pepper.** Cook the **cauli. florets** (from a small cauli) as usual, and toss in the dressing. This is one which really benefits from freshly-cooked cauliflower. Add some of **30g toasted almonds**, and use the rest to sprinkle on top.

Three C's Twice Salad The first three c's are cauliflower, Caerphilly, and cashew nuts. The second 3 C's is the Australian sauce, which adds a little heat to the dressing. Unfortunately this 3C's sauce isn't made any more. I haven't found a really satisfactory substitute;

probably the best is a moderately hot salsa, or try a mango hot sauce, though this is really too sweet.

This is one in which to try raw cauli, cut up small. My version has cooked florets from a **medium cauliflower, 150g Caerphilly**, cut into sticks, **100g toasted cashew nuts**. Mix them, and dress with **6 tbsp. mayonnaise** with sauce to taste, (or maybe 3 tbsp. mayo, 3 tbsp plain yoghurt, 1 tsp. French or grainy mustard with sauce to taste) and the **juice of a lemon** mixed in.

La Belle Vaughan Salad.

A French composed salad, with potatoes, cauliflower, green beans, and asparagus, with hard boiled eggs. You can make a production of this, making a dome with the mixed vegetables, coating with mayonnaise, and decorating with hard-boiled egg slices and using egg yolk and whites to make a central daisy. Don't. This sort of production is way out of date, but it doesn't mean the basic flavours are not truly delicious. Cook, separately, florets from a **medium cauli**; **500g salad potatoes**; **500g French beans**; and **250g asparagus tips**. They should all be cooked lightly. Cube the potatoes and mix with the other veg, being careful not to squash anything unduly. Add a dressing of **10 tbsp. extra-virgin olive oil, 3 tbsp. white wine vinegar** (maybe tarragon vinegar), **salt** and **pepper**, and mix in lightly. Hardboil **3 eggs** while the salad is cooling, peel, slice, and mix in very carefully. Put in a large flat bowl, and sprinkle with chopped **parsley**. Serve with **mayonnaise** in a separate bowl – must be home-made here, if not, give it a miss. This needs nothing with it but bread, and certainly the mix is too heavy to take green leaves. It makes a lot, but it is almost as good the next day as well.

Cauliflower a la Grecque.

This is one of my standbys when I have used half or more of a cauliflower, and what I have left isn't enough to use as a dish. The cauliflower florets are cooked lightly first, then cooked again in an oily, lemony, winey spicy marinade. It's then a splendid component of a spread of small salads. Cook the florets from **half a cauli** for just 3 mins. Make the broth by mixing **250 ml. dry white wine, juice of 2 lemons, 5 tbsp. olive oil, 1 tsp. each coriander seed and black peppercorns**, lightly crushed, **1 tsp. salt**, and **thyme** and **bay leaf**. Bring this to be boil and simmer 5 mins, to blend the flavours, then immerse the florets in the liquid. Cover, simmer 5 mins, then let the mixture cool together. If you like, you can strain off most of the broth and use it to cook other vegetables, such as baby leeks, small onions, courgettes, or mushrooms. Mushrooms, especially, respond to a tinge of tomato, so add 1 tsp. tomato puree to the broth. This is a very good method to know, since it applies to so many vegetables, and the sharp flavour is refreshing in warm weather. It also helps the vegetables to keep.

Simplest Cauliflower Soup.

Blanch the florets of a **medium cauliflower** for 3 mins., and drain. Peel, quarter, and slice thinly **200g potatoes**. Put both into **600 ml milk** – full-fat best – with **1 tsp. salt**. Bring to the boil, cover, and let simmer 25-30 mins, or till soft enough to puree. Note; if you're cooking in milk, here or elsewhere, always rinse the pan in cold water before you start. The thin water film left reduces any singeing of the milk, which otherwise happens very easily. Puree – mouli-legumes, blender, stick blender, whatever. Add **up to 200 ml more milk** to reach your preferred consistency, and reheat. Taste for **salt**, and add a little grated **nutmeg** to taste. No pepper here. Swirl in **30g butter** and add some chopped **chervil**, for preference, otherwise **parsley.** Serve with **croutons fried in butter**. Pure, rich, bland – it has to be early 20th-century French bourgeois cooking.

Cream of Cauliflower and Watercress Soup.

This is made on a different principle, with no potatoes and the soup thickened with flour. The milk is replaced by stock and the soup enriched with cream at the end. Cook **200g sliced leeks** in **50g butter** till soft but not coloured. Add **30g flour** and stir in, and cook 1-2 mins. Add **800 ml. stock or water**, and bring to the boil, stirring. **Salt and pepper**. Add the florets from a **medium cauliflower** and simmer 10 mins. Add a **chopped bunch or bag of watercress**, keeping some leaves back for garnish. Simmer 5-10 mins. more, and puree the mixture by your preferred method. Taste for seasoning. Just before eating, reheat, stir in **150 ml. double cream**, and sprinkle the reserved leaves on top.

Cauliflower and Sorrel Soup

This is a variation on the cauli-and-watercress one, using **2 good handfuls of sorrel** instead of the watercress. Wash the sorrel, and let it collapse in **30g butter** on low heat, covered. . Cook **200g sliced** leeks in **50g butter** till soft but not coloured. Add **30g flour** and stir in, and cook 1-2 mins. Add **800 ml. stock or water**, and bring to the boil, stirring. **Salt** and **pepper**. Add the florets from a **medium cauliflower** and simmer 15 mins Add the sorrel. Puree, taste for seasoning. To my taste, this needs very little **cream – 3-4 tbsp.** – and **30g butter** swirled in just before eating. Sorrel and cauli are a terrific combination; I don't know why it's not classic.

Persian Cauliflower Omelette (Kuku)

Cook the florets from half a **medium cauliflower** lightly – it should still be crunchy. Chop the florets till no more than pea-sized. Cook **3 finely chopped cloves garlic** in **2 tbsp. oil** in a large frying pan, then add **6 sliced spring onions**. Stir and cook briefly, then add the cauliflower, **½ tsp. salt**, and **black pepper**. Stir and cook till the cauliflower has some light brown bits. Let it cool, then mix with **6 beaten eggs**, with a little **salt**, and chopped **parsley** (say, half a supermarket packet, but this really is up to personal taste and what you have. If you have **dill** or fennel herb, this would be even nicer and more Persian) Wipe out the large frying pan, melt **15g butter** in it, and add the cauli-egg mix. Cook on LOW heat until slightly crisp at the edge and brown on the bottom. Turn over; my break-up and turn bits technique is fine. Cook again on low heat, till the bottom is brown and the centre is set. The kuku should be quite deep, rather like a thick pancake, and can be eaten straightaway or as a snack when cold.

Cauliflower Cheese.

This is my own, down-home, comforting winter supper. It will be disapproved of by chefs and those who wish to make food more elegant, or more expensive. It's much more to my taste, and that of my family and friends, than anything using cream and Parmesan (good though these are in other contexts, just not here). Start by cooking a **medium cauliflower**, broken into florets, with sliced stem and inner white leaves. Little boiling water for 8-10 mins. Meanwhile, melt **40g butter** in a flat-bottomed pan, add **30g flour**, blend, and let cook on low heat for 2-3 mins without colouring. If it doesn't spread out to cover the pan base, but is lumpy, add more butter. Pour in, all at once, **300ml cold milk**; stir well, and turn up the heat. Stir frequently while it's coming to the boil, but you can leave it enough to add **1 tsp. salt**, quite a lot of **pepper**, and a good grating of **nutmeg**. As it approaches the boil, it will start to thicken, and at that point keep stirring, getting into the pan corners. It's a very simple way to do it. Cook 5 mins on a low heat once it's thickened, adding more milk if it's too thick. Then take off the heat, and beat in **120g strong Cheddar**. Drain the cauli well, (you might even roll it in a clean teatowel), spread out in a shallow dish, and cover with the sauce. Sprinkle **more grated cheese on top** – my family likes lots, and I can easily use more than 50g. If all is hot, put under the grill until everything is bubbling and the top is golden brown. If it has been waiting, put into the oven at 180 to heat through, finishing under the grill if necessary. We eat it just with hunks of bread, saving anything else for a separate course.

Cauliflower Gratin.
I owe the idea of this to Gregg Wallace; it's much simpler than the cauliflower cheese, and goes better with, for example, baked potatoes. Cook florets from a **medium cauliflower** as usual; drain, and put in large flat baking dish. Mix **150 ml plain Greek yoghurt, 1 tsp. French mustard,** and **100g grated Cheddar**, and drop spoonfuls over the cauli, spreading out to cover it all. Sprinkle with **breadcrumbs** and **25g butter** in small pieces, and grill until gold.

Cauliflower Hash.
Peel, boil and cube **500g potatoes**. Cook the florets from a **medium cauliflower**, cut them a little smaller, and mix with the potatoes. Add **1 small chopped onion, salt, pepper** and **nutmeg**. Add **100 ml. double cream** to the mix, stir, and pour into a large frying pan in which you've heated **2 tbsp. olive oil**. Cook fairly slowly, breaking up, turning, and squashing the mix as it browns on the bottom. You should end up with a flat cake full of crunchy brown bits. It's possible to play around with this – add cheese, add beaten eggs to the pan when it's nearly done – but it's very good just as it stands.

Pasta with Cauliflower.
This is one of those pasta dishes that are really a first course not a meal, and you need something after it – an omelette or a dryish dish with chick peas or dried beans. It couldn't be simpler; make **cauliflower with garlic, ginger and chili** (p. 67) without the ginger, and mix with just-cooked **pasta**. Keep some of the pasta water to moisten the pasta mix, if you like. Grated **Parmesan** if you like.

Cauliflower and Eggs with Pasta.

Obviously a version of carbonara, but if you call it that any meat-eaters will be disappointed. It's good in its own right. Much more of a meal than the above, but very similar. When making **cauliflower with garlic and chili**, make sure that the cauli florets brown a little. Add to the **just-drained hot pasta**, and pour over **3 beaten eggs** with **salt** and **pepper**. Stir through the pasta/cauliflower mix so the eggs cook lightly, add grated **Parmesan**, and serve immediately.

Cauliflower Pastitsio. (4-6 people, depending on hunger)

Add macaroni cheese to cauliflower cheese, and get pastitsio. Cook **200g pasta**, and drain. Cook a **medium cauliflower**, cut in florets; drain and mix with the pasta. Cook **1 large chopped onion** in **50g butter** till soft, add **40g flour**, and cook a couple of minutes. Add **500 ml milk**, and bring to the boil, stirring. **Salt, pepper, nutmeg.** Cook 5 mins, take off the heat, and add **150g grated strong Cheddar**. Mix the sauce with pasta/cauliflower mix. Tip into a large baking dish, sprinkle with **more grated cheese**, and bake at 200 until the top is browned in places. These dishes are not good if there isn't enough sauce, but that's about the only thing to go wrong. If you are really in a hurry, you can use 1 can of Campbell's condensed soup + 1 can milk. (Celery, mushroom, cream of onion).

Cauliflower and Rice Casserole.

In the (unlikely) event that you have run out of pasta but have some rice, you can adapt the above dish. Cook **200g** rice in boiling salted water till JUST done, drain, and add to it **2 chopped shallots** sweated till soft in **30g butter**. Add chopped **parsley**. Cook the florets from a **medium cauli**, drain well. Make a sauce as above, using stock instead of milk (**40g butter, 30g flour, 400 ml stock, salt, pepper, nutmeg.**) Grate **200g Cheddar**. In a buttered deep baking dish, layer 1/3rd rice, 1/3rd sauce, 1/3rd cheese, half cauliflower. Repeat, twice, ending with cheese. Bake in a hot oven till bubbly and browned. Saying "if you've run out of pasta" doesn't sound very positive about this, but in fact it has a taste, texture and virtues of its own. Do try it!

Cauliflower Sformato.

This is a slightly cut-down version of a souffle – with less respect, but also can hang around longer. See Broccoli for a full souffle recipe. Cook a **medium cauli**, in florets, with the stem sliced thinly.

Preferably use the default method and let the bottom layer toast a little – even with the lid on, your nose will tell you this is happening. Make a thick white sauce with **20g butter, 15g flour,** and **250 ml. milk. Salt, pepper, nutmeg.** Whizz cauli and sauce in a food processor, and whizz in **3 large eggs.** Then whizz in **80g grated Parmesan,** (more Italian) **or 120g grated strong Cheddar** (cheaper, tastes very good). Turn the whole into a buttered baking dish; low and wide gives more crust, deeper helps the sformato to rise. Both work. Sprinkle the top with **more grated Parmesan or Cheddar,** whichever you used first. Bake at 180 till risen, set, and gold on top – depending on dish, it will take 30-40 mins. Let it cool a few minutes before eating.

Curries. All the dishes above – especially the main courses – have been full of cheese and rich and bland. This is one of cauliflower's strengths, but the other is its response to curry spices. In fact I've probably done more curries with cauliflower over the years than I've cooked the cheese-y ones. The following is a selection of favourites in different styles, but there are many more possibilities out there.

Cauliflower with Fennel and Mustard Seeds. Strictly, this isn't a curry, which is a liquid dish, but it uses Indian spicing and cooking methods. Cut a **medium cauli.** into florets a little smaller than usual – no more than 2 cm. across and 5 cm. long. You need a large frying pan with a lid. Heat **4 tbsp. vegetable oil** in this, and add **1 tsp. whole fennel seeds** and **2 tsp. whole black mustard seeds.** When the mustard seeds start to pop, add **4 finely-chopped cloves garlic.** Cook 1 min, then add **¼ tsp. ground turmeric** and about the same of **cayenne pepper.** Add the cauli florets, stir, then add **4 tbsp. water** and **1 tsp. salt.** Stir again, cover the pan, and cook for 5-10 mins, depending how crisp you like your cauliflower. At the end, if any water is left, take off the lid and turn up the heat to evaporate it. Chopped **fresh green coriander** if you have it and aren't using it elsewhere in the meal.

Cauliflower with Ginger and Fresh Coriander.
This doesn't just use fresh coriander as a garnish, but the cauliflower is cooked in it. You need a **large bunch of fresh green coriander – equivalent to about 3 supermarket packets** – so make this when you've been to an oriental shop where it's comparatively cheap to get a lot. You also need a piece of **fresh ginger weighing 30-40g,** which

must be peeled, then reduced to a puree – grated on a microplane, pounded in a mortar, or whizzed in a blender with 4 tbsp. water. (This last idea is often used by Madhur Jaffrey for onions, garlic, ginger, which need to be pureed for their proper effect in Indian food) Cut a **medium cauliflower** into small florets. Heat **4 tbsp. vegetable oil** in a large frying pan with a lid, and add the ginger and **½ tsp. turmeric**. Cook gently, stirring, about 2 mins, then add **1 chopped deseeded green chili** and the green coriander, chopped. Stir, then add the cauli florets. Cook gently about 5 mins, stirring. Add **1 tsp. cumin, ground, 2 tsp. coriander ground, 1 tsp. garam masala, 1 tsp. salt, juice of 1 lemon,** and **4 tbsp. water.** (If you get spices ready on a saucer first, this is easier) Stir again, cover, and let it cook very slowly for 30-40 mins (this isn't critical). Stir every now and then, and add a little more water if it's needed.

Cauliflower with Onion and Tomato.
Cut a **medium cauliflower** into florets. Whizz **1 medium onion, 4 cloves garlic**, and **30g ginger** in the food processor to a paste. (All these should be peeled and cut coarsely first) Heat **4 tbsp. vegetable oil** in a large frying pan with a lid, and add the onion paste and **½ tsp. turmeric**. Fry until the mixture starts to brown a little. Add **2 chopped tomatoes, tinned or fresh, 1-2 fresh chilis, seeded and chopped, a little chopped fresh coriander, and a spice mix made of 1 tsp. each cumin seeds, coriander seeds, black peppercorns,** and **½ tsp. cardamom seeds, ground together.** Add **1 tsp. salt**, and the **juice of ½ lemon**. Stir all this to a uniform paste, then add the cauliflower. Stir again to mix, add **4 tbsp. water**, cover, and cook 30-40 mins. It's interesting to compare this and the last recipe; they have a lot in common, but taste quite different. This is also a good one if you might have extra people turning up; you can add frozen peas at the last minute, with a bit more water, and provide for more people without visible effort.

Cauliflower with Potatoes.
Heat **2 tbsp. vegetable oil** in a large pan with a lid – ideally that frying pan again. Add **1 chopped onion**, and fry on moderate heat till it starts to brown. Add **300g potatoes**, peeled and cut into 1-cm cubes, and cook till they start to brown. Add a **chopped deseeded fresh chili, 1 tsp salt**, and a **spice mix of 1 tsp each coriander seeds, fennel seeds, and black peppercorns, ground with 2-3 cloves. Juice of 1 lemon,**

½ tsp. turmeric, and stir together. Add **1 medium cauliflower** cut into florets, then **1 small carton yoghurt, 4 tbsp. water**. Stir again, cover, and cook till the potatoes are done.

Cauliflower with Potatoes and Peas

This comes from Maharashta, the area surrounding and inland from Mumbai, whereas the last recipe is much less localised. Again, see how much difference the spicing makes to a basic dish using the same ingredients. Cut into small florets **half a medium cauliflower**; cube **250g potatoes**. Heat **4 tbsp. vegetable oil** in a large frying pan with a lid; when hot, add a **pinch asafoetida (hing)**, then **1 tbsp. black mustard seeds**. When these start to pop, add **10 dried curry leaves**, if available. If not omit this step. Now add potatoes, cauliflower, **125g peas, 2 small hot green chilis, chopped with seeds, ½ tsp turmeric, 1 tsp. salt, ½ tsp. sugar**. Stir-fry for 2 mins. Add **4 tbsp. water**, cover, and cook for 15-20 mins, or till the potatoes are just done (I find that potatoes cooking with not much liquid and spices take much longer than you'd expect) Sprinkle with **2 tbsp. grated fresh coconut** and chopped **fresh green coriander.**

Channa Dhal and Cauliflower Stew.

Definitely a main dish. Wash **200g. channa dhal**, and put in a saucepan with **1 chopped onion, 40g ginger, grated, 6 cloves garlic, chopped**, and **1 litre water**. (If you chopped onion, ginger, garlic in the food processor, it would only improve the transfer of flavour) Add **½ tsp. turmeric, 2 dried hot red chilis**, and bring to the boil, Simmer, covered, for 15 mins. Fish out chilis and bay leaf. Now add **200g potato**, peeled and cubed, **quarter of a medium cauliflower** cut into florets, **2 tsp. salt**.. Cook another 20 mins, or till the potatoes are done and the dhal has collapsed to a puree. It should not be too thin – if it is, boil hard for a few mins. to evaporate some water. The last touch is the enrichment with fried spices, called Tarka. Heat **4 tbsp. vegetable oil (or ghee, if you have some)** and add **2 tsp. cumin seeds**. When they turn brown, very quickly, add **2-4 seeded chopped chilis**, swirl, and tip the whole into the lentil pan, where it will sizzle and hiss and transfer the odours to the lentils, etc. Add the **juice of ½ lemon** (more, if to your taste), **1 tsp. garam masala**, tip into a serving dish, and sprinkle with chopped **fresh green coriander.**

Cauliflower and Peas in Yoghurt.

This is what I'd call a raita, but a bit more substantial than the standard cucumber version. It needs very little to turn into a light meal – a few spiced fried potatoes, maybe. Cut **half a medium cauliflower** into florets, and steam/boil in little water for 5 mins. Drain. Add cauliflower, **60g defrosted frozen peas, ½ tsp salt, 1 tsp ground roasted cumin seeds** to **500 ml yoghurt**, a large carton. Taste for **salt**; season with **black pepper**. Chill.

And, last, **Anglicised Vegetable Curry including Cauliflower.**

Chop finely **6 cloves garlic, 30g ginger, 2 fresh deseeded chilis**, and cook them gently in **2 tbsp. oil**. Add a spice mix of **2 tsp coriander seed, 1 tsp. cumin seed, ½ tsp. fenugreek, 1 tsp. black pepper,** and **a 5 cm stick cinnamon**, all ground together, with **1 tsp. turmeric** and **1 tsp. salt**. (If you haven't all the spices, use 2 good tsp. garam masala) Stir and cook 2 mins. Add **2 tins crushed tomatoes**, and **200 ml stock or water**. Add **1 tbsp. tamarind** from a jar. Then add **1 medium cauli**, cut into florets; **2 medium potatoes**, peeled and cubed; **¼ swede**, peeled and cubed, and a **drained and rinsed can of chickpeas**. Simmer covered 30 mins or more, till the potatoes and other roots are done. Add **100g defrosted frozen peas, 150 ml. plain yoghurt**, and stir in well. **Juice of 1 lemon**, or to taste Chopped **fresh green coriander**. Serve with boiled rice, chutneys, pickles . . .it's delicious. Obviously you can vary the veg – sweet potato, parsnip, winter squash. Add some shredded green leaves to the dish at the end – or even at the beginning; India has lots of curries involving long-cooked spinach, so you're not doing something strange.

New Carrots

This can mean anything from the thinnings from your home-grown carrots to the bunches with foliage in supermarkets. The smaller they are, the less chance they have had to develop the rounded flavour of mature carrots, but they have their own charms, so fresh and delicate and crunchy. I'd definitely say don't peel these, just scrub. And they don't need to be grated or cooked with strong tastes. Cook lightly, cook with spring flavours, eat raw and simple, and celebrate them as one of the joys of spring.

Note; the packets of "baby" carrots sold in supermarkets are often larger ones trimmed and shaped, and not new at all. Taste to judge the texture and sweetness, before using any of these methods for them.

Default.
Trim the tops, leaving maybe a little tuft of green to hold them by, scrub, and eat raw, rather like radishes. The fresher the better here. It's really more like grazing; if you leave a plate of garden thinnings around while people cook, lay the table, and so on, there probably won't be any left. You could also have them with a dip, but keep the flavour mild. The exception here is garlic, which complements them well, either as a wild garlic dip or the Greek Skordalia

Skordalia.
Basically a garlic mayonnaise without eggs, but with breadcrumbs and ground almonds, this is tricky to make by hand, but very easy in a food processor.
You need **half a roasted head of garlic**, ideally done when the oven is on for something else. Squeeze the garlic cloves into the food processor. If this doesn't suit for some reason, peel and blanch **4 cloves garlic**, and drain. Put these in the food processor. Soak **a crustless slice of good bread** in a little water, squeeze out the water, and add to the processor. Add **60g ground almonds, salt, 4 tbsp. olive oil, 4 tbsp. hot water,** and **the juice of a lemon**. Whizz. If it's too stiff, add a little more hot water. taste, and add more oil or vinegar to adjust. This can be a dip for any crudites, fritters, falafel, new potatoes, beetroot, green beans . . Or a dressing for hard-boiled eggs. Done like this, it's a beautiful balanced sauce. If you'd like more garlic hit, use

raw garlic; no roasting, no blanching. This isn't really balanced, but it will open your sinuses and taste amazing.

Cooked New Carrots.
There is one way of cooking here, and several ways of finishing to make the final vegetable dish taste a little different. Top, tail, and scrub or peel **500g new carrots**, cut them up as necessary, and put in a pan with **a few tbsp. water, a knob of butter, a little salt,** and **a little sugar**. Cook gently, uncovered, for 10-15 mins. or until the water is gone.

Lemon carrots, Finish 1. Add the **juice of a lemon** and some chopped **mint**, and heat about 1 min. longer

Thyme flowers, Finish 2. Just add some **thyme or marjoram flowers** when the carrots are cooked and just before serving.

Capers, Finish 3. Use **olive oil instead of butter** when cooking the carrots, and add a **clove of garlic**, chopped. Toss with **capers** to taste before serving

With Toasted Nuts, Finish 4. Ideally with **pine nuts**, toasted lightly. Other toasted nuts, like hazelnuts or almonds, are also very good, and pistachios would look amazing, but I'd steer clear of walnuts as having too strong a taste.

With Butter Sauce, Finish 5. This is really a mini-course to eat alone, with bread. Cook the carrots just with water and salt. For the sauce, a version of beurre blanc, chop **a shallot** finely, and put in a pan with **120ml. white wine** and **½ tsp. salt**. Bring to a boil, and reduce to about 1 tbsp. Divide **125g room-temperature butter** into 8 cubes while this is happening. Add one cube at a time to the reduced wine mix, stirring quickly and moving the pan on and off the heat, so that the butter doesn't melt but emulsifies. When you get it right, you end up with a uniform, thick-liquid, pale and lukewarm sauce, permeated with flavour of shallot and wine, with a light texture. It is one of the most delicious sauces around, and an amazing transformation of three basic ingredients. Anyhow, finish the sauce with some chopped **tarragon**, if you have some, and eat with the carrots. Some excellent new potatoes would be good here, too.

Cooked Grated New Carrots.
Very fast, after the carrots are grated. Grate **400g new carrots**, and put in a pan with **20g butter, salt** and **pepper**. Cover and cook 5 mins, turning the mass now and then, until done. Add **a squeeze of lemon** to

taste. **Herbs** can be added – not needed, but nice. Try chives, fennel, dill, mint, tarragon, or basil – just one, not all. Perhaps chervil is nicest, but also hard to come by unless you grow it, because it's so fragile and wilts so fast.

These go well with other seasonal veg, lightly cooked, like new potatoes, asparagus, broad beans, new turnips, peas, and so on. In fact a platter of fresh lightly-cooked veg like this makes a splendid meal, warm with butter and bread, or cold with a dressing of mayo/mustard/plain yoghurt on the side. If the carrots are to be eaten cold, cook them with olive oil (1-2 tbsp) not butter.

Carrot and Broad Bean Pilau.
Very much a springtime dish, with both vegetables young and fresh. Don't try it any other time. Scrub or peel **500g young carrots**, and cut into pieces about twice the size of broad beans. Shell **750g broad bean pods**; blanch the beans, drain, and peel. Sweat **2 chopped shallots** in **2 tbsp. olive oil** till soft, then add the carrots and sweat 2-3 mins more. Add **200g long-grain rice**, and cook, stirring, until the rice has become translucent. Add **400 ml. stock or water**, **salt** if needed, a **bay leaf** and **a couple of sprigs of oregano or marjoram**. Bring to the boil, cover, turn the heat right down and let the rice cook till all the liquid has vanished. Then turn off the heat, put a folded teatowel over the pan and put the lid on top, and leave it to sit quietly for 10 mins. or more. Heat **1 tbsp. extra-virgin olive oil**, add the beans, and warm through gently. Add the **juice of a lemon**, and stir all into the pilau. **Pepper** if liked; taste for salt and add more if needed; take out the oregano sprigs, and sprinkle chopped **herbs** – marjoram or dill or fennel or parsley – over the top. If you have marjoram in flower, use some flowers as wall as leaves – a lovely effect.

"Root and Leaf" Soup.
The tops of the bunched young spring carrots look so tempting, but I've hardly ever come across a use for them in the kitchen. This is one; the soup is sludgy-coloured, and it's not obvious that it's a carrot soup. Challenge people to guess. It does taste very good, and the recipe was used by someone else within a few days of them tasting mine.
Trim the **tops from a bunch of new carrots** – about 10, about 15 cm long, if you're picking not buying. The carrots weigh about 500g without tops. Cut off the tough bases of the stems, and chop the rest

roughly. Grate the **carrots**, or leave a couple aside for garnishing and grate the rest. Sweat **a small chopped onion in 30g butter**. Add grated carrots, carrot tops, **3-4 sprigs thyme (lemon thyme if you have it)** and sweat, covered, a few mins. more. Add **700 ml stock or water** and **3 flat tbsp. long-grain rice**, and **1 tsp. salt if your stock is unsalted**. Simmer, covered, 20 mins. Let it cool a bit, and make smooth by whichever means you prefer – blender, mouli, hand-held blender, food processor. It's a good idea, though not quite necessary, to fish out the woody stems of the thyme. Reheat, thin with more stock/water if necessary or to your taste, taste for seasoning. Garnish and serve. The garnish can be **thin matchsticks of the carrots held back from grating, or a dribble of cream in a pattern, and/or croutons**. The cream can be added to the soup and stirred in. The spiral dribble uses less cream and sets off the colour; the cream stirred in makes it taste fuller in the mouth. It's good cold, too.

New Potatoes

What a treat at the right time of year! How we love them! Plain, simply boiled, scraped or not as you like, with butter, they are as English a treasure as asparagus.

Why do we esteem new potatoes so highly, when other countries just see them as part of the yearly run of vegetables? Partly, I think, because of the Jersey Royal, but mainly because, until recently, none of our potatoes were waxy. If you wanted to make a potato salad with non-floury potatoes, new potatoes in season were the only game in town. It's hard to remember that forty years ago writers could be astonished by the fact that in France you could get potatoes for salad for most of the year.

The Jersey Royal I think is still better than any other new potato, but it ain't what it used to be. All my friends of a certain age, and me, agree that Jerseys don't have the taste and texture they used to. Maybe there are so many more grown now that cultivation has become more intensive and more labour-saving. I've heard it said that part of the original method included using seaweed for fertilisation, and this has been superseded by modern fertilisers. This is a story one would like to believe. Certainly organic Jersey Royals are much closer to the old style, if not identical But even the modern Jersey Royal is a joy for ever, particularly if you never knew the old. And small fresh Cornish or Boston new potatoes can be as good as modern Jerseys, when fresh. Try growing them yourself. I've only grown Sutton's Foremost, which was marvellous.

Scraping. Scraping or scrubbing as preferred technique probably depends on age. When I was a child, new potatoes came dirty. After a quick rinse, I, or any other child about, was sat down with a bowl of water and a blunt knife, to scrape the potatoes. The very thin skin came off so easily, leaving a beautiful white potato. I still believe that a potato that won't scrape isn't a new potato, whatever the label says. I am so used to scraping that it doesn't seem like a chore, but I could never get my children to do it. So the modern way is to wash, scrub lightly, and boil in their skins. It saves time; it is probably marginally healthier, but to my mind it does slightly shade the pure pleasure of eating new potatoes. If they are freshly dug, however, there isn't a skin to come off; this gradually develops over the next few days.

Don't leave the potatoes hanging about before they are cooked, and certainly don't (EVER) soak them in water. It takes away the freshness of taste, and the vitamins. It's better for new potatoes to be added to boiling water, rather than putting them in cold water and bringing to the boil, but it's not a big deal if you do it the other way. Salt the boiling water. Everyone I know puts a sprig of mint in the pan when boiling new potatoes. This is really a bit of kitchen magic; you may get a little flavour of mint when the potatoes are scraped, but if they are in their skins there is no way the mint can flavour the potatoes. But the scent announces to the family that there will be new potatoes soon.

When it comes to eating the plainly boiled new potatoes – they take 15-20 mins, depending on size – I still prefer the childish way. Unadorned potatoes on the (cold) plate, and butter smeared into a small wedge on the side of the plate. Only a limited amount of butter, because it was rationed. Take a potato on the fork, take a small piece of butter on the knife, smear the potato with butter, and eat before it melts. I used to eat tiny amounts of butter with most of the potatoes, and save the smallest potato and the largest piece of butter for the end. Often this last mouthful had more butter than potato! An early introduction to the pleasures of delayed gratification.

This is not the modern way. The cooked boiled new potatoes are drained, put into a warmed serving dish, butter added and mixed in, and chopped herbs added. It's probably a better way, especially if whatever else you're serving benefits from a warmed plate, but childish habits are powerful and I still prefer the first way.

The few recipes here are those which can only be done with real new potatoes. Those for salad potatoes, or waxy potatoes generally, or imported new potatoes from Egypt or Cyprus, have their place in the main potato section. The distinction obviously isn't absolute, though.

Fondant Potatoes (Pommes de Terre Fondantes)
Beautiful, and unexpected. **500g new potatoes**, as close to the same size as possible, and not too big. Scrape, rinse, and dry them. **40g butter**. And, most important, a lidded pan in which the potatoes fit in

one layer, quite tightly. Melt the butter in the pan, add the potatoes and shake and roll them around, clamp on the lid, and cook over very low heat till the potatoes are done. Shake the pan with the lid on from time to time. There should be a gently bubbling noise going on inside, and the butter mustn't burn. **Salt** when cooked. The potatoes are golden on the outside and melting and tender within; there is not meant to be any crispness, as if they were roast potatoes.

Provencal Potatoes.

Start as for fondant potatoes, same pan, same preparation, only using **3 tbsp. extra-virgin olive oil** instead of butter. When the potatoes are cooked, add **2-3 cloves garlic**, finely chopped, and **a handful of parsley**, chopped. Mix them in but don't cook any more, so you get the full meridional hit of the garlic.

Potatoes in a Bag.

Scrape, rinse, dry **24 small new potatoes, golf-ball size or smaller**. Cut a large sheet of foil which will enclose them, and put the potatoes on the foil, with **50g butter, ½ tsp salt, 2 mint leaves**. Fold over the foil and fold the edges together, leaving the whole thing baggy rather than tight. Put the parcel in a 180 oven, and cook 20-25 mins. Perfectly cooked, buttery, no trouble, no watching – and if you have more people, you simply make more bags.

Two Sauces for New Potatoes.

1. Cream Sauce. Put **50g butter** and **4 tbsp. double cream** in a small pan, and heat gently, stirring, till it thickens. **Salt (quite a lot), pepper, nutmeg**. Either pour it over the potatoes, or, if you want to reheat previously cooked potatoes, slice them and add to the sauce.

2. Metz Sauce. Make it in a double boiler, or a bowl balanced on top of a pan of simmering water. Work **1 level tsp plain flour** into **50g butter**. Chop **a small handful of parsley and tarragon and chervil**, if possible, with **2 shallots,** and put these with the butter mix in the bowl/top of double boiler. Add **1 tsp. Dijon mustard, a little grated lemon peel**, and **300 ml. double cream**. Heat over the simmering water, stirring now and then, until very hot but not boiling. **Salt** and **pepper**, and a **squeeze of lemon juice** to taste. Put **sliced boiled new potatoes** in this, and let them heat through. In fact, the sauce is so good that it enhances many other things – try adding French beans with the potatoes, or having the sauce with hot hard-boiled or poached eggs.

New Potatoes with Goat's Cheese.
The cooked new potatoes are mixed with a dressing of soft goat's cheese and milk. The little cylinders of rindless Welsh goat's cheese, found encased in plastic at supermarkets, are just right for this. Crumble up **50-60g of soft goat cheese** – half a packet – and mix with **30g butter** and **6 tbsp. milk**. Warm this together, stirring, till all is well-blended. Cook **700g new potatoes**, drain when cooked, and halve or quarter if they are not small. **Salt** and **pepper**, then add the cheese mixture and mix all well. Chopped **chives**. This is quite rich, and goes very well with one or more plain-cooked vegetables.

New Potato Salad.
As simple as possible; just the **cooked potatoes**, dressed while hot with a dressing of **extra-virgin olive oil** and **wine vinegar**, **salt** and **pepper**. Add a judicious amount of onion flavour, from **spring onions or chives**, and maybe some **radish** slices. Slices of **hard-boiled egg**, maybe. But don't get fancy in this case – leave it for when the main ingredient needs more support.

Smashed New Potatoes.
This is an ambiguous dish, in that it can be made just as well with seasonal new potatoes and year-round small salad potatoes. It's very new and fashionable (2008-9) for reasons I don't understand. It seems to me that it's the product of a yearning for mash when suitable potatoes aren't available.
Boil and drain **500g new potatoes**. Press each potato with a wooden spoon or similar, until it bursts, and add **25g butter, 3 tbsp. double cream, salt, pepper, chopped chives** and **parsley.** Mix very well with the wooden spoon, breaking up the potatoes further in the process. They are crumbed rather than mashed. Other things to try – green sauce; oil-and-vinegar; oil, capers, olives and sun-dried tomatoes.

More – much much more – on potatoes in the Year-Round chapter. I wanted to put something here, though, to celebrate the joys of a truly seasonal vegetable.

New Turnips

Little white turnips are a completely different vegetable to the winter version of the same name. Different flavour, different treatment. The late spring/early summer turnips are neat, pretty, shining white, tasty and crunchy eaten raw; maybe we should rename them. If you grow them, and they are very reliable, you can count about 8 weeks from sowing to eating, in Sheffield. These first turnips are about an inch across – more the size of radishes. If you get them this young, leave a tuft of green on top, to emphasise their youth.

Default: Glazed New Turnips.
Peel **500g new turnips** if you need to, and put in a pan with a **knob of butter, salt**, and **1 tsp sugar**. Water to cover, and boil briskly with the lid half off until the water has evaporated. Shake them so they are covered with the mixture of butter and sugar, and let them brown a little. **Pepper** and serve, with chopped **parsley if you like**. You can vary this by adding a few fried mushrooms, or even peas.

Punch-nep.
A Welsh dish of surprising deliciousness. Peel, cut up, and boil separately **500g young turnips** and **500g old potatoes**. Drain and mash them together, with **30g butter, salt**, and **lots of black pepper**. Smooth the top, and make small holes with a spoon end. Put **small pieces of butter, up to 60g**, in the holes. That's it; the flavour is unidentifiable but delicious. If you have the turnip greens, cook them like spinach and mix into the puree for a turnip version of **Colcannon**. (see Cabbage chapter for the original)

Turnips with Mustard and Honey.
Peel **500g new turnips** and slice fairly thinly, and boil for 5 mins in salted water. Drain. Meanwhile, melt **30g butter** in an oven dish, add **1 dsp light brown sugar, 1 tbsp. honey**, and **1 level dsp powdered mustard**. Work them together, and season with **salt** and **pepper**. Add the turnip slices, and mix so all the slices are coated. Cook at 170, covered, for ½ hr. Usually cooked mustard loses its bite, but not so here. So reduce the amount if you aren't fond of mustard, but the tang goes well with the sweetness and turnip flavour.

Roast turnips alone, or with other vegetables.

Roast **turnips** like any other vegetable, that is, peel, cut in chunks, put in roasting tin, pour over some **olive oil** and mix with your hands, **salt, few cloves garlic**, maybe a **sprig of rosemary**, and roast at 170 for 30-40 mins. A good early summer combination is turnips, red onions, red sweet peppers, potatoes, and courgettes, but the delightful thing about roast mixed veg. is that almost any combination is super. And troublefree.

New Turnips braised with spinach.

This version uses Japanese ingredients for an unusual effect. Peel **500g baby turnips**, halve, and cut in thin slices. Mix in a pan with **1 tbsp soy sauce, 1 tbsp honey, 1 tbsp mirin (Japanese rice wine), sherry, or white wine**. Add enough **water** to just cover, and simmer about 5 mins. Turn up heat and add **250g young spinach**, pushing down and stirring, until cooked. Sprinkle with **toasted sesame seeds** or other seeds like pumpkin or sunflower to serve. If you want to use the turnip greens in this, cook them first in a large amount of boiling water, drain, squeeze dry, and cut up roughly.

Turnip and Carrot Salad.

Grate **250g each turnips and carrots**, peeled. Mix with a dressing of **3 tbsp extra-virgin olive oil, 1 tbsp. lemon juice, salt** and **pepper**, and chopped **fennel**. This is so simple that its goodness is surprising – and, even more surprising, my kids liked it.

Lettuce, Turnip and Pea Salad.

Peel, halve if necessary, and slice thinly **8 small (5 cm) turnips**. Cook them in boiling salted water till just tender, and drain well. Cook **250g shelled peas**, or defrost frozen peas. Wash **1 soft-headed lettuce**, and tear the leaves. Mix all in a large bowl, and dress with **3 tbsp. extra-virgin olive oil, salt**, and **pepper**, mixing well. No acid in this. The contrast of textures, and the sweetness of the peas and turnips, is enough.

Green Turnip Soup.

Peel and quarter **700g new turnips**, and cook them by the glazing method with **25g butter, 1 tsp each sugar** and **salt**, and **water to cover**. Wash **350g turnip greens or spinach**, shred, and cook in **25g butter** till softened, about 2 mins. Puree the turnips and leaves in the blender with **some of 1 litre stock**. Mix **3 tbsp. ground rice** with a **little more of the stock**, and put the rest of the stock, the pureed veg, and the ground rice to boil, stirring. Cook gently about 20 mins., until the rice has thickened the soup. Add **300 ml. milk**, and add **salt, pepper**, and **lemon juice** to taste. A lovely soup, well worth the effort.

Cream of Turnip Soup
Call it **Potage Freneuse** if you think people may be put off by turnips. Sweat **1 onion**, peeled and chopped in **25g butter**, and add **500g new turnips**, peeled and chunked. Cook another 5 mins or so, then add **1 medium potato**, also peeled and chopped. Add **750 ml. stock**, and simmer about 40 mins. Blend, mouli, or sieve the soup, taste for seasoning, and add **4-5 tbsp. cream**. This needs **croutons**, either fried, nicer but calorific, or toasted, which are fine. You could also add some salted peanuts, in which case be very sparing with the salt earlier.

Turnip Curry.
Turnips make splendid curries. The best, by some way, is in Dharamjit Singh's Penguin Indian Cookery, Korma Shalgam, but it is long and fiddly. This is my usual curry using turnips, simpler and very good.
Peel **700g. turnips** and slice them vertically. Heat **60g ghee or 4 tbsp. vegetable oil**, add **2 onions**, peeled and chopped finely, and fry briskly until browning. Add **3 cloves garlic, chopped, a knob of ginger, finely chopped, 1 tbsp coriander seed ground with 1 tsp cumin and 1 tsp black pepper, ½ tsp turmeric, and ¼ tsp. cayenne pepper**. Stir briefly, then add the **tomatoes from 1 tin**, drained and squashed, **or 500g fresh tomatoes**, peeled and chunked. Cook about 5 mins more. Add the turnips, and **½ pt. water. 1 tsp salt**. Cover and cook gently till the turnips are done; reduce the liquid by boiling hard if necessary, as there shouldn't be too much sauce. Finish with garnish of chopped **green coriander**.

Turnip Goulash.
Fry **1 chopped onion** in **2 tbsp oil**. Add **1 red pepper**, seeded and cut into strips, and cook 5 mins more. Add **250g each turnips and potatoes**, peeled and chunked, stir round, then add **1 tbsp. Hungarian paprika** off the heat. (If you can't find Hungarian paprika, as I haven't been able to for some time, use Spanish smoked pimenton.) Add **300 ml water** and **salt**. No pepper. Cover and cook slowly till done. Then add **4 tbsp. double cream**, if it suits the rest of your meal, and lots of chopped **parsley** in either case.

125

If you are growing turnips, don't forget the turnip tops. In Italy these are called cime di rape, and are highly thought of. It may be a special variety of turnip that they use in Italy, however. They can be cooked by any recipe for strong greens, or try **Orecchiette con Cime di Rape.** In a large pan of boiling water, cook **350g. orecchiette** (pasta shaped like little ears) for 15 mins. Halfway through, add **500g. turnip tops,** washed and destalked. Meanwhile, warm **4 chopped garlic cloves** and **1 chopped deseeded fresh chili** in 4 tbsp. olive oil. Dip a cup of water from the pasta/greens pan, then drain when ready. Return to the pan, tip in the oil with garlic and chili, and add reserved pasta water so the mix is not too dry. Serve with **grated pecorino or Parmesan,** and **extra extra-virgin olive oil** so the eaters can add it to their taste. For 4.

Purple Sprouting Broccoli

This is so good, don't mess with it! I feel about this as I feel about asparagus; it's precious, it shows that spring is really here, and it's most enjoyable at its simplest. You can grow it, when you really get it at its best; or buy from farmer's markets, greengrocers, supermarkets. Just make sure it's English and as fresh as possible. You can buy it all year round, imported, quite often from Zimbabwe. It's not bad, but I just avoid it out of season.

Purple sprouting has had a precipitous career in public esteem over the last thirty years or so. It used to have no status at all – it occurred in spring, chucked at random into a greengrocer's box, with many tired leaves and very few flowering heads. Then came calabrese, with big dark green heads – it's hard to imagine that this is such a new vegetable in England, that it simply wasn't available until around 1980. As this moved rapidly from novelty to staple, purple sprouting also moved up in esteem. Because the yield is less than for calabrese, and it occupies the land for longer, it had to become more expensive to survive in competition. And because it was more expensive, people could notice its merits, which they hadn't when it was cheap. As grown, harvested, marketed now, it can take the comparison with asparagus – with which I fully agree. But the story does show us that taste isn't the only criterion by which a vegetable is judged, becomes fashionable or not, is expensive or not. You see a different twist on the same themes with cavolo nero, which would never have made it big as dinosaur kale.

Recently the supermarkets are selling "Tenderstem" broccoli. Just the same as sprouting broccoli for flavour and ways to use, but available for longer. It seems all of it is grown in Kenya and flown in, so I shall give it a miss no matter how persuasive the advertising. Breeders have also produced autumn-sprouting broccoli, which I would love to like. I've grown it and bought at a farmer's market, and it has been nowhere near as good as the spring kind. I may have been unlucky; try it and see what you think.

I have treated purple sprouting broccoli, and "normal" broccoli, as separate vegetables. This isn't right botanically, but is definitely right

127

in the kitchen. If you come across white sprouting broccoli, treat it just as purple.

Default Plain boiled. Allow 500g for 4 people, unless experience shows you need more. Trim the sprigs of any large, wilted, or tough-looking leaves, and any tough stalk. You can tell whether a stalk is tender or tough by pushing a fingernail into it; if the nail goes in, the stalk will be tender when cooked. If you have central heads which are more than 5 cm across, halve them lengthwise. Boil in plenty of salted water for 2-5 mins, depending on freshness and your taste. Hover and keep trying. Drain well, and serve on hot plates. Melted butter with it; or any of the egg/butter sauce, such as Hollandaise, Bearnaise, Breton . . I like to have it as a separate course, and pick it up with my fingers, dip into the butter or sauce, and then eat.

Purple Sprouting Broccoli with Garlic and Almonds.
Boil 500g broccoli, and arrange on a hot serving dish. Saute **50g almonds** in **50g butter** till golden, and add **2 chopped cloves garlic**. After 30 sec, pour over the broccoli, and take to table at once.

Purple Sprouting Broccoli with Pine Nuts and Raisins
A Sicilian-style recipe, in tribute to where the vegetable was first developed. Soak **25g raisins** for 10 mins or so in warm water if they are not juicy and sticky. Drain and dry. Toss **40g pine nuts** in **2 tbsp. extra-virgin olive oil** until starting to brown, then add raisins and cook just to heat through. Scatter over **500g cooked broccoli shoots.**

Roast Purple Sprouting Broccoli.
Trim **500g spears**, discarding tough stems, then cut into 10 cm lengths (This only applies to bought; most of my garden stuff is cut at about that length) Mix with **salt** and **4 tbsp. olive oil**, and roast in hot oven for 10 mins. You can, but need not, drizzle on **balsamic vinegar** before eating.

Stir-Fried Broccoli.
Trim and cut into bite-size pieces **500g purple sprouting**. Trim and slice **a dozen spring onions**. Stir fry for 2-3 mins in **3 tbsp. vegetable oil**. Then add a mix of **2 tbsp. soy sauce, 2 tbsp. wine (rice wine, dry sherry, or whatever; I wouldn't open a bottle of sherry specially),**

½ tsp. **sugar,** and **4 tbsp. water.** Cover and cook for about 5 mins. Eat straightaway.

Purple Sprouting Broccoli Salads.

Basic; dress plain-cooked broccoli while still hot with oil and vinegar or lemon, salt and pepper. Let it cool. Lukewarm is OK, fridge temperature isn't, really. You can vary this with other things; **Purples Salad with Red Pepper; Purples Salad with Walnuts and Black Olives** (and walnut oil if you have it); **Purples Salad with Radish and Spring Onion**

Marinaded Purple Sprouting.

This is close to, but not quite the same as, the a la Grecque method (p. 384). Mix **2 tbsp. olive oil, 75 ml dry white wine, 1 tsp. salt, juice of ½ lemon, thyme and bay leaf, 1 chopped clove garlic, 1 chopped shallot, ½ tsp.each crushed black peppercorns and coriander seed, 1 small dried chili, 150 ml. water** in a large frying pan with a lid. Simmer together for 10 mins. Add **500g purple sprouting**, well-trimmed, cover, and cook for 10-15 mins, or till the broccoli is done to your taste. Let it cool in the liquid. One virtue of this kind of recipe is that it is useful when, somehow, you have more fresh produce than you can use before it gets tired. Vegetables a la Grecque keep without deteriorating for 2-3 days.

Orecchiette with Purple Sprouting Broccoli. *****

I don't often specify what sort of pasta to use for a pasta dish, but in this case the small, hard southern-Italian "baby ears" are absolutely right. Supermarkets stock them, in the premium range. You need **350g orecchiette** for 4 people. Start with the sauce. Trim **500g sprouting broccoli**, and boil for 3 mins in salted water. Drain. Soak **25g sultanas** in warm water; drain. Saute **1 chopped onion** in **4 tbsp. olive oil** till soft, add **1 chopped fresh deseeded chili** and cook 1 min more. Add the sultanas, the broccoli, and **25g pine nuts**, and cook very gently for 10 mins, while the orecchiette are boiling. Drain the pasta, and turn into the pan with the broccoli mix. Mix gently; you don't want to break up the broccoli. Serve with **grated Pecorino** – just right for this, cheaper than Parmesan, and almost as easy to find. This is a five-star dish.

If you are a vegetarian who occasionally eats fish, then now is the time to do it. The orecchiette dish is even better with half a tin of anchovies, pounded, added to the sauce

Sprouting Broccoli with Scrambled Egg.
You don't really need a recipe for this; toast; scrambled egg; cooked broccoli spears on top. The combination of the creamy egg and the stalks is terrific.

Sprouting Broccoli Pesto.
Really a use for leftover cooked sprouting broccoli, should you ever have some. If you don't, cook a little – **150-200g purple sprouting–** specially for this. Cook lightly, and drain. Put in the food processor with **basil, parsley, chopped garlic, pine nuts, grated Parmesan, salt**, and **olive oil**, and whizz. Taste, and adjust the quantities of any to make it to your taste. Goes with pasta and gnocchi.

Sprouting Broccoli with Puree of Dried Broad Beans.
This is based on an Italian original which uses *cime di rapa,* also called *rapini.* These are the flowering tops of a special variety of turnip, and can easily be found in the US and Canada. I haven't seen them here, but in my experience sprouting broccoli is more tender, less tough.

You can make the puree of dried broad beans – butter beans – either from the dried beans, or use 3 tins of butter beans for 4 people. The dried beans may be marginally better, but the tin route is much less hassle. So, for dried, soak **300g butter beans** overnight, then boil in water to cover for 5-10 mins. Drain them, cool in cold water, and PEEL. Put the peeled beans in a pan with water to cover well, add **1 tsp. salt**, and simmer covered till the beans are pulpy. You want to end up with moist beans and no surplus water. For the route using tins, drain **3 tins butter beans**, rinse, and pick through to remove any skins. Now break into chunks **100g good white bread**, crusts removed before weighing, and pour over **4 tbsp. hot milk**. Let it stand 5 mins, and squeeze out and discard excess milk. Put beans, crumbs, and **75 ml (5 tbsp) extra-virgin olive oil** in the food processor, and whizz smooth. It should be quite thick, so you can lift a heaped spoonful; if it isn't, add more soaked crumbs. Leave to stand.

Trim and boil **700g sprouting broccoli** for 2-3 mins, and drain. You can do all this any time in the day.

When you're ready to eat, heat the bean puree in a double boiler or in the microwave. Chop **3 cloves garlic**, and cook gently in a frying pan with **2 tbsp. extra-virgin olive oil**. When it starts to change colour, added the drained sprouting broccoli, and cook, turning often, so that it heats through and mixes with the garlic. Taste both components for salt. Spread the pureed beans on a dish, and put the sauteed stalks on top. Dribble over **2-3 tbsp. extra-virgin oil,** and serve. Crusty bread needed, but little else. Note; there is no pepper, and this is intentional.

Radishes

This is only about "summer" radishes, the red or red-and-white, round or cylindrical, fast-growing spring and summer crop we all know. Winter radishes – larger, hardier – have their own section. Books will tell you that you can pick summer radishes 3 weeks after sowing. I've never found them grow that quickly, but they are indeed the fastest-growing crop. Mostly they are eaten raw, fresh, and crunchy, but there are ways of cooking and treating them which are often useful.

Default. The simplest of all possibilities – just eat! Wash and serve with a little tuft at the top, and eat alone, with salt, or, the French way, with butter and salt. For this, you smear a little butter on the radish, dip in salt, and eat. It's a nice, slow, meditative start to a meal.

Radishes in Sandwiches.

This isn't a recipe, more a reminder. Radish sandwiches by themselves are light. Slices of radish can enliven other sandwich material, like bean spreads or hummus. Simple radish sandwiches can be a side dish for dishes with sauce – try them with hard-boiled egg mayonnaise, for example.

Radish, Cucumber, and Spring Onion Salad.

These are all components of a mixed English salad, but isolating them like this brings out their separate virtues. It's surprising and addictive. Slice **a bunch of radishes, ½ a cucumber**, and trim **a bunch of spring onions**. Dress with **sour cream, salt**, and **lemon juice.** I like to leave most of the vegetables undressed, with a blob of dressing on top and more on the side, and let people muddle in the dressing themselves or eat the mixture. neat.

Tunisian Radish Salad.

Top and tail **a bunch or a packet of radishes**, and slice them thinly. Sprinkle over **1 tsp salt**, and mix in. Leave to stand an hour or so. Tip the mix into a sieve and rinse under the cold tap. Dry them. Add **1 tsp. capers** and **1 chopped salted lemon, juice of 1 lemon**, and **1 tbsp. extra-virgin olive oil.** This has strong and unusual flavours which may not be to everyone's taste, but I love it.

132

Radish and Cucumber Salad.

Trim and quarter **a bunch of radishes, or a packet**. Quarter lengthways and seed **a cucumber**, then cut into 1 cm. slices. Mix with the radishes. Heat **2 tbsp. sunflower oil** in a small frying pan, add **1 tsp. each black mustard seed and cumin**, and continue to heat until the mustard seeds pop. Add **1 finely-chopped chili**. Stir, and pour over the veg. Add the **juice of a lime, 30g roast peanuts**, and **salt** to taste. Chopped **green coriander** if you have it; otherwise parsley.

Radishes with Sour Cream.

Trim and slice **a bunch of radishes, about 250g**. Mix with **150 ml, or a small carton, of soured cream**, and **pepper**. Part of a spread of small salads. The first time I did this, someone said "Ah, radish raita!". It all went – and always does.

Radish, Apple, and Cheese Salad.

Cut **a bunch of radishes, 2 tart eating apples**, and **200g cheese** into pieces of about the same size. This is a good way to use different cheeses; Sage Derby is really good here, so is Wensleydale or white Stilton. But ordinary Cheddar, not too strong, is fine. Dress with **4 tbsp. extra-virgin oil** (quite a peppery one, if you have a choice) mixed with **2 tsp. grainy mustard**. No acid; no salt; no pepper.

Potato Salad with Radish and Feta.

Boil **500g new potatoes**, drain, and dress with **3 tbsp. extra-virgin olive oil** and **1 tbsp. red wine vinegar. Salt and pepper**. Let it cool. Add slices from **a bunch of radishes, ½ a red onion, chopped, 2 tbsp. capers**, and **150g feta**. Stir gently. Chopped **herbs**.

After this selection, it's clear that you can make many more salads using radishes. Fennel? Cress (water or mustard-and-)? However, there are times when you have radishes which are not so spanking fresh that they can be eaten raw. Or maybe you want to cook them just for a change, or maybe your meal needs a hot something. In these cases, it's worth knowing a couple of things to do involving cooked radish.

Saute of Radish and Spring Onions.

Slice **a bunch of radishes**, and trim and slice **6 spring onions**. Cook both these in **20g butter** in a small frying pan, until the radishes are tender. Add chopped **parsley, salt,** and the **juice of ½ a lemon**. This is a small dish – enough for 2 as the only vegetable – but you could expand it with, for example, mushrooms, or cooked potatoes.

Radish and Carrot Puree.

Slice **2 small onions, 200g carrots,** and **200g radishes,** and boil in **a little water** till they are soft. Drain, keeping the liquid as stock. Put the vegetables in a food processor. Add **1 tsp. salt.** Warm **3 tbsp. vegetable oil,** and add **1 tsp. black mustard seeds** and **1 tsp. cumin.** When the mustard seeds pop, add **a small knob of ginger,** peeled and chopped very fine, and stir briefly. Empty into the food processor, and whizz. If you want to let down the puree a little, use **yoghurt or milk**.

Baked Radishes.

Trim and blanch **a bunch of whole radishes** for 3 mins. Mix **1 tbsp. honey or maple syrup, 1 tbsp. vegetable oil, salt** and **cinnamon,** and roll the radishes in this. Cook in a medium oven for 30 mins or so, till tender. These are delicious, and you eat many more than you'd ever eat if they were raw.

Pasta with Radishes.

This is nicer and more of a dish if the radish leaves are fresh enough to be used – as they would be if you grew them. But it's perfectly OK simply with bought leafless radishes. Sweat **a medium chopped onion** in **2 tbsp. olive oil** while **200g pasta** is cooking. Add about **20 sliced radishes,** and **their chopped leaves,** if you have them, and **2 chopped cloves garlic**. More radishes if there are no leaves. Stir around and cook 2 mins. or so. Scoop out **a little of the pasta cooking water** and use to make the radish mixture more like a sauce. Add this to the drained pasta, add chopped **parsley,** and serve with grated **Parmesan**.

Radish Fritters.

Beat **1 egg** and **5 tbsp. milk** together. Stir in **50g flour, salt, 120g grated cheese,** and **200g grated radish**. Drop spoonfuls into **hot deep fat,** and cook till browned. Drain on kitchen paper, and serve as soon as possible.

Radish Leaves.

You can cook the leaves on a bunch of radishes, if they are fresh and perky, like any other greens. See spring greens or cabbage for ideas.

Radish Seed Pods.

If your garden radishes get away, flower, and produce seed pods, these can be pickled with sugar and vinegar. There is even a radish variety specialising in pod production. When I tried this, no-one liked it, and the jar hung on for several years before I threw it out, still nearly full. So I can't recommend this, but if you are fond of pickles you probably won't agree with me.

Rocket and Wild Rocket

Ever so popular, ever so trendy, and a pleasure to eat. It turns up everywhere in green salads or as a garnish for practically anything. Sandwiches, main dishes, bruschetta, snacks, beans on toast . . .For a time, it seemed as if it would push out watercress, but watercress has made a comeback, and now you find them both everywhere.

I find watercress more versatile, myself, and seldom buy rocket. It's not that I don't like it, but given the choice . . .However, it is possible to grow rocket yourself, which is much in its favour. It needs to grow quickly, with some warmth. I once grew it over winter, in a dark dank corner, and the result was strong-tasting, rank and tough. It put me off for years.

I'm only giving one recipe for rocket. Use it like watercress; put it in salads; strew some over the top of anything that benefits from the green and the taste of rocket. If you really have a lot, you can put it in soups, risottos, pasta sauces. It's really very versatile.

Poor Man's Soup with Potatoes and Rocket.
This is based on a recipe in Marcella Hazan's Second Classic Italian Cookbook. Rocket grows wild in Italian fields, and both potatoes and stale bread are staples. And it is really good!
Peel and cut up **4 medium potatoes**, and start to cook in **700 ml stock (or water)**. Add **4-6 peeled whole garlic cloves**. Wash **60g rocket**, and add to the pot after 10 mins or so. Add **salt** if your stock isn't already salted. When the potatoes are done, add **100g stale good bread**, cut up, leaving crusts on. Let the pan rest, covered, for 10 mins or so. Break up roughly with a hand blender, or whizz briefly in a blender. Not smooth, but not plain with lumps either. Taste for salt. Stir in **4 tbsp. extra-virgin olive oil** and **quite a lot of pepper**.
It is less of a soup of the poor if you have **small slices of bread** , brushed with **oil**, and toasted in the oven with grated **Parmesan** on top, but I do like the effect.

Samphire

There isn't much to say about this, except to note its existence. If you live by the sea, you might be able to forage for some. If you don't, it's a question of buying some when you see it -- normally at a fishmonger. In 2011, Waitrose have started to sell it, on the fish counter; in 2012, I've seen it in Tesco. It is strongly seasonal, late spring/early summer. It isn't a seaweed, though it looks as if it might be, but a salt-marsh plant. Having got some samphire, wash and boil for 5 mins, then drain and eat alone, or with butter, or let it cool and eat with a salad dressing. Its flavour is so unusual that I don't think it mixes with anything – though it will go with raw mushroom slices when cold. Do try some if you see it. The flavour is salty, unusual, delicious.

In East Anglia, pickled samphire can be found. Try some of this before you decide whether you want to vinegar-up some of your precious samphire. Categorically, I don't. If you do, I read that it's pickled like everything else, from onions to red cabbage.

Sorrel

I don't really see sorrel as a staple, but it is a comforting presence in the garden from early March through to October, and it means I'm never at a loss for a simple evening meal for one, (a sorrel omelette), when I don't feel like cooking, or a sorrel and lentil soup to add substance for unexpected guests. My sorrel patch keeps trying to flower, so I shear and cut off all the flowering stalks from time to time, and take quite a lot of leaves at the same time to make a puree, which I then freeze in small quantities for spontaneous use. I wouldn't want to be without it.

While you are gardening, you can nibble leaves from the sorrel. A few leaves can go into a mixed green salad. To me, though, it isn't something you'd use to make a salad on its own. You may disagree; try and see.

Sorrel Omelette.
For 1 person. Wash **a small bunch of sorrel, approximately 20g**, and chop. Take out any tough stalks, but most of the stalks of young sorrel are OK. Melt about **10 g – or a nut – of butter**, and let the sorrel and **a little salt** melt in this. About 5 mins. Make a **2 or 3 egg omelette**, and fill with the sorrel. A truly delicious combination. If you use more sorrel, put the cooked sorrel on oval ciabatta toasts, and add a poached egg you'd have a bruschetta.

Sorrel Puree, for keeping.
Take **as many sorrel leaves as will fit in a large pan**. Weigh them, to give a guideline for the butter to be used later. Wash, removing any long stalks, and put in the pan with the water that clings to the sorrel. Put on a high heat, covered, for 2-3 mins, turning over a couple of times, so that the sorrel collapses. Beat in the pan to a puree, and add **1/3rd of the weight of sorrel in butter**, (not fridge-cold), which you beat in. Freeze in small bags, putting 2-3 tbsp. in each. It's then ready for soup, sauce, omelette, or anything else that occurs.

Sorrel-Stuffed Eggs.
Here is a use for one of the freezer bags of sorrel puree, or a **puree freshly made with a double handful of sorrel.** Hard-boil **8 eggs**, cool under running water. Shell, halve, and scoop out the yolks. Mix the

yolks with the sorrel puree, **season**, and taste. It's sharp and almost lemony. Stuff the hollows of the egg whites with the puree, mounding as necessary, and serve on **a bed of mild salad leaves**. You might want to decorate with criss-crosses of roasted red pepper, or black olives, or even chives; it will look prettier, but the sorrel stuffed eggs are just fine on their own.

Sorrel and Pea Pate.
Another use for frozen puree. Thaw 300g frozen peas, and put in the food processor with **2-3 tbsp. sorrel puree**, thawed if frozen. Add some chopped **parsley** and **chives, 50g soft butter**, and **4 tbsp. yoghurt or sour cream. Salt** and **pepper (5-pepper blend good here)**, and whizz smooth. Serve with toast as a starter.

Lentil Soup with Sorrel.
Sweat **1 small onion, 1 small carrot**, diced in **25g butter**. Add **400g Puy lentils**, washed, and **parsley, thyme**, and **½ a bay leaf**. Swirl round to mix well, then add 1½ **litres water**, bring to the boil, and simmer till the lentils are cooked, 30-45 mins depending on their age. I have specified Puy lentils here; there are other posh lentils, Canadian and Italian, but Puy is by far the nicest to my taste. Meanwhile, pick over **150g sorrel**, wash and shred, and let them collapse in **40g butter**. When the lentils are cooked, puree the soup – food mill, blender – and add the sorrel. **Salt** to taste. It is an old French touch to pour the boiling soup onto 2 egg yolks, mixed with a little of the puree, in the serving bowl, This thickens and enriches it. This last bit is entirely optional; I hardly ever do it.

Asparagus, Sorrel and Leek Soup.
A considerable contrast to the last recipe, which is cheap and uses stored lentils and growing sorrel. This soup has special, and expensive, spring vegetables, and is more suited to weekends and entertaining than everyday use.
Peel the stalks of **500g asparagus**, and cut into 3 cm lengths, keeping the tips separate. Wash, trim and slice **2 small or 1 large leek**. Sweat the leeks in **40g butter** in a large pot. When they are soft, add **30g plain flour**, and stir in. Add 1½ **litres water or stock** and the asparagus stems (not tips yet).Bring to the boil, stirring, and cook 15 mins. Add **300g sorrel**, destalked and washed, and cook 5 mins more. Don't let anyone see it at this stage, as it looks very unappetising. Let

cool slightly, then push through a foodmill. Better than a blender in this case, as it holds back any fibres. Just before serving, reheat the soup, **salt** and **pepper** to taste. Add the asparagus tips, and cook 3 mins. Then add **150 ml double cream, 100g. thawed peas** (or fresh, if you are lucky enough to have them), and check the seasoning again. Serve.

Sorrel with Chick Peas.
Inspired by a Nigella original, but I think nicer.
Heat **2 tbsp. olive oil**, and add **1 tsp. cumin seed**. When they start to change colour, add **1 small chopped onion, 1 deseeded chopped chili**, and **3 chopped cloves garlic**. When the onion is soft but not coloured, add **2 handfuls sorrel**, destalked and shredded, and let it collapse (If you have puree, this is a good time to use it.) Add **a tin of chick peas**, drained and rinsed, and let it warm through. If you have ready cooked chick peas you made earlier, these would be better. Let the whole warm through, taste for **salt**, heat (more chili?) and sharpness (**lemon juice?**) Eat with bread or rice.

Sorrel Quiche.
You need a **23 cm (9")** part-baked pastry case, or **2 smaller ones (18 cm)** for this amount of filling. Sweat **1 large sliced onion** in **50g butter** for about 15 mins. Add **200g sorrel**, roughly sliced, and turn till the leaves collapse. Let cool. Beat **3 eggs, 300 ml double cream, salt** and **pepper**, and add the onion mix. Pour into the pastry cases. Sprinkle the top with **30g grated strong Cheddar**, and bake at 150 for 30-40 mins, or till done. Let it cool a little before eating.
I always use double cream, and only double cream, in quiches. It makes them so rich and delicious, and miles away from the commercial sort. It wouldn't be good for an everyday item, but I think of pastry items as occasional treats, not for every day.

Sorrel and Spinach Custard.
Take **700g mixed sorrel and spinach**, destalk and wash, and put in a large pan with only the water that clings to them. Cover, and cook on high heat for about 3 mins, stirring from time to time, until all the leaves have collapsed. Drain, squeeze dry, and chop finely. Beat together **3 eggs, 3 egg yolks, 300 ml milk**, and the greens. **Salt, pepper, nutmeg, chives**. (Alternatively, you can whizz eggs and greens in the food processor, and omit the chopping stage. Stir in milk

and seasoning. Tip the lot into a buttered souffle-type dish, and bake, surrounded by warm water, at 170 for 40 mins or till set. This needs something like mixed roast veg – especially potatoes, tomatoes, peppers – to set off colour and texture.

This last recipe illustrates how sorrel can go into a spinach recipe, but it must be one where the lemony effect of the sorrel is welcome. There are a lot of these.

Spinach

Spinach is admired and respected in France, Italy, Persia, India, China among others. Is it a coincidence that those I've named have the most admired styles of cooking in the world? I don't think so. Meanwhile, in English-speaking countries spinach had a bumpy ride. Boiled for a long time and not well drained in Victorian times, spinach was so disliked by the generation brought up eating this that it was their most hated vegetable. Popeye was introduced to encourage spinach eating – from tins. But the rebirth of spinach cooking for English speakers came with the admiration for foreign cooking postwar, and now everyone likes spinach. (Well, all the people I know like spinach) I think now that the least esteemed veg. would be marrow, but no-one collects data on this. You can only tell with hindsight, as, for example, parsnips and rhubarb have recently had an upswing in England.

It's strange that spinach is so fashionable, and at the same time it's more difficult than ever to get spanking-fresh, crackling spinach bought loose. Partly it's difficult to grow at its best in England, as it runs to seed in warm weather and is killed by frost. Guy Watson, in the Riverford Farm cookbook, tells us how difficult it is to grow spinach organically. But true spinach is much nicer than any of its cousins – spinach beet, perpetual spinach, New Zealand spinach, Good King Henry – in dishes designed for spinach, so it's really worth the effort.

And cooking raw spinach does involve some effort. First you pick it over, taking off any long tough stalks. Then you wash it, at least once. There are places where 3 washes for spinach is prescribed. Lift it from the bowl of washing water, rather than drain through a colander, to leave the earth behind. Then jam handfuls into a pan, over high heat, until the pan is full. Turn over with a wooden spoon so all the spinach is exposed to the heat, and it will collapse to a much smaller volume. When it is collapsed, about 10 mins for a large panful, take off the heat, and drain in colander. Press with plate edge and/or teatowel to get it as dry as possible. Then it's ready for a final heating, with butter or oil or cream, or it can be left to cool and used later. You can also stir-fry – see below. I like the packets of baby spinach from Sainsbury's which can be microwaved in the packet, which taste very good and save a lot of hassle. Whichever, you need an enormous amount of spinach – 4 people can eat 1 kg of fresh spinach, and look round for more.

When you've gone through this, you have one of the most flexible ingredients possible. I don't think it's possible to overcook spinach from this first-cooked state, and I've tried versions where it's cooked for a couple of hours. It goes into an enormous number of main dishes, pies and stuffings and pancakes and souffles and dumplings and frittate and ……

Given that local fresh spinach is distinctly seasonal, there's no wonder that frozen is popular. Frozen leaf spinach is admitted as useful by almost everyone. Frozen chopped spinach is derided, and I agree. We did a family comparison tasting, and we all said that fresh spinach is better than frozen leaf is much better than frozen chopped.

Default. Buttered Spinach.
Cook and drain **spinach, 1 kg for 4 people**. Or defrost frozen leaf spinach and squeeze dry. Cut up roughly. Add to **30g butter**, and cook, stirring, over moderate heat until the spinach is drier. Season with **salt, pepper, freshly grated nutmeg**. (Nutmeg is almost always part of the seasoning for spinach) Add **another 30g or more of butter**, turn the heat low and cover, and let it absorb the butter for 5-10 mins. The more butter you use, the nicer the spinach, but the more you use the less healthy it becomes. There is an old French recipe in which spinach is persuaded, over several cooking sessions over 4 days, to absorb half its own weight in butter. I don't care how good this tastes, I'm not going to eat it!

Spinach with Cream.
As for buttered spinach till it's seasoned. Then add **100-200 ml double cream**, depending on your conscience, and cook covered over low heat, stirring from time to time. It amazes me every time how the cream amalgamates with the spinach and disappears from view.

Spinach with Seville Orange Juice.
You can only do this in January/February, when Sevilles are available. They can be frozen if you have enough freezer space. But there is a charm to something you can only eat occasionally, so I tend to keep it for deep winter. Cook **1 kg spinach** as for buttered spinach; add the

juice of **2 Seville oranges** when seasoning. Leave out the nutmeg in this case, and up the quantity of **pepper**. This is nice with something crisp. Adults might like fried bread triangles, curls of Melba toast (which can be bought) or crostini (ditto) Most children would love garlic bread.

Spinach with Pine Nuts and Currants.
Soak **30g currants** in warm water for 30 mins, to rehydrate a little. Drain. Wash, cook and drain **1 kg. fresh spinach** (or defrost and drain 600-700g frozen leaf spinach) Squeeze as dry as you can. Heat **2 tbsp. extra-virgin olive oil**, and add **50g pine nuts**. Cook a little till they start to colour, add the spinach and currants, and stir well. **Salt** and **pepper**, cover, and leave on low heat 5 mins or so.
You can use other nuts when reheating the spinach, just as for pine nuts, but leave out the currants. Walnuts with walnut oil and garlic. Hazelnuts with hazelnut oil. Cashews and olive oil. These are non-traditional, improvised dishes which are adapted to go with the rest of the meal and the tastes of the eaters.

Basic Stir-Fried Spinach.
Fast, easy, a very good way to do it. This is only for fresh spinach. YOU NEED A BIG PAN. And you need to do it in batches, if you're cooking for more than 2.
Wash **1 kg. spinach** as usual, and dry as far as possible. Heat **1 tbsp. sunflower oil** in your large pan, and add **1 clove garlic** chopped with **1 slice ginger**. Put handfuls of spinach into the pan with your left hand while stirring with your right, and stir till the leaves begin to collapse. Tip out into a warm serving dish. Repeat till you've used all the spinach. It's obviously worth doing all the chopping of garlic and ginger for, say, 4 batches in advance, and just scoop a fraction into the hot oil each time. This may be the best way of cooking spinach as a lone vegetable.

Stir-Fried Mixed Vegetables with Spinach.
Suppose you choose **onion, mushroom, and water chestnuts** as your other vegetables. You need less spinach here, say 200g for 4 people. Wash it and shake dry. Peel and slice **1 halved onion** very thinly. Slice **150g button mushrooms** thinly. Slice thinly **12 or so water chestnuts**, from a tin. Chop together **1 clove garlic, 1 slice peeled ginger. Maybe a chili** if you like?. Heat **1 tbsp. sunflower oil** in a

wok/pan, and stir-fry the onion till soft and colouring on high heat. Add garlic/ginger, stir, add mushrooms. After stirring these, pile in the spinach, and stir this on high heat too till it collapses. Add the water chestnuts, stir briefly, and add **1 tbsp. soy sauce mixed with 1 tbsp. sherry/rice wine/white wine.** There will be a great burst of steam; mix well, and serve very quickly. This is just an example, and the vegetables can be varied as you like. I'd avoid anything which needs long cooking, and you obviously don't want another green. But peppers, courgettes, bean sprouts, mange-tout, very thin slices of kohl-rabi, are all possibles. So is tofu to make a main dish, if it's stir-fried with flavourings beforehand, or you use a ready-flavoured tofu.

Indian Spinach.
This is only for fresh spinach. You need **1 kg. spinach**, washed, drained and chopped. Heat **5 tbsp. sunflower oil** in a large pan, and add the **tip of a tsp. of ground hing, or asafoetida.** Straightaway add the spinach, and stir around till it starts to collapse. Add **1 tsp salt, ½ tsp. turmeric**, and **up to ½ tsp cayenne pepper**. If you can get ground Kashmiri chili, this is better – not as hot as cayenne, and much more flavour. Add **250 ml. water** when the spinach has collapsed, and cook on medium high heat, uncovered, for 25-30 mins, till the liquid is gone. Stir and mash the spinach from time to time. When dry, sprinkle over **½ tsp. garam masala**, mix in, and serve. It should be quite chili-hot, but how hot depends on your eaters. With chapattis and yoghurt, this makes a meal.

Spinach with Indian Spices.
This can be made with frozen spinach. It's a bit more complicated than the last one, but still quite simple. Defrost **500g frozen leaf spinach**, and squeeze dry. Slice **2 medium onions**, halved, in thin slices, like half-rings. Chop **a walnut-size knob of fresh ginger** and **2 fresh chilis** finely. Heat **2 tbsp. sunflower oil** with **30g butter**; when hot, add **½ tsp. fennel seeds** and **1 tsp. black cumin seeds**. After 30 sec, add the onions, and fry till the onions have browned. Add the spinach and stir to mix. Add ginger/chili mix and **½ tsp salt**, stir again, turn the heat down to low, cover, and cook for 20 mins. If there is any liquid left after this, raise the heat again and boil it off.

Wilted Spinach Salad.

We are currently lucky in being able to buy baby spinach leaves for salads using raw spinach, something which was not available even 20 years ago. I admit they come in plastic packets, but nothing's perfect. This salad, based on one in the Greens Cook Book, has croutons, olives, and feta.

Start with the croutons; cut **slices from good bread**, cut off the crusts, and cut into squares about 3 cm a side. Brush these with **olive oil**, and bake on a sheet in a moderate oven till browned, turning to brown both sides. You could fry them, but they take more oil. Wash **200g baby spinach leaves**, dry as far as possible, and put in a metal bowl. (Metal is important, as it doesn't absorb the heat of the oil as a pottery bowl would. Plastic is OK but will melt if any of the hot oil gets to it. If you don't have a metal bowl, use a large saucepan) Add **1 clove garlic**, finely chopped, **a few sprigs of marjoram or mint or parsley, chopped, a dozen black olives,** and **1 tbsp. sherry vinegar**. Mix all in. Heat **4 tbsp. extra-virgin olive oil** till very hot but not smoking, and pour over the spinach leaves. Quickly turn the salad over so that the hot oil gets to as many leaves as possible. Taste to see if more vinegar is needed. No salt is needed, because of the olives and feta. Turn into a serving bowl, mix in the croutons, and sprinkle **4 oz crumbled feta** over the salad. Eat quickly.

There are obviously many variations possible on this basic principle of wilting the spinach with hot oil. I think the croutons are essential, and olives are always to my taste. The vinegar can be red wine vinegar or balsamic. Thin slices of red onion, or chopped spring onions, can be added, The feta can be dropped and grated Parmesan or another hard cheese used, like Manchego. Strips of roasted red pepper? Sprouted fenugreek seeds?

Warm Spinach Salad with Poached Egg and Mushrooms.

For 4 people, **200g baby spinach leaves**, washed and dried. **Croutons,** as above. Arrange these on 4 large plates. Poach **4 eggs**. While the eggs are poaching, heat **1 tbsp. olive oil**, and fry quickly **150g sliced closed-cup mushrooms** (chestnut mushrooms if you like) **Salt** the mushrooms when they are just cooked, and distribute them over the spinach. Put a poached egg, drained well, on each salad. To the mushroom pan, add **1 tbsp. red wine vinegar**, swirl over heat, then add **3 tbsp. extra-virgin olive oil**. Swirl again, and pour this hot dressing over the salads. **Pepper**. Chopped **chives** if you have them. You might prefer this with a mixture of greens as a base; try with the spinach, rocket, watercress mixture that comes in supermarket bags.

Spinach with Yoghurt.
This salad/meze dish uses **cooked spinach, from 400-500 g fresh or 300g frozen** (but use fresh here if you can) Fry **a chopped onion** in **2 tbsp. sunflower oil** till brown. Crush **a clove of garlic** with **salt**, and add to **600 ml. Greek yoghurt**. Add the spinach, the onion, and **pepper** to taste to the yoghurt. Chill. Just before serving, sprinkle with **paprika, or black cumin seeds**. The ideal and authentic is ground **sumac**, so use this if you have some.

Spinach Dip.
100g spinach, cooked, drained, squeezed dry. **100g cream cheese**. **Juice of 1 lime or ½ lemon. 4 spring onions,** trimmed and cut into ½ cm lengths. **1 dsp. crème fraiche or soured cream or double cream. ¼ tsp salt.** Put all these in food processor and whizz together. Taste and adjust; scrape out and serve. As well as a dip, this can be sandwich spread, dressing for baked potatoes, used for stuffed hard-boiled eggs, and anything else your imagination comes up with.

Spinach Soup.
Sweat **1 small chopped onion** in **30g butter** until soft, and add **2 chopped cloves garlic**. Stir in, leave a minute or so, then add **1 heaped tbsp. plain flour**. Stir to blend, then add **600 ml. stock or water**. Bring to the boil, stirring. Add **500g fresh spinach**, washed and drained, **salt (unless your stock is salty)**. If you have some **sorrel**, this can be added at the end of cooking. Cook about 20 mins, and let cool a little. Make the soup smooth in a blender, by putting it through a mouli, or with a hand-held blender. Thin with water if needed. Taste for **salt**, and add **pepper**. Reheat. Stir in **100 ml. double cream**, or pour the soup into plates/bowls and add a swirl of double cream or a dollop of sour cream. Add chopped **chives**. I think it needs **croutons**. If you cover toast slices with grated cheese and melt this under the grill to go with the soup, it can be a light meal.

"One-Eyed Bouillabaisse".
This is a joke name, like Welsh Rabbit, and served the same function; it's what you eat if your hunter/fisher comes back empty-handed.

Cook and drain **1 kg. fresh spinach**, or defrost 500g frozen leaf spinach. Chop the spinach roughly. Heat **4 tbsp. olive oil** and add **1 large chopped onion**. Cook over moderate heat till it is yellow, not at all brown, and add the spinach. Stir and let the mixture cook until the water from the spinach has evaporated. Add **4 chopped cloves garlic, 500g waxy potatoes**, peeled and cut into small dice, and stir about. Then add **1 litre boiling water, bay leaf, sprig of thyme, chopped herb fennel, a strip of orange peel, salt** and **pepper**, and simmer vigorously until the potatoes are done. At this point, to be correct, you should poach **an egg for each person** in the soup. I recommend poaching the eggs separately instead. Instead, give a final taste and adjustment to the soup, bring it to a vigorous boil and stir in **2 tbsp. extra-virgin olive oil.** Pour into soup bowls/plates, and add a poached egg to each. Serve with crusty bread. Or you could miss out the eggs and serve toasts with **Rouille.** (For rouille, whizz **mayonnaise** with **chopped garlic, chopped chili, a little roasted red pepper** (probably from a jar), and **basil or oregano.**)

Cold Spinach Soup.

Soak **2 thick slices decrusted bread** in a little cold **water**, squeeze dry, and put the soggy crumb in a large bowl. Add **200g spinach**, lightly cooked (could be leftover?), **a handful of rocket roughly chopped, ditto of watercress or salad cress, 1 cucumber** in coarse dice, **2-4 cloves roughly chopped garlic**, and **4 spring onions**, sliced. Whizz batches in the food processor with judicious amounts of **water from 600 ml**, in a jug. When they have all been pureed and turned into another bowl, add the rest of the water, **3 tbsp. extra-virgin olive oil, the juice of a lime**, and **1 tsp. salt** Stir together. Taste and adjust – more salt? Pepper? More lime juice? Maybe a chopped chili would improve it? When pleased, put the soup to chill, and serve very cold with crusty bread. If this is nasturtium season, you can use a handful of leaves instead of cress – or as well as – and garnish the soup with nasturtium flowers. Worthy of a photograph!.

Spinach Omelette.

If you make French, rolled omelettes at all, then a spinach omelette is just a variation on the theme, filled with a little warmed buttered spinach, almost certainly leftover. If you want a reminder, see Techniques. However, the spinach omelette I'm giving here is a little different and fancier – not better, just different. You need **200g**

spinach, cooked, drained well, and chopped. Beat **4 eggs** with a little chopped **parsley, salt** and **pepper**, and beat in the spinach. Chop **6 spring onions** and add. Preheat the grill. Melt **30g butter** in a frying pan, tip in the egg mix, and cook on moderate heat, lifting the edges and letting the liquid flow underneath until there is little liquid left. Sprinkle the top of the omelette with **30g grated Cheddar**, and put the whole pan under the grill until the cheese is bubbly. If you have some **croutons**, sprinkle them over the omelette top before adding the cheese. This makes a main dish for 2; for more, make more than one omelette. This isn't a frittata or a classic omelette, but halfway between, and very nice indeed.

Eggs Florentine. Poached eggs sit on a bed of spinach, and the whole is covered with cheese sauce topped with grated cheese and grilled till the cheese top is crusty and brown. Very rich and gooey, and it needs plain things – like boiled potatoes – to go with it. There are times, though, when it just hits the spot, and if you use frozen leaf spinach, it comes entirely from stores.

So, for 4 people, **a bed of buttered spinach, about 1 kg frozen.** Hot when it's put into the wide flat dish. **4 poached eggs**, drained and put into hollows in the spinach. **300 ml cheese sauce (40g butter, 30g flour, 300 ml milk, salt, pepper, nutmeg, 60g grated cheese.) Another 30g grated cheese**, or more, to sprinkle the top.

Spinach Sformato Parma style (alla Parmigiana).

Defrost **600g frozen spinach** (chopped is OK here, because of all the other tastes and texture) and dry out slowly on a low heat. Meanwhile, sweat **a medium chopped onion** in **30g butter** till soft, add **1 rounded tbsp. flour**, and let cook till the mix bubbles. Add **120 ml milk**, and bring to the boil so it thickens. **Salt, pepper, nutmeg** – quite a lot of seasoning, for the mass of spinach and the eggs to come. Let the sauce cool a little, then mix in **60g mascarpone**, the spinach, **50g grated Parmesan**, and **2 beaten eggs**. This is very easily done in the food processor. Pour the whole into a buttered souffle dish. Stand the dish in a roasting pan, and pour in enough boiling water to come halfway up the sides. Bake at 180 for about 45 mins, or till a skewer stuck in the middle comes out clean. Take out of the oven, and CAREFULLY lift the souffle dish from the water and turn the sformato onto a dish. The best way is to put the serving plate upside down on the top of the dish, and hold them together while turning over

-- but 3 hands is helpful for this. You can eat it alone or with carrots or with tomato sauce.

Pancakes Stuffed with Spinach and Cheese.
This is still on the Italian theme, but adapted. Italians would use cannelloni for stuffing, usually, or put the mixture into stuffed pasta like ravioli or tortellini. Indeed, supermarkets are full of stuffed pasta shapes with spinach and cheese. I like a higher proportion of filling to wrapper, so use pancakes.

Make the filling first. You want **200g cooked spinach**, either fresh or defrosted frozen, and dried out with **20g butter** over a low heat. This means starting with 300g frozen or 400-500g fresh. The quantity isn't critical, though. Chop the spinach finely, and mix with **200g ricotta or Philadelphia, 30g grated Parmesan, 2 eggs, salt, pepper,** and **nutmeg**. This filling should be delicious when you taste it. Make a pancake batter with **250g flour, 2 tbsp. olive oil, salt, 2 eggs, and 300 ml. each milk and water**.

Set up for cooking pancakes and stuffing them as they are made, which means a bowl of batter by the stove, a cup standing on a saucer for adding batter to the pan, the filling, a plate on which to roll the pancakes, and a large flattish baking dish to hold the stuffed pancakes. Heat your pancake pan with **a very little oil**, swirl it round, and pour off any excess. Add just enough batter to make a thin pancake, and swirl round to cover the base of the pan. It cooks in less than half a minute. When the top shows no liquid, slide a metal slice under the pancake and turn it. (These pancakes are too thin and delicate to toss) Just a few seconds on the second side, then slide the pancake out on to the plate. Pour in batter for the next one, and while this is cooking on the first side, stuff the pancake. Put a good dsp. filling just to one side of. the centre of the pancake. Fold over the smaller side, turn over the sides, roll to take up the larger side, and put the rolled pancake in the dish. Now turn the next pancake, and repeat until either batter or filling runs out. I usually get 18 pancakes from this amount of batter, and there's often a bit of filling left. (See stuffed eggs) You don't have time to do anything else while cooking the pancakes, but the whole batch is done in 25-30 mins. Once the pancakes are in the baking dish, you can leave them (even freeze them in this state) or go straight on. When you want to eat in 20-30 mins or so, pour **200 ml. stock** over the pancakes, sprinkle the top with about **30g grated Parmesan** and **dots**

of butter. Put in a 180 oven till the stock is absorbed and the top slightly crusty, and serve. You don't need anything with it.

Spanokopitta, or Greek Spinach Pie.

This is made with filo pastry, which you buy frozen. Don't even think of making it, as it's a job for professionals to get it thin and uniform. You need a metal oven dish, about 28 x 18 x 8 cm (13"x 7"x 3" in old money) A medium roasting tin will probably fit the bill. You also need **20 sheets filo**, this size or a bit bigger. They often come about twice the size, in which case halve them and use 10 sheets. Defrost the filo. If exposed to the air it really wants to dry out and become brittle, so while you are using filo keep unused sheets under a layer of foil and then a damp teatowel.

Make the filling: fry gently **1 medium chopped onion** in **1 tbsp. oil** until soft. Add **2 finely chopped spring onions, 500g raw spinach** washed dried and chopped (or 300g frozen leaf spinach, defrosted and chopped), **a small bunch of parsley** and **leaves from 5-6 sprigs mint**, chopped, and **1 tsp. salt**. Cook until the mixture seems dry. Let it cool a little, then add **2 eggs, pepper**, and freshly grated **nutmeg**. Then cheeses; **150g each filo and ricotta or curd cheese**, and **60g hard cheese – pecorino romano or Manchego** are better here than Parmesan, but use Parmesan if that's what you have. Let the filling cool. Now melt **120g butter**, and brush the base of the tin with it. Add a sheet of filo, brush with butter, and continue till you have 10 layers. Add the filling, spreading to the edges. Cover with a further 10 sheets filo, brushing each with butter, including the top of the top layer. Any excess should be tucked in down the sides. Mark the top layers into squares with a sharp knife, making sure not to cut through the bottom. Bake this whole confection at 180 for 40 mins, till golden brown. Eat warm or cold.

This makes enough for 8-10 people as first course, or part of a spread. Any left over can be eaten cold as snack, picnic lunch -- it will get eaten.

You can make small appetiser pastries by wrapping the filling in strips of filo. I don't recommend this; the proportion of wrap to filling is high, and the time it takes to produce these attractive little objects is out of all proportion to the time they take to eat. I think you can see all these small, starchy-wrapper + little filling, objects as a way of stretching a filling while filling people up with carbohydrate. Not what we want to do nowadays.

151

Spinach Fritters with Sour Cream.

Use about **150g leftover cooked spinach, or** cook **250-300g fresh spinach**, drain, and squeeze. Put this in the food processor, with **2 eggs, 6 chopped spring onions, 250 ml buttermilk, 120g plain flour, 1 tsp. baking powder, ½ tsp. salt** and **pepper**, and whizz. Pour into a bowl, and add **50g melted butter**, stirring in. Heat **½ tbsp. oil** in a non-stick frying pan on medium heat, and fry small dollops of the batter in this. How many you get in depends on the size of the pan and the size of the dollops; don't crowd them. Fry till lightly browned on both sides, then transfer to a plate in the warming drawer while the rest are cooked. Add more oil if needed. Serve with **soured cream** mixed with chopped **herbs** (dill or fennel and chives are best, but parsley and spring onion will be fine), **salt** and **lemon juice** to taste. These aren't as pretty as the spanokopitta above, but if anything they go faster. The charm of fried food, I think.

Pasta and Spinach.

The simplest way to include spinach in any pasta dish is to add spinach leaves, washed and trimmed, to the pasta water just before the pasta is done. About 30 sec boiling, then drain pasta and spinach together and add any sauce. Simple things like chili and garlic, or creamy sauces, respond best. You can also buy green pasta, which is coloured by spinach. This looks pretty, but I can't taste any difference from normal pasta – in fact, there isn't a lot of spinach in there, so you wouldn't expect to. In terms of pretty dishes, there is an Italian dish called Paglia e Fieno – straw and hay, in translation, so don't – which has equal amounts of egg noodles and spinach noodles with a creamy sauce with mushrooms. Very attractive.

Lasagne with Spinach, Cheese and Tomato.

Lasagne are very useful dishes for parties and larger numbers, because they can be prepared ahead, cooked at the last moment, everyone likes them, and they are very filling. Most lasagne dishes are not at the top of the gastronomic scale (I'd except the asparagus lasagne in that chapter from this), but they are pretty good. So here is another variant.

You need **precooked or no-cook lasagne sheets, tomato sauce, spinach and cheese filling, either the one below or the Spanokopitta filling, white sauce, and Mozzarella or Lancashire**

cheese. Also 1 or 2 large flattish baking dishes. The quantities I give are for 5 layers of lasagne in a dish 28 x 18 cm at the base.

Tomato sauce: in a blender or food processor whizz **2 tins whole tomatoes** and their juice with **1 small chopped onion, 2 cloves garlic, salt** and **pepper, fresh marjoram or dried oregano**, and **2 tbsp. olive oil**. Boil down to sauce consistency; taste, and add **1 tsp. red wine vinegar**. Let cool.

Spinach-cheese filling. Definitely a place for **frozen spinach, defrost about 400g**. Fry **1 small chopped onion** in **2 tbsp. olive oil**, add **2 chopped cloves garlic**, the defrosted chopped spinach, **salt, pepper, nutmeg**. Stir now and then till pretty dry. Let cool a bit, then add **200g ricotta, 2 eggs, 60g freshly-grated Parmesan**, and the **finely-chopped peel of 1 lemon**. Taste and adjust.

White sauce: 40g butter, 30g flour, 600 ml. milk.

Grate **120g Mozzarella, or 120g creamy Lancashire**, crumbled

Butter the baking pan. Spread a thin layer of white sauce on the bottom. Layer of lasagne, layer of half tomato sauce, grated cheese, lasagne, half spinach-and-cheese, thin layer white sauce, lasagne, tomato sauce, grated cheese, lasagne, other half spinach-and-cheese, lasagne, rest of white sauce. Cover with foil, and bake 180 for 20 mins. Remove the foil and bake another 15-20 mins, till the top is puffed and browned. Let it rest a few minutes before eating.

Indian Rice with Spinach.

Can go with almost anything, or be eaten alone, or with yoghurt and pickles. It's mildly but tellingly spiced. It's also fine to use frozen spinach in it.

Soak **500g Basmati rice** (for 6-8 people) in water to cover for 30 mins. Cook **250-300g frozen spinach**, and dry out over moderate heat. Chop very finely. Cut **1 small onion** in half, then in very thin crosswise slices. Cook this onion in **3 tbsp. sunflower oil** over moderate heat till it browns as uniformly as possible. Drain the rice, keeping the soaking water. Add the rice to the onion, and fry about 2 mins. Now add spinach, **250g tomatoes**, chopped fine, **½ tsp each coriander and cumin**, roasted together and ground, **½ tsp. turmeric**. Make up the soaking water, if necessary, to 500 ml, and add **1 tsp. salt**. Bring to a boil, cover tightly, and cook on low heat for 20-25 mins, till there is no visible water and there are little holes on top of the rice mix. Put a folded teatowel between pan and lid, and leave for 10 mins on turned-off burner. If you have a flat warm plate, as on an

Aga, keep it there; it doesn't need to cook, but it needs to adjust itself. Then eat. If there is a crust at the bottom of the pot, this is for eating, and Indians think of it as a delicacy.

Palak Dhal.

Unmistakably Indian, though it uses green lentils. These don't collapse as masoor dhal or channa dhal do when cooked, which is good here.

Put **250g green ("Continental") lentils** in a pan with **250g chopped fresh or frozen spinach**, add **½ tsp. turmeric** and **600 ml water**, and cook gently till done. Add more water if needed, but it should end up dry. The lentils should take 30-40 mins, but it depends on their age. Heat **1 tbsp. sunflower oil** in a frying pan, and add **1 tsp. ground cumin, a thick slice of fresh ginger** peeled and finely chopped, and **2 fresh chilis**, deseeded and chopped. Cook about ½ min, and tip into the dhal. Stir, add **1 tsp. salt,** taste. If you would like it hotter, use a little (very little) cayenne. Finish with the **juice of a lemon**, and eat hot, with rice, yoghurt, vegetable curries, pickles, etc. Or not; just dhal and chapatti or naan is terrific.

Spinach with Chickpeas and Potatoes.

This is a fast assembly job for a quick supper, using tinned chickpeas and washed spinach from the supermarket.

You need **400g peeled cooked potatoes**, which can be leftovers. Make a spice mix with **½ tsp. coriander, ½ tsp. allspice, a blade of mace** ground together (or add some nutmeg after grinding if you don't keep mace) Add **½ tsp salt** to the mix, and a **little chopped fresh marjoram or dried herbes de Provence**. Now fry **1 medium chopped onion** in **2 tbsp. olive oil** in a large pot which has a lid. When the onion is golden, add **2 chopped fresh deseeded chilis** and the spice mix. Stir a few secs, then add **1 can chickpeas**, drained and rinsed. Half a minute more, then add **200g baby leaf spinach** and the potatoes, cut in dice. Cover and cook on low heat about 5 mins, stirring a couple of times, so the spinach is done. Add **2 tbsp. sun-dried tomatoes in oil** and the **juice of a lemon**, and taste. You can eat this as is, or pretty it up with chopped **parsley**. If you have **sumac**, sprinkle the top with it – a good idea because it tastes good. Chopped dill is also delicious. Only one of these, though. I'd eat alone with **plain yoghurt** on the side.

Tex-Mex Spinach and Beans.
Soak and cook **200g red beans or pinto beans**, and drain, **or open 2 tins**, drain and rinse. (There isn't much advantage in using the dried beans here, unless you have some already cooked) Fry **2 large chopped onions** in **3 tbsp. sunflower oil**, add **2 chopped cloves garlic** and **2 deseeded fresh chilis**, then add **300g fresh spinach**, washed, dried, chopped. Cook until the spinach is wilted, stirring, about 5 mins. Add **1 tbsp. American-style chili powder** (as for chili sin carne; buy it, or see my version there), the drained beans, **salt if using your own beans** (tinned ones have enough salt already), **100g grated Cheddar**, and **50 ml. stock or water**. Turn into a baking dish and cook at 180 for 20 mins or so. If following up the Tex-Mex theme, this could go with flour tortillas, grated cheese, shredded lettuce, slices of avocado, sour cream, salsa . . . people do like these roll-your-own dinners. Otherwise just rice or even chips.

Elizabethan Sweet Spinach Tart.
This is a curiosity, as we never think of using spinach in sweet dishes nowadays. I did it several times for historical dinners when I was catering, and it always went down well; try it and see what you think.
Have ready a **20-cm (8") pastry shell, baked blind**. The pastry can be ordinary shortcrust or German pastry (see Basics) Wash and trim **1 kg spinach**, and pack into a large pan with **4 tbsp. white wine**. Cover and steam 5 mins, turning a couple of times. Drain spinach well and chop finely (or process) Mix **60 ml rosewater, 80g sugar, 1/3 tsp ground cinnamon, pinch of salt** in a pan, bring to the boil, and add the chopped spinach. Cook on low heat, uncovered, stirring now and then, until all the liquid has evaporated. Let it cool. Fill the pie shell with this mixture. Now decorate, with either **sliced strawberries or flower petals**. Rose petals, if in season, should be brushed with egg white and allowed to dry. The rose, and the rose tree, MUST NOT have been sprayed at all. Or you can buy little scrunched-up crystallised rose petals and scatter them over the top. Serve cold.

Spring Greens and Other Greens

"Spring greens" is a fairly broad category. Originally, it meant a cabbage which didn't form a heart and could be cut in late winter or spring. It easily extends to cabbages which will form a heart if left alone, but can be cut as greens before that stage. These are also what is meant by collard greens in books on soul-food or Southern States cooking. So far, so defined. But there are also other greens which can be cut in spring – turnip tops, mustards, even dandelions – and since these are treated in the same way as spring greens, they are generally included in the category.

So I've divided this chapter into two parts, the first for fairly tender greens like the non-hearting cabbages, and a second for tougher, more demanding leaves. The recipes aren't limited to one category or the other; in fact, many of the recipes for kale, spring greens, cabbage, Swiss chard are interchangeable. The trouble with letting it all blend into "greens" is that it encourages the idea that all dishes with them are much the same, and this doesn't help to maintain interest from cook or eaters. Insist on the differences between the different kinds, give the dishes different names, and aim to add distinction to a despised peasant vegetable. Dishes with greens don't deserve to be despised, but even in a foodie world where peasant is good, greens have a struggle for respect. Look for spring greens in the River Café books, and you'll see what I mean. Fashionable cavolo nero, imported, yes; local spring greens, no way. At least at home, one doesn't have to follow fashion.

Basically there are two ways of dealing with the stronger flavours of greens. You can soften the flavour with eggs, milk, cream, cheese, or you can complement and balance the flavour with other strong tastes, like chili, ginger, or garlic. There are examples of both here.

Default Spring Greens.
Trim **500g bunches of spring greens** and cut out the stalks. Slice the leaves crosswise. Put in a pan with **25g butter, 2 cm water**, and **½ tsp salt**. Cover, and cook on moderate heat for 20-25 mins, stirring from time to time. Halfway through, add some chopped **strong herb** – rosemary, thyme, or sage. Finish with **a little more butter** and **the juice of half a lemon**. It's interesting that these greens don't have a

cooked-cabbage smell even though they are cooked for a comparatively long time, because there isn't much water.

Spring Greens with Garlic and Soy.
Wash and chop **2 small bunches greens** crosswise, 1 cm wide, cutting down almost to stump. Discard the stump. Heat **2-4 tbsp. oil** in a large frying pan or wok, add **2 crushed garlic cloves**, after 20 sec add greens. Cook on high heat, stirring, about 2 mins. Add **2 tsp. soy sauce**, stir for 15 sec more, and serve. You can add ginger, chili, and lemon, just one of these or all of them. .

Spring Greens with Cumin and Chili.
Wash and cut up **500g spring greens**. Heat **4 tbsp. sunflower oil**, and add **1 tsp. cumin seeds** and **3 small dried red chilis**. When the cumin has darkened, add **1 sliced onion** and **4 chopped cloves garlic**. Fry till softened, then add the greens, **½ tsp. salt**, and **2-3 tbsp. water**. Cover, and cook on low heat 20-25 mins. Chopped **fresh green coriander** to finish, if you have some.

Spring Greens with Mustard.
Trim and chop roughly **500g spring greens**. Heat **2 tbsp. sunflower oil** in a large frying pan, add **1 tsp. cumin seeds** and **2 chopped cloves garlic**. Stir once, then add **1 small chopped onion** and **a knob of ginger** finely chopped. When this is starting to colour, add the leaves, **2 chopped tinned tomatoes or 2 large fresh chopped tomatoes**, ½ tsp salt, and **2 tbsp. water**. Cover and cook for 20 mins. Stir in at least **1 tbsp. wholegrain mustard**, to taste, and **a pinch of sugar**. Serve quickly, while the mustard still has its bite.

Spring Greens with Coconut and Chili.
Trim and slice thinly **500g spring greens**. Heat **1 tbsp oil**, add **3 garlic cloves** crushed with **½ tsp salt** to make a paste, and **2 small dried chilis**. After 1 min, add **400 ml coconut milk**, and simmer 10 mins till reduced to half. Add the spring greens, and cook gently, covered, 15-20 mins, or until the sauce is very reduced and coating the greens. Add **lemon juice to taste.**

Spring Greens with Horseradish.
Wash, trim and chop roughly **500g spring greens**. Heat **2 tbsp. sunflower oil** in a large frying pan, and add **1 tbsp. black mustard**

seeds. When these pop, add **2 chopped cloves garlic**, stir a couple of times, then add the greens, **salt**, and **2 tbsp. water**. Cook gently, covered, 20 mins or till done. Add **4-5 tbsp. double cream**, and stir to coat the leaves, reducing if necessary so there is no visible liquid. Stir in **1 tbsp. grated horseradish, fresh or from a jar** (not horseradish sauce). Taste; adjust with more horseradish or more cream, till it's as you like it. Serve quickly.

Bubble and Squeak. Use the cabbage recipe.

Spring Green Rice.
Use **equal weights of spring greens and long-grain rice – say 300g of each for 4 people**. Wash, clean and shred the greens, and mix with the (washed) rice. Put in a heavy pan with a lid, add **300 ml. water, salt**, and **30g butter** dotted over the top. Bring to the boil, and cook very slowly, covered, for 12 mins. Lift the lid, stretch a teatowel across the top of the pan, replace the lid, turn off the heat, and let it steam for another 12 mins. This is so simple and cheap. If eaten on its own – and it could be, maybe with an egg each to make a full meal – it needs strong pickles or chili sauce, for a modern English palate. If you've been pushing the boat out, entertained too much, eaten and drunk too much, then this helps you return to balance, sobriety, and solvency. Quite some claims!

"Seaweed". Deep-fried shreds; see cabbage.

Spring Green Soup with Stilton.
Fry **2 chopped onions** in **50g butter** in a large pan. When they are starting to soften, add **2-3 chopped carrots, 2 outside sticks celery**, chopped, **3 chopped cloves garlic**, and **(optional) 1-2 leeks**, sliced finely. Put on the lid and let these sweat for 10 mins. on a low heat. Add **300g potatoes**, peeled and diced, **bay leaf** and **thyme**, and **1 litre stock. Salt if stock not salted already**. Simmer 15 mins, then add **250g spring greens**, washed and cut up. Simmer 15 mins more, till done. Crumble in **100g Blue Stilton.**
This is an outline for a soup which can be varied a lot. Different vegetables – celeriac, kohl-rabi, turnip – not, I think, tomatoes. Green beans, cooked dried beans, peas at the end. Different herbs chopped to finish. You could even puree it before adding the Stilton, but I'd say

you should only do this if your eaters REALLY dislike bits in their soup.

Spring Green Custard.
Wash, trim, slice **500g spring cabbage**. Soften **a chopped onion** in **50g butter**, then add the spring greens, stir, cover, and cook 15 mins or till tender. Remove the lid, **salt**, turn up the heat, and cook till all the moisture has gone. Turn into a bowl, and mix with **crumbs from 3 slices good bread, decrusted, 4 eggs, 100g Wensleydale cheese, 250 ml. double cream**, and **quite a lot of freshly ground black pepper. (1/2 tsp peppercorns, ground in coffee mill, is about right for me)** Turn into a buttered souffle dish, stand the dish in a baking pan of near-boiling water, and bake at 150 for 45-60 mins, or till done. A skewer in the centre will come out clean. Let it stand for 10 mins out of the oven, then run a knife round the edge and turn onto a large plate. (Cover the dish with the upside down plate, and holding both with teatowels turn the lot upside down. A short sharp shake will dislodge the custard from the souffle dish, so it falls onto the plate). Alone, or with a tomato sauce or salsa. You can bake the custard in ramekins, for a shorter time, and have one for each eater. Prettier; no difference in taste.

Greens, Miscellaneous

I am including here things like Brussels sprout tops; kohl-rabi tops, dandelions; indeterminate bags sold in supermarkets as "greens". It also includes the sort of foraged greens that Cretans are so good at, turning them into the staple part of their diet called "horta". Most of us in England don't do this, because we just don't have the knowledge to go foraging. Still, we may come across an unknown "green" in market or garden often enough to need a procedure, particularly if we grow vegetables.

Most of these greens are challenging. They have strong flavours, unpleasant amounts of acridity or bitterness or tannin; their texture is often tough. In these cases the solution is boiling water, and often lots of it. Some Cretan recipes involve 3 separate blanching stages, before the final treatment. "Tops" of garden vegetables aren't usually so difficult, and one blanching is enough.

Whatever your green, pick it over and trim. Stems are often tough and undesirable, as they are in more conventional greens like kale and even spinach. Remove thick stems from the leaves. Cut the leaves crosswise into ribbons, and wash well. Then dunk the shredded leaves into boiling salted water. It helps to have a nibble of the raw leaf before you do this, so you can estimate how tough, how bitter, and so on it actually is. Blanching for 5 mins. is probably enough for most cultivated greens. Drain well. You will probably need to chop further before finishing the preparation.

Default: Cretan Horta.
Wash, trim and cut the leaves roughly – **any greens you happen to have**. Blanch them once, twice, or even more if they are still tough after the first blanching. Drain, squeeze out the water, and chop. Season with **salt** and **pepper**, and reheat the chopped mass gently – there will still be enough water to stop it catching – and add **lemon juice** and **extra-virgin olive oil** before serving. The hot greens warm the oil and lemon, and the smell is lovely. It's another of those "I thought I didn't like greens" moments.

Bruschetta.
A very simple way. Warm some **olive oil** with chopped **garlic**, and add the prepared, blanched, **chopped greens**. **Salt, pepper or chili in some form** – chopped fresh, flakes, Tabasco. Let the green absorb the flavours, covered, on a low heat for 5-10 mins. Taste, and adjust. **Lemon** may be a good idea. Meanwhile, toast **slices of good bread**. Griddling can produce texture and flavour superior to the toaster, but is more hassle. Pile the green and juices onto the toast, and eat as a starter. It is surprisingly good.

Gingered Greens.
Prepare, boil, drain and chop the greens. Then saute **2 chopped shallots** and **50g ginger**, grated or finely chopped, in **2 tbsp. sunflower oil** till softened. Stir in the greens, season, and heat through. This is also good with **toasted sesame seeds** on top, and **maybe a dribble of toasted sesame oil**. Or cut the ginger to half, and use toasted pumpkin seeds and pumpkin seed oil to finish.

Greens with Spicy Red Paste.
Put **6 shallots, 3 cloves garlic, ½ red pepper**, and **2 seeded chilis** in a small food processor with **4 tbsp. water**, and whizz to a paste. Wash and shred **500g greens**. Heat **3 tbsp. sunflower oil** in a large frying pan which has a lid. Add the spice paste, and stir until it goes dark. The water has to evaporate before it can start to cook. Add the greens and **1 tsp salt**, and **a couple of tbsp. water**. Cover, turn down the heat, and cook for 15-20 mins. If you have some Thai curry paste, red, green or yellow, use this instead of the home-made paste. Some commercial Thai pastes don't have fish sauce in; some do, so read the ingredients.

Pasta with Turnip Tops. These are the leaves of turnips, and best when the turnips are young. You need about **700g. turnip tops for 4.** In Southern Italy, it would be made with orecchiette, which are little ear-shaped pasta, quite hard, and also quite easy to find and quite pricy. But any standard pasta can be used. Tear the turnip tops into smallish pieces, suppressing tough stems, and boil or steam them till tender, 5 mins. or so. Drain. Peel and chop **500g. tomatoes, or use the tomatoes from a tin**, drained and chopped. Cook **3 chopped garlic cloves, 1 chopped fresh chili** in **3 tbsp. olive oil** for a couple of minutes, add the tomatoes, and cook a few mins. Add the drained greens to reheat. Meanwhile, cook **350g. pasta**, drain, and mix with the sauce. Serve with grated **Parmesan**.
You can do this with sprouting broccoli, Swiss chard, spinach, kale, spring cabbage . . .it's quite general for greens with pasta.

Spring Onions

It's a case of always the bridesmaid, never the bride with spring onions. We, in Britain, enjoy them, expect them to be there, and assign them a supporting role. And quite a limited one at that. I don't plan to abandon old habits – I too use spring onions as supporting players most often – but I do want to enrich the tradition.

Default.
This has to be the supporting role. I tend to trim them (or sometimes not) and stand in a glass on the table. This means that those who want them can take; those who don't, needn't. And there are two reasons for not trimming; one is that this way the unused ones can go back in the fridge, without deteriorating; the other is that individuals trimming their own adds to the slow-paced quality of a good meal. Of course, it's also easier.

Barbecued Spring Onions.
I read, in Colman Andrews book on Catalan Cuisine, about the feast called the calcotada, where hundreds of spring onions are barbecued and eaten with romesco sauce. English spring onions won't give the same effect; they are smaller, stronger, and grown differently However, Colman Andrews suggests that spring onions, at least 2.5 cm in diameter, can be used, and will give an approximation. Trim at both ends; roast till the outside is blackened, and wrap in several layers of newspaper. When they are all cooked, wrap the parcels in a large plastic bag, and leave to steam for 1-2 hrs. Slip off the blackened outsides, dip the onion bulb into romesco sauce, and bite. This is a messy operation, no two ways about it, but for onion lovers it's amazing.

Romesco Sauce.
This is used a lot in Catalan cooking, but this is one of its more important uses. Put **2 roasted red peppers**, cut-up roughly, **2-3 fresh chilis**, deseeded and chopped, **300g tomatoes**, skinned and chopped, **3 chopped cloves garlic, 30g hazelnuts, 120 ml. olive oil, 2 tbsp. red wine vinegar,** and **1 tsp salt** in a food processor, and whizz smooth. Taste and adjust. This makes quite a lot; any leftovers can be a dip, go with hard-boiled eggs, or go as a sauce with a fried dish.

Spring Onion and Garlic Puree.

Trim **4 bunches of spring onions**, leaving on a length of green about half that of the white. Chop roughly. Put in a baking dish with **3 tbsp. olive oil, 5 cloves garlic**, and **½ tsp salt**, cover tightly, and bake at 160 for 30-40 mins. Whizz in a food processor with the **juice of a lemon**. Taste for seasoning. Eat warm or cold. If cold, dribble a **little extra-virgin olive oil** over the mound in its bowl, and use as a dip. Warm, it can be spread on toasts of sourdough or ciabatta, and make bruschetta.

Mushroom Cheeseburger with Spring Onions.

You need **1 large mushroom per burger bun**. Take out the stem, and put gill-side-up on an oven dish. Dribble **a little olive oil** into each, and spread it over the surface as much as possible. Roast in a moderate oven, or cook the mushrooms on a barbecue. It is important to cook them all the way through. Chop **1-2 spring onions per mushroom**, and sprinkle them on top. Cover with **thin slices of Cheddar**, and cook again until the cheese is melting. Put into **toasted buns** – buttered if you like. Dribble any juices over the top half of the bun. It doesn't actually need ketchup, but I think ketchup is part of the burger experience.

Braised Spring Onions Nicoise.

You need **4 bunches of spring onions**, large preferred. Trim, and arrange in one layer in an ovenproof dish. Whizz together **a tin of crushed tomatoes, 2 cloves garlic, 150 ml stock, 2 tbsp. olive oil, salt, pepper, thyme**. Pour over the spring onions, and cover the dish with foil or otherwise. Bake in a low oven (150) for 20 mins., or until the spring onions are tender. Take out the spring onions and arrange on a plate, then boil down the braising liquid over high heat until it's reduced to about half. (Obviously, transfer the liquid to a pan if the baking dish won't go on the cooker top) Pour over the spring onions, decorate with **black olives**, and let cool.

Scrambled Eggs with Spring Onions, Indian Style.

Simple scrambled eggs with spring onions is such a simple idea that it doesn't need a recipe. This is a bit more complicated, and worth the extra effort. Trim and slice a **dozen or so large spring onions** (more if they are thin). Deseed and chop **a chili**. Toast **1½ tsp cumin seed**. Heat **4 tbsp. butter (or ghee, if you have it)**, and gently cook the spring onions and chili in it for 5-10 mins. Add **8 eggs**, beaten with a

little salt, lower the heat still more, and scramble gently. When starting to set, add **60 ml double cream**, the cumin seed, and stir until the eggs are done. Add some chopped **fresh green coriander**, and serve at once. Indian style would mean eating with chapattis; in an English context, toast is just right.

Stelk, or Spring Onion Mash.

An Irish dish. Trim and cut **250g spring onions** into 2 cm lengths. Simmer in **300 ml. milk** while you boil **750g old potatoes**, peeled. Strain the milk from the spring onions, and use it to mash the potatoes, with **salt** and **pepper**. Beat the potatoes, then add the spring onions and **50g butter**. Beat until the mash is pale green and fluffy. The Irish way of eating is to make a hollow in the top of each helping, and add **a piece of butter –15-30g.** The butter melts; you eat from the outside of the mound, dipping each forkful (or spoonful) into the melted butter. This way it has to be a dish on its own. Alternatively, you can simply eat as mash with whatever else you want.

Potato and Spring Onions Patties.

If you have some stelk leftover, this makes a good starting point for this recipe. Otherwise, boil and mash (without additions) **500g potatoes**. Trim **2 bunches spring onions** and blanch for 3 mins. Drain and chop. (If you like a stronger taste, leave them raw, and just chop) Mix with the mashed potatoes, **2 eggs, salt, pepper** and **nutmeg**, and **4 tbsp. fresh bread crumbs**. Shape into small potato cakes, about 5 cm. across, and fry these in **oil or butter** till golden brown on both sides. The breadcrumbs make a surprising difference to the texture; don't miss them out.

Spring Onion Tart or Flan.

Trim and chop **2 bunches spring onions**, and sweat in **20g butter** for 5 mins or so. Mix **125g curd cheese, 125 ml. yoghurt, 4 egg yolks, 4 tbsp. double cream**, and **salt** and **pepper**. Beat the **4 egg whites** till stiff, and fold them in. Now, if making a flan, mix in the spring onions, pour into a buttered baking dish – can be 25 cm diameter and low, or a souffle dish. Sprinkle top with **a little grated cheese**. Bake at 170 till risen and (nearly) set; time depends on dish.

If you are making a tart, you need a **25 cm tart tin lined with shortcrust pastry and baked blind** (Basics). Spread the onions on the bottom, and cover with the egg/cheese mixture, Sprinkle top with **a little grated cheese**; bake at 180 for 25-30 mins. Serve warm or cool.

Two very different breadstuffs, one Chinese, one Italian, but both depending for their oomph on spring onions.

Chinese Spring Onion Pancakes

have no yeast, and need no oven. Make a dough from **250g plain white flour** with **1 tsp salt**, mixed with **250 ml boiling water**. use a wooden spoon to mix, then knead the dough until it is smooth. With this small quantity of dough I often knead from hand to hand while walking round the house, but a floured surface would be more normal. Let the dough rest, covered, for ½ hr. In a small bowl mix **a bunch of spring onions**, trimmed and chopped finely, **1 tsp. salt**, and **80g soft butter** (the Chinese would use lard not butter, but the mix has to be solid and spreadable) Form the dough into a 30 cm log, and cut into pieces of 2.5 cm (12 altogether) Keep the rest of the pieces covered, while rolling one of them into an oval about ½ cm thick. Brush the top of the oval with **toasted sesame oil**, then spread with 1/12 of the spring onion mix. Fold the oval lengthwise in thirds to enclose the filling, pinch the open ends close, and beginning at one end, roll this strip into a spiral coil. Flatten it gently and roll into a round, about 12 cm across. Cover this pancake, and make the rest in the same way. In a large, heavy frying pan heat **enough vegetable oil to make at least 1 cm. depth**, until very hot but not smoking. Slide in a pancake, turning once, till golden and bubbly. It should take 30-40 secs if the oil is hot enough. Drain on paper towels, and serve while hot. These go very well with any Chinese meal, especially a Northern one. They can also be a snack or appetiser.

Spring Onion Foccaccia

You can make this with wholemeal, white, or in-between flour, depending on your taste. The dough is made by the 2-stage method. Start by making a sponge or starter, from **200g strong flour, a packet of fast acting dried yeast, and 150 ml. warm water.** Knead smooth, and let rise till it has doubled in size (For breadmaking in general, see Basics) Knock back, and add **4 tbsp. olive oil, 1 tsp. salt, 120 ml. warm water**, and a total of **200g flour**. Depending on your flour, you may need more flour or more water to make a stiff dough. So add only half the flour when you are mixing oil, water, flour into the knocked-

165

back sponge, and add the rest as needed. Knead smooth, and let rise again. Knock back a second time, and roll out to about 10 mm thick. Put on a baking sheet. Spread over it a chopped bunch of spring onions, pressing them into the dough. Dribble over 2 tbsp. olive oil, and sprinkle with ½ tsp coarse sea salt. Bake at 400 till done, and eat while fresh and warm.

There are no precise indications here of time taken for rising or baking. I find the total process takes about 3 hrs, but it will depend on the flour used, the rising temperature, and too many other factors to list. Here, as in all bread-making, it is easier to adapt to the process rather than try to control it. Professionals have to control the process; that's why their recipes are much more complicated.

Spring Onion Dip

Mix **equal quantities of yoghurt and (bought) mayonnaise**, then flavour with **mushroom ketchup or soy sauce**, chopped **spring onions**, and chopped **parsley**. **Salt** and **pepper**, Especially good with crudites.

Celestial Soup

There is that moment when you've done several things for a Chinese meal, and realise that an extra dish of soup would be a good idea. This fits the bill nicely.

Boil **1 litre water**; add **2 tbsp soy sauce, 3 tbsp. Marigold stock powder, several chopped spring onions,** and **1 tsp. dark sesame oil**. It's very convincing. You can add a few watercress leaves, or coriander leaves, if you have them, but it's OK in its basic form.

Spring onions also make very good fritters/tempura, but you wouldn't be doing these using just spring onions. However, they can well be added to a dish of mixed deep-fried vegetables, whether Japanese-style or Mediterranean.

Stinging Nettles

You may have some inner resistance to using nettles. Try to overcome it, because nettles taste good, they are impeccably organic, they are free, and they are different. If you think your eaters may object, don't tell them.

The best time to pick nettles is in early spring, when the new shoots are about 15 cm high. Wear rubber gloves, and take a bag. Try to avoid roadside patches; there is no lead in petrol anymore, but there are other forms of pollution to avoid. The nettles cook down, but not as much as spinach does. Never pick them after 1st June, as they become old and fibrous and laxative. When they are cooking, they have a quite distinct and pleasant scent. Boiling even for a short time gets rid of any sting.

DEFAULT. Nettle Soup (or Potage des Orties for the sceptical).
Wash **about 200g. young nettles**. Cook, with about **200g peeled and cut-up potatoes** and **1 chopped onion**, in **600 ml. salted water**, for about 15 mins. Let cool a little, then whizz in blender. Reheat, and add **a good slug of double cream** and a **few small pieces of butter**. Stir in and serve. A beautiful colour, and puzzling though delicious taste. I think garlic bread goes well with it.

Chopped Nettles.
Wash and boil **200g young nettle shoots** in plenty of salted water, 5-10 mins. Drain, squeeze, and chop finely. Reheat in **20g butter**, with **salt** and **pepper**.
Maybe melt **a chopped onion, or some chopped garlic**, in the butter before adding nettles.
OR reheat, add **olive oil and lemon juice**, for a Greek island version.
OR You can make an Indian dish by frying **cumin and mustard seeds** in some **oil** till the mustard seeds pop, adding a **chopped chilli and chopped garlic**, and stirring in the chopped nettles.

Wild Green Risotto
Allow **about 50g nettles and 50g risotto rice per head**. Boil the washed nettles in plenty of salted water for 5-10 minutes, then drain and chop. Melt **a chopped onion** (for 4-6) in **30g. butter,** and add the

167

rice. Let it cook gently for a couple of minutes, then start adding **stock from 1½ litres** in small doses (see general risotto recipe in Techniques) After 2 doses of stock, add the chopped nettles, and stir well. When the risotto is almost done, add **chopped salad greens – I used a packet of rocket, watercress, and spinach, --** and let these just wilt. Any wild or garden greens can be used instead; I fancy radish leaves, though I haven't tried this. Some chives or dill or parsley is also good if you have them. Stir in **50g grated Parmesan** and serve. You don't need to tell people it's nettles, and they'll know. But this fresh green risotto *feels* as if it's doing you good.

There are many more possibilities. A friend makes a quiche with nettles, as if they were spinach. In fact, almost anything involving cooked spinach can also be done with cooked nettles, so look at spinach for more ideas,

Swiss Chard

Swiss Chard is a handsome and useful vegetable, and I can't think why it isn't more generally available and generally used. It can also be available for most of the year, depending on when the seeds are sown. I've always sown late in July-August, let the vegetable grow through the winter, and then used it when growth takes a spurt in early spring. Others see it as harvested in early autumn or winter, and at least one person says it's best in summer because it can stand dryness and heat without running to seed.

Actually, it's more like two vegetables in the classic form, with broad white stems and dark green leaves, because in many cases the stems and leaves are cooked separately. Ruby chard is a variety which doesn't grow so strongly, with spectacular deep vivid red stems, and this is almost always cooked as a whole. In the UK, it's a matter of taking what you can get, or growing it. People also vary in which part they prefer; some compare the stems to asparagus or seakale, and some laud the leaves, with more body than spinach and, they say, a better flavour. Try both, together or apart, and decide what you think.

I have arranged this as dishes using just stems, those using just the leaves, and then those using both. If what you have is Ruby chard, concentrate on the last section. The leaves need using almost as soon as you get them. The stems can survive for several days in the fridge.

Chard Stems

These are sometimes just called chards, mostly in American books, but read recipes from other books carefully to see what is meant. Wash first. Start by separating leaf and stem, either using a knife and making a V-shaped cut into the leaf, or using scissors. What happens next depends on the precise type and condition of the stem. Broad white stems of a certain maturity usually have a thin tough film on either side of the stem, which should be peeled off. Cut partway through the top of the stalk from inside, leaving a thin piece attached to the film; hold the thin piece, and pull towards the bottom of the stem, detaching the film. It's rather like stringing celery, except this is a complete film you are removing. Turn the stem over, and repeat on the inner side. If you can't detect a film with the first cut, you are lucky with your chard and can omit this entirely. You can miss it out anyway, but it's like peeling vegetables or stringing celery; the end result is much nicer if you take the trouble.

Default; Glazed Chard.
Cut the trimmed stems crosswise into pieces about 1 cm long. If the stems were very broad, you might want to cut these lengthwise into 2 or 3 pieces as well. For about **500g stems**, warm **4 tbsp. olive oil**, and add the stems. Stir round to coat them with oil, then cover and cook very slowly, stirring from time to time, for 15-30 mins, till very tender. **Salt and pepper**, and the **juice of half a lemon**, and they are ready to eat as a side dish.

Braised Chard
is the same, with a bit more elaboration. Sweat **2 chopped shallots** and **a chopped clove garlic** in the oil before adding **500g stems**. When the stems are coated with the oil, add **100 ml. stock**, and cook gently, covered, about 20 mins, or till tender. Uncover, and raise the heat to evaporate the remaining liquid. **Salt and pepper**, and chopped **parsley**. Or other herb to taste. Or omit the shallot and use **3-4 cloves garlic** – this tastes much more Italian.

Chards with Parmesan.
For this, and subsequent more complicated recipes, it's often better to boil the chard stems before further treatment. They can take 30 mins to cook, though 15-20 is more normal. Taste to make sure they are done to your liking. Drain well. For **500g stems**, you need **60g each butter and Parmesan**. Smear a baking dish with a little of the butter, then layer stalks, sprinkle of **salt** and Parmesan, dots of butter, until all the stalks are in. The top layer should be well sprinkled with Parmesan and dotted with butter. Cook at 180 until there is a light cheesy crust on top, and let it cool a little before eating.

Chards in Cheese Sauce, au Gratin.
Like cauliflower cheese with another vegetable; some people, like my husband, prefer the chard version. Trim **700g stems**, and boil until tender, up to 30 min. Meanwhile, melt **40g butter** in a flat-bottomed pan, add **30g flour**, blend, and let cook on low heat for 2-3 mins without colouring. If it doesn't spread out to cover the pan base, but is lumpy, add more butter. Pour in, all at once, **300ml cold milk**; stir

well, and turn up the heat. Stir frequently while it's coming to the boil, but you can leave it enough to add **1 tsp. salt**, quite a lot of **pepper**, and a good grating of **nutmeg**. As it approaches the boil, it will start to thicken, and at that point keep stirring, getting into the pan corners. This is a very simple way to do it. Cook 5 mins on a low heat once it's thickened, adding more milk if it's too thick. Then take off the heat, and beat in **120g strong Cheddar**. Drain the chard well, (you might even roll it in a clean teatowel), spread out in a shallow dish, and cover with the sauce. Sprinkle at least **50g more grated cheese** on top – my family likes lots, and I can easily use more than 50g. If all is hot, put under the grill until everything is bubbling and the top is golden brown. If it has been waiting, put into the oven at 180 to heat through, finishing under the grill if necessary. We eat it just with hunks of bread, saving anything else for a separate course.

Chards in Blue Cheese Sauce.
Very rich, very delicious, and you don't need very much. A first course, or mean main to follow plentiful nibbles. Cut **12 broad chard stems**, peeled, into pieces about 8 cm by 1 cm, and boil them for 15 mins. Meanwhile, heat **200 ml double cream** gently, and add **100g blue cheese** broken up when it's warm. Not too strong a blue – Stilton, mild Gorgonzola, Saint-Agur, for example. Stir till the cheese melts, then season with a little **salt** (cheese is salty), and dashes of **Tabasco** to taste. Add the drained chard pieces and mix well. Turn into a buttered flat oven dish, sprinkle the top with **breadcrumbs**, and bake at 180 till the top is golden.

Chards with Tahina Sauce.
Cook **500g stems**, cut into 1 cm squares, till just tender, 10-15 mins or more. Meanwhile, make the sauce. I usually do it in a mortar, which gives better control of the end result, but you can mix everything all at once in a food processor. Pound **2 cloves garlic**, peeled, with ½ **tsp. salt** in a mortar, and add **3 tbsp. tahini paste**, stirred well if the oil is sitting on top in the jar. Stir it in, then add lemon juice (up to **2 lemons**), and water to thin down. If using the processor, start with the juice of 1 lemon and 3 tbsp. water. Mix the sauce into the drained chard stems; you may not need it all. Leftover tahina is not a problem; it will probably be eaten quickly by people passing and dipping fingers in, but it goes with many many veg and falafel as well.

Chards with Tomato Sauce.

A simple tomato sauce, with garlic but no onion (see p. 234). **Cooked chards.** Add the chards to the sauce, simmer for 10 mins or so, and add **either capers or basil leaves**. Alone or with pasta.

Pancakes Stuffed with Chard.

First make the filling. Cut **400g prepared chard stems** into 1 cm dice, and blanch for 2 mins. Drain. Cook **1 chopped shallot** gently in **20g butter**, and add **250g sliced mushrooms** – can be closed-cup, buttons, large (in which case cut the slices crosswise into 2 or 3) or any form of wild mushroom you've laid your hands on. Turn and cook about 5 mins, then add the chard dice and **½ tsp. salt**, and stir. Cover and let cook gently about 10 mins. Make a white sauce (**30g butter, 25g flour, 250 ml milk, salt, pepper, nutmeg**; see Basics), and stir the mush/chard mix into this. Add **60g grated tasty hard cheese** – Cheddar, probably. Taste; it should be well-seasoned and not too salty. Now make **2 batches pancakes** (see Basics). As each pancake is cooked, transfer to a plate and start cooking the next one. Put a rounded dsp of filling on the cooked pancake, smear out, and roll, turning over the top, tucking in the sides, and rolling into a compact cylinder. It's easy to do this before the pancake now cooking is ready to be turned, with practice. As the cylinders are made, put them in a large low baking dish smeared with **butter**. You will get 12-16 stuffed pancakes out of the mix. You can now go straight on with the last stages, or leave it (covered, in the fridge) for some hours, or freeze. If freezing, let it defrost before going on. Pour **300 ml. stock** over the pancakes, and sprinkle the top with **40g grated Parmesan**. Cook in a 200 oven for about 20 mins, until the cheese has crusted lightly. The pancakes absorb the stock and swell gently, and the whole combination of textures and flavours is superlative.

Chards in Salad.

The chards cooked as glazed chards, default recipe, make a fine salad if left to cool, and chopped herbs added. Alternatively, if boiling chard for a dish, boil a few extra stems, drain, and dress with a mustardy vinaigrette. Let it cool in the dressing. Serve it alone or on a bed of greens.

Other. Chard stems, previously blanched, can be added to a mixed stir-fry. Chard stems can also be used when making a vegetable stock.

The stems of ruby chard give the stock some of their colour, which helps it to look appetising.

Swiss Chard Leaves

The dark green leaves, full of body and presence, need to be used quickly after picking or buying. Fortunately they are very easy to cook simply, and many ways of using these leaves involve a preliminary blanching. So you can cook a lot of leaves when you first get them, and use the cooked leaves in different ways over the next couple of days.

They are similar to spinach and can be used in many spinach recipes, but they need more cooking and are actually preferable to spinach in many made-up dishes. The flavour is more delicate, and the texture more positive. Maybe most of the time you will want to cook the leaves simply, but I've given a selection of more dressed-up dishes which bring out the special character of chard leaves.

Default. Chard Leaves

Wash the **leaves** carefully. Put in a large pan with the water clinging to the leaves, **salt**, cover, and cook over medium heat for 10-20 mins until the leaves are tender. Stir often. Drain very well, and chop roughly (or finely, to your taste, or even not at all!) Reheat in **butter**, and sprinkle with grated **Parmesan** to serve. Or cook some chopped garlic gently in extra-virgin oil, add the greens, and stir till is all hot; season with lemon, salt if needed, pepper. Or use the greens as a salad, dressing with oil and lemon while still warm.

Chard Leaf and Parsley Frittata.

Wash, cook, drain and chop **200g chard leaves** (or use some already cooked) Fry **a small chopped onion** in **1 tbsp. olive oil**, and add **100g sliced button mushrooms**. When these have become golden, add **a chopped clove of garlic** and the chard leaves, stir well, and leave on a low heat. Sprinkle with **1 tsp. wine vinegar**, and let this evaporate. Beat **6 eggs** with a **large bunch of parsley**, chopped, **30g Parmesan**, grated, **salt** and **pepper**. Pour this over the onion/mushroom/leaf mix, stir to mix, then cook over a very low heat until the eggs are set, which should take 10 mins. or more. Turn the frittata over, probably by breaking into pieces and turning these, then pressing to reunite the

173

pieces, and let it brown on the bottom for a couple of mins. more. Slide it out onto a platter, and eat warm or cool.

Pasta with Chard Leaves and Goat's Cheese.

400g chard leaves, washed, cooked, drained, and roughly chopped. Saute **2 chopped onions** in **2 tbsp. olive oil**, until they start to colour. Add the chard leaves, and sprinkle with **1 tbsp. balsamic vinegar** and a little **salt.** Stir well, and cook a few mins. Meanwhile, boil **400g pasta** of your choice, and drain, reserving some of the **cooking water**. Mix the drained pasta with the green mixture, using cooking water as needed to let down the sauce, and add **150g soft goat's cheese**, crumbled. Mix all well, and sprinkle with **50g pine nuts**, toasted. The goat's cheese/greens effect is unusual and lovely.

Buckwheat Noodles with Chard Leaves and Lentils.

In this the chard leaves are not precooked but are cooked as part of the overall preparation. Start by boiling **100g lentilles du Puy** or other very good lentils, in water to cover with a **bay leaf** and a little **salt.** Simmer till just done, usually about 30 mins. Drain them, keeping the water for stock for another use. Add **1 dsp.extra-virgin olive oil, salt**, and **pepper** to the lentils, and keep for the next stage. Wash **400g chard leaves**, and cut into strips about 2 cm. wide. Warm **2 chopped cloves garlic** in **4 tbsp. olive oil** in a large pan. Before the garlic colours, add the lentils, **2 carrots**, peeled and cubed, **a diced stick of celery**, and **1 leek**, cleaned and chopped. Stir, and cook for 1-2 mins. Then add the chard leaves, and **150 ml.** stock. Simmer gently, covered, until the leaves are tender. There should be a little liquid left at the end. In a separate large pan, boil **300g buckwheat noodles.** When they are done, scoop them out and add to the lentil/leek mix. Mix all well, add a small handful of **parsley**, chopped, and a good sprinkling of **pepper.** Finish with grated **Parmesan** to taste, dribble over a little more **extra-virgin oil**, and serve. It isn't as heavy as you'd expect, but is still a warming dish for a chilly evening.

Risotto with White Wine and Chard Leaves.

Wash, cook, drain and chop **200g chard leaves** (or use some already cooked) If you have other greens – beet tops, turnip tops, even sprouting broccoli – you can use these instead of, or as well as, the chard. While the risotto is cooking, warm the greens with **10g butter** and **1 chopped clove garlic.** For the risotto itself, heat **1½ litres stock**, and keep warm for adding to the risotto. **Salt** the stock lightly. Heat **40g butter** in a large pan, flattish for preference. Add **1 very finely chopped shallot**, and cook gently to "melt" the shallot for 2-3 mins. Add **300g risotto rice**, and stir until the rice becomes opaque. Add **100 ml. white wine**, stir, and cook gently until the wine has nearly evaporated. Start adding stock by the ladleful, stirring after each addition, and letting each addition nearly evaporate before adding the next ladle. The risotto will be done after 20-30 mins; taste when the grains seem swollen. They should be tender but not squashy. There may be leftover stock. Add the greens and chopped **parsley**, let it all come to temperature, and taste for seasoning. Sprinkle with grated **Parmesan** and eat as soon as possible – risottos don't wait.

Pancakes with a Green Filling.

This is the same type of dish as the stuffed pancakes made with the chard stems, but the filling is very different, and the whole dish is hardly recognizable as using the same vegetable as the stem dish. Wash, cook, drain and chop **400g chard leaves**. Warm **20g butter** in a small pan, add **2 chopped cloves garlic**, and tip into the chard leaves before the garlic colours. Mix well; season well with **salt, pepper, nutmeg**. Mix together **200g each cream cheese and cottage cheese** – or use 400g curd cheese, if you can find it. Add **2 eggs, 50g Parmesan**, grated, and blend, then mix in the green mixture. (Parmesan really is best here, but you can use Pecorino or 100g grated strong Cheddar if necessary). Now make **2 batches pancakes** (see Basics). As each pancake is cooked, transfer to a plate and start cooking the next one. Put a rounded dsp of filling on the cooked pancake, smear out, and roll, turning over the top, tucking in the sides, and rolling into a compact cylinder. It's easy to do this before the pancake now cooking is ready to be turned, with practice. As the cylinders are made, put them in a large low baking dish smeared with butter. You should get 12-16 stuffed pancakes. Now dot the top with **butter**, and warm through at 160 for about 10 mins. Serve them with **sour cream**. It may seem odd, but slices of pear or halved plums go very well with this – try it and see.

Chard Leaves with White Beans.

The dried cannellini or haricot beans are cooked from scratch; tins can't be used here, because the beans absorb the flavours of garlic and sage as they cook. Soak **250g of the chosen dried beans** overnight (or quick-soak; see Basics). Drain them, and put into a pan with **10-12 fresh sage leaves, 7-8 cloves garlic**, peeled but whole, **2 tbsp. extra-virgin olive oil**, and water to cover by about 2 cm. DO NOT SALT. Bring to the boil, cover, and simmer till the beans are tender. While they are cooking, wash and shred **200g chard leaves**. Add **1 tsp. salt** to the beans, and the shredded leaves, and cook very gently until the chard leaves are tender. Drizzle with at least **1 tbsp. extra-virgin olive oil, pepper** with enthusiasm, and add **lemon juice** to taste, from at least 1 lemon. Serve warm or cool. You can also do this with chickpeas, which are not so melting as the beans but therefore give a dish with more texture. I'd like to add croutons to the chickpea dish, but they aren't appropriate for the cannellini one.

Filo Pie with Swiss Chard Leaves

Make the filling; **200g chard leaves**, washed, cooked, drained, and chopped. Mix with **2 eggs, 150g Caerphilly cheese, grated, 4-5 sprigs mint**, leaves chopped, **salt and pepper**. Oil a round 20 cm baking dish, and put in the first of **4 leaves filo pastry** (bought frozen, defrosted, kept under slightly damp towel, rest refrozen). Brush this with **olive oil**. Add another leaf, brush with oil, and so on till all 4 leaves have been used. Put the filling in the pie. Fold the filo leaves to the centre of the pie, trimming off excess pastry. Brush the top of the pie with **oil**, and bake at 180 for 20-30 mins, until the pastry top is brown and crisp.

Quiche with Swiss Chard Leaves.

Make a **batch of pastry using 250g flour**, (Basics) and use it to line a 21-22 cm pie tin that's 3 cm. deep at least. (That's 8-9" and 1" in old measurements; many of us have pie tins bought before everything was so determinedly metric) Bake blind until golden brown (Basics again). While this is happening, wash, shred, cook till tender, drain, and chop **200g chard leaves**. Beat **2 eggs** with **200 ml. whipping cream**, season with **salt, pepper, nutmeg,** and add the chard leaves and **100g grated hard cheese**. It would be Gruyere style in France; in England use a Double Gloucester or Cheshire or Cheddar. Bake at 170 for 20-30 mins till the filling is cooked and a little puffed. Let it rest a few mins before eating, so the filling can settle.

Chard Leaf and Lentil Soup.

Wash **200g good lentils** – lentilles du Puy are always my favourites, but there are good Italian and Spanish varieties too. Boil them with **2 litres water, 1 tsp salt**, and **a small diced potato**, until nearly done – 20-30 mins, usually. Meanwhile, prepare about **200g cleaned shredded greens**. Mostly Swiss chard leaves, but they can include watercress, rocket, spinach, young kale, beet greens, and others you might have. Start frying **1 medium chopped onion in 3 tbsp. olive oil**. Add **6-8 chopped cloves garlic**, and a **handful of fresh green coriander**, chopped, to the onion in the pan, and cook until the scent of garlic rises from the pan. Add the greens and stir well. Cover, and let the greens wilt and reduce in volume, about 5 mins. Stir the lot into the simmering pan of lentils, stir, and simmer all, covered, for about 20 mins, stirring from time to time. Finish with the **juice of 2 lemons**, or more to taste, and eat hot, warm, or cool. You can tell that this is a Middle Eastern soup, and you also feel it is so good for you, as well as very good to eat.

Cold Polish Swiss Chard Soup.

The details of this soup, and its provenance, could hardly be more different from the last one, and they illustrate the range of countries where Swiss chard is popular. For this, you need **250g chard leaves**, washed, and shred them finely. Mix with **6 chopped spring onions** and **1 litre stock**, and simmer 15 mins. Pour into a serving bowl, and let it cool a few mins. Beat **2 eggs**, and add a **small carton (150 ml approx) of sour cream or plain yoghurt**. Slowly stir this into the chard mixture. Then start to adjust the taste for the balance you prefer, with **lemon juice, chopped dill, salt if needed, and Tabasco**. Chill well

Swiss Chard – Stems and Leaves Together.

As I say in the introduction to this section, these recipes are especially useful for ruby or rainbow chard, where the stems are quite thin and not suitable for cooking alone. Scissors here are much better than a knife, because you want to remove the thick stem going up into the leaf. Only if the vegetable is very young can you avoid separating stem and leaf. It can't be denied that preparing these is quite time-consuming, but the ease of growing and the beauty in the garden of ruby or rainbow chard make it worthwhile.

Default: Stir-Fried Ruby Chard or Swiss Chard.
Wash, and separate the leaves from the stems. Cut the stems in 2 cm pieces; likewise the leaves, lengthwise and crosswise. For **500g chard**, heat **2 tbsp. sunflower oil**, add the chard stem pieces, and stir-fry on high heat for 1 min. Add **120 ml. water** and ½ **tsp. salt**, cover, turn down the heat to medium, and let it cook for 5 mins, or until a piece tastes nearly tender. Take off the lid, turn up the heat to maximum, add the leaf pieces, and stir-fry for 2 mins more. It's good and simple just as it is; I prefer it with **1 tbsp. soy sauce** and a squeeze of **lime or lemon juice**, and some **pepper**.

Braised Ruby Chard with Garlic and Chili.
Prepare about **500g ruby chard**, slicing the stalks and cutting up the leaves separately. Cook the stalks in boiling salted water till tender; scoop them out, and add the leaves. Cook these about 5 mins, drain, and cool. When nearly ready to eat, warm **2 tbsp. extra-virgin olive oil**, and add **4 chopped cloves garlic**. After about 30 sec, before the garlic starts to colour, add **1 deseeded, finely chopped chili**, and stir. Add the chard stalks and leaves, and stir about until the vegetable is heated through. **Salt and pepper, lemon juice to taste**, and maybe a **chopped herb** – basil, fennel, parsley.

Swiss Chard Crumble.
Cook **500g Swiss or ruby chard** as in the preliminaries to braised ruby chard, separating stems and leaves. Warm **150 ml. double cream** with **1 chopped clove garlic**, and set it aside to infuse. **Salt and pepper** it just before use. Butter a baking dish, add the chard stems and then leaves, and pour over the cream. Sprinkle the top with **60g grated Cheddar** and **30g breadcrumbs**, or more if you have a very shallow dish. A moderate but complete coating is the idea. Put the dish under the grill until crumbs are toasted, cheese is melted, and everything is hot.

Swiss Chard, Rice, Beans and Cheese.
This is an amazing dish for using up leftover rice and cooked dried beans, and you'd never guess it from the taste. You need about **150g raw rice, cooked** – or say 300g cooked rice. Brown, white, jasmine, red, whatever. Also **50-100g cooked dried beans** – they can be plain, but a sauce on them won't detract from the dish. Separate and chop the

stems from **500g chard**, and blanch them until nearly cooked. Then fry them gently with **2 finely chopped onions** in **2 tbsp. oil** until transparent, add **1-2 chopped cloves garlic**, and stir. Add the cooked rice and beans, put the chopped leaves on top, and cover the pan. Cook on low heat until the leaves are done, and stir them into the mixture. Add **100-150g grated Cheddar** and **soy sauce** to taste – start with 1 tbsp. if the beans didn't have a sauce. Stir well, and eat while the cheese is still melted into the mixture. Not, alas, good cold.

Moroccan Chard Stew. Chop finely **500g Swiss or ruby chard**, stalks and leaves. Put these in a pan with a good lid with **1 medium chopped onion, 50g chopped fresh green coriander, 5 tbsp. olive oil, 1 tsp. ras-el-hanout spice mixture, salt and pepper, and 4 tbsp. water.** Cover, and cook gently for 30 mins. Then add **50g white rice**, stir, and cook tightly covered 20 mins more. Stir from time to time in the last 10 mins, and add a tbsp. or so of water if it's getting too dry. The rice should absorb the juices from the chard as it cooks. It goes well with couscous. I also like some Indian pickle here, but you may not.

Swiss Chard, Bean, and Barley Soup.
From the mountains of North-East Italy, where they eat, and need, a lot of warming food. The barley for this soup is cooked separately, and can be done in advance. Boil **1 litre water**, and add **120g pearl barley**. Simmer, covered, about 40 mins or till the barley is soft. Drain, keeping the cooking water. Wash and shred stalks and leaves of **500g Swiss chard**. Fry **1 large finely chopped onion** in **3 tbsp. olive oil** until lightly coloured, then add **1 medium carrot,** chopped, and **2-3 stalks celery**, chopped. Cover and sweat 5 mins, then add a **standard tin tomatoes**, broken up, with the juice. Leave to simmer covered 5 mins more, then add the chard stalks and leaves and **1 tsp. salt**. Mix and cook very gently, covered, until the chard stalks are very tender. Add the contents of **1 tin cannellini or other beans**, drained and rinsed (or dried beans cooked earlier) and the barley, and stir well. The soup will be very thick at this point; thin it down to your preferred state with the water from cooking the barley. Taste for **salt**; you will certainly need some more. **Pepper**. Serve with grated **Parmesan**. If you are reheating this soup, you will probably need to thin it some more, as it thickens on standing.

Watercress

The buyer's experience of watercress is in flux at the moment. In old-fashioned greengrocers, it was sold in bunches, with its stems in water. Recently, (last 5-10 years?) supermarkets have put it in packets, all tangled up and not so convenient if you want to trim off the leaves. And much more expensive. About the same time, rocket came into fashion as a sharp, strong-tasting leaf, and it's still fashionable. But the backlash, growing in strength, is saying that we English have a traditional, strong-tasting, peppery leaf, grown in quantity, and watercress can be used in place of rocket in many dishes. The supermarkets' compromise is a salad packet of watercress, rocket, and spinach – which I don't want to knock, it's a good salad.

Watercress is not something you can grow yourself; it needs pools of clear pure water. And you are always warned against eating watercress found wild, because the water upstream may be – probably is – polluted by sheep, which can give you diseases carried by liver fluke. I know people who don't worry about this, and eat watercress when they find it wild. I wouldn't myself, and I'd advise strongly against it.

But having talked about these non-gastronomic aspects, oh, how **nice** watercress is. Green and fresh and peppery and lively. And it preserves these aspects whether raw by itself, in salads, cooked, put into soups, risottos, souffles. . . It feels as if it's really good for you, too (though to get one of the 5-a-day you have to eat a whole packet). Eat more watercress.

Default.
The simplest possible way; heap the sprigs, simply rinsed and dried, in a bowl in the centre of the table, and encourage people to take sprigs and eat. You can dip it in oil, melted butter, dressings, sauces – but you don't need to. Just munch.

Watercress and Cucumber Salad.
Cut a **cucumber** into thick half-moons, scooping out seeds if they are prominent. Chop **a packet of watercress** coarsely, including stalks. Dress with **oil and vinegar, salt** and **pepper**. Goes well with goat's

cheese, feta, Cheshire. Lovely for eating outside on a warm day; even a picnic, if you take the dressing separately.

Watercress in Green Salads.
Unused watercress from a packet, not enough to make a salad alone, can go with any other salad greens – lettuce various; chicory (witloof), lamb's lettuce (a particularly good combination), baby spinach . . .Just be cautious with the dressing; too much makes watercress sad almost instantly.

Oriental Watercress Salad.
Toast **1 tbsp. sesame seeds** under the grill. Wash and pick over **a packet of watercress**. Make a dressing from **1 tbsp. soy sauce, 1 tbsp. wine vinegar, ½ tsp. sugar,** and **1 tsp. dark sesame oil**. Pour over the watercress, toss, and sprinkle the sesame seeds on top. If you've bought some Szechwan peppercorns and not used them much, use some here. You can add other things to this, like cucumber, or radish, or sprouted seeds. Sprouted fenugreek is really good and adds to the Oriental flavour.

Watercress and Orange Salad.
½ packet each of watercress and lamb's lettuce. Lightly dressed with **oil** and **lemon, salt** and **pepper**. For four people, use **2 oranges** – big ones are easier to get segments from. Peel the oranges thoroughly, so no pith is left. I like the French term "a vif" for this, roughly translated as "to the quick" Then slide a knife between membrane and segment, and turn the knife to flick the segment out. When you have as many segments as you can get, squeeze the membraneous skeleton over the orange segments. Blood oranges (sorry, ruby red oranges) are lovely here, for colour and taste; don't even try to segment these, but peel aggressively, so no pith is left, and slice crosswise. In either case, arrange the dressed greens on a platter, and lay the oranges on top. **A few black olives** add to the colour contrasts.

Watercress and Walnut Salad.
Watercress, walnuts, dressing using **walnut oil** and **wine vinegar or sherry vinegar, or balsamic vinegar**. You can also fry some cubes of bread in walnut oil, and add these; this is getting a bit heavy for my taste, but lots of other people like it. Try it with other nuts, too;

hazelnuts and hazelnut oil; almonds, toasted, with olive oil dressing; even toasted cashew nuts – olive oil dressing again.

Locket's Salad, (Watercress, pear, blue cheese)

These are the ingredients of Locket's Savoury (below) **Watercress** base; slices of **good dessert pear**, peeled and cored (not Conference); chunks of **blue cheese, preferably Stilton**; dressing of **extra-virgin olive oil** and **wine vinegar**, with **a little salt** and **lots of pepper**. I prefer this to the savoury.

Watercress, Watermelon, Salted Almonds.

Just a mixture of these ingredients, with a light dressing of oil and lemon. **1 packet watercress, a wedge of watermelon, 2 tbsp. salted almonds, 1 tbsp. extra-virgin olive oil, juice of half a lemon.** Part of the pleasure is the colour combination. Add cubed **feta cheese** and **black olives** to make a whole-meal salad.

Watercress Puree.

Pick over the **watercress from 3 packets**, taking out any tough stalks – there won't be many. Boil **1½ litres water** with **20g sea salt**, and blanch the watercress for 3 mins. Drain, and run cold water through to stop any further cooking. Put in the food processor, and whizz smooth. Transfer to a small saucepan, and add **50g butter, juice of ½ lemon, 4 tbsp. double cream, salt** and **pepper**. Serve as soon as it's really hot. If kept waiting, it will gradually change colour from a beautiful green, and look much less appetising.

If you have some ageing watercress – not good enough to eat raw, too good to put on the compost heap – blanch it as above, drain, squeeze, and puree. It can then be used for adding to mayonnaise, yoghurt and raitas, soups – even a version of pesto with watercress. But the main thing is that it has an extra couple of days of life so you have a chance to use it.

Stir-fried Watercress with Chinese Mushrooms and Bamboo Shoots.

Wash **2 packets watercress**, and pick over to take out any tough stems. Drain and dry in a cloth. Soak **8 dried Chinese mushrooms** by pouring over boiling water to cover, and letting them stand 10-15 mins. Drain, cut off and discard stems (or keep for stock), and slice the caps thinly. Shred **half a bamboo shoot** from a tin. Heat **2 tbsp. oil** in a wok or large frying pan, and add the mushrooms and bamboo shoots. Stir for about 1 min, then add the watercress. Stir, then add **½ tsp salt** and **1 tsp. sugar**. Stir-fry again for 1 min. Lift the vegetables out on to a serving dish, and reduce the liquid left behind over high heat. When this liquid is almost gone, add any accumulated liquid from the vegetables, and reduce again. Pour the liquid over the vegetables, and eat immediately.

Mash with Watercress.
Not a recipe, a good idea. Chop **watercress** and add to **mashed potato**. The more watercress the better – either none or a lot, is my feeling. Not a mimsy in-between amount.

Watercress and Potato Soup.
Wash and pick over **a packet of watercress**, and select about a palmful of leaves only (no stalks) for the final addition to the soup. Sweat **a leek**, cleaned and chopped, in **30g butter** till soft but not coloured. Add **300g old potatoes**, peeled and chunked, and the remainder of the watercress. Add **1 litre water, salt**, and simmer till the potatoes are done. Let cool a little, then blend – a blender is better than a food mill for this one. Taste for seasoning, add a grate of **nutmeg**. Just before serving, reheat, add **100-150 ml. double cream**, and the reserved leaves. Delicate, rich and lovely.

Fermented Watercress Soup.
After a very conventional soup, we have a real oddity. Don't be put off it on that account, however. It's obviously useful if you have overbought watercress – say for a party – but worth trying for itself.
Wash thoroughly **2 packets of watercress** and dry. Then put in a glass (or non-metal, anyway) bowl, add **1 tbsp. salt**, cover with water, and leave in the fridge for 3 days. Drain and chop. Sweat **2 leeks**, chopped, in **30g butter** till soft. Add **300g potatoes**, peeled and cubed, leave about 2 mins, then add **750 ml stock**. Simmer till the potatoes are cooked, and add the watercress. Bring back to the boil. Cover, let cool a little, blend or puree by the way you prefer, thin if necessary, taste for seasoning. Reheat when needed. Croutons nice but not necessary.

Green Eggs.
I am always surprised how popular stuffed eggs are. They aren't difficult, though it's not worth doing them for fewer than 4 people.

Hard-boil **6 eggs**, cool, and peel. Halve and take out the yolks. In the small bowl of the food processor, or in a mortar, blend the yolks with **1 tsp French mustard, 1 tbsp. mayonnaise**, and **¼ packet chopped watercress**. Taste for **salt**; I think ¼ tsp is right here. No pepper. Fill the hollows in the egg whites with this mixture, and arrange on a bed of **watercress from the rest of the packet**. You can, if you like, serve this with mayonnaise with more watercress blended in, but I prefer it without. Those of us who have endlessly read Dr. Seuss out loud, and are not vege, would love to eat green eggs and ham.

Watercress Roulade.

A roulade is very much an 80's dish, but none the worse for that. It's spectacular to look at, and very good to eat; it's not difficult; and it's cheap. It also tastes very spring-like and light, even though it isn't particularly light. What you are doing is making a flat souffle omelette, then rolling it up round a filling. I would hate to do this without baking parchment paper, which is extremely and reliably non-stick, and reusable. (I'd find meringues much more difficult, if not impossible, without this paper.)

For the filling, hardboil **2 eggs**, cool, peel, and chop. Add **3 tbsp. mayonnaise, preferably home-made, 1 packet chopped watercress, 50g grated best Cheddar, 1 tsp. French mustard, salt** and **pepper** to taste. Line a flat, "Swiss-roll" baking tin with baking parchment. Separate **4 eggs**, and mix the yolks with **another packet of watercress**, chopped, and **30g grated Cheddar**. Add **a pinch of salt** to the 4 egg whites, and beat until stiff but not dry. Fold a dollop of these into the yolks, then tip this mixture back on top of the whites and fold in gently. Tip onto the baking parchment, spread it out, and bake for 15-20 mins at 180. The top must be set. Spread the filling over the top, and roll up, using spatula, palette knife and paper itself to help. This is the only tricky bit; comfort yourself, because it doesn't have to be perfect. Again use the paper to transfer to an ovenproof platter, and pop it back in the oven to reheat for a couple of mins. Eat as soon as possible. It looks good with a red (tomato or pepper) or purple beetroot salad to go with it.

Locket's Savoury.

Introduced by a 70's restaurant called Locket's, and very popular on the dinner-party circuit of the time. Now I couldn't contemplate it at the end of a meal, but it makes a really good lunch.

Toast and decrust **1-2 slices bread per eater. Butter**, and put on a baking sheet. Put sprigs of **watercress** on each (a packet will do 6-8 pieces toast from large loaf) Peel, core, and slice **a dessert pear for each 4 toasts**, and distribute the slices over them. Then **1-2 slices Blue Stilton** on top of each toast – or small thin chunks – and bake in a moderate oven until the cheese begins to melt. Not too long, or the watercress will wilt, but there is a fairly large window of about 5 mins where these are both OK (that is, cheese melting, watercress perky)

Watercress Tart.
If you have **a cooked tart case**, no further cooking is needed. For a 18 cm. pastry case, mix **350g cottage cheese, most of a packet of watercress**, chopped, (keep a few small sprigs for decorating the top), **10-cm cucumber**, chopped, **a few sliced raw mushrooms, some sliced radishes, celery, spring onions** if you like . . . what you want is a lively fresh-tasting mix. Pile the filling into the tart case, decorate with the reserved watercress, eat.   If you have some leftover puff pastry, leave out the flan case, and serve a mound of cottage cheese mix accompanied by a brown, risen, warm slice of puff.   What a combination of wholesome and decadent!   Even if you go the tart route, it needs something crisp, and something green to go with it; toast and cabbage, at a minimum.

Watercress sandwiches
Most important here is **good bread. Butter, lots of watercress**. Try eating these sandwiches with soups instead of plain bread – with tomato soup, for example.

Watercress Dip.
1 packet chopped watercress, 200g curd cheese (or cottage + cream cheeses), juice of ½ lemon, a few walnuts, chopped not too fine. **Salt** and **pepper**. Easiest in the food processor, where you should add walnuts after scraping out; perfectly possible by hand. For crudites, sandwiches, baked potatoes, spread on toast before poached eggs, and more.

Wild Garlic, or Ramsons

This has become extremely fashionable over the past few years among chefs and top restaurants, and is touted in foodie columns in magazines. Along with fashion goes expense; I've seen figures of £20/kg, which is not unreasonable if you are paying people to gather from the wild. If supermarkets took it up it would be unsustainable, and wild supplies would suffer and vanish. The woodlands in which wild garlic grows would be poorer for it. So I won't encourage anyone to buy this. If, on the other hand, you have a local wood where it grows plentifully – and it tends to grow in quantity if it grows at all – then a few leaves from different plants, in season, isn't going to hurt, provided that not everyone is doing it. You don't need very much for the flavour and scent to come through – 25 leaves, weighing about a gram apiece, is enough for most uses.

The season is quite short, March to May at most. After May the leaves become more fibrous and stronger, even ranker, in flavour. It's fine to pick before flowering, but the presence of flowers helps with identification. New leaves without flowers can be confused with lily-of-the-valley, which is poisonous. So pick only if you are sure of identification. The smell helps. As you approach a patch of wild garlic the air is scented with the characteristic smell.

To discover for yourself how much you like the flavour, and how much of the flavour you like, **Wild Garlic Soup** is the easiest vehicle. Sweat **1 chopped onion** in **30g butter**, add **200g potatoes**, peeled and cut up, and **500 ml stock/water**. Simmer. If you add the wild garlic leaves before simmering, you will get less flavour than if you add them when the potatoes are cooked. Use **25-50 leaves** for this quantity soup. Let cool a little, puree, season. Reheat, thinning if needed, and add **cream** to taste just before serving. If the flavour is too strong, you can use milk instead of stock, which softens the flavour considerably. For the strongest flavour, use 50 leaves; add just before pureeing; and shred a few leaves to add directly to the soup. This is emphatically not a one-recipe-fits-all-tastes soup, and you know your eaters better than anyone else.

Wild Garlic Pesto.

A nice simple use, and it has the advantage of keeping much better than the fresh leaves. Take about **100g leaves and flowers**, and blanch for 1 min in boiling salted water. Drain and dry. Put in the food processor with **50g walnuts or hazelnuts, salt, 100 ml. extra-virgin olive oil,** and **the juice of a lemon**, and whizz to a puree. Add more oil if it is still paste-like and lumpy. Turn out of the bowl, and stir in **50g grated Parmesan.** This can be made in a mortar, pounding everything with a pestle, but it's much harder! This is fierce, no doubt about it, but I love it. Goes with pasta, gnocchi, baked potatoes, in an omelette, spread on toast for garlic toasts . . . And it freezes, but not for long.

Wild Garlic, Potato, and Leeks Gratin

Comparatively tame, but delicious. Sweat **300g leeks**, trimmed and slice, in **50g butter**. Add **30 leaves of wild garlic**, washed and shredded, and cook 5 mins more. **Salt** and **pepper**. Add **100 ml. each milk and double cream**, and bring to the boil. Leave while you peel and slice THINLY **500g old potatoes**. Arrange potatoes and milk mixture in layers in a wide buttered baking dish, finishing with potatoes. Cover the dish with foil and bake at 180 for 1 hr. It should be done after that – use a knife blade to ensure the potatoes are soft throughout – and cook more if they need it. When done, take off the foil, and allow the top to brown. A green veg. or green salad makes this into a meal.

More Ideas.

You can immerse wild garlic leaves in olive oil, and leave to soak for a few days. Then use the oil in salad dressings, tomato sauce, with roast tomatoes . . .

Chefs have suggested making a mint and wild garlic sauce as a spring salad dressing; deep-frying the flowers in a light batter; in spring minestrone; in risotto; in a dressing with mustard, wine, and sunflower oil . . . As you can see, the field for invention is wide open. Me, I'll stick with pesto, soup, gratin, and infused oil for the brief time wild garlic is around.

Summer, Early Autumn

Fennel

Aubergines
Courgettes
Cucumber
Fennel
French Beans
Globe Artichokes
Kohl Rabi
Lettuce
Marrow
Peas
Peppers
Pumpkin and Squash
Runner Beans
Shallots
Shell Beans
Sweetcorn
Sweet Potatoes
Tomatillos
Tomatoes

Kohl Rabi

Shell Beans

Globe
Artichokes

Peppers

Tomatillos

Aubergine

Eggplant is the American name. Apparently aubergine also comes in an ivory, egg-shaped form. I've never seen it. But aubergines are instantly recognisable and very beautiful; deep purple, taut, shiny – you could even say sexy. And it must grow so well and easily in Mediterranean climates. There are so many recipes for it, and this is usually a sign of an abundance – even a glut -- to use in one form or another. People's creativity is sparked off . . . For me, it doesn't have a strong and distinctive flavour, but the texture and presence aubergine adds to dishes is remarkable.

For all that, it isn't an English vegetable. My seed catalogue has 8 varieties, including one for growing in a sunny sheltered spot outside, so home-grown aubergines must be possible. In a good summer you might even have too many. Practically every vegetarian and Mediterranean book has many ways of using aubergine. So I have limited myself to just a few aubergine recipes I like very much. Should you have a glut, you might need to look elsewhere. But if, like most of us, you are buying aubergines one or two at a time, for a known purpose, try these first.

The most famous use of aubergine is in **Ratatouille**, and I think this is probably also the default.
For it, you need **1 aubergine, 2 medium onions, 2 red peppers, 500g tomatoes**, and **garlic** and **olive oil.** You will see recipes telling you to cook the vegetables separately, and simmer together just for a few minutes before serving. I can't believe this is the basic peasant recipe, and to me it doesn't taste sufficiently better to be worth the extra effort. There is also a tradition of salting the cut-up aubergine before cooking. This is supposed to extract any bitterness. Modern varieties of aubergine aren't bitter, so from this point of view you can miss it out. However, salting the aubergines also means that they absorb less oil, and this must be a good thing. So cut your aubergine in cubes – taking off the top and bottom, but leaving the skin on – and sprinkle with **1 tsp salt**. Mix the salt in with your hands, and leave the mix in a colander or sieve for 30 mins. or more. After this, squeeze the cubes, and dry on paper towels. Most of the salt will be removed in the liquid

they exude, or be wiped off with the towel, so don't worry about the quantity. Peel and slice the onions, and sweat them in **3-4 tbsp. olive oil** until transparent. Add the aubergine cubes and the peppers, seeded and cut into strips, along with **3-4 cloves garlic**, peeled and sliced. Sweat 20-30 mins more, until the veg. are cooked. Add the tomatoes, peeled and chopped, and sweat 10 mins more. Look at it now; if there is a lot of liquid, turn up the heat and cook on medium heat until it has evaporated. If not, sweat 10 mins more. It should be a thick stew. Taste for salt, and add some if needed. Finish with fresh **basil**, slivered; fresh **parsley**, chopped; or both. It's wonderful hot or cold. Or reheated. You can add **2-3 medium courgettes,** cubed, with the aubergine and peppers, to your ratatouille, which will extend it without diluting the effect, but they aren't necessary. This is a true classic.

For my daughter's wedding buffet, I made an **Upside-Down Ratatouille Tart** inspired by a Tarte Tatin. I baked rounds of puff pastry, put them on serving dishes, spooned lots of ratatouille on top, and sprinkled with crumbled goat's cheese. It was a great success.

Fried Sliced Aubergine.
I don't peel, but simply slice about ½ cm thick. If eating just as fried slices, you might want to halve the aubergine before slicing, as then more fit into a pan. Allow **1 medium aubergine** per head. **Salt** and dry them. Dip into **flour**, and fry in **olive oil** – the oil flavour goes very well with aubergine. They will absorb a remarkable amount of oil. You may need to cook them in batches. Drain on kitchen towel, paper or cloth, and serve, alone or, wickedly, with garlic mayonnaise or skordalia. (p. 385) You can elaborate on fried whole slices by making "sandwiches", with a filling of crumbled cheese and herbs, and baking them under a coating of tomato sauce. This makes a main dish.

An Indian variant on this, **Spiced Fried Aubergine.**
Don't salt them this time. **1 medium aubergine** per head. Dip the slices in a mixture of **1 tsp. salt, ½ tsp turmeric, ¼ tsp ground cayenne pepper**, and about **½ tsp. freshly ground black pepper**. Fry the slices in **vegetable oil** till reddish-brown on each side, and serve with **lemon quarters** or with a fresh Indian chutney, such as coriander or mint. It goes with any Indian dishes, and lots of Western ones as well.

Chinese Braised Eggplant

has lovely strong flavours, well balanced, and is distinct from any of these other recipes.

Start by soaking **6 dried shitake mushrooms** in boiling water for 10-15 mins. Drain (The soaking liquid from shitake never seems to be used in Chinese cooking, and I'm not sure why) Cut off the mushroom stems and discard, and sliver the mushrooms. Cut into squares **2 seeded green peppers.** Make a sauce mix with **3 cloves garlic, 2 seeded green chilis, 1 tbsp. soy sauce, 2 tbsp. dry sherry or white wine, 1 tbsp. red wine vinegar, 1 tsp. sugar, ½ tsp. salt.** This is best whizzed briefly in the blender, or you can pound the garlic, chilis and salt in a mortar and then mix in the liquids. Cut about **500g aubergine**, topped and tailed, into cubes, and fry them in **4 tbsp. oil** until lightly browned. Keep pressing them as you stir, to release the oil they absorb. You may need more oil. When done, tip into a sieve and press again to release any oil. This can all be done in advance. About 10 mins before eating, heat **2 tbsp. oil** and add the sliced shitake mushrooms and peppers. Stir-fry about 2 mins, then add the aubergine; reduce the heat and stir-fry about 5 mins. Add **100 ml. water**, stir in, then add the sauce. Reduce the heat, and cook, stirring, about 3 mins. more. Serve straightaway. Any leftovers are good cold, as a salad, but this isn't orthodox Chinese.

Aubergine and Pickle Salad is based on one in Claudia Roden's Middle Eastern Food.

Salt **1 kg aubergines**, cubed, dry, and fry in oil till cooked and lightly browned on both sides. Mix with **500g tomatoes**, skinned and chopped, and about **400g piccalilli**. Start with half the amount and taste till it pleases you. People who like pickles will love this. Mrs. Roden's version layers the fried aubergine and the raw tomatoes, sliced, and stews gently for ½ hr before adding the piccalilli. This has the virtue that it can be kept, under a thin layer of oil in the fridge, but hasn't the freshness of my version.

Potato and Aubergine Curry.

This is a main dish. Fry **1 chopped medium onion** in **1 tbsp. oil**, add **3-4 chopped cloves garlic** when transparent, then add **1 cubed aubergine** and about **250g potatoes**, peeled and cut into small chunks. Fry a little, then add a mix of **1 tsp. turmeric, 1 tsp. garam masala, ½ tsp. cayenne, and 1 tsp. salt.** Turn over to mix, add **a tin of**

191

tomatoes, whole or chopped, and cook 30-40 mins. until the potato is cooked. Sprinkle with chopped **fresh green coriander** to serve. This is a basic everyday curry, very easy, but delicious anyhow.

Aubergine Parmigiana

is very far from an everyday dish. Rich, oily, succulent and with a scent that permeates the house and calls everyone from cellar to attic. In Southern Italy you can buy it from cooked-food shops; would we could here! It's basically a layered dish, with tomato sauce, fried aubergine slices, and cheeses, authentically Mozzarella and Parmesan. It must be Parmesan, but in England I prefer to use a mild English cheese – creamy Lancashire or Wensleydale – instead of the Mozzarella. I have a recipe using fresh sheep's milk cheese, made richer by mixing with cream.

Start by making the tomato sauce; fry **1 medium chopped onion in 2 tbsp. olive oil**. When transparent, add **3 cloves garlic**, chopped fine, then **2 tins chopped tomatoes**, and **2-3 tbsp. tomato paste**. Simmer vigorously for 30-45 mins, adding **salt, pepper**, and **dried oregano** to taste after 15 mins or so. When done, it will not be watery. Meanwhile, prepare **1½ kg aubergines**; top and tail, slice, salt and let drain ½ hr, then dry. Fry the slices lightly in **olive oil** without letting them colour, and drain on kitchen towels. Slice **200g chosen cheese**, and grate **80g Parmesan**. Lightly oil a wide shallow baking dish; put in a layer of tomato sauce, a layer of fried aubergine, and some cheese and a sprinkle of Parmesan. Sprinkle this layer with plenty of **pepper**, then repeat until the aubergines are used up. There may be some tomato sauce left over; it will be useful another time. Finish the top with the rest of the Parmesan and a dribble of **olive oil**, and bake at 150 for 45-60 mins, until the top is crusty and the sides are bubbling. Serve hot. This makes a lot, enough for 6-8 hungry people. If you are feeding fewer, it freezes well, so make 2 dishes and freeze one for the future. (Note; Elizabeth David says she prefers a version with courgettes, which is less rich and oily. Also cheaper, if you are buying the vegetables)

Aubergine and Bean Gratin

is American, and a very warming dish for winter.

Start by soaking **100g dried white beans, such as haricots or cannellini**, overnight (I'd recommend doing twice this amount, so then you have beans cooked ready for another dish) Drain. Cover the beans with fresh water, add **2 bay leaves**, the **leaves from 2 sprigs sage**, chopped, **2 whole cloves garlic**, peeled, and **1 tbsp. olive oil**. Bring to the boil and simmer till the beans are done, 45 mins at least. Add ½ **tsp. salt** when done. Drain the beans, keeping the liquid.

Cook **2 large chopped onions** in **4 tbsp. olive oil** with **3 chopped cloves garlic**, more **sage**, about the same as before, and some **thyme leaves**. Add **1 tsp. salt**, and cook slowly, covered, until the onions are soft. Add **1 aubergine**, cubed, stir together, and cook covered 10 mins more. Add **1 tin tomatoes** with the juice, cover again, and cook till the aubergine is tender. Add the drained beans. Add more salt if needed, lots of **black pepper**, ground, and more sage and thyme if you think it's needed.

Pour the whole mixture into a large oiled flat dish. There should be enough liquid to come about halfway up the vegetables; if not, add some of the bean cooking liquid. Crumb **2 thick slices decrusted bread**, spread them over the top, and dribble with **olive oil**. Bake at 180 till the top is browned.

Aubergine and Nut Crumble.

I once cooked this for a party of 20 vegans, and they loved it. It's good on a domestic scale, too; no-one misses meat or dairy when the flavours are as good as this.

Top, tail, slice, salt and dry **350g aubergines**. Fry gently till cooked through in **2 tbsp. olive oil** – you may need more oil, and you may need to cook them in 2 batches. Just use the minimum of oil. Drain the slices on kitchen towels. Add a little more **oil** to the pan, and cook **2 medium onions**, chopped, and **3 cloves garlic**. Add **1 tin chopped tomatoes, 250 ml. stock,** and **1 tbsp. tomato puree**, and simmer 10 mins. Season with **salt, pepper, fresh basil or dried herbes de Provence**. Oil a baking dish, and spread half the aubergine slices on the bottom (ideally, they will just fit, but put some on top if necessary). Add half the tomato sauce, then a mix of **60g pine nuts and 60g broken-up walnuts**. Then add the rest of the aubergines, and the rest of the tomato sauce. Make a mix of breadcrumbs from **1 thick slice bread, 4 tbsp. wheatgerm,** and **2 tbsp. sesame seeds**. Spread this over the top. Bake at 170 for about 30 mins, till top is brown and crisp. Obviously you can vary the nuts according to what you have.

A couple of these dishes, and others you'll find elsewhere, involve frying the salted aubergine in olive oil before going on with the recipe.

It does make them succulent; it also uses a lot of oil. (I have a counter-intuitive feeling that if you start with enough oil, you use less in total than adding dribs and drabs as needed. The surplus can then be drained off.) If this worries you, quite reasonably, try brushing each side of the slice with olive oil, and then grilling. Much less oil is used. It may not be quite as much to your taste, but it's better for you, and it may turn out that you prefer it.

The rest of the recipes use baked whole or halved aubergines, and include some of the most useful ones, the puree which can be a salad or a dip. First, though, the simplest is **Baked Herbed Aubergine.**
For each **aubergine**, chop the leaves from **2 sprigs oregano or marjoram** (or parsley at a pinch), and mix with salt and pepper. Cut **4 peeled garlic cloves** into slivers. Then dip each sliver in the herb mixture, make a small slash with the point of a knife in the aubergine, and insert the garlic. This can look quite messy, but don't worry. Put in an oiled baking dish with a lid, cover, and bake at 170 for about an hour. If eating hot, have some **extra-virgin oil** on the table so that the eaters can mash the inside of the aubergine and dribble with the oil. **1 aubergine per person**, and don't expect to eat the skin. You can also serve them cold, again with oil for mashing.

Baked Aubergine with Marinated Feta.
Based on a Thomasina Miers recipe. Ideally, set the feta to marinate the night before you want to eat the dish. Crush **2 peeled cloves garlic** in a mortar with **½ tsp. salt**, and add **3 tbsp. extra-virgin olive oil, juice of ½ lemon, a finely-chopped seeded chili,** and **some chopped mint.** Put in a **packet of feta, (200g or thereabouts)** loosely broken into chunks, and add **black pepper.** Next day, halve **2 aubergines** lengthways, and cut criss-cross slashes in the flesh side. Rub with **salt** and **1 tsp cumin seed, toasted and ground,** and bake skin-side up in an oiled dish at 170 for 45 mins. Let cool. For serving, arrange the halves flesh-side up on a serving plate, and scatter with the marinated feta. Chopped herbs for decoration, if liked. Thomasina added pomegranate seeds for colour; not for me, I don't think it helps the taste.
The marinated feta is good in all sorts of contexts as well as this. When you try it, you will think of everything from green salads to hard-boiled eggs to lentils which would benefit from it.

Both the following puree/salads start in the same way, by roasting a whole aubergine. Prick the skin in several places before cooking. They don't often explode in the oven, but even the once it happened to me was once too many. Then put in roasting tin and cook at 180 for 40-50 mins. This can also be done on a barbecue, if there is one going. Let it cool, when it will seem to collapse.

Mock Caviar.

A bad name, partly because it doesn't taste anything like, and partly because of associations. But that's what they call it in Romania and other Balkan countries; rename it if you like. Peel **2 cooled roasted aubergines**, and mash up the insides with **4 tbsp. extra-virgin olive oil (Greek, ideally), juice of 1 lemon, ½ tsp. salt,** and **black pepper**. This can be done in a food processor; it must be smooth. Add **1 very finely chopped onion**, stir in, and chill. Best with black bread, watercress, and lemon quarters.

Baba Ghanouj.

2 aubergines, roasted, cooled, and peeled. Whizz (or mash) the flesh with **3 tbsp. tahini, 1-2 crushed cloves garlic, juice of at least 1 lemon, to taste, 1 tbsp. extra-virgin olive oil, ½ tsp. salt or more to taste**. This is perfectly good as it is, in a mound with a sprinkle of **paprika or stronger dried chili**. I like it even more when I add some **caramelised onion**, 1 tbsp. or so. This is fine if you have some ready, but isn't practical to do on a small scale. In this case I'd use 1 tbsp. of caramelised onion from a jar. All these variants go well as part of a simple meze table, with toasted pita bread, olives, radishes, and whatever other crudités or salads you gather from stock. As I've said in the introduction, this sort of table of little dishes makes a smashing meal.

Broccoli

The large dark-green heads, as opposed to sprouting broccoli. This has rapidly become such a staple in our kitchens that it's hard to remember how new it is. When I was in the US in 1961, I fell for this vegetable I'd never seen before, and when I came back to England, was disappointed not to find it. The yearning for broccoli was one of the reasons I started (trying to) grow vegetables, and discovered sprouting broccoli because there were seeds for that. Jane Grigson's Vegetable Book, published in 1978, mentions broccoli as just appearing in supermarkets, as a luxury. I think we have to thank the supermarkets for the spread and increased availability of broccoli. It's now got to the point, in the US, where children are expected to dislike broccoli as they used to be expected to dislike spinach. Once again, we see how little fashion and taste have to do with each other. And broccoli does taste good, mild for a member of the cabbage family, sweet, and a pleasing texture.

In English contexts, the large blue-green heads are sold without much of the large thick stalk, and hardly any leaves. Don't buy it, or use it, if the blue-green shows any hint of yellow, and any sign of flowering. These bring on a bitterness which is not pleasant. If there is a lot of stalk, it's possible to treat stalks and florets as two different vegetables. The crucial thing about using broccoli stalks – alone or with florets – is that they must be PEELED. There is quite a thick fibrous layer round the outside of the stalk, sometimes extending even to the little stalks in the head. When preparing broccoli, cut off the florets, breaking them up to be 3-5 cm across the top. Then peel the stalk, cutting off a slice at the bottom, and then stripping the skin from the stalk from the bottom up. So prepared, the stalk can be cut into small pale green/white sticks, which cook in pretty much the same time as the florets. If you don't peel, you'll find a lot of plates with discarded stalks, because they are not pleasant to eat.

Unlike cauliflower, broccoli is seldom eaten raw. But it takes very little cooking.
Default. Plain boiled, with butter. It's better boiled than steamed, as steaming takes longer and fades the bright colour to a darker sludgy green. So prepare your head or heads of broccoli, wash, and dump into

a lot of boiling salted water. I like it cooked only about 5 mins, so it's possible to cook the broccoli while the rest of the meal is being served. It is said that the colour stays brighter if the pan is uncovered, but I don't like the smell and the clouds of steam, so I cover the pan. It doesn't seem to me to affect the colour badly. Drain well, put in a heated dish, and serve with butter on the table so people can add their own, as taste and conscience allow. If you also have wedges of lemon, anyone dieting or simply cutting down can have broccoli with lemon, salt, pepper, which is very good.

Broccoli Braised in Butter.
If there is some reason why you want your broccoli hot but can't do it at the last minute, this enables you to do so. Cook **700-800g raw broccoli** for 4-6 people in boiling water for 3 mins.. only, then drain, and spread out on a clean teatowel to cool quickly. Put the broccoli in a buttered baking dish, and pour over **60g melted butter**. **Salt** and **pepper** lightly. Seal the dish with foil. About 20 mins before serving, put in a moderate, 170, oven, and leave till broccoli is hot. Serve as soon as possible. There aren't many circumstances in which you NEED to do this, but it is very nice indeed.

There are several variations on the theme of parboiled broccoli finished with butter or oil, and other flavours. **Broccoli with Butter and Parmesan** can hardly fail; heat the cooked, drained, cooled broccoli in melted butter in a frying pan (40g butter to 700g raw broccoli), and when it is heated through, add 50g grated Parmesan. Stir in and eat, probably alone. **Broccoli with Garlic;** cook 2 finely-chopped cloves garlic in 3 tbsp. extra-virgin olive oil, add the broccoli and cook gently till it's heated through. **Broccoli with Chili and Garlic;** cook 2 finely-chopped cloves of garlic and 1 chopped deseeded fresh chili in 3 tbsp. olive oil, add the broccoli, and cook gently till heated through. Finish with the juice of half a lemon.

Stir-Braised Broccoli.
Cut up a **400g head of broccoli**. The florets should be small, and the stem chiplets even thinner than usual. This way no pre-cooking is needed. Heat **2 tbsp. sunflower oil** or other bland oil in a wok or frying pan, and add the dry broccoli (That is, after washing, dry with a teatowel) Stir over high heat until the broccoli florets start to brown a little, about 5 mins. Add ½ **tsp. salt, 1 tsp. sugar**, and **250 ml. stock**.

Stir, and keep cooking on high heat until almost all the liquid has gone and the broccoli is done. Sprinkle with **1 tbsp. soy sauce**, turn over to mix, and eat.

The stir-braising method, modified, can be used for broccoli with other vegetables – onions, or mushrooms, or bamboo shoots, or beansprouts, or peppers, or . . .. Add tofu, plain or smoked or marinated, to the plain broccoli or one of the mixtures, and you have a meal. If doing one of the mixtures, think about adding some chopped garlic and ginger to the oil.

Broccoli Stewed in Red Wine.

Cooking broccoli this way loses the bright colour and light texture. It has to be good to compensate for this, so overcome your initial dismay and taste it. Once tasted there are no problems; it's a complete new set of flavours for broccoli. Prepare **700g broccoli**, cutting large florets in two and making chiplets from the peeled stems. Wash, and mix with **2 medium chopped onions**. Spread a layer of about half of this on the bottom of a large lidded frying pan, and sprinkle with **60g black olives**, pitted, **20g capers**, and slivers from **50g Parmesan**. Dribble over **2 tbsp. extra-virgin olive oil**. Add the rest of the broccoli/onion mix, and dribble over **another 2 tbsp. oil**. Pour over all **200 ml. red wine** – ideally, a not-too expensive Shiraz –and cover tightly. Cook on low heat for about an hour, until all the red wine has evaporated or been absorbed. Eat hot; it doesn't reheat.

Broccoli Puree.

Sweat **2 shallots, 1 chopped clove garlic** in **40g butter** till soft. Add **700g prepared broccoli**, cut smaller than usual, and stir. Add **120 ml stock, salt** and **pepper**, and simmer, covered, until the liquid has been absorbed or evaporated. Puree all this in the food processor. Reheat in a double boiler just before serving. When the puree is hot, stir in **20g butter, 20g grated cheese**, and **3-4 tbsp. double cream**. **Nutmeg** is another good addition. Delicious as a vegetable; and halfway to being a soup.

You may wonder why I don't suggest broccoli in cheese sauce. I think, and all my friends agree, that they simply don't go. This is odd, because cauliflower and cheese sauce is so good, but it seems to be a fact.

Salad of Broccoli, Sun-dried Tomatoes, and Pine Nuts.

Prepare and boil **700g broccoli** for 4-5 mins, drain, rinse with cold water, and shake as dry as possible. Make a dressing with **4 tbsp. extra-virgin olive oil, 1 tbsp. sherry vinegar, 1 garlic clove finely chopped, salt** and **pepper**. Add the broccoli to the dressing. Also add **3-4 sun-dried tomatoes**, drained if in oil, or soaked to rehydrate if very dry, and sliced. Toast **1-2 tbsp. pine nuts** under the grill, add, and stir all gently. Eat, if possible, as soon as it's cool. This is compulsive salad.

Broccoli Salad with Roasted Peppers, Capers, and Olives.

Really, the name says it all. **700g broccoli**, prepared and lightly cooked and drained. **2 roasted and peeled peppers, ideally red and yellow** for the colour, cut in strips. **1 tbsp. capers. A dozen or so stoned olives**, halved unless very small. **3 chopped spring onions**. Dressing of **4 tbsp. extra-virgin olive oil, balsamic vinegar to taste, salt** (caution, because of olives and capers) and **pepper**. Chopped **parsley**. Maybe a sprinkling of **chili flakes**?

Broccoli Cocktail. (by analogy with prawn cocktail)

Mayonnaise with tomato ketchup and horseradish to taste added. Shredded lettuce as a bed; cooked broccoli florets on top; a dollop of mayonnaise mix on the broccoli. This looks lovely and tastes better.

Broccoli Salad with Blue Cheese and Toasted Walnuts.

This is a time to use walnut oil if you have it; if not, extra-virgin olive oil. Make a dressing with **4 tbsp. chosen oil, 1 tbsp. white wine vinegar, a finely chopped clove of garlic, several shakes of Tabasco, salt** with caution. Cook and drain **700g prepared broccoli**, and add to the dressing. When it's cool, add **100g mild and creamy blue cheese**. Creamy Gorgonzola, or even blue Brie is the strength to have in mind. Toast **50g chopped walnuts** under the grill, let cool, and add to the salad. A meal in itself, with good bread.

Broccoli Stem Salad with Cheese.

Generally, with bought broccoli in the UK you don't get enough stem to be worth keeping separate. If there's a combination of circumstances where you can accumulate **4 or more thick stems of broccoli**, try this salad. Peel the stems and cut into small chiplets, and blanch in boiling water for just 1 min. Drain and dry. Make a dressing with **½ tsp. French mustard, 1 tsp. cumin seeds** (ideally toasted and) ground, **1 tbsp. white wine vinegar, 3 tbsp. extra-virgin olive oil, salt** and **pepper**. Mix the stems into this, and add **100g mild hard cheese** also cut in strips, as far as possible. Cheese can be Gouda, Gruyere, creamy Lancashire, Cheshire - that sort of texture. When you've tried this, you might start working out how to get more stems!

Broccoli Floret and Potato Soup.
This is one way of getting stems, by using up florets. Adapted from Marcella Hazan's recipe in Marcella Cucina. Chop **1 medium onion** finely, and sweat in **1 tbsp. olive oil** until it turns golden. Add **1 chopped clove garlic**, stir a minute or so, then add **2 large potatoes**, peeled and cubed in 1-cm dice. Cook for 2-3 mins, turning over to mix the flavours, then add **300g broccoli florets**, cut from the stem. The florets should be about the same diameter as the potato dice. A quick stir, then add **400 ml. stock**. Bring to the boil and simmer till the potatoes are well done and breaking up. Stir well, taste for salt, pepper, and finish by swirling in **20g butter** and some chopped **basil**. Have a bowl of grated **Parmesan** on the table.

Broccoli, Barley Couscous, and Bean Soup (3B's Soup)
Inspired by Marcella Hazan, but in this case I used some barley couscous, which makes the whole soup quicker and lighter. The soup is a quick assembly job, where the components are cooked separately and then simmered together briefly with lots of lightly fried garlic. Prepare and boil **500g broccoli**, stems and florets, and drain. Cook **150g dried beans** (cannellini in the original, but use haricots, flageolets, or borlotti beans depending what you have.) Or use a tin of the appropriate beans, drained and washed. Cover **50g barley couscous** with boiling water, and leave to stand at least 5 mins, till all the water is absorbed. Chop **6-8 cloves garlic**, depending on size, and add to **3 tbsp. extra-virgin olive oil** in a soup pot. Stir. As soon as the garlic seems to be changing colour, add the cooked broccoli, and stir to mix with the oil and garlic. Add the beans and barley, stir again, then add **stock** to cover by 3 cm. or so. Simmer about 5 mins, taste for **salt**, add a good few grinds of **pepper** to taste, and serve. I like it with grated **Parmesan**; one friend said it made it too rich, so the choice is yours.

Iced Broccoli Cream Soup.

American in inspiration, this time, and obviously a derivation of Vichyssoise; I prefer it. Heat **1 litre stock**, and add **2 medium onions**, peeled and chunked, **2 small carrots**, peeled and chunked, **2 outer celery stalks**, strings removed and chunked, and a small handful of **parsley**. Cut up and trim **500g broccoli**, and add to the pot. **Salt, ¼ tsp. cayenne pepper**, and a sprig each of **thyme** and **rosemary** if convenient. After 5 mins cooking, fish out a few broccoli florets, and keep them aside for garnish. After 15-20 mins, when all is tender, fish out the woody herb stems, and let it cool a little. Blend (in blender, food processor, or mouli) to a cream. Chill. Finish by stirring in **6-8 tbsp. double cream** (or less, according to taste; a swirl of cream uses much less and looks prettier, but doesn't give that creamy mouthfeel.) Garnish with small broccoli florets, kept from the first cooking. **Chives** if you like.

Pasta with Broccoli.

As with many other pasta-with-vegetable dishes, there are many variations. Here, you cook the broccoli in the large pan of boiling water you will later use for the pasta, thus saving fuel for the expenditure of little more time. Prepare **500g broccoli** for **500g pasta**, 4-5 people. Drop the broccoli in the boiling salted water, and cook 5 mins. Meanwhile, cook **6-8 cloves garlic**, chopped, in **4 tbsp. extra-virgin olive oil**. Don't let it get brown; if it starts to change colour, whip the pan off the heat. Scoop out the broccoli pieces from the pan of boiling water, and add to the oil/garlic pan. Turn and fry on medium heat, mashing until the broccoli is quite soft. As soon as you can, tip the pasta into the boiling water, and cook till it's at the stage you like. I find the times on the packet are pretty good. Just before the pasta is cooked, dip in a mug and get some of the pasta water. When done, drain the pasta, and add to the broccoli pan. Stir and mix, add a few tbsp. of the reserved cooking water so it's not too dry. Serve with grated **Parmesan**. Variations I like; add a chopped chili to the garlic at the beginning; or add 3 tbsp. Tapenade with the water at the end; or add some pesto at the end; or add about 20 halved cherry tomatoes at the end, which makes it look lovely.

Broccoli with Couscous and Walnuts.

Cook **200g broccoli** as for broccoli with chili and garlic, above. Toast **50g broken-up walnut pieces**. Pour boiling water to cover over **150g**

201

couscous, cover, and let it stand for 5 mins or till the water is absorbed. Mix all these together, and serve hot Taste and adjust with **lemon juice, salt, pepper**. (It will reheat in the microwave if people are late) I like a dollop of plain **yoghurt** on the plate with this, but you may not.

Broccoli and Cashew Pilau.

Start by soaking **200g Basmati rice** in **250 ml**. water for ½ hr. While this is happening, toast **100g raw cashews** under the grill, and blanch **500g broccoli**, trimmed, peeled, and cut small. Blanch for 3 mins only, as it will finish cooking in the pilau. Drain the broccoli and leave to one side. Drain the rice, keeping the soaking water. Heat **3 tbsp. sunflower or other neutral oil** in a pan with a lid, and add **2 tsp. cumin seed**. When this starts to brown and smell delicious, which takes about 30 sec, add a **6-cm cinnamon stick**, broken in several pieces, **2 small dried hot chilis**, and **2 bay leaves**, broken a little. Swirl round, then add **1 medium onion**, chopped, and **2-4 cloves garlic**, also chopped. Stir for 2-3 mins, until the onion is softening. Add the drained rice, stir round so it absorbs the flavours, then add the soaking water and **½ tsp. salt**. Stir once, bring to the boil, put on the lid, and turn the heat as low as possible. After 10 mins, have a look -- the water should be entirely or nearly absorbed. Add the broccoli and cashews, stir in. If there is more water, cook on low heat till it is gone. If not, cover the pan with a clean teatowel, put the lid on top, and let it sit with the heat turned off for another 10 mins, so that the steamy heat completes the cooking of the rice and broccoli. Turn it out and eat. It can be garnished with more toasted cashew, or crispy fried onion slices, or slices of hard-boiled egg, or chopped fresh green coriander. The Indian tendency is to go over the top with presentation, so they would probably use most of these and maybe some silver leaf as well, for an occasion. But you don't need to garnish at all, if you don't want to. I like a raita, or just plain yoghurt, with this. Or sometimes, the strong and vulgar kick of lime pickle is just right.

Broccoli Quiche.

Have ready a lightly baked tart shell (Basics), either 25 cm diameter, or 2 of 18 cm. (That's 10" and 7" in old measurements) Trim **200g broccoli** and cut into small pieces; blanch 2 mins and drain. Cut **100g Gruyere or Emmenthal** into small cubes, and scatter these over the prebaked pastry. Put in the broccoli, arranging it evenly with florets up. Beat **3 eggs** with **250 ml double cream**, **salt, pepper**, and **nutmeg**, and pour this carefully over the broccoli. Bake at 150 for 30-40 mins, till almost firm; take out, and let cool a little before serving. Quiches are really so much nicer made with double cream; this way, you can actually see why they caught on and became so fashionable. If you prefer/have some, use caramelised onion instead of the cheese.

Broccoli Souffle*****.

I really want to recommend this to you. It's been the dish of choice at my Christmas dinner, when feeding some vegetarians and more meat-eaters, for more than 15 years. And probably more people have asked for the recipe than for any other recipe of mine. Celebratory, pure, and very good.

Trim well **700g broccoli**, cut into small pieces, and boil in plenty of salted water about 12 mins. Drain. (Cook longer if using sieve to puree) Make a thick white sauce with about **40g butter, a heaped large tbsp. flour (40g)** and a **good 300 ml. milk. Salt, (about 1 tsp) fresh ground pepper** and **nutmeg**. Cook very slowly for 5 mins or so. Let it cool 5 mins or so. Put in food processor with broccoli, and **5 egg yolks**. Whizz till smooth. If no food processor, then blender, Mouli-legumes, or sieve in order of preference. In this case beat in egg yolks after blending broccoli and sauce. Add about **180g strongest Cheddar** and beat in well. The whole thing can rest at this point for up to 24 hours -- or I have frozen it for 3 days. Add **pinch of salt** to **5, 6 or 7 egg whites** (more than matching is better, but only if the extra egg whites are available) and beat to soft peaks. Beat about a quarter of the egg whites into the broccoli mix, then turn this on top of the egg whites and fold in gently but thoroughly. Turn into 2 buttered souffle dishes (1 large, 1 medium) and sprinkle with more **grated Cheddar**. Run little finger round the mixture about 1 cm from the edge. (This piece of magic is supposed to help the centre to rise, and does seem to work) Cook at 180 for 40 mins or till done. Have everyone waiting for it!

As indicated, quantities are not really critical. (I often say that the point of my Christmas dinner is that I can cook it when drunk, and usually do) If the egg whites are well beaten, and the other mixture is about the texture of mayonnaise, it will rise properly. This amount serves 2 vegetarians and 4-8 others as side dish.

Courgettes and Other Summer Squash

Almost the whole range of cooking methods can be applied to courgettes, and they will be lovely. And you will be thankful for this if you grow them, because you *will* have too many. I know of at least two books just on cooking courgettes. So what I have here is what I think of as the best and most rewarding (i.e. balance of taste to effort and cost) recipes, but there are many many more.

There are various forms of summer squash you may come across. Yellow courgettes are very little different, in my experience, from green ones, and these themselves vary in colour from dark to pale green. Dark green round courgettes are better for some uses, like baking halved, and not so good for other uses that need slices. Pattypan squash, or custard marrow, is an interesting shape, but can be cooked just as courgettes when small. Large courgettes overlap with marrow, also a summer squash, but this has its own section.

Default. If you are in a hurry, and don't want to think too much about it, slice the **courgettes**, and fry at a moderate heat in **butter or oil**. **Salt, pepper. Garlic** maybe, at start. Keep stirring, so you get some brown bits, but no burnt ones. Chopped **herbs** at end if you have some. About 10 mins from start to finish. This is hard to better.

Raw Courgette Salads These are really for tiny courgettes from the garden, spanking fresh.

Grated Courgette with Mustard Dressing.
Grate 3-4 tiny courgettes. Make a dressing of 1 tbsp. extra virgin olive oil, ¼ tsp mustard, Dijon or seedy, and ¼ tsp salt. Mix with the courgettes. Taste – do you want a squeeze of lemon? Eat quickly.

Courgette and Radish Salad
Grated raw courgette can also be mixed with grated radish. **3 largish radishes per small courgette**. Make a dressing first with **1 tsp. sherry vinegar, ½ tsp French mustard, and 4 tsp. walnut oil**. Mix well. Grate the vegetables into this, add **¼ tsp salt** for 4 courgettes, and a few pieces of **walnut**. Lovely!

Simple Green Salad with Courgettes
This takes **4 medium courgettes** for **2 assorted heads of lettuce** (not Webbs) or equivalent in other salad greens. Wash and tear the lettuce. Slice the courgettes fairly thinly, crosswise, and steam or cook in salted boiling water about 4 mins. Drain well and dry. Mix courgettes with lettuce in a salad bowl, and dress with a **vinaigrette with a little garlic, parsley, chives, and a few capers.**

Three-Colour Salad.
Trim, halve, and slice **4 medium courgettes**, and blanch for 2 mins. Mix **6 tbsp. extra virgin olive oil** with **1 tbsp. sherry vinegar, juice of 1 lemon**, and **2 cloves garlic** very finely chopped. Add the courgettes, **1 each red and yellow peppers**, quartered, seeded, and thinly sliced. **Salt** and **pepper**, and quite a lot of chopped **parsley** and slivered **basil.** Cover, and let marinate for a couple of hours. Taste and add more lemon if needed.

Zucchini Fritto all'Aceto (or Courgettes Soured)
Cut **500g. prepared courgettes** (top-and-tail, and remove any marked pieces of skin) into small chiplets, about ½ cm thick and 2-3 cm long. Sprinkle with **1 tsp. salt**, mix it in, and leave in a sieve to drain for about ½ hr. Dry them. Heat a deep-sized frying pan with enough **oil** to be about ½ cm. deep. Dip the courgette sticks into **flour**, and fry them, in batches and not too many at once, until they are brown. Take them out, roll on kitchen paper, and then put in a serving dish. Add a total of **3 tbsp. best white wine vinegar** in proportional amounts to each batch. Squash **2 cloves garlic** and bury these in the courgettes. **Pepper.** Leave to cool. This is probably more an appetiser or part of a buffet than a strict salad, but it's really good.

Courgette Celery Radish and Cheese Salad
Cut **1 courgette** into chiplets as in the last recipe. Blanch them for about 30 sec, drain, and dry. Cut **4 stalks celery**, destringed, and **100g. hard cheese** (Cheshire is good here) into strips about the same size. Slice **a dozen radishes**. Mix them all, and dress with a mixture of **4 tbsp. extra-virgin olive oil, 1 tsp mustard with seeds, the juice of a lemon**, and **¼ tsp. salt**. You may not need all the dressing. Add a **few pieces of walnut or almond** as a garnish on the top.

In the default method, I have suggested cooking them quickly, without a lid. This can obviously be very much varied, by changing the oil, the presence of absence of garlic, the herbs used (any of basil, mint, tarragon, marjoram or others). The effect is remarkably different if you cook them more slowly, with a lid on the pan. These are **Braised Courgettes.**

Heat **20g butter** in a frying pan with a lid, add **2 cloves garlic** very finely chopped. When this starts to cook, add **4-5 young courgettes**, trimmed and sliced thinly. Stir round, **salt** and **pepper,** then turn the heat very low, put a lid on the pan, and leave 20 mins. or so. Stir from time to time. If there is any liquid, turn up the heat and let it boil away. Add chopped **basil**, or another herb.

Braised Courgettes with Onion.
A variation on the last recipe. Sweat **a sliced onion** in the butter first, gently, just so it is transparent. Omit the garlic. Add the courgettes and some chopped **parsley** and **thyme. Salt** and **pepper.** Cook as above, with lid.

Courgettes and Tomatoes.
Cook **braised courgettes, or braised courgettes with onion**. Add tomatoes, fresh or tinned, after the courgettes have cooked at least 10 mins. If you are using **500g fresh tomatoes**, peel and chop them, and let them cook for about 10 mins until they have softened and become a sauce. I often use tinned tomatoes – **a whole tin of whole plum tomatoes**, roughly torn up – and let it cook to a thick consistency. My children called this courgette mush, and ate it hot or cold with gusto. (For non-veggies, it's great with sausages) You can also let it go cold and add the **flesh of a lemon**, peeled, seeded, and cut up, with **lemon juice and herbs**; this is yet another dish, **Courgettes with Panache.**

Courgettes with Thyme and Sour Cream.
Cook **3-4 small courgettes** in **20g butter**, with **thyme** leaves, with a lid as for braised courgettes. When they are tender mix in **a spoonful of sour cream or crème fraiche.** A very worthwhile variant.

Stir-braised Courgettes
uses Chinese seasonings to vary the flavour. For **500g courgettes**, thinly sliced, heat **3 tbsp. oil** in a large frying pan. Add **1 clove garlic** and **2 slices ginger**, peeled and finely chopped, and stir for a few

moments. Add the courgettes, and stir-fry for 2 mins. Add **4 tbsp. stock or water**, and cook gently 2 mins more, stirring. Add **1 tbsp. soy sauce, ½ tbsp. hoisin sauce, ½ tsp. salt**, and **½ tsp. sugar**. Put on a lid, and let it simmer for 5 mins. Serve in a bowl, with other Chinese dishes. Or let it cool and eat as a salad.

Calabacitas with Chili Verde

has Mexican flavours, adapted to English ingredients. In a saucepan, cook **1 small chopped onion** in **3 tbsp. sunflower oil** (or other; just not olive) until soft. Add **2 medium courgettes**, cubed, **1 cut-up green pepper** (seeded), **100g corn kernels**, and **2 plump green chilis**, also seeded. **Salt, about ½ tsp**. Cook the mixture, stirring, a few minutes. Add **5 tbsp. milk, pepper**, and simmer covered for 10 mins or till done. Taste for seasoning – if it's too hot there's not much you can do except add more courgettes, but with these proportions it shouldn't be. You can always make it hotter by adding some more strips of chili, or let people hot it up as they like it with Tabasco or similar sauce. Anyhow, add **100g grated Caerphilly or Wensleydale**, and stir in. Can be wrapped in tortillas by itself, or served with other Mexican-style dishes.

Roast Courgettes.

As part of roast mixed veg, particularly with a mix of **onion, aubergine**, and **peppers**, when it is a kind of roast ratatouille. Cut the **courgettes** into 5-cm chunks to roast.

Potatoes can be added, too, when it is an easy one-dish meal. Add **olive oil, salt, woody herbs, cloves garlic**, and mix in with your hands, so that all the veg. are coated with olive oil. Roast at 180-200 for about 30 mins.

Slow-Roasted Courgette with Balsamic Vinegar.

This is an ideal use for "the one that got away"; hidden under leaves, or found after a few days away. You want **1 or 2 large courgettes weighing about 500g. each**. Cut them in quarters lengthwise, and sprinkle the flesh surface with salt. Cover with paper towel to absorb the liquid, and leave about ½ hr. Wipe the salted surface. Rub the surfaces with **2 tbsp. olive oil**, and put in a heavy roasting pan. Roast in a 150 oven for 1 to 1½ hrs, turning from time to time. It will shrink and brown on the edges; the cut surface should go a golden colour. Sprinkle with **1 tbsp. extra-virgin olive oil**, and **½ tbsp. best balsamic**. Eat!

Griddled Courgettes.

Cut the trimmed **courgettes** into long, thin slices, about ¼ cm if you can manage it Brush them with **oil**, or pour a little oil onto a plate and rub each side in it. Cook them on a ridged griddle at moderate heat, until they are soft and pliable, and marked with stripes from the griddle. Sprinkle with **salt** and **lemon juice**. On a diet kick, I tried this without dipping in oil, and didn't like it a bit. They became leathery.

Courgette Fritters.

Everyone likes these. I don't eat them as often as I'd like because they are deep-fried and therefore nutritionally sinful, but once in a while . . .. Use thin slices of **courgette**, dip them in **frying batter** (see Basics chapter) or cut chiplets and dip in flour, deep-fry until they are crisp and brown, drain on kitchen paper, and eat as soon as possible. Mixed with other vegetables also battered and deep-fried, this makes a really delectable dish. Other veg should certainly include cauliflower, mushrooms, and onions, but there are many more.

Summer Minestrone

In a large pot warm **3 tbsp. olive oil**, and add **1 medium chopped onion** and **2 chopped celery stalks**. Let it cook gently till transparent, and add **1 medium courgette, diced**, and **2-3 chopped cloves garlic**. Stir around for about 10 mins, still on a low heat, then add **500g. tomatoes, peeled and roughly chopped**. Tomatoes can be fresh or tinned. Another 10 mins, then add **2 small potatoes, peeled and diced**. If you are using tinned tomatoes, add the potatoes first, so they can absorb the oil-based flavours of the other veg. Stir again, and add **1 litre water.** Cook 20 mins, till the potatoes are nearly cooked, and add **100g. broad beans, 30g soup pasta, salt** and **pepper.** Cook until the pasta is done, and serve alone or with traditional **basil pesto.** I think I prefer it alone; others might not.   I am told that in Italy a summer minestrone is often eaten lukewarm, as this makes it more refreshing. We seldom get hot enough weather in England for this to be a good idea.

Spicy Courgette and Corn Soup.

First, tear apart **a dried ancho chili**, remove and discard the cap and seeds, and soak the rest in boiling water for ½ hr. Whizz the chili and its soaking water in a blender with **1 cut-up plump fresh chili,** deseeded. Then cook **1 large onion**, chopped, in **2 tbsp. sunflower oil** till soft. Sprinkle in **2 tbsp. flour**, and stir it in. Let it cook a couple of mins. Add the chili puree, **a tin of crushed tomatoes**, a good sprinkling of **thyme**, and **300 ml. water.** Simmer for about 10 mins, then add **2 medium courgettes**, diced, and **100g. frozen corn. Salt**. Cook about 5 mins more, and serve. The unusual nature of this soup comes from the ancho chili. These can sometimes be found in supermarkets, or bought by mail-order. They are not hot, but have a lovely rounded fruity warmth. Because they are dried, they keep very well – I did once have some for 10 years, and they were still good at the end. So grab some when you see them.

Courgette Frittata.
Make some **braised courgettes, with garlic**. Beat **eggs** with **salt** and **pepper**, pour over the courgettes, and cook slowly till done. Ideally it should be turned over as a unit, to gild the second side, but I usually break it into convenient chunks to turn over individually, and let them meld together again while the second side cooks. Proportions**; for 1, 1 small/medium courgette and 2 eggs; for 4, 4 courgettes and 4 eggs.** The courgette should be a substantial part of the dish. You can also add some cooked cubed **potatoes,** to make it more substantial. Chopped **herbs** added with the eggs are good. You can eat it hot or cold, if cooked in oil; cold it makes good picnic food.

Courgettes with Pasta.
As made in Italy, this is a very variable but always simple dish, meant to act as a first course. One good version: about **500g. courgettes**, quartered and cut into thin slices. Cook them quickly in **2 tbsp. olive oil**, **salt** and **pepper** at the end. Boil **350g. pasta**; at the end, dip out a cup of the water, to moisten the pasta if needed. Drain. Mix with the courgettes, **a large handful of mixed herbs or just parsley**, chopped, and **2 tbsp. more extra-virgin oil. Grated Parmesan or Pecorino.**
This is probably a bit stark for most English tastes, which tend to use pasta as a main-course item. It is delicious in its own right, IF you have really good pasta, courgettes, oil, herbs. However, to bulk it out a little, try adding **100-200g. cheese**. In order of authenticity, ricotta, Mozzarella, feta, Caerphilly or Wensleydale, mild Brie cubed, or a soft creamy blue. If you are using cheese, cook the courgettes in butter, and add butter instead of oil at the end.

OR You can make the cooked courgettes into a sauce with more pizzazz with toasted **pine nuts**, a little **onion** fried with the courgettes, and **chopped sun-dried tomatoes**. **OR** make them more child-friendly by adding a strong-flavoured **tomato sauce**. It is only the French who go in for one and only one correct way to make a dish; everyone else allows much more room for improvisation, even if the name stays the same.

Courgette Lasagne.

I am a fan of the no-pre-cook lasagne available almost everywhere now. They may not be the best of pasta, but in the complexity of a lasagne it's hard to tell. And it cuts out a messy stage, of boiling the lasagne a few at a time and finding somewhere large enough to lay them out to drain. If you prefer the traditional or the egg lasagne, or even home-made, prepare them as on the packet, or by boiling briefly for home-made. The amount of lasagne needed varies with the size and depth of the baking dish; but will be **about half a supermarket packet of no-cook lasagne**. Apart from the lasagne, there are 3 components to this lasagne dish, as there are in most lasagne. You need courgettes in a tomato sauce, mushrooms cooked with garlic, and a rather thin white sauce in larger quantity than traditionally specified. This is because the no-cook noodles absorb more liquid, and a dish made using proportions for pre-boiled lasagne will be dry and stodgy. So, for 6-8 people, make a **white sauce with 60g butter, 60g flour, and 1¼ litres of milk. Salt, pepper and nutmeg. 500g courgettes, made as for courgettes and tomatoes above, with garlic. 300g. mushrooms, finely chopped, fried in butter with garlic**. You also need cheese; an Italian version will say 200g. Parmesan, but I don't think the expense is justified here. Use about **350g. mature Cheddar** is my recommendation. Smear the bottom of a large flat dish with some of the white sauce; a thin layer of mushrooms, a layer of lasagne, more white sauce and a sprinkle of cheese. A layer of courgettes, white sauce, lasagne, mushrooms, white sauce, lasagne , white sauce and cheese, and so on until all is used up. Top layer should be white sauce, and topped with a good fraction of the grated cheese. Bake at 150 for about ¾ hr, or until the whole is bubbling hot and the cheese topping is golden.

You can make **a different version** using spinach with the courgettes instead of tomatoes; in this case add nutmeg to the spinach mix as well as the white sauce.

Courgette Risotto.

Cook the courgettes first, some hours ahead if you like. Clean **4 medium courgettes** and slice into 1-cm. rounds. Fry **1 small chopped onion** in **3 tbsp. oil** till translucent, add **1 clove garlic**, chopped, then the sliced courgettes and **½ tsp. salt**. Turn down the heat, and cook, turning now and then, to a rich gold.

Scoop the courgettes into the risotto-cooking pan, leaving behind as much oil as you can. You could even drain the courgettes in a sieve. Add **30g. butter**, and heat till it starts to sizzle. Add **250g. risotto rice**, stir round till coated, and cook 2-3 mins. Start adding ladles of stock from a pan of **1½ litres simmering (really good) stock**, letting the rice absorb it and the pan nearly dry out before adding the next. Stir often, after adding stock and sometimes in between. When the rice is done, taste for **salt**, add **pepper, a knob of butter, 30g or so grated Parmesan**, and chopped **herbs** – maybe just parsley, maybe some mint or marjoram as well. Stir again, and eat as soon as possible with more grated **Parmesan**.

Tian of Courgettes

A tian is a baked dish from Southern France. Actually "tian" is the name of the shallow, rectangular, earthenware baking dish, and it is filled with a mix of vegetables in season, usually some form of starch such as rice or potatoes, and often cheese. It is one of the dishes that used to be taken to the baker's oven, when few people had ovens at home, and can therefore rest before cooking and cool a little afterwards.

Cut **1 kg. courgettes** into quarters lengthwise, and then slice thinly. Cook **2 large chopped onions** in **3 tbsp. olive oil** till translucent, add the courgettes and **3 cloves garlic**, finely chopped. Raise the heat and cook for about 15 mins, turning often. Add **2 tbsp. flour** and blend into the oil, and cook 2 mins. Then add **600 ml. milk**, and bring to the boil, stirring. so that the vegetables are coated in a white sauce. **1 tsp salt**, and **pepper**. About ¼ tsp **dried herbes de Provence**. Meanwhile, boil **150g. white rice** for 5 mins, or the same of brown rice for 25-30 mins, and drain. Add this to veg. and sauce. Add also **80g. Gruyere** or other hard cheese, grated, and stir in. Taste for seasoning. Tip the whole into the oiled baking dish, and flatten if needed. Sprinkle with more grated cheese, and dribble **1 tbsp. olive oil** over the top. It can rest for several hours at this point. Bake at 180 for about 40-45 mins, until the rice is cooked, the milk absorbed, and the top browned. Eat with a green salad and country bread.

As I've said, this is a variable dish, so you can add spinach, or mushrooms, or broccoli, or various fresh beans, to the mix. But it's very good as it is, especially on a cool summer evening.

Courgette and Tomato Custard

Cook **1 chopped onion** gently in **20g butter**. Add **500g. grated courgettes** and cook gently, stirring. **Salt**. Add **1 large tomato, at least 150g, peeled and chopped**. Cook about 5 mins, add some **basil** slivered, and turn into a buttered baking dish. Beat **2 eggs** with **150 ml. scalded milk, minimal salt,** and **pepper**, and pour over the courgette mix. Bake at 150 for 25-30 mins, or till the custard is set. Serve warm or cold with a salad. Obviously, this could be baked as the filling in a 22 cm. pastry case, which I would recommend unless you have reasons to avoid pastry.

Courgette Tart.

Bake blind a **22 cm pastry case**. (Basics) Cook **300g cubed courgettes** with **1 small onion, chopped, 15g. butter, some chopped tarragon, salt** and **pepper**, in a covered pan for 10 mins. Beat together **2 eggs** and **200 ml crème fraiche or soured cream**, add **60g grated Cheddar or 30g grated Parmesan**, and mix into the courgettes. Pour into the pastry case, and bake at 150 for 30-40 mins. Best warm or cold rather than straight from the oven.

Sformato of Courgettes

Cut **700g. courgettes** into quarters, then into ½ cm slices. Cook these quite quickly in **20g. butter**, with a sprinkle of **salt**, till they are slightly browned and barely tender. You may need to do this in more than 1 batch, depending on the size of your pan; in this case you may need more butter.

In a separate pan, melt **40g. butter**, add **30g flour**, and cook gently 2 mins. Add **300 ml milk**, and bring to boil, stirring. **Salt, pepper, nutmeg**, and **60g strong Cheddar**, grated. Off the heat, beat in **2 eggs**, then add the courgettes and fold together gently. Butter a 22-cm. round baking dish, and sprinkle with **fresh bread crumbs**. Pour in the courgette mix, sprinkle with **30g. more grated cheese**, and bake at 170 for 30 mins, or until a knife inserted in the mix comes out clean. Serve warm.

Courgette Souffle.

The ingredients are very much the same as those for the sformato. Make the **white sauce with seasoning and cheese**, and cook the **courgettes** as above. Whizz the two together in a food processor, and add the **yolks of 3 eggs** and whizz again. Beat the **whites of the 3 eggs**, with a **pinch of salt**, till stiff, and fold into the courgette mixture. The best way is to take a dollop of the stiff egg whites and beat into the puree, to lighten it a little, and then tip this on top of the remainder of the beaten whites and fold in gently. Pour into a buttered straight-sided dish, no crumbs. Sprinkle the top with **cheese**, and run a finger through the mixture close to the edge of the dish. This bit of magic helps it to stick to the dish and rise high in the middle. Bake at 180 for 30 mins or so.

Courgette Muffins.

Savoury muffins are fairly new, but very useful. They are quick to make, can take lots of strong flavours, and are impressive. Grate a **200g courgette**, and have ready **3 chopped spring onions**. Prepare a 12-hole muffin tin, or cases. I am lucky enough to have a non-stick one, so all I do is wipe round with an oily paper towel. Beat **2 eggs** with **200 ml. milk** and **150 ml. sunflower oil**. Add the vegetables and stir. In a separate bowl, mix **350g. flour, 3 tsp. baking powder, 100g. grated hard tasty cheese, ½ tsp. salt**, and quite a lot of fresh ground **pepper**. (Treble what you would normally use) Add the flour mixture to the egg mix, stir gently, until well mixed. Divide among the prepared tins. Bake at 180 for about 20 mins, until firm but springy. Let them cool a few mins in the tin, then turn them out onto a cooling tray. These take about 10 mins to prepare, so the reward/time ratio is pretty high!

There are also courgette patties, courgette cakes, curries including them . .. . but I think that's enough. I haven't said anything about stuffed courgettes; they are a hassle, and pleasant without being outstanding. For Mediterranean countries, stuffings meant a little meat could flavour a lot of veg, but that isn't relevant for vegetarians.

Cucumbers

What's long and green and goes up the motorway at 150 mph? Answer: the E-type cucumber. This sixties joke illustrates how deeply the idea of cucumber fits into our culture. So does "cool as a cucumber"; so does cucumber sandwiches as shorthand for a way of life that includes tea on the lawn. How did a Mediterranean vegetable come to hold this place?

As well as the familiar long, thin greenhouse product, often English grown and available year-round, there are ridge cucumbers, seldom available to buy and only in season. Australians have "Lebanese" cucumbers, which is a variety not an import. Americans refer to ours as "English" cucumbers, and are full of instructions about removing the wax with which they are treated there. Any cucumber can be used in the following recipes, though the ridge ones may be better for the more elaborate cooked dishes, and the greenhouse one for the salads. Not much in it.

Simple, reliable, fall-back ways of using cucumber are sliced, in mixed salads. When I have some small length left over from whatever, I make raita or tsatsiki, both cucumber + yoghurt where the seasoning changes it from India to Eastern Med. I'd like to promote the **simplest possible use of cucumber, peeled, cut in sticks, and served with aperitifs**. Maybe a few olives and radishes as well, and this is wonderful hot-weather food.

I have several favourite salads, like the **Middle-European Cucumber Salad.**
Slice **1 large cucumber** thinly (I would say if you're slicing 2 or more cucumbers, set the food processor up, but one is more easily done on the slicing side of a box grater). Add **6 tbsp. each cider vinegar and water**, with **salt** and **pepper** to taste. Chill for a couple of hours, and serve with a slotted spoon. Wonderful diet food!

Chinese Cucumber Salad
Also terrific on a diet. Quarter the **cucumber** and slice not quite so thinly. Add **1 tsp salt, 2 tbsp. soy sauce, 2 tbsp vinegar, 1/2 tbsp sugar,** and **½ tbsp dark sesame oil**. You can serve it immediately or let it stand 30 mins or so. It's OK the next day as well.

Seedy Cucumber Salad.
Toast, separately, **1 tbsp sesame seeds, 2 tbsp pumpkin seeds.** I always toast seeds on an enamel plate under the grill, but they can also be done in a dry frying pan or in the oven. Whichever, watch carefully, so they brown but don't burn. Quarter a **cucumber** lengthwise, scrape out the seeds, and cut into small sticks. Mix with **1 tsp salt**, and leave to stand 1 hr or so. Tip into sieve, rinse, and dry on teatowel. Mix with cooled seeds, **1 tbsp soy sauce, few dashes Tabasco, 1 tsp dark sesame oil**, and mix. You can use finely chopped chilli instead of the Tabasco; or add chopped fresh coriander; or spring onions.

Cucumber/Pineapple Salsa.
Fruity, sweet, refreshing, and very summery. **Half a cucumber**, and about ¼ **of a medium pineapple.** Cut the cucumber into small dice; peel, core and chop the pineapple. Add ½ **tsp. salt, 1 chopped fresh green chili**, and the **juice of 1-2 limes**. Mix well; it's best when freshly made. If you have **mint or basil**, a little chopped and added makes it even better. No oil at all.

Turkish Cucumber in Walnut Sauce.
The sauce is the important bit here, and it also goes well with lots of other veg – French beans, courgettes, marrow, beetroot, salsify – and probably more. Put **100 g walnuts** in the food processor, and grind. Add **3 cloves garlic**, roughly cut, **1 good slice bread,** decrusted and crumbed, **1 chopped chilli** or several dashes Tabasco, **1 mean tsp salt**, and the **juice of 2-3 lemons**. Whizz. Add **water**, whizzing it in, to make the right consistency, and adjust the taste with lemon juice, salt, and Tabasco so that it is sharp, the chilli tang comes through but isn't positively hot, and, unhelpfully, it's really good. (By this I mean that a taster's verdict will change from "very nice" to "Yum") Put **1 diced cucumber** in a dish, with **2 tbsp olive oil**, and toss. Pour some sauce over; keep the rest on the side. The sauce can be varied by using hazelnuts, almonds, or a mixture of both with walnuts, but whichever, it's very more-ish. If there's a little sauce left, it can be used in sandwiches or as a dip.

Tahitian Cucumber Salad.

My most elaborate salad is really a buffet item, and always goes down very well

Soak **2 thinly sliced cucumbers** with **2 tbsp salt, 150 ml. wine vinegar** for ½ hr, then drain. Grate **120g creamed coconut** (the packet sort) and cover with **150 ml. boiling water**. Stir until the coconut is dissolved. Whip **150 ml. double cream**, and mix with the coconut, the cucumber, and **1 tbsp sugar**. Stir in **1 tbsp dark sesame oil**. Serve garnished with **chives or toasted sesame seeds**. This is enough for 10-12; 6 cucumbers will do 30-40 people . This can't be described as slimming, or in any way good for you, but it is nice.

Raita/Tsatsiki.

You will have noticed that in some of the salads above the cucumber is salted and drained before use, which concentrates its flavour and makes it less likely to lose water in the salad. This is especially a good idea for either of these salads. For either, you need **1 cucumber**, cut into small cubes, salted, drained, and dried. (unless you haven't time, when the salad will still be OK, but a bit less toothsome) For **Raita**, mix simply with **thick yoghurt** (I like Greek) and **pepper**, and sprinkle top with **black cumin seeds**. You can add chopped **mint**, or chopped **tomatoes**, but in any case it's almost indispensable with Indian food. I don't add chilli, because I like the cooling effect; I don't add fresh coriander, because that flavour is almost always somewhere else in the dishes. But they are both authentic additions if you want to. For **Tsatsiki**, pound **2 big cloves garlic** with a little **salt** in a mortar. Stir in **2 tbsp extra-virgin olive oil, 1 tbsp lemon juice**, and **pepper**, and then **300 ml Greek yoghurt**. Add **1 large cucumber**, diced, salted, rinsed, drained and dried. It can be peeled, but I don't. It can be grated, which is a good idea sometimes. Salt, drain and dry the grated cucumber just as for cubes. Chopped **mint**, or **dill**, is a great addition. After this you will never again want a commercial version, which are comparatively very expensive and tasteless and have the wrong texture.

Cucumber and Feta Salad

is more substantial, but still light. Make a dressing with **3 tbsp. extra-virgin oil, 2 tbsp. lemon juice**, and **pepper** to taste. Add **1 large cucumber**, peeled, seeded and diced, **1 small red onion**, chopped fine (or a few spring onions), and **1 packet Feta**, crumbled. Mix, eat. You could use a young goat's cheese instead of the Feta, or a salty crumbly Caerphilly. Or Wensleydale for Wallace and Grommit, who never seem to eat any vegetables!

I haven't run out of lovely cucumber salads, but I think that's enough. Consider now cooking cucumbers; it was fashionable in 18th-century England and France, and their food was very good.

Sauteed cucumbers

The simplest way. Halve **2 cucumbers** lengthwise, then cut into ½ cm slices. Melt **25g butter**, add the cucumbers, **salt** and **pepper**, and a **pinch of sugar**. Sir around, then add **5 tbsp water**, cover, and simmer about 7 mins, or till the cucumbers are tender. Take off the lid and evaporate the water, stirring so the cucumbers glaze. Add a chopped herb, such as **dill or parsley**. I haven't tried basil, but my mind's taste says it would be good.

Cucumber Ragout

This uses much the same method, but more vegetables. Fry **1 large sliced onion** in **2 tbsp oil**, till soft and gold but not browned, then add **4 medium carrots**, peeled and sliced, **1 cucumber** halved lengthways and sliced, and **1 green pepper** seeded and diced. Season, cover, and cook gently about 15 mins, till the carrots are cooked Good hot or cold.

Cucumbers are also good in cold summer soups. **Gazpacho** is the best known, and can be found under tomatoes.

Hungarian Cucumber Soup

Mix the following in a large bowl: **1 cucumber peeled and chunked,** leaves from **packet watercress, 1 green pepper**, seeded and chunked, **2 chopped spring onions, 3 tbsp mayonnaise, 3 tbsp yoghurt, 3 tbsp white wine vinegar, 2 tbsp chopped dill or parsley, 1 tsp salt, pepper**. Add **600 ml. water**. Blend it all in batches, thin if necessary, taste and adjust seasoning, and chill.

Cold Cucumber Soup

A more conventional way. Saute **2 shallots** in **25g butter**, add a cut-up **cucumber**, and cook on low heat for a couple of minutes. Add **25g flour**, stir in, and cook a little more. Add **1 litre stock or water**, and some **watercress or land cress leaves** if you have them. Bring to a boil, and cook gently about 20 mins. Blend the soup, and cool. Stir in **150 ml. plain yoghurt**, and chill. Serve with chopped **herbs**, or a sprinkling of **toasted almonds or seeds**. If need be, this can be reheated and served hot.

Cucumber Dip

This is probably best made for at least 6 people, as the recipe makes quite a lot. Mix together **250g cream cheese, 2 tbsp sour cream, 1 minced clove garlic, salt** and **pepper, 2 tsp wine vinegar, ¼ cucumber finely chopped, 1 tbsp tomato paste, 2-3 tsp paprika** to taste, and chopped **parsley**. Use as a dip with vegetable sticks, and any leftovers make good sandwiches.

Cucumber Quiche.

You need a **ready-baked 23 cm (9") shell of short pastry**. Make **a batch of sauteed cucumbers**, and mix with the **juice of 1 lemon, 2 eggs** and about **5 tbsp. double cream. Salt** and **pepper**. Pour the mix into the shell, and scatter the top with **flaked almonds**. Bake in a moderate oven for about 20-25 mins, till set. Meanwhile cut a **slice of decrusted bread** into dice, and fry in a little **butter** in a small frying pan, till golden. Spread these croutons on top of the flan, and serve warm.

You can stuff cucumbers, hollowing out cylinders, stuffing, and garnishing the top with something coloured, and they look very tempting as part of an appetiser spread. I wouldn't bother; I don't think the taste is worth it. You can also pickle your own cucumbers, but the French do marvellous little cornichons in jars and the Poles brilliant dill pickles, so this is one case where I rely on the commercial product.

What is very much worth doing is **Bread-and-Butter Pickle, ******* which is American in origin. Everyone always asks about the name, and I simply don't know. It is good enough to eat by itself in a sandwich, brilliant with cheese or other spreads, and useful in many ways. And if you give some to your meat-eating friends, it is THE pickle to go on hamburgers. I even made this commercially, in small quantities, selling to David Mellor for his kitchen shop.

3 large cucumbers, 500g white onions, 1 green pepper, 4 tbsp salt, 350g light brown sugar, 450 ml cider vinegar, 1 tbsp. white mustard seed, ½ tsp turmeric, ½ tsp celery seed, ¼ tsp ground cloves. Slice the cucumbers thinly, and the peeled onions. Seed and slice the green pepper. Mix all these in a large bowl, add the salt, mix in with your hands, and leave for 3 hours. Mix the other ingredients in a preserving pan, and boil 5 mins. Drain and rinse the vegetables, and add to the syrup. Bring just to the boil, stirring, and put into warmed jars and seal with vinegar-proof lids. (Old washed instant-coffee jars are good) This makes about 6 jars of the size that hold 100g instant coffee, or 8 jamjars. It keeps very well indeed, but seldom needs to. Please try this one.

Fennel

Truly, fennel is unique among vegetables. The strong aniseed flavour when raw. The bulbous shape made up of overlapping layers, bending back slightly at the top for sprightly green fronds. The pale green and white colours, so clear they are refreshing in themselves. A painter's delight just from its appearance. There are times when I think that doing anything other with fennel than breaking it into its leaves, and dipping them into oil and salt at the start of a meal, is a shame. **Raw Fennel,** then, is the default mode for this vegetable. But then it's easy to start elaborating. Add some cucumber sticks, and some radishes, to this starter. Elaborate a little more, and make these three components into a simple salad.

Fennel, Cucumber and Radish Salad.

Cut a **bulb of fennel** into thin slices, then halve or quarter the slices to make bite-size pieces. Cube **half a cucumber**, into smaller dice. Slice **half-a-dozen radishes** thinly. Dress this mixture with **2 tbsp. olive oil, juice of ½ a lemon**, and **salt** and **pepper**. The flavours of this are so clear that I think any of the normal additions – garlic, herbs – detract from the overall effect.

Fennel, Watercress, and Orange Salad.

Make a vinaigrette with **6 tbsp. extra-virgin olive oil, 1 tbsp. white wine vinegar, 1 tsp. balsamic vinegar, a shallot very finely chopped, the peel and juice of an orange,** and **salt.** No pepper in this one. Taste and add more vinegar if needed. Toast **a small handful of skinned almonds** under the grill. (Almonds are better bought in their skins and blanched and skinned as needed, but easier bought ready skinned) Trim **2 medium fennel bulbs**, and slice as thinly as you can. Add the chopped fennel tops and 2 tbsp. vinaigrette, and leave. Peel and remove the segments from **2 oranges**, add 2 tbsp. vinaigrette, and leave. Wash **2 packets/bunches watercress**, dry and pick over. When ready, toss the watercress with the rest of the dressing, and mix with the fennel and the oranges and the almonds. Enough for 6, easily. If you can buy blood oranges, use 3 or 4, and cut them in rounds rather than segmenting.

Fennel and Blue Cheese Salad.

This is full of sharp, enlivening, strong winter tastes, and you can almost feel it reviving you after a lot of heavy food. Trim and slice **a large fennel bulb**; trim and slice **2 heads of chicory**; peel and slice thinly **3-4 stalks celery**. Mix all these, and add **80g crumbled blue cheese**. I'd use picante Gorgonzola, or Stilton. Add **2 tbsp. extra-virgin olive oil or walnut oil**, and mix. The vegetables should not be dripping with oil. Add **a few drops balsamic vinegar**, mix again, then add **a couple of palmfuls of toasted hazelnuts or walnuts.** Taste for **salt** and **pepper**. I don't think it needs either, as there's enough salt in the cheese.

Fennel and Oyster Mushroom Salad.

2 fennel bulbs, trimmed, sliced very thin, then cut smaller to match the oyster mushrooms. Sprinkle with **2 tbsp. sherry vinegar, 3 tbsp. extra-virgin olive oil, salt** and **pepper**. Cook **200g oyster mushrooms**, torn into strips, in **1 tbsp. olive oil**, with **1 finely chopped clove garlic**. Tip over fennel and mix well. Eat when it's cooled. Garnish the top with **Parmesan shavings** just before serving.

Fennel, Apple and Walnut Salad.

A version of Waldorf salad with the fennel substituted for celery, and a lighter dressing. Mix **1 tsp. Dijon mustard, 1 tbsp. mayonnaise (can be Hellmann's),** and **2 tbsp. plain yoghurt**. Add **2 medium fennel**, trimmed and diced, **3 apples** cored not skinned and diced, and **100g walnuts**, broken a little. Mix well. Sprinkle with the chopped **fennel fronds or** another herb – **tarragon** would be lovely, but is out of season in winter.

Fennel Coleslaw.

Cut **2 medium fennel**, trimmed, into thin strips; ditto an **apple**. Mix these with a **small shredded cabbage**, green or white. Dress with a vinaigrette of **4 tbsp. extra-virgin olive oil, 1 tbsp. white wine vinegar, 1 tsp. Dijon mustard or whole-grain mustard, salt** and **pepper**. Let it stand for an hour or so, so the vegetables soften a little. (This is also convenient, since you don't have to make it at the last minute)

Fennel and Potato Salad.
Not really a recipe, more an idea. **Small cooked waxy potatoes, chopped fennel, hard-boiled eggs sliced or quartered, vinaigrette dressing**, and **some salty, piquant addition, like olives or capers. Or a seedy addition, like za'atar or dukkah or toasted seeds like sunflower or pumpkin**.

Cooked fennel seems to me to lose a lot of its aniseed taste and sharpness. If you want to keep the taste of aniseed, add a few fennel seeds or aniseeds to any oil the fennel is cooked in.

Roast Fennel
The simplest way of cooking the vegetable, this is truly delicious either alone or in a mixed vegetable roast. Cut the **bulb or bulbs** in chunks, each with a little root end to hold them together. Turn them with a **little oil** in a roasting dish, with **salt** and maybe **some garlic cloves**, with **fennel seeds** if you like. Bake at 170 for about 30 mins. You get lovely crisp caramelised edges and soft delectable middles. You don't need to worry about doing too much, as any leftovers can go into salads of beans, lentils, rice, potatoes . . .

Braised Fennel.
Fennel can also be cooked by the reduction method. Trim and quarter 2 fennel bulbs, and put in a pan with a **couple of whole, peeled garlic cloves, a knob of butter or a little olive oil, a little sugar, salt**, and **enough stock to cover.** Cover the pan, and cook gently for about an hour, until the fennel is really tender. Raise the heat and boil down until only a little glaze is left. Delicious just as it is, and also a good way to start on more elaborate cooked fennel dishes. You can add grated Parmesan when the fennel has its glaze, and turn a few times to incorporate the Parmesan. Or, for example, **Fennel in cheese sauce** takes fennel cooked like this, adds cheese sauce, top sprinkled with more grated cheese and maybe breadcrumbs, and brown the top under the grill or in the oven. You can add baby onions to the pot after about half-an-hour, for **Ragout of Fennel with Baby Onions.**

Fennel Braised with Honey and Balsamic Vinegar
This tastes deceptively rich. It uses a slightly different technique to the above braised fennel, as the fennel is browned before adding any liquid. Trim and quarter **4 small fennel bulbs,** and brown them slowly,

in one layer, in **50g butter**. Turn over to get all sides browned. This is a slowish stage, as it can take 10-15 mins to brown the fennel without burning the butter. Drizzle on **4 tbsp. balsamic vinegar**, not necessarily the best, and turn the fennel in this liquid. Add **1 tbsp. honey**, mix in, then add a little **water**, to cover the pan base but not the fennel. Add **a bay leaf**, and **a couple of sprigs of thyme. Salt** and **pepper**. Cover the pan, and cook on low heat until the fennel is really tender, about ½ hr. Reduce the cooking juices to a glaze, and serve.

Fennel with Mushrooms and Tomatoes.
Trim **2 fennel bulbs**, keeping the **fronds**, and cut into thin strips. Cook these in **2 tbsp. olive oil**, with a finely-chopped **clove of garlic**, for about 5 mins. Add a **tin of tomatoes**, and some **thyme leaves**. Cook for 5-10 mins, until the mixture is nearly dry. Add **350g white mushrooms**, sliced, and **4 tbsp. stock or water. Salt** and **pepper**. Simmer till the mix is nearly dry. Sprinkle with the chopped fronds, and serve hot or as a salad at room temperature.

Fennel Soup with Egg and Lemon (Fennel Avgolemono)
Couldn't be simpler. The idea is that you flavour stock with the vegetable, then thicken the mix with eggs and lemon. The vegetable can stay in the soup or be removed; the stock can also be used to cook small pasta or rice before it is thickened. So, for 4 people, cook **1 trimmed and chopped large bulb of fennel** in **1 litre stock** for 10 mins, or until well-flavoured. Beat **3 eggs** with the **juice of 2 lemons**, and pour into the soup OFF THE HEAT. Stir, and return to a low heat, stirring, until the soup has thickened slightly. DO NOT BOIL, or the eggs will scramble. Taste for **salt, pepper, acidity**. Sprinkle with the chopped fennel fronds, and also garden herb **fennel or dill.**

Fennel and Celeriac Soup.
Full of positively-flavoured vegetables, but smooth and soothing. Start by improving **2 litres vegetable stock** – whether home-made or Marigold – by boiling in it **trimmings from 2 medium fennel bulbs, a small celeriac, the greens from 3 leeks,** and ½ **tsp. each of celery seed and fennel seed** for about ½ hr. You need to end up with 1½ litres stock Strain. Taste for saltiness, and add up to **1 tsp. salt** as needed.
Sweat **3 trimmed leeks**, sliced into rounds, the **2 medium fennel** cut into chunks, and the peeled **celeriac** cut into chunks in **30g butter**.

After 10-15 mins, add the strained stock, bring to a boil, and cook 15-20 mins, till the vegetables are cooked. Puree, in a blender after cooling slightly, or with a blender wand, or by passing through a mouli-legumes. Heat to boiling again, and stir in **150 ml. double cream**. Taste for **salt;** add **pepper**. Then add the **fennel fronds**, chopped, and some chopped **watercress**, and serve. Making this soup obviously falls into 3 stages, which can be separated in time to suit your convenience. Only the reheating, cream, and addition of watercress need to happen just before eating. This is enough or more than enough for 6 people.

Pasta with Fennel

A first-course pasta, not a whole meal. Coarsely chop 1 medium fennel bulb, and cook in **2 tbsp. olive oil** on moderately low heat for 5 mins, so the fennel is tender but still crisp. Cook **200g pasta** in boiling salted water with **1 tsp. fennel seeds**. Drain, reserving a little of the cooking water to moisturise the dish. Add to the fennel, with **50g chopped black olives, dried chili flakes to taste**, and the **juice of 1 lemon**. Add the reserved water as needed. Sprinkle with the **chopped fennel fronds** – supplemented by herb fennel from the garden if convenient – and serve with **grated Parmesan**.

Pasta e fagioli

This is my version, which is a little elaborated on the standard in Italian books. Soak **150g dried beans (cannellini, borlotti, haricots)** overnight or by the quick method (Basics). Put them to cook with **2 litres stock or water, NOT salted**, and cook for 1 hr. or till nearly done. (Unsalted stock implies it has to be yours, not Marigold, here. If you have no home-made stock use water) Add **3 medium potatoes**, peeled and cubed, **1 leek**, trimmed and sliced, **3 sticks celery**, sliced small, **1 large or 2 medium fennel bulbs**, trimmed and chopped, and **4 cloves garlic**, chopped fine. Cook another 30 mins or so till the veg. are tender, turn up the heat, salt, and add **120g pasta** – penne, for example. Not long ones here, as it makes the soup-like dish impossible to eat tidily. Not soup pasta, either. When the pasta is done, taste for **salt**, and add chopped **parsley** and **fennel fronds**. Serve with grated **Parmesan**. This sounds so simple that the goodness of the result comes as a surprise.

Fennel Risotto

Chop finely **3 medium fennel bulbs**, reserving the **green tops**. Mix these tops, chopped, with **4 tbsp. vodka** and the **juice of 1 lemon**. Grind **2 peeled cloves of garlic, 2 tsp. fennel seeds**, and **1 fresh green chili**, seeded, with **1 tsp. salt** in a mortar. Cook **1 small chopped onion** in **40g butter** in a large pan till transparent, then add the fennel seed mix from the mortar. Stir and cook till the smell rises, then add the fennel. Cook another 5 mins. Add **200g risotto rice**, and let cook for a couple of minutes so the rice grains absorb the butter. Add a ladle of warm **stock from 1½ litres**, stir, and continue to add ladles of stock as the last lot of stock evaporates/is absorbed. When the rice is just done, add the vodka mix and **another 25g butter**, stir vigorously, and serve with grated **Parmesan**.

Fennel and Potato Gratin

This is not low-calorie, low-fat, or particularly quick to make. It <u>is</u> spectacularly rich and delicious, and well worth any compensating reductions in tomorrow's food. This is true of most creamy gratins, but this, with the clear aniseed note added, may be the best of them all. A centrepiece, and probably all that's needed for a meal, along with a green salad.

There are 4 components. A leek and fennel ragout; flavoured cream and milk; potatoes; and cheese. For the ragout, start by adding **3 leeks**, trimmed, washed and thinly sliced, to **15g hot butter** in a large frying pan. Add **1 tsp. ground fennel seed, salt** and **pepper**; when all is sizzling, put on the lid, and sweat on low heat for 5-10 mins. Quarter **2 large fennel bulbs,** and slice very thinly. Add to the pan with **4 finely chopped cloves garlic**, and cook till the fennel is tender. Mix in a small palmful of chopped **thyme** and **parsley**, and let cool. Heat **300 ml each milk and double cream** together with **a bay leaf, ½ tsp. fennel seed, parsley stalks**, and **2-3 sprigs fresh thyme**. Cover, and keep warm for about 20 mins. so that the milky mix is flavoured by the additions. Pour through a sieve to remove the aromatics, and add salt. Slice very thinly **700g potatoes**, peeled.

Start to assemble: butter a large baking dish, and layer with a third of the potato slices, **salt** and **pepper**, half the fennel mix, and one-third of **200g grated Cheddar**. Repeat these layers. Finish the top with the final third of the potato slices. Pour over the hot cream mix. Cover the dish, and bake at 150 for 1 hr. Test the potatoes for doneness with the point of a knife; there should be no resistance anywhere. If there is, continue to cook. When the potatoes are done, sprinkle the top with the remaining third of the grated cheese, and cook at 170 until the cheese has melted and the gratin is golden and a little crisp on top.

Pizza with Fennel

Make **pizza dough with 250g flour** (Basics). Make the tomato sauce for spreading: saute **1 very small onion**, chopped, in **1 dsp. olive oil**, with **½ tsp. fennel seed**, ground. After about 5 mins, add **3 chopped cloves garlic**, stir, and add **1 tin crushed tomatoes, salt** and **pepper**. Simmer down to a thick sauce. Cook **1 bulb fennel**, trimmed, quartered, and finely sliced in **another dsp olive oil**, in another pan, till just done, about 5 mins. **Salt** and **pepper**. Roll out the pizza dough into 2 discs, and put on oiled baking sheets. Brush with **olive oil**, spread on the cooled tomato sauce, then distribute the fennel slices over this. Distribute **150g sliced Mozzarella** (or, my preference, Lancashire) over the pizzas, **pepper**. Leave to stand 10 mins or so. Bake in a very hot oven till done, probably 15-20 mins. Take out of the oven and sprinkle with grated **Parmesan**.

Concluding, the fennel trimmings can be used in vegetable stock.

French Beans

We know what we mean by French beans. They are dark green, about 4" long, cylindrical and quite thin, and in supermarkets often come ready trimmed in packets from Kenya. (I do wonder why this happens, when in summer on Bruges market you can buy beautiful, thinner, local delicate beans from heaps at 1 euro/kg, but I expect it's because the supermarkets can't get them in winter as well.) If you're a gardener, there are many other possibilities – bush, climbing? Yellow beans called wax, purple ones called Blue Lake (which lose their colour on cooking, but are easier to see when picking.) There are varieties with flat pods, sometimes available to buy, which seem halfway to runner beans. All of them taste much the same when boiled till just right, which is to say very good indeed.

I did wonder whether or not to put runner beans in with this section, and call the whole thing something like summer beans. But I find that taste and texture are different, and so are the more dressed-up ways of cooking them. In fact, I think that runners should be elevated as a typically English vegetable, in the same way that sweetcorn, while available everywhere, is at its best grown, picked, and cooked in the U.S. So runners have their own section, and I was confirmed in this when I found that runners are actually not the same species as French, etc beans.

Back to French beans. They all need topping and tailing. Many of them have been bred to be stringless, and will be unless they are middle-aged. But it never does any harm to check, by breaking a bean at the top and seeing whether you can pull off a string down the side. If so, I find a swivel-action potato peeler is what is needed for destringing. Small French beans are mostly cooked whole, while the larger, ribbon beans can be sliced crosswise or cut diagonally into smaller pieces.

Default is plain boiled. This is one of the cases where a lot of rapidly-boiling salted water is needed. First, it comes back to the boil more quickly; second, cooking the beans in a little water exaggerates the discolouration that takes place on cooking. I have read that this is due to them releasing acid into the water, which then affects the colour. I don't know if this is so; I do know they are more attractive if cooked

227

in a lot of water. It's impossible to give an exact time; it depends on the age of the beans, their freshness, and also on how you like them. Start tasting after 3 mins; you don't want them to squeak when you bite, but you don't want them overdone either. Drain well, put into a warmed dish, and add a little butter. You can elaborate on this very easily, obviously; herb butters or oil or more elaborate sauces. Here are several less obvious ways of dressing up plain beans.

French Beans with Cream and Lemon.
Turn **500g cooked beans** briefly in **20g butter**, and add **3 tbsp. double cream** and **juice of ½ a lemon**.

French Beans with Hazelnuts.
Cook a finely chopped **shallot** in **20g butter** till transparent, and add **50g roughly broken hazelnuts** and cook for 3 mins. Add chopped **parsley**, and mix into **500g cooked beans**.

French Beans Lyonnaise
Cook **1 medium onion**, chopped fine, in **30g butter** in a frying pan. Add **500g cooked drained beans, a little thyme, salt** and **pepper**, and cook for about 5 mins., stirring to mix the onion and beans well.

French Beans with Genovese dressing
Cook **1 finely chopped clove garlic** in **2 tbsp. extra virgin olive oil** briefly, and add **2 tsp. drained capers**. Add **500g cooked drained beans**, and turn them about for a couple of mins. Add slivers of **basil** and serve.

French Beans with Broccoli.
Mix equal volumes of cooked small **broccoli florets** and **very good cooked beans**, and add **extra-virgin olive oil** to taste. **Pepper**.

French Beans Greek-Style
or cooked with tomatoes. Sweat **1 medium onion**, chopped, and **1 clove garlic**, chopped, in **5 tbsp. olive oil**. Add **500g green beans**, topped, tailed, and halved. For ribbon beans, cut them diagonally into lozenges. Stir, and add **250g tomatoes**, peeled and chopped, **salt** and **pepper**, and **2 dozen leaves oregano**, chopped. Failing fresh oregano, use marjoram, dried oregano, or rather more chopped parsley. Cook slowly at least ½ hr, until everything is tender and there is a little thick

tomato sauce. Taste for seasoning. Eat hot, warm, or cold. You can use less olive oil, but this detracts from the Greek effect. Perhaps use less to start with, and dribble with extra-virgin oil when finished. This is one of the dishes that illustrates the importance of using good ingredients. Old, tired beans, cheap tasteless tomatoes – hardly worth eating. Fresh beans, good tomatoes – excellence.

French Beans and Water Chestnuts.
This is a truly admirable vegetable dish, Chinese in style, but because there is no soy sauce, it can go with any kind of food.
Prepare **500g beans**, cutting the beans into 2" pieces, ideally on the slant. Mix **1 mean tsp. cornflour** with **1 tbsp. stock**. Slice **a dozen or so water chestnuts**, almost certainly tinned. Heat **1 tbsp. vegetable oil** in a large frying pan or wok. Add the beans, and stir-fry for 3 mins. Add **1 tsp. salt, 1 tsp sugar**, and the water chestnuts, and stir about 30 sec. Add **3 tbsp. stock**, cover the pan, and cook on a moderate heat for 3 mins or till the beans are tender. Add the cornflour mix, stir till thickened, and serve.

French Beans in Egg Sauce.
Boil **500g beans** in salted water till just done. Reserve **1 tbsp. of the water** for the sauce, and drain the beans. Beat **2 eggs** with **1 tbsp. wine vinegar**, the bean water, **1 tsp. French mustard, 1 shallot chopped very finely, salt** and **pepper**. Pour over the beans, and cook over a VERY low heat until the beans are covered with a thick creamy sauce. Avoid any hint of the egg scrambling; if worried or distracted, it would be worth thickening the sauce in the top of a double boiler, with regular stirring. Sprinkle with chopped **parsley** to serve.

Salads.
The simplest salad of all means dressing the **cooked green beans**, still hot, with **oil and vinegar or lemon, salt** and **pepper**, and leaving them to cool. This is so simple and so delectable that it's worth boiling more green beans than you need for one meal, so you have the salad ready for the next. This scores on so many saving fronts – time, energy – that it seems almost unfair that it should be so good as well. Chopped **tarragon** is an unexpected but delightful addition to the plain salad.

French Bean, Olive, and Preserved Lemon Salad.

Cooked and dressed green beans as before, cut into 1-2" lengths. Use lemon in the dressing. Add **black olives, about 12 to 500g. beans**, and some finely chopped **preserved lemon**. The amount depends on how much you like preserved lemon; a quarter of one or even less adds an almost indefinable savour; I like them a lot, and use at least one, so the presence is positively felt.

French Beans with Walnut Dressing.

Plain boiled beans, drained, lightly oiled, and cooled; walnut dressing. I've given a recipe for this under cucumber, but repeat it here because this is such a good combination. Put **100 g walnuts** in the food processor, and grind. Add **3 cloves garlic**, roughly cut, **1 good slice bread**, decrusted and crumbed, **1 chopped chili** or several dashes Tabasco, **1 mean tsp salt**, and the **juice of 2-3 lemons**. Whizz. Add **water**, whizzing it in, to make the right consistency, and adjust the taste with lemon juice, salt, and Tabasco so that it is sharp, the chili tang comes through but it isn't positively hot. Serve the beans with a dollop of the sauce on the side.

French Beans with Sweetcorn.

I have strong views about sweet corn bought in England, so suggest here **200g frozen corn** to **500g green beans**. Cut the beans into 2- cm lengths before cooking. Drain both veg, mix, and dress with **2 tbsp. extra-virgin olive oil** and **1 mean dsp. sherry vinegar. Salt, pepper**, and quite a lot of **chives**. I think this is more than the sum of the parts, unlike the next recipe..

French Beans and Tomatoes.

I don't think either of them adds to the other in a salad; I would far rather have two separate salads. If you disagree, the mixture is obvious enough. Cut the **beans** into short lengths to give them the best chance of mixing with the chunks – not slices – of **tomato. Oil-and-vinegar dressing**.

French Bean, Grapefruit, and Peanut Salad.

An unlikely but delicious combination. Cook **500g French beans** as usual, drain. Get the segments from **1-2 grapefruit** – in summer, they are often smallish where I buy them, so I'd use 2. 1 really large one is easier to deal with. Cut a thick slice from top and bottom, then stand it on a chopping board and slice downwards all round to expose flesh with no pith at all. Cut along the membranes to release the segments, ideally over a bowl to catch the juices. Add grapefruit segments to the French beans, add **40-50g roast peanuts**, and **2 spring onions**, trimmed and sliced. Dress with a mixture of the **juice of a lime (or ½ lemon, if necessary), 1 tbsp. soy sauce, 1 tbsp. soft brown sugar,** and **1 mild red chili**, deseeded and chopped finely.

Roast Green Beans.
I came across this idea in Anna Thomas' book, felt fairly dubious, but tried it. Surprise; it's really good. You need **1 kg. tender young beans**, stringless. Trim them, and mix them with the **cloves from 1 head garlic, peeled; 2 tbsp. olive oil; ½ tsp. salt**. Spread them out on 2 baking sheets and roast at 200 for about 40 mins, until they smell toasty and have brown patches. Hot or cold; eat them with fingers or more respectably. You can add a **little more extra-virgin oil** and a **little balsamic vinegar**.

Pasta with Green Beans.
A good one for flat beans. Cut **500g.beans** into 5-cm diamonds, and boil for 10 mins. or till tender. Drain. Cook **4 finely-chopped garlic cloves** in **4 tbsp. olive oil** until the smell starts to change, add the beans and **salt** and **pepper**, and cook, stirring, for 3 mins. Meanwhile cook **500g pasta**, and reserve a **little water** before draining. Mix pasta and bean mix, reserved pasta water till it's not too dry for your taste, and add the **leaves from 2 sprigs basil**, cut into slivers. You could also add toasted pine nuts or almonds, but the plain version is surprisingly good. To my taste it doesn't even need **Parmesan**, but you may not agree.

Fresh Pasta with Green Beans, Walnuts, and Crème Fraiche.
If you make your own pasta, this would be a good place to add herbs to the dough. Cut into ½ cm noodles. If buying, you need **250g pasta**. Boil **350g green beans**, topped and tailed, and drain.. Gently cook **4 finely chopped shallots** in **30g butter** for 1 min. in a large frying pan, add **2 finely chopped cloves garlic, 150 ml. stock or water, salt**, and chopped **basil leaves from 2 sprigs**. Cook 10 mins, then add **300 ml crème fraiche**, and cook till the sauce thickens. Taste for **salt**; add a good sprinkle **chili flakes, or black pepper**. Add the beans. Boil the pasta, about 2 mins for shop-bought fresh, while leaving beans/cream

mix on a low heat. Drain pasta and add to pan with quite a lot more chopped **basil**. Turn about to mix as well as possible, and add **80g chopped walnuts**. Serve with grated **Parmesan**.

Green Bean Risotto.

As always for a risotto, the better the stock the better the end product. Don't go overboard, however; dried porcini generally improve a vegetable stock, but in this case the competing flavour would be too heavy. Some tomato flavour, restrained, would be a good idea. (See Stock in Basics chapter) For **300g rice**, for 6 people, you need **1½ litres stock**, lightly salted, and hot.

Boil **200g French beans** till just tender, drain, and keep aside. Cook **1 small chopped onion** in **50g butter** in a large frying pan. When the onion is soft, add **2 finely chopped garlic cloves**, cook another min, and add 300g risotto rice. Turn this about for 3-4 mins, add **a dozen strands of saffron soaked in hot water** and pounded, then start adding ladles of the stock. Let each evaporate before adding more, stirring very often. When the rice is nearly done, add the beans. Taste for **salt**. Just before serving, add **2 tomatoes**, cut into chunks. Serve with grated **Parmesan**.

I'm giving recipes for two different green bean curries, so you can see what they have in common and how you can produce a different curry to your own taste. The beans in these are deliberately overcooked, to allow the spices to permeate the beans. Lightly cooked is not authentic, but if you prefer it, then do it!

Green Bean Curry 1.

Trim **500g green beans** and cut into 2-cm
 pieces. Ribbon beans are fine here. Chop finely together **1 small onion, 2 cloves garlic**, and a **3-cm piece of fresh ginger**. Heat **2 tbsp. oil** in a frying pan which has a lid, and add **1 tsp. each whole cumin and fennel seeds**. Stir. After a few seconds, add the onion mix, and cook till lightly browned. Add the green beans and stir for another 2 mins. Add **1 tsp. each coriander, cumin, and black pepper**, ground together, and ¼ tsp each **turmeric and cayenne pepper**. Stir again, then add **150 ml water** and ½ **tsp. salt**. Bring to boil, cover, and simmer 15 mins. Add **1 peeled chopped tomato** and some chopped **fresh green coriander**. Simmer 5 mins more, then serve.

Green Bean Curry 2.

Trim **500g green beans**, and slice into thin rounds. Mix **3 tbsp. plain yoghurt** with **1 chopped deseeded green chili, a small handful of fresh green coriander, chopped, 1 tsp. each salt and sugar, 1 tsp. dry mustard powder, 1 tsp. cumin seeds, ground, the juice of ½ lemon,** and **3 tbsp. water.**

Heat **3 tbsp. oil** in frying pan which has a lid, and add **½ tsp cumin seeds** and **½ tsp. black mustard seeds**. When the mustard seeds start to pop, add the green beans, and fry for 5 mins. Add the yoghurt mixture, and stir. Cover the pan, and cook on very low heat for 30 mins. or more. Taste for **salt**, and serve.

Sformato of French Beans

Trim **500g French beans**, and cut into 3-cm or shorter lengths. Blanch for 3 mins in boiling salted water, drain, and set aside. Make a plain white sauce with **30g butter, 30g white flour**, and **300 ml. milk. Salt, pepper, nutmeg**. Turn off the heat, and add **80g grated Cheddar**. Beat **3 eggs** in a large bowl, and add the cheesy sauce and the French beans. **Butter** a souffle mould or deep cylindrical dish (e.g. Pyrex), then sprinkle with fresh dry **breadcrumbs**. Pour everything from the bowl into the dish, and smooth the top. Bake for 40 mins at 180. I like to sprinkle the top with more grated cheese for the last 10 mins, but this isn't strictly orthodox. Let it cool several minutes before serving. You can turn the dish out onto a plate, but I prefer it served straight from the dish. Definitely a main dish.

French Bean Crumble.

Prepare **500g French beans** as usual; that is, top, tail, cut into short lengths, blanch, drain. Make a white sauce using thin yoghurt instead of milk; melt **30g butter**, sweat **1 chopped shallot** in it till transparent, add **25g white flour**, then add **300 ml thin yoghurt** and stir while bringing to the boil until it thickens. Add **100g grated Cheddar**. Stir in the beans. Spread the mix in a shallow baking dish. For the crumble, mix **120g flour, brown or white, 60g rolled oats**, and rub in **80g butter**. (Or use the food processor) **Salt, pepper, chopped fresh herbs**; if you have **chives**, these should be one of the herbs. So should **tarragon**. But **parsley** will be fine if that is what you have. Spread over the bean mix, and bake at 180 for about 25 mins, or till the crumble is crisp and brown.

Globe Artichokes

I haven't given many recipes for globe artichokes, because they are an expensive vegetable and something of a treat. Also, other vegetarian cookbooks use them a lot. The artichoke plant is perennial, and does grow well in parts of the UK. Most of the artichokes we can buy, however, are imported. The artichoke is the immature bud of a thistle-like plant; each plant gives several buds a year.

Default; Boiled, with Melted Butter.
Allow **one globe artichoke per person**; a vegetable with built-in portion control. They should look dull green and lively; avoid any with browning on the outside leaves. First break off the stem, if there is one several inches long, by bending it close to the head until it snaps. Sometimes fibres come away from the bottom of the artichoke with the stem. Don't discard the stem. Break off the two lower rows of leaves, by holding the top of the leaf and bending it out and down until it snaps off. Occasionally, there are little spikes on the top of each leaf of the remaining globe; if so, trim them off with scissors. Have a LARGE pan – or even 2 – of **salted water** ready boiling, and drop in the artichokes right way up. They should be able to bob about freely. Boil steadily, covered, for 30-45 mins depending on size, but anyway until a leaf from the bottom pulls away easily. Scoop out the artichokes and drain them upside down. Have a small bowl or ramekin of **melted butter** for each person. At least 30g per head. I now melt the butter in the microwave, which is very easy.

How to Eat an Artichoke. This is such an unlikely process that no-one will discover it for themselves, and a lot of people have sad tales of misadventure. Starting with the outer, lowest leaves, pull off one. Dip the fleshy base of the leaf into the melted butter. Put the leaf base upside-down between your teeth, and gently draw off the fleshy part at the bottom of the leaf. Discard the leaf. (You will need a large bowl on the table for the detritus. In French it's called a *poubelle de table*, or table dustbin, and is useful for all sorts of foods where there is a lot to discard.) Continue with the next leaf, and so on. As you get higher up and further into the artichoke, the leaves get thinner and softer, and there is progressively less flesh on them. The centre leaves, forming a little cone, can usually be discarded. Now you come to the booby trap, or choke, which would be the prickles if the thistle was allowed to develop. This bit is NOT for eating. It lies above, and is attached to, the saucer-shaped base or heart of the artichoke, which is the most delicious part. So scoop out and discard the choke, using a teaspoon. The heart will have a dimpled top surface where the choke was connected. Pour a little of the remaining melted butter into the heart, and eat this solid nugget of delicious tender flesh. Proper people use a knife and fork, but since you've been using your fingers so far . . .

The process of eating an artichoke takes time and concentration, but it is satisfying, absorbing, and very physical. To my surprise, children enjoy the ritual too. It was a bad day for my budget when I first let mine try an artichoke!

Above, I said keep the stalk. If you peel it to get rid of the outer fibres, and trim the dried-up bit from the bottom, you can cook and eat the stalks as if they were hearts. Sometimes; sometimes they are too fibrous. Even if they are fibrous, it should go into stock.

You can also let the artichoke go cold, and eat with vinaigrette. This is what to do when you buy them ready-cooked, in all their dark-grey-green glory, from a French charcuterie. I prefer the butter route, but only marginally. Since I have been trying to eat less butter, I've found that 15g. per artichoke is enough, and I eat most leaves as they come. For most people, allow 30g butter. It is, after all, a ceremonial occasion.

Fritedda *****
This is a light braise of artichoke hearts, peas, and broad beans. At its best, it is a celebration of spring, and deserves a feast to set it off. Even with careful substitutions for fresh peas and beans, it is a feast. It is also expensive, which is another reason for reserving it for special occasions. Don't even THINK of substituting anything for the fresh artichokes, as this deprives the whole dish of its point.
You need at least **one artichoke per person**, and more is better, up to two per head. The tedious and wasteful part is that the artichokes are stripped down so that only the heart is left. Before you start doing this, have a bowl of salted water with the juice of a lemon squeezed into it. This is to stop the cut surfaces of the artichokes blackening. Remove the stalks, and then start to bend back the leaves around the base to

snap them off. Keep doing this until you have just a cone of inner leaves above the heart, and cut this cone off with a knife. Then quarter the artichoke heart, and trim each quarter to get rid of the choke, the outer scars from the leaves, and anything else that spoils the heart, so that what you have left is just heart. Drop into the lemony water. (If the waste offends, keep the outer leaves and boil them tomorrow; you can then eat them as for a whole artichoke, or make soup with them – see below. The rest is for the compost heap.)

Peas and beans; for 6, you need about **150g each of peas and broad beans**. If the peas are fresh, taste and assess about how long they need to cook, between, say, 2 mins and 20 mins. If the broad beans are your own, use only small ones, good enough to eat raw. You don't want any which should be double-shelled. If using frozen peas and beans, defrost the peas, and defrost 200g. broad beans. Then slip the broad beans out of the outer skin, so they are little bright green nuggets.

After the preparation, the cooking is very easy. Warm **6 tbsp. extra-virgin olive oil** in a pan with a cover, and cook **1 medium sliced onion** gently in it. When the onion is soft, add the drained artichoke hearts, and some fresh **dill** if you have it. Otherwise add a sprig of **thyme.** Add **3 tbsp. water**, cover, and cook gently for 15 mins or to the halfway point for the artichokes. Add fresh beans if using, and cook for another 15 min. Add the peas if you judge it appropriate. If the heat is really low, you shouldn't need more water; add another couple of tbsp. if the pan is really dry. After a total of 30 min. since the artichokes went in, add the frozen veg. if that's what you're using, and fresh peas if very young. Add **1 tsp. salt**. Cook another 5 mins, then let it rest 5 mins before serving.

You can see that this makes considerable calls on your judgement, but it's going to be fantastic even if it's not exactly right. Your only remaining problem is going to be making sure that the non-veggies at the table, who presumably have something else as well, don't take more than their fair share. I can truly say that this is one of the nicest dishes in the book.

After that blow-out, let's come down to earth and talk about forms of artichoke other than fresh. None of them do more than remind artichoke lovers of the real thing, but some of them do have virtues of their own. Frozen artichokes are OK; tinned I keep trying in case they have improved, but they never have. The various appetiser preparation – jarred in oil, char-grilled in oil, and so on, are perfectly respectable components of a salad-y spread, as appetiser or main part of the meal. But I think you'd find it hard to tell that they were artichokes if you were blindfolded.

Artichoke Frittata

can quite well be made with frozen artichokes. If you live in California, you could use the hearts of 1 artichoke per person, but in the UK, cook about ½ **a packet of frozen artichokes** according to the packet instructions. Or drain a packet of char-grilled artichokes. In a large frying pan, cook **2 finely chopped shallots** in **30g butter** until they have softened. Add the cooked, sliced artichoke hearts, and stir to coat them. Beat **6 eggs** in a bowl with chopped **parsley** and **basil** (a small handful parsley, leaves from 2 sprigs basil), **salt and pepper.** Pour this into the pan, and cook slowly without stirring until the frittata is nearly set. Sprinkle the top with grated **Parmesan**, and put under the grill, not too close, until the frittata is completely cooked and the Parmesan is melted. Serve in wedges. You could add some cooked new potatoes to the vegetable mix, which would make it even more substantial.

Pasta with Artichokes, 2 versions.

The first version has artichokes in cream, and the second has them in a tomato sauce with olives. For both, cook **fresh or frozen artichokes, ½ packet frozen, or ½ to 1 heart per head.** You can even use tinned; drain the liquid from 1 tin. In all cases cut into pieces easy to eat.

Version 1, with cream.

Warm the artichokes in **2 tbsp. olive oil** with **1 clove garlic**, finely chopped. Cook **500g pasta**, for 6 people, and drain. Add **30g butter, 75 ml (or 5 tbsp) double cream**, the artichokes, **salt and pepper** to taste, and grated **Parmesan.** Mix well and serve straightaway.

Version 2, with tomatoes and olives.

Make a tomato sauce, with **1 small onion** sweated in **2 tbsp. olive oil**, with **2 finely chopped garlic cloves** and **1 finely chopped deseeded chili** added when the onion is soft. Add a **small glass white wine**, and cook till it has evaporated. Add **2 tins tomatoes**, crushing the tomatoes between your fingers, and cook the sauce about 20 mins. Add the artichokes, and **1 or 2 dozen black olives** (destoned if you like, but they taste better with the stones in) **Salt and pepper,** maybe **lemon**

juice, and simmer a few mins. Serve over **500g cooked pasta**, for 6. The chili and wine go very well with the artichoke taste. **Parmesan** if you like; it's not necessary, but it adds to the symphony of delicious tastes.

Artichoke Soup.

I cannot deny that this is a hassle, but you feel so frugal and virtuous while making it! It is also good soup. Boil the **leaves from making the fritedda, or 4 whole artichokes**. The leaves will not take very long, 5-10 mins. Then sit down with a teaspoon and some music, and scrape the artichoke meat from the bottom of each leaf. If using whole artichokes, slice the hearts (or keep them for another use?) Cook **1 small minced onion** in **30g butter**, and add **30g flour**. Stir into a roux, and add **800 ml. stock** and the artichoke puree (and chopped hearts). Bring to the boil, stirring, add **salt, pepper and a little grated nutmeg**, and simmer 10 mins. Blend or sieve. Reheat the soup, and thicken with a mix of **2 egg yolks** and **6 tbsp. double cream**. Beat the yolks and cream in a bowl; add a ladle of soup, take the soup off the heat and stir in the mix. If it does not thicken straight away, heat very cautiously, to avoid the eggs scrambling, until it does thicken. Taste; you might want a **little lemon juice** to bring out the tastes.

As a final frugal note, you can't use the water artichokes have boiled in for anything else in the kitchen, but it can be used for watering garden plants.

Kohl Rabi

Kohl rabi (sometimes with a hyphen, sometimes without) is an unusual and unloved vegetable in England – we haven't even bothered to give it an English name. It has its virtues; it's easy to grow, it looks impressive (now we have all seen the dragon fruit the supermarkets are trying to introduce, the appearance may seem less strange) and its taste is rather nuttier than that of turnip. IT HAS TO BE SMALL, no bigger than a tennis ball. Larger ones get hollow, woodier, and stronger in taste. Its stronghold is Germany and Eastern Europe, and existing recipes for it have the flavours of those areas. This is not to say that there aren't many other ways waiting to be discovered, one of which may be the one which flatters its individuality and makes people go Wow. I can't say any of these are quite that good, but they all arouse enthusiasm.

Default. Glazed. Peel **1 small kohl rabi per head**, and cut into small slices; barely cover with water, and add **salt, tsp sugar for 4 small ones**, (slightly more than for carrots or turnips), and about **15g butter**. Boil with the lid half off until the water is evaporated and the sauce starts to sizzle; toss the vegetable to spread the glaze, and let it caramelise slightly.

Kohl Rabi with Cream and Lemon
Cook **4 small kohl rabi** as for glazed, and add **2-3 tbsp. cream, good squeeze lemon juice,** and **some chopped fennel or dill**. Cook until the cream clings, and serve straightaway. You can add sour cream, 6-8 tbsp., instead of the cream, and leave the sauce more liquid. If you then add chopped chives, it becomes **Kohl Rabi Country Style**. You can see the scope for varying this according to what is available. Horseradish added to the cream at the end, not heated, makes a very good dish. If you are short of kohl rabi, you can add peas, broad beans (which is very good) or freshly cooked new potatoes.

Roast Kohl Rabi.
Roast in the standard way, with **oil, salt and pepper**, and a tough herb like **thyme or rosemary**. Alone or with other vegetables.

Kohl Rabi and Apple Salad.

Peel and grate **2 small kohl rabi**, and **½ Granny Smith apple. Salt, pinch sugar, 1 tsp. grainy mustard, juice of 1 lemon,** and **1 good dsp. crème fraiche**. Mix all together. A slightly nutty flavour, which would be increased by adding some young fresh filberts. For 2-4 depending what else is on the table.

Grated Salad of Kohl Rabi.

For the dressing, mix **1 dsp mayonnaise, 2 dsp Greek yoghurt, salt, quite a lot of black pepper, ½ tsp cumin seed, ground,** and **½ tsp. smoked pimenton**. Grate **1 small kohlrabi**, peeled, and **1 medium carrot**. Cut **½ red pepper in slivers**, about the size of the other vegetables. Cut up **1 spring onion**. Mix all these into the dressing.

Seedy Kohl Rabi Salad.

Grate **2 small peeled kohl-rabi**, and mix with **2 tbsp. thick yoghurt, juice of ½ lemon**, and **salt** and **pepper**. Toast **60g sunflower seeds** (yes, this is a lot), and mix into the salad. Chopped **parsley**. (A note: make sure you have hulled sunflower seeds and toast them yourself. You can buy handsome, toasted, salted seeds with stripy hulls, which are fine eaten alone, but in this salad will give you a mouthful of inedible splinters)

Austrian-Style Kohl Rabi Soup.

This is a clear soup with small pieces of vegetable, so the vegetables should be cut small. If you or your family don't like soup-with-bits, then it can be pureed, but that's a shame in this case. **5-6 kohl rabi, 2 leeks, 2 medium carrots, 50g butter, 1½ litres stock** (the better the stock the better), **100g shelled peas**, and **100-200g spinach**. Prepare the vegetables; peel and dice the carrots and kohl rabi, wash and thinly slice the leeks. Sweat the leeks and carrots in the butter for about 5 mins, and add the kohl rabi. A few mins more, then add the stock, **salt** and **pepper**, bring to a boil, and simmer, partly covered, about 30 mins. This reduces the stock somewhat, so be cautious with the salt. Add the peas, and the spinach washed, stemmed, and sliced in ribbons. Cook about 3 mins more; taste for seasoning. Serve hot. I feel sure the Austrians would add dollops of sour cream to each serving, but I don't think it adds. **Toast cubes** do; and not fried croutons in this case.

Gratin of Kohl Rabi and Potatoes.

Peel **2 kohl rabi, 2 medium potatoes**, and slice thinly. (Slicing blade of grater; food processor, or just a knife. The thicker the slices the longer the gratin takes to cook, and the less it melds into a rich and succulent whole) If the outside of the kohl rabi is fibrous when you peel it, grate rather than slice it. Chop **a clove of garlic** finely, and mix with the potatoes. Grate about **150g Cheddar or other strong hard cheese** – not Parmesan, though; it's wasted in gratins, in my view. In a buttered baking dish layer kohl rabi, potatoes, cheese, seasoning each layer with **salt** and **pepper** as you go. If you want to avoid black specks use freshly ground white pepper; for an interesting variant use the 5-pepper mix now easily available. Pour round the sides **300 ml single cream, or half-and-half double cream and milk**. Bake at 150 for 1-1 ½ hrs, or until a knife meets no uneven resistance when pushed in.

Kohl Rabi and Potato Goulash

If you want this to taste Hungarian, you must use Hungarian paprika. It's good with Spanish, but not as good. Sweat **1 onion**, thinly sliced, in **50g butter**. Off the heat, add **2 tsp Hungarian paprika** – sweet or hot, depending on the effect you want and the one you have. Add **500g kohl rabi**, peeled and chunked, **500g potatoes**, peeled and chunked, **1 tsp caraway seeds, 150 ml stock, 1 tsp salt**, and **2 bay leaves**. Simmer till the potatoes are cooked. Add **1 tbsp. cider vinegar**, or to taste; fish out the bay leaves, and stir in **4 tbsp. sour cream**. Don't boil after this. Add quite a lot of chopped **parsley**, and eat. This goes well with sausages, vegetarian or otherwise. It can also be a soup with the potatoes cut smaller and more stock.

And, if you want more things to do with kohl rabi, all the new turnip recipes can be used for them. And vice versa; all these recipes can be used for new turnips, if you haven't got kohl rabi.

Lettuce

Once upon a time there was soft, floppy lettuce, and that was all. Then came Iceberg, gradually superseded by Webbs Wonder; crisp and tightly wrapped. The occasional Cos in high summer has swelled to year-round availability. And now there are Little Gems, probably the most popular, green frilly lettuces, Lollo Rosso, packets of mixed salad stuffs, packets of individual greens like rocket and lamb's lettuce; a veritable cornucopia in the supermarkets and at the seed merchants. And this is all very much to the good, when it comes to making an interesting green salad.

And an interesting green salad will seldom be the same twice running; it's spontaneously put together with what you have, in garden or bought. It's probably a good idea to keep the textures fairly close; Webb's doesn't mix easily with other, softer leaves, but is fine with chicory, Chinese leaf, or shredded cabbage. Given a mixture of green leaves, good extra-virgin olive oil and either lemon juice or vinegar (usually said to be proportions of 3 oil to 1 vinegar, but I often use less of the acid element), salt and pepper, and you have the simplest of all salad dishes. Add herbs? Mustard in the dressing? Walnut oil instead of olive? You can make a green salad every day of the year, and not repeat yourself.

Lettuce Hearts with Butter
Very good salad, and not often seen. If you are worried about using butter, note that you actually use less than the equivalent in oil. And it's so good for a change!
You need very good, soft lettuces, and only use the hearts. **1 lettuce heart per person**. Break the hearts apart into fork-size pieces, and put in a bowl. Sprinkle with **salt.** For 4, warm **30g butter** with **1 sliced clove garlic** in a small pan, without letting it even think of cooking. Trickle it gently over the lettuce, putting the last few drops through a sieve to retain the garlic. Squeeze over the **juice of ½ lemon**. Eat quickly.

Iceberg Lettuce with Blue Cheese Dressing
An American standard, and worthy of it. For the dressing, take **150 ml. Greek-style yoghurt,** and stir in **2 tbsp. extra-virgin olive oil. Salt, pepper, lemon juice** to taste. Add **50g crumbled blue cheese**, and stir

in. A piquant blue cheese is good here – piquant Gorgonzola, Stilton, Bleu d'Auvergne. Roquefort would be extravagant but super. Taste; adjust to your taste. Shred or break into pieces as much **iceberg lettuce** as you need for your numbers, and dress with cautious amounts of the dressing. Taste as you go. You want the lettuce shreds or pieces lightly coated, without a pool of leftover dressing at the bottom of the bowl.

Don't worry if you have too much dressing. It can be a dip with crudites, a sauce for plain vegetables, or a side sauce with fritters, vegetable cakes, etc.

Classic Caesar Salad

The best salad to give those English people who don't like salad. There are still a few around, often elderly, but they will all eat a Caesar. So will everyone else, with great gusto. The classic does NOT have anchovies, but does, alas for vegetarians, have Worcester sauce. In this version I have replaced the Lea & Perrins with mushroom ketchup.   3 or 4 hours beforehand, put **1 cut-up clove of garlic** to soak in **8 tbsp. extra-virgin olive oil**. Sometime between then and serving, fry **2 slices crustless day-old bread**, cut in cubes, in **olive oil**, and drain on paper towels. Take **2 large Cos lettuce**, and tear all but the very outer leaves into smallish pieces. **Salt, pepper**, and **30g Parmesan**, grated. Toss. Squeeze over the **juice of 2 lemons**; toss. Break over the salad **1 egg, boiled for 1 minute** – or stood in a cup with boiling water poured over for 5 mins – and toss. Pour on about half the oil through a sieve, and toss again. Add a few drops, **up to ½ tsp, mushroom ketchup**, toss. Finally, pour the other half of the oil over the croutons, add them to the salad and toss one last time. And 6 people will eat this much as a first course.

Modern versions tend to make the dressing up beforehand, often blended, sometimes omitting egg or using a raw yolk, adding anchovies. The ones I've tried have been quite pleasant, but are not superlative like the real thing. And fast food outlets now add all sorts of meat, or chicken, or other protein, thoroughly bastardising the dish. Don't do it – or if you do, call it something else.

Cos and Avocado Salad

Tear all but the outer leaves of **1 Cos lettuce**, and put in large bowl with **½ avocado, cubed, 3-4 thinly sliced radishes**, and **1 tbsp.**

sunflower seeds toasted. In a small bowl mix **2 tsp. fresh lemon juice, 2 tsp. soy sauce**, and **2 tbsp. sunflower oil**. Toss and serve. I'm partial to this dressing with soy sauce on all sorts of salads, often with a little dark sesame oil added. But this salad is better without it.

I could go on giving ideas for simple green salads, but the possible variation is so large that you are better off experimenting with what you have. One thought; many books will speak about the *chapon*, which is a heel of French bread rubbed with garlic and tossed with the leaves. It is supposed to add a hint of garlic, without requiring you to eat the stuff. If you want garlic, I'd say it's better to be more positive; I've never noticed any influence from the chapon. Maybe our dried garlic in England isn't juicy enough?

A note. If you have leftover dressed green salad, you can make a **Salad Soup** from it. **For each helping of leftover salad**, you need **150 ml. milk** and **150 ml. stock**. Whizz the salad and dressing with a little milk, tip into a pan with the rest of the milk and the stock, and warm just to boiling. Taste for seasoning. Serve sprinkled with chopped **parsley**, and maybe croutons. I can't say this is brilliant, but it's OK, and the only thing I know to do with leftover salad apart from composting. You never know; your family might prefer to eat up all the salad in the first place.

Green Salads with Cheese

The simplest possible version of this adds a few small cubes of cheese to lettuce leaves, with a dressing mainly oil and very little, very good wine vinegar. 50g cheese to 1 head soft lettuce, and the cheese can be any firm but not too strong type. The original is Gruyere, but Cheshire, Caerphilly, Wensleydale, medium-mature Gouda are all good. This is great as a pause in a meal, after the main course and before the dessert.

Stronger-tasting leaves can take stronger cheeses, even Webb's with a mild blue. The blue can be blended into the dressing, or in cubes. Or you can have a green salad with a slice of goat's cheese, grilled alone or on a toast. Or a wilted salad, where you fry small pieces of halloumi in olive oil, put the pieces on the leaves, tip a small slug of vinegar into the pan and swirl, and pour the hot dressing over. Mix quickly and eat before the cheese is cold.

You may notice I haven't mentioned salad cream, mayonnaise, cream dressings, sour cream. They have their place, but not in a green salad.

I think the general problem with lettuce is not the making of salads; it's what to do with the outside leaves, or whole heads when there is a glut. There are suggestions below for soup, stir-fried lettuce, pasta sauce, braised lettuce, a creamy puree, and dhal.

Lettuce Soup 1

Sweat **a chopped onion** in **20g butter** for 2-3 mins, and add **lots of chopped outside lettuce leaves**. Let the heap collapse for a few mins, then add **1 medium potato**, peeled and diced, and **stock or water** to cover, **salt** if needed, and simmer for 15-20 mins. Puree in blender or food processor. Reheat, and swirl in **2-3 tbsp. double cream** and some chopped **herbs**. You could also finish it with herbed butter instead of the cream, or add **green peas**. Several **cloves of garlic** added at the beginning make the soup taste completely different. You could also spice at the beginning, with chopped fresh chili and ground cumin, and finish with chopped oregano or marjoram.

Lettuce Soup 2; Potage Vert

This is a more elegant version, and hence has more specific quantities. Shred the **white of a medium leek** very finely. You need the equivalent of **2 Little Gems in lettuce leaves, leftover greens from mixed salad packets, celery leaves, and spinach** -- don't use lettuce alone in this. Shred the greens finely. Sweat leek and greens in **30g butter**, without letting the leek colour. Add **600 ml water or stock**, and **1 tsp salt if stock unsalted**, or you are using water. French country cooking used to use the water from boiling dried beans, with flavourings, here, and it's a good idea if you have cooked dried beans recently.. Boil slowly about 20 mins. You can blend or not at this stage. In a small bowl, beat **2 egg yolks** with **6 tbsp. double cream**. Take a ladle of soup and beat into the egg/cream mix, to warm it gently. Take the soup off the heat, and stir in the egg/cream/soup mixture. Taste for seasoning, and swirl in **another 30g of butter** before serving. You can't reheat this soup, because of the eggs. On the other hand it is delicate, unctuous, and nourishing; the above amount serves 4-6.

Sweet-and-Sour Stir-Fried Lettuce

Tear **½ a crispy lettuce** into large pieces, and wash. Heat **4 tsp. oil** in a wok or large frying pan, and stir-fry **3 cloves garlic, finely chopped, and 1 chopped deseeded red chili** for 1 min. Add the lettuce, turn up heat, and stir-fry 3 mins. Add a mix of **3 tbsp. sugar, 4 tbsp. rice vinegar or cider vinegar**, and **1 tsp salt**, stir to mix, and eat as soon as possible.

Stir-Fried Lettuce with Mushrooms

Cut into chunks and wash **1 crisp lettuce**. Slice **200g. button mushrooms** thinly. Stir-fry **3 cloves chopped garlic, 1 knob ginger** peeled and finely chopped, in **4 tbsp. oil** in a wok or large frying pan. After 1 min, add the lettuce chunks, and **½ tsp salt** and **1 tsp. sugar**. Stir for about 1 min, then add the mushrooms. Add **6 tbsp. stock**, and simmer 2 mins. Thicken with **cornflour, 1 tsp.** mixed with **2 tbsp. water**. Pour onto serving dish, taste for salt and sugar, and add more if needed. Dribble over **1 tsp. dark sesame oil**

You will notice that neither of these uses soy sauce, so the lettuce colour is clear and tempting. However, you can add soy sauce if you like, at the seasoning stage towards the end. Indeed these are very variable recipes, which can take onion, other kinds of mushrooms, other sorts of greens, . . .

Pasta with Cos Lettuce Sauce

Use about **300g of the outside leaves of Cos lettuce, or Little Gem, or one of the leafy chicories**. Chop finely **1 onion, 2-3 cloves garlic, and 1 green chili, deseeded**. Sweat these in **2 tbsp. olive oil**. Add the lettuce, shredded, and **1 tsp. salt**. When the lettuce has collapsed, add **½ tin chopped tomatoes**, and cook gently 10 mins. Meanwhile boil **300g pasta** for 4, drain, and add to the sauce. Some **torn basil leaves** at this point can only be good, if you have them. Turn and cook gently 1 min, dribble over **2 tbsp. extra-virgin olive oil**, and serve with **grated cheese, Parmesan or Pecorino**.

Braised Lettuce

This is predominantly a French idea. In high-grade Victorian cookery, braised lettuce hearts, along with braised carrots, baby onions, turnips, would be served as a garnish to a ceremonial roast. Lower down the scale, braised lettuce was simply a vegetable, and a proper vegetable braise is always a surprise and a delight.

Use **8 round lettuce for 6 people**. Trim them, taking off any unsightly leaves and cutting the stem level with the base. Wash them. Plunge them, head up, into a large pan of boiling salted water. Cook 5 mins. from the time that the water boils again. Lift them out and drop into a lot of cold water. When cool, lift out and squeeze to remove as much water as possible. Open them out on a teatowel, and season each heart with **salt, pepper**, and **thyme**. Fold over the outside leaves, and shape into a cylinder. Tie this round with string. Take a pan in which the squashed and tied lettuce fit snugly, and butter the bottom generously with **50g. butter**. Add **1 chopped onion, 2 chopped medium carrots**, and rest the lettuce parcels on this bed. Tuck **bay leaves, parsley, sprigs of thyme**, maybe **celery leaves** between the lettuces. 1½ hours before you want to eat it, cover the pan, and put on a low-to-moderate heat for 10-15 mins. What you are doing is gently toasting, without browning at all, the vegetables at the base. Don't stir. When this point is reached, add **300 ml. stock**. Tuck a butter wrapper, or circle of Bakewell paper, on top, and cover the pan. Cook for 1- 1¼ hrs, basting from time to time, in a low oven. When this is complete, lift the lettuces out onto a serving dish, and take off the strings. Pour the juices through a sieve into a small pan, and boil down until there is only a few tbsp. juice left. Salt cautiously, and swirl in **30g butter**. Pour over the lettuces, and serve. There is no doubt that this is a hassle, but I think the end result is worth it from time to time.

Simpler Braised Lettuce.
Designed for Little Gems, or similar small compact lettuces. Butter a lidded pan which can also go in the oven, about **10g butter**. Arrange on this **1 chopped shallot, a diced carrot**, and **a chopped clove of garlic**. Quarter **4 Little Gems** and arrange them in one layer (as far as possible) on top. Tuck in some **sprigs of thyme** and **a bay leaf.** Cover, and put on moderate heat to toast the lower veg. without browning. Don't stir. When the steam from the pan changes colour (it really does; stops being white and becomes grey-blue) add **stock** to cover, **salt** and **pepper**, and cook covered in a low oven (130) for about 1 hr. Finish like the braised lettuce above; take out the lettuce, sieve the juices, and boil them down to a syrup. Swirl in **30g butter** and pour over the lettuce on their serving plate. They won't look beautiful, so maybe some chopped **parsley** to cheer them a little. However, they taste good

and different. In a way, the first method has much to commend it, if you have a glut of lettuce in the garden, whereas Little Gems are almost always bought. But the second way is simpler.

Buttered Lettuce.

This is essentially petits pois French style without the peas Wash and trim **6-8 young lettuce, or the equivalent in outer leaves**, and shred crosswise in strips of about 1 cm. Trim **6 spring onions**. Using altogether **60g butter**, layer lettuce strips, 1/3 butter, in 3 layers. Snuggle the spring onions, and a **bouquet of parsley, thyme and ½ bay leaf** in the middle, with **1 tsp sugar**. Sprinkle with **1 tsp salt**. Cover tightly, and cook on a low heat for 45 mins. The lettuce will have produced quite a lot of liquid, thicken it with **cornflour or arrowroot**. Remove the herbs. Serve with **sugar** to sprinkle on, to taste.

Lettuce Cream

This uses the **outer leaves of 8 round lettuces**, for 4 people. Wash the leaves well, then put them in a large pan of boiling salted water, and boil for 5 mins after the water reboils. Drain, rinse in cold water, and squeeze as dry as possible. Process the leaves with **4 tbsp milk**, to make a puree. Then put in a pan with **150 ml double cream, 50g butter, salt** and **pepper**, and cook over a high heat for 10 mins, stirring all the time. Serve with fried or toasted triangles of bread. Alternatively, it can go with poached eggs. Or, when the puree has reduced, you can add **4 beaten raw eggs** and cook, stirring, till the eggs are thickened. You could serve it in a cooked tart shell. And that's before you even think of adding a cheese; 50g blue cheese crumbled in at the end of the basic recipe gives considerable added punch and savouriness. When I use blue cheese where it melts, I almost always like some heat with it – like **Tabasco.** These additions have taken the dish a long way from its delicate, creamy, subtle roots, but you may prefer something with more oomph.

Dhal with Shredded Lettuce.

Make the dhal as usual, (boil **250g lentils, any sort**, in about 5 cm water with flavourings. I usually use **a slice of ginger, a couple of dried chilis**, and **1 tsp turmeric**) When the lentils are ready, add **1 tsp salt**, and **shredded outside lettuce leaves** – what you have. Stir well. When the lettuce has collapsed, heat **2 tbsp. oil** in a frying pan, and add the finishing spices – usually **3-4 cloves garlic, sliced**, and **1 tsp. cumin seed**. **Maybe 1 tsp. black mustard seeds** also, which will pop just before they are ready. When these are sizzling, pour into the dhal, stir, and serve immediately.

Red-Cooked Lettuce.
This is a Chinese home-style dish. You can eat it alone, or add some tofu cubes to make it into a main dish. Excellent, simple, and very cheap either way.

You need **enough lettuce – whole, or outside leaves – to half-fill a 2-litre pan** with a lid. Cut about 4 cm thick – whole lettuce – or put leaves together and slice across.   Stir-fry **1 large chopped onion, 2 chopped cloves garlic** in **2 tbsp. oil** in a large pan which has a lid. After 3-4 mins, sprinkle with **1 tsp. Marigold stock powder, 5 tbsp. water**. Stir, cook 2 mins, add **2 slices ginger**, peeled, and the lettuce slices. Turn to coat all the lettuce with the onion mixture. Add **5 tbsp. soy sauce, 2 tbsp. wine, 2 tsp. sugar**, and **pepper**. Cover the pan and cook on low heat for 15-30 mins, turning the lettuce over a couple of times. You can take out the ginger – it's not to be eaten. Taste and serve. It can be reheated if there is any left.

Marrow, or Vegetable Marrow

A confession; before I started working on this book, I had a long-term prejudice about marrow, dating back to childhood experiences of it boiled, or boiled in a white sauce. Overcooked and tasteless and slimy, it put me off and probably put off many thousands of other children of the same vintage. An adult look at marrow has changed my mind. There are many tasty things to make with it. Even more surprising, if you microwave marrow, it has a delicious taste of its own. How can I have missed out all these years on something so good, cheap, and plentiful?

All my recipes avoid letting marrow come in contact with water. If you have other recipes where it is boiled or steamed, try microwaving it instead, and I bet it will be an improvement. The recipes are based on a marrow of about 1 kg, about 30 cm long.

Default: Buttered Marrow.
Peel **a 30-cm marrow** if necessary. Cut out the centre seeds, and cut into chunks. Soften **a finely chopped shallot** in **50g butter** (for 4) and add the cut-up marrow. Add chopped **marjoram, salt** and **pepper**, and cook gently, covered, for 20-30 mins. Add **2 tbsp. water or stock**, and **juice of 1 lemon**. You can also add a little **cream**, which is nice but not essential. Try other herbs, like **basil** or **sage**, or even **parsley** if that's all there is.

Marrow from the Microwave.
Cut **a 30-cm marrow** in 1-cm discs, and cut out the seedy centre. Microwave till tender and seeming dry on the surface. 3 rings took 5 mins in my 800w. microwave. Fewer take less time; lower powers take longer; you will have experience with your own oven that helps you to judge. This is mostly a preliminary process, so time isn't critical. The rings can be cut up and served cold with, e.g. the walnut sauce in the cucumber section, or a soy dressing with sugar, vinegar, and a little dark sesame oil. Or they are ready to be stuffed, or griddled.

Griddled Marrow.
Use microwaved rings. Brush each side with **olive oil**, or pour a little oil on a plate and dip each side in it. Cook the rings on a barbecue or a

ridged griddle, until both sides are marked with griddle lines. Sprinkle with **salt** and **lemon juice**; and eat them hot or cold. I think this is a 5* method, and so far removed from the stereotype of my childhood you wouldn't know it was the same vegetable.

Roast Marrow.

It can be roasted alone or with other vegetables; I prefer the second. Chunk **peeled red onion, seeded peppers of any colour, seeded marrow**, and mix with **small potatoes**. Add **olive oil, chopped garlic**, and **salt**, and mix the whole with your hands. Tip into a roasting tin (or mix the lot in the tin from the start) and cook at 180 for 50-60 mins. You want everything to be tender, with browned edges. This is a meal in itself, particularly with a salsa and a green salad.

Deep-Fried Marrow.

Peel and quarter **a 30-cm marrow**, deseed, and cut into cubes of about 2 cm. Dip these in **seasoned flour**, and deep-fry in batches. If you have a thermostatted deep-fryer, the temperature should be 190. If not, either use a thermometer, or adjust the heat so that the cubes take about 4 mins to become crisp and golden (Not as hot as for chips, that is, but hot enough so the marrow doesn't absorb fat) Drain on kitchen paper or newspaper, and **salt** lightly. I'd use this with a spread of dishes which was a bit short on crispness.

Marrow with Tomatoes.

A version of the favourite summer vegetable mush. (see Courgettes)
Quarter **a 30-cm marrow**, scoop out the seeds, and cut into cubes. Sweat **1 large chopped onion** in **4 tbsp. olive oil** for 10 mins, then add **2-4 cloves chopped garlic**. Add the marrow cubes and mix well, and let cook about 5 mins. Add **500g. tomatoes**, peeled and chopped, **or 1 tin tomatoes** Add also **2 tbsp tomato puree, 1 tsp sugar, salt** and **pepper**. Cover the pan and cook for 20 mins. Add chopped **basil**, and serve hot or cold. If cold, **wine vinegar** to taste can be added, to make it more salad-like. You could add peppers or mushrooms, before the marrow, to make vegetable dishes which call out for a proper name.

Marrow Curry.

Sweat **1 medium chopped onion** in **2 tbsp. sunflower oil** in a large pan with a lid. After 5 mins, add **4 sliced green peppers**, and **a small**

marrow, seeded and chunked, and sweat, covered, 5 mins more. Add **3 chopped cloves garlic, 2 seeded chopped green chilis, 1 tsp. turmeric, 1 tsp garam masala**, and **1 tsp. salt**. Cook covered 5 mins longer or until you are sure the marrow is cooked. Take off the lid, raise the heat, and cook until the pan is almost dry.. Add the **juice of 1 lemon**, and sprinkle with chopped **fresh green coriander** to serve. A good complement to dhal, rice, raita.

Marrow Rings with Soy and Sesame.

For this, you start with **microwaved rings of marrow**. Brush them VERY lightly with **dark sesame oil** on the top surface. Mix **2 tbsp. tomato puree, 2 tbsp. soy**, and **2 tbsp. sesame seeds**, and spread this over the top surfaces. Bake at 200 for 10-15 mins.

Stuffed Marrow.

Once again, start with **microwaved rings of marrow**. Here are 3 possible stuffings:

1. **Sage and Onion Stuffing**. Sweat **2 medium onions**, chopped, in **40g butter** till tender. Add **10-12 chopped sage leaves**, (or more if you like), and **30g fresh breadcrumbs. Salt** and **pepper**. For about 4 rings.
2. **Walnut and Mushroom Stuffing**. Fry **500g large dark mushrooms**, cut fairly small, in **30g butter or oil**. Let them cook a few mins, then add **salt** to release the juices, and let them cook till dry. Add **2 very finely chopped green chilis, 100g walnuts, ground, 50g breadcrumbs**, and enough **stock** to make it of stuffing consistency. **Salt** and **pepper**, and chopped **herbs** if liked. Taste; it takes quite a lot of salt. For about 8 rings
3. **Apricot and Nut Stuffing. 100g breadcrumbs, 50g ready-to-eat apricots, 50g cashew nuts, 1 stick celery diced, ½ tsp. ground cinnamon, 50g melted butter. Salt** and **pepper**. About 8 rings.

The procedure with all of these is the same. Spread the rings out on a baking dish, and fill the hollows with stuffing and mound on top. Bake at 180 for 20-30 mins. The crumbs should brown slightly. Incidentally, the stuffings are all breadcrumb-based, rather than using cooked rice, couscous, or another grain, because the stuffing is not enclosed and steamy, but open. If you have too much stuffing, put it in a small dish and bake with the marrow rings. All the stuffings are delicious alone.

Curried Marrow Soup.

Sweat **1 large chopped onion** in **30g butter**, and when transparent add chopped **garlic (anything from 1-6 cloves, depending on your mood), 2 chopped deseeded green chilis, ½ tsp turmeric, 1 tsp. garam masala, ¼ tsp (or even less) cayenne pepper.** Stir around and let sweat 2 mins more, add **1 marrow**, peeled, seeded, and cut into small pieces, and let sweat covered about 10 mins. Add **600 ml. stock, 1 crumpled bayleaf**, and **1 tsp. salt**. Cook gently, covered, 15-20 mins. Let cool a bit. Blend, either in blender or with hand-held version. Reheat. Garnish with a spoonful of **yoghurt** in each plate, and chopped **fresh green coriander**.

Marrow and Ginger Jam

In one sense, this is the last resort when you are overcome by marrows. On the other, it's really very good jam, and reminiscent of the delicious melon-and-ginger jam that came in tins from South Africa 40 years ago. Not since the EU, alas!

Peel, deseed and cube **enough marrow to give 1 kg. cubes**. You need a total of **750g. granulated sugar, the rind and juice of 3 lemons**, and a **3-cm piece of root ginger**. Sprinkle the marrow cubes with one-third of the sugar, mix in with your hands, and leave overnight. Chop the ginger finely, and tie into a cheesecloth bag with the lemon rind. Mix the marrow, the remaining sugar, and the lemon juice in a preserving pan (or other large pan), and bring to the boil, immersing the bag in the mixture. Boil for 15 mins, and taste. If the ginger flavour is strong enough, take out the bag. Continue boiling until setting point is reached. Pot in clean warm jars. Yields 2½ to 3 kg.

Peas – Garden, Mange-Tout, and Sugar Snaps

For the best peas, you must grow them yourself, and eat them very young. One year, we were off for three weeks holiday, so I picked all the peas on the allotment that were not quite ready. They would be too old when I got back. Shelled, these peas gave a heap of tiny, intensely green balls. They were too good to cook at all; we just ate spoonfuls raw from the bowl, and I remember them with intense pleasure. Neither bought peas nor frozen come anywhere near this. But bought peas, and frozen, are what we have most of the time. And, between these two, I think frozen (best frozen, i.e. organic petits pois) usually come closer to the ideal than bought. And you can buy them all year round. However, peas bought carefully, in season, and local, can outshine the frozen.

The **default** method of cooking peas is simply boiling in salted water– minimally for frozen, where I just let them come back to the boil and drain, and a variable time for fresh. You just have to taste a middle-sized pea from your pot; smaller will be a little overdone, great big ones not quite done. Add butter, amount according to conscience, maybe a little mint or other herb. DON'T buy frozen peas with mint added.

Sweated Peas.
If you want to seem more elegant, call them petits pois a l'etuves. A little more complicated than the default, with less hanging over the pan and tasting at the last minute. Shell and wash the peas, then put **500g peas** in a pan with **50g butter, 2 tbsp water, salt and pepper, 1 tsp sugar**, and maybe **a few chopped fresh mint leaves**. Cover tightly, and cook over low heat for 15-20 mins. Don't defrost if frozen. If there is any liquid left at the end, raise the heat slightly to boil it off. You can turn this into **peas in cream** by adding double cream + a squeeze of lemon, or crème fraiche, at this stage. In this case omit the mint. Jane Grigson suggests adding a good grating of nutmeg at the beginning; I think I would prefer a few leaves of lemon thyme, or some chopped chives at the end.

Petits Pois a la Francaise.
This includes lettuce, spring onions or baby onions, and young carrots. Better for older peas, if you have let some get away in the garden. I

wouldn't buy peas specially for this. Wash and trim **a head of floppy lettuce**, quarter, and wrap some string round each quarter to keep it together. Boil **50g butter** with **150 ml water** with **1 dsp sugar, salt** and **pepper**, and add **500g shelled peas**. Add some stems of **parsley**, also tied together, the lettuce quarters on top, **2 young carrots**, sliced thinly, and **12 spring onion bulbs**, trimmed and peeled. Baste the lettuce with the liquid. Cover tightly and cook slowly 20-30 mins. Turn the vegetables over several times during their cooking. At the end, the water should be almost evaporated. Take out the parsley, de-string the lettuce, and toss with **another 25g butter**. Taste for seasoning, and serve. I think it should be eaten with a spoon. As an aside, this is a good thing to do if you have surplus lettuce.

You can also combine your cooked peas with young cooked carrots, sauteed mushrooms, or raw spring onions or radishes. This may be helpful if you have just a few peas; this would mean they were from the garden, so probably better alone. However, the combinations go very well with pasta; **pasta with peas and mushrooms; pasta with peas and roast red peppers; pasta with creamy peas and spring onions, pasta with peas and asparagus tips.**

Peas are also delicious in salads. If you are using fresh peas, boil them first till nearly done, then drain and rinse with cold water. If using frozen, just let them thaw, don't cook at all.

Mustardy Pea Salad. (also for sugar snaps, mange-tout)
Make a dressing with **1 tsp Dijon mustard, 1 good tbsp mayonnaise**, and **2-3 tbsp Greek yoghurt** (I find that mayonnaise on its own is too heavy for me now, and much prefer this mixture for everything where I would have used mayo before) Add **500g peas, about 50g Cheddar or other hard cheese** cut into small pieces, **1-2 sticks finely chopped celery**, and **a slice of red onion** finely chopped. **Salt** and **pepper** to taste. You can serve it in a bowl on its own, or plated on dressed green salad leaves. This would be splendid with cooked sugar snaps or mange-tout, as well; I would use a smoked cheese, slivered, in that case. Halved **radishes** would look good, add texture and a compatible taste, but are strictly optional.

Pea and pickled-lemon salad.
For about **500g peas**, use **½ a pickled lemon**, discarding the pulp if orthodox, or using all as I do. Chop quite finely, and add to peas with some chopped **mint** and **2 tbsp extra-virgin olive oil**. That's it.

Pea, olive, and ginger salad.
An elaboration on pea/pickled lemon. Add some sliced **stuffed green olives, a little very finely chopped ginger**, and **parsley** not mint. Soak **1 clove garlic** in the **oil**, which can be less distinguished – ordinary olive oil or sunflower oil, if you prefer – for a couple of hours beforehand. **Pepper**, but there will be enough salt with the olives and pickled lemon.

Greek-ish pea salad.
Only because there is **feta** in this, along with **peas, spring onion or red onion, mint**, and **oil-and-lemon dressing**. Proportions to taste. Another good one for mange-tout or sugar snaps.

Andalusian Rice salad.
Any pea salad can be mixed with cooked rice to make it more substantial, but this is a specially good pea/rice combination.
Boil **350g long-grain rice** in plenty of salted water; when done, drain, rinse, and spread on a teatowel to cool and dry. When cold, put in a bowl with **100-200g small raw, or defrosted frozen, peas, 50g sultanas, sliced artichoke hearts** as you feel able (if fresh, cooked, reduced to heart; if tinned, drain; if frozen, cooked; if chargrilled in supermarket pot, drain) and some finely chopped **chives**. Add about **8 tbsp vinaigrette**, and leave to marinate. Make the sauce; pound **1 clove garlic** with **salt**, and pound in **basil leaves**, finely chopped first. Stir in gradually **4 tbsp extra-virgin olive oil**, then **1 tbsp tomato paste**. Work in **a small packet (100 g) cream cheese. Pepper** to taste. It can also be made in the food processor. Put some of the sauce on top of the rice salad, and leave the rest by the side for those who want more. This is enough for 8-10 people. You can use sliced **raw button mushrooms** as well as, or instead of, the artichokes. Filling, and impressive for a buffet.

Green Pea Soup
The best pea soup, by far, comes from Elizabeth David's French Provincial Cookery. I do it regularly for dinner parties; no-one has ever refused seconds, and everyone asks for the recipe. I've tried lots

of others, but none has the intense flavour of peas and the unctuous texture and the superb green colour. In outline, shred the **heart of a soft lettuce**, and put into **125g melted butter** in a pan. Stir, then add **800g best peas** (fresh or best frozen), **1 tsp. salt**, **1 tsp. sugar**. Sweat, covered, 10 mins. Add **1 litre water**, and cook till the peas are tender (hardly any time). Puree by your favourite means – blender when cooled a little, mouli, sieve. Warm through, taste for seasoning. Eat.

Peapod Soup.
From the sublime to the very useful. You need good, shiny, healthy peapods. (Probably your own growing, or possibly a farmer's market) Start the soup, up to or including puree-ing, the day you shell the peas; no sense in letting the pods get older. Sweat **1 small chopped onion** in **25g butter**; add about **500g peapods**, stir, and add **600 ml water**. **Salt** and **pepper**, maybe **sprig mint or thyme or other herb**. Cook till soft, about 25 mins. Take out herbs. Then push through mouli, or whizz in food processor and sieve. You must do one of these, as otherwise there will be stringy lumps which are unpleasant to eat and spoil the whole effect. Dilute with water to right consistency, and finish with **a slurp (4-6 tbsp) double cream**. **Croutons** are good but not essential.

Peas can also be turned into a **sformato**. See French beans.

The whole other area for use of peas is in Indian food. They go well at all levels, from my standard vegetable curry (see potato section) to Mrs Balbir Singh's Paneer Channa Biryani, than which there is little more rich and compulsive. Here I will offer peas pilau, and mattar Paneer – peas with Indian cheese, or similar.

Peas Pilau.
2 tbsp oil or ghee or butter, 1 tsp green peppercorns, 1 tsp whole cumin seeds, 1 tsp black mustard seeds, 350g long-grain rice, 200g peas, fresh or frozen and defrosted, 1 tbsp. ground coriander, ½ tsp ground turmeric, 1 tsp salt.

Heat the oil in a heavy pot which has a lid, and add the green peppercorns, cumin, and black mustard seed. After a little while, the mustard seeds will pop. Add the rice, the peas if fresh, and the ground spices. Stir well for about 2 mins. Add 750 ml water and the salt, bring to the boil, and cook covered over low heat for about 25 mins. Add the

257

peas if using frozen. Cover with a folded teatowel over the pot, replace lid, and leave to stand with heat off for 5-10 mins. Stir peas in, and serve.

Mattar Paneer (Peas with Indian cheese)

A note on Paneer. This can be bought from Indian groceries, and in supermarkets from time to time. It is a typical cheese of hot countries, rather like halloumi or Mozzarella, and not to my taste. I almost always use Philadelphia or other cream cheese, and much prefer the effect. Straying from authenticity even further, you can use cubes of tofu, and this is a really good idea.

60g ghee or butter. 1 medium onion, 6 cloves garlic, 2 knobs ginger. 1 tsp turmeric, 1 tsp ground coriander, ¼ tsp cayenne pepper, 2 tsp garam masala, 1 tsp salt. 1 tin chopped tomatoes, or 500g fresh, chopped. 250g peas, fresh or frozen. 200 g Philadelphia or paneer. Fresh coriander to garnish.

Heat the ghee in a large frying pan, add the onion, and cook gently for about 10 mins, until it starts to brown. Add the garlic and ginger, peeled and finely chopped (people HATE getting a chunk of ginger) Cook for another minute or so, then add the spices and salt, and stir in. Add the tin of tomatoes, and simmer 10 mins. Add the peas and cook till done, covered (for most frying pans, which don't have lids, an enamel plate works well.) Cook uncovered for 5 mins or so, and add the cheese, cut into smallish cubes. Replace lid to let the cheese heat through, then turn into serving dish, and garnish with chopped coriander if liked. It is authentic, but there are still lots of English people who don't like it, or you simply might not have any. Mint is worth trying on a subsequent occasion.

Risi e Bisi

A famous Venetian dish, which may be superlative with Venetian ingredients. In England, I find it's best as comfort food; bland, quite subtle, warming and filling. In most versions it is done as a risotto. For the risotto technique see the techniques chapter. In outline, sweat **1 small chopped onion** in **25g butter**, add **250g risotto rice**, and turn for 1-2 mins in the butter. Add **200g peas** now if they are fresh. Gradually add **stock from 1½ litres**, kept nearly boiling on the side, in ladle-fuls, stirring often, and letting one lot be absorbed/evaporate before adding the next. If you're using defrosted frozen peas, add them when the rice is nearly done. When done, you want it to be almost but not quite soupy, but you can still eat it with a fork. Add **grated Parmesan, more butter, pepper, herbs if you like** but not authentic, stir well, and serve straightaway.

Mange-Tout and Sugar Snaps

Mange-tout are the flat pods, sugar snaps are sweeter and have small peas in the pods. They both grow better in slightly warmer climates than the "English" peas-in-pods; my daughter in Australia can't grow English peas, but does well with both these. Both are often treated in the Chinese style, stir-fried alone or with other vegetables. Or they can be boiled briefly. The pods almost always need stringing on both sides. I am told they are easy to grow, but haven't myself had success, which may be a consequence of living too far North, in Sheffield. Most of the year the ones you see are imported, and I tend to avoid them for that reason. When you do see English mange-tout or sugar snaps, you can have real peas instead, which I prefer. All the same, there are times when sugar snaps, particularly, are just what you want to eat, plain boiled, and eaten with the fingers. I'm not giving any other recipes for sugar snaps, but if you have a lot, try boiling them briefly and using in salads based on these for peas, or with a dip for scooping.

Home-Style Mange-Tout (Chinese)
Stir-fry **3 cloves garlic, a knob of ginger** and **1-2 chillies**, all finely chopped, in **4 tbsp. oil** for 1 min. Add **350g mange-tout**, strings removed, stir, cover, and cook 1 min. Add **1 tsp each salt and sherry**, and cook, stirring, 1 min. more Serve at once.

Stir-fried Mange-Tout with Szechwan Preserved Vegetable
String **500g mange-tout**, and shred finely **2 or 3 pieces Szechwan vegetable**. Heat **4 tbsp oil**, add the Szechwan vegetable and **½ tsp salt**, turn for about 30 sec, then add the mange-tout. Stir-fry briefly, and add **1 tbsp. dry sherry** and **1 tsp sugar**. Cook about 1 min, and serve immediately.

Mange-Tout and Cucumber Salad.
Boil or steam **200g mange-tout** briefly and drain. Quarter **a cucumber** lengthwise, scrape out the seeds, and cut into small sticks (a bit smaller, a bit shorter, than the mange-tout) Mix. Dress with a mixture of **1 tbsp. olive oil, juice of ½ a lime, ¼ tsp. sugar, salt,** and

pepper. You might sometimes add 1 tbsp. soy sauce and miss out the salt; try it both ways.

Pea Shoots.

These are new, and expensive to buy. Sarah Raven, in her gardening book, is very persuasive on the ease of growing these in halved drainpipes. They are delicious, they taste of peas, and you can use them in salad, as a garnish, or stir-fried. I found a recipe in a Chinese book where they are used "as a spinach", and stir-fried with mushrooms, carrot, and bamboo shoot. No soy sauce, just salt and pepper, and cornflour in water to thicken the juices. Mostly, they are used as a garnish, heaped up to give height to a restaurant-style dish.

Peppers

These used to be a seasonal vegetable, and expensive. Now they are grown year-round, often hydroponically, in Holland, and are still quite expensive. Even these Dutch peppers add a flash of colour and an intimation of sunnier climates to our meals. They are not the same as peppers grown in the South, in full sun, but the difference is less painful than with many other vegetables. They come not only in green and red, but nowadays in orange, yellow, purple. In all cases the unripe pepper is green, and it gradually turns colour as it ripens. If peppers ripen off the plant, they are often a little wrinkled. Now we are starting to see different shapes, like the long conical Ramiro.

I usually buy peppers with a definite dish in mind, and any not used for that are chopped up and go to cheer up salads - almost any salads. They are very enlivening with a salad of dried beans, for example. However, if you have some peppers without anything specific in mind, or have bought more than you immediately need on the market, I'd say the default is either in a mixed vegetable stew, or a mixed vegetable roast. There are lots of variation of the mixed vegetable stew, from different places with different names, and I go through some of them below.

Default: Mixed Vegetable Stew with Peppers
Prepare the peppers; quarter through the top, and pull or cut off the cap; scrape out the seeds and white membranes to which the seeds are attached; cut in strips. One or two missed seeds don't matter. Sweat **200g onions** in oil; add **3-4 peppers** in strips, and **1-4 garlic cloves**. Sweat, covered, about 15 mins. Add **a tin of tomatoes, salt, pepper, herbs**, and **any other vegetables you want to put in** – courgettes, marrow, etc, and cook uncovered until the tomatoes have reduced and the resulting mixture isn't too liquid. Quantities for this depend on what you have, but all my versions have been gratefully received.

Mixed Vegetable Roast
This can include small potatoes, or chunks of larger ones, so it has the virtue than it can be a complete meal with a salad and/or some cheese. Components again are variable, but usually include **onions** cut into chunks vertically (so each chunk has a bit of the root end and hence they stay together), **potatoes**, and seeded **peppers** cut into squares.

Some **garlic**, of course. What you add to this makes the differences:- **courgettes, chunked, or aubergine, chunked, or squash, peeled and chunked, or tomatoes.** I wouldn't put in leafy or green vegetables, but florets of **cauliflower** are fine. Mix your selection in a roasting tin with **olive oil** and **salt**, and cook at 180 for 30-45 mins. Keep an eye on it; turn the veg. at least once in the middle of cooking. And there you are – dinner.

You can use peppers raw or roasted. For raw, most people use them as they are. Marcella Hazan, in all her books on Italian food, recommends peeling the pepper to be used raw. Cut in quarters and peel with a swivel-blade peeler, she says. I've tried it; it does make them nicer, but it's fiddly and I don't always bother. Try it and see what you think.

Roasting as a stage in preparation. Roasting isn't for green peppers, only for fully ripe red, yellow, etc. It transforms the texture and the taste, to the point where it's hardly recognisable as the same thing. And many, perhaps most, prefer the roasted peppers. What I do is roast the entire pepper, with the stalk in, under the grill – not too close. My daughter quarters them and roasts them inside-down in the oven. You will have read about the idea of skewering them and toasting in a gas-burner flame; this seems like macho cookery to me, but it is also more economical on fuel. If you have a barbecue going, pop peppers on it after the rest of the cooking is finished, and let them roast there, turning now and then – possibly the nicest product. The result of any of these is skin which is black and bubbly, as close to all over as can reasonably be managed. It is easier to get the skin off if you let the peppers cool in a steamy atmosphere. I put them in a bowl and cover it with a cloth; strong brown paper bags were good when these were given away; you can put them in a plastic bag, or cover the bowl with clingfilm, but this really isn't necessary and isn't environmentally friendly. When the peppers are cool enough to handle, lift them out, and pull off the black skin, which is a very thin detachable layer, and discard it. Take out and discard the stem, and seed them if you roasted them whole. DON'T skin them under a tap, as sometimes recommended, as you will wash a lot of juice and flavour away. And a tiny bit of skin left isn't going to spoil your dish.

I've said above that raw peppers, cut into squares or strips, can add to most salads. Here are a few specific ones, where peppers are more of a main ingredient.

Autumn Salad
2 green peppers, 2 large green apples (English eaters if possible), 50g. raisins, and **50g. hazelnuts**. Deseed the peppers and cut into rough squares. Chop apples in pieces around the same size as the pepper pieces, both a bit bigger than the hazelnuts. Dress with a **nut oil – hazelnut if possible, or walnut –** and **cider vinegar**, with **salt** and **pepper**. Chewy, crunchy, full of early-autumn tastes.

Fennel, Pepper, and Olives
This is autumnal and more Italian in nature. Slice **2 fennel bulbs** very thinly crosswise, after trimming and halving them, and soak in cold water about 10 mins. Drain and dry. Mix with **1 red pepper**, cut lengthwise into slivers, and about **a dozen black olives,** stoned and sliced. Dress with **extra-virgin olive oil** with **a very little wine vinegar, salt** and **pepper**. If you have any **preserved chilis** – Italian, Mexican-style, or indeed other -- a little goes very well with this salad. So does a soft cheese, like **Mozzarella, feta (my choice) or even cottage cheese**. In any of its forms, this is a very crunchy salad, so avoid it for people who prefer their food soft. You can make it less crunchy by blanching the fennel for 1-2 mins, and using roasted red pepper.

Italian Salad of red peppers with cucumber and lemon.
Slice **2 whole unwaxed lemons** as thinly as you can, with the skin on. Pick out and discard the pips. Sprinkle the lemon slices with **1 tsp. salt**. Prepare **a red pepper**, and slice very thinly lengthwise. Slice **a cucumber** very thinly too, on the long slit of a grater. Put the cucumber on a large plate; drain the lemon slices and arrange on top, letting the cucumber show round the edge. Then heap the pepper slices in the middle. Drizzle over **2-3 tbsp. extra virgin olive oil**, and **a few grinds of pepper**. There is enough salt in the lemon.

Simple Salad with Roasted Red Peppers.
Roasted red peppers make a salad by themselves, with an **oil-and-lemon dressing**, and maybe **a few capers or olives or roasted garlic cloves**. Anchovies are terrific here if you eat them.

Salad of Hearts of Palm and Roast Red Peppers.

Drain the **tin of palm hearts**, and slice into thin rounds. Scatter over **6 roasted peppers**, cut in strips. Dressing of **3 tbsp. extra-virgin olive oil, juice of a lemon, salt** and **pepper**. Beautifully red and cream; any other colour you introduce shouldn't spoil the harmony. Black olives would be fine; so would the pale green of cucumber or the cream of raw mushrooms, but I think the bright green of chopped parsley wouldn't go.

Roasted Red Pepper and Halloumi Salad

This is as complicated as I want to get with a roast-pepper salad. Cut **roasted peppers – 1 per head –** in strips, and dress with **oil and lemon**, and **capers**. Divide between individual plates, with **green leaves** plentifully on each. Then slice about **200g halloumi** into 8 pieces, and cook in **a little olive oil** in a frying pan till both sides are golden. (Or, if a barbecue is going, toast them on the hot plate after dipping in oil) 2 slices per plate. I'd like some **black olives** along with this. The whole effect is salty, filling, and appetising.

Roast Peppers Piedmont-style

These are not roasted as above, so that the skin can be removed, but are semi-stuffed. Halve and deseed **1-2 green peppers per head**, and arrange in a flat roasting dish. In each half put **2 or 3 thin slices garlic, a halved cherry tomato**, and **a dsp. of extra-virgin olive oil**. Sprinkle with **salt**. Bake at 150 for about 30 mins, and let cool. They can be a salad, an appetiser, a snack – but are, alas, too oily to be eaten with the fingers. Leftovers, obviously, aren't a problem, so you may as well fill up the roasting tray and do a lot, when green peppers are on offer.

Rajas

These are Mexican or Tex-Mex, and come in many forms. My favourite is this simple fry of green peppers and onions. Cut **3 green peppers**, cored and deseeded, into strips, and cut **1 large onion** into lengthwise strips. **A finely-chopped green chili** can be added if you like. Cook in **2 tbsp. sunflower oil** on moderate heat till softened to taste, and **salt** when done. Use as part of a tortilla or wrap filling, with refried beans, guacamole, salsa, and limes to squeeze over. Or with any other combination of dishes you think they will enhance; they may originate in Mexico, but aren't limited to Mexican food.

The mixed dishes, cooked in olive oil and usually garlic, and using a selection of Mediterranean vegetables, have many names, originate in different places, and are distinguished by different seasonings and finishes. Summarising:

Pisto Manchego, Spain, with onions, courgettes, green peppers, tomatoes

Pistouille, South of France; onions, courgettes, peppers, tomatoes, and pesto

Lecso, Hungarian; onions, green peppers, tomatoes, and paprika

Corsican peppers; green peppers and tomatoes

Piperade, Basque country; onions, green peppers, and tomatoes, with egg scrambled into the mix

Peperonata, Italian; onions, red/yellow peppers, tomatoes

Chakchouka, Tunisian. Onions, red peppers, tomatoes, and finished with whole eggs.

Ratatouille, the most famous of all, needs aubergines, and I have put it in that section.

I think it's important to give different dishes, even slightly different, their own names, and keep them distinct. It adds interest to the daily round, and respects the origins of the dish. I seem to be swimming against a tide here, where pesto now means anything that might be pounded in a mortar, not the original mix of basil, garlic, pine nuts, Parmesan, and olive oil, and Tarte Tatin is not just an upside-down, caramelised, apple tart, but is often not even fruit. Names and distinctions are important and civilised; smearing out is a step towards barbarism.

Pisto Manchego

Coarsely chop **2 large onions** and **3 cloves garlic**, cut **2 medium courgettes** into small cubes, and chop into 5-cm pieces **2 large green peppers**, topped and seeded. Heat **4 tbsp. olive oil**, add the vegetables and stir. Add **1 tsp salt**. Reduce heat to lowest, cover the pan, and sweat for 30-40 mins. Uncover, and add **500g peeled chopped tomatoes (or the contents of a tin)**, and cook fairly quickly, uncovered, until most of the moisture has evaporated. Taste for seasoning.

265

Pistouille

Slice **1 kg courgettes**, and fry briskly till tender and lightly browned in **2 tbsp. olive oil** in a large frying pan. Meanwhile, gently fry **1 chopped onion** and **1 green pepper**, seeded and cut in small squares, in **another 2 tbsp. olive oil**, till tender and not brown. Add to this mix **1 kg. tomatoes**, peeled and chopped, **or 2 tins tomatoes**, and **1 tsp. salt**, and cook briskly uncovered until juices have almost evaporated. Add the courgettes, and cook together 5-10 mins, until the mixture is a thick mass. Pound **2 cloves of garlic** with ½ tsp salt and the **leaves of 2 sprigs basil**, and mix into the hot vegetables. Serve straightaway, with the lively aromas of garlic and basil at their best.

If any of this is leftover, it can be freshened with some fresh chopped tomato and olive oil to taste.

Lecso

Cook **2 medium chopped onions** in **2 tbsp. sunflower oil**, with **1 chopped clove garlic**, till lightly coloured. Off the heat, add **2 tsp. sweet Hungarian paprika, 4 medium green peppers**, seeded and chunked, and **500g peeled chopped tomatoes**, or 1 tin, and **1 tbsp. tomato puree** from tube or can. **½ tsp. salt.** Cover the pan, and cook 30 mins on medium heat. It should be quite liquid. It can be served alone, or with fried eggs.

Corsican peppers

Cut **2 green or red or other-colour peppers** in strips, and cook gently, covered, in **2 tbsp. olive oil** for 10-15 mins. Add **1-2 chopped cloves garlic, a tin of tomatoes, salt** and **pepper**, and cook uncovered until fairly thick. Add slivered **basil leaves** to taste, and serve straightaway.

Piperade

Cook **1 thinly sliced large onion** in **2 tbsp. olive oil** till wilted, and add **6 green peppers**, seeded and cut into strips. Cook, covered, about 15 mins, and add **2 chopped cloves garlic, 2 tins chopped tomatoes, salt** and **pepper**, and **a few thyme leaves, or a pinch of dried mixed Mediterranean herbs**. Cook until fairly dry, then add, on low heat, **4 beaten eggs**, and stir until they begin to thicken. They should not get dry. Serve very quickly, as the eggs will go on cooking. This goes very well indeed with triangles of fried bread.

Peperonata

Cook **1 small chopped onion** in **2 tbsp. olive oil** until it starts to brown. Add **2 cloves garlic**, chopped, and **2 red and/or yellow peppers**, cover, and simmer 15 mins. Add **500g tomatoes**, peeled and roughly chopped, **salt** and **pepper**, and cook uncovered, fairly briskly till sauce is thick. Add **2 tbsp. wine vinegar** and cook a minute more, then taste for seasoning, and add **2 tbsp. extra-virgin olive oil**. Hot or cold.

Chakchouka

Soften **1 large chopped onion** in **2 tbsp olive oil**, in a frying pan, and add **2-3 cloves chopped garlic**. Add **3 red peppers**, seeded and cut into chunks, and **1 tin tomatoes**. **Salt, pepper, thyme**, maybe **a few crushed coriander seeds**, and cook briskly to reduce to a chunky puree. **4 eggs** Make 4 hollows in the mix, and drop an egg into each one. Cover the pan and let cook till the eggs are done.

All of the above, except the lecso, would respond to 1 or more fresh chilis, deseeded and chopped, added with the peppers.

Chilled Roasted Red Pepper Soup

A very simple soup which celebrates the pepper flavour. You need **6-8 red peppers, roasted and peeled**. Whizz ¾ of them in the food processor, and tip into a pan. Add a **small bunch of dill**, chopped, **300 ml stock**, and **300 ml tomato juice**. **Salt** and **pepper**. Bring slowly to the boil, then let cool. Taste for **seasoning**. Chop the rest of the peppers, put in the bottom of the serving dish, and pour over the cooled puree. Chill well. Just before serving, chop **½ green pepper** into small dice, and sprinkle on top. A lovely, light, colourful summer starter.

Peppers, raw or roasted, can also go into any summer minestrone or mixed vegetable soup, without being the main ingredient.

Pepper Frittata

For this you start by making a soft stew with **1 medium onion**, chopped, **2 tbsp. oil, 4 cloves garlic**, chopped, and **4 red and/or yellow peppers**. Cook covered about 15 mins, then let cool. Mix with **8 beaten eggs, 60g. Fontina cheese (or Wensleydale)** grated, and the chopped **leaves of 2 basil sprigs**. **Salt** and **pepper**. Tip the mix into a large frying pan with **1 tbsp. olive oil**, heated, and cook over low heat. Turn over halfway through, when most of the egg is no longer runny. The orthodox way is to cover the frying pan with a large plate and turn both over, taking care that the hot oil doesn't run onto your hands, arms, etc., then slide the frittata back into the pan. The coward's way, which I always use, is to turn chunks of the frittata over on the pan and let it meld together. It's even easier but less fuel-efficient to finish cooking the top under the grill. Anyhow, when the frittata is cooked on both sides, sprinkle with a little grated **Parmesan,** and, **optionally, a few drops balsamic vinegar**. Eat warm or cold; it makes a fine picnic item. I see no reason why you shouldn't make a smaller frittata with leftovers of peperonata.

Peppers make marvellous pasta sauces. Any of the pepper stews above would go well with pasta, but here are 3 specific sauces; two Italian-inspired and one which specifically uses buckwheat pasta.

Pasta with Sauteed Red Peppers

For a sauce for **400g pasta**, prepare **5 fine meaty red peppers**, and cut first into lengthwise strips, and then halve the strips crosswise. Cook briskly in **3 tbsp. olive oil** for about 15 mins, until tender but not overdone. Add **a chopped clove garlic** and **salt** to taste. When the pasta is cooked and drained, put in a serving dish with the peppers and their oil, **50g. melted butter, the shredded leaves of 2 sprigs of basil**, and freshly grated **Parmesan** to taste. This is another of those Italian dishes which is really a first course, and should have another course, like an omelette or a filling salad, next. Or you could thoroughly mix cultures and go on to a hefty pudding.

Pasta with Peppers and Peas.

This sauce, again, is proportioned for 400g pasta, but if it's a main dish you might want to increase the proportion of sauce. Roast **3 medium red peppers**, skin, and cut into square pieces. Heat **50g butter** in a frying pan, and add **100g thawed frozen peas**. When the peas have warmed through, add the pepper squares. Add **300 ml double cream, salt**, and **quite a lot of ground black pepper**. Cook till the cream thickens, and pour over the cooked drained pasta. Freshly grated **Parmesan**. I like a few shakes of **Tabasco** with this, added when the cream is reduced.

Buckwheat Pasta with Peppers and Walnuts
For **300g buckwheat spaghetti**. Cook **2 green peppers**, cut into squares, and **1 chopped clove garlic**, in **50g butter** in a covered pan for about 10 mins. Maybe cook **a chili** with the peppers, if you like warm food. **Salt** and **pepper**. Add **100-150g cheese in small chunks – Cheshire is good, so is goat cheese, hard or soft.** Mix well with the cooked drained pasta, and sprinkle **100g broken walnuts** on top. I think, but haven't tried it, that the softish cheese crusted with walnuts would be good here as well.

Risotto with Peppers and Lettuce
What will make this really good is a really good stock. If you already have some vegetable stock, or have made some with Marigold powder, simmer **1½ litres simple stock** with **1 chopped-up pepper, a stick of celery**, and **a chopped leek**, to strengthen these flavours in the finished dish. Keep the sieved stock, lightly salted, warm. Sweat **1 small chopped onion** and **2 red peppers**, seeded and cut in 1-cm squares, in **30g butter**, for rather longer than usual so the red pepper starts to soften. Add **250g risotto rice**, and let it absorb the fat and flavours for a few minutes while stirring from time to time. Start adding the stock in ladlefuls, cooking over low/moderate heat, and letting each ladle be absorbed before adding more, stirring each time. The risotto takes 25-35 mins to cook. Just as it is done, and still a little liquid, add **1 green pepper**, cut into small squares, **the heart of a Cos lettuce**, shredded finely, and grated **Parmesan**. A real triumph.

Like Shirley Conran in Superwoman, I think life is too short to stuff a mushroom, or a courgette, or a tomato, or a leek. Peppers are different; they cry out for that hollow to be filled with something delectable, and baked to blend the flavours. Two versions of **Stuffed Peppers**, one with rice, one with bread.

Allow **one pepper per person, with 1 or 2 extra** (like the teaspoon of tea for the pot). They can be any colour. They can be stuffed whole or halved, and I prefer them halved. This way the stuffing and pepper seem to meld together better, it cooks more quickly, and it is also easier. Don't listen to anyone who tells you to blanch the peppers in boiling water before stuffing them; it is a waste of flavour and makes them floppy. So halve your peppers, deseed them, and arrange in an oiled roasting tin. If you want to do them whole for the appearance, make sure they will stand up, cut off the top, extract the seeds, and stand in an oiled baking dish just big enough to hold them.

Stuffing 1, with rice.
Sweat **1 small chopped onion** in **2 tbsp. olive oil**, and add **80g long-grain rice**. Turn it over so it turns white, and add **300 ml vegetable stock**, and salt if needed. Cook covered on a low heat till the rice is done. Let cool somewhat, then mix in **120g crumbled Cheshire or Lancashire, 30g. grated Parmesan, pepper**, and some chopped **herb**. Oregano is conventional, dill would be good, parsley if nothing else. Taste for seasoning. Fill the peppers; this should be enough for 6 whole or 12 halves, and bake at 150 for 30-40 mins for halves and up to 1 hr. for whole ones.

Stuffing 2, with bread.
Decrust and dice **4 slices from a large loaf of white bread, homemade-style** (NOT sliced). Fry these dice in **3 tbsp. olive oil** until they are crisp. Drain on kitchen paper, and turn into a bowl. Mix with **18 or so black olives**, stoned and chopped, **2 tbsp. capers, 1 chopped clove garlic**, and **6 leaves basil**, chopped. Stir well and fill 4 peppers or 8 halves. Sprinkle some **breadcrumbs** over the top of each, and drizzle with **a little extra-virgin olive oil**. Bake at 150 for about 30 mins. If the breadcrumbs on top are not crisp and coloured, finish the dish under a hot grill. Once, cooking for a friend who doesn't like olives or capers, I missed these out and put in 2 small packets of oyster mushrooms, sauteed in oil, with lots of pepper. No basil. A lovely variation.

Roasted Red Pepper Pancakes
These are so good and surprising that it's hard to believe how easy they are, once you've roasted 2 large red peppers and peeled them. Since you only need 2, they may well have been part of roasting peppers for another meal.
Mix **2 roasted peppers**, broken up into squares, with **3 egg yolks** in a food processor, and whizz till smooth. Add **350 ml milk, 1 small shallot**, peeled and chopped, and whizz again. Pour this onto a mix of **180g plain flour, ½ tsp salt, ½ tsp. baking powder**, and add also **30g melted butter**. Stir together until mixed, but don't overmix. Heat a large frying pan with a **skimming of oil**, and cook the batter in large tbsp. or small ladle-fuls, in batches. Cook on both sides, and keep

warm as they are cooked. Serve with butter on the table for those who want it. You can let people help themselves from the serving dish, or arrange 2 or 3 pancakes on a plate for each eater, and pretty it up with – say – asparagus, or peas, or cooked corn kernels, and sprigs of parsley or dill.

Roast Pepper Tart with Goat's Cheese
Have **1 large, or 2 small, partly baked pastry shells** ready (see Basics) Trim and clean **2 large leeks**, halve lengthwise, and then slice into thin slices. Sweat these in **30g butter** for about 10 mins; **salt** and **pepper**. Let cool. Whizz in a food processor **2 roasted red peppers** with **3 eggs**, then add **150 ml double cream**. **Salt** and **pepper**. Put the leeks on the bottom of the pastry shell, spreading them out, and pour over the pepper/egg/cream mix. Bake at 150 for a total of 35-40 mins. For the last 5 mins, sprinkle **100g goat's cheese**, crumbled, over the top, and allow to melt and spread for these few mins. Let the tart rest 5-10 mins before serving. Very rich, only an occasional indulgence, but delicious and impressive.

Pizza with Peperonata.
For the method of making pizza dough, and a general pizza, see the Basics chapter. And, in general, almost any pizza you're making will be improved with some presence of peppers, whether it's rings of green or slivers of roasted pepper. This one needs **a batch of peperonata**, above; so make 2 batches, use one as planned, and save the other half for this pizza. Spread out the **pizza dough from 250g flour** on the baking tray, and brush with **oil** – garlic oil is good if you have some. Spread a batch of peperonata over, for a 30 cm (12") pizza. Distribute about **150g sliced Mozzarella** over the pizza, then halve **6 cherry tomatoes** and place on top. (On a test comparing Mozzarella and Caerphilly, my friends marginally preferred the Caerphilly. Up to you) **Salt** and **pepper**. Bake at 220 for 10-15 mins, or till done. Sprinkle with shredded **basil**, and serve. You can easily wait this long for a delivery, and it's so much nicer.

Chili sin Carne
The secret of my chili is the spice mix; make this first. (Actually, you need to have some dried red beans ready first; tin or cooked yourself) Mix **1 tsp. allspice, 1 tsp cumin, 4 cm cinnamon stick**, and grind, in

coffee grinder or otherwise. Add **¼ tsp. cayenne or plain chili powder**, and **½ tsp dried oregano**.

Sweat **1 medium chopped onion** in **2 tbsp. sunflower oil**, and add **4 chopped cloves garlic** when it has become yellow. Add **2 peppers, slivered**, and cook 5 mins more. Add the spice mix, and stir about 1 min. Then add **red beans, 120g. of the dried beans cooked, or 2 tins drained and rinsed**, followed by **1 tin tomatoes**. **Salt**. Simmer 20 mins or so to let the flavours blend, and serve with plain boiled rice.

Curried Beans with Green Peppers

The method for this is very similar to that for the chili sin carne above; only the spices are different. For the spice mix, grind together **1 dsp. coriander seed, 1 tsp cumin seed, 4 cloves, 2" cinnamon stick, and the seeds from 4 brown cardamoms**. Add **¼ tsp. cayenne pepper**. Have ready **150g raw red beans, cooked, or 2 tins, drained and rinsed.**

Fry **1 medium chopped onion** in **2 tbsp. non-olive oil (or ghee, if you have some)**. When starting to brown, add **4 chopped cloves garlic**, stir, then **2 medium green peppers**, seeded and chunked, and **1 fresh chili**, seeded and chopped. Add **2 slices ginger**, chopped fine. Stir and cook for a few mins, then add the spices. Stir and inhale. Add the beans, **salt** if you cooked them yourself, and **1 tin tomatoes**. Stir well, and simmer 30 mins. or so (this isn't precise; if your family or guests are a bit late, keep simmering) Taste for salt and heat. Sprinkle with chopped **fresh green coriander** just before serving. A yoghurt dish – cucumber or other – and some plain rice makes up the meal. You could also add a vegetable curry if feeling energetic. Note; they don't have to be red beans; black-eyed peas, chick peas, or any other bean will be fine.

Roasted Red Pepper Dip.

Assume you have **2-3 red peppers** left from a roasting session, or roast these specially. Put into the food processor with **3 chopped cloves garlic, parsley and basil, 1 tbsp. extra-virgin olive oil, juice of ½ lemon, 100g Philadelphia or substitute, salt** and **pepper**, and whizz. (Or you could use a garlic-and-herb cheese, if you have some to use up) Taste and adjust seasoning. Use either as a dip, or spread on toasted diagonal slices of ciabatta as a version of bruschetta. You get another terrific dip, the Greek **strofilia**, if you use **feta, 100-150g**, instead of the Philadelphia, and **a chopped fresh chili**, deseeded.

Red Pepper Salsa

Chop **1 raw seeded red pepper** and **1 red or green chili** finely. Mix with **2 tbsp. wine or cider vinegar, half a small packet of fresh coriander**, chopped, **1 peeled finely chopped shallot**, and the **juice of 1 lime or lemon. Salt**. Taste and adjust quantities, and chill. Will add freshness and kick to anything from salads to winter root casseroles, served on the side. This makes 8-12 servings, but it's hard to cut it down.

Pumpkin and Winter Squash

We are used to pumpkins, and for some reason the many many other varieties that the Americans call winter squash have been strange to us till recently. They are all forms of the same species, and historically were grown because of their yield and because of their storage capability. A ripe pumpkin/squash has matured in the sun and the skin has hardened – it's one of the signs of a winter squash that you can't easily push your thumbnail into the skin. It will then keep for some months – in the right conditions, even through to March. Unfortunately, flavour didn't go along with these virtues. Some varieties have a better flavour than others, but you can't simply go by variety. If they haven't been well grown they won't have developed flavour either. Still, I do get the impression that pumpkins as grown in England have even less flavour than the average squash. There is a reason why they are now mostly used for hollowing out and carving into Halloween lanterns, and that is because it's very hard to make something appetising with them. Hence, I think, the recent popularity of butternut squash, which really does have flavour. I read that Kabocha, onion squash, and Buttercup all taste even better; Buttercup may, but not the ones I've tried, grown in England. I'd certainly say I've had better and more consistent results from butternut than any other squash, and it can be grown in England (under glass, usually). Incidentally, I assumed at first that butternuts with larger bulb ends were better; I've recently discovered this is wrong, and what you want are large top ends. My favourite seed catalogue has 25 varieties of winter squash, so someone must be growing all these different kinds.

Whatever you are going to do with your winter squash, you face the problem of getting inside it and then, often, peeling it, and the bigger, the harder. An authoritative article in Gourmet, Sept 1990, says " "A heavy cleaver or giant knife is sufficient for some of the less sturdy squash, such as Acorn, Butternut or Calabaza. Some tougher-shelled specimens need extra attention: in which case, cut off the stem end, place your biggest, sharpest knife lengthwise in the squash, and with a wooden mallet or rolling pin gently hammer the part of the blade that joins the handle until the squash splits in two. Scoop out and discard the fibre and save the seeds for roasting. Cut the squash into smallish pieces, about 3" square, remove the rind with a paring knife or vegetable peeler, then cut the squash to suit the recipe."

I'm trying to cover squash in general, so whatever type you acquire – homegrown, veg. box, market – the guidelines apply. They come in so many forms, and the forms are changing all the time as new varieties are bred and marketed, that it's impossible to cover them all. I got a selection of 12 different sorts from my local organic shop. But the microwave can be used for almost all. Small ones, individual serving size, only need piercing, microwaving, and then halving, seeding, and seasoning to serve. In fact, you can pierce and cook them whole up to about 3 lb. weight. Larger ones should be pierced and microwaved for a few minutes, to help with hacking them into manageable chunks. You can use the microwave to soften a squash just enough to make it easier to hack up and peel. If cooking thoroughly, microwave the chunks, skin side down, covered, until they are tender. Or, again up to about 3 lb., oven bake at 150 until they are tender, then halve and seed. Oven-baking preserves the most flavour and is least trouble.

Whatever means you use, winter squashes, and especially pumpkin, are extremely flexible. They can be used in appetisers, soups, main dishes, side dishes, desserts, and sweet baked goods. This is largely a function of their smooth texture, when cooked, and their weak flavour which can be brought out (or swamped) by other, stronger-tasting ingredients. And, on the flexibility side, pumpkin seeds are delicious toasted on their own, or in savoury dishes, and pumpkin oil is dark and strong and has a splendid flavour when used in cautious amounts at the end of a process. The flowers are also edible, like those of courgettes.

Default.
Roast, alone or as part of mixed vegetable roast. Cut, or hack, the **squash or pumpkin** into chunks, removing the seeds, and peeling if practicable. Add **a little oil** – type depending on what else is being served, but olive is almost always good – and mix in with your hands. **Salt and pepper**. Roast at 170 for 30-45 mins, until the edges are slightly caramelised. **A few cloves of garlic** mixed in would always be to my taste.

Roast Butternut with Tarragon.

Melt **30g butter** in a roasting dish, and add cubes from **1 small butternut squash**, halved, seeded, peeled, and cut up. **Salt, pepper, ½ tsp. brown sugar**, and some chopped **tarragon – leaves from 2-3 sprigs**. Roast as usual, and finish with a little **more chopped tarragon**. If you have a small squash, sized for 1 or 2 people, cut in half, scoop out the seeds, put a nut of butter and the other seasonings inside the hollow, and roast at a slightly lower temperature – say 150 – for 45 mins. or so. Finish with chopped tarragon.

Roast Squash with Olives.

For small, single-serving squash. Halve the **squash** and deseed. In each half put **a few stoned black olives, ¼ of a small garlic clove peeled and slivered, a small sprig of thyme,** and **a little chopped chili.** Use a whole chili if you're cooking for 6; if for 2, this is the time to use ¼ tsp of instant chili. No salt. Then add **1 dsp. olive oil** to each half. Put in an oiled baking dish and cover, with lid or foil. Bake at 180 for 30 mins, then take off the lid, reduce the heat to 150, and cook till tender, probably 10-15 mins. more.

Butternut Squash in a Parcel.

The parcel can be made of baking parchment or foil. Whichever, the little single-person parcels can be made up some hours ahead, and then put to bake 30 mins. before they are needed. This can be very convenient. Halve, seed, peel and cut **1 small butternut squash** into small cubes. Trim and clean **3 medium leeks**, halve them, and cut into thin slices. Mix butternut and leeks, and add **3 cloves garlic**, chopped, and **2 tbsp. olive oil. Salt** and **pepper.** Oil the foil or paper, cut into 30 cm squares. Divide the squash mixture among the squares, and stick a small sprig of **rosemary** in the middle. Wrap up the parcels, folding the edges together tightly. When needed, bake 30 mins at 170. It's worth opening one parcel a little just to check the squash is cooked through. Let everyone unwrap their own packet.

Braised Garlicky Winter Squash

Cut up **enough squash to give you about 500g smallish chunks.** Halve, seed, peel first, obviously. Melt **15g butter** in a small pan with a cover, and add **8 cloves garlic**, peeled, and **2 tbsp. white wine.** Cover, and cook on VERY low heat for 15 mins. The garlic must not burn. Mash the garlic a little with the back of a spoon, and pour the mix over the squash in a larger pan. Add **another 15 – 30g butter**, stir well, cover, and cook until the squash is tender, stirring now and then. About 20 mins for butternut; others will vary. **Salt and pepper** to taste – maybe a dash of Tabasco or sprinkle of ground chili – and add chopped **parsley** before serving. If you have some roasted garlic, you can use this instead of cooking the garlic as in the first step above. If you like garlic, this is gorgeous.

Winter Squash Stew with Chilis.
This makes a lot, but reheats well. The first stages are a bit fiddly, because you toast many of the flavourings to bring out their taste. So: roast separately, either in a dry frying pan or on an enamel plate under the grill, **3 tbsp. sesame seeds; 3 tbsp. or more pumpkin seeds; 2 tsp. cumin seeds**. Grind the sesame seeds, the pumpkin seeds, and the cumin in a coffee mill. Keep the cumin separate. Halve, seed, peel and cut up **a squash weighing 700g – 1 kg**.
Now the easy bit. Saute **2 coarsely chopped onions** in **2 tbsp. vegetable oil** until they start to soften. Add **2 chopped cloves garlic**, the cumin, **1 tsp. dried oregano** and the chili element, and cook 1 min more. The chili element can be **3 tsp. Kashmiri garam masala, OR 2 tbsp. ancho chili powder, bought off the net, OR 3 tsp. smoked pimenton**. Add the squash, **200g large mushrooms**, broken into chunks, **1 tsp. salt**, and **600 ml. water or stock**. Cover, and cook slowly till the squash is tender. If it dries out, the heat is too high; add more water or stock. Then add the ground seeds, **1 small cauliflower** cut into florets, **100g. frozen corn**, and **1 tin crushed tomatoes**. Bring to the boil, and taste for salt and chili; add more if needed. Cook till the cauli is tender, and add **100g frozen peas**, and cook a few mins more. Sprinkle with chopped **fresh green coriander**. Serve with **sour cream**.
This is obviously capable of lots of variation with the other vegetables, but I really like the cauliflower in there.

Winter Vegetable Stew. Much plainer than the last stew, but warming and comforting. Again, this makes a lot. The second half could be covered with pastry and turned into a pie. Start with **1.5kg. squash**, of whatever kind. Halve, seed, peel, dice it. Fry quite quickly in **2 tbsp. olive oil**, with **2 chopped onions** and **2 sliced fennels**, for about 10 mins, stirring often. Add **2 medium potatoes**, peeled and diced, and fry another 5-10 mins, until the vegetables are starting to colour.

Meanwhile, heat **1 tbsp. olive oil** in another pan, add **2 sliced cloves garlic**, and soon afterwards **500g. mushrooms**, sliced. Ideally these should be wild mushrooms, otherwise use large ones. Add **salt** and **a pinch of cayenne pepper**, and cook until the juices have been released and dried up, and the mushrooms are starting to brown. Add these, and **1 tin tomatoes with their juice**, to the squash mixture, and stir well. Add also **½ the tomato tin of water**. Simmer the lot, covered, for 20 mins or until the potatoes are done. Add a little water if needed, but it shouldn't be too wet – it's a stew, not a chunky soup! Slice crosswise **half a head of Chinese leaf**, and toss it in **1 tbsp. olive oil** over high heat just till it wilts. Stir it into the stew. Now add **cider vinegar, honey, Tabasco, and mushroom ketchup** to adjust the taste to your liking – start with 1 tbsp. vinegar, 1 tbsp ketchup, 1 good tsp. honey, and a few splashes of Tabasco. Adjust salt, and sprinkle well with freshly ground **black pepper**. I'd prefer this with crusty fresh bread, but it can also go with rice or couscous.

Squash Tagine with Aubergine.
I call it a tagine because of the Moroccan spicing, not because of the pot it cooks in. If you have a tagine, then use it; if not – as I haven't – then any large cooking pot, with tight lid, which goes on a burner. Halve, seed, peel, chunk a **1 kg. squash**. Chunk and salt **2 aubergines**. Make a spice mix; **2 tsp. each of coriander, cumin, caraway, 2" cinnamon stick,** and **1 tsp black pepper**, ground together. Add to this mix **¼ tsp. cayenne pepper, 1 tsp. ground ginger**, and **1 tsp. smoked paprika**. Fry quite quickly **2 large chopped onions** in **4 tbsp. olive oil**, adding **4 chopped cloves garlic** as they start to brown. Add the spice mix, and cook about 1 min more, enjoying the fragrance of the spices as it rises. Add the squash, **2 tins of tomatoes and their juices, 6 whole green chilis, 1 tsp. salt**, and **1 tbsp. honey**. Add **300 ml. water**, and let the whole cook slowly, covered, for 20 mins. Meanwhile, drain and dry the aubergines, and cook in **2 tbsp. olive oil** (or more if needed) until they are browned outside. Add them to the stew, with **100g chickpeas, cooked (or 1 tin, drained and rinsed)** and **80g. black olives**. Simmer a little more, making sure everything is cooked. **Lemon juice or preserved lemon, and/or chopped green coriander**, are great additions, but not really essential. Serve with rice or couscous, a bowl of plain yoghurt, and harissa. The chilis need not be eaten, but probably some macho eater will do so. Adding them whole adds flavour without much heat.

Squash Curry.
This is similar to the tajine, and only the spices are different. The taste is also different. The spice mix should have **2 tsp. each cumin and coriander, 1 tsp. black pepper, 12 green cardamoms, 2" cinnamon stick, and 5 cloves ground together**. Add to this **a mean ¼ tsp. cayenne, 2 tsp. paprika for colour, 1 tsp. turmeric**. Cut up, seed, peel **a squash weighing 1 kg or a bit more**. Cut into chunks. Fry quite quickly **2 large chopped onions** in **4 tbsp. sunflower oil**, adding **4 chopped cloves garlic** and **3 seeded cut-up fresh green chilis (the fatter kind)** as they start to brown. Add the spice mix, and cook about 1 min more, enjoying the fragrance of the spices as it rises. Then add the squash chunks, and stir. Add **1 tin of tomatoes, 1 tsp. salt**, and **150 ml. water**. Cover and cook for about 45 mins, or till the squash is done. This makes enough for 6 people, with plain rice. Its only problem is that it's easy to make it really hot, so be careful with the cayenne unless you know your eaters like it hot. Chopped **fresh green coriander** to garnish, unless you are using it elsewhere in the meal. And this would be good with a raita, either cucumber or banana in yoghurt.

Thai Butternut Curry.
Yet another variation on the stew theme, but distinct in its tastes. This assumes you have some Thai green curry paste, either homemade from a previous meal or bought. Cook **1 large sliced white onion** in **2 tbsp. vegetable oil** till browning, then add **1½ tbsp. Thai green curry paste** and **4 chopped garlic cloves**. Stir 1 min., then add **2 handfuls roast peanuts**, roughly chopped, and **1 lemon grass stalk**, peeled and thinly sliced. (Lemon balm makes an excellent substitute for lemon grass; use the leaves from 3 sprigs, chopped) Add **450 ml. coconut milk, about half as much water**, and **2 sliced chilis** (seeded if you don't want it very hot) Bring to the boil, then add chunks from **1 kg butternut squash**, and **1 tsp. salt**. (If not vegetarian, you would add 2 tbsp. fish sauce instead of the salt, which is more authentic.) Simmer, covered, till done, about 20 mins. Add **100g. frozen peas**, and **200g baby spinach**. When the pot comes back to the boil, turn off the heat. You can sprinkle with either **fresh green coriander or fresh basil**, chopped.

Squash Risotto.

Only do this if you have a flavourful squash. If you don't, it will come out simply dull Cut up, after the usual preliminaries, **enough squash to give you 500g. weight**. Then proceed as for a normal risotto; sweat **a small chopped onion** in **50g butter**, add **1 finely chopped clove garlic**, then **350g. risotto rice**. Stir this until opaque, and add **60 ml. dry white wine**. When this has evaporated, add the first ladle from **1½ litres stock**, kept simmering very gently in another pan, and the squash. Keep stirring, adding ladles of stock as the previous batch is absorbed/evaporates, until the rice is cooked. Beat in **50g butter** and **80g grated Parmesan**, and serve straightaway. You could use Gorgonzola instead of Parmesan if you are a fan of blue cheese.

Squash Salad.

Do this when you have roasted some **squash** and have some leftover. Peel, quarter, core and slice an appropriate amount of **pears** – about half the volume of squash. Mix the pears and squash, and toss with some **oil-and-lemon dressing**. Arrange on **watercress**, and crumble some **blue cheese**, Stilton, Gorgonzola, or similar, on top. Roquefort is too strong, and anyway I'm loath to use Roquefort for anything but eating by itself. And Danish Blue is just too sharp and unsubtle. This makes a smashing lunch.

Basic Squash Soup.

There aren't many salads for squash; but there are almost too many soups. I think this happens because the texture of squash, cooked and blended, is so smooth, filling and comforting, without being full of calories. Allow about **250g unprepared pumpkin or squash per eater** – but it doesn't matter if there is too much, as it can always be reheated. I think a good-tasting squash is better here than pumpkin, which comes into its own in desserts. Prepare the squash, cutting in small chunks. For 6 people, using 1.5 kg squash, melt **50g. butter** in a large pan, and tip in the chunks. Cook moderately fast, uncovered, for 10-15 mins, until light gold, stirring now and then. Pour in a **slurp of white wine**, and cook till it has evaporated. Add **1 litre light stock, ½ tsp. salt**, and **2 bay leaves**. Simmer 10-15 mins until the squash is completely tender. Gordon Ramsay says that dropping some **Parmesan rind** in for the simmering stage really adds to depth of flavour, and I agree. Do it if you have some Parmesan rind in store. Take out the rind and bay leaf, and whizz the soup, either in batches in a blender or with a hand-held blender. Reheat, thin with more stock if necessary, taste for seasoning, adding **salt** if needed and freshly ground black **pepper**. You can finish it with a swirl of butter or cream, have croutons or cheesy toasts to eat with it, or simply eat unadorned and golden.

Squash Soup with Leeks and White Wine.
The soup has characteristically French flavours. Sweat **1 large leek**, cleaned and sliced thinly crosswise, and **2 crushed cloves garlic** in **2 tbsp. olive oil**. Add **2 bay leaves, the leaves from 4 sprigs thyme**, and a little chopped **parsley** to the pot, and cook 2 mins more. (The French would tie the herbs together in a bouquet garni, and remove them; I prefer them left in, and avoid the hassle of tying.) Add **150 ml. white wine**, and reduce to a syrup. Add the **squash; chunks from 1 kg.**, prepared, **1 tsp. salt**, and **1 litre stock**. Simmer till the squash is tender, 20 mins or so. Whizz smooth, taking out the bay leaves. Reheat, adding **up to 150 ml each milk and double cream** to adjust the thickness. Taste for seasoning and serve.

Roast Squash Soup with Autumn Nuts.
In this soup, you make efforts to get maximum flavour from the squash, and complement it with other rich autumn flavours. Not an everyday soup, but astonishingly good.
Hack up **1 kg. squash**, removing the seeds, but leaving the skin on. Toss with **2 tbsp. olive oil**, and roast at 170 for 1 hr or more. It should have browned edges, and have shrunk while roasting. Let it cool, scrape off the flesh, and discard the rind (Or save it to go into stock)
Gently cook **2 leeks**, trimmed and sliced, in **2 tbsp. olive oil**. When they are soft, add **4 tbsp. Marsala or other dessert wine**, and reduce to a glaze. Add **100g chestnuts** (fresh peeled; vacuum-packed, which I prefer; or dried, soaked and cooked till done) and cook 5 mins more. Add the squash, **1 tsp. salt**, and **300 ml. stock**. Cook 10 mins, or longer if using fresh chestnuts. Puree in blender, in batches. Reheat, adding **more stock** if needed to thin out, and **150 ml. yoghurt or sour cream**. Taste for seasoning. Add some chopped **fresh sage** to taste – I use 4 leaves, but sage is not one of my favourite herbs – and **a little chopped fresh marjoram if you have it**. Serve sprinkled with **100g. chopped walnuts**.

Spaghetti Squash stands on its own. Usually it's oval and pale yellow, and weighs 1½ to 2 kg, and its flesh when cooked falls into bland, slightly sweet strands which resemble spaghetti. Basic cooking can be done by many of the main methods; boiling, but you need a very large pan. Steaming; ditto, though you can quarter it first. Microwaving; halve or quarter, leave the seeds in, and wrap in clingfilm (This is one of the few times where clingfilm is needed; normally I try not to use it) Microwave at high power for 8-10 mins, until soft when pressed, and then let it stand for 5 mins. Baking; pierce and bake whole at 170 for up to 1½ hrs, till a skewer shows it is tender. After one of these, scoop out the seeds and use a fork to scrape out the strands.

The temptation, having got these spaghetti-like strands, is to treat them like pasta with tomato sauces and Parmesan. They are actually better other ways, as they seem to have no affinity with tomatoes.

Spaghetti Squash with Apples and Ginger.
Use **about half the strands from 1 squash**. While it is cooking, peel **2 slices of fresh ginger** and chop finely, then heat ginger in **150 ml double cream** to infuse. Let it cook very gently 10 mins, then strain and discard the ginger. Melt **50g butter** in a large frying pan, and add dice from **2 apples**, peeled and cored. When the apples are tender and gold, add **1 dsp. brown sugar**, and cook till the apples are glazed, about 1 min. Add the strands of spaghetti squash, and mix gently. **Salt, pepper, nutmeg**. Then add the cream, and cook gently till it is absorbed.

Spaghetti Squash Pancakes.
Use **strands from half a cooked squash**. Mix with **3 chopped spring onions, 50g plain flour, 1 tsp. baking powder, 2 eggs**, and **salt and pepper**. Cook tablespoons of this batter in **clarified butter or oil**, in a large frying pan. Flatten them as they are put into the pan, and brown on both sides over medium-low heat. Serve with **sour cream and chopped fresh green coriander, or with applesauce**.

These are the best things I can find to do with spaghetti squash. My main feeling after this is that I won't cook spaghetti squash again. You might acquire one somehow; you might not agree with me.

Pumpkin Seeds. Every time you prepare a squash there will be masses of seeds mixed with fibre. It seems a pity to waste them, and fortunately pumpkin seeds make a truly tempting snack or nibbling food. Separate the seeds from the fibre, and boil each half-litre of seeds in 1 litre. water, with 2 tbsp. salt, for 15 mins. If the squash has been cooked before you get the seeds, miss out this stage. Drain them, mix with 1 tbsp. vegetable oil, spread them out on a baking sheet at 150 for 30 mins, turning often. When done they are crisp and golden.

The pumpkin seeds you buy are suitable for eating as they are, but are better lightly toasted, in a dry frying pan, or on an enamel plate under the grill. Watch and turn them to get them all toasted and none burnt. If you do it yourself, it's fiddly but free; bought are easier and much pricier.

Pumpkin Seed "Pesto"

This uses pumpkin seeds and also pumpkin seed oil, dark and flavourful and intense, and it is useful as dip or sauce or dolloped into soups, or anywhere you would use any sort of pesto. You probably shouldn't eat too much unless you're trying to put weight on, but it's so strongly-flavoured you don't need to. My recipe is very close to one in Sainsbury's Magazine, Nov. 2002.

Roast **60g pumpkin seeds**, then put in a food processor with **2-3 cloves garlic**, slice, and the **leaves from ½ packet basil and ½ pkt parsley. ½ tsp. salt.** Pulse the mixture till it is blended, then pour in **60 ml pumpkin seed oil** through the feed tube with the machine running. Finally, add **70g. grated Parmesan** and pulse again till blended.

Pumpkin seed oil can also go on salads, finishing soups and stews and Western-style stir-fries, even with scrambled eggs.

And now to desserts and baked goods. All I have tried use pumpkin, not squash; many need puree, dried out. And while it's possible to do this if you have lots of pumpkin, I find a tin of Libby's solid-pack pumpkin in the larder means I don't have to buy pumpkin and prepare it. A really good, cheap, and useful tin to keep in stock. (In 2009 I can't find it in supermarkets; let's hope it becomes available again.)

Pumpkin Gelato.

Prepare **enough pumpkin to give you 400g.**, and simmer it in **300 ml. milk** till done. Add **100g. dark brown sugar**, and stir to dissolve. If using a tin, just blend with the milk and warm to dissolve the sugar. Add **6 crushed amaretti biscuits**, and **3 tbsp. Kirsch**. Freeze. Simple, unexpected, good.

Brandied Pumpkin Pie.

I've felt many times that I ought to do pumpkin pie, and I've often been disappointed. This is the first one I have tried which is really good. If you can't find tins of pumpkin puree, steam or microwave cut-up pumpkin. Remove from skin, and cook over low heat to dry out, stirring to puree. You need 400g dry puree.

Make **2 batches of shortcrust pastry, each with 250g. flour, etc**. (see Basics) and line 2 x 23 cm (9") pie dishes or rings with it. You will probably have some pastry left for another day. Chill the pie shell while mixing the filling: **400g dried-out pumpkin puree or 1 tin solid-pack pumpkin, 150g. light brown sugar, 2 tsp. ground cinnamon, 1 tsp. ground ginger, ½ tsp. salt, 300 ml. double cream and 150 ml. milk, 2 eggs**, and **4 tbsp. brandy**, all mixed till smooth. Pour into the pie shells, and bake them at 160 until the filling is mostly set but the centre still shakes a little. Let them cool on a rack. Serve with **whipped cream** to which you add finely chopped **candied ginger**. This would be just as good with rum not brandy. I've seen, but not tried, a recipe using maple syrup as the sweetener; this should also be excellent.

Pumpkin Rolls.

Make a sponge*: mix:**1½ tsp dry yeast, 1 tsp. sugar, 4 tbsp. warm water**, and **60g. flour**, and leave it to rise. In another bowl, mix **200g or ½ can pumpkin puree, 2 tbsp. light brown sugar, 30g. melted butter, 1 egg, ½ tsp. salt, ½ tsp. cinnamon**, and **4 tbsp. maple syrup**. Add this to the risen sponge and mix well till smooth. Then knead in **200g whole wheat bread flour**, and **enough white bread flour, probably 200-250g,** to make a firm dough. It's impossible to be exact here, because it depends on how dry the pumpkin puree was. . Let the dough rise till doubled in size – it may be slow because of the sugar in it. Knock back, knead briefly on a work surface, and divide into 20-24 small pieces. Shape these into rolls, let them rise, covered with clean teatowels, till they look light and puffy, brush with **melted butter** to keep the crust soft, and bake at 200 for 15 mins or till done. If you are a habitual breadmaker, this will work; if you're not, don't start here!

*A sponge, in breadmaking, is an initial mix to get the yeast working and active, so that it's ready to go fast when mixed with the main body of ingredients for the dough.

This is the merest skim through all the possibilities with winter squashes and pumpkins. I haven't covered pasta sauces, fillings for ravioli (one regional Italian speciality has pumpkin and amaretti as a filling), gratins, bakes, and more. And all my recipes are subject to variations, as well. I hope there's enough to keep you going, unless you have grown LOTS.

Runner Beans

The liking for runner beans seems to me characteristically English, and is not universal even here. I think that the eating pleasure depends, more than any other vegetable, on how they are cut. In all cases, they need to be destringed; peel off both edges with a potato peeler. One school of thought tops, tails, and strings the beans, and cuts them into diagonal lozenges. In this case, if the beans are longer than, say, 20 cm, the skin is perceptibly rough, and this puts a lot of people off. The other way of cutting, which I wholeheartedly recommend, tops, tails, and strings them, and then slices them into very long, thin, slices. There is a gadget for doing this, which used to be on the handle of many potato peelers. At the moment, Lakeland sell a slicer for runner beans. This means that there is not enough surface for the roughness to be noticeable, and allows the flavour to be enjoyed.

To cook them this way, they have to be FRESH. Which means not from a supermarket, but from a farmer's market or, even better, from the garden. When they are fresh, they are firm enough to go through the bean slicer. When they have been picked for some time, they go floppy, and won't go through. Cutting them this way means that even 30-40 cm beans are delicious. Any infant beans in the pods are also sliced, and also tender. Allow 4 runners, 25-cm or thereabouts, per person.

Having got your heap of long thin strings, all you need to do is boil them, in plenty of salted water, boiling hard when they go in. Cook them for 5-7 mins from the time the water comes back to the boil, hovering over the pan for the last couple of minutes and tasting for doneness. Drain well, and serve the tangle on hot plates with cold butter ad lib. They deserve to be eaten by themselves, like fresh asparagus, and are at least as delicious to my taste.

Only when you've had them like this several times should you even think of doing anything else. And then there is a question of form; a tangle of long thin strings doesn't mix very well with other ingredients. I have, for example, tried them with spaghetti, which is often recommended. They do not want to mix, so you end up with separate clumps. Not a pleasure to eat. So, for other dishes, take the strings after cutting, in bundles, and cut into shorter lengths, about 5 cm. Then proceed with whatever you are planning to make with them.

Runners with Cream and Thyme.
Simmer **150 ml. double cream** with **1 chopped clove garlic, thyme leaves, salt** and **pepper**, so that it reduces and thickens. Pour through sieve, over **500g. just cooked runner beans** Toss and serve in warmed dish.

Runner Beans with Almonds.
Use about **50g. flaked almonds** to **500 g. runner beans**. Toast the almonds under the grill, and mix with **50g. melted butter**. Pour over the beans and toss.

Runners with Cheese.
Keep **500 g. beans** slightly underdone while cooking them. Drain. Put the beans into **50g. melted butter** in a large frying pan, and toss for a couple of minutes, till completely done. Sprinkle with **100g. grated cheese**, ideally one of the less hard English cheeses like Wensleydale or mild Lancashire. The cheese will have enough salt. Mix well, add **pepper**. Some of the cheese will make a crust on the pan bottom; scrape it off. Definitely one to eat on its own, in something like a tasting menu of lots of small dishes.

Runners with Tomato Sauce.
Have some **thick tomato sauce** ready, like the quick easy tomato sauce from the Tomato section, and mix the drained **cooked runners** into it. This is a very easy version of the Turkish Runners below, but not noticeably worse.

Turkish Runners.
Prepare (top, tail, destring) **500 g. beans**, cutting them, for this, in diagonals to make lozenges. Sweat **1 large sliced onion** in **2 tbsp. olive oil** till soft, and add **2 chopped cloves garlic**. After half a minute, add the beans, **500 g. tomatoes**, chopped, **3 cloves (the spice)** and **2-cm stick cinnamon, salt** and **pepper**. Cover the pan, and cook slowly for 1 hr. or so. They are meant to be soft and overcooked. Garnish with chopped **dill or parsley**. Eat hot, warm, or cold. They can be served with a dollop of **yoghurt** on top, or mixed in.

Stir Fried Runner Beans.

Top, tail and destring **250g. runners**, and cut into thin diagonal slices. Heat **4 tbsp. oil** in wok or large frying pan, and add **2 shredded deseeded red chilis** and **1 small knob root ginger**, peeled and chopped very fine. Stir 30 sec. Add the beans and stir-fry 2 mins more. Add **2 tsp. soy sauce, 1 tsp sugar, 1 tsp salt**, and stir to mix. Taste. If more cooking needed, cover the pan and leave 1 min more. Serve at once.

Runner Bean Puree.

More baby food, but don't knock it! All these vegetable purees are nice in themselves, and also good to know if you have a sore throat or toothache. Trim and string **500g runners,** slice crosswise, and boil till tender in stock or salted water. Drain, keeping the stock for other uses, and puree in a food processor. It will make the puree better textured and flavoured if you squeeze out some water, by tipping the puree into a clean teatowel, wrapping, and squeezing. Add to the puree **30g butter, 2 tbsp. double cream, salt** and **pepper**, and chopped **basil** or **parsley** to taste. Reheat in microwave or double boiler.

Runner Bean Salad.

Not so much a recipe, more a collection of possibilities. In every case **oil** the **beans** lightly when they are still warm. Then they can be dressed with a straight **vinaigrette, with vinegar or lemon**. Chopped **spring onions or chives** are a very good addition. So is **garlic,** soaked in the oil beforehand and strained out. Instead of vinaigrette, you can add **yoghurt, alone or mixed with mayo, or sour cream**; this will depend on what else you are serving. The **walnut dressing** (in French bean, cucumber) is also good, but don't try to mix it in; serve on the side. A nest of runner strings with **hard-boiled egg slices and mayo/yoghurt/mustard** is also a good way to go.

Runner Bean and Mushroom Soup.

Soak **a few dried porcini** by pouring boiling water over them and leave to stand 30 mins. Only a few; you want to complement the taste of the runners, not swamp it. Drain the mushrooms, keeping the soaking water as stock. Trim and cut finely **300g runners**. Sweat **1 medium chopped onion** in **2 tbsp. olive oil** till transparent. Add **1 medium potato**, peeled and cubed. Then add **1 litre stock**, including the mushroom-soaking water, the beans, and the cut up soaked mushrooms. **Marjoram or oregano** if possible, ideally fresh but dried better than nothing. Simmer for 20 mins. Taste for **seasoning**. Puree if you like – I do. Garnish the top with hammer shapes of **button mushroom**, and maybe a dollop of **sour cream**.

Pasta with Runners.

You need short lengths of runners for this, so they will mix well with the pasta. So, after cutting long thin strings from **300g runners**, gather them into bundles and cut into 5 cm. lengths. Boil them till tender; boil **300g pasta**. Cook gently **2 cloves garlic**, finely chopped, in **50g. butter**, and mix all together in one of the pans you've used for cooking. Add **3 beaten eggs** with **salt, pepper, ½ tsp Tabasco**, and mix well. Depending on how well you like the eggs done, and how hot the mixture was, you may want to heat the pan. Mix in **50g grated Parmesan** and serve immediately. This is obviously based on pasta carbonara, and it works very well.

Curried Runners with Cashew and Coconut Milk.

Trim **500g runners**, and cut into long thin diagonals, aiming to have the long side about 10 cm and the thickness about ½ cm. This cutting does make a difference to the final dish. Blanch them for 2 mins only in boiling salted water, drain, and run cold water over them to cool quickly. Dry on a clean teatowel or kitchen paper. Fry rather quickly **1 small chopped onion** in **2 tbsp. oil**, adding **1 chopped chili, 1 tsp. black mustard seeds** and **100g. raw cashews** as the onion starts to brown on the edges. Let cook 1-2 mins, then add **1 tsp garam masala, ½ tsp. turmeric, 1 tsp cumin seeds**, ground, and **1 tsp. salt**. Stir, and add **300 ml. coconut milk**. (see Ingredients). Simmer 5 mins, add beans, and simmer 5 mins. more. Garnish with finely chopped **fresh green coriander**, unless other dishes are already using it. A fast, easy, not-very-authentic, and delicious curry.

Runner Bean Custard.

Prepare **500 g runners**, cutting into long strings and cutting across to get short strings. Blanch for 3 mins in boiling salted water. Drain, and mix with **15g butter**, chopped **parsley** and **chives, salt** and **pepper**, and **lemon juice**. Beat **4 eggs** with **150 ml double cream**, pour over the beans, and mix. Pour into a buttered shallow baking dish, and cook at 200 for about 20 mins or till set.

This is, essentially, a quiche without pastry, and you can turn it into a quiche by baking in a ready cooked pastry shell. Many people would prefer it with some grated **cheese** on top, to go brown and crisp.

Gado-Gado (my version).
This is a one-platter meal, where people can choose what they like from an assortment. There is a hot peanut sauce to eat with all of this, and the difference is that the sauce in my version is Chinese, not Indonesian. It is also so good that I can't resist dipping my finger in every time I pass if there are leftovers.

Sauce: **about 1/3 jar peanut butter, 3 tbsp. soy sauce, 3 tbsp. wine vinegar, 3 tbsp. sunflower or other bland oil, 1 tsp. dark sesame oil, 1 tsp sugar, Tabasco.** Whizz all these in the food processor, and then adjust the flavour to taste. Ideally it should not taste of peanut butter, or coat the roof of the mouth; and the vinegar, salt from the soy, heat from the Tabasco, and sesame flavour should be so balanced that it's irresistible. It's not easy to get right, but when you have you will know, provided you keep tasting.

On the platter arrange **plain bean curd, hard-boiled eggs, cooked runners, sliced cucumber, shredded lettuce**, and **bean sprouts** if you can get good ones. The last few times I've bought them, they have smelt stale and starting to rot when I opened the packet, even well within the sell-by date. If no bean sprouts, use another sort you have sprouted yourself, like fenugreek or alfalfa. This whole dish is subject to a lot of variation; you can use any plain boiled vegetables. Shredded Chinese leaves can be used instead of lettuce. Bok choy would be good . . . and so on. Dribble some of the sauce over the bean curd on the platter, and have the rest in a bowl alongside for people to help themselves. I haven't given quantities, because it depends so much on the number of people to be fed. This is a smashing buffet dish.

Shallots

Shallots are small, slightly elongated, members of the onion family, distinguished by having two or three "cloves" in one bulb-like head. They have had something of a renaissance recently. When I was learning to cook, they were almost exclusively used in rich sauces, where they were boiled down in wine and/or vinegar to give a reduction which flavoured Bearnaise sauce, beurre blanc, sauce Bercy, and more. And very good these sauces are too. Books of the time have warnings that shallots shouldn't be browned, as it makes them bitter. Now shallots are used roasted and caramelised, and much appreciated in this form. A larger kind, the banana shallot, has appeared, which makes the task of peeling a lot of shallots much easier. And they are often used when only a very small amount of onion flavour is needed. They are most often used as an ingredient for other dishes rather than by themselves, but there are a few dishes where they shine by themselves.

Default. Caramelised Shallots.
To achieve this, they can be roasted or fried, depending whether the oven is on for other things or not. Peel them. For oven roasting, toss **500g peeled shallots** with a **little salt** and **oil**, and roast for about 30 mins in a moderate oven. To fry, peel and halve, and fry quite quickly in **oil or butter**, adding **salt** and **a little sugar** to help the browning process. Continue frying till they are a rich dark brown.

Glazed Shallots.
A vegetable in themselves, or a useful garnish. Peel and halve **500g shallots**. Turn them in **20g butter plus 1 tbsp. oil** till they are lightly browned all over; add **stock to cover, salt, a little sugar**, and cook at moderate speed until the stock has evaporated and a light glaze remains, turning from time to time.

Crisp Deep-fried Shallots.
An Asian garnish, for almost any Thai or Indonesian or South Indian dish. Peel and slice thinly **250g shallots**. Heat enough **oil** for the shallots to move freely. When hot, add the shallots, and cook till gold. Scoop out and drain well on kitchen paper; let cool. They can be stored for several days in a screw-topped jar in the fridge.

Shallot Tarte Tatin.

First cook 500g shallots for 7-10 mins in boiling salted water. Drain. Heat **50g butter** with **1 tbsp. light brown sugar** in an ovenproof pan, and cook the shallots, with **salt** and **pepper**, gently in this until they are caramelised. Take off the heat, and let cool. Roll **all-butter puff pastry** into a rectangle, and cut a round a little larger than your pan, and lay it over the shallots. Tuck the edges underneath. Bake at 200 for 30-35 mins, until the pastry is risen and browned. Turn it upside-down onto a serving plate. There's no point in giving an amount of puff pastry, because it depends on your pan. When rolled, it should be about 5 mm thick. If it's bought, or bought ready-rolled, you'll obviously have the weight of the packet, and will probably have some left over. Leftovers make terrific cheese straws, or can be sugared to make palmiers

If you want to elaborate this, add 250g Camembert, sliced thinly, over the shallots and under the pastry, which makes the dish taste really rich. Or you can garnish the browned shallot top, after turning out, with goat's cheese and sun-dried tomatoes, or simply scatter some rocket over it.

Sauces. Most of these sauces were originally designed as meat accompaniments, but they are so good it would be a shame not to adapt them for vegetarian purposes. Since they are rich in butter and/or eggs, they go extremely well with a simple baked potato, where you can appreciate the delicious taste and texture. They go with broccoli, asparagus, runner beans . . They can be used as warm dips. They go well with plain bakes, which have a tendency to be dry. In fact, if you can make these sauces, you can serve them with old shoes and your eaters will still be ravished.

Bearnaise Sauce.

Chop **2 shallots** finely, and put in a pan with a **couple of sprigs of tarragon, chopped.** Cover with **6 tbsp. each white wine and white wine vinegar** Boil down until there is only 1 tbsp. or so of liquid left. Strain this unto **3 beaten egg yolks**, salted, and stir well. You can now go the classic route or the easy route. For the easy route, put into a blender, and whizz while adding **120g. melted and cooled butter** slowly through the hole in the lid. For the classic route, put the mix into a double boiler, and add 120g butter cut into 8-10 pieces. Beat each in well before adding the next. I can't taste any difference between the two ways, and the first is easiest and most reliable. You may, though, find yourself in a holiday home without a blender, when it's useful to know of the classic way. (A bowl over simmering water makes a fine double boiler) When the sauce is thickened, scrape into a bowl, and add **pepper** to taste and chopped **tarragon**. Don't try to heat it, or it will split or scramble. It SHOULD be lukewarm.

Beurre Blanc (White Butter). *****

This is renowned as difficult to make; I haven't found it so. Peel and chop very finely **3 shallots**, and add **3 tbsp. each white wine and white wine vinegar**. Boil it down almost to a paste. Divide **200g softened best butter** into 8 cubes; add the first cube to the shallots. Whisk over the heat a few seconds; you are trying to get the butter to emulsify, not to melt. Keep adding cubes of butter and whisking, so that the final sauce is cream-like in consistency and pale in colour. It will never be more than tepid. The ingredients are simple, the success is all in the technique. And it's one of the most delectable things I have ever made.

Pickled Shallots

My friends assure me these are an improvement on pickled onions. I really don't like either – I don't much like anything with malt vinegar – but pickled onion eaters love these. Peel **a quantity of shallots; probably not worth doing less than 1 kg**. Soak them overnight in a **brine of 100g salt per litre water**. Drain and rinse well. Pack into jars. Boil **malt vinegar** with black peppercorns, coriander seed, mustard seeds, dried chilis, and bay leaves. Quantities; for 1 litre vinegar, use 1 tbsp. black peppercorns, 1 tbsp. coriander seed, 3 bay leaves, 1 tbsp. mustard seed, and 4 small hot dried chilis. Let the vinegar cool, pour it into the jars to cover the shallots, seal, and store for a couple of months before using. Mostly used with bread and cheese, but a pickled shallot can be chopped and added to many strong-flavoured and piquant salads.

Shell Beans

What I mean by this is the fresh form of dried beans, mostly borlotti (cranberry beans in America and Oz), cannellini, and flageolets. They look like succulent dried beans. If you grow them (alas, I've had very little success, because snails eat the plant) then you pick the ripe or even semi-dried pods, and shell them like broad beans. From 2008, you can buy frozen flageolets, at the moment exclusive to Booths, which is centred in Lancashire. The River Café books say that frozen borlotti are available, but I haven't seen them. In 2011, I found fresh borlotti, in their pods, at a farmer's market. Availability is increasing. Practically all these recipes have been tried with the frozen flageolets.

Traditionally, these beans were grown for drying, so few if any were eaten fresh. The same was true for peas, I believe, until the seventeenth century. With the spread of a market economy, dried beans as winter food are not as necessary to subsistence as they were, and new ways of using the fresh beans are springing up. They are now a coming fresh autumn vegetable, and well worth a try. If they are fresh, cooking time depends on the state of dryness they have reached; it can be as little as 15 mins or as much as 1 hr.

The most common traditional uses are in soups, the Soupe au Pistou of Nice and its area, and various forms of minestrone from North Italy. This is not necessarily where you want to put your carefully-grown, or hardly-acquired, fresh beans. If you get them frozen, the simplest thing to do is follow the packet instructions, and they are really good simply as a plain veg, maybe with a bit of butter. But what I'd choose as the default is **Tuscan Beans.**

In a heavy pot put **350g. beans, 150 ml water, 4 tbsp. extra virgin olive oil, 3 crushed cloves garlic, 5 fresh sage leaves, salt** and **pepper**. (Note that salt doesn't act on these fresh beans as it does on dried beans, where you should never add salt before the end). Cook at a slow simmer, on top of the stove or in a low oven, for 1½ hrs, stirring from time to time. Add **2 tbs. water** from time to time, just enough to prevent sticking. If your simmer is slow enough, you won't lose any water. At the same time, you want to finish up with no liquid water left in the pot, just swollen beans which have absorbed the oil. Serve with **more olive oil** to dribble over the beans, to taste. The first time you do this, a certain amount of watching over the pot is needed;

after that, you'll have a pretty good idea of how much attention is needed next time. If you don't have sage, try rosemary, or thyme for the flageolets.

Puree of Shell Beans.
Use **plain-boiled beans, or leftover Tuscan beans**. Add **1 or 2 pieces cooked potato**, depending on the amount you have, and mash through a food mill or with a masher or fork. Beat in **double cream**, to give the consistency of a sloppy mash; taste for **salt** and **pepper**, and finish with grated **Parmesan**. You could even brown this under the grill or in the oven, but it's not needed; super on its own.

You can also vary the Tuscan beans by adding 2 tomatoes, skinned and cut-up, at the beginning. If using flageolets, I would also add 1 chopped shallot and use thyme not sage – the flavours are then reminiscent of the Breton dish of haricots, eaten alone or with roast lamb.

Shell Beans with Celery and White Wine.
Fry **a chopped onion** in a **little oil** till transparent; add **350g beans, 3-4 sliced stalks of celery, thyme, 3 tbsp. more oil,** and **a glass of white wine. Salt** and **pepper.** Cook very slowly for 1 hr, adding **water** – not more wine – if needed. You could also try this braise using butter, about 30g. overall, instead of oil; a more Northern flavour. If using butter, I might well add some cream and chopped parsley at the end, to make something you'd need to eat from soup plates, though certainly not a soup. Using oil, though, means it can be eaten cool.

Shell Bean and Squash Stew.
Warming, comforting, autumnal, variable. Start by frying **1 chopped onion** in **2 tbsp. sunflower oil**, adding **2-3 chopped cloves garlic** and **1-2 chopped fresh chilis** when the onion is starting to go yellow. Add about **500g. prepared squash** –I used Delicata when doing this, because that's what I had – **600 ml. stock**, and some **dried herbs – oregano, Italian mix, Provencal mix – or just thyme**. After about 10 mins, add **250g beans, cooked**, and **a tin of tomatoes, or 500g. fresh tomatoes** peeled and chopped. Cook another 15 mins, so all the flavours blend. When nearly ready to eat, add **200g. spinach**, roughly chopped, **or 2 packets of spinach/watercress/rocket** as sold in supermarkets, also roughly chopped. Stir in the greens, taste for salt

and pepper, and serve. I like pesto with this, but it isn't necessary. You can also add in any vegetables you have, like corn, peppers, potatoes – but probably not all at once.

Mushroom and Flageolet Stew.
This is elegant and refined and will impress anyone. First, soak **a small handful of dried porcini** by pouring over boiling water and leaving for ½ hr. or so. Meanwhile, cook **250g. beans** with **extra-virgin olive oil, 2 crushed cloves of garlic, thyme** and **salt** and a little **water,** as for Tuscan beans Leave with a little more liquid than if you were eating them alone.   Also meanwhile, saute **200g. large mushrooms**, sliced, in 2 tbsp. olive oil. When they start to release their juices, add the drained porcini and their soaking water, either sieved through kitchen paper in a sieve, or simply poured on leaving the sediment at the bottom of the soaking basin. **Salt**, and go on cooking the mushrooms till the liquid has been absorbed. Mix beans and mushrooms, and eat with rice or good bread. (Or couscous or pasta, but the first two are better)

Shell beans also lend themselves to filling salads with seasonal flavours – endives of various sorts, fennel, celery, shallots. You can also adapt any of the broad bean salads; I'm particularly fond of the bean/cheese/raw mushroom combination, though there's not much seasonal about it.

Flageolet and Endive Salad
250g beans plainly cooked in water; an **equal volume of some form of endive – Belgian, Batavia, Sugar Loaf chicory**; -- and a dressing of **extra virgin olive oil, wine vinegar, salt** and **pepper**. Very simple and very good. It makes a lovely easy meal with cheese, olives, and good bread.

Flageolet and Celery Salad with Preserved Lemon.
Cook **250g. fresh or frozen flageolets or other beans** in water with **thyme, bay leaf, salt**, and **2 crushed cloves of garlic**. Drain, and remove the seasonings. Mix with **6 chopped stalks of celery, 250g. tomatoes, chopped, ½ a preserved lemon**, diced (you are supposed to use only the rind, but I eat the lot), and **a dozen or so halved stoneless green olives**. Dress with **extra-virgin olive oil, lemon juice**, and

pepper. Taste for **salt** before adding any; there may be enough from the preserved lemon and the olives. Chopped **parsley** if you like.

Flageolet and Roast Fennel Salad.
Cook **250g. flageolets** in salted water, and drain. Leave aside. Cut **1 large or 2 small fennel bulbs** into chunks, keeping the fronds to one side for garnish. Cut ½ a red onion into wedges. Mix these with **½ tsp. salt, the cloves from a head of garlic**, separated but not peeled, and **2 tbsp. olive oil**. Roast until the veg. are soft and lightly browned. When they are cool, mix with the beans, and dress with **oil and lemon**, squeezing the cloves of garlic into the dressing. **Salt** and **pepper**. Garnish with the **fennel fronds**, and **black olives** if you like.

Soupe au Pistou.
Seasonal South-of-France, and variable; no two recipes are the same. This is mine, originally derived from Elizabeth David and Jane Grigson.

Sweat **1 peeled chopped onion** in **2 tbsp. olive oil**, adding **a chopped leek** and **2-3 cloves sliced garlic** after a few mins. Add **500g. tomatoes**, peeled and chopped (or a tin), and then **1 litre water**. Add **200g. green French beans** cut into short lengths, **2-3 stalks chopped celery with the leaves, also chopped, 100g flageolets (or whatever other fresh shell bean you have), 2 small potatoes**, peeled and diced, and **1 medium courgette**, diced. **Salt**, and a **little chopped basil**. When the shell beans have a few mins. to go, add **50g. soup pasta** of whatever sort you have – not too large, but ideally not tiny either. Cook till the pasta is done. Serve with **pistou**, the Nicois version of pesto. Pound, or whizz, the **leaves from a good bunch of basil** with **3-4 cloves garlic**, peeled, **½ tsp salt**, and **50g. grated Parmesan**. Add **3 tbsp. extra-virgin olive oil,** or enough to make a paste. Serve in a bowl so people can spoon this elixir into their soup. Both my authorities recommend grated Gruyere with the soup; I can't agree, and wouldn't have any cheese other than that in the pistou. Chunks of bread on the side seem good to me.

Tuscan Winter Soup.
This is for later in the season than the soupe au pistou, and much heartier. It needs cavolo nero, or Tuscan black cabbage; you can substitute with kale or Savoy cabbage if that's what you have, and call it something else – a Northern soup.

Sweat **3 chopped onions, 3 cloves garlic, sliced, 2 diced carrots** and **2 diced stalks celery** in **4-5 tbsp. olive oil** till soft. Add a **chunk of Parmesan rind, 1 tin chopped tomatoes, 250g flageolets or other, 2-3 peeled diced potatoes, salt, pepper, bay leaf, thyme**, and **1 litre stock or water**. Simmer ½ hr, then add **100-150g. of cavolo nero or other green**, shredded, and simmer 20-30 mins. Pick out the herbs and the Parmesan rind, and taste for seasoning. Serve with grated **cheese**, and **extra-virgin olive oil** to dribble into the soup. It's very comforting.

Rustic Pasta and Beans.

The Italian influence here is clear, but in this form it is Italian-American, and very hearty. The beans are prepared in advance, then mixed with strips of mi-cuit tomato and just-cooked pasta, garlic in oil is poured over, and the whole is topped with Mozzarella and smoked Mozzarella. Given my prejudice about Mozzarella, I'd use Caerphilly or Wensleydale, and smoked Cheddar, but you don't have to agree with me or conform.

Cook **250g beans** as for Tuscan beans, using **thyme** not sage, and adding **a strip of lemon zest, ½ tsp ground allspice**, and **a whole dried chili**. If you have dried chipotles, this is very good here. Leave it a little wetter than usual, to moisten the pasta. When done, mix in **6-8 mi-cuit tomatoes** (or your own roasted tomatoes, cut in strips), and **350g. pasta (spirals, shells, butterflies), cooked**. Reserve a little cooking water to thin the mix, if needed. Heat **2 tbsp. olive oil**, and cook in it **12 (or more) sliced cloves garlic**. When the garlic starts to brown, tip the lot over the pasta/bean mix, and mix in. If too dry (taste), add enough reserved pasta cooking water to let down. Add cubes of **100g each Mozzarella and smoked Mozzarella**, and quite a lot of chopped **parsley**.

Non-vegetarians can cook sausages, cut them up, and mix in – chorizo is good. But it's not necessary.

Pasta with Shell Beans, Walnuts, and Crème Fraiche.

Another pasta dish, but this is mild, gentle, subtle, rich .

Cook **4 chopped shallots** in **25g butter** till soft. Add **2 finely chopped cloves garlic**, some chopped **herb** . .thyme, basil, tarragon, or parsley if that's what you have, **200g flageolets**, and **150 ml. stock or water**. Cook gently about 10 mins, then add a **small carton of crème fraiche** and stir in. **Salt, pepper, chili flakes** if you like. Add **50g chopped walnuts**, and stir. Meanwhile, cook **350g. pasta** of your choice, drain, and mix with the sauce. Serve with grated **Parmesan**.

You can make shell beans into risotto, tarts, add them to savoury bread puddings, bake in savoury custard. I think their flavour is good enough, and delicate enough, that they are better in simpler dishes.

Sweetcorn

I love good corn on the cob. I also have strong views about corn in England, so I will allow my prejudices, built on experience, free rein. In the US, they say that you can walk down the garden to pick your corn, but you should run back – to the pan of boiling water waiting for it. Corn bought in the US from a farm stand, picked that morning and eaten in the evening, is brilliant; you can make a meal of 2, 3 or more cobs of corn, and want nothing better. In an English supermarket, the poor cob is picked, stripped of its protective husks, wrapped in plastic, and trucked about the country for an unknown number of days. It is just a token of what corn should be, and barely worth eating when you've tried the real thing. And the supermarkets know it. I've heard that there will be corn picked on the day of sale; I haven't seen any yet. At its best, corn on the cob is one of the best vegetables in the world; try to get it as close as you can to this state. It must stay in its green fresh husks until just before you cook it. It must be picked that day, or at worst the day before. And it needs – o nutritional theorists – lots of butter and salt to eat it with.

Once you have your **fresh corn in its husk**, bring a large pan of **salted water** to the boil. Strip the cobs of their husks, and pull off the "silk" threads that cling to it. Drop it in the water, and boil 5-7 mins depending on how long it's been picked. Lift out, serve with hot plates, **butter**, **salt**, and a plentiful supply of paper napkins or towels. There are little skewers you stick in either end; have no truck with them. Eating corn on the cob is a physical, hands-on experience, and you should abandon manners and wallow in it.

I believe that corn barbecued in its wrappers reaches the same gastronomic heights, and I'm really sorry that I have never managed to try it. I hope you will be able to. My best sources tell me that corn should be barbecued for 15-20 mins, after folding back but not removing the husks, taking off the silk, and folding the husks back over. You can also wrap corn, husked or not, in heavy duty foil for barbecuing.

A frugal note; corn cobs make a very good addition to a stock. Even if you're roasting or sweating the stock vegetables, don't do this to the corn cob. Just add to the simmering liquid.

American cookbooks are full of corn dishes where the kernels are cut from the fresh cob with a knife, spurting juices the while. Don't kid yourself that we can do it here – unless you grow it in the one summer in five or more that it will ripen. (I am basing this on experience in Sheffield; maybe it's more frequent in the South of England) Unless you can get truly fresh corn, you are better off making these dishes with frozen corn, which is prepared and frozen very quickly after picking. It is more like the real thing than anything you'll buy from a supermarket or a veg. box. If you have fresh corn cobs and want to strip the kernels, then hold the trimmed corn upright and run a knife down the rows of kernels at a low angle, pressing quite hard. When you've done this, use the knife to extract any further kernels still stuck. A moderate cob will give you about 100-120g kernels. There are American gadgets specifically for stripping kernels from the cob; ask a visiting friend to bring you one as a present, or find a kitchen-gadget shop if you are there yourself. They are full of useful gadgets we don't have here; my favourite is a tiny box grater for nutmeg.

As for baby corn, I think it's a joke. Sure, it looks pretty, and its texture isn't bad. Taste? Well, none. Dishes can look tempting to eat without this expensive and pointless garnish.

Succotash.
One of my favourite things to do with corn kernels. This is a cut-down version of what started life as a very macho, meat-and-veg cauldron for large gatherings, but in this cut-down form it's both good and useful. Cook, separately, **200g each broad beans and frozen corn**. Soften **a small onion** in **20g butter**, add the drained veg, and cook gently for a couple of minutes while turning them to mix well.

Sauteed Corn and Green Peppers.
You need about **350g. corn kernels**, fresh from the cob or defrosted frozen. Cook **2 large onions**, chopped, in **50g. butter** over fairly high heat until they are softened. Add **1 chopped green pepper**, and cook another 5 mins or so. Add the corn, reduce the heat, cover, and cook about 8 mins more. Add **salt, pepper**, and **paprika** to taste.

Indonesian Fried Sweetcorn.
Mix **1 small chopped onion, 2 –3 sticks celery**, finely chopped, and **250g corn kernels**. Heat **3 tbsp. oil** in large frying pan, add mixed veg, and stir-fry for 3-4 mins. Add **1 egg**, beaten with **salt**, and continue to stir until the egg is nearly cooked. Turn onto serving dish and sprinkle with chopped **green coriander leaves. A little fresh chili** can go in with the veg. at the beginning.

Corn with Tomatoes and Herbs.
First make a tomato stew as follows; cook **a dozen spring onions**, thinly sliced, and **1 chopped clove garlic** in a **mix of 1 tbsp. oil and 15g. butter**. When they are soft, add **500g tomatoes**, peeled and chopped, and **thyme, parsley, and tarragon**, all chopped. **Salt.** Cook gently about 5 mins. Stir in **350g. corn kernels**, cover, and simmer 10-15 mins. Taste for **salt**, add **pepper**, add **another 15g butter**, and more chopped **parsley**.

Yellow Corn and Courgette Saute.
Ideally, this is made with yellow courgettes or other yellow summer squash, so the whole dish is golden-coloured. If you only have green courgettes, don't worry; it is only the appearance, not the taste, which is affected.
Heat **25g butter**, and add **1 finely chopped, seeded, green chili**. Before this browns, add **4 thinly sliced small courgettes**, **salt**, cover, and cook 5 mins. Add **200g corn kernels**, stir to mix, then add **50 ml. double cream**. Turn up the heat, and cook until the cream has thickened and coats the vegetables. **Pepper**, taste for **salt**, and garnish with chopped **chives** and chopped **fresh green coriander**.

These last 4 recipes all have corn kernels with other vegetables, and there is no limit to the number of veg. that can be used this way. Mushrooms are obvious, peas, broccoli, carrots or braised shallots are all possibilities.

You can also make lovely salads with corn kernels. If you have fresh corn, cook extra cobs when boiling, and scrape off the kernels when cool. If frozen, cook the kernels briefly, and drain well.

Spicy Corn Salad.

You need **500g. corn kernels** for this, which serves 6 or more. If frozen, defrost. Heat **1 tbsp. oil** in large frying pan, and add **1 or 2 green chilis**, seeded and diced, the corn, and **a little salt**. Cook at medium heat till the corn is tender – about 8 mins for fresh, 4-5 for frozen. Put in a bowl and toss with **2 tsp. white wine vinegar, the juice of a lime, ¼ tsp or less of cayenne or other powdered chili**, and **salt** to taste. Let cool. Add **1-2 spring onions**, thinly sliced in rounds, and **18 or so halved cherry tomatoes**. This can be finished with chopped **herbs**, parsley or fresh green coriander, or maybe fennel. As well as a salad, it can be a relish or salsa with Mexican or other dishes.

Corn and Feta Salad.

A very simple mix; **cooked corn kernels, spring onion in rounds, radishes ditto, chopped peeled (or not) tomato**, with a dressing of **extra-virgin olive oil, vinegar, salt** and **pepper**. Crumble the **feta** on top – about ½ the weight of the corn.

Sweet Potato and Corn Soup

Many sweetcorn soups are too sweet and bland to my taste, especially the Chinese ones. This recipe balances the sweetness with heat from the chilis, but, though good, it still isn't in my top rank. See what you think.

Cook **1 large chopped onion** in **25g. butter** till it is brown. Add **1 tsp. cumin, ground**. Peel and dice **1 kg. sweet potatoes**, and cook, separately, in **1 litre vegetable stock** till tender. Add the onions, and deglaze the frying pan with a little of the liquid. Puree in a blender or food mill. Add **500g corn kernels, 1 diced red pepper**, and **2 chopped seeded green chilis**, and **1 tsp salt**. Add **300 ml. milk**, and simmer till corn is tender. (5 mins or less for frozen) Add **juice of 1 lemon, 2-3 tbsp. cream**. Taste; if hot and sweet are not balanced to your taste, add **Tabasco**. This is enough for 8, and only needs a sandwich or salad to complete a meal.

Corn Risotto.

All these corn dishes are improved as the corn you use is better, but this risotto depends on good corn for its quality. You need about **1 litre lightly-salted vegetable stock**, and it will help the corn flavour if you have used corncobs in the stock. Or just simmer cobs in already-made stock for 20 mins or so. You need **200g corn kernels**; whizz half

303

of them in the food processor until roughly chopped, then mix with the remainder. Now proceed as for any risotto; soften **a small chopped onion** in **25g. butter**, add **200g risotto rice** and stir a couple of mins. Add **150 ml. dry white wine**, and let it be absorbed/evaporate. Add a ladle of the stock, and all the corn, to the rice, and let it be absorbed. Continue adding stock and stirring regularly till the rice is done. Finish with grated **Parmesan** and **a knob of butter**, and eat straightaway.

Corn Pudding.

This, like corn on the cob, really needs fresh corn. If you haven't got good corn, do something else. Scrape the ears from **4 corncobs, giving you about 500g. kernels**. Mix with **300 ml. whipping cream, 1 tsp. sugar, salt** and **pepper**. Pour into a buttered baking dish, and dot **25g. butter** over the top. Cook at 130 for 40 mins or so, until lightly browned on top. Serve alone.

Corn and Chili Pancakes.

As well as corn kernels, these also use cornmeal, or polenta flour. See below for more on this. Mix **250 ml. coarse cornmeal** with **60 ml. milk**, and stir till mixed. Bring **120 ml. milk** to the boil in another pan, add the cornmeal mixture, and stir till the mixture thickens, 2-3 mins. only. (It's reminiscent of making Horlicks; the powder has to be wetted before the hot liquid is added.) Pour into a mixing bowl, and let cool a little. Then add **25g. butter, 1 tsp. baking powder, 1 tsp. salt, 2 eggs, ½ a chopped red pepper, 6 spring onions finely chopped, 1 seeded chili finely chopped**, and **4 tbsp. plain flour**. Stir. Add **100g. corn kernels**, processed to break them a little. Stir again. Cook small ladlefuls of this mixture in a non-stick frying pan with a little oil, on a moderate heat. Turn when the bottom is lightly browned, and brown the second side also. If you make small pancakes, several can be cooked at a time. Keep them warm, and serve with **sour cream**.

Corn Fritters.

Make a fritter batter. For the one I use, separate **1 egg**. Mix **80g. flour, 1½ tsp baking powder, the egg yolk**, and **4 tbsp. each milk and water. Salt** and **pepper**. Beat the **egg-white** stiff and fold in. Then mix in **100g. corn kernels**. Don't leave this to stand, as the baking powder starts to work as soon as it is wetted. **Deep-fry** tablespoons of the mixture until gold. This go well as an accompaniment to many sorts of dishes, -- try them with a lentil-based stew, for example -- or can be eaten alone with a relish or salsa. If you make more fritter batter, and divide, you can dip onion rings in the non-corn part to go with the corn fritters.

Corn, Bean and Squash Stew

A combination of three basic foods of pre-Conquest America, though not as they would have made it. Roast **2 tsp. cumin seeds** under the grill, or in a small dry pan. Grind with a **5-cm piece cinnamon stick,** and **4 cloves (the spice)**. Add **1 tsp dried oregano, 1 tsp. salt**, and **1 tbsp. ancho chili powder**. Fry **a large chopped onion** briskly in **4 tbsp. sunflower oil** for 2-3 mins, then add **4 chopped cloves garlic** and the spices. Cook for 1 min or so, then add **1 tin tomatoes**, broken up, and cook 5 mins. more. Add **500g. squash, probably butternut**, peeled, seeded and chunked. If it becomes too dry, add a little water. Cook 40 mins, until squash about half done, and add **1 tin red beans or pinto beans**, drained and rinsed, **350g. corn kernels**, and **2 fresh chopped green chilis**. Continue to simmer until the squash is cooked. Thin with more stock if needed, or boil down a little if there is too much liquid. Taste for **salt**, sprinkle with **fresh chopped green coriander**, and serve.

Corn Custard.

Melt **1 finely chopped shallot** in **15g. butter**. Add **1 finely chopped green pepper** and **3 green chilis**, seeded and finely chopped. Cook gently 5 mins, and add **half of 350g. corn kernels**. Cook uncovered another 5 mins, stirring often. Whizz, in blender or food processor, **the other half of the corn** with **2 flat tbsp. flour** and **60 ml. milk**. Beat **3 eggs** in a large bowl, and add both parts so far, the pepper mix and the blended mix. Add **salt, pepper, grated nutmeg, 150 ml. double cream**, and **100g grated strong Cheddar**. Pour into a buttered souffle dish, and bake this standing in a dish of boiling water for 45 mins at 130, or till set. Let it stand before serving warm or cold. Bread with texture is needed with this for contrast, and a green salad is good as well. If you separate the eggs, whip the whites after everything mixed and fold them in, and bake at 150 for 30-35 mins, you have **Corn Souffle**.

Chili Corn Bread.

Although called a bread, it's really a rich bake, and can be eaten alone with just a salad or accompanying vegetable. Whizz **250g. corn kernels** with **200 ml. milk**, to break them up a little – you don't want a puree (Alternatively, you can use a tin of cream-style corn, in which case add the milk to the eggs.) Mix the corn mix, **2 eggs, 100g. strong Cheddar cut into small cubes, 200g. cornmeal or polenta meal, 50g. melted butter, 3 seeded chopped green chilis**, and **2 roasted red peppers** cut in strips. Add **½ tsp. bicarbonate of soda**, and about **1 tsp. salt**. Tip into a buttered baking dish, and sprinkle with **60g. grated Cheddar**. Bake at 170 for 40-50 mins, till a skewer comes out dry. You can eat it hot from the oven, or cooled.

New Mexico Quiche.
Line a 23-cm (9") tart tin with shortcrust pastry and bake blind. (Basics). Cook **1 small onion** in **20g butter** on moderate heat till transparent, and add **200g. corn kernels. Salt, little chili powder**. Cook 5 mins or till the corn is cooked. Let cool, and mix in **2 chopped fresh green chilis**, and **quite a lot of chopped oregano** – by that I mean about twice what you'd normally put in as a herb. Beat **3 eggs** with **150 ml. double cream**, and **salt**. Sprinkle **a little grated Cheddar** over the bottom of the tart shell, put in the corn mix, and pour over the egg mix. Sprinkle with **more grated Cheddar – about 50g. overall**. Bake at 130 for 35-40 mins, till the quiche is set and the top lightly browned.

Almost all these recipes are based on North or South American recipes, because this is where the creativity has been. You can look for Italian recipes, or French, and find nothing. Apart, of course, from Italian uses of cornmeal or polenta. Cooking polenta, or its equivalent, to make a form of cornmeal mush is common across Southern Europe; mamaliga in Romania, for example. I've only given recipes in this book for polenta/cornmeal as an auxiliary ingredient, but there could be whole books on using it.

Sweet Potatoes

I have some doubts whether sweet potatoes belong in this book. They CAN be grown here -- the Organic Gardening catalogue sells slips of 2 varieties, but emphasises the need for warmth. They are really a sub-tropical crop, but then, honestly, so are tomatoes. I think my dubious feelings about sweet potatoes come from the relentless pushing they are receiving from supermarket magazines and TV chefs, who seem to want us to think that they are a more stylish substitute for potatoes. Most of the supplies I see are imported from the US. I really don't want to contribute to a move to supplant a basic staple, which grows well and easily here, for a globally-traded import. This is politics not gastronomy. But even gastronomically, do we need encouraging to have more sweetness in our food? Sweet potatoes are noticeably sweet even when cooked simply, and lots of American recipes add sugar or maple syrup or other sweeteners. You can even have a Thanksgiving casserole of sweet potatoes baked with marshmallows.

So, with reservations, a few recipes for sweet potatoes treated simply, just in case you live in the South of England and grow them, or know someone who does. Or just think that sometimes, this flavour and texture is exactly what you want.

Default. Baked Sweet Potatoes
Bake them, as for baked potatoes. Allow **1 sweet potato per head, or 2 if small**. Scrub clean, prick the skin, and cook at around 170 till soft when squeezed Time depends on size; they take a bit less time than ordinary potatoes, so say 40-60 mins. Split open and eat with **butter, and/or cheese, or soured cream with chives**. Greek yoghurt, alone or with vegetables in it – some form of raita, in fact. Sweet potatoes respond to the warmer spices, like cinnamon and nutmeg, or chili.

Roast Sweet Potatoes.
Peel and chunk the **sweet potatoes**, and mix with, as a minimum, **1 red onion per large sweet potato**. Peel and quarter the red onion. Add **2 or more unpeeled garlic cloves per sweet potato** – you can go as far as a whole head, halved crosswise. Mix these with **2-3 tbsp. olive oil per sweet potato, salt and pepper**, and roast at 180. They will be done earlier than you'd expect, probably in about half an hour. So far

so good, but roasted vegetables are better when there's a mixture. Try **red peppers**, seeded and quartered, and **carrots**, peeled and chunked, for a brilliant-coloured psychedelic effect. Or try them with chunks of **large mushrooms and cauliflower florets. Or courgettes** – often lots around in a late-summer garden.

Mashed Sweet Potatoes.
Peel and chunk, and boil, steam or microwave the sweet potatoes. Do not discard the cooking water if boiling, as you'll need it to thin the mash. Mash as for potatoes – in order of preference, mouli, ricer and fork. Add a **big lump of butter, salt** and **pepper, ground cinnamon or nutmeg or mace or allspice** to taste, and beat with **some of the reserved water or milk** until they are the consistency you like.

Roasted Sweet Potatoes in Salad.
1 medium sweet potato per person. Peel and cut into bite-sized pieces, and toss in roasting dish with **½ tbsp. olive oil for each potato. Salt** and **pepper**. Roast at 180 for about 30 mins, until the cubes are tender and the outsides brown. Meanwhile, make the dressing. Put in a food processor or blender **6 tbsp. extra-virgin olive oil, for 4 potatoes**, and add the **zest and juice of ½ an orange (or 1 mandarin or similar), juice of 1 lemon**, and **1 tbsp. sherry vinegar**. Add **a red pepper**, seeded and chunked, **a fresh chili**, seeded and cut up, and **3 chopped spring onions**. Add **½ tsp. allspice, ground (or a mix of black peppercorns and cumin, ground, if you don't have allspice) Salt**, but not pepper. A **small bunch of parsley or mint**, leaves only, roughly cut up. Whizz the whole lot together to a puree. Taste and adjust for salt, acidity, heat -- you might like another chili if the first was mild. When the sweet potatoes are cooked, put in a bowl and add 6 tbsp. of the dressing, and mix. Add more dressing if needed. You can eat it hot or cold. This is a terrific dressing, and any leftover from this salad will easily find a home with another. Try it with beetroot, for example. Or with cooked white dried beans.

Sweet Potato Salad with Couscous.
Prepare **150g couscous** according to the packet – that is, simply cover the couscous in a bowl with boiling water or stock, cover, and let it stand for 5 mins until the liquid is absorbed. Peel and dice about **400g sweet potato**, and steam, microwave or boil until tender. Drain well, and mix with the couscous. Add **1 red pepper**, seeded and diced, and

1 red onion, chopped. (I like red onion for salads to be mellowed by soaking in cold water for 15-20 mins before draining and adding to the salad.) Make a dressing with **6 tbsp. extra-virgin olive oil** and **2 tbsp. balsamic vinegar (or other good vinegar), salt** and **pepper**, and dress the salad with most or all of this. You can simply sprinkle with chopped **parsley or chives,** or you could add some **toasted nuts or seeds.** Toasted pecans or Brazil nuts would go with the American origin of the sweet potato, as would toasted pumpkin seeds.

Sweet Potato, Butternut, and Coconut Soup.

Full of exotic flavours, and very good. Heat **2 tbsp. sunflower oil** in a large pot, and add **2 tbsp. green Thai curry paste.** Stir for 3-4 mins, then add **1 medium chopped onion, 2 outside sticks of celery**, peeled and cut up, **2-3 tomatoes**, chopped, or half the contents of a tin. Let these sweat gently, covered, while you prepare **500g each sweet potato and butternut squash**, that is, peel, seed the squash, and cube. Add to the pot, add **½ tsp. salt**, and sweat 10 mins more, stirring now and then. Add **500 ml stock**, and simmer, covered, for 20 mins or until the sweet potato and squash are cooked. Let it cool a little, and blend to a puree in liquidiser or food processor or mouli. Put back in a clean pan, reheat, and stir in **400 ml. coconut milk**. Taste for **salt,** add **pepper if needed**, and sprinkle with chopped **fresh green coriander** to serve.

Sweet Potatoes and Beans from the Baker's Oven (Boulangere)

Cook your own dried beans, **200g. borlotti beans**, for this, or use part of a double batch cooked for something else. (See Basics for soaking and cooking dried beans). Drain them, keeping the liquid for stock. Add the **leaves of 5-6 stems of thyme** to the beans – that is, a lot. **Salt** and **pepper**; if you've cooked them yourself there will be no salt, so you need ½ tsp or more. Add **1 tbsp. mushroom ketchup**, and **½ tsp. ground cinnamon.** Put the beans in a baking dish. Peel **3 medium sweet potatoes**. Halve them lengthwise, and cut into thin half-moon slices. Arrange the slices over the beans, overlapping, and making a pattern. Pour over **250 ml stock**, and dot the top with **30g butter**. Cover the top with foil and bake at 150 for 60 mins or more, until the sweet potato slices are cooked and the stock is mostly absorbed. Let it cool a little before serving, or you can eat it cool.

Tomatillos

Or Mexican green tomatoes. They are not tomatoes at all, but are related to Physalis. They come as rather sticky green or yellow spheres surrounded by a papery husk. They are usually 2-5 cm. across. Perhaps they don't really belong here, as you can't yet buy them here – though maybe you can in London. But they grow so willingly and easily for me, and they produce such lively dishes, that I can't resist.

In Mexico, they are always cooked before using them, but you don't have to do this. If you decide to cook first, strip off the husks, and simmer gently in salted water for 10-15 mins, depending on size. Drain. Because they are usually cooked, tins are OK if you can find them. In the US, you can buy cans of "green tomatoes" quite easily. I think these will gradually become available here. You can substitute ordinary underripe – not entirely green, but starting to turn – tomatoes, and add lime juice to give that acid quality that tomatillos have. But do try growing them; many pretty yellow flowers, brownish husks on the fruit, and a really unusual product. They don't seem to have any pests – well, they won't, as they are so unusual.

Default; Tomatillo Salsa.
Rinse about **500g tomatillos**, and chunk them.   Whizz in the food processor with **1 small chopped onion, ½ cup green coriander, ¼ tsp sugar, 2 green chilis chopped, 1 tsp. salt,** and the **juice of 1-2 limes**. Taste; it may need more lime juice. Serve chilled. You can use this as a dip; with avocados; with rice; with Mexican-style chili beans; or as part of the spread for a **Tortilla Meal**.
What I do for this is have various fillings ready on the table, like **refried beans, sliced avocado, tomatillo salsa, grated cheese, shredded lettuce, maybe pickled jalapenos from a jar**, and **sour cream** for topping. Toast the tortillas (corn or wheat) on a griddle, so they become pliable and get brown patches on each side. Sometimes they puff up, which is great, even though they collapse again before eating. Then each person can take a tortilla and fill it as they like, putting sour cream on top or not. It makes a very convivial meal, as foods involving the diners often do.

Tomatillo Salsa with Ancho Chilis.

A variant, well worth trying. I have referred to ancho chilis elsewhere, for their moderate heat, deep fruity flavour, and long-keeping qualities. Tear apart **3 ancho chillies**, removing stem and seeds. (There are so many seeds it is worth keeping them, and using them for heat in other dishes). Soak the chili pieces in **boiling water to cover**, letting them stand ½ hr or so. Then whizz in blender with their water. Put in frying pan, to encourage evaporation. Add **1 chopped onion, 250g. tomatillos halved, 3 garlic cloves**, and **1 tsp. salt**, and simmer until the mixture seems slightly thickened. Add **1 tsp cumin seed, ground**, and some **fresh green coriander**, roughly cut-up, and whizz the whole lot in the food processor. If it is too thick, let it down with a little water. Same uses as the other salsa.

You can also make an unusual and delicious **Chili con Queso** with this. When it is smooth in the food processor, whizz in **a packet. Philadelphia cream cheese**. A large packet softens the taste more; a small packet gives you more oomph. My family dotes on this, scooped up as an appetiser with bread, tortilla chips, or crudités.

Potatoes in Tomatillo Sauce.

Boil **500g. baby potatoes** till nearly done, and drain. Whizz **500g. tomatillos** with **2 deseeded green chilis, 1 tsp salt, handful of green coriander** in the food processor. Fry **1 chopped onion** in **1 tbsp. oil**, add **2 chopped cloves garlic** and **1 tsp cumin seeds, ground**, then add the puree. Cook for 10-15 mins, then add the potatoes and cook 5 mins. more. **Lemon or lime juice** to taste. This will go with rice or, cross-culturally, with couscous, as well as being eaten alone.

Tomatillo and Squash Soup.

This is based on a recipe from Anna Thomas' book, "From Anna's Kitchen". Roast **700g tomatillos, husked and halved**, with **500g. halved red tomatoes, 2 large onions** cut in wedges, and **a dozen cloves of unpeeled garlic** at 200 until the veg. are soft and starting to blacken in spots. Quarter and seed enough squash to give **700g. prepared squash** – Anna Thomas says Kabocha, but whatever squash you can get is fine, and it will probably be butternut. Roast the squash on another tray . When the roasted veg. have cooled a little, scoop the soft squash from its skin, skin the tomatoes, and squeeze the garlic from its skin. Chop **2 fresh seeded chilis**. Whizz squash, onions, tomatillos, tomatoes and garlic with the fresh chilis and some fresh **green coriander** in a food processor, in 2 batches if necessary. Turn into a pan, and thin down with **½ to 1 litre. vegetable stock or water**. **Salt** to taste, probably about 1 tsp for this amount if there is none in the stock You might like some **lemon or lime juice**. Reheat and serve. If you are not using fresh tomatoes, 1 tin chopped tomatoes, not roasted, is a good substitute.

Tomatillo Pizza.
Slice horizontally **6 large tomatillos,** and **salt** and **pepper** them. Have ready 1 **batch of fast easy tomato sauce** (in Tomato section), or other tomato sauce, reduced till thick, and with **extra chopped garlic** added after reduction. (Try 1 clove of garlic to start with, but I like about 4) Grate **100g. Cheddar** with **100g. smoked cheese**. Have ready a **12"** **pizza base** (see Basics chapter). Pour **1 tbsp. olive oil** on to the dough, and spread it all over with your fingers. Then spread with the tomato sauce, and lay the tomatillos dispersed over the top. Spread the cheeses over the top. Bake the pizza, 15-20 mins at 220.

If you have more tomatillos than this, look in cookbooks from California, and on Mexican food.

Tomatoes

Tomatoes are so familiar, and come in so many forms, that hardly a day goes by without using them in some way. And even raw tomatoes come in a host of varieties and sizes, from cherry and currant tomatoes to giants weighing 1 kg.. or more. My seed catalogue has 51 varieties, and there is a small book available covering 100 of the best varieties. And this just for the UK! Think, though; each tomato variety has a slightly different taste, and probably a different balance of micro-nutrients, which we don't yet know enough to specify. An argument, at least, for eating lots of different kinds when possible.

Organic tomatoes, as bought, are one of the foods where I can't say the taste is superior. There are other arguments for buying organic, but for me taste is one of the most important. It's probable that the tastier varieties yield less, and with the premium on organic veg, a lower-yield variety isn't seen as commercially viable. It's a pity; my own organic-grown, when I do get any, are superior in taste to any shop-bought.

Practically every cookbook will moan about the flavour of supermarket tomatoes, especially in winter. I disagree strongly. I find that if I choose among the most expensive tomatoes in the supermarket, I can have flavourful tomatoes all through the winter. And I eat a tomato salad almost every day. Yes, cheap ones are symbols of tomato, even in summer, rather than the real thing, so don't buy them. Encourage the growers producing good ones.

As for tomato products, I would feel badly understocked if I didn't have tinned whole tomatoes, tinned (or Tetrapacked) crushed tomatoes, tomato paste, tomato ketchup (the new expensive ones, like Tiptree, are preferred to Heinz by my family.) Sometimes I also have passata and sun-dried tomatoes. They are a staple in my cooking, not just an ingredient.

Tomatoes sometimes need peeling. Generally, I like tomatoes with skins for raw dishes, and peeled tomatoes for cooked ones. To peel tomatoes, pour boiling water over the tomatoes in a basin. Let them stand 10 secs if very ripe, 1 min if red but under-ripe. Pour off the water and pull off the skin; it hardly ever needs a knife even to start the process.

If you have cherry or small tomatoes, think before doing anything. Piled up on a plate or in a bowl, they encourage people just to nibble, without any seasoning or dressing. More than one colour is even more appetising.

Tomato Salad.
Simply slice the **tomatoes**, in half vertically and then into wedges, sprinkle with **salt** and **½ dsp. extra-virgin olive oil per large tomato (or 8 cherry)**, stir around, and eat. Amounts: I eat 150-200g by myself, but hardly anyone else does. If you allow about 80g per head, that should give about the right amount. More conventionally, you can add a drop of vinegar, pepper, a little sugar – but my way gives you most tomato flavour. I find that I eat this with a spoon when I'm alone. You can add herbs; basil is classic, mint is good and a bit unusual, parsley is fine, chives are good. But for everyday what I want is tomato, oil, and salt.

Tomato Salad with Fried Almonds.
Cut up **500g tomatoes** and mix with chopped parsley. Fry **40g split almonds** with **1 tsp lightly ground coriander seed** in **2 tbsp. olive oil**, just till the almonds brown. Tip into the salad, and add **a little oil and vinegar dressing**. This is a good party buffet item.

Three absolute classics: salsa, Greek salad, and salad with melon, cucumber and avocado.

Tomato Salsa.
Chop about **500g. tomatoes**. Chop finely **½ red onion, 3 cloves garlic, some fresh green coriander**, and **2 chopped seeded green chilis** with **½ tsp salt**. Or whizz in the food processor, adding a little tomato to help it all pulp. Mix the pulp into the tomatoes. Taste. You might want a little cider vinegar to sharpen it, but I usually prefer it without. It can be very liquid; drain it if you want a conventional salsa. Goes, as a side relish, with almost everything. Just don't taste too much so it's all gone before the meal!

Greek Salad.

The way I ate it every day on holiday in Crete. In a bowl assemble a layer of sliced **cucumber**, a layer of sliced **green pepper**, a thin layer of sliced **red onion**, and a lot of sliced **tomato**. Put a lump of **feta** on top, and sprinkle the feta with **dried oregano**. Have **extra-virgin olive oil and lemon** ready to dress the salad, but let people do it themselves. It's better with Mediterranean ingredients and a Mediterranean ambience, but it's pretty marvellous at home with the best ingredients you can find.

This has attracted the attention of the creative cook, and I've seen suggestions to substitute fennel for cucumber, or use roasted peppers. These are probably good, but they are not the accepted version in Greece.

Tomato, Melon, Cucumber, and Avocado Salad. ***

For 6 people you need **500g cherry tomatoes**. Cut in half. Cut up **half a medium-size ripe melon** into chunks about the size of the tomatoes. Likewise ½ **a cucumber**. Halve, peel, and cut into chunks **2 or 3 ripe avocados**. Put them all into a bowl, and add **6 tbsp. oil-and-vinegar dressing**. Stir well, and chill for a couple of hours. Eat from soup plates with spoons. This is an excellent starter for a summer dinner for friends.

Panzanella

I'm very fond of this salad, which is basically tomatoes with soggy bread. Depress your friends' expectations by calling it this, and they will be so relieved and pleased when they get to taste it. You need **good bread which has gone stale – about 250g**. It can be wholemeal, country bread, ciabatta, but DON'T use white sliced. Anyhow, break this bread into chunks. You can decrust it if you like, but I don't. If it's really hard, you should soak it in water for a few minutes, then squeeze out the excess. If it's 2-3 days old, you don't need to soak. Add **1 thinly sliced red onion, ½ cucumber**, cubed, and **700g to 1 kg. tomatoes**, cut up roughly. Add **a dozen leaves basil**, cut into strips, and **2 tbsp. capers**. Mix together, then add **5 tbsp. extra-virgin olive oil, 2 tbsp. wine vinegar, a little salt**, and **pepper** to taste. Because this is a country salad for using stale bread, it is enormously variable. You can add garlic, or green olives. Chopped celery is a good addition. At the River Café they add roasted peppers in 2 colours to their

Panzanella. If you aren't vegetarian, 2-4 anchovy fillets are very good. Serve in soup plates with spoons.

People wishing to avoid the peasant connotations of using-up-stale-bread started making this salad with fried or toasted bread cubes. Use a little less bread, say 150g., cut into crustless squares, and fry them in olive oil; reduce oil in dressing almost to nothing. Or toast bread, decrust, and cube. Otherwise proceed just as for Panzanella. I prefer chopped spring onions to red onion in both these salads. This refined version hasn't yet got a proper name. Call it **Tomato Salad with Croutons.**

Tunisian Salad.

The name indicates that harissa is used in the dressing; otherwise I doubt its authenticity. But it's very nice. Slice **1 kg. tomatoes** crosswise, and chop the end pieces. Arrange the slices on a plate or shallow bowl. Put **1 thinly sliced red onion**, separated into rings, on top, and scatter with **a few sliced radishes**. Make the dressing in a small bowl; mix **1 tsp. French mustard, ½ tsp harissa, 1 tbsp each wine vinegar and lemon juice,** and **8 tbsp. extra-virgin olive oil.** Add to the dressing the chopped tomato end pieces, **2 chopped spring onions, salt** and **pepper**, and quite a lot of chopped **parsley**. Drizzle it over the salad.

Italian Tomato and Cheese Salad.

The classic among these is Italian, and its colours of red, white and green remind Italians of their flag. **Sliced tomatoes, sliced Mozzarella, green basil slivers,** and **oil and vinegar.** I've said several times I am not enamoured of Mozzarella, but here no substitute makes sense.

English Cheese-and-Tomato salad

Use **500g. tomatoes, 100-200g. cheese – Cheshire, Wensleydale, Caerphilly all better than Cheddar here – 6 spring onions.** Cube the cheese, cut the tomatoes into pieces about the same size, chop the spring onions. Mix well, dress with **oil-&-vinegar**, and serve surrounded by **watercress.** Doing a little fusion, it also goes well stuffed into warmed pitta breads!

Red Bean and Tomato Salad.

Cook **100g dried red beans** as usual, drain, let cool. Or use a tin; drain and rinse well. Add **1 chopped red onion** and **200-400g tomatoes**, chopped. Dress with **oil-and-vinegar dressing**, with few dashes **Tabasco** added, and garnish with fresh **green coriander**, chopped. Very good, very filling; a main-dish salad. **Olives** and **celery** would both go well; so would **pickled jalapeno chilis**, for those who like them.

Tomatoes and bread come in enough different forms to deserve a special section. Most often you read about the Catalan **Pa amb Tomaquet,** which is probably best on its home ground. There they have better and more suitable ingredients than we do. Even with English bread, tomato, garlic it's worth a try, however.

You need **large slices of a rough-textured country loaf** – not wholemeal, not white, but in between. Soak some **chopped garlic** in **extra-virgin olive oil – should be Spanish.** Toast the bread, brush or otherwise distribute the garlicky oil on it. Then take **a large halved very ripe tomato** and rub onto the toast – you see why it has to be coarse textured bread, because it's almost like a grater. You should end up with saturated toast, and just the skin of the tomato. A marvellous starter for barbecue meals.

Pan Bagna

French Mediterranean in origin, it was designed for picnics. I usually use **baguettes**; if you get the half-baked ones in the supermarket, on average one per person is about right. Bake and split in two lengthwise. You can use a large round country loaf for 4-6, or chunky rolls halved. If using the loaf, halve across the middle and scoop out quite a lot of crumb to make room for the filling. Rub the inside of whatever you are using with **garlic**. Mix **chopped tomatoes, chopped stoned black olives**, and chopped **red or green pepper. Salt, not much, pepper; 1 tbsp. olive oil per baguette, and 1 tsp vinegar for each**. Spoon onto the baguette, cover with the other half, and roll tightly in foil or tie with string. Put them under a weight (bread board + few tins) for an hour or so, or just transport to your picnic. There are many possible additives well in the spirit of the dish, such as gherkins, celery, prepared artichokes from a jar, capers, a few thin French beans . . just not all at once.

317

English Tomato Sandwiches.
You need good bread; the kind matters less than the quality. Do you want them thin and refined, or coarse and chunky? Refined sandwiches need peeled tomatoes, cut very thin. Chunky sandwiches can take unpeeled tomatoes in thicker slices and be rather messy to eat. Butter or mayo? I like to use mayo with horseradish added. Salt will help the juices to run, which will be absorbed better by the bread if you only spread one slice with butter/mayo. A thin sandwich with butter, little Marmite, tomatoes, is very much an English taste – don't give them to Americans, none of whom (of those I've met) can stand Marmite. A sandwich with tomatoes and hard-boiled egg is another classic. But like so much in the English repertoire, they are good if you have good materials, whereas a sandwich with cheap sliced bread, margarine, and cheap tasteless tomatoes will be awful. Though there are probably people who like the latter because "it's like my mother made it"

Tomato Toasts with Grilled Goat's Cheese.
Roast **cherry tomatoes** and smear them onto **ready-toasted slices of French bread, roll, or small round loaf.** Sprinkle with **salt**. Put **a round slice from a goat's cheese on top of each slice,** and put briefly under the grill until the cheese starts to melt. Drizzle with **extra-virgin olive oil, pepper**, and eat straight away. A good lunch with a green salad.

Roast Tomatoes
These are so easy to do, and so delicious. You need quite a lot of tomatoes – the best time to make them is when you have bought lots of tomatoes reduced in price. Lightly **oil** one or two roasting dishes. Halve the **tomatoes**, lengthwise for plum tomatoes and crosswise for everything else, and lay them cut side up and close together in the dish. Sprinkle with **salt, pepper**, and **a little more oil**, and bake at 140 for 1-2 hours. Let them cool, and you have a stash of rich-tasting tomatoes for almost anything you want to cook, that won't go off as quickly as the raw ones would. Be sure not to waste any juices or sediment, though in my experience there is very little.

English Fried Tomatoes
These are an essential part of the "full English breakfast", which most people only eat on holiday. I find that a full English breakfast is too much even for lunch, but makes a supper that's very popular with the

family. It is fatty, especially with the fried bread that's also needed, but once in a while that's OK. Cook the tomatoes towards the end of the process, after eggs, mushrooms, potatoes, and fried bread, all of which are keeping warm. Thick slices, cooked fairly quickly on both sides, until cooked all through – it takes longer than you expect, every time. Salt only when done.

Talking of the fry-up, when I was a child I loved the very last component in a fry-up, which was fried cheese. Thin slices of Cheshire or Lancashire were put in the pan, in the flavoured oil left behind after everything has cooked, and allowed to melt and ooze. It isn't healthy, but the memory makes my mouth water, and I've never come across this since I grew up.

I like fried tomatoes by themselves, on unbuttered toast, as well.

Spicy Tomatoes on Toast.
Cook **1 finely chopped clove garlic** gently for 1 min. in **25g. butter** in a smallish frying pan. Add **3 medium tomatoes**, cut in half, cut side down, and cook 10 mins, turning a couple of times. Sprinkle with ½ **tsp garam masala.** You could cook a chopped **chili** with the garlic, if you are really fond of spicy food. Meanwhile, toast a **thick slice of bread**, and spread with **mango chutney**. Tip the tomatoes and their juices over the toast, and eat. This is obviously for 1 person yearning for a snack or fast light lunch.

Indian Fried Tomatoes.
Authentic, and using small amounts of several whole spices. Have ready **12 fenugreek seeds, ¼ tsp cumin seeds, ¼ tsp. fennel seeds, ¼ tsp. black mustard seeds**. Peel and chop **1 kg. ripe tomatoes**. Heat **3 tbsp. oil** in a heavy pan with a cover. The oil should be mustard, but the last few years I've found this hard to get hold of. Use sunflower oil if no mustard oil. Add the spices. When the mustard seeds pop, tip in the tomatoes, shake, and cover. After 1 min, add **1 tsp salt, ¼ tsp cayenne pepper**, and **1 tsp dark brown sugar**. Replace lid, and cook on low heat for 10 mins. This is a splendid, quick, side dish for a curry meal. Or, for a snack, eat on toast or with naan bread.

Broiled Devilled Tomatoes.
Cut **4 medium tomatoes** in half, and grill them skin-side up, then cut-side up, in a dish one notch down from the grill. When well-cooked, spread them with a mixture of **3 cloves garlic**, pounded to a paste with

a little salt, **1 heaped tsp. Dijon mustard**, and **1 tbsp. olive oil**. Grill again till the top is bubbly and golden. This is good if you have to deal with large but unripe tomatoes.

Tomatoes a la Provencale.

Obviously best with large, juicy, misshapen Mediterranean tomatoes, but still very good with large commercial tomatoes sold on the vine. Halve **eight large tomatoes**, and put cut-side up in an oven dish, lightly **oil**ed. **Salt** and **pepper**, and sprinkle with **2 tbsp. olive oil**. Cook in the oven at 170 for about 30 mins. Meanwhile, chop finely **4 cloves garlic** and **a good handful of parsley**. Mix with **1 thick slice of bread**, crusts cut off, and made into breadcrumbs. Take the tomatoes out of the oven, and put the breadcrumb mix thickly over each top. Grill until the topping is gold and slightly crisp.

Chinese Stir-Fried Tomatoes.

Tomatoes only caught on in China during the 20th century, and they treat them in a characteristically Chinese style. As with all stir-fried dishes, everything is prepared before any cooking starts.

Skin and quarter **8 medium tomatoes**. Cut **a 10-cm piece of cucumber** lengthwise into slivers. Chop **2 peeled spring onions**. Finely chop **2 cloves garlic** and **2 slices ginger**, peeled. Mix **3 tbsp. soy sauce, 1 tbsp. hoisin sauce**, and **2 tsp sugar** together. Chop some **fresh green coriander** for garnish.

Now heat **2 tbsp. oil** in a wok or large frying pan, and add the garlic, ginger, and spring onion. Stir 30 sec, then add the cucumber, and stir-fry for 2 mins. Add the tomatoes, with the soy sauce mixture, and stir gently for 2 mins. Add **2 tbsp. dry sherry or white wine (or rice wine if you have any)**, cook another min. or so. Stir in the chopped green coriander, and serve as one of the several dishes making up a Chinese meal. Or, if you are not being so authentic, with an omelette or a baked dish of beans.

Tomato Soup.

I have difficulty with my family about tomato soup; they all prefer Heinz. This is not that the soup you/I/one makes isn't often nicer/better, but Heinz is the way they think tomato soup should taste, and they reject all deviations. So the limited number of soups here aren't even the same sort of thing. For more tomato soups, and more tomato recipes than you will ever get round to, Lindsay Bareham's Big Red Book of Tomatoes is the place to look.

Gazpacho

Assemble in a large bowl **1 cucumber**, coarsely chopped; **1 onion**, peeled and coarsely chopped, **1 green pepper**, seeded and chunked, **4 cloves garlic**, peeled and slice; **2 thick slices good bread**, decrusted and broken up; **700g tomatoes peeled and chunked, or 1 tin tomatoes**; **3 tsp salt**; **600 ml. water**; **3 tbsp. wine vinegar**; **2 tsp tomato puree**; **3 tbsp. extra-virgin olive oil.** Whizz this in batches in a blender, filling a serving bowl with the puree. When all is done, stir the soup in the second bowl well, and taste for seasoning. If too thick, add a little more water. Chill, covered. One is always told to serve it with garnishes of bread cubes, cucumber, and onion, all finely chopped. I never bother, and I don't think the soup is any worse for it. Unbeatable for lunch on a really hot day; excellent at any time.

Acquacotta.

Or "cooked water", but don't let that put you off, as it is thoroughly flavourful and restoring. The most authentic versions are a thin vegetable soup with toast and egg added at the last moment, but more modern versions miss out the toast and eggs. This is a peasant version; change as you will. Peasants, after all, use what they have, and don't have written recipes.

Fry **2 chopped onions** in **5 tbsp. olive oil** till golden. Add **a stalk of celery**, diced small, and **a small dried chili or 2. Salt** and **pepper**. Cook another 5 mins, then add **1 kg. tomatoes**, peeled and chopped. Cook 15 mins more, then add **1 litre water**; bring to boil, and simmer 20 mins. Poach **4 eggs** in the soup, and scoop each out on to **a slice of toasted country bread** in each soup plate. Add chopped **basil** to the soup. Pour the soup over the bread, and sprinkle with grated **Pecorino or Parmesan**.

Standard variations: 1. Add other vegetables with the celery, such as **courgettes and/or peppers.**

2. Use **15g. dried porcini**, soaked beforehand in hot water for ½ hour. Add the chopped porcini with the celery; use the soaking water, filtered through a kitchen towel or cheesecloth, as part of the cooking water.

3. Add chopped mint instead of, or as well as, the basil.

4. Omit the eggs.

Italian instant tomato soup.

This is based on, but not identical to, Elizabeth David's Minestra di Pomodoro in her Italian Food. I find it most useful for unexpected guests; something to eat, quickly available, reassures them that they are welcome, and that a meal is coming. It also means that no-one drinks too much while waiting.

Cook **2 chopped cloves garlic** briefly in **1 tbsp. olive oil**. Add **a tin of chopped tomatoes** and some fresh **basil or parsley**, chopped. Cook 5 mins, then add **600 ml. vegetable stock, or water + Marigold. Salt** and **pepper**. Cook 5 mins, and it's ready. Meanwhile toast lightly some **bread, English, French, Italian, or what-have-you**; cover thinly with grated **cheese, ideally Parmesan**, and toast under the grill until the cheese is melted. Cut into smallish pieces and serve with the soup. The toasts are meant to go IN the soup.

Tomato Sauces.

Oh dear. Lindsay Bareham, in the Big Red Book of Tomatoes, has at least 35 tomato sauces. Marcella Hazan has a good dozen in her various books on Italian cookery. I will assume that you would like a standard, fast, easy tomato sauce for pasta; a more complex one for other dishes as well; and a raw sauce for pasta. But remember, there is a whole world of variation out there as well as these.

Fast Easy Tomato Sauce.

Put the **contents of a tin of tomatoes** in the blender. Add **a slurp of olive oil, 1-4 cloves garlic, peeled, salt** and **pepper**, and **dried oregano or fresh basil or fresh parsley**. Whizz. Cook quite quickly, stirring every now and then, for about 10 mins. while the pasta cooks.

Raw Tomato Sauce for Pasta. You need **700g best tomatoes**; ripe, sun-ripened indeed. Peel them. Add **6 tbsp. best extra-virgin olive oil, some chopped basil, salt** and **pepper**. Stir, and let it sit for at least 30 mins. When the pasta – for 6 – is cooked and drained, stir the tomato mixture into it and serve immediately. This does not need grated Parmesan.

Long-Cooked Complex Tomato Sauce.

Chop **1 large onion, 1 carrot**, and **a stalk of celery**, and sweat them in **2 tbsp. olive oil** for 10-15 mins on low heat. Add **2 cloves chopped garlic**, and some **thyme** and chopped **parsley**. Leave another few mins, then add **1 kg. tomatoes**, peeled and cut up, and **2 tbsp. tomato paste. Salt** and **pepper**. Cook very slowly, covered, for up to an hour, stirring from time to time. If not thick enough by then, turn up the heat a little and reduce to the right consistency. Taste. You might need not only more salt and pepper, but a little sugar.

Tomato Omelette.

Use **leftover tomato sauce**, and boil it down till really thick. Cook a 1-person omelette (**2 or 3 eggs**) in olive oil, and spread about **1 tbsp. of the warm reduced sauce** over it when nearly ready. Roll and serve immediately.

If you want to have the zing of raw tomatoes with an omelette, I'd make a salsa, and serve it by the side rather than inside. A herb or vegetable omelette would be good, one with tiny fried croutons and herbs as filling would be even better.

Tomato Risotto

For this, for 4 people, you need **a batch of fast easy tomato sauce**, above. If you have super tomatoes, make the sauce with 700g of them, peeling and chopping in the blender as if tinned. Keep the sauce hot while making the risotto. Also keep hot about **1 litre vegetable stock**; you may not need it all. Warm **1 tbsp. olive oil** in a heavy-bottomed frying pan, and cook **1 small chopped onion** in it until it is transparent. Add **200g. risotto rice**, and stir for about 3 mins. Pour in **100 ml, or a small glass, of white wine**, and stir as it is absorbed. Add a ladle (or half mug) of the heated stock, and keep the pan just simmering as the rice absorbs the stock. Then add a ladle of tomato sauce. Keep adding the stock and the sauce alternately, stirring often; if the sauce runs out, just add the stock, until the rice is ready. If it is completely dry, add a little more stock, and some grated **Parmesan** and **25g. butter**. Stir vigorously, scatter with slivered **basil leaves**, and serve immediately. This tastes rich, subtle, and comforting.

Tomato Charlotte

The principle of this is that tomatoes are layered with flavoured breadcrumbs and baked. Top breadcrumbs become crisp; lower down the juice penetrates and is thickened.

Melt **50g butter** in frying pan, and in it cook gently **100g. fresh breadcrumbs**, from decrusted bread. **Salt** and **pepper, herbs – thyme or oregano** are good here. When the breadcrumbs have absorbed the butter and it starts to separate, it's ready. Peel and chop **700g. tomatoes**. Layer crumbs and tomatoes in a baking dish, starting and finishing with crumbs. Add **a little sugar** to the tomatoes unless they are really ripe. Dot the top with **butter**, and bake at 160 for 30-40 mins. If you use brown breadcrumbs, it becomes **Brown Tom.**

You can vary the breadcrumbs in any way you'd make a stuffing – onion, lemon rind, or lots of chopped parsley.

Tomato Bread and Butter Pudding.

This can also be called Tomato Strata if you want to sound American.

Make tomato sandwiches with **thin slices good bread, butter, tomato slices**, and **tomato ketchup**. Layer them in a baking dish with chopped sauteed **mushrooms**. For 3 rounds of sandwich and 350g mushrooms, beat **3 eggs** with **300 ml milk**, and pour over the sandwiches. Let it stand at least half an hour, and then bake at 150 until done and gently browned on top. You can, obviously, add cheese to this, either in the sandwiches or sprinkled on top, or indeed both. A homely dish that's surprisingly good.

Tomato Tart.

There are many ways of making this. You can do it quiche-style, with the tomatoes in a rich custard. You can use puff pastry rolled thin and cut individually, and top with slices of tomato. This is my favourite way.

Start with **a cooked tart shell, 23 cm (9") diameter** (see Basics chapter) Brush the base with **1 tbsp. Dijon mustard**. Spread some fairly thick tomato sauce, about **1 recipe of fast easy tomato sauce**, over the mustard, and then cover this with **thin slices of 300g tomato**. Sprinkle with **salt** and **pepper**. Grate **100g Gruyere or middle-aged Gouda**, and sprinkle over the top. Bake at 160 for about 20 mins, until the cheese is bubbling and slightly brown. This can be a main-course tart with lots of vegetables or salads, or it can be cut up into small pieces as appetisers. Or, of course, you can make tartlets for appetisers; in this case use raw pastry rolled thin, mustard, sauce, and grated cheese. Whichever way, it is always enormously popular.

Mixed vegetable dishes using tomatoes as a main ingredient are all over the book. Look there for **Ratatouille, Pisto Manchego, and Lecso,** among others.

Green Tomatoes.

If you grow tomatoes successfully, you'll have quite a lot of green tomatoes at the end of the season. If you grow tomatoes unsuccessfully, or we have a bad summer, you will have even more. The most I ever had was after summer 2003, where they ripened on windowsills till the end of November, were eaten as below, made every preserve I knew . . .I must have had about 20 kg, from two dozen plants.

If you only have a (comparatively) few green tomatoes, let me urge you to try **Green Tomato Mincemeat.** This is for Christmas mince pies, and it tastes fresher and fruitier than the conventional kind. Also, impeccably vegetarian, without the little drops of fatty stuff in shop-bought vegetarian mincemeat meant to imitate suet. Mince pies made with this green tomato preserve are actually nicer! I've made this almost every year for at least 30 years.

2 kg green tomatoes, 1 tbsp. salt. 3 kg. cooking apples, 2 large oranges, 700g sultanas, 700g light brown sugar, 500g. white sugar, 3 tsp. ground cinnamon, 1 tsp. each ground nutmeg, ground cloves, and ground ginger, 150 ml. wine vinegar.

Wash, drain, hull and chop the tomatoes into pieces about 1 cm. cube. (so a 2-cm tomato will give you eight). Add the salt, and mix well with your hands. Let them stand about an hour, then pour over boiling water to cover. Let them stand 5 mins, then drain.
Wash, peel, core and chop the cooking apples. Mince the oranges. Mix both with the tomatoes, and add all the other ingredients. Cook gently about ½ hr in a preserving pan, until there is no visible liquid. Pot into clean warm jars. Makes about 6½ kg., which will do 21 dozen mince pies of the small size I make. If you don't make that many, a jar of mincemeat is a good little present for friends.

Fried Green Tomatoes.
This is the famous one. I say famous because of the film, not because many people in this country have tried it. Thickly slice **500g large green tomatoes**, crosswise, and use only the centre slices. **Flour** the slices, and fry them in **butter** till browned on both sides. Take them out, and keep warm. Add **150 ml. double cream** to the pan, and cook

gently, scraping any brown bits from the pan bottom. Add **salt** and some chopped **parsley.** When the cream is smooth and thick, pour it over the tomatoes. I bet that at the Whistle Stop Café they used cornmeal, not flour, but it isn't a staple for us as it is in the Southern States. Eat on **toast, or with crusty bread**.

Grilled and Marinaded Green Tomatoes.

4 large green tomatoes, about 600g. Same thick crosswise slices as for fried, discarding top and bottom. Brush with **olive oil**, and sprinkle with **salt** and **pepper**. Cook on a preheated griddle, or under and close to the grill, until browned on both sides. Put in a serving dish, and add **2 tbsp. red wine vinegar, 1 clove garlic thinly sliced, some chopped basil,** and **3 tbsp. extra virgin olive oil**. Stir about. Let it rest 6 hours, or overnight, in the fridge, and eat as part of a spread of salads.

Roast Squash with Green Tomatoes.

1 kg. squash, like butternut or acorn. 700g green tomatoes. 500g each red onions and small potatoes. 4-5 cloves garlic, 2 tbsp. olive oil, salt and **pepper**. Cut all the veg into chunks after peeling, etc. (see notes on cutting squash under that heading) Mix them all together with the oil and seasoning in a large roasting tin. Cook at 180 for about 1 hr. Look from time to time; if they start to look overcooked and charred, stop now. Or, if they are not done, leave them a bit longer. Roast veg. are hard to predict, because it depends on the accuracy of the oven thermostat and the size of the roasting pan. They are always delicious, though.

Green Tomato Quiche

You need a **ready-baked 22-cm tart shell**, (Basics). Chop **200g onion**, and cook gently in **1 tbsp. olive oil**. After 10 mins or so, add **500g chopped green tomatoes**, and cook another 5 mins. Then add **200g grated Cheddar, 200g Hellmann's mayonnaise, 1 tsp. caster sugar, leaves from 6-8 stems basil**, chopped, and **pepper**. Taste; I don't think it needs salt. Spread into the tart case, and cook at 170 for 30 mins till set. Best with several salads, as it's quite rich.

Green Tomato Compote.

This is very sweet, and needs to be eaten with sharp **plain yoghurt**. For each **350g. tomatoes** you need **500g. granulated sugar**. Make the sugar into a thick syrup with **150 ml water**, add the sliced tomatoes, and cook for about 10 min. Serve chilled. One of the last summer fruits.

Green Tomato Pie
This originated in Vermont, and is eaten there with wedges of local Cheddar. (just as apple pie is eaten in Yorkshire with cheese) It's a double-crusted pie. You need **short pastry made from 250g flour** (see Basics) Line a 23-cm (9") pie tin with part of the pastry. Wash, hull, and chop **500g green tomatoes**, and mix with **180g. sugar, 2 tbsp. cider vinegar,** and ½ **tsp each of ground cinnamon and ground allspice**. Put into the pie shell, dot with **25g butter**, and cover with pastry. Seal the edges, trim, and pinch the edge decoratively. Slash the top, and brush with egg or milk. Bake at 160 for about 40 mins. Serve cool, with slices of cheese I prefer yoghurt or sour cream to the cheese; try both.

Green Tomato Chutney.
Most people have a version; this is mine. It is quite a hot chutney.
1 kg. green tomatoes, 500g. dark brown sugar, 300 ml. malt vinegar, 15 cloves garlic (more if they are small) (It doesn't taste garlicky; it does need this much) **4 tsp grated fresh ginger, 15g salt, 1 tsp. black peppercorns, 2 tsp. cumin seed, 10 brown cardamom pods, ½ tsp. whole cloves, 2 tsp coriander seed, 1 tsp cayenne pepper.**
Bash the cardamoms in a mortar or otherwise, and extract the seeds. Grind them together with the whole spices, in a coffee mill or in the mortar with a pestle. Wash and chop the tomatoes. Mix everything in a pan, and cook slowly, covered, until the tomatoes are really soft, about an hour. Stir often, crushing the tomatoes slightly. Put into clean warm jars with vinegar-proof lids – instant coffee jars are good. It keeps well, up to 2 years, and doesn't dry out.

Late Autumn, Winter

Bok Choy

Celeriac

Kale, Cavolo Nero

Beetroot
Bok Choy, etc
Calabrese Broccoli
Brusseld Sprouts
Cabbage
Carrots, Mature
Celeriac
Celery
Chicory
Chicories, Endive
Chinese Leaves
Jerusalem Artichoke
Kale, Cavolo Nero
Lamb's Lettuce
Leeks
Parsnip
Red Cabbage
Salsify
Sauerkraut
Swede
Winter Radish

Chicory

Jerusalem Artichokes

Salsify

Beetroot

We all know beetroot, its regal colour and its usual disgusting taste of malt vinegar. I assure you that none of the following recipes uses malt vinegar, but bring out the sweet, earthy taste of the vegetable itself. The sweet taste is no accident; roots across the family are grown for their sweetness, and local European sugar is derived from a beetroot variety.

Beetroot used to be cooked by greengrocers, boiled in quantity. If you went at the right time, there was a cloud of steam and a distinctive scent, and large beetroot ready to peel and use. As far as I know, this doesn't happen any more. Now you can buy loose roots, bunches with leaves, cooked beetroot without vinegar, and many variations on beetroot with malt vinegar. Foodies will pour scorn on you if you use the supermarkets' ready cooked **plain** beetroot (no vinegar), but I find them good and useful. They have a very long use-by date, so you can keep a packet in the fridge for an emergency for about 4 months. There are also stripy beetroot, very pretty when raw, and golden beetroot, which don't bleed and stain other food on the plate as much as the red. These are usually sold uncooked, and often in bunches with leaves. I've also come across white beetroot, which I find very odd in the discrepancy between its beetroot taste and off-white colour. Flavours of these variants are much the same, perhaps with a bit less sweetness.

Sometimes beetroot is eaten raw, but not often. Usually it's cooked, either boiled or baked. There is some disagreement among cookery writers as to the best method for flavour, which suggests to me that there isn't much difference, and I can't say that it affects the end result much to my taste. I mostly boil small ones and bake large ones, but it depends on convenience. Because baking large beetroot takes a long time, it's better done when the oven is being used for something else. Whichever, you want to avoid the beetroot bleeding, so leave on the leaf bases at the top of the root, and the long trailing root. Cutting these allows the juices to flow out. Wash the raw beetroot, but don't scrub, as the skins are much more fragile than you'd expect. For baking, wrap each beetroot in foil. Oven temperature doesn't much matter, but avoid too hot or really cool. Test for doneness with a skewer, which should meet no resistance. When the beetroot is done, by boiling or baking, the skin will slide away when pressed sideways with a thumb. Not all of it, so you'll probably need a knife to peel it with, but I find the moment of slide and wrinkle really a pleasure. Cooked beetroot is soft all the way through.

The leaves from bunched beetroots are also good for cooking, but they need to be fresh, not wilting. So use the leaves first if you buy a bunch, and let the beetroot, with the bottom 3-cm of leaf stalks left on, wait a little. The root keeps quite well uncooked. Leaf recipes are at the end of this section, and you can also use the leaves instead of chard leaves in any of the recipes for Swiss Chard leaves.

Default. Cooked Beetroot Salad.
Cut **250g peeled cooked beetroot** into cubes or matchsticks, and dress with **extra-virgin olive oil, lemon juice, salt and pepper**. Proportions of 4 tbsp. olive oil to 1 tbsp. lemon juice. This is perfectly good as it is, but better with the addition of **1 tsp. ground cumin** or other spice before dressing. Finish the salad, if you have time and ingredients, with **chopped fresh green coriander or mint**, and **1 small red onion**, peeled and sliced very thin. This is one of those delightful salads which you can eat often, and vary a little every time without altering the essential goodness.

The default salad is fine alone, but can be varied still further by serving it on or alongside other vegetables, suitably dressed. Lambs' lettuce. Chicory (see chicory for more details) Celeriac matchsticks, blanched briefly, in a mustardy vinaigrette. Broccoli florets, for the amazing colours. Or carrots

Beetroot and Carrot Salad with Moroccan Spices.
Cut **250g each of cooked peeled beetroot and raw peeled carrot** into matchsticks. Blanch the carrots about 5 mins in boiling salted water, if you like. Make the dressing from **1 tbsp. pomegranate molasses, the juice of an orange, a knob of ginger** and **a clove of garlic** chopped very finely, **½ tsp. each cumin and coriander**, freshly ground, **½ tsp salt**, and **1 tbsp. extra-virgin olive oil**. Mix dressing with carrots and beetroot, and sprinkle with chopped **parsley**.

Beetroot, Apple, Celery and Watercress Salad. This is a colourful salad, and is even more so if you can mix red and golden beetroot. If you can't the taste is unchanged.

Boil or roast **500g beetroot**, and peel. Make a dressing; crush **1 clove garlic** in a mortar with **½ tsp. salt**, add **½ tsp. garam masala** and **½ tsp. dry mustard**, then add the **juice of ½ a lemon**. Then beat in **6 tbsp. extra-virgin olive oil**. Mix 2 tbsp. dressing with the beetroot, cubed or cut into wedges, and add **6 chopped trimmed spring onions**. Trim, peel, and slice finely **a celery heart**, and mix with **2 large apples,** peeled, cored, and sliced. Add about **50g walnut pieces**, then 2 tbsp. dressing, and mix. Pick over and wash **80-160g watercress** (that is, 1 or 2 supermarket packets, or 1-2 old-fashioned bunches) Spread the watercress out on a plate or platter, and arrange the beetroot and the celery mix in separate heaps over the watercress. The rest of the dressing can be on the table if anyone wants more.

Beetroot, Walnut, Yoghurt and Horseradish Salad.

250g peeled, diced beetroot; 50g walnuts, dressed with **100ml. yoghurt mixed with 1 tsp. grated horseradish, ½ tsp. salt**. Taste; you may like **lemon juice** with this. Sometimes I do, sometimes I don't. But the beetroot/horseradish combination is classic, and turns up in many different forms. Such a pity that the roots of horseradish are seldom on sale, and you have to grow it to get it fresh.

Sweet and Sour Beetroot Salad.

Most beetroot salads have some sweet-sour element, but they are exaggerated in this, and set off by the bite of horseradish. Make a dressing from **1 mean tsp freshly grated horseradish, or a rounded tsp. preserved horseradish (NOT sauce), 1 tbsp. pomegranate molasses, 1 tbsp. white wine vinegar, ¼ tsp. salt, and 2 tbsp. yoghurt**. Taste and adjust. Add **250g cooked beetroot**, peeled and cubed. You can eat straightaway or leave for some hours. I once used elderflower vinegar instead of white wine vinegar, and this added a flowery scent, so hopeful in midwinter.

Melbourne Market Dip.

This is a dip rather than a salad, and it's lovely. Just don't have a precious tablecloth on when people are leaning over to dip crudités or crisps, etc, into this. Whizz **250g cooked beetroot** in a food processor with **300 ml. yoghurt, juice of a lemon, 2 tbsp. extra-virgin olive** oil, ½ tsp. salt, ½ tsp. **each freshly ground cumin, coriander, and cinnamon, and ½ tsp. paprika or <u>mild</u> (pure) powdered chili**. Taste and adjust. It would keep quite well if it got the chance.

Beetroot, Feta and Mint Salad.

A salad for lunch on one's own; easy and good, filling and hardly fattening. Quantities given are for 4, though. Dice **250g cooked peeled beetroot**, and dress with **2 tbsp. extra-virgin olive oil** and the **juice of ½ a lemon. Pepper**, but no salt because of the feta. Mix in 2/3rds of finely chopped **mint from 4 good sprigs**. Break **200g feta** into lumps and dispose them on top of the beetroot. Sprinkle the feta with the rest of the mint. This lends itself to additional ingredients to make it a more substantial meal; cooked drained lentils are good, and so is couscous. In both cases, mix in the beetroot first, and put chunks of feta on top. You can also add oranges, in slices or segments, to the basic salad, which turns it into a Cretan dish. In this case, sprinkle the feta with dried wild oregano instead of the mint.

Warm Salad with Beetroot, Potatoes, and Blue Cheese.

Start with about **500g raw beetroot**, peel, and cut into chunks – 4 to a small beet, and appropriately depending on size. Wear rubber gloves while doing this. Mix with **3 tbsp. olive oil, 1 tbsp. white wine vinegar, 1 tsp. Demerara sugar** in a small roasting dish, and cook at 200 for 40-45 mins, or till done. Baste 2 or 3 times while cooking. If the pan starts to get dry, cover with foil and turn the oven down a bit. The beetroot becomes quite crisp, and loses whatever makes it respond to acid; it's lovely, and different. After the beet has been in the oven for 20 mins, scrub **250g small waxy potatoes**, and boil them in their skins. Drain when done, and cut into 2 or 4, roughly the size of the beetroot pieces. Mix, and add **50g walnuts, 2 tbsp. walnut oil, about ½ tsp. salt**, and a good grinding of **black pepper**. When it has cooled a little, add **100g (or so) mildish blue cheese – Blue Shropshire or creamy Gorgonzola**, for example. Eat before it gets cold. Enough for 2 as main dish, 4 as side salad.

Beetroot and Potato Salad Dome.

There are times when it's good to present dishes formally, with some ceremony and shape; this dish is one for those times. This sort of presentation is so old-fashioned that it can seem like an up-to-date novelty. It's also prepared well in advance; potatoes and beetroot marinate for 2 days before assembling a dome an hour or more before eating. Cook **350g each salad potatoes and beetroot**, peel, and cut in ½ cm thick slices. Mix them with **6 finely chopped shallots, 150 ml. dry white wine, 2 tbsp. white wine vinegar, salt and pepper** to taste. Leave all for 2 days. On the day of serving, make the sauce/filling. Grate **2 cucumbers, salt,** and let stand in a colander for 15-20 mins to drain. Rinse with cold water, then squeeze them dry. Hard-boil **2 eggs,** shell, and chop finely. Whizz in food processor **200g Philadelphia cream cheese** with the eggs, the cucumber, **2 tbsp. tomato concentrate** from tube (or small tin), **1 finely chopped clove garlic, 3 tbsp. drained rinsed capers, small handful of parsley, chopped, ½ tsp. salt, pepper, Tabasco.** Taste and assess – more Tabasco? More salt? You can add 2 tbsp. brandy at this point, if you like. The sauce should have the consistency of mayonnaise. If making this by hand, you need to add some single cream to the Philadelphia, to thin it slightly. (This sauce is useful for all sorts of other things; a dip, a general salad dressing (not lettuce), with hard-boiled eggs.) Back to the beetroot/potato mix. Drain. Pick out slices of beetroot and potato, which are now pretty much the same colour, and use them to line a medium pudding basin. It will take up to half the veg. to do this. Dice the rest of the beetroot and potato and mix with about half the sauce, adding chopped **chives** and **tarragon**, if you have some. Taste. Pack the salad tightly into the bowl, cover, and chill for ½ hr. at least. Tip out onto serving dish, and use a little more sauce to dribble over the top and down the dome's sides.

Rest of the sauce on the table – or tuck it away for another time.

Of course, you don't have to do the decorative bit; just dice beetroot and potatoes before marinading, drain after 2 days, and mix with the sauce and more chopped herbs. Simpler, less rich because you use less sauce, but, you will admit, not as impressive.

Beetroot and Butter Bean Salad.

120g dried butter beans, soaked and cooked. No salt until they are tender. Drain. Or use the contents of a tin, drained and rinsed; these are salted. Separately, dice about **250g beetroot**, cooked and peeled. Make a dressing with **3 tbsp. extra-virgin olive oil, juice of half a lemon, salt and pepper**, and dress beans and beetroot in their own bowls. When you're ready to eat, mix them very lightly, and serve on platter or on salad leaves. Some onion flavour – **shallots, chives, spring onions** – is a good idea with this; put your choice in with the beans.

Herbs, too, can only enhance the salad. If you want a sumptuous-looking dish, use black beans instead of butter beans, mix beans and beetroot, and add orange segments and chopped green pepper.

I said at the start of this section that raw beetroot is not much eaten, but it's recently been quite fashionable after Nigella endorsed it in How to Eat. Nonetheless, it can have an aggressive taste when raw, which can be good in small quantities, with a sharp dressing to balance the sweetness, or when softened with yoghurt. Try small quantities of these; if you like them, then variations will suggest themselves.

Raw Beetroot with Orange and Cumin.
Add the **juice of an orange** to **3 small raw beetroot**, freshly peeled and grated, just enough to moisten. Toast a few **cumin seeds**, and add to the beetroot with **salt**. Serve as part of a number of small salads.

Raw Beetroot with Yoghurt
Grate **4 small raw beetroot**. Chop finely a small handful of **fresh green coriander**, and **leaves from 4-6 stems of mint**. Mix these into the beetroot, and then mix in **5 tbsp. Greek yoghurt. Salt to taste**. You'll probably find you can eat more beetroot like this than in the last salad. In fact, this is leaning towards a relish, For the full-blown relish experience, try the Central European beetroot/horseradish relish.

Chrain (Jewish horseradish-beetroot relish)
This is a traditional recipe, and proportions of the ingredients vary wildly in different sources. I have settled on **100g horseradish root, 250g cooked beetroot, 1 tbsp. honey or sugar,** and **6 tbsp. white-wine vinegar**. Peel and grate the horseradish; the fumes will make you weep and penetrate nose and sinuses. Grate the peeled cooked beetroot, and mix both with honey and vinegar. **Salt** to taste. Serve in a glass bowl, and store in a glass jar. A Czech friend used to make a week's supply, and it kept well in the fridge. It goes with anything savoury that needs a lift, especially pastries.

Beetroot is mostly used as a salad, but can make a fine hot vegetable with different seasonings. Most versions, but not all, start from cooked beetroot.

Beetroot with Lemon Juice and Capers.
Start with **250g cooked beetroot**, and cut into cubes or matchsticks. Heat the cubes in **30g butter** with the **shredded rind of a lemon**. When hot, add the **juice of the lemon, 2 tbsp. drained rinsed capers**, and chopped **parsley**. No salt needed because of the capers. This can also be done with a salted lemon substituting for both lemon rind and juice.

Beetroot with Ginger and Cumin.
Cut **250g cooked peeled beetroot** into matchsticks, and heat them in **30g butter** with a **knob of ginger**, peeled and finely chopped. A little **salt**, and **½ tsp. ground cumin** seeds. It's slightly nicer if you toast the cumin seeds before grinding, but you might feel that this is too much hassle for such a small amount. Eat as it is, or add a little Greek yoghurt just before serving.

Beetroot with Yoghurt and Juniper.
Cut **250g peeled cooked beetroot** into chunks. Warm **5 tbsp. yoghurt** in a small pan with the **juice of ½ lemon, pinch salt**, and **12 or so crushed juniper berries** (mostly these are soft enough to crush with finger and thumb, saving on washing-up, but a pestle and mortar do a better job.) Add the beetroot, warm through on low heat, eat. Divine scent of gin! If you are doing this in summer, and have the plant, a very little **angelica leaf**, chopped, aids the resemblance still more.

Beetroot with Pistachio Sauce.
Wrap about **700g whole beetroot** individually in foil, and bake. Oven temperature here depends on what else you are cooking, and time on size of beetroot, but a rough guide would say that medium beetroot will take about an hour at 180. Unwrap just enough to test with a skewer; if there is no resistance, the beetroot is done. Meanwhile, heat **4 tbsp. sunflower oil** in a small frying pan, and add **4 cloves of garlic**, peeled and roughly chopped. Add **150g pistachios** – not the shell-on salted cocktail sort, but shelled and green. Cook gently 2-3 mins. Let cool. Add **1 tsp. salt**, then whizz in food processor, adding **4 tbsp. more oil**, and more if needed. You are aiming for a paste which is just pourable. When the beetroot are done, peel and chunk, salt and pepper, and spoon the pistachio sauce on top. Warm or cold.
This recipe has lots of variations; the vegetables can be any winter root, like carrot, swede, parsnip, Jerusalem artichokes; the nuts can be

335

walnuts, hazelnuts, almonds. The nut sauce keeps well and can be used with almost any roast veg. or with pasta.

Beetroot a Russian Way.

Start by poaching **10-12 baby onions**, peeled, in **250 ml. stock**. Fish them out when done. Thicken the stock; melt **20g butter** in a small pan, add ½ **tsp. caraway seeds**, then **1 tbsp. flour**. Blend into roux and cook gently 5 mins; the aim is to colour the roux without burning, but this is much harder with such a small quantity. When your nerve breaks, or when there is the first sign of burning, add all the stock at once, stirring vigorously. Simmer 5 mins or so. Then add **600g cooked beetroot**, peeled and chunked, the onions, and **2 tbsp. red wine vinegar**. Taste for salt (depends on your stock). Finish with ½ **tsp. sugar. 1 tsp. or more finely grated horseradish,** and **2 tbsp. sour cream.**

Beetroot and Cranberries.

The cooked beetroot are reheated in a spicy cranberry sauce. The amount of sauce given here is far too much for the amount of beetroot, but it isn't possible to make less, and the rest can be used with many other dishes. For the sauce: **200g cranberries**, picked over, washed and put in a saucepan with the **zest and juice of an orange**. Add **60g sugar** and **1 tbsp. clear spirit – vodka, gin, white rum** – what you have. Cook gently. When the cranberries start to pop, add **1 seeded chopped chili**, and cook about 5 mins, stirring. Taste; I think it needs a little **salt,** about ½ tsp. It may need another chili, depending on the heat of the first. Take about **4 tbsp. of this sauce** for reheating **250g beetroot**, and keep the rest in the fridge (to go with potato cakes, stuffed pancakes, gratins?) Taste the reheated dish; it may need lemon juice, or possibly a little sugar if you have a sweet tooth. If you have pickled damsons, sieve some of these and use instead of the cranberries. Because there is no butter in this, it can be eaten cold, but hot is nicer.

Beetroot Crisps.

Commercially available in packets at a ridiculous price, and very nice. You can do better, fresher, cheaper. Peel thin slices from raw peeled beetroot with a swivel-action peeler (rubber gloves) Deep-fry, a few at a time, drain well, and eat. This is not difficult.

Beetroot Soups. One of the uses most associated with beetroot, and for good reason. The word Borscht springs to mind, and this Eastern European soup comes in multiple variants. The most wintry variants are meat-heavy, but there are many lighter versions which are, and should be, impeccably vegetarian.

Vampire's Passion (Blender Borscht)

Mix in a bowl **500 ml tomato juice, 600 g cooked beetroot**, peeled and chunked, **3 pickled cucumbers (the large, dilled, Polish kind)**, chunked, **1 small chopped onion, few shakes Tabasco**. Whizz in a blender in batches. Chill. Serve with chopped **hard-boiled eggs** and **sour cream** to garnish.

Winter Borscht.

In its best form, this is for people who brew their own beer and occasionally find some has gone sour. What we have then is alegar, or vinegar made from ale – tasty and not too acid. If you haven't got this, use mostly water with cider vinegar to taste. As for me, once I'd tried this soup I used to let some beer sour every time I brewed.

You need **16 young raw beetroot, or about 700g**. Peel them (rubber gloves) and cut 12 of them small. The chipping disc of a food processor is ideal for this, but when I made it regularly I didn't have a food processor and did it by hand. Cover these beetroot with **600 ml. alegar**, and let them soak several hours. Then sweat **2 onions** chopped finely, **2 medium carrots** ditto, and some chopped **parsley** in **40g butter**. When they are soft, stir in **30g flour**, turn up the heat a little, and colour the vegetables and flour. Add **2 litres good stock, 2 bay leaves**, and **salt** depending on stock's saltiness. Bring to the boil. Drain the beetroot, keeping about 200 ml. of the marinade to one side. Put the beetroot in the soup, and simmer all till the vegetables are cooked. Now grate the remaining 4 beetroot, mix with the reserved vinegar, add to the soup, and serve fairly promptly. The last-minute addition of the alegar and the raw beetroot brighten the colour. Lots of **sour cream** with this.

If you haven't got sour home-made beer, use cider vinegar. The 600 ml. alegar is replaced by 150 ml cider vinegar, made up with water to 600 ml. Otherwise proceed as above.

In its Polish home, winter borscht goes with little stuffed patties, pirozhki. I've never got on with these, good though they can be, because the soup seems to me enough. If you want to try the effect

337

without too much effort, try some mushroom ravioli cooked separately and added to the soup by those who want it. For the whole number, Anna Thomas' first book, The Vegetarian Epicure, has a good version of pirozhki.

English Beetroot Soup.

Not all beetroot soup is borscht, and sometimes one wants a more conventional flavour. Try this one. Peel and chop **1 medium onion, 2 cloves garlic**, and a **small knob of ginger**. Sweat them in **20g butter**. When soft but not coloured, add pounded **seeds from 2 green cardamoms**, and **700g raw beetroot**, peeled and chunked. Stir well and leave a moment, then add **1 litre water, 2 bay leaves, 2 sprigs thyme, parsley stems,** and **1 tsp. salt**. Simmer till the beetroot is done. Let cool, pick out the herbs, and make the soup smooth in your favourite way -blender, hand-held blender, mouli. Now add the **juice of an orange**. Assess the thickness, it may well need thinning with more water to your favoured consistency. Taste for salt and sweetness and adjust if necessary. Reheat, and serve in hot plates with a swirl of **cream** and **croutons**. You could add the cream to the soup, but in this case I think the swirl looks so good that it's preferable.

Beetroot is seldom used as the chief component of a main dish, and this seems a great shame. Here are some examples. They are all good, but I wouldn't say they have reached their classic form yet. (An example of a new classic is broccoli and Stilton soup. Perhaps you know something has become classic when debased commercial versions appear?)

Pasta with Beetroot.

Have ready **700g beetroot**, cooked, peeled, diced. You also need some caramelised onions, from **1 lb. onions**. If you're doing this from scratch, see Onion section for detail; in outline, peel and slice 1 lb onions, sweat in a covered pan with **30g** butter on low heat until they start to turn gold and are soft, which will take 45 mins or more. Then take off the lid, raise the heat, and let the onions brown, stirring often. Because this takes time, though not much effort, I tend to make a lot at once, use some, and freeze the rest in useful-size batches. So you may have some in stock. Or you can sidestep the process and buy them in jars. Whichever, warm the onions through and add the beetroot while the **pasta (400g for 4 people)** is cooking. Just before the pasta is ready, dip out a mug of water from the pot, to thin the sauce if you like. Drain the pasta, return to the pan, and mix in the onions and beetroot. Lots of freshly ground black pepper. Serve with grated **Parmesan**. If you prefer – and I do – omit the Parmesan, and add small pieces of **soft goat's cheese or ricotta** to the pasta and sauce. This is thoroughly unexpected, and very good indeed.

Beetroot and Celery Risotto.
Cook gently **a small chopped onion** in **40g butter** in a large frying pan. Add **300g raw beetroot**, peeled, quartered, and finely sliced, and **4 stalks celery**, peeled and sliced. Stir and let cook 3-4 mins, then add **300g risotto rice**. Cook, stirring, for 2-3 mins, then add **100 ml. dry white wine**. Let this evaporate, then add a ladle of stock from a simmering pan of about **1.5 litres stock**, barely salted. Stir and cook over moderate heat. When the pan is nearly dry, add another ladle of stock, and go on until the rice is cooked. You may have some stock left over. When very nearly ready, add **pepper, a knob of butter, and a handful of grated Parmesan**, stir vigorously, and serve. The **rind of a lemon chopped with parsley** sprinkled on at the last moment improves it, but it's fine even without this. A green salad on the side is almost necessary, preferably with rocket for this combination. The risotto's colour is simply amazing with raw beetroot, but I've made it with ready-cooked, where the colour doesn't bleed but the taste is still terrific.

Red Flannel Hash (American)
I assume the name relates to the colour being like that of red flannel underwear. Cook **500g potatoes**, peel if you didn't do it first, and cube. Cube **250g cooked beetroot** and add to the potatoes. Add **1 finely-chopped large onion. Salt, quite a lot of pepper, and 100 ml. double cream**. Mix the lot, and tip into a deep frying pan with **30g butter** already melted in it. Cook slowly, turning every now and then (turning portions, rather than the whole mass), until it is brown on both sides and shot through with browned bits. Serve with a fried or poached egg on top, and either tomato ketchup or HP sauce. This is a meal for family and children's friends?

Beetroot and Potato Gratin.
You need a large shallow ovenproof dish for this. Peel **300g raw beetroot**, and slice thinly. Peel **500g baking/boiling potatoes**, and

slice thinly. Arrange in layers in the buttered gratin dish, seasoning each layer with **salt and pepper** as you go. Pound **1 clove of garlic** with ½ **tsp. salt** in a mortar, and add **150 ml. double cream** to the mortar. Tip into **500 ml. milk**, and stir well. Pour this mixture cautiously over the layers in the dish. It should just cover the top layer; you may not need it all, depending on your dish. If you need more, just add more milk. Bake, uncovered, at 150 for up to 2 hrs, until a knife point slides through the layers with no resistance. The top should be richly brown   I know that gratins should be done with all double cream, but I find this far too rich. The use of milk is not meanness, but actually makes the dish better for modern tastes. It's pretty good as it is; have some fruity chutney with it. If you put a sprinkle of ground spice – nutmeg or cardamom – in with the pepper, this really ups its rating.

Beetroot and Stilton Quiche.

Line a 22-cm (9") pie tin with **short pastry from 250-g flour** (Basics), and bake blind (Basics) Cut up **250g cooked beetroot** quite small, and spread over the bottom of the pastry case. Beat **2 eggs** with **150 ml. double cream** and **up to ½ tsp. Tabasco or crumbled dried chili**. Crumble in **100g blue Stilton**. Pour this mix over the beetroot, and cook at 150 for 30 mins, or till set. Eat warm and fresh. You will note there's no salt or pepper here; the cheese is salty, and I don't think chilis and pepper go together in the same dish.

Beetroot Curry

Peel and grate **500g raw beetroot**. Rubber gloves are a good idea; so is wearing an apron, and grating on the draining board so splashes can be easily washed away. Heat **2 tbsp. sunflower oil** in a pan which has a lid. When hot, add ½ **tsp. black mustard seeds**, and let them start to pop. Then add **1 chopped onion, 4 chopped cloves garlic**, and **2 seeded chopped chilis** (red are better here, just for the colour). Fry till the onion is starting to brown. Add the grated beetroot, stir, and add a spice mix of **2 tsp. coriander seed, 1 tsp. cumin seed, 3-cm cinnamon stick, and 1 tsp. black peppercorns**. Stir again, add ½ **tin of chopped tomatoes, ½ tsp. salt**, and **100 ml. water**. Simmer, covered, till the beetroot is cooked, probably 15-20 mins. Stir in **100 ml coconut milk**, and cook a few mins. more. Add the **juice of a lime**. Taste and adjust if necessary. If you have no raw beetroot, you can make it with 2 packets, 400g, cubed. Either way, I like it so much I try to have some left over, for a lunch salad, cold, the next day.

Beetroot Greens. Beautiful, reddish-green leaves with crimson veins. As I've said above, these have to be used when really fresh – otherwise they go sad and droopy, faster than most greens. Fortunately, they need only brief attention to turn them into a cooked form which can then be used for all the dishes below. So when you get your beet greens from the garden, or home from the market, wash them, strip out the thick stalks. Boil about 3-cm depth salted water, and stuff the greens into the pan. Cover, and cook 2 mins. only. Drain, rinse with cold water, drain again, squeeze dry in a teatowel, and chop roughly or finely according to taste. They don't cook down as much as spinach; you get about half the volume of the original leaves. To eat them as greens, cook **1 small chopped onion** in **30g butter**, add the **cooked greens from 1 bunch beetroot** and warm through, **salt and pepper**, and serve. Or use garlic and olive oil, or shallot and butter. Beet greens are one of the nicest of the dark green leaves, mild, with almost a sweet edge. To make more of a main dish from them, try the following, but they are very good alone.

Beet Greens in Cheese Sauce.
For **blanched chopped greens from 2 bunches beetroot**, make cheese sauce with **30g butter, 20g flour, 200 ml. milk**. (Basics) **Salt, pepper, nutmeg.** Let the sauce cook on a low heat for about 5 mins after it has thickened, then take it off the heat and add about half of **100g grated Cheddar**. Mix this sauce with the greens, and spread out in a gratin dish. Sprinkle the top thickly with the other half of the grated cheese, and cook under the grill until the top is bubbling, and goldeny-brown. If you've made the mixture in the gratin dish ahead of time, it's better cooked in a hot oven –200 – for 15-20 mins.

Beet Greens Soufflé.
White sauce and cheese again, but transformed by the magic of air expanding in beaten egg whites. Make a white sauce as above, with **30g butter, 30g flour, 200 ml. milk, salt, pepper, nutmeg.** Put this in a food processor with **chopped cooked beet greens from 1 bunch beetroot**, and whizz. Add **50g. grated cheese** (usually Cheddar, but I once tried Sage Derby and it added greatly to the complex flavour) and **3 egg yolks**, and whizz again. In another bowl beat **3-5 egg whites** with a **pinch of salt** till stiff. Put the puree from the processor into a bowl, add about ¼ of the beaten whites to the puree and blend

341

together, and then mix the lightened puree back into the egg whites. Tip and scrape the soufflé mix into a buttered dish, and run a finger round the edge of the mix, which helps the rise. Bake at 180 for 30 mins, till it is puffed and golden.

Beet Greens and Goat's Cheese Tart.

This is a simple assembly job. Roll puff pastry (Basics, or bought) into a rectangle about 20 x 30 cm, and turn over the edges to make a low wall. Brush the tops of the edges with **egg** or milk, and bake at 200 till fully cooked. Have ready **cooked greens from 2 bunches beetroot,** and heat through in **2 tbsp. extra-virgin olive oil** with **2 finely chopped cloves garlic**. Spread these over the tart. Dot over this **100g or so soft goat's cheese**, probably a little French or English log. Drizzle over a little more **oil,** sprinkle with chopped **marjoram or parsley**, and warm through in the turned-off oven. A green salad may seem redundant with the greens in the tart, but I think it's needed.

As well as all these, if you have a glut of beetroot you can make cakes with it or make preserves. Nigel Slater has a beetroot and chocolate cake which sounds really good.

Bok Choy and Other Chinese Greens

It seems to me that bok choy, and similar greens like choy sum, are one of the best new vegetable introductions to this country. They grow well here, and English-grown ones can be found in supermarkets. They are mild-flavoured, tender, non-challenging, exotic, fast and easy to cook, good to eat. And pretty, the sight of tender green leaves on succulent stems is enough to make one's mouth water.

Bok choy (also known as pak choy) is probably the commonest, and can also be found as baby bok choy, which are even more pretty and tender and sweet. One of the few baby vegetables for which there seems to be good reason (Baby spinach is another) There is choy sum, which has longer green leaves and tight little flower clusters. This can be found in Sainsbury's, though not other supermarkets round here so far. There are shungiku, or chopsuey greens; mizuna and mibuna, "green in snow" or mustard greens, tatsoi, Chinese broccoli, and more. These have the potential to become very fashionable, as well as being tasty and nutritious, and I expect to see ever more kinds coming from gardeners, growers, getting into vegetable boxes, available from supermarkets . . . in fact, becoming a regularly available vegetable in England. And this is good news for vegetarians as well as everyone else. The best place to find out more is Joy Larkcom's book "Oriental Vegetables", which gives ways of growing them organically, and recipes for using them.

Most of them are better for cooking than salads, though young greens of any sort can go into a mixed salad. Flavours and textures strengthen as they grow up a little, so cooking is more appropriate. And most of these greens are cooked in very much the same way, so you only need to apply one of two techniques, steaming or stir-frying. In Oriental restaurants, they also appear as "fondue", poached in broth. Grow or grab as many sorts as you can -- though if you grow, don't let them get old and coarse and large, as I have on occasion. I'm still very enthusiastic about them.

Most of the recipes here show their Chinese/Oriental background, and you may want to play that up, especially in the main dishes. But we are still waiting for the definitive English treatment of these new introductions.

Preparation is much the same for all these vegetables. Wash very well in the form you will cook it in, whole, halved, or cut-up. Lift them out of the washing water to leave any dirt, etc, behind, rather than pouring leaves and water through a colander.

Default. Steamed, following the instructions on the packet.

Better Default: Stir-fried Bok Choy.

This is a little more trouble than steaming, but ends up tasting much nicer. Allow **300g bok choy** for 4 people. Separate the leaves from the bok choy stems, which take longer to cook. Cut the stems crosswise in pieces about 3-cm; slice the leaves across to roughly the same size. Heat **1 tbsp. oil** in wok or large frying pan, add the stems and stir and toss for 1-2 mins. Add the leaves, and stir till the leaves wilt. Add a little **water or stock –2-4 tbsp**, depending on pan size – and a **splash of soy sauce** or a little salt, turn again, cover, and cook on moderate heat for 1-5 mins., depending on the age of the vegetable. The stems should be crisp and tender when done. Eat IMMEDIATELY. Any other of these Asian greens can be stir-fried in the same way with minor adjustments to timing.

Bok Choy with Mushrooms.

Pour boiling water over **6 medium dried Chinese mushrooms** – more if small, less if large – and let stand 20 mins. at least. Lift them out, cut off and discard the stem, and slice the caps thinly. Slice **100g fresh closed-cap mushrooms** thinly crosswise. Clean and slice thickly **300g bok choy**, fairly young and no more than 20 cm long. (They are cooked less than usual, so need to be young) Chop **1 medium shallot**. Mix **2 tbsp. soy sauce, 2 tbsp. sherry or white wine, 4 tbsp. mushroom-soaking liquid, 1 tsp. sugar, 1 tsp. cornflour** in a cup for the sauce. Action: heat **2 tbsp. sunflower oil** in a wok or large frying pan. Add the shallot and cook for 1 min. Turn up the heat, add the bok choy, and stir-fry 1 min. Add the mushrooms, fresh and dried, and toss and stir 1 min. Add the sauce ingredients, stirring first to disperse the cornflour, stir in the pan, turn down the heat and cook covered 2 mins. more. I like a small fresh **chili**, sliced, in with the shallot, but it's not necessary.

Bok Choy with Black Bean Sauce.

For this, you need Chinese dried black beans. They are a small variety of soybean, and they are sold in large packets in Chinese shops. They have a very savoury effect wherever they are used, and they seem to last indefinitely in the larder. Once you've tried the unique flavour they give to stir-fries, it's unlikely you'll ever want the commercial pots of "black bean sauce" again. For **250-300g bok choy**, you need **1 tsp. of the black beans.** Soak them in hot water for 10 mins, then mash them with **3 cloves garlic**, peeled and chopped. The black beans, and the garlic, are soft enough to be smeared out together on a chopping board, or pounded in a mortar, to make a paste. Slice the bok choy thickly, crosswise, and wash. Also have **a chopped fresh chili** ready. Heat 1 tbsp. oil in a wok or large frying pan, add the black bean paste and stir-fry for 30 secs. Add the sliced bok choy, stir to coat, then add the chili, **1 tsp. sugar**, and **4 tbsp. water**. Cover, reduce heat, and cook 2-3 mins.

Hot and Sour Bok Choy.

Allow **1 small bok choy per head**. Quarter and wash well. Mix the sauce materials in a cup; you need **1 tsp. cornflour, 1 tbsp. sugar, 2 tbsp. soy sauce, 2 tbsp. rice vinegar or white wine vinegar,** and **1 tbsp. sherry**. You also need **2 fresh chilis**, deseeded and chopped finely. Heat **1 tbsp. sunflower oil** in a wok or large frying pan, add the chili and stir ½ min, then add the bok choy. Stir and fry to coat with the oil, till nearly done. Add the sauce ingredients from the cup, mix well, and let it bubble to thicken the sauce. Turn into a serving dish. Unlike most stir-fried dishes, this is good cold.

Bok Choy with Mediterranean Tastes.

This moves away from the Oriental style, to very pleasing effect. Prepare **250-300g bok choy**. Make a mix of **2 tbsp. chopped capers, 12 or more olives**, pitted and chopped, and **3 cloves garlic**, peeled and chopped. Have **half a lemon** next to the stove. Heat **1 tbsp. extra-virgin olive oil** in a wok or large frying pan, add the bok choy, and stir-fry for 2-3 mins. Add the caper mix, and stir-fry for 1 min more. Squeeze over the juice from the lemon half, stir quickly, and serve.

Bean-Thread Noodles with Vegetables.

This dish uses a selection of vegetables, which can be widely varied. They are all almost cooked in advance, mixed, and stir-fried rapidly to blend the flavours. Then the cooked noodles are added, and the mix is fried together until all is hot. Bean thread noodles (also known as transparent noodles, or glass noodles), are an Oriental speciality which I much like from time to time, but many people don't. They are made from ground mung beans, not a starch at all. Any Chinese shop will have them in transparent packets, and they keep very well in pantry or cupboard. They aren't eaten alone. Their texture is smooth and slippery, which is what can put people off. I'd recommend trying a dish with these noodles in a restaurant before making a family meal from them. If you are not using bean thread noodles, use 100g Chinese egg noodles instead.

Soak **50g bean thread noodles** in hot water for 5 mins, and drain. Soak **6 dried Chinese mushrooms** in hot water to cover for 20-30 mins, lift out, cut off and discard the tough stems, and slice thinly. Blanch **200g bok choy** for 1 min, drain, squeeze, and slice thickly. Cut **1 carrot** and **1 small courgette** into matchstick pieces. Trim and slice thickly **6 spring onions** (fewer if they are large). All the vegetables can be put into a single bowl, and mixed well. Chop finely **3 cloves garlic**. Mix in a cup **2 tbsp. soy sauce, 1 tsp. sugar**. Have **2 tsp. dark sesame oil** in another cup.

Heat **4 tbsp. sunflower oil** in a wok or large frying pan, and add the garlic. Stir and fry for a few seconds only,. Then add all the vegetables. Stir and fry 3-4 mins, till the vegetables are tender but still crisp. Add the drained noodles, mix, then add the soy sauce mix. Stir well, and cook over low heat until all is hot. Dribble the sesame oil over, and serve.

I've varied this with defrosted edamame beans (p. 99) instead of carrot and courgette, and finished the whole thing with chopped fresh green coriander. A very worthy variation.

Bok Choy and Mushrooms with Buckwheat Noodles.

Buckwheat noodles are, at the moment, only found in natural-foods shops. Sometimes they have their Japanese name of soba. Whichever, they have a different and lovely taste and texture compared to wheat noodles, and I like to keep some in stock. You wouldn't want to eat them all the time, but they are great as a change. If you can't get them, use ordinary, rather thick pasta. As usual, about **300g noodles for 4**

people. Soak **6-8 dried Chinese mushrooms** in hot water for 20-30 mins, lift out, cut off and discard the tough stems, and slice thinly. Slice **2 small heads bok choy** thickly, crosswise. Slice **100g closed-cap mushroom** lengthwise. Chop finely together **3 cloves garlic, peeled, a knob of fresh ginger, peeled,** and **2 fresh chilis, deseeded**. Mix in a cup **2 tbsp. sherry, 2 tbsp. soy sauce,** and **2 tsp. dark sesame oil**. Start to boil the noodles. Meanwhile, heat **2 tbsp. sunflower oil** in a wok or large frying pan, add the garlic/ginger/chili mix and stir-fry 30 sec. Add the bok choy and the slices of dried mushroom. Stir-fry for 3-4 mins, then add the raw mushrooms. The noodles now should be ready – if not, leave the wok aside off the heat, and return it just before you drain the noodles. Drain the noodles, add to the hot vegetables, and add the soy/wine/oil mix. Stir together well, turn into a serving dish, and sprinkle with chopped **fresh green coriander**.

Anglicised Bok Choy and Mushrooms with Pasta.
Fry **200g large dark mushrooms**, sliced, in **30g butter**. **Salt** halfway through their cooking to bring out the juices. When they are almost cooked, add **3 chopped cloves garlic.** Steam **2 small bok choy** till just cooked, slice, and add to the mushrooms. Add **100 ml. double cream**, bubble a little till the sauce thickens, and add freshly ground black **pepper**. Taste for **salt**. Meanwhile, boil **300g pasta**; drain when cooked. Pour the sauce over and mix. Serve with grated **Parmesan**.

Brussels Sprouts

Brussels sprouts are the vegetable with a bad name in England. Most people say they dislike them; the rest sound apologetic about their liking. Why? Bad, overblown and overboiled Brussels sprouts are horrid, but if we hated all the vegetables which can be badly chosen and badly cooked there wouldn't be much left. A campaign to rehabilitate the Brussels sprout? Maybe a new name would help; they should be cavolini, which sounds Italian and endearing. (Actually, it *is* the Italian name of Brussels sprouts) Meanwhile, cook them carefully and not too much, and people will say -- I don't like most Brussels sprouts, but yours are different.

If you are buying Brussels sprouts, you want small, neat, tidy ones. They are supposed to be better after a frost – I think this is because so many other vegetables disappear with a frost, and it's a way of talking them up. Even so, I wouldn't want to eat Brussels sprouts in summer – unlike my son-in-law, who insists on them on Christmas Day in Australia, at 40°C. If you grow them, then you may find that no matter how careful you are, they are loose-leaved and not compact. As long as they are fresh, this can be coped with.

Default. This *has* to be boiled and buttered. Trim the outer leaves from the sprouts. If you have reason to think there may be wildlife in there, put them in a bowl of salty water for 10 mins or so, to encourage the bugs to leave. Comfort yourself that there will only be bugs if they are impeccably organic and healthy. If you have compact sprouts, use them as they are. If they are loose leaved even after trimming, then cut a small cross in the stem to encourage the stem to cook through at the same time as the leaves. Drain them, and cook them in 3 cm. boiling salted water in a covered pan. They will take 5-10 mins. As for doneness, I cannot do better than quote Jane Grigson: "The base part should be nutty textured, not exactly crisp, but slightly resistant in an agreeable way." That's what you want. Drain well, and serve with butter dotted over them and lots of pepper.

A bit more elaboration, a better taste (to me, anyhow) **Brussels Sprouts with Noisette Butter.** Drain and keep the sprouts warm briefly. Heat **50g butter** in a small pan until it turns light brown – not black – and add **1 tbsp. white wine vinegar**. It should hiss and spit. Swirl round to mix, add **chopped herbs** – parsley or a mix – and pour over the sprouts, ideally while still sizzling. Eat IMMEDIATELY.

If you want to go really over the top, serve the plain sprouts with Hollandaise Sauce (see Basics). If you also have some poached eggs and toasted muffins, which also go well with the Hollandaise, you have a super light meal.

Brussels Sprouts with Cumin and Mustard Seed.

Indian flavours, non-Indian ingredient. For **500g hot cooked sprouts**, heat **1 tbsp. sunflower oil** in a small frying pan. Add **1 tbsp. black mustard seeds** and **1 tsp. cumin seeds**, and wait for the mustard seeds to start popping. Drizzle the mixture over the sprouts, **salt**, and serve. You could vary this by adding garlic slices when the mustard seeds have popped.

Brussels Sprouts Reheated in Butter.

Sometimes – like Christmas Day – it is helpful to cook the sprouts in advance. If you are going to treat them in any of the following ways where the sprouts are cooked first, leave them a little less done – 6-8 mins, in fact. Cook and drain 500g sprouts, or fish them out of boiling water, and spread them out in one layer on a cloth until they are cold.

Now you just need a few moments work to reheat and serve. Smear **15g butter** over the base of a baking dish which has a cover. If no lid, then foil will do fine. Arrange the sprouts in it in one layer. **Salt** and **pepper**, then pour over **30g melted butter** Cover the pan and leave till 20 mins before serving. Heat on the stove top until the butter can be heard to sizzle, then put in a moderate oven for 15-20 mins, until hot. Oven temperature here doesn't much matter, provided it's not so hot it burns the sprouts and butter. If you want **Brussels Sprouts with Chestnuts,** add ready-cooked chestnuts to the baking dish before reheating. I'd always use vacuum-packed chestnuts at Christmas; there is so much else going on that no-one will taste and appreciate the virtues of fresh chestnuts peeled by you, and you can probably do without the hassle.

Brussels Sprouts with Crème Fraiche, Chili, and Lime.

Cook **500g Brussels sprouts**, drain, cool, and halve. When nearly ready to eat, fry **2 chopped shallots** in **15g butter** until soft, not coloured. Add **1 chopped seeded chili**, then **150 ml crème fraiche** and **½ tsp. Marigold stock powder**. Stir, then add the sprouts, and cook very gently until the sprouts are heated through. Add the **juice of a lime**, turn into a serving dish, and sprinkle with **chopped fresh green coriander** if you have some. Otherwise, oregano/marjoram, or parsley.

Brussels Sprouts with Sesame Seeds.
Toast about **2 tbsp. white sesame seeds** – on an enamel plate under the grill, or in a dry frying pan. Boil, drain, cool **500g Brussels sprouts**. Just before serving, heat **1 tbsp. sunflower oil** in a frying pan, add **1 chopped clove garlic**. Swirl, then add the sprouts. Let them warm through over a low heat; **salt** and **pepper**, and **1 tsp. toasted sesame oil**. Turn onto a dish and sprinkle with the sesame seeds.

Fricassee of Brussels Sprouts with Onions and Peppers.
This dish, with its Mediterranean flavours, really asks to have cavolini named in its title instead of Brussels sprouts. Boil **500g Brussels sprouts**, drain, cool, and halve. In a heavy frying pan with a lid, fry **3 sliced red onions** in **3 tbsp. olive oil**, stirring now and then. When they start to brown, add **2 peppers, ideally 1 red, 1 yellow**, but 2 of one colour if that's what you have. The peppers should be deseeded and cut into thin strips. Add **2 chopped cloves garlic**. **Salt** and **pepper**, cover, and sweat all on low heat for about 20 mins, till the vegetables are soft. So far, it's like the early stages of peperonata; if you have some of this left over from something else, use it here. Anyhow, add the halved Brussels sprouts to the vegetable mix, cover again, and sweat 10 mins or so, till the sprouts are hot. Drizzle with **another tbsp. extra-virgin olive oil** just before serving, if you like.

The next batch of recipes is for braised Brussels sprouts. These are easier and the timing is less critical than for boiled sprouts, and it's easy to add different flavours.

Brussels Sprouts with French Mustard.
Trim and halve **500g Brussels sprouts**. Put them in a pan with **150 ml. stock, 15g butter, salt** and **pepper** (salt depending on the stock; if using Marigold powder, no salt is needed), and some chopped **parsley**.

Cover and cook gently 15 mins, or till the sprouts are tender. Stir in **1 tsp. French mustard**.

Paprika Brussels Sprouts.
Trim and halve **500g Brussels sprouts**. Put in a pan with **150 ml. stock, 1 tsp. smoked paprika, 1 tsp. tomato puree, 15g butter,** and **salt**. Add a little chopped fresh **chili** if you like. Cover and cook gently 15 mins. Taste for seasoning.

Brussels Sprouts with Shallots
Trim and shred **500g Brussels sprouts**. Chop **3 shallots**, and saute in **2 tbsp. olive oil** until they are softened. Over moderate heat, add the shredded sprouts, stir well, and add **100 ml. water, salt**. Cook for 5-8 mins stirring often. Add **pepper** to taste, and **2 tsp. balsamic vinegar.**

Brussels Sprouts with Leeks.
Trim and halve **500g Brussels sprouts**; clean and slice **6 small leeks**. Put in a pan with **30g butter, 4 tbsp. stock**, and ½ tsp salt. Cover, and cook on moderate heat for 10 mins. Finish with **1 dsp. grainy mustard or horseradish,** , depending what else you're having,. Really good for something so simple.

Glazed Brussels Sprouts with Walnut Oil and Red Wine.
These sprouts are browned and cooked in a liquid that is reduced down to a glaze, just as the sprouts are cooked. This is tricky to get absolutely right, so you may need to adjust. If the liquid has evaporated too soon, add a little water, and reduce that down; if there is too much liquid when the sprouts are done, scoop out the sprouts and boil down the liquid alone. When it's a glaze, put the sprouts back and roll them round to cover with the glaze. Start by mixing **250 ml. red wine** with **250 ml. stock**, and boil down to half. Trim **500g Brussels sprouts**. Heat **2 tbsp. walnut oil** in a frying pan large enough to take the sprouts in one layer. If it won't take all the 500g, leave a few sprouts out. Add the sprouts to the oil, and fry quite quickly, rolling them about from time to time, till they darken and brown a little on the edges. Add the stock/wine mixture, **salt** if needed, and boil at a moderate speed, uncovered, until the liquid has become a glaze. Turn the sprouts from time to time. Eat them hot.

Brussels Sprouts with Carrots.

Melt **40g butter** in a large wide pan, and add **1 chopped onion**. Let it sweat while you prepare **500g Brussels sprouts** and peel and slice thickly **500g carrots**. Add these to the onion, stir, and add **200 ml. stock or water. Salt if needed, ½ tsp. dried herbs**. Simmer covered for 30 mins, then take off the lid, raise the heat, and reduce the stock to a glaze. Eat hot.

Brussels Sprouts Sauteed with Almonds.

Trim and shred finely **500g Brussels sprouts**. Heat **2 tbsp. olive oil** in a large skillet, and add the sprouts. Stir, sprinkle with **4 tbsp. water, salt** and **pepper**, and cover. Cook on medium heat about 5 mins. Take off the lid, raise the heat, and evaporate the liquid, stirring, until there is no water left. Meanwhile, toast **50g whole blanched almonds** under the grill (almonds you blanch yourself are juicier (for blanching almonds see Basics) but bought blanched almonds are more convenient. Your choice) Add the almonds to the cooked sprouts, sprinkle with **1 dsp. balsamic vinegar** and some chopped **dill or fennel**, and eat.

Brussels Sprouts Fried with Garlic and Sage.

Trim **500g Brussels sprouts**, and shred them finely. Wash the shreds. Heat **2 tbsp. olive oil** in a pan large enough to hold the sprouts, and add **2-3 chopped cloves garlic**, and **6 shredded sage leaves**. Stir, and add the washed shreds. Stir again, cover the pan, and cook quite quickly for 5 mins or so. Stir from time to time. Take off the lid, season, evaporate any remaining liquid, and serve.

Brussels Sprouts with Onion, Garlic and Chili.

Trim and quarter **500g Brussels sprouts** – or in more pieces if they are large. Heat **3 tbsp. sunflower oil** in a wok or large frying pan, and add **1 medium onion**, sliced. Fry quickly until it starts to change colour, stirring, then add **2 cloves garlic**, chopped, and **1 fresh deseeded chopped chili**. Stir again, and add the sprouts. Reduce the heat a little, and let them fry with frequent stirring for about 10 mins. or till done. **Salt** to taste. The sprouts should have brown edges, at least, which are always delicious.

Roast Brussels Sprouts with Garlic.

These are partly fried, partly roast, and they should turn dark brown in the cooking. Trim and halve **500g sprouts**. Heat **4 tbsp. olive oil** in a large flat pan which can go in the oven, and add the sprouts, in one layer if possible. Add **6 whole cloves garlic**, peeled, and sprinkle with **salt.** Cook till the sprouts start to brown on the underside, and then put in the oven at 200. Cook, shaking the pan from time to time, until the sprouts are brown and tender, probably about 30 mins. Drizzle with **1 tbsp. balsamic vinegar**, plenty of **pepper**, and eat.

Sweet Roast Brussels Sprouts

Mix **500g Brussels sprouts**, trimmed and halved, **2 sliced shallots, 4 tbsp olive oil, 1 tbsp honey**, and roast 30 mins at 200. (If you don't like them brown/black, stop before they get to that stage) Sprinkle with **1 tbsp toasted pine nuts, 1 tbsp balsamic vinegar,** and serve.

This is an example of sweetness with Brussels sprouts, which some people really like. If you do, try this recipe using maple syrup instead of honey, or use maple syrup mixed with the butter for sprouts and chestnuts.

Brussels Sprout Puree.

A good way to disguise the vegetable, if you need to. People who don't like sprouts like this, and so do people who do like sprouts. But only do it when you have some other components of the meal with texture, as purees can be too much like baby food for comfort. Trim and cook **500g Brussels sprouts**, by boiling in a little water, as in default recipe. Whizz them in the food processor, or put through a mouli. Add **salt, pepper, ¼ tsp sugar**, and **3-4 tbsp. sour cream or crème fraiche**. Reheat, and serve very hot.

Brussels Sprouts, Chestnuts and Nutmeg Cream.

Trim and cook **500g sprouts**, and whizz to a puree and season, as for the last recipe. Add **100 ml crème fraiche, salt, pepper**, and a good grating of **nutmeg**. Mix **250g cooked chestnuts** into the puree, and reheat in a double boiler.

Brussels Sprouts and Potato Puree.

Trim, blanch for 5 mins, and drain **500g Brussels sprouts**. Fry **1 large chopped onion** in **20g. butter (preferable) or oil**. When it's softened, add the sprouts, and **500g potatoes**, peeled and diced. Shake around, and add **500 ml. stock or water. Salt if needed, pepper, little nutmeg**. Cook slowly, covered, for 30 mins or till everything is very tender. Drain off and keep the liquid, and puree the vegetables with mouli or potato masher or fork. Beat in **50g butter** and a little **milk**, to taste.

Simple Brussels Sprout Soup

The last recipe is obviously more than halfway to a soup. When the veg. are cooked, don't drain, but puree the whole in blender, food processor, mouli. Reheat with more stock to get the thickness you like, and finish with **double cream**, either mixed in (uses more, better mouthfeel) or swirled in a pattern on the top (uses less, looks prettier, lets taste of soup come through more strongly). **Croutons** are almost essential with this, for contrast of texture.

Brussels Sprout Soup with Walnuts.

A variation on the plain soup above. Use **2 tbsp. walnut oil** to cook **1 large chopped onion**. Add **300g peeled diced potatoes, 250g peeled diced swede**, and sweat 10 mins. Add **1 litre stock**, cook 20 mins, and add **500g trimmed Brussels sprouts**, quartered. Cook 10 mins more; the potato and swede should be done. Puree in your favourite way. Taste, and adjust seasoning and thickness if needed. Sprinkle each serving with **toasted crumbled walnuts, probably about 60g for this** amount of soup. **Cheesy croutons** are lovely – toast **bread** lightly, cover with grated **cheese** (Wensleydale or Caerphilly best here), and let the cheese melt under the grill. Cut the slices into shapes, or let the eaters do this.

Brussels Sprouts and Fennel Chowder.

Cook **1 medium chopped onion** in **50g** butter till starting to colour. Add **1 clove garlic**, finely chopped, and stir a little. Add **300g Brussels sprouts**, trimmed and sliced, and **1 fennel bulb**, trimmed and chopped. Add also **½ tsp. crushed anise seed**, or, if you don't have anise, caraway seed. Sweat covered 10 mins. Add **600 ml. stock**, and simmer until the sprouts are in the state you like – can be 5 mins, can be 30. Taste for seasoning. If you are serving this with lumps, then take care to cut the vegetables tidily to start with. It's only a chowder if not pureed. On the other hand, you can puree it and call it Brussels and Fennel Soup. Lots of people are sensitive to bits in their soup, and only you know what you can get away with. Myself, I think this is better with the bits, and **croutons** too. If pureed, try adding small chunks of **blue cheese** to each plate.

Brussels Sprout Souffle.

This is a souffle made with a potato base instead of a white-sauce base. You can adapt other soufflés to use potatoes; you can adapt this one to use white sauce, on the model of broccoli souffle. Cook **250g each trimmed Brussels sprouts and peeled diced potato** in boiling salted water. You can cook them together, in which case start the potatoes 10 mins before the sprouts. Whizz sprouts and potato together in the food processor, maybe in 2 batches depending on the processor size. Add **150 ml. double cream**; whizz in. Add **3 egg yolks, 100g grated cheese**. I like Wensleydale or young Lancashire here, something with a slightly acid edge. Season with **salt, nutmeg, a few shakes of Tabasco**. You can use this immediately or let it go cold. About 45 mins before eating, butter a souffle dish. Beat till stiff **4 or even 5 egg whites**. Dollop about ¼ of the beaten egg whites on the puree, and mix in. Then tip this back on top of the egg whites and fold in carefully and thoroughly. Tip and scrape into the souffle dish, run a finger round near the edge, and bake at 200 for 30-35 mins.

Wild Rice with Brussels Sprouts.

I came across this suggestion in an American vegetarian book, and the writer said this was a great and unexpected combination. He/she is absolutely right; try it. Put **250g wild rice** into a pan with **750 ml. stock, a bay leaf, 1 tsp. salt**, and **pepper**. Bring to the boil, and cook on low heat for 40 mins. While this is cooking, make **250g Brussels sprouts** into Roast Brussels Sprouts with Garlic, above, p353. Taste the wild rice; if it's done, drain off any excess stock. If it's not done (and it is variable), go on cooking, adding water if needed. As the rice is just ready, stir in the Brussels sprouts, and eat hot. This is ideal as the precursor to a dairy-heavy dessert, like baked custard or cheesecake.

Brussels Sprouts, Butter Beans, and Miso.

Start with **200g dried butter beans**, or 2 standard tins. If using dried beans, soak them overnight (or quick-soak, see Basics), and then cook in boiling water till almost done. Drain if necessary. Peel and dice **700g potatoes**, not new or a salad sort, but something like Desiree. Sweat **2 large chopped onions** in **2 tbsp. oil** for about 10 mins, then

355

take the pan off the heat and work in **2 tbsp. miso**. Add **800 ml. stock**, and bring to the boil, stirring. Add the potatoes and the butter beans, and put all into an ovenproof casserole with a lid. Cook at 150 for 1-2 hrs – sorry not to be more precise, but the potatoes should be soft and collapsing and the beans done. If using tinned beans, just cook until the potatoes are done. There will be a lot of liquid; pour some off, so the remainder will just come to the top of the mixture when the sprouts are added. Now add **salt** to taste, not much because of the miso, and add **500g Brussels sprouts**, trimmed and halved. Stir till the sprouts are submerged, and persuade the potatoes to make a layer on top, as far as possible. This is so you can brown the top, which always makes a dish look and taste better. Put back in the oven at 180 with no lid, and leave about 20 mins or till the top is browned and the sprouts cooked. Sprinkle with chopped **parsley** and serve. It is impolite to suggest that, if you have no miso, Marmite can be used with similar effect. Mix 1 dsp. in after adding water to sweated onion, instead of before water as for miso.

Curried Brussels Sprouts.
Trim and shred **500g Brussels sprouts**. Chop together, with knife or in the small bowl of a food processor, **2 fresh seeded chilis, 4 cloves garlic**, and a **small knob of ginger**, peeled. Heat **2 tbsp. oil** in a wide pan with a lid, and add **1 dsp. black mustard seed** and **1 tsp. cumin seeds**. When the mustard seeds are popping well, add the chili/garlic/ginger mix, and stir for about ½ min. Add the shredded sprouts, stir, and let cook 5 mins or so, stirring often. Add the spicing; maybe **1 tsp. garam masala**, your own or bought; or 2 tsp. curry paste of any kind. If using a Thai curry paste, omit the chili mix, and add at that time. Stir to blend everything, then add **200 ml. coconut milk**, and **½ tsp. salt**. Simmer 5-10 mins, raising the heat if necessary to reduce the coconut milk. Taste, add **the juice of a lemon**, sprinkle with chopped **fresh green coriander**, and serve.

Cavolini Salad with Blue Cheese.
Trim and slice thinly **250g really good, small, nutty, fresh Brussels sprouts**, the nicest you can find. Cube **100g blue cheese** – Blue Stilton or other English blue, and mix with the sprouts. Dress with **mayonnaise** with **garlic** added – about 3 tbsp. mayo – or the mayo/yoghurt/mustard mix. No prejudice will be excited if people

don't know what they are eating, because they won't guess from the taste.

There are many other possible salads if you've got these desirable fresh, nutty, small sprouts. Slice them thinly. Try with watercress and citrus – grapefruit segments or satsuma segments, even sliced kumquat, and a dressing with oil and lemon juice. Mix the shreds into other green salads.

Brussels Sprouts a la Grecque.

An expensive marinade for a delicious appetiser plate, to nibble with olives, nuts, dips and crudites. Put **300 ml. water, 150 ml. olive oil – extra-virgin best –** and the **juice of 4 lemons** in a pan. Add **1 bay leaf, 2-3 sprigs thyme, 1 tsp. cracked – not ground – coriander seed** and **½ tsp cracked black peppercorns, ½ tsp. salt.** Simmer for 5 mins, then add **500g small nutty sprouts**, trimmed, and simmer uncovered about 10 mins, till sprouts just tender. Let the whole thing cool. Fish out the bay leaf and thyme sprigs, taste for salt and pepper, and add more if needed. Sprinkle with chopped **parsley.** You could also add a **dried chili** with the other aromatics; I prefer this variation.

Before finishing with sprouts, let me warn you against jars of sprouts bought in Belgium. They look pretty in a clear liquid, but when you open the jar you find no flavourings, just sprouts tasting cabbagey and overcooked. And they are quite expensive. Not a good buy!

If you grow your own, or get an organic box, there are Brussels Sprout Tops. These are a very worthwhile extra. They can be cooked like any other fairly tender green, like spring greens, for example. Or try this recipe, which I think brings out their best.

Creamed Brussels Sprouts Tops.

Brussels tops if bought have some stem, and a few top sprouts left on them. These, cut or picked from the stem, improve the mix. If you are cutting your own, you will probably just take the loose, leafy head, and in this case you need one head per person. Trim and shred **enough Brussels tops for the number of people** you're feeding. Blanch for 4-5 mins in boiling salted water. Reheat in a knob of **butter** in a large frying pan, **salt** and **pepper**. Mix in roughly **a small tub of crème fraiche** (for 4-6) mixed with **1 tsp. Dijon mustard.**

Cabbage

Spring, Green, Savoy, White
And Sauerkraut

Cabbage and other greens are, in a sense, the heart of this book. They are very much for home consumption, and largely ignored by restaurants – to be fair, two of the most memorable cabbages I have ever eaten were in posh French restaurants, but it's rare. If you are trying in your home cooking to imitate a restaurant, then cabbage will be low on your agenda too. But restaurants and home cooking have different priorities. Restaurants have a large throughput at unpredictable times; they want foods which can be cooked or finished at the last minute, they want to impress, and, in general, your nutrition is not their concern. At home, there is a small number of people, mostly eating at defined times, and your priorities are nutrition, budget, taste and practicality, all at once. Cabbages fit in with this impeccably; good nutrition, cheap, always available, easy to prepare, and capable of being delicious.

Think how beautiful some cabbages are. Slice through the middle of a red cabbage or a Savoy, and just be amazed at the interwoven complexity. A natural analogue of the knotwork in the Lindisfarne gospels. The colours of a January King, all blue-green and maroon. These are the incidental rewards of the domestic cook.

Cabbages come in different varieties at different seasons; my seed catalogue has 19 varieties, for spring, summer, autumn and winter. I think that in most cases it is hard to tell the variety of cabbage from its taste; they are bred for different growing properties. Savoy is a bit different, and is specified in many recipes; apart from this, use "green", "white" or any. I haven't tried to include all sorts of cabbage here. Red cabbage, Chinese leaves and other Chinese brassicas, kales including cavolo nero, and spring greens all have separate chapters, because that's what their cooking needs dictate.

Cabbage on the whole is a Northern vegetable, and some kinds, like Savoy, are better for being frosted before cutting. Therefore many of

358

the recipes are for warming, comfortable food, best in winter, but not amiss in parts of an English summer. Mountainous areas in India, Italy and Greece have also given rise to ways of cooking cabbage. Indian ways of stuffing cabbage are particularly varied and ingenious. Don't look for cabbage recipes from California or Mexico.

Cabbage can be cooked in 2 major ways – and eaten raw. It can be cooked quickly, mostly around 5 mins. and certainly less than 10. Or it can be cooked long, slow, with little liquid, and covered; more than an hour here. It is lots of water, and long cooking times, that allow cabbage and other brassicas – Brussels sprouts, cauliflower -- to release the sulphur compounds that make cooking cabbage smell bad.

I can't deny that there is prejudice about cabbage, partly, but not entirely, because of memories of school dinners and grandmother's cooking, where the cabbages were boiled to death. You may well – as I do – have a mindset which means you often don't think of cabbage when there are more tempting veg. available. I heartily recommend you try to get over this. All the recipes below have been tried on people who think they don't like cabbage, as well as those who do, and have been approved.

There are so many I have divided them up under headings of cooked side dishes, salads, soups, and main dishes. Other chapters work this way without being explicit, but aren't as long.

COOKED CABBAGE SIDE DISHES

Default. Shred the cabbage, whichever sort, and put in a pan with a knob of butter, a few tbsp. water, salt, pepper, and a little of a tough herb (for example, rosemary or thyme or sage) or spice (for example, caraway or cumin or coriander) Only one of these. Bring to the boil, cover, and cook for 5-7 mins on a medium heat. If you haven't used spice or herb at the start, finish with a chopped fresh herb like parsley or chives or tarragon or . . .. Just this one dish gives an amazing amount of variety in detail, and it's reliably lovely.

Cabbage with Garlic and Juniper.
John Tovey's original of this swept the dinner-party-giving classes in the late 70's. It was briefly roasted at a high heat, and I found that

there was a mix of raw and burnt shreds. Now I do it cooked briefly in a covered pan, and much prefer my variation. Heat **2 tbsp. olive oil** in a pan with a lid; add **3 chopped cloves garlic** and **a dozen or so juniper berries,** crushed in a mortar or otherwise. Almost immediately, add **shredded white cabbage, about 200g**, but it's not critical. Splash of **water, salt**, stir to mix well, cover, and cook 5 mins. **Pepper** at end.

Savoy Cabbage with Chili and Ginger.
Chop finely **3 cloves garlic, 1-2 chilis**, depending on your tolerance for heat and their heat. Leave the seeds in if you want it really hot. Heat **2 tbsp. oil**, and add the garlic and chili. After a few seconds, add **half a medium Savoy**, trimmed and shredded, a splash of **water**, and a little **salt**. Bring to the boil, cover, turn down the heat and cook about 7 mins, or till done to your liking. Add **1 tsp. soy sauce** and stir in.

Cabbage with Garlic and Shallots.
Cut a **bunch of spring onions, 6 shallots, 3 cloves garlic,** and **1 seeded chili** into long strips. Not chopped, you taste them separately. Cut up the **leaves from a head of celery.** Shred **400g fresh green cabbage**. Heat **2 tbsp. oil, not olive**, in a wok or wide frying pan, and add shallots and garlic. Stir. After a minute or so, add the chili. Almost immediately, add the cabbage, spring onions, and celery leaves. Stir on quite high heat until the volume has reduced quite a bit. Add **4 tbsp. stock, 1 tsp salt**, and continue to stir-fry on medium heat until the cabbage is done.

Cabbage in Cream.
You can use this for any cabbage, Savoy, green or white, and other greens as well. The unctuousity of the cream has a terrific effect on the taste and texture in the mouth. Shred **500g of whichever cabbage** you are using, and blanch for 3-4 mins in boiling salted water. Drain, put in pan, and add **150 ml. double cream**. (In real life, give it a good slurp.) Cook 2-3 mins, stirring to coat with the cream and let it thicken a bit. It needs a lot of **pepper**; possibly the 5-pepper blend.

Cabbage with Dill and Sour Cream.
Basically Hungarian, with adaptations. Cut **half a white cabbage** in slices 5-10 mm thick, after coring it. Boil these slices in salted water, with a pinch of **caraway seeds**, till just tender, 7-10 mins. Drain.

Thicken a **cup of stock** with **arrowroot or cornflour Salt** if needed, **pepper**. (Hungarians would use some of the cabbage water, and thicken with a roux, but I think that's a step too far) Add the cabbage to the sauce, with **3-4 sprigs dill or fennel**, chopped, and **2-3 spring onions**, cut into thin rounds. Reheat. Add **2 tbsp. soured cream** and stir in. This seems to me to call out for triangles of toast or fried bread, but these aren't authentic or necessary.

Normandy Cabbage.
Use **half a large green cabbage, or a small whole one**, for example the pointed cabbage found in late winter. Slice it 5-10 mm thick, removing the core. Blanch these slices in boiling salted water 5 mins, and drain well. Put in a pot with a lid, and add **2 medium apples**, peeled, cored, quartered, **6 tbsp. dry cider** (or white wine; it may not feel worth buying cider just for this), **3 tbsp. water, salt** and **pepper** and **nutmeg**. Cover the pan, and let it cook slowly for 45 mins to 1 hr. If it is too wet at the end, turn up the heat and leave the lid off to evaporate the excess. Taste. Add **50g butter** in small pieces, and swirl to blend it with the juices and coat the cabbage.

Cabbage with Apples and Peanuts.
Shred **half a Savoy or white cabbage**, and put in a pan with **1 chopped clove of garlic, 3 tbsp. olive oil** and **2 tbsp. white wine vinegar.** Cover, and cook for 7-8 mins. Peel, core and slice **an eating apple** – I like russets – and stir into the pan with **100g salted peanuts**, and **pepper**. (The peanuts are why the dish doesn't need salt) Cook 2 mins more, covered, and serve. The apple should still have crunch.

Spicy Tomato Cabbage.
Shred the **inner part of a small Savoy**, and put in a pan. Blend **150 ml. stock** with **2 tsp mushroom ketchup, 1 tbsp. tomato puree, 1 tbsp. non-olive oil, a few shakes of Tabasco, and ½ tsp. garam masala. Salt** as needed. If you have **2 firm tomatoes**, save them till the end; if not, add 2 tbsp. tinned crushed tomatoes to the mix. Pour over the cabbage, mix, bring to the boil, and cook moderately for about 10 mins, stirring from time to time. If using fresh tomatoes, add them at the end, so they are not cooked.

Long-cooked Sweet-sour Cabbage.
Shred ½ **a white cabbage**. Peel the **zest from a lemon**, avoiding the pith as far as possible, and squeeze the **juice**. Melt **50g butter** in a pan with a lid, add the cabbage, lemon zest, **2 tsp. sugar, salt** and **pepper**. Stir, then cook on low heat for 1 hr (or in a low oven, if it's on). When done there should be no liquid; if there is, take off the lid and let it evaporate. Add the lemon juice, stir, and eat. You wouldn't believe how different this tastes if you use a lime (or 2 if small) instead of a lemon. This – and other sweet-sour cabbage dishes – go particularly well with couscous.

Italian Sweet-and-Sour Cabbage (Cavoli in Agrodolce)
Shred **a green (pointed) cabbage**, removing the core. Fry **a small chopped onion** in **2 tbsp. olive oil**, and add **1 tbsp. tomato paste** mixed with **4 tbsp. water**. Add the cabbage, stir, then add **salt, pepper**, and **2 tbsp. wine vinegar**. Cook covered for 5 mins, stirring often, then add **1 dsp. sugar**. Cook 5 mins more, taste, eat.

Pennsylvania Dutch Sweet-and-Sour Cabbage.
This one is cooked plainly and has a sweet-and-sour sauce added. Trim **500g green cabbage**, and shred. Put in a covered pan with enough **stock** to cover the bottom, bring to the boil, then simmer covered for 5-7 mins. Meanwhile make the sauce: beat an **egg yolk** with **2 tbsp. sugar, 4 tbsp. red wine vinegar** and **1 tsp. French mustard** and put into a double boiler. Warm, beating, as if making a Hollandaise sauce. When the mixture is warm and shows signs of thickening, beat in **30g butter** in bits, and when this is incorporated, add **100 ml. double cream, salt** and **pepper**, and **chopped dill**. (Or fennel, or even parsley if that's what you have.) Mix cabbage with about half the sauce, and serve the rest in a bowl so people can take more as they want. Truly delicious; this is a party veg.

Oriental (ish) Sweet-and-Sour Cabbage.
This incorporates marmalade along with Oriental seasonings, and the bitter note is surprisingly good. Shred **500g white cabbage**. Mix **2 tbsp. white wine vinegar, 2 tbsp. sugar, 2 tbsp. marmalade with peel**, and a **pinch of salt** in a bowl. Heat **2 tbsp. oil** in a wok or large frying pan, add **2 slices ginger**, chopped, and stir. Immediately add the cabbage, and stir-fry over high heat for 2-3 mins. Add the sauce, turn down the heat, and stir-fry 1 min more. Add **2 chopped cloves of**

garlic, stir, cover, and let cook for 2 mins or till done to your taste. Drizzle over **1 tsp. dark sesame oil**, and serve.

Red-Cooked Cabbage.

Going from Oriental-ish to the real thing, this is a Chinese home-style dish. You can eat it alone, or add some tofu cubes to make it into a main dish. Excellent, simple, and very cheap either way. Cut a **large cabbage – green, white, Savoy –** into slices about 2.5 cm thick. Stir-fry **1 large chopped onion, 2 chopped cloves garlic** in **2 tbsp. oil** in a large pan which has a lid. After 3-4 mins, sprinkle with **1 tsp. Marigold stock powder, 5 tbsp. water**. Stir, cook 2 mins, add **2 slices ginger**, peeled, **1 star anise** (the whole star shape) and the cabbage slices. Turn to coat all the cabbage with the onion mixture. Add **5 tbsp. soy sauce, 2 tbsp. wine, 2 tsp. sugar**, and **pepper**. Cover the pan and cook on low heat for 50-60 mins, turning the cabbage over a couple of times. You can take out the ginger – it's not to be eaten. Taste and serve. It can be reheated if there is any left.

Green Cabbage with Miso.

Shred **a medium green cabbage**, discarding the core and tough stems, and blanch for 1 min. Drain and squeeze. Mix **2 tbsp. miso, 1 tbsp. wine vinegar, ½ tsp. each salt and sugar**. Let down with **2-3 tbsp. hot water**, to improve mixing. Add the cabbage and mix well. Sprinkle with **toasted sesame seeds**, and **either ground Szechwan pepper or dried chili flakes**.

Green Cabbage with Spices.

Shred **half a medium Savoy or other green cabbage**. Heat **4 tbsp. non-olive oil** in a wide and heavy pot with a lid. Add **1 tsp. whole black mustard seeds** and **2 bay leaves**, broken up into 2 or 3 pieces. When the mustard seeds are popping well, add the cabbage, and stir it about. Add **salt, 1 tsp sugar**, and **1 chopped green chilli** (deseeded), Stir again, reduce the heat, and cover with the lid. Cook for 5-7 mins. Turn off the heat, and sprinkle with chopped **fresh green coriander**. My son looked up while taking his third helping of this, saying "But I don't even like cabbage!"

Indian Smothered Cabbage.

Shred **a medium cabbage, green or white**, removing the stem. Heat **2 tbsp. sunflower oil** in a large frying pan with a cover. Add **2 tsp.**

cumin seeds, and almost immediately, when the seeds change colour, add the **tip of a tsp. of asafoetida (hing).** Miss this out if you don't have any (but get some for next time). Immediately add the shredded cabbage. Sprinkle **¼ tsp. turmeric** over, and turn and stir until mixed. Add a **knob of ginger**, peeled and finely chopped, **2 green chilis**, ditto, and **½ tin of chopped tomatoes**. Stir again and cook about 5 mins. Add **1 tsp. salt, 5 tbsp. water**, cover, and cook on low heat for about 10 mins, till the cabbage is tender. Check from time to time that it isn't burning. When done, sprinkle with chopped **fresh green coriander**, and serve.

Savoy Cabbage with Celery.

Put **50g butter** in a lidded pan. Add the **inner leaves of a Savoy cabbage**, shredded, **2 medium leeks**, sliced thin crosswise, **a head of celery**, stalks separated and peeled and sliced thinly crosswise, a **couple of sprigs of rosemary** or chopped oregano, **salt** and **pepper**. Pour over **100 ml. stock, 3 tbsp. wine vinegar**. Put on the lid and cook slowly for 40 mins or more, till all is very tender. Taste and serve.

Green Cabbage with Green Peppers.

Shred **half a small green cabbage** – spring or summer for preference. Chop **1 green pepper, 6 spring onions,** and **a clove garlic**, and mix with the cabbage. Heat **2 tbsp. olive oil**, add the veg., **salt** and **pepper**, and **3 tbsp. water**, cover, and cook on very low heat about 30 mins. Taste and serve. This has a mild and almost sweet flavour.

Braised Cabbage with Baby Onions and Mushrooms.

For this, the three components are started separately, and cooked together so the flavours blend. It takes time from start to finish, but not an enormous amount of attention in between. Start with **a green winter cabbage**; trim and core, and cut into wedges about 5 cm wide at the outside. Sweat **a sliced onion** in **2 tbsp. olive oil**, covered, for 5 mins, then add the cabbage wedges, **salt, 1 tsp. sugar**, and **100 ml. stock**. Cover tightly, and cook for 1 hr on a very low heat or in a low oven, if on. During this hour, peel **12 pickling onions or shallots**. Brown them in **1 dsp olive oil** in a small pan, rolling them round, and add **100 ml stock, 1 tsp sugar, salt** and **pepper**, and cook gently, uncovered, until the stock is evaporated and the onions glazed. Add them to the cabbage, stir, and leave the mix to go on cooking. Now slice **250g mushrooms**, wild or cultivated, and cook them in **1 tbsp. olive oil**, adding **2 chopped cloves of garlic, the leaves from a sprig of thyme,** and **salt.** When the pan has dried out, tip these over the cabbage, and go on cooking. The cabbage needs a minimum of 1½ hrs, but can go longer. I prefer to add the mushrooms about 15 mins before eating, but they can be cooked whenever it suits you and reheated just before adding them to the cabbage. If you add some dried cepes to the mushrooms, it bumps up the savoury character a lot, but it is excellent without them. (To use the cepes, start soaking 15g in boiling water as you start to cook. Use some of the soaking liquid for the stock in cooking the cabbage. Add the soaked cepes to the frying mushrooms, and pour in and evaporate the remaining soaking water as the mushrooms cook. This really makes a whole new dish; 2 recipes in one!) Anyhow, when the dish is ready, taste for seasoning, sprinkle with fresh chopped **parsley**, and serve.

Stir-Fried Cabbage with Carrot and Spring Onions.
Trim **½ medium green cabbage**, and slice it lengthwise into long thin shreds. Peel **1 carrot**, and cut in small matchsticks. Trim **12 spring onions**, cut across, then cut these lengthwise into strips. Heat **4 tbsp. sunflower oil**, and add **2 slices ginger**, peeled and pounded lightly to squash the fibres and release the flavour. Add all the veg. and **1 tsp. salt.** Stir-fry for about 3 mins, till well wilted, then add **3 tbsp. wine or stock**, turn down the heat, and cook covered 4 mins. Then take off the lid and give a blast of heat while removing the ginger. You can, but need not, sprinkle over ½ tsp toasted sesame oil, depending what else is in the meal. Serve immediately. This is one of these dishes which are unmistakably Chinese, even without soy sauce, and yet will fit into almost any other context. It's great with a pie, for example.

"Seaweed".
It's usually kale which is used for this, but cabbage makes very good seaweed. Simply shred green cabbage finely, and drop small amounts into hot deep-frying oil. It will sizzle and dry very quickly. Fish it out and drain on kitchen paper. An excellent garnish which goes not only with Chinese meals but almost any hot dinner.

SALADS

Many cabbage salads are variations on cole slaw, with shredded cabbage, sometimes other vegetables, and a dressing which can be thin, or creamy, or mayonnaise-based. Having said that, there is a great range of tastes and textures possible, and you need never be bored by making the same thing too often.

Basic Coleslaw.
Actually there is no such thing as a standard recipe for this American favourite. In all cases, you start with **white cabbage**, quartered, cored, and shredded to give amounts suitable for your need. The cabbage used to be soaked in ice water for up to an hour, then drained and dried; I don't do this. There may be, but don't have to be, additions – **carrot or onion and/or pepper**. Sweet tooths (teeth?) will like the cabbage mixed with crushed pineapple. The dressing can be vinaigrette, sour cream dressing, mayonnaise, or "cooked salad dressing", which is the homemade version of salad cream. You can use bottled salad cream if you like it; the homemade version is nicer, doesn't have additives or preservatives, but is still very sharp. The following is the version I would make most often, with ingredients I always have available.

Default Coleslaw.
Shred **a quarter of a hefty white cabbage**. Mix the shreds with **3 grated carrots** and **half a green pepper**, shredded. **Salt** and **pepper**. Mix well with **4-5 tbsp. vinaigrette, made with 1 tsp. French mustard, 1 tbsp. wine vinegar, 4 tbsp. extra-virgin olive oil.** Leave an hour or so before serving.
If you like it with a more weighty dressing, use a mixture of **1 tsp. French mustard, 2 tbsp. mayonnaise (homemade or bought),** and **2 tbsp. plain yoghurt.**

American Cooked Dressing. Mix together **1 rounded tbsp. plain flour, 2 tsp. sugar, ½ tsp. salt, 1 tsp. dry English mustard powder,** and **a very little cayenne pepper**. In the top of a double boiler, beat this mix into **1 egg**, then add **200 ml milk, 50 ml. wine vinegar**, and add **30 g butter**. Heat over boiling water, stirring from time to time, until the dressing has thickened slightly. Let it cool. If this is too acid for you, it can be let down with double cream! You can use tarragon vinegar, when it becomes an admirable dressing for appetisers made with slices of Granny Smith apple. In the original form, use it to dress coleslaw, with or without other ingredients.

Luxury Coleslaw. Shred **enough white cabbage for 4**, and stir with the **juice of ½ lemon** and some chopped **parsley** and **chives**. Beat **150 ml. double cream** till thick, and add **½ tsp. each celery seed and sugar**, and **salt** and **pepper** to taste. Add **100g green grapes**, turn over the cabbage, and mix well. Garnish the top with **toasted flaked almonds.**

Barbecue Coleslaw.
This has the flavours used in barbecue sauces. Mix **4 tbsp. mayonnaise, 4 tbsp. plain yoghurt, 2 tbsp. tomato ketchup, 1 tbsp. wine vinegar. Salt** and **pepper**. Add **6 chopped spring onions**. Add dashes of **Tabasco** to taste. Use this mixture to dress enough **shredded cabbage for 8**, with grated **carrot** and slivered **green pepper** added.

Coleslaw with Blue Cheese
The dressing uses a **small pot of sour cream (150 ml)**, with **1 small chopped shallot, salt** and **pepper**, and **about 50g blue cheese** mashed into it. I find both Roquefort and Danish Blue too strong here, and would use Stilton or mild Gorgonzola. Grate an apple into the cabbage shreds, add the juice of a lemon, and mix well with the dressing. The dressing is enough for 6-8 helpings.

Russian Coleslaw.
Soak **enough cabbage shreds for 6** in ice water for 30 mins, drain and dry. Add **2 tsp. sugar,** mix, then **salt** and **pepper**, and mix again. Add **½ green pepper**, slivered, and **12 ready-to-eat prunes**, slivered. Make the dressing: put **150 ml double cream** till into a bowl, and gradually stir in **3 tbsp. white wine vinegar**. (Or you can use sour cream and reduce vinegar to 2 tbsp.) Add **3 tbsp. grated horseradish**, and **1 small shallot**, chopped very finely. **Salt** and **pepper** to taste. More horseradish if it needs it. Turn the salad in the dressing, and serve.

Coleslaw with Emmenthal. (or Gruyere, old Gouda, Cheddar, etc)
Mix **shredded cabbage for 4, 5-6 stalks celery**, peeled and finely chopped, and **120g Emmenthal** in small strips. Dress with a garlicky

vinaigrette; pound **1 clove garlic** to a paste with **½ tsp. salt**, in a mortar or on a chopping board. Mix with the **juice of ½ a lemon** and **4 tbsp. extra-virgin olive oil**. Just before serving the salad, put **2 quartered hard-boiled eggs on top**. I actually prefer this with Cheddar; its stronger, less subtle flavour stands out against the dressing better, I think.

Nourishing Cole Slaw.
Shredded cabbage, with grated **carrot**, grated **apple**, **roasted sunflower seeds** and **salted peanuts**, and **currants**. Proportions to your taste. Make the dressing with **100g cottage cheese, 4 tbsp. plain yoghurt, ½ banana** in a blender and add **apple juice** to thin down to dressing consistency. (I can't tell you how much; it depends which yoghurt and cottage cheese you are using) (I once used white wine when I had no apple juice, and that was also very good) **Salt** (remember the salt in the peanuts) and **pepper** to taste. Children really like the lucky-dip quality of this.

Asian Coleslaw.
Shred **½ a medium white cabbage** (or other if that's what you have). Add **3 coarsely grated carrots, 1 shredded red pepper, 2 grated apples,** and **50g crushed roasted peanuts**. Dress with a mix of **1 tbsp. soy sauce, 1 tbsp. brown sugar, juice of a lemon** (or 2 limes), with **2 cloves garlic** and **1 deseeded chilli** finely chopped. Taste, and adjust till you like it.

Other cabbage salads tend to be simpler than coleslaw, and use other cabbages than white. Take the Italian **Savoy Cabbage Salad.**
This uses garlic crusts, about which I was doubtful with lettuce; here, they show their potential. Shred the **centre of half a Savoy cabbage**. Take **2 pieces of CRUSTY bread crust**, each about the size of half the end crust of a large English tin loaf. Rub each with a **peeled and lightly crushed clove of garlic**, so that the crust absorbs as much flavour as possible. Add to the cabbage, mix, and let stand covered about an hour. Ten minutes before serving, toss the salad with **oil, vinegar, salt and pepper**. Remove the crusts before serving – or, if you like the taste of garlic, break into smaller pieces and leave in, which is what I do. It could hardly be simpler or more classy.

Sour Summer Salad.

Use a **small spring or summer cabbage, of approx. 500g**, for this. Take off the coarse outer leaves and any core, and shred the remainder. Add **half a medium iceberg lettuce**, also shredded, and **1 grated carrot**. Then add **1½ tsp. salt, 2 tbsp. red wine vinegar, 1 tbsp. olive oil, 1 tsp. dried oregano or herbes de Provence**, and the **tip of a tsp. of cayenne pepper**. Mix well. Let it sit, covered, at least an hour, possibly better overnight.

Moroccan Cabbage Salad.

A **small young spring or summer cabbage**, cored and shredded. Add **3 medium oranges**, peeled so no pith remains, and segments only used, **5 tbsp. orange juice** – mostly from peel and skin, but make it up if necessary from more oranges – the **juice of a lemon, 2 tsp. sugar, a small handful of raisins, 1 tsp. salt**, and a pinch of **ground cinnamon**. Mix well and chill, covered, 2-3 hrs. I actually prefer it after it's stood overnight. You may need to drain off some juice before serving.

Greek Winter Salad.

Even in Greece it is not perpetual summer, and Greeks adapt their salad to what is available. In winter, use about **500g green or white cabbage**, shredded. Dress this with **4 tbsp. extra-virgin olive oil** and **juice of 1 lemon**, about an hour before you want to eat it. Or longer, if more convenient. Just before eating, mix with a **handful of salad greens** as available, such as watercress, rocket, Cos lettuce, in small pieces. Arrange these on a large plate, and sprinkle over **a small red onion**, cut into rings, about a **dozen black olives**, and some shredded **green pepper** if available. Small not-too-hot **pickled peppers** can be arranged on top, as well. Crumble **250g feta cheese** and heap in the middle, and sprinkle with **dried oregano**. Sprinkle quite a lot of chopped **parsley** all over the salad, then dribble over **2-3 tbsp. extra-virgin olive oil**. Squeeze over **lemon juice** to taste. **Black pepper**. Salt is provided by olives and feta, but taste to see if you want more. I can't say it's as good as the high summer version, but on its own terms it's an excellent salad.

Shredded Cabbage with Tahina.

I dote upon tahina salad; it's one of the items I daren't leave around the kitchen because I dip my finger in every time I go past, and it's very soon gone. So this salad, which uses a whole batch and is compulsive – tahina tastes with bulk and texture – has a lot going for it. For the tahina salad, crush **1-2 cloves garlic** (or more) in a mortar with **1 tsp. salt**. Add about **quarter of a jar of tahini**, the unmixed paste, and stir. Work in the **juice of 2-3 lemons**; as it thickens, let it down with a little water, until consistency and acidity are right. Ideally, it's left for some hours to mellow, but I'm happy to eat it straightaway. To this amount of sauce add **500g white cabbage**, finely shredded, and mix well.

SOUPS.

Quick Cabbage and Ginger Soup.
Quarter, core and slice **a medium green cabbage**, and start to cook it in **50g butter** on a low heat. Add **50g root ginger**, peeled and grated or chopped finely. When the cabbage is somewhat wilted, add **1 litre vegetable stock**, and cook for 10 mins. or till softened. Let it cool, and whizz in a blender or puree otherwise. Taste and season. Serve with **sour cream**. It's a thin soup, and croutons go well, but they needn't be more than toast cut into squares. This is about the simplest soup you can imagine, and very good with it.

Cabbage and Apple Soup.
Shred **half a white cabbage**. Chop coarsely **3 onions** and **4 cooking apples**. Put all of these in a pot with **50g butter**, and sweat for 15 mins. Stir from time to time to make sure nothing catches. Add **2 chopped cloves garlic, 1½ litres stock, salt** and **pepper**, and simmer for 5-10 mins. Let it cool and whizz smooth. Serve with a little grated **horseradish**, or a dollop of horseradish cream, in each bowl. I'd also like croutons, but they aren't necessary. This isn't a pretty soup, but it's simple, cheap, and disguises the presence of cabbage for those doubtful.

Savoy Cabbage Soup with Asian Flavours.
Finely shred **half a Savoy cabbage**. Chop **500g onions** finely. Cook the onions gently in **2 tbsp. sunflower oil** for 10-15 mins, stirring and avoiding browning, then add the cabbage shreds. Fry another 5 mins, stirring often, then add **4 chopped cloves garlic, 2 chopped seeded green chilis, a knob of root ginger** peeled and chopped, and **2 tbsp. coriander seeds**, ground finely. Cook another 5 mins, stirring. Add

800 ml. vegetable stock, simmer for a couple of minutes, then add **a tin (400 ml) of coconut milk**, the **juice of 3 limes or 2 lemons**, chopped **fresh green coriander** to taste, and **salt** and **pepper**. Serve while the cabbage is still crisp.

Main-Meal Cabbage Soup.

Really a cabbage-heavy version of a minestrone, and the vegetables can be varied according to what you have. Heat **4 tbsp. oil** in a large pot which has a lid, and add **2 large chopped onions**. Let them fry slowly while you prepare and add **4 large celery stalks**, peeled and sliced thin; **2 medium carrots**, peeled and diced; **4 cloves garlic**, finely chopped; **3 medium potatoes**, peeled and diced. Stir in about **800g green cabbage**, quartered, cored, and shredded – in this case, if the shreds are too long to eat conveniently, cut them in half. Let the cabbage cook until it is wilted and the volume reduced. Add **1½ litres stock, a tin of crushed tomatoes, 1-2 bay leaves**, some **thyme** –fresh or dried, and **salt.** Simmer 5 mins, add the **beans (cannellini or borlotti or haricot or flageolet) from 1 tin (or your own home-cooked beans)** and leftover or specially cooked rice. For this quantity, ideally you would have 100g raw rice, cooked, or around **200g cooked rice** – but it depends what you have. The soup should be thick. You can use small cooked pasta instead; I don't think the pasta should be cooked in the soup, as it would mean the cabbage would be overcooked. Taste for seasoning, and serve with spoonfuls of **yoghurt.** I'd like **pesto** with it, but it's not authentic.

Shchi

Shred **700g white cabbage**, and chop finely **200g onion, 1 small celeriac, 1 small parsnip.** Cook the onions gently in **50g butter** for about 10 mins, till they are soft but not coloured. Add cabbage, celeriac and parsnip, turn down the heat, cover the pan, and cook 15 mins more. Meanwhile, peel and dice **500g potatoes**. Add **2 litres stock**, simmer 20 mins, then add the diced potato. Simmer 20 mins more; add **4 tomatoes from a tin**, chopped. (This is winter, and you need tomatoes with flavour) Cook 10 mins more, then taste and add **salt** and **pepper**. In an ideal world, this would be eaten with little pastry tartlets filled with cottage cheese mixed with eggs, but I have to admit that for me, **sour cream to dollop in** is enough, and I've never made the tartlets. If you want to add a slightly sour cheese flavour and a crisp texture, toast some grated **Caerphilly** on toasts, to make cheese croutons.

Savoy and Cannellini Bean Soup.
This soup, from the Romagna region of Italy, cooks the cabbage long and slow in very little liquid with onions, bringing out a deep and mellow flavour. **250g cannellini beans, cooked.** You can obviously use other beans than cannellini if that's what you have. If using dried beans, they need to be soaked overnight (or quick-soaked) and boiled without salt till done. Cook **75g chopped onion** in **4 tbsp. extra-virgin olive oil** on medium heat until the onion is golden. Add **3 chopped cloves garlic**, and stir. Then add the shreds from **1 large Savoy cabbage** and **½ tsp. salt**. Turn to coat the cabbage with oil and onion. Then add **100 ml. water**, cover, and cook VERY slowly for 3 hrs. Add a little more water if needed, but there should be none left at the end of this process. Add the cooked beans, or beans from 2 tins, drained and rinsed. Cover all with about 3 cm. water, and add **1 tsp. Marigold stock powder** (or use stock, but the flavour difference doesn't come through here) Simmer about 30 mins, and add **salt** and **pepper** to your taste. Serve with a drizzle of **extra-virgin oil** on each plate, and grated **Parmesan** on the table. It needs crusty, chewy bread on the side, which can also be dunked in the soup.

I've only given 6 soup recipes, but it will be clear they are all pretty variable. I've tried to cover the main ways of preparation. However, there are none of the heavy, main-meal soups of France, Spain and Russia in particular, because these all depend on a meaty stock, and meat in the soup, and they lose their character if converted to vegetarian versions. Historically, there probably wasn't much meat, and what there was was preserved, but the flavour of the soup needed this. If you are not vegetarian, I urge you to look for these soups and try them.

Cabbage Main Dishes.

Bubble and Squeak.
A traditional English dish from leftovers, but much much nicer than that implies. It is the crispy brown bits interspersed among the cake that make it so good; so cook it long and slow, in a large frying pan. Use approximately **equal volumes of mashed potato and leftover,**

stirring, about 2 mins, till lightly browned. Add **a mug of the bean cooking water** and stir, scraping off any sticky deposits in the pan. Tip the whole lot back into the main pan, and go on cooking. Wash and drain the **contents of a jar of sauerkraut**, and add this to the soup pan. Go on cooking until the beans are done, probably another hour.. Mash the potatoes roughly, and stir them into the soup pot. Add **salt** and **pepper** to taste. You can eat it now, but it is better chilled for a day or so, and reheated. Serve with grated **Parmesan**.

Sauerkraut-Stuffed Pancakes.

These pancakes can be eaten as soon as they are ready, or reheated some time later with a little stock in the oven, or reheated later by frying. I don't like the last option, but it's nice to know it's there.

First make the sauerkraut filling: start by frying **3 large onions**, finely chopped, in **2 tbsp. oil** till lightly browned. Add **250g mushrooms**, roughly chopped, and fry, stirring now and then, about 5 mins. Add the **contents of a jar of sauerkraut**, rinsed and drained well, and **1 tsp caraway or cumin seeds**, and cook over moderate heat for about 10 mins, stirring now and then. Add **80 ml sour cream, cautious salt** – taste – and **pepper**. This is the filling. Make **2 batches pancake mix** (in total 250g flour, salt, 2 tbsp. neutral oil, 2 eggs, 300 ml. each milk and water; see Basics). Start to make the pancakes, filling each with a good rounded tbsp. of filling as you cook the next one. To roll the pancake, fold one side over the filling, which should be off-centre; turn in the sides, and roll up. They end as compact cylinders. I get 17-18 pancakes out of this mix. If using immediately, keep warm as you make them, and serve with **more sour cream**. If reheating, put in a dish as they are rolled. To reheat in the oven, arrange in a lightly buttered baking dish in one layer, and pour over **enough stock to come ½ cm up the sides**. Cover with foil and heat in a medium (170) oven for 10 mins or so, and serve with **sour cream**. For frying, use clarified butter, enough to be ¼ cm deep, and turn to brown on all sides. Refrying pancakes is better with a richer pancake mix, but the whole thing then is suitable for people doing heavy work outdoors in winter – lumberjack stuffed pancakes, you might say.

Carrots

Carrots are second only to onions in the range of dishes they are used in, and in their versatility alone or with other veg. They get used in sweet dishes as well as savoury, Asian dishes as well as Western, and on top of all this they are cheap to buy. You owe it to yourself to have a range of carrot dishes at command, for everything from simple snacks to complicated meals. Chefs and restaurants don't do much with them – too cheap, too common – all the more reason for cherishing them.

Default.
This is carrots as a simple vegetable accompaniment to a main dish. Wash if needed. Top and tail **6 medium carrots** for 4 people, and peel. I always peel mature carrots, even organic or the sort sold as "no-need-to peel", but you may feel differently. Slice into thinnish rounds, less than ¼ " or ½ cm. Cover with **water**, and add **½ tsp salt**, **15-30g butter**, and **1 tsp sugar**.   Bring to the boil, and simmer 10 mins or so with the lid on. Take off the lid, turn up the heat, and boil off the liquid. You can tell when it's gone because the sound changes to a sizzling, frying noise. Shake round well. You don't need them to brown, but they are also good if lightly browned. These would be proper **Carottes Vichy** if cooked in Vichy water not tap; as it is they are **Glazed Carrots.** I would never simply boil them when I can do this.

Peasant Carrots, from the South of France.
A slight variation on the recipe above. Use **1 tbsp. olive oil** not butter, and add **1 or 2 finely chopped cloves of garlic.** Finish with lots of chopped **parsley**. I'm not sure I don't prefer this to the default, but the garlic makes it maybe less friendly to other things you're eating.

Roast Carrots with Barbecue Sauce.
Chunks of carrot are a fairly constant presence in my mixed vegetable roasts, but I seldom do them alone. If they are roasted alone, (peel and chunk **500g carrots**, roll in **olive oil** with a little **salt** and **unpeeled cloves of garlic**, cook at 170 for 20 mins or so) and you want to fancy them up a bit, they respond well to coating with a sticky barbecue-type sauce when they are nearly done; try this one. Soften **1 chopped onion** and **2 chopped cloves garlic** in **1 tbsp. oil**. Mix in the food processor

with **300 ml. tomato ketchup, 2 tbsp. cider vinegar, 4 tbsp. maple syrup, 1 tbsp mushroom ketchup, 1 mean tsp. chipotle chilis in adobo (or other chili; 2 fresh, seeded; or crushed chilis from a jar; or even good few dashes Tabasco)**, with the **peel and juice of an orange**. Process till smooth, and simmer uncovered for 10 mins. Pour some of this, at least 4 tbsp., over the roast carrots, stir, and cook another 10-15 mins. This is not as sweet as most commercial or home-made barbecue sauces, but it will go sticky and caramelised for all that. The recipe makes much more than you need, but a barbecue sauce is always useful to have around.

Steamed or Butter-Cooked Grated Carrots
Another simple way of cooking them starts by grating the prepared carrots. Then you can either steam the grated tangle, or sweat them in butter under a lid. They don't take long. If using the butter, keep turning them from time to time, and season early. The only trouble I know with steamed carrots is that you have to season at the end, and it's not easy to distribute the salt evenly into the tangle. Apart from this minor hiccup, steamed grated carrots are great, especially as garnish or bed.

Carrots flamed with Pastis
Strictly, for this, you should cut the carrots into matchsticks, or julienne. It's easier just to grate them, unless you have a julienne disc on the food processor. Whichever, prepare **8 medium carrots**. Heat **15g butter** with **1 tbsp. olive oil**; when hot, tip in the carrots, add ½ **tsp. salt**, and saute for about 10 mins, stirring often. When they are done, add **2 tbsp. white wine**, increase the heat, and cook till all the liquid is gone. Take the pan off the heat, add **3 tbsp. Ricard, Pernod, or other version of pastis**, and light cautiously. Swirl the pan until the flames die out, taste for seasoning, and serve quickly in a warm dish. I often find it difficult to light the pastis; if you do, don't worry, just bubble till the alcohol has evaporated and left the flavour behind. A little **chervil** would pick up the aniseed notes.

Carrots with Garlic, Ginger, and Cumin
Cut **500g carrots**, prepared, into small cubes, or grate them. Blend together a **5-cm piece ginger, peeled and chopped, 4 cloves garlic, peeled and chopped**, and **2 tbsp. water**. Heat **1 tbsp. sunflower oil** and add **2 tsp cumin seeds**, and cook ½ min. Add the ginger/garlic puree, and cook over moderate heat for 1 min. Add the carrots, and

stir so they are coated with the spicy mixture. Add **150 ml water** and **salt**, and cook covered till the carrots are just tender – about 20 mins for julienne, 10 for grated. **Pepper**, and cook till the liquid is evaporated. Add the **juice of a lemon**, and serve. Sprinkle with chopped **green coriander** if you have some.

Carrot Puree.

This is one of the purees that came to prominence with Cuisine Minceur in the 1970's, and is very virtuous and easy to eat. It needs positive flavouring to avoid the baby-food connotations.

Boil the **carrots**, drain, and puree in food processor or through a mouli-legumes. Beat in **a small piece of butter**. Add ½ to 1 tsp. **brown sugar**, to bring out the sweetness of the carrots. **Salt** and **pepper; nutmeg** is good; or quite a lot of chopped **herb**. Chervil is delicious if you have it, so is tarragon, but parsley is fine.

Carrots with Soy-Lemon Butter.

Prepare **6 carrots** and cut into thin rounds. Boil or steam them, and drain. Turn into a warm bowl, and add **15g butter, 1 tsp soy sauce, the juice of ½ a lemon**, and **1 chopped spring onion. Salt** and **pepper**. Because the seasonings are sparse, eaters tend to think that these are normal carrots which happen to be extra-delicious.

Carrots with Marsala.

An Italian dish, moving towards something you could eat by itself, and would want to. For about **8 medium carrots**; prepare them, and cut them lengthways, then crossways, to give 4 pieces. Then cut each piece lengthways once or twice, to make sticks of approximately uniform size. Start them in **30g butter** in a lidded frying pan, without its lid at the moment, and cook on a low heat for about 5 mins, turning now and then. Add **salt** and **pepper, 1 tsp sugar**, and **120 ml. Marsala**, and simmer gently about 5 mins. If no Marsala, try another rich sweet fortified wine – Bristol Cream sherry, or cheapish port, for example. Then cover the carrots with **water**, put on the lid, and cook gently till done. Take off the lid, and boil away the liquid, until there is a small amount of rich sauce. Serve sprinkled with chopped **parsley**. You could also try using red wine with 2 good tbsp. redcurrant jelly; this isn't Italian any more, but still makes a good dish.

Carrots with Parmesan.

Also Italian, obviously, and one of my favourite vegetable dishes. But it is neither fast nor trouble-free, so it doesn't turn up very often. Prepare **700g. carrots**, and slice into rounds of 1-cm thickness or a bit less. If the tails are thin, the discs can be a bit thicker there. Put the carrots with **50g butter** in a large frying pan – or 2 if needed – so they fit in a single layer. Add enough **water** to come half-way up the carrots, and cook uncovered over medium heat until the water has evaporated. Add a splash of water, and **1 tsp salt, ½ tsp sugar**. Go on cooking over a low heat. You're aiming to get the carrot pieces well-browned, shrunken, and wrinkled – so keep adding a little water as the pan gets dry, and turning the carrots. If you've used two pans, you'll be able to get them all into one as they shrink; if one pan, you might want to transfer them to a smaller one. This stage takes 1½ to 2 hrs, and you need to keep your eye on them. When they are cooked and the liquid is gone, add **30-40g grated Parmesan**, turn them over in it, and serve immediately. I always feel I could eat the lot by myself, but I'm unlikely to be allowed to. Believe me, it's worth the effort.

Turkish-Style Carrots.

Boil **500g carrots** in **salty water**, trimmed, peeled and cut in thinnish rounds. When nearly done, drain, leave a little, then toss in **flour**. Fry them in **2 tbsp. olive oil** till brown, and turn into a serving dish. Pour over **300 ml. warmed yoghurt**, and sprinkle with **toasted cumin seeds** and ground black **pepper**. Chopped **dill** wouldn't come amiss, either, if you have some.

Chinese Sweet-and-Sour Carrots.

I am always astonished how Chinese this tastes, even though there are no obvious Chinese seasonings. It's an ideal extra dish if you are doing a Chinese meal of several dishes served together.

Cut **6-8 medium carrots** into oblique slices, and stir-fry in **2 tbsp. sunflower oil** for 1 min. Add **1 tsp salt** and **150 ml. water**, cover, and let boil until the carrots are cooked , 5-10 mins depending on age. Mix **2 tbsp. white wine vinegar or rice vinegar, 2 tbsp sugar, 1 tbsp. cornflour** with **300 ml. water**, pour over the carrots, and stir until the sauce is thick and translucent. That's it.

Basic Carrot Salad.

Carrot salad can be so varied, convenient, and cheap, that I tend to eat some version most days through the winter. It can be made with chunks of carrot as well as grated, and seasonings from many countries are responsible for the many forms. And that's not to mention the carrot sticks for dipping, or the many times it turns up in other salads, of which cole-slaw is only one. The basic version has **grated carrot, extra-virgin olive oil and lemon, salt** and **pepper**, and **a few currants**. Vary the dried fruit (I like cut-up dried ready-to-eat apricots), replace fruit with nuts, leave out fruit and add herbs . . .Really, look round the garden, fridge and cupboards, and see what needs using, which will complement the carrots.

In my experience, it isn't worth setting up a mechanical gadget to grate ½ a kilo of carrots, and washing it up afterwards. Do it by hand. If you are doing carrot salad for 30, they will need around 3 kg. carrots, and then a mechanism is marvellous.

Moroccan Carrot Salad

This shows what I mean about variation of seasoning. Grated carrots, **lemon juice** and **a little olive oil, salt,** and **orange-flower water** to taste. This is better if left for an hour or so for the flavours to mingle. Decorate with **black olives**.

Nigella's Carrot and Peanut Salad.

This is in Forever Summer, and in my view it is unimproveable. Grate **4 medium carrots** very coarsely, mix with **80g salted peanuts**, and dress with **2 tbsp. red wine vinegar, 2 tbsp. sunflower oil**, and a **few drops dark sesame oil**. That's it. How can it be so good?

Carrot Salad with Balsamic Vinegar.

Grate **4-6 carrots**, and dress with **1 tbsp. balsamic vinegar, 2 tbsp. olive oil, salt** and **pepper**. Add **sultanas** and **blanched almonds** to taste.

Carrots with Apple and Horseradish.

Grate **6 medium carrots** and **2 Granny Smith apples**, peeled if you like. Mix a **small tub of sour cream** with (ideally) **fresh horseradish, or grated horseradish from a bottle**, to taste. NOT horseradish sauce. **Salt, 1 tsp sugar, juice of ½ lemon**. Mix the carrot and apple into the sauce, and also mix in some chopped **parsley**. Sprinkle the top with more parsley. It may seem obvious, but I've only just realised that if you want your dish to have the parsley taste, mix some in and then sprinkle more on top. You can also vary this by using French mustard instead of horseradish, but the sauce should taste less of mustard than it should of horseradish. The mustard can swamp the flavours; the horseradish points them up. Let this stand at least an hour; it's still fine next day.

Carrot Salad with Mustard Seed Dressing.
Grate **4-6 medium carrots**, and add a **palmful of sultanas. Salt,** and the **juice of 2 limes.** Heat **3 tbsp. sunflower oil**, and add **1 tbsp. whole black mustard seeds**. Cook till they are popping vigorously. Pour all over the carrot mix, stir, and serve.

Carrot Salad with Garlic and Ginger.
Grate **4 large peeled carrots**. Add little **salt, walnut-sized knob of ginger**, peeled and chopped finely, and **1 large clove garlic**, ditto. Add **1 tbsp. extra-virgin olive oil**, and mix lightly with your hands (OK, spoon would do, but hands don't compress the mix.) Leave to stand at least ½ hour. The ginger and garlic flavours permeate the carrots, and it's lovely and also unusual, when most carrot salads bring out the sweet side with currants, etc.

Carrot Salad Thai-Style.
This is adapted from a recipe from Stephanie Alexander's Cook's Companion, and she was aiming to replicate Thai green papaya salad. It's very good, strong-tasting, compulsive – and very low in fat.
Start by chopping together **3-4 cloves garlic, a lump of ginger the size of a walnut-with-shell, peeled, a mild chili, seeded**, and a **few sprigs of fresh green coriander**. Scrape these into a bowl, and add **1 tsp brown sugar, (dark for preference), the juice of 1 lemon or 3 limes, 1 tbsp. soy sauce**, and a **palmful of chopped salted peanuts.** Trim and peel **4 medium carrots**, grate into the mixture, and stir well. You can eat it straight away, but it's better left a couple of hours, or even overnight. Two people tucking in can easily eat all of this, but conventionally it would serve 4-6.

Carrot Salad with Hijiki (Sea Vegetable).
OK, sea vegetable is a less off-putting way of saying seaweed, and hijiki is even more obscure. It comes as a dried mass of black threads, usually from Japan.

Soak **15g hijiki** in **150 ml warm water** for 10 mins or so, drain, rinse, and simmer in water to cover for 10 mins more. Let cool, and drain Mix with **6 medium carrots**, grated, **2 chopped spring onions, 1 tbsp. sunflower oil**, and **1 tbsp. soy sauce**. Mix in **50g. roasted sunflower seeds**. It doesn't need salt, as the hijiki and the soy sauce are both salty.

Carrot Salad with Bay Leaves
The form of the carrots is part of the pleasure of this salad. Ideally, make it the day before you want to eat it.

Peel **6-8 medium carrots**, and then use the vegetable peeler to cut long strips from head to tail of the carrot. Be careful – I almost always graze myself when doing this. When you get near the carrot's core, you can't get the width of the strips any more, so keep the middles for stock. Dump the carrot ribbons, with **2 bay leaves**, in boiling **salted water**, and cook for 1 min. only after it comes back to the boil. You want to soften the ribbons without depriving them of all their crunch. Drain, keeping the bay leaves, and run cold water through them to cool. Dry them on a clean kitchen towel. Mix the carrot ribbons with **5 tbsp. extra-virgin olive oil, 1 clove garlic very finely chopped, salt** to taste, and black **pepper**. Press the mixture down, cover, and leave to marinate 8 hours at least. Fluff up the ribbons before serving.

Carrot Salad with Harissa.
Peel and slice **8 carrots** into thick rounds. Mix **2 tbsp. olive oil, the juice of a lemon, ½ tsp. salt**, and **2 tsp. harissa**, and pour over the carrots in a pan. Add **water** almost to cover, and simmer, covered, for about 30 mins, taking off the lid for the last 10 mins. to reduce the liquid. Let it cool. Roast **2 tsp. cumin seeds** in a dry pan, or under the grill. Mix chopped **fresh green coriander** and ½ tsp. (yes, a lot) of **freshly ground black pepper** into the carrots, and sprinkle the cumin seeds on top. Let it stand a couple of hours before eating. The seasoning here is so dominant that you can use this for any root vegetable – potatoes, turnips, swedes – and it will still be great and warming.

Carrot Salad with Hazelnuts and Feta.

You can make this with any cut of carrot – grated, matchstick, half-rounds. Matchsticks probably give the best effect but are also a bit more hassle; I tend to use half-rounds. Whichever, boil **8 medium carrots** until just tender, and drain. Dressing of **oil, lemon, very little salt**, and a **herb** –oregano, ideally. Let it cool. Mix in **hazelnuts**, roasted a little and rubbed in a towel to get rid of (most of) their skins. Put broken-up chunks of **feta** on top, and dribble these with **a little more extra-virgin oil**.

Carrot and Green Pepper Salad.

Heat **4 tbsp. sunflower oil**, and add **2 tsp. mustard seeds**. When they have popped, turn down the heat, and add **2 tsp. cumin seed**. Let this toast a little also, then add **3 carrots**, thinly sliced, **3 green peppers**, seeded and cut into squares, **2 tsp. garam masala** and **¼ tsp. cayenne pepper**. Put on the lid, and cook over low heat 5-10 mins, stirring sometimes. Stir in **1 tbsp. brown sugar, salt** and **pepper**, and the **juice of 2 lemons**, and let cool. Taste for seasoning before eating. This is half-way between a salad and a pickle. If your conscience lets you use more oil, it helps the mix keep better -- but it probably won't need to. Delicious strong curry-type flavours; it's very good with plain rice and dhal, but it will also add zip to any amount of hot or cold Western foods.

French Country Carrot Soup, or Potage Crecy a l'Ancienne Mode.

This carrot soup, thickened with bread, is an example of how attention to detail makes a delicious soup from almost nothing.

You need about **150g. of bread crusts**, with about 1 cm. crumb left on. Say, the 2 crusts of a home-made style loaf, or make up the weight from the bottom of a baguette. Wholemeal adds to the flavour but makes the soup look brown and murky; I prefer white bread here for this reason, but there isn't a lot in it. Cut the bread in large dice, and dry out in a low oven, without browning. Meanwhile, cut **500g carrots** in slices, and chop finely **1 large onion**. Sweat the carrot and onion in **40g butter** for 10-15 mins. on low heat, covered. If you have a **leek**, slice this and put in with the carrot and onion. Add the bread cubes, **1 litre stock**, and some **parsley stalks** tied together for ease of removal. (Or drop them in and have flecks of green in the soup, which is what I would do) **Salt** if needed, **1 tsp. sugar**. Simmer gently about 40 mins, then let cool a little and blend. Reheat the soup, thinning with more stock if it needs it. Taste for **salt**; add a good grinding of **pepper**. Just before serving, stir in **50g. butter**, sprinkle with chopped **chervil (ideal) or parsley**, and serve with little crisp **croutons**. It is the quantity of butter that gives this soup its quality; if you don't want to use this much, do another soup. This isn't the most delicious of soups, but it's quite good, and feeding 4 people for less than £1 is amazing!

Three-Colours Italian Soup.

This is delicate, subtle, and easy to do Start by peeling and dicing roughly **700g potatoes**, and cook them in **salted water** to cover. When they are done, push potatoes and liquid through a mouli-legumes, or blend them. Meanwhile, fry gently **2 chopped shallots in 20g. butter** till transparent; add **1 carrot**, peeled and diced, and **2 stalks celery**, also peeled and diced. Cook for about 2 mins, then empty the mixture into the potato puree. Add **30g Parmesan**, grated, **300 ml. milk**, and **300 ml. stock**. Bring to the boil, stirring, and cook about 5 mins. Mix in chopped **parsley** as the soup is served, and have little **croutons** and more grated **Parmesan** on the table.

Spiced Carrot Soup.

Carrot and coriander soup seems to have become a modern classic in England, so that you can buy it in packets, in tins, and even as Cup-a-Soups. So try this slightly more elaborate, and spicier, version.

Grind together **2 tsp. cumin seed, 1 tsp. coriander seed, ½ tsp. black peppercorns**, and the **seeds from 6 green cardamom pods**. Fry **1 medium onion**, roughly chopped, in **1 tbsp. sunflower oil** for 5 mins, then add **2 cloves garlic**, chopped, a   **2-cm knob ginger**, peeled and chopped, **1 chili**, seeded and cut up, and the spices. Cook 5 mins more, stirring so that it doesn't stick. The smell at this stage is wonderful. Add **1 kg. carrots**, peeled and sliced, and **1 small chunked sweet potato**, like a N.Z. kumara, or half a more normally sized one. Add **1 litre stock**, and **1 tsp. salt**. Simmer till the carrots are cooked, then work through a mouli-legumes or blend. Add the **juice of 3 oranges**, freshly squeezed, and thin with **stock** to get the consistency that pleases you. Taste; you may want more salt, or to increase the heat with a dash of **Tabasco**. Sprinkle with chopped **fresh green coriander**, and serve with **sour cream** on the side, so that people can swirl in a spoonful or so to taste. This makes 6-8 helpings, but can be reheated next day if some is not eaten.

Carrot and Cashew Soup.

Nearly a whole-meal soup, this is derived from Recipes for a Small Planet. This 70's book worked on the principles of increasing the protein content of vegetarian dishes by using complementary sources of incomplete protein; the reason I keep on using it is that almost everything I've tried from it has been delicious. For the last 25 years we have thought that getting enough protein isn't a problem; now I think I see the first swing of fashion towards emphasis on protein again. But remember, you are not eating nutrients, but food. Enough hobbyhorse; to the soup.

The soup is not pureed, so it's important to cut the vegetables small and neat. Chop **2 medium onions**, and sweat them in **4 tbsp. oil (your choice)** for 5 mins. Add **10 medium carrots**, peeled and grated, and sweat with the lid on another 5 mins. Add **2 chopped apples**, peeled and cored; **a small tin tomato paste, 1 litre stock**, and **1 tsp. salt**. Bring to the boil, and add **50g. brown rice**. Simmer, covered, for 40 mins, or until the rice is done. Add **50g. raisins or sultanas**, and **100g cashew pieces** – bought like that or roughly chopped if you have whole ones. The cashews should be raw, not roasted. This is either a very thick soup or a thin stew; whichever, it's really good. Serve with a bowl of **yoghurt or soured cream** to swirl into each plate.

You may have leftovers from this soup. On reheating, it will probably have thickened because of the rice, and you will need to add more stock or, possibly, milk.

Now we come to main dishes based on carrots. Souffle, gnocchi, pudding, curry, fricassee – and there are more, like a sformato, which can be adapted from other sformatos like French beans

Carrot Fricassee.

Gentle, subtle, warming. comforting; an ideal winter centrepiece. Peel and slice **2 medium onions**, and peel and slice thinly **8 medium carrots**. Sweat them in **30g. butter**, covered, till tender but not browned, about half-an-hour. Add **2 cloves finely chopped garlic** for the last 5 mins. Then add **1 rounded tbsp. flour**, stir it in, and cook a few mins. more, again avoiding browning. Add **150 ml stock, 150 ml. milk**, and bring to a boil, stirring. **Salt, pepper, nutmeg**. Simmer uncovered until the sauce is the consistency of single cream. Just before serving, beat **2 egg yolks** with **4 tbsp. double cream**, and fold into the carrots OFF THE HEAT. Stir until the egg yolks thicken the sauce a little more; you may need to put back on a low heat, but don't let it get even one bubble. Sprinkle with **parsley**. If you serve it in a vegetable dish, it's nice to stick **triangles of fried bread or toast** round the edges; if not, have them on the table. Some crunch is good with the mellow unctuousness of the dish. You can elaborate on this – adding turnips, celery root, etc; or leaving out the egg-yolk/cream thickening, and covering it with pastry and baking for carrot pie; or even serve with dumplings. Try it as above first, though.

Carrot Pudding, or Liberated Stuffing.

Grate **3 peeled medium carrots**, and mix with **450 ml fresh breadcrumbs**, made yourself, not commercial. I do mine in the coffee/spice grinder. Saute **1 small chopped onion, 2 stalks celery** finely chopped, and **2 chopped cloves garlic** in **30g. butter** till soft, and add to carrot/crumb mix. Add **80g sultanas (or raisins or currants)**, and some chopped fresh herb. Oregano, thyme, fennel, parsley – one of these. **Salt, pepper, 2 eggs**. Mix together well. Turn the mix into a greased baking dish, Pyrex for preference, scatter the top with **flaked almonds**, and bake at 170 for 30 mins, or till well-browned. It needs gravy or sauce, such as tomato or mushroom.

Carrot/Potato Gnocchi.

Maybe this should be in the potato leftovers section, as you need to start with about **250g leftover mashed potato**, not too wet. Mix in **2 medium carrots**, grated, **1 small onion**, finely chopped, **2 eggs, 50g grated cheese, salt, pepper** and **nutmeg**. Now add **flour, about 150g.**, to make a soft dough. It's impossible to be precise; it depends on the consistency of the potato. Chill for 1 hr or so. Then divide the dough into 4, and roll each part by hand on a floured surface to a rope about 1 cm thick. Cut into gnocchi about 3 cm long. Cook them, 10-12 at a time, in boiling salted water until they float; scoop out and drain. Arrange in a buttered baking dish, dot with more **butter**, and bake at 150 for 15-20 mins. Serve with grated cheese, ideally **Parmesan**. A wow of an elegant first course for an Italian or any meal; fills you up; very cheap; and uses leftovers. How much more housewifely virtue do you need?

You can stop at the soft dough stage, and fry it as carrot/potato cakes, and eat with tomato sauce and maybe a fried or poached egg to make a whole meal. Not so elegant, but easier.

Carrot and Brazil Nut Souffle.

Trim, peel and grate **2 medium carrots**, and squeeze them dry in a tea-towel. Chop **an onion** finely, and sweat them both in **30g. butter** till soft. Work in **30g flour**, then add **120 ml. milk** to make a thick sauce. Season; I like some **fennel seeds** as well as **salt** and **pepper**, but you may prefer nutmeg or lots of black pepper or herbs. Grind **60g. Brazil nuts** in the food processor, then add the thick sauce and whizz together. Add the **yolks of 4 eggs** and whizz again. Separately, whisk **4 egg whites** with a **pinch of salt** until they are firm. If you have a spare egg white from something else, include it here. Beat about a quarter of the whipped egg whites into the sauce, then turn this mix on top of the rest of the egg whites and fold in carefully. Turn into a buttered souffle dish, and cook at 200 for 25-30 mins, or till done. The best way to test is to give the souffle, still in the oven, a small sharp push; if the centre, only, trembles, it's done.

Carrot and Pea Curry.

Fry **2 medium onions**, finely chopped, in **2 tbsp. oil** till brown. This always takes longer than you expect – 15 mins at least – but keep stirring from time to time. Add **2 cloves garlic, a walnut-size lump of ginger**, and **a green chili**, all finely chopped, and cook 2-3 mins more. Add ½ **tsp turmeric, 1 tsp. ground coriander, 1 tsp. ground cumin, ½ tsp. garam masala, tip of a tsp. cayenne pepper**, and ½ **tsp cumin seeds**, and cook 2 mins. more. Add **4 tbsp. water** and **2 tomatoes** from a tin, broken up, and cook 2-3 min. again. Now add **250g carrots**, peeled and diced, and **150g frozen peas, salt**, cover, and cook gently till done. Squeeze over the **juice of ½ lemon**, and sprinkle with chopped **fresh green coriander** if not using it elsewhere in the meal.

As if all this isn't enough, carrot can go into sweet things too. I've come across muffins, "coffeecakes", breads . . but can't really recommend them The two below, carrot cake and Indian carrot halwa, I can and do urge you to try.

Carrot Cake.

Another modern classic, American-derived. You can make this very rich, and there are many recipes out there for more elaborate cakes than my version. It's a staple of cathedral tea shops, vegetarian restaurants, and supermarket cake displays. Anyhow, try my version, which is comparatively simple, easy to make, and cheap.

Mix **150g. self-raising flour, 150 g. brown sugar** (I like light brown here), a **tiny pinch of salt**, and **½ tsp. each of ground cinnamon and mace**. (You can grind 3-cm cinnamon stick and the mace pieces that will fit on a teaspoon, and the cake will be better for it.) Put in food processor, add **150 ml vegetable oil** and **2 eggs,** and whizz until well-mixed. Turn out into bowl, and stir in **3 medium carrots**, trimmed, peeled and grated, and **50g roughly chopped walnuts**. Turn into an oiled 18 cm (7") cake tin, and bake at 170 for 45-60 mins (testing for doneness with a skewer). Cool in tin before turning out. The normal topping for a carrot cake uses **60g. cream cheese, 150g. icing sugar**, and **30g. soft butter** whizzed in the food processor. Add **vanilla EXTRACT, a few drops**, to taste, and spread over the cake. If this icing is too rich for you, as it is for me, just sprinkle the top of the cake with **icing sugar mixed with a little cinnamon**, and rubbed through a sieve over the cake.

Indian Carrot Halwa.

Bring **1 litre. milk** to a boil, and add **350g. prepared grated carrot (5-6 medium)** Simmer till it thickens. At first you have to watch and turn down the heat to stop the milk boiling over; after a while this doesn't happen, though I don't know why. When the milk is much reduced and the mixture thickens, add **180g. soft brown sugar, 3 heaped tbsp. flaked almonds, 1 tbsp. clear honey**, and **30g. unsalted butter**. Go on cooking this until very thick. Add **¾ tsp. kewra water**, and spread in a flattish dish. Decorate the top with **green unsalted pistachios**. Indians would also add very thin pieces of edible silver sheet, but this is tasteless, not easy to come by, and you'd have to keep explaining it to your guests. The amount given above makes quite a lot, 12 or more helpings, but it does keep, covered, in the fridge. It is an oddity for most English tastes, but once tasted, almost always enjoyed.

Celeriac

Celeriac is that roughly-spherical, creamy-coloured veg with a tangle of roots at the bottom and a pattern of small scars all over the rest. It looks, and behaves in the kitchen, like a root; botanically it isn't a root but a corm, but this doesn't affect the way you treat it. It is celery-flavoured, but with a completely different texture to bunch celery. It used to be quite rare, and something to be grabbed whenever possible; now it's available all through autumn and winter, and this is a real advance to be welcomed. Mostly English, as well. I think of it as a treat which you can often have.

Default. In this case, there are two possibles, one where it's a salad and one where it's cooked.
Celeriac remoulade is the salad. Peel the **celeriac** thickly, and remove any spongy bits in the middle. I find the easiest way to peel is to quarter vertically first, and then you can see better how much you need to take off. The peel can be used in stock. When peeled, cut it into matchstick slivers, either with a knife or using a food processor. Grated isn't right for this. When you have the slivers, you can blanch them in boiled salted water for 1 min or less, or miss this out. I prefer the minimal softening you get with blanching, and think it improves the taste. You may not agree, and it's certainly easier not to blanch. If blanching, drain well and dry, and mix with very mustardy mayonnaise. Not very much; **2 good tbsp. mayo**, with **1 tsp French mustard**, smooth or whole-grain, will do slivers from a quarter of a celeriac. You can garnish with **capers, gherkins, olives, or herbs**, or just have it alone. A really smashing classic winter salad. **Celeriac and salt lemon salad** isn't classic, but this is a very worthwhile variation. For the amount above, shred **½ a salted lemon**, and mix in.

Celeriac and Potato Mash
This is the default method where I want to use it hot. Peel and chunk a **celeriac**, and peel and chunk **a roughly equal volume of potatoes**. (A whole celeriac will make mash for 5 or 6, and you may not have that many to feed) Boil them together in salted water till done – about 20 mins, then drain. Ideally, push through a mouli-legumes with large holes. Not a food processor, which makes potatoes gluey. If nothing else, just use a fork to mash. **Salt, pepper, butter,** and **hot milk** to

reach your preferred consistency. Beat the hot milk in well. (Mash is always supposed to be made with hot milk, but I don't always bother to heat the milk, and it's hard to tell the difference.) You can get a more intensely tasty puree if you omit the milk, and hold back some of the water the veg. were boiled in for the mash.

Another delicious mixed puree is **Celeriac and Carrot Mash.**
Peel **a medium celeriac** and **500 g carrots**, and boil or steam the veg. till just done. Drain, and mash with **salt, pepper, nutmeg, 50 g butter**, and **milk or single cream** to get a pleasing mash. As I've said elsewhere, my favourite mashing tool is a mouli-legumes, but this mix can be mashed in the food processor without going gluey. It is more apt to leave recalcitrant lumps than the mouli, however. You can obviously use other vegetables instead of, or as well as, the carrot, such as swede or beetroot.

Celeriac, Chestnut and Potato Puree

This is the best of these mixed purees, and is definitely one for a ceremonial meal. I have used it for a Thanksgiving meal, and people had two or more helpings. It's done a little differently, as the veg. are braised rather than boiled. Sweat **1 large onion**, finely chopped, in **40g butter** till soft, about 10 mins. Add **500g celeriac**, trimmed, peeled and chunked, **1 kg potatoes**, ditto, and **300g vacuum-packed chestnuts**. (This is a bit of a cheat; if you want to prepare fresh chestnuts, it can only be good) Add **½ litre stock**, and enough **water** to cover. **Salt** if there is none in the stock. Simmer till the potatoes are done, and push everything through a mouli-legumes. Add **butter, salt if needed, pepper**, and enough of the **cooking liquid** to make a fairly soft consistency. This puree reheats very well in the microwave, making it convenient if you are doing an elaborate and celebratory meal.

Any leftovers from any of these purees can be shaped into patties, floured, and fried in a little oil till browned on both sides. The plainer purees can be enriched by adding walnuts or hazelnuts. Or, more elaborately, made into croquettes by coating with flour, egg, and crumbs, and deep-frying.

Roast Celeriac

This is a simpler method of cooking celeriac, and is excellent alone or with other vegetables. I usually do several vegetables together; chunks **celeriac, potato** and/or **sweet potato, onion,** and **squash** or **other roots** if these are around. Add some cloves **garlic**, unpeeled, and **olive oil** and **salt**, mix, and roast at 160 for 40 mins or till done.

Spicy Celeriac.

Peel and cut **a large celeriac** into chips. Cook these in a large pan (which has a lid) in **3 tbsp. sunflower oil** for about 10 mins, till lightly browned. Add **1 tsp fennel seeds, 1 tsp. black pepper** roughly crushed, **¼ tsp cayenne, ½ tsp. salt**. Stir again. Add a **few tbsp. water** and the **juice of 2 lemons**, cover the pan, and simmer till done. Add **chopped herbs** if you have some.

Celeriac Crisps are more of a snack than part of a meal. Peel the **celeriac**, and cut into very thin slices. Deep-fry these till golden brown, drain well, and **salt**. One book I have suggests eating these dipped into garlic mayonnaise; it sounds delicious but thoroughly unwise.

Celeriac Braised with Orange

This is really a variant on the reduction method of cooking. Put **250g prepared diced celeriac** in a pan with the **juice of 2 small oranges (Seville if you have them), 1 tsp honey, 10g butter, ¼ tsp salt,** and **6 tbsp. water**. Simmer partially covered until the liquid has reduced to a glaze. Good alone or with chopped **chives**. Normally I'm quite casual about orange or lemon pips getting in to the dish when I squeeze them – it does show it's the real thing! If you use Sevilles here, though, do use a squeezer to take out the pips, as there are so many of them that practically every mouthful will have a pip in it if you don't. That apart, this is a 5* way of cooking celeriac, especially if you let the celeriac toast a little at the end.

Celeriac Gratin.

Peel and chunk a **celeriac**, and blanch for 15 mins in salted water. Drain, and chop a little in a buttered ovenproof dish. **Salt** and **pepper** and **nutmeg** to taste, then add a **good slurp of single cream** – not awash, but visibly present. Bake at 180 for 20-30 mins, till lightly browned. You can add a sprinkle of cheese to the top, if your meal doesn't already have enough cheese in it.

Celeriac and Potato Gratin.

Peel and trim **½ medium celeriac** and **500g potatoes**. Slice both very thinly. Layer in a buttered wide baking dish, adding **salt** and **pepper** to each pair of layers. Heat **300 ml milk** with **2 chopped cloves garlic**, and let it stand for a few mins. Add **100 ml double cream**, then pour over the sliced veg. layers through a sieve. (or not, if you've chopped the garlic finely and don't mind finding bits) Bake at 130 for an hour or so, until the layers are very tender and the top is browned. In the original, Dauphinoise, version of this, cream is used for all the liquid. This is too rich for me, and most people who try it. Because this gratin is an adaptation of the original, there is no reason not to vary it if you like, for example by having 1 or 2 layers sliced onion in there. But as written it is delicious, filling, warming, and makes a meal with only a green vegetable or salad.

Salads.

Most celeriac salads have a thick dressing, based on mayonnaise or cream. Celeriac remoulade (default, above) is one of these, and this can be played with by adding other ingredients. **Celeriac, carrot and cress salad** has grated carrot added to the celeriac/mayo mix, and is garnished with cress. That's cress as in mustard-and-, or watercress, or landcress if it grows in your garden. (I grew some 25 years ago, and it is still around, self-seeded and not much wanted). A bit less mustard in the mayo for this one. I prefer this with the mayo/yoghurt/mustard mix I use such a lot.

Celeriac, Apple and Walnut Salad.

This is a variation on the American Waldorf Salad, and I prefer it. It can be dressed with mayonnaise, but I use the mix of **1 tsp. French mustard, 1 tbsp. Hellman's, and 2 tbsp. plain yoghurt** that is my regular substitute. This amount of dressing is enough for **½ smallish celeriac**, peeled, shredded, and blanched 1 min; **1 grated apple**, and **50g or so broken-up walnuts**. It's best when eaten within an hour or so, as it can go soft if kept overnight.

Celeriac and Green Bean Salad.

If you are being purist about local and seasonal, opportunities to make this are infrequent. It is delicious, and worth stretching a point for occasionally. Peel and shred **a medium celeriac**, and blanch. Lift the shreds out with a slotted spoon or skimmer, keeping the water to cook **200g thin French beans** (can even be frozen). Drain these and cut into shorter lengths. Chop finely **2-3 shallots**, and cut **a green pepper** into slivers. Mix in a salad bowl. Pound **2 cloves garlic** with a little **salt** in a mortar, and add **1 tsp. French mustard, the juice of a lemon**, and **5 tbsp. extra-virgin olive oil**. Add finely-chopped fresh **basil** to taste. When well mixed, pour over the salad and mix well. Scatter **black olives** over the top, and decorate with more **basil** leaves.

Double Celery Salad.

There's something a bit showy about combining celeriac and celery, but it is a very good salad. Shred and blanch **½ a medium celeriac**, drain, and mix with **4 tbsp. olive oil, 1 tbsp. white wine vinegar, salt** and **pepper**. Let it marinate for an hour or so. Cut the **inner part of a head of celery**, stalks destringed, into shreds about the same size as the celeriac. Cut into pieces of the same size **100g hard goat's or sheep's cheese** – Manchego, Ossau Iraty, something like that. There are good English versions, but they tend to be available only where they are made and in London. Drain unabsorbed dressing from the celeriac – it can be used for dressing another salad, and the celery flavour will improve it. Mix celeriac, celery, and cheese. In yet another bowl, mix **1 heaped tsp. French mustard** with **100 ml. double cream**, whisking. **Salt, pepper, chopped parsley**. Add the dressing to the salad, taste, and eat.

Celeriac, Mushroom and Cheese Salad.

There is a well-known Italian salad, consisting of raw mushrooms, cheese, and a little celery. I substituted quite a lot of celeriac for the celery, and found a superb winter salad. You want equal volumes of sliced raw mushrooms and celeriac – say **100g mushrooms** and **200g celeriac**, or a quarter of a medium specimen. Slice the mushrooms, and dress with **2 tbsp. extra virgin olive oil, the juice of ½ a lemon**, and **salt**. Cut the celeriac in shreds, and blanch for 1 min. in boiling salted water. Drain, let cool, and mix with the mushrooms. Add **50-75g firm but mild cheese**, cubed. In Italy this would be Fontina, in France Gruyere. I use mature Gouda. The point is that it should not be crumbly, nor too strong; mild, nutty, solid and creamy are the properties. But if you only have Cheddar don't let this stop you.

Celeriac and Hard-Boiled Egg Salad.
Peel and shred a **500g celeriac**, and blanch the shreds as usual. Drain well. Mix with **1 shredded green pepper, 120g small black olives**, and **6-8 shredded cornichons** (or half a dill pickle) . Dress with some of a tomato vinaigrette; **2 tbsp. red wine vinegar, 1 tbsp. tomato paste, 1 tsp. French mustard, 8 tbsp. olive oil, salt** and **pepper.** Arrange on top of **green salad leaves**, decorate with **halved hard-boiled eggs**, and sprinkle a little more vinaigrette on each egg. Note: celeriac salads never contain fresh tomatoes, but the flavour here is really enhanced by the tomato paste.

Cream of Celeriac Soup.
Boil together a **small peeled celeriac** and **300g potatoes**, both cut in chunks, in **1 litre. water or stock**. When the potatoes are cooked, puree the soup – blender, stick blender, mouli-legumes – and thin with a little **milk**. Reheat, taste for seasoning, and add a knob of **butter** and a dollop of **cream** before serving. This soup is so simple that its quality and purity come as a real surprise. **Croutons** are an enhancement.

Celeriac and Cepe Soup.
The idea for this soup came from Jane Grigson's Vegetable Book, and the dried cepes add remarkably to the flavour, as they usually do. Just cover **15g dried cepes** with boiling water, and leave to stand until needed. Sweat **100g onion**, chopped, in **50g butter** until it starts to soften. Add **150g prepared celeriac**, in small chunks, and **100g peeled chunked potato**. Cook 5 mins longer, on a low heat. Lift the soaked cepes from their water, and add to the pot. Pour in the soaking liquid, leaving behind the last drops and the sediment. Add **600 ml. water** and **salt,** bring to the boil, and cook gently till done. Puree the soup by your favourite means. Thin down if necessary, taste for **salt. Pepper** at this stage. Serve with dollops of **sour cream** in the soup bowl, and **croutons**.

Split Pea and Celeriac Soup.
Soak **100g split peas,** green or yellow, whichever you have, overnight. Next day, warm **3 tbsp. olive oil** in a soup pot, add **3 bay leaves, a**

sprig of rosemary and **2 cloves sliced garlic**. Add **1 large onion**, chopped, **1 medium celeriac**, diced, **2 outer celery stalks** chopped, and cook gently about 10 mins. Add **100ml dry white wine**, raise the heat, and let the wine evaporate. Add **1 litre stock or water**, and the drained split peas. Cook, salt-less, until the split peas are very soft. You can now puree all the soup or just some of it. Pureeing part of the soup leaves some texture in the soup while thickening it; do it if you like bits in your soup. (In this case, you need to cut the vegetables smaller and more neatly than if you're pureeing completely) Drizzle each serving with **extra-virgin oil**, and serve with **croutons**. Really an excellent and unassuming winter soup.

Celeriac Nicoise.

A stew which can be eaten hot or cold. Cook **a chopped onion** in **olive oil** for about 5 mins or till slightly softened. Add **2 chopped cloves of garlic**, then, after a few moments, **300g (half a medium) celeriac** trimmed and cut into small chunks. Add a **tin of tomatoes** and a **sprinkle of dried mixed herbs** (herbes provencale for preference) Cook, covered, until the celeriac is done, and taste for seasoning. This is a good place to use a **5-pepper mix**. Add the **juice of a lemon**, stir, and eat. If serving cold, drizzle with a little **extra-virgin olive oil**.

Celeriac Loaf.

Prepare **enough celeriac to give 350g prepared**. Put in a food processor with a **handful of parsley, 80g walnuts, 1 medium chopped onion**, and **a fresh seeded chili**. Whizz. Mix with **2 beaten eggs, 80g breadcrumbs** (brown for preference), **2 tbsp. olive oil, 1 tbsp. mushroom ketchup, salt,** and **350 ml. milk**. Put in an oiled loaf tin, and bake slowly at 150 for 1 to 1¼ hours. Serve sliced with **tomato sauce or mushroom sauce.**

Celeriac Stew with Lentils.

Sweat **1 small chopped onion, 1 small chopped carrot, 2 chopped celery stalks, 2 chopped cloves garlic**, and **a bay leaf** in **2 tbsp. olive oil** for 5-10 mins. Add **½ medium celeriac**, peeled and cut into small cubes, and **300g lentils**. Puy lentils are best, but ordinary brown lentils will do. Add **stock to cover**, and simmer gently, with a lid, until lentils and celeriac are cooked. If there is free liquid, boil until it has evaporated. **Salt** and **pepper**. Add chopped **parsley, 2 tbsp. extra-**

virgin olive oil, and **1 tsp. sherry vinegar**. Eat it alone or with plain rice or couscous.

Celeriac Souffle.

This is an unusual souffle, in that there is no white sauce involved, just a puree of celeriac. Peel and steam (preferable) or boil **1 large celeriac**, cut in chunks. Put in a food processor with **a good knob of butter, 1 tbsp. French mustard, 2 egg yolks, salt, pepper**, and **nutmeg**. Whizz smooth, and transfer to a bowl. Beat **4 egg whites** to soft peaks. Beat about a quarter of the egg whites into the celeriac puree to lighten it, then tip all on top of the remaining egg whites and fold in. Scrape into a buttered souffle dish, and bake at 170 for about 30 mins. Easy and spectacular.

There are many more things to do with celeriac, but they seem mostly to be variations on the above. Just play with the possibilities. I haven't found a bad one yet.

Celery

There has been a great change in the growing of celery over the past 30-50 years. It used to be an autumn vegetable; now it's available year-round. And availability has meant that it's possible to keep a head of celery in the fridge, so it's always ready as a flavour base for dishes like pasta sauces, soups, stock, and more.

Celery used to be earthed up; it came very dirty, almost white, and very tender. Modern self-blanching celery, which is the kind almost exclusively available, is larger, clean, pale green, and is much more stringy than the old sort. You could eat most "dirty" celery raw, after washing. With modern celery, only the inner stalks are tender enough, and they need peeling thinly to get rid of the strings. Self-blanched does have a stronger and more characteristic flavour. Cookery books haven't really caught up with this change; for example, they will still give dishes using whole celery hearts, which are impractical when you need to peel or chop the stalks to remove the strings. I think you need to peel even if you are going to slice and cook your celery. And the best way to do this is with a swivel-action potato peeler. Don't rely on cutting one end nearly through and pulling off the strings this reveals, because it won't get them all. You may not mind strings as much as I do, but I think most people prefer their celery string-free.

In most of this book, I haven't been very precise about measurements, because a little more or less isn't crucial to the working of the recipe. Well, it isn't here, either, but celery does vary a lot in size. At one extreme, I've seen celery in Australia that's about 1m long, and sold in quarters. At the other, a "dirty" celery head may be not much more than 10 cm. A standard supermarket head weighs about 600g, and after taking the inner stems and heart, and destringing, you get around 150g. of celery usable raw. This is the size I've standardised on; if your celery is different in size, adjust accordingly. And always keep any leaves, as they can go into stock and even be used alone (see deep-fried leaf fritters below.)

Default. In spite of all I said above, this has to be celery sticks, peeled of their strings, and eaten raw with cheese or as part of crudites. Use only the central part. The outer stalks are a mainstay of vegetarian stock. Celery with hard, strong English cheeses is classic at midday or evening meal (call it dinner and tea, or lunch and dinner, depending on your background)

Waldorf Salad.
Everyone agrees that this American salad should have apples, celery, walnuts, and mayonnaise. After that everyone disagrees on proportions. Americans like more – sometimes much more—apple than celery; English versions have about equal amounts. My version is even quirkier, because I prefer more celery than apple – by volume, about 3 parts celery to 2 parts cubed apple, but do it by eye not measuring. String and slice finely the **inner part of a head of celery**, and use **a sharp, firm apple**. Cox, Russet, Granny Smith, Jazz apples all give a different effect. Core the apple and cube, but leave the skin on to look prettier. I use my mayo-substitute mix of mayonnaise, plain yoghurt, and mustard, in quantity to bind not swamp the solids. (For 1 medium apple, 1 celery heart, that's **1 dsp mayo, 1 rounded dsp Greek yoghurt, and 1 mean tsp. French mustard**) **Pepper** well, and taste to be sure it's as you like it. Add a **small handful of broken walnut halves** before serving. It's a chewy salad, and I think eaten most easily with a spoon – though this is strictly for domestic meals.

Celery, Walnut and Blue Cheese Salad.
Strong and delicious flavours, served on a **bed of greens** – lettuce, or other salad greens in season. I like a bitter flavour, as from endive (Belgian endive) or Batavian endive or chicory. Prepare and slice the **inner parts of a head of celery**, and mix with about **a quarter of its volume in walnut pieces**. Dress with **3 tbsp. walnut oil, 1 tbsp. white wine vinegar, pepper, very little salt**, and let chill. (If you happen to have **walnut ketchup**, add some of this to the dressing to taste) Let the salad chill for about 1 hr, then add **100g cubed blue cheese** of your choice – I think Stilton is best here, but I'm happy with most kinds. Turn over gently and spread over a bed of greens.

Celery, Mushroom and Cheese Salad.
The **inner parts of a head of celery**, stringed and sliced crosswise very thinly. Slice **100g button mushrooms**, and add to the celery. Vinaigrette: **3 tbsp. extra-virgin olive oil, 1 tbsp. wine vinegar, salt** and **pepper**. Mix and add **100g cheese** cut in small sticks or cubes. Which cheese? I can't think of any hard or semi-hard cheese which

wouldn't be good. Tasty Lancashire? Aged Gouda? Pont l'Eveque? Crumbly acid Caerphilly? Sage Derby? Spanish sheep's milk Manchego? If all else in the fridge fails, Cheddar will be as good as – but no better than – any of these. Note: raw mushrooms tend to soak up oil, and you may want to add some more as you serve it.

Celery and Cashew Nut Salad.
In fact there are other vegetables here which make it really colourful, but it's the dressing that's really distinctive. Put **1 tsp. juniper berries** and **½ tsp peppercorns** in a mortar, and pound them well. Mix in **2 tbsp. olive oil, 1 tbsp. gin**, and then **3-4 tbsp. mayonnaise**. Taste, **salt**, and adjust. Mix the **inner parts of a head of celery**, sliced; **50g cashew nuts**, lightly toasted, **1 grated carrot, 1 diced red or yellow pepper**, and mix with the dressing. Sprinkle with chopped **parsley**. If you have some, add some grated **mooli** (long white radish) or **half a (Belgian) endive** – this adds something white to the composition, and makes it taste even more agreeable.

Chinese Marinated Celery.
You need **2 inner portions of celery** for this, say **300g peeled stalks**. Cut into 5-cm lengths, and mix with **½ tsp salt** and **1 tsp sugar** in a bowl. Leave for 10 mins. Mix **2 tsp. sugar, 2 tbsp. sunflower oil, 1 dsp. toasted sesame oil, 1 tbsp. soy sauce, 1 tbsp. cider or wine vinegar, 1 clove garlic**, very finely chopped, and **1 small fresh chili**, deseeded and chopped. Rinse, drain and dry the celery, and mix with the dressing. Let it chill for at least 3 hours and up to a day. (Ideal make-ahead stuff) You can, but needn't, add chopped **herbs**, like fresh green coriander, parsley, or a tiny bit of lovage if you grow it. I say "if you grow it", but if you start with a small lovage plant, before you know where you are you have a 2m monster spreading about 1m wide, and you are desperate to find ways of using it. It grows like a very vigorous weed. And it's perennial, so it does the same every year, starting in April. Its flavour is so strong, to me at least, that 2 leaflets are as much as you can use at once. It tastes like a mix of celery and Marmite.

Celery, Rocket, and Pickled Lemon Salad.
Not much to say; quantities as you like them; no acid in the dressing. Brilliant side salad, especially with Mediterranean food.

Celery, Apple, Beetroot and Potato Salad.

Make a dressing with the **yolk of a hard-boiled egg, 3 tbsp. walnut oil, the juice of a lemon, salt** and **pepper**. Add to this the **middle part of a head of celery**, destringed and sliced thinly; **1 apple**, peeled, cored and cut into small cubes, and about **100g cooked potato**, cut into small cubes. Just before serving, add **a cooked beetroot**, cut into small cubes, and stir gently. You can garnish with chopped herbs, but the pallor of the other ingredients with the brilliance of the beetroot seems to me enough. It will keep overnight, but will go the colour of a bowl of berries; pretty enough, but not what you expect as a savoury.

Celery and Potato with Blue Cheese Dressing.

Cook **700g salad potatoes**, boiled or steamed as you prefer. Peel and cube or slice, depending on the size (come to that, leave them whole if they are small. However, I do think potatoes in salad should be peeled) Peel while they are hot as you can manage, ideally; hot potatoes absorb flavours better. Sprinkle **2 tbsp. white wine vinegar** and **1 tsp. salt**, mix, and let them cool. Add the **inner part of a head of celery**, destringed and sliced, and **6 spring onions**, sliced, and **6-12 radishes**, washed, dried and sliced, and mix all together. Make the dressing, which is a flavoured mayonnaise: put **1 egg** into a blender, and add **salt, pepper, 1 tbsp. white wine vinegar**, and **½ tsp. French mustard**. Have ready in a jug **120 ml. sunflower oil**, or other mild-flavoured oil. Also have ready **100g mild blue cheese** – creamy Gorgonzola, Blue Shropshire, for example. Start to whizz the egg mix, and pour in through the lid about half the oil. Stop, and add the broken up blue cheese. Add a few shakes of **Tabasco**. Replace the lid, and continue to blend while adding the rest of the oil. Taste and adjust to your liking before persuading the dressing out of the blender. Put dressing on potato mix, turn it in, and eat. I see no reason why the dressing shouldn't be made in a food processor or by hand; it's just that I'm used to using the blender for this type of thing.

Celery Boats.

The sort of thing you might want to nibble with drinks when being elegant. **Inner stems**, destringed, and cut into lengths. The easiest filling, and very nice too, is cheese of some sort; **Boursin with garlic and herbs, or blue cheese mashed with cream cheese** are the ones that come most easily to mind. You could really go OTT with a tapenade stuffing and a toothpick with a slice of radish standing upright.

After that selection of salads – there could be many more – let's move on to cooked celery. I can't remember the last time I was offered cooked celery outside my home, and it's deeply unfashionable. Partly, I am sure, it's the fact that it used to be boiled, and it was soggy and stringy at the same time. Whatever the reasons, though, cooked celery offers a range of tastes, depending on the method of cooking, and combines with many other flavours in more filling dishes. Just make sure the stems are thoroughly stringed, and the outside stems can be used and enjoyed. It can be stir-fried, roast, braised, and cooked in combination with other veg.

Stir-Fried Celery.

This uses truly remarkable quantities of garlic to complement the celery flavour. Prepare **500g celery stalks**, destringing thoroughly. Slice them thinly lengthwise, then cut the lengths into pieces about 2 cm. Peel and chop **12 large cloves garlic**, or a head. Have ready **120 ml. stock**. Heat **2 tbsp. sunflower oil** in a wok or large frying pan. Add the garlic, and stir briefly –10-20 secs. Add the celery and **1 tsp. salt**, and cook on high heat, stirring, for 2 mins. Then add the stock, reduce the heat a little, and keep stirring until the stock has reduced to a glaze. Eat IMMEDIATELY. No soy sauce, nothing which isn't European – but it tastes very Chinese and savoury.

Roast Celery.

Clean, destring and slice about 5cm long the **outside stalks from 2 heads celery**. Put in a roasting tin, and add **1 red onion** cut in wedges, a halved **head of garlic** (take away any white membrane that comes away, but don't peel), **2 sprigs thyme, 2 tbsp. olive oil**, and ½ **tsp. salt**. There should be more than one layer in the roasting tin; if there isn't, turn the lot into a smaller tin. Turn all this over with your hands to mix. Roast at 200 till tender and done, probably 40-50 mins. Turn every 15 mins or so. You can, as usual with roasting vegetables, add any others you have around. I like celery roast with winter squash, for example.

Deep-Fried Celery Sticks.

An appetising nibble, perhaps going with vegetable crisps. Destring **outer stalks of celery**, and cut into the shape of small chips – say, 5 cm long, along the length of the stalk, and ½ cm wide. Soak them in **milk** for 30 mins or more, till you're ready to fry them. Heat **oil for deep frying**. The originator of this method of cooking, John Tovey, dipped the drained sticks in flour mixed with curry powder. I don't use curry powder; I use **50g plain flour** and **2 tsp. garam masala**. (The main difference, it seems to me, is that curry powder is often heavy on fenugreek, and garam masala doesn't use it) Anyhow, put flour, spice mix, **extra ground black pepper**, up to 1 tsp, into a bag, and add the drained celery chiplets. Shake to coat, and tip into a sieve (over a plate, so the flour doesn't fly everywhere) Shake to get rid of excess flour. Then drop small handfuls of strips into the oil, spreading them out as far as you can, and trying to keep separate with a skimmer. They will brown in a few minutes, not a quick in-and-out. When brown, lift out, drain, sprinkle with **salt**, and eat.

Celery Leaf Fritters

If you get passionate about using every bit of food, you'll eat a lot of these. Even if you don't, eat some sometimes. There's a reason why deep-fried food is so popular, and this is a good example. Put **200g flour, ½ tsp salt, 200 ml. milk, 1 egg**, and **15g melted butter** in a blender and whizz. Add to the blender **30g blue cheese**, and **celery leaves from a large head**, washed and chopped. You should have about 50-60g celery leaves, but this is just a guide. The mix should be green. Anyhow, blend again, and pour and scrape the mix from the blender. Heat oil for deep frying, and drop dessertspoonfuls of batter into the fat. Not too many at once. Fry till golden brown, scoop out, drain on paper, kitchen or news-, and serve straightaway. I've never eaten these with deep-fried celery, but it could be a witty combination.

Oven-Braised Celery

Prepare (wash and destring) the **outer stems from 2 heads of celery**. Cut into 5-cm lengths. Heat **2 tbsp extra-virgin olive oil** in an ovenproof dish, and add the celery. Turn and cook gently for 2 mins. Add **250 ml stock, salt** and **pepper** (and a sprig of **thyme** if you have one), stir, and put in a 150 oven Cook for 20-30 mins, stirring now and then, until the stock is reduced and the celery tender. You can cook it, covered, on top of the stove as well.

Celery with Parmesan.

This starts off much the same as the last recipe. The shallower the layer of celery in the pan, the better, so use as large a pan as you have. Before adding the celery, cook **1 small chopped onion** in the **oil** until it starts to colour. Add the **celery**, fry 2 mins, then add **250 ml stock** and oven-braise until the celery is tender and the stock much reduced. Turn up the oven to 200. Now fiddle with the dish a little, so the top layer is pieces of celery with the inner side up. Sprinkle the top with **60g grated Parmesan**. Put back in the oven for 5-10 mins, until the cheese has melted and turned slightly crusty. Let it stand out of the oven a few mins before serving, just so it's not likely to burn mouths.

Celery with Potatoes and Olive Oil.

This is ridiculously easy, and the only unknown is the cooking time. It can be anything from 30 to 50 mins, but it will keep warm. Prepare the **outer sticks from a head of celery**, and cut into 5 cm lengths. Put in a saucepan with **6 tbsp. olive oil** and **water to cover**, and cook, covered, 10 mins. Peel **500g waxy potatoes**, and chunk them. Your normal boiled-potato size is what's wanted. Add to the pot with **1 tsp salt** and the **juice of ½ lemon**. Cover and cook gently till done. If there is still some water left, uncover and boil it away; there should only be oil left at the end. Serve hot.

Celery, Leeks, Tomatoes.

Wash, destring and slice thinly the **outer stems of a celery head**. Trim, clean and slice **4 small leeks**. Sweat these, covered, in **40g butter** for 5-10 mins. Add **4 medium tomatoes**, peeled and chopped (or use the whole tomatoes from a tin, chopped), and **100 ml stock or water**. **Salt**. **A small sprig of rosemary**, if convenient. Cover and cook slowly for 20-25 mins, till the celery is tender. Take out the rosemary, taste, **pepper**, and sprinkle with chopped **parsley**.

Celery Soup.

Wash and destring **200g outer celery stalks** (If you don't destring here, you can sieve the soup after liquidising. I think thoroughness at first is preferable) Chop roughly, with some **celery leaves** if you have some. Also chop **a medium onion** and **100g peeled potato**. Sweat all of these in **50g butter**, covered, for about 10 mins. Add **1 litre stock**, and simmer 30 mins or so. Let cool a little and blend. Taste for seasoning. Now finish according to taste, time, purpose, and conscience. (i) Add **250 ml milk** and top with chopped **herbs** of choice; (ii) Pour a **few tbsp. double cream** in a swirl on the top; (iii) Particularly if entertaining and wanting to be luxurious, thicken with **2 eggs yolks** and **150 ml. double cream** (see Basics) (iv) Add and stir in **3-4 tbsp. double cream**, then crumble some **blue cheese** on top.

Celery and Tomato Pasta Sauce.
Makes enough for 400g pasta, for 4 moderate appetites. Peel and finely chop **a small onion,** and cook on a moderate heat in **40g butter** and **1 tbsp. extra-virgin olive oil** till it starts to brown. Add **3-4 prepared celery sticks**, chopped, and as many **leaves** as you can muster (well, within reason. No more than half the volume of the celery sticks) Cover, turn down the heat, and cook about 10 mins, stirring now and then, Add **1 tin (400g) whole tomatoes** with their juice, and mash the tomatoes about with a wooden spoon to break them up. **Salt** and **pepper**. Add **herbs**, fresh or dried, at this point if you like, but the sauce is purer and fresher without. But I am a fan of rosemary or thyme with celery, so sometimes I do and sometimes I don't. Cook gently, uncovered, until the sauce has reduced to – well, sauce consistency -- 10-20 mins. Meanwhile cook and drain the pasta, and mix with the sauce and grated **Parmesan** to taste.

Celery Risotto.
You want this to be permeated with celery flavour, and it has celery in several forms to show off the variations. First make sure that the stock is strong on celery, and add a few lovage leaflets as well if you have it. Allow **1-1½ litres of stock** for **300g rice**, for 4-6 people. The stock should be cautiously salted – I think about **½ tsp salt per litre of stock** is about right, because the flavour concentrates as the stock evaporates. Have the stock nearly boiling next to the risotto pan. Cook a **small finely chopped onion** in **50g butter**, until changing colour. Add **5-6 outer celery stalks**, destrung, and chopped finely, and stir. Add the chopped **inner leaves of the celery head**. Cook a few mins more, stirring, then add 300g risotto rice and stir this to coat with the butter. Start adding ladle-fuls of stock, one by one, as the last one nearly dries up. Stir often. When the rice is nearly done, add the **finely chopped heart of the celery**; this should still be crunchy when the risotto is cooked. You may not need all the stock. When the rice is cooked but still a little firm, add a small lump of **butter** and **30g Parmesan**,

412

grated, and stir well. Note this has no wine, no extra flavours except the Parmesan – pure and beautiful.

Celery Souffle.

I am devoted to vegetable soufflés for entertaining and formal meals. Not enough people make them, in my view. They still have a whiff of skill and difficulty overcome about them, but this hasn't been true since we got thermostatted ovens. I would blench at doing a souffle in a coal or wood-fired oven, but not many of us have to do this. Celery souffle is a bit unusual, because it has potatoes for its base instead of bechamel sauce, but it rises just as well as any other.

Start by preparing the **inner 300g of a head of celery**, destringing those stalks which need it, and chopping finely. Boil with **400g potatoes** in **salted water** until tender, about 20 mins. Drain. Put in a food processor with **100 ml double cream**, and whizz. When smooth, add **100g grated Cheddar**, whizz in, then **3 egg yolks**. Transfer to a bowl and taste for seasoning. It certainly needs **pepper**, and maybe **nutmeg**. Whisk **4 egg whites** with a **pinch of salt** in a separate bowl till stiff. Dollop about a quarter of these onto the celery mix, and beat in. Then tip the lightened celery mix onto the rest of the egg whites, and fold in carefully but thoroughly. Put into a buttered souffle dish, sprinkle the top with a **little more grated cheese**, and bake at 200 for 35-40 mins, or till done. It should be a little firmer than other soufflés.

Celery with Lentils.

Wash **300g lentils** (ideally, lentilles du Puy, but certainly a kind that stays whole when cooked) and put in a pan with **1 litre stock, 2 bay leaves, ½ tsp. salt**, and **a dried chili.** Cook till done, aiming to have almost no liquid left at the end. Chop finely **a celery heart and a couple of the stalks next to it** - all destringed as needed – and fry the celery with **2-4 large cloves garlic**, chopped, in **4 tbsp. olive oil.** They should start to brown. Tip the pan into the lentils, and season with **soy sauce**, starting with **2 tbsp.** and going on till you like the taste. Goes with rice or other grain or couscous; if you use couscous, this is a quick, easy, tasty meal.

Celery, Lemon and Herb Bake.

This was originally a stuffing, but baked alone it is lighter and nicer. Easy to do, and a lovely toasted brown top. Prepare **250g each chopped onion, and chopped outer stalks of celery** (destringed), and cook them very gently in **100g butter** for 15 mins, covered. Off the heat, mix with **400g fresh breadcrumbs, 2 eggs, grated rind and juice of 1 lemon**, a lot of chopped **parsley, salt** and **pepper**. Leaves of **lemon thyme** go well in here, too, if available. Or you can use marjoram instead of parsley and thyme. Put into a buttered dish, squashing down a little but not much, and bake at 180 about 20 mins. This is really good by itself, but the family may like HP sauce or fruity chutney with it.

Celery and Chestnut Loaf.

Vegetarians are always associated with nut loaves, in a negative way. Ignore the associations, because this is good. Open **a pack, 300g, of vacuum-packed chestnuts**, which are one of the innovations I am really thankful for. Chop them well. Fry **1 large chopped onion, 1 chopped clove garlic, 200g outer stalks of celery**, destringed and chopped, in **30g butter** till gold. Add **150 ml. stock** and the chestnuts, and simmer 10 mins. Add the **grated rind and juice of a lemon**, chopped **herbs** – a few sprigs each of parsley, thyme, and marjoram is ideal, **2 tbsp. soy sauce, salt** and **pepper** to taste. Add **1 beaten egg**. (This is a good place to use a 5-pepper mix rather than straight black pepper. Or go way-out and use ground Szechwan peppercorns.) Pack into a buttered dish, and bake at 180 for 20-30 mins. This needs a green vegetable and some mild liquid sauce – could be thickened good stock, tomato-y sauce, or a thickened stock with miso.

Chicories and Endives

These are almost the least recognisable vegetables in the book, and I wish I could have pictures. There will be pictures on the blog, as soon as possible.

These winter salad vegetables have many virtues. They give a fresh, green, distinctive salad in late autumn and early winter, though home growers can have them at other times. They look beautiful, with acid greens, pale yellows and reds, and their textures are also crisp and interesting. They deserve to be much more popular and widely available than they are. One reason for their unpopularity is that older varieties were often bitter, but this has been bred out of newer varieties. The other is the confusion over names, which I will try to sort out. If in doubt, however, just point when you see them! And do try growing them; I would specially recommend Sugar Loaf chicory varieties. They are all sown late for autumn/winter heads, so can grow in a patch of ground vacated by an early crop. Joy Larkcom, in "The Salad Garden" is excellent on growing these, as on other salad crops.

Names. There are two major types of endive, the curly leaved, also known as frisee, and the flat-leaved, also known as Batavia or escarole. A curly endive really is frizzy, with acid-green outside leaves and a blanched, whitish-yellow heart, all made up of the wildly curled and jagged leaves. Batavia, or escarole, looks more like a tall conventional lettuce, but is unlikely to be confused with one because its leaves have a twist at the base and leaves with some curl and even fringing at the edges. It's hardier than the curly endive, and lasts longer outside in late autumn.

The chicories are a closely-related group, and include all the rest of the "chicory/endive" group. I've mentioned Sugar Loaf chicory already, with a tall pale-green blocky head that can be blanched but often blanches itself by folding over the outside leaves. There are all the Italian red chicories, like radicchio and Treviso. There are other Italian varieties, like catalogna, sometimes called asparagus chicory in seed catalogues, grumolo, monk's beard, . . . If you want to grow these, look at a good seed catalogue. And then there are the types that give forced heads in winter, like "chicory", the modern name for "Belgian endive" (you see what I mean about confused names!) or witloof, the Belgian name. It has a separate chapter; as a forced vegetable, it comes later in the winter, and has a different texture and different ways of cooking to the other chicories.

Chicories and endives have one huge obstacle to surmount before they become popular. They still have a certain amount of bitterness, varying with variety. Blanching reduces this, but doesn't get rid of it entirely. And bitterness in food is an adult and sophisticated taste, at least in England. Those who like it find it refreshing and stimulating. If you like pink gin and chocolate high in cocoa, you'll take to these salads like a duck to water. Cooking reduces the bitterness. The supermarkets' answer is to introduce a few leaves from a bitter chicory or endive among a lot of mild leaves, in various mixed salad packs. The last one I tried had leaves of "multileaf Red Batavia", which was not bitter at all, but firm and mild-flavoured. It would be great if we could buy this in heads. .

Meanwhile, try growing Sugar Loaf chicory, and grab any of the others when you see them to try out these recipes. A winter salad green is a great thing to have, just for winter, to mark the season.

As always, I've only included recipes which I have tried and liked myself. This means no Treviso, no catalogna, no puntarelle. Italian books are the place to look for these recipes, if you live in London and can find the vegetable.

Note on use of endives, and occasionally chicories, in salads. If you find the leaves of Batavia/escarole, or frisee (curly), too tough, blanch in boiling salted water for 1 min, then drain well and spread out to cool. It softens them without making them unfit for salad.

Bitter Greens Salad with Citrus Fruit
The greens are a **mix of heart of Batavia or Sugar Loaf chicory, radicchio, watercress or frisee – enough greens for 4.** Pick over, break up, wash and dry them. A supermarket packet of watercress, rocket and baby spinach mixed with chicory hearts does fine. For the citrus, **a red grapefruit, 2 blood oranges or oranges, 2 satsumas or clementines or similar, and some kumquats** if you come across them. Peel the citrus – except the kumquats – thoroughly. The French

say "a vif"; in English I expect it would be "to the quick". There should be no white pith left. Slice thinly crosswise, first cutting the grapefruit in half lengthwise. Slice the kumquats thinly. Make a dressing with **4 tbsp. olive oil, 1 tbsp. white wine vinegar, 2 tbsp. orange juice**, and **salt** to taste. Toss the greens with half the dressing, and lay out on plates. Arrange the citrus slices over them, and sprinkle with the rest of the dressing. Refreshing to the eye as well as the tastebuds.

Batavia with Apple and Walnuts.
Use **a large head of Batavia (escarole, broad-leaf endive) or some Sugar Loaf chicory**, number depending on their size. Use only the inner, light green leaves. Mix with the **leaves of a bunch of watercress**, and **a shredded chicory (witloof or Belgian endive)**. Cut **an apple**, peeled or not as you like, into quarters, core, and slice thinly. Put these in a large bowl and add **50g. crumbled walnuts**, and **50-100g. cubed Brie**. For the dressing, mix **1 tbsp. sherry vinegar, 2 tbsp. walnut oil, 2 tbsp. mild oil** and **salt**. Pour the dressing over the salad and mix, and grind **pepper** over it at the table.

Frisee (Curly Endive) with Black Olives and Croutons.
Take **as many leaves of a curly endive**, starting from the centre, as you need for 4 people. Probably not as many as you would of a softer salad green, as chewiness soon satiates. Fry **2 slices of bread**, decrusted and cubed, in **olive oil** till browned, and add **1 chopped clove garlic** for the last 30 sec. Tip this over the leaves, mix, and garnish the top with **black olives**, preferably stoned. However, the nicest black olives come with stones in, so I use these and let people spit the stones out. You can stone the olives, with a knife or a cherry stoner, and thus get the best of all worlds. This salad doesn't need salt, pepper, or acidifier, because it's well-balanced just as it is.

Frisee Salad with Apricots and Peanuts
Make a dressing with **4 tbsp. extra-virgin olive oil, the juice and zest of half an orange, 1 tbsp. white wine vinegar or cider vinegar, 1 crushed clove garlic, salt**, and **1 tbsp. chopped mango chutney**. Pour over the **centre leaves of a head of frisee**, washed, dried and cut up. Mix **40g chopped ready-to-eat dried apricots** and **a large handful dry-roast peanuts**, and mix half of this into the salad. This

417

can be left to stand for an hour or two. Just before serving, sprinkle the rest of the apricots and peanuts over the top.

Basic Sauteed Batavia/Sugar Loaf Chicory.

Break **a head** into leaves, and blanch the tougher outside leaves for 2 mins in boiling salted water. Break up into smaller pieces. Cook **2-3 chopped cloves garlic** in **4 tbsp. olive oil** gently, without letting them brown, and add the leaves. Cover. Cook 5 mins, stirring now and then, till soft.

I say this is basic because all sorts of things can be added. If you have a few good mushrooms – cepes, shitake, chestnut – left over from something else, saute these briefly and add to the cooked leaves. Alternatively, a few chopped spring onions, with or without some toasted sesame seeds. Pine nuts? Olives? Toasted pumpkin seeds? I haven't tried all of these, but they would all add liveliness to the dish.

Radicchio Braised with Blue Cheese.

Take **1 radicchio per person**, trim, and halve. If the radicchio are larger than a large grapefruit, allow 1 for every 2 people. Wash well. Melt **40g butter** in a pan that will just hold the vegetable in 1 layer, add it, and add freshly-ground **black pepper**. Turn it and cook gently, covered, for 10-15 mins, depending on size, till the radicchio has shrunk and changed colour. Sprinkle with **2 tsp. balsamic vinegar**, and turn pieces over in this. Transfer to a grillable pan, if need be, with juices. Assuming 4 people, put **100g thinly sliced creamy blue cheese** on top – Gorgonzola is ideal, though difficult to slice tidily. Put under a preheated grill till the cheese has melted. Serve straight away.

Radicchio Braised with Leeks

1 head of radicchio per person, trimmed, quartered, and washed. Use **1 leek per person**, trim, wash, halve, and cut into chunks. Cook the leeks gently, covered, in **4 tbsp. olive oil** till nearly done and gently coloured. **Salt** and **pepper**. Add the radicchio, with **1 chopped garlic clove per head**, and fry until the radicchio is done, turning often. Add **lemon juice**, and drizzle over a little **extra-virgin olive oil**.

Batavia with Beans.

It's easiest to start this with **leftover cooked dried beans**, with various flavours added – particularly garlic, onion, herbs, tomato, maybe chili. If you don't have these and still want to use the escarole in this way, use a tin of beans, and add them to fried onion and garlic with herbs as you like. I like thyme; sage is a good complement to the flavours. Using warm beans, add **shredded Batavia**, and cook gently till the leaves are done. If you are using a heart (recommended), then use the leaves as they are. If using outside leaves, shred and blanch 2-3 mins before adding. I'm sorry this isn't more precise, but it is a very variable dish. You can serve this on toast rubbed with garlic, to make a version of Bruschetta. In this case, add **thin slices of tasty cheese** – Parmesan is obvious, Old Amsterdam or other mature Dutch-type cheeses are very good, or even a blue. You can also drizzle it with a little truffle oil if you have some, or more extra-virgin olive oil with lemon, or a strong seed oil like pumpkin or dark sesame.

Sugar Loaf and Rice Soup.
You can do this with batavia or the outer leaves of frisee, but I do it with Sugar Loaf. There are a lot of outside leaves on all of these, and you use a lot of them in this soup. You need about **500g. of leaves**. Wash them and cut into thin strips. Saute **a small chopped onion** in **40g butter** till transparent, and add the leaves and a little **salt**. Stir the pot for a couple of minutes, then add **150 ml stock**, cover, and cook on very low heat for about ½ hr. You can stop at this stage and finish the soup just before eating. Add **750 ml. stock**, bring to the boil, and add **80g risotto rice**. Bring to the boil again, cover, and cook gently until the rice is done, about 20 mins. Taste for seasoning, add about **30g. freshly grated Parmesan**, stir, and serve. This is a soup which can't be reheated if there are leftovers, because it becomes almost solid on cooling. But, done as above, it's surprisingly good.

There is a Southern Italian dish of stuffed batavia/escarole, and a pizza or pie using this. I have had no success at all in making this, and I'd recommend giving it a miss. If you ever find it in a restaurant, give it a try, and see if you think it's good and worth the effort.

Chicory, or Belgian Endive, or Witloof

Chicory is a forced vegetable, and this is the key to its character and its differences from the other forms of chicory. The plants are grown in summer, with large leaves, and, I'm told, pretty sky-blue flowers. The leaves are very bitter. In autumn, the roots are dug up, the parts above ground cut off, and the roots buried in the dark. The process is very similar to forcing rhubarb for winter use. The roots sprout, giving (surprisingly) this tight torpedo-shaped head of ivory leaves, in which the bitterness is reduced to a very pleasant level. As the chicons – their proper name – are exposed to light, they get darker yellow tinges at the top of the leaves; with more light these go green. With light the bitterness grows stronger. Chicons used to come wrapped in dark blue paper to protect them from light, but they were a luxury then. Now, in supermarkets, they are sealed in transparent plastic and put under bright lights; it's a wonder any get to the consumer without turning green. When buying, look for the palest you can find. They shouldn't have brown edges or bruises, either. They are still expensive. When you get them home, take them out of their plastic, and put in a paper bag in the fridge, to avoid any more deleterious changes.

There has been a long confusion in England about the name. The vegetable is in fact a chicory. However, the French called it "endive Belges", and when it first appeared in England the French name was translated as Belgian endive. You'll find it with this name in American and older English books – though not very old, because the forcing technique wasn't discovered till the early twentieth century. The Flemish, who should know best, call it "witloof" or white leaf, which is at least unambiguous. I'd like to see this name catch on, but the supermarkets seem to have settled on "chicory". This leaves other chicories without a distinctive name, so radicchio is sold as radicchio with no hint of its kinship with other leaves like Sugar Loaf chicory. If we ever start growing the two or three other types popular in France they will have to be renamed, too.

You can buy seed to grow the plant from scratch. Much of the chicory available in supermarkets is British-grown. In many ways this is likely to be better than you can grow yourself, because it's hard to keep the control of forcing conditions on a domestic scale. The only advantage of growing it yourself is to keep the chicons away from light.

Chicory is a marvellous winter vegetable, and I can't decide whether it's better in salads or cooked. For salads, it has crispness and texture unlike any out-of season lettuce, and it has taste too, lively and refreshing.

Salad Default. Chicory and Beetroot Salad.
For 4 people, allow **2 medium heads chicory, 250g cooked beetroot** Cut a thin slice from the base of the chicory heads, to remove the brown. Trim or remove any browned outside leaves. DON'T WASH. Halve and cut in slices, and dress with **extra-virgin olive oil, lemon juice, salt** and **pepper** all mixed. Cube cooked peeled beetroot, and dress this separately with the same dressing. Put the beetroot in a heap in the centre of a large plate, and the chicory around it. Sprinkle the lot with chopped **parsley.** You can eat the chicory alone, but it's really best with the contrast of sweetness from the beetroot. For a third note and contrast of texture, add a few sliced **raw button mushrooms** over the top of the chicory.

Chicory, Watercress and Walnut Salad.
Toast **30g walnut halves** under the grill until they smell toasty. You won't see a change of colour. Make a dressing with **2 tbsp. walnut oil, 2 tbsp. extra-virgin olive oil (not too tasty), 1 tbsp. sherry vinegar, 1 small shallot** chopped finely, and **salt.** No pepper. Mix **3 chicories**, trimmed, halved, and sliced, with **80g watercress**, picked over and large stems discarded. Add the walnuts and about half the dressing, and mix well. Add more dressing if you think it's needed.
This is a lovely salad on its own, and it also lends itself to variations. Croutons, for example. Or pear cubes and blue cheese cubes, and it's a whole-meal salad. Or a citrus variation; use lemon juice and only olive oil in the dressing, not sherry vinegar and walnut oil, and add segments of orange, or satsuma or clementine, or grapefruit, or even sliced kumquats.

Chicory and Chinese Leaf Salad.
The difference here is the dressing. Make it from **50 ml. plain yoghurt** and **1 tbsp. white wine vinegar.** Add **1 clove garlic**, crushed with ½ **tsp. salt** on a chopping board. Add **pepper** to taste. Trim, halve, slice

2 **heads chicory**, and shred **¼ head Chinese leaves.** Mix and dress. Fine alone; even better with **1 bulb fennel**, trimmed and chopped, and **2 small apples**, cored but not peeled, and cubed.

Chicory with Caesar-style Dressing.

Make the dressing. Boil **an egg** for 1 MINUTE ONLY. Then crack the egg into a liquidiser, and use only what comes out without using a teaspoon. Add to the liquidiser **1 tsp. French mustard, a crushed garlic clove, 1 tsp. mushroom ketchup or vegetarian Worcester sauce,** and the **juice of a lemon.** Put **4 tbsp. extra-virgin olive oil** in a cup. With the liquidiser running, dribble this in through the hole in the top. It doesn't thicken like mayonnaise, but emulsifies. Cube **1-2 slices decrusted bread**, and fry the cubes in **olive oil** till brown and crisp. (If you do this early, hide the croutons, to stop passers-through nibbling till they are gone) Trim, halve, slice **3 heads chicory**, add the dressing to them in a salad bowl, add the croutons and **30g Parmesan**, grated, and toss. Taste and adjust flavours.

Chicory with Kiwi Fruit.

Trim and slice **2 heads chicory**. Add to them **2 kiwi fruit**, peeled and diced, **4 cut-up ready-to-eat apricots, 1 roasted red pepper**, cut in squares. Heat **2 tbsp. sunflower oil** in a small frying pan, and add **1 tsp. cumin seeds** and 1 tsp. mustard seeds. When the mustard seeds start popping, add **2 tbsp. desiccated coconut**, and cook gently till the coconut starts to brown. Add **½ tsp. salt**, and pour the lot over the salad. Mix well and serve. You can use any other tropical fruit instead of kiwi, or leave it out altogether and use raisins/sultanas instead.

Chicory and Baby Spinach Salad with Fried Halloumi.

This can take a positive dressing; **3 tbsp. extra-virgin olive oil, 1 tbsp. balsamic vinegar, 1 clove of garlic pureed with ½ tsp. salt, 1 tsp. French mustard.** Soak thin slices from **1 small red onion** in cold water for 10-15 mins, drain, and dry. Add to a mix of **200g baby spinach leaves** and **3 heads chicory**, trimmed and sliced. Add a **few sliced radishes**, if available. Cut **a packet of Halloumi cheese** into thin slices, and fry them quickly in sunflower oil on both sides. Dress the salad while the Halloumi is frying. When done, put the slices on kitchen paper to absorb excess oil. Put the slices on top of the salad, and serve as quickly as possible, while the cheese is still warm. This makes a lot; enough for 6 as main dish.

Chicory, Fennel, Celery and Stilton Salad.
This is a pale salad, with three items of similar colour and very different tastes. **2 heads of chicory**, trimmed, halved and sliced; **1 bulb fennel**, trimmed, halved and sliced as thin as you can; **a heart of celery**, destringed and sliced. Mix them all. Add **100g (or less) cubed Blue Stilton** or other blue cheese, and mix in. Dress with a mix of **2 tbsp. extra-virgin olive oil, ½ tbsp. balsamic vinegar**, and **a very little salt**. Sprinkle the top with **toasted flaked almonds**. Ideal around Christmas, but good any time in winter. If you want to brighten it, add some shredded radicchio to the mix. There is a salad very similar to this in the Fennel section; it's so good I didn't want you to miss it!

Chicory Leaves.
This is a very pretty appetiser, and makes **one head of chicory** go a long way. Trim the base and any damaged leaves, and separate the head into long individual leaves. Put a teaspoonful of **any creamy salad mix** at the base of the leaf, and arrange the leaves on a plate like a flower. I like a mix of grated celeriac, mayonnaise, and chopped walnuts, but don't be limited by this. A blue cheese dip would be good, so would any salsa.

Cooked Chicory.
Cooking chicory softens both taste and texture, and adds richness and succulence. This usually comes from butter, but can be oil. Butter suits the Northern character of the vegetable better, I think.

Default; Buttered Chicory.
Cut off the brown base of **4 chicory**, and cut crosswise into 3-4 slices. Melt **80g butter** in a frying pan, add the slices, and stir to coat. **Salt** and **pepper**. Cook gently for 5 mins or more, until cooked and soft, add the **juice of a lemon**, sprinkle with chopped **parsley**, and eat straightaway. For **Chicory with Cream,** add 50-100 ml double cream at the end, and let it bubble to a sauce -- high days and holidays, only, because it is nutritional overkill, but it is so good. **Chicory with Raspberry Vinegar** leaves out the lemon juice and adds 2 tbsp. raspberry vinegar when the chicory is cooked. Stir and let the vinegar dry out, then add 50 ml. crème fraiche. Other flavoured vinegars work too; I specially like elderflower vinegar, when I've made some the previous spring.

Chicory Polonaise.

Start by making buttered chicory, until they are cooked. Hard-boil **3 eggs**, peel, and chop. Mix in some chopped **parsley**. Also, fry fresh breadcrumbs from **a large slice of decrusted bread** in **20g butter** till crisp. Put the cooked vegetable in a serving dish, spread the egg mix over it, and tip over the crisp buttered crumbs. This is a substantial vegetable, or a light lunch on its own. There are lots of vegetables which can be dressed-up in this style, and the garnish is always good. Cauliflower, broccoli, cabbage, leeks, runner beans, French beans, etc. etc.

Caramelised Chicory.

Trim **4 heads chicory**, and halve. Butter the bottom of a baking dish which will just hold the chicory, pack the halves in, and dot with **20g butter**. Mix **2 tsp. runny honey** with the **juice of ½ a large orange**, and distribute over the top. **Salt** and **pepper.** Put into a 180 oven, and cook for about 1 hr, turning every 15 mins. When it is done, the juices will have reduced and thickened, and the chicory will be browned. If it looks as if it will burn, turn the oven down – we want caramel not char.

Chicory Bruschetta.

Make caramelised chicory as above. When it's done, spread a little **Gorgonzola** on the **prepared bruschetta** (slices of French bread cut at an angle, brushed with garlicky olive oil. and baked in the same 180 oven for about 10 mins). Then put a chunk of chicory on top, and serve. Snack or first course.

Chicory and Apple Braise.

Peel, core and cut into matchsticks **2 large or 3 small apples**. Cook them in **30g butter** in a large frying pan, on moderate heat, turning till brown. It takes about 5 mins. Sprinkle with **1 tsp. sugar**, if needed. Put in a dish and keep to one side. Meanwhile, trim and slice thickly crosswise **4 heads chicory**. Add another **30g butter** to the pan (without cleaning), and add the chicory slices. **Salt, pepper, 1 tsp. sugar**. Stir and cook over fairly high heat until the chicory pieces are slightly browned.   Add the apples, mix well, and add **3 tbsp. stock/water**. Cover and cook gently about 5 mins.

Chicory in Cheese Sauce.

The non-vegetarian, standard version of this dish wraps cooked heads of chicory in ham slices, covers them with cheese sauce, sprinkles with breadcrumbs, and browns the dish. Much of this is very good, but the ham is a weak point in this dish -- it gets stringy and hard to cut. However, I can't be confident I've found the best vegetarian way of improving this dish. I don't know a vegetarian sheet which could wrap the chicory heads. I use **a bed of cooked spinach** in the base of the (flattish) dish. Blanch trimmed **chicory heads, one per person**, in boiling salted water for 10 mins. (I'm told that putting a heel of rye bread in with the boiling water reduces bitterness) Drain and squeeze, to get out all the possible water. You could braise them instead, as in buttered chicory, but keeping the heads whole. Tastes better, many more calories. Embed them in the spinach as far as possible, without them touching the base. Make cheese sauce (Basics) from **30g butter, 1 tbsp. flour, 200 ml. milk, salt, pepper** and **nutmeg;** when thickened take off the heat and beat in **50g grated Cheddar**. Pour the sauce over the chicory, spreading it out to cover all the spinach as well. Sprinkle the top with **fresh breadcrumbs and/or grated cheese**, and heat in 180 oven till top is brown and bubbling. This needs crusty fresh bread, though the reckless might prefer chips!

You could also try a bed of lightly cooked slices of large mushroom, a bed of courgette slices lightly cooked, or a mash of celeriac and potato. Just remember it's got to be good with cheese sauce.

Chicory "Tarte Tatin"

For this you want **4 heads of caramelised chicory**, and **200g carrots**, cubed and cooked with water, **a little sugar, a knob of butter**, and **salt**, until glazed. Mix the two vegetables, and sprinkle with **1 tbsp. balsamic vinegar**. Put these in a buttered tin, spread **120g grated Cheddar** over them, and cover with **shortcrust pastry** (Basics), rolled so that there is enough pastry to tuck down the sides of the vegetables. Bake at 200 for 20-25 mins, until the pastry is cooked, and invert the whole onto a serving dish.

Chicory Risotto.

Trim and shred **2 heads chicory**. Sweat **1 small chopped onion** in **30g butter** in a large frying pan. When soft but not coloured, add the shredded chicory, and stir. Add **300g risotto rice**, cook for a minute or two, stirring, then add **100 ml white wine**. Let this bubble away, then add a ladle from 1½ litre stock, simmering. Again, let this bubble gently, stirring often, till the pan is nearly dry, then add another ladle of stock. Keep on doing this until the rice is cooked to your taste. It usually takes 25-35 mins. Taste for **salt** when the rice is nearly done; the amount needed depends on the saltiness of the stock. Add **50g grated Parmesan, 30g butter**, beat well, and serve straightaway.

Pickled Chicory.
Cut **15g fresh ginger, ¼ medium-hot red chili** into thin strips, put into pan with **40g granulated sugar, 150 ml white wine vinegar**, simmer 5 mins. Let cool. Halve crosswise and break into leaves **a head of chicory**, and toss with **1 tsp salt**. Leave in colander for 2 hrs. Stir into vinegar mix, chill 24 hrs.

Chinese Leaves or Chinese Cabbage

What a lovely vegetable! About a kilo of cream or pale yellow, densely packed, frilly leaves in cylinder form. Mild tasting, brilliant in salads and in stir-fries, as well as more exotic dishes. Available almost all the year, though best in late autumn. It keeps well in the fridge – I've had one up to a month, and still been able to use it for salad. Not expensive. And grown in England too. I can't think of any disadvantages, just a line-up of highly desirable qualities. So why don't we use it more?

Most of the recipes below have some obvious Chinese derivation, simply because this is a vegetable originating in China and not yet assimilated (I have to admit that many foreign dishes are not exactly assimilated but altered to suit English tastes, while still retaining their ethnic connections. Chicken tikka masala is an obvious example here, as it originated in Birmingham, uses Indian tastes, and is England's favourite dish in surveys) Salads in China are rarely raw, because of health concerns; adapted salads can be raw, because our health concerns are different. Quite a lot of the salads here use exotic fruit, which is not Chinese and again part of naturalisation.

Default
A simple salad. Shred the leaves (**about half a head**) by cutting crosswise from the top, and use this simple Chinese dressing: **1 tbsp. each of sunflower oil, soy sauce, wine vinegar (red or white, doesn't matter); 1 tsp. dark sesame oil; ½ tsp. sugar**. If you have some **ginger**, shred a very little into the dressing, **or** add a couple of dashes of **Tabasco**. These are to enliven not to dominate.

You can add almost anything to this basic salad, and it particularly responds to fruit. The salads following are particular combinations that I've really liked, but don't let me limit your creativity. With new vegetables – which this still is – there is no agreed way to make the best of it, to bring out its special qualities.

Chinese Leaf and Broad Bean Salad.
Defrost **250g frozen broad beans**, and pop them from their skins, to give beautiful tender bright green inners. Shred **½ head Chinese leaf**.

Mix, and dress with mix of **3 tbsp. extra-virgin olive oil, 1 tbsp. white wine vinegar, ½ tsp. Dijon mustard, salt** and **pepper**. Sprinkle with chopped **parsley**. Very pretty, and lives up to its looks.

Chinese Leaves, Celery and Pepper Salad.

Shred **¼ head of Chinese leaves**. Add **3-4 stalks celery**, destringed and sliced thin, **1 roasted red pepper**, deseeded and cut in strips, **sprouted seed** (especially bean sprouts, if you can get good ones). Dress with a mix of **3 tbsp. sunflower or other neutral oil, juice of ½ lemon, salt** and **pepper**. Sometimes I leave out salt and add 1 tsp. soy sauce instead; just as good, but not better. Sprinkle the top with **roasted seeds – sunflower, sesame or pumpkin, or even salted peanuts**.

Grand Salad with Chinese Leaves.

Start with **½ head Chinese leaves**, shredded. Add whatever you have which is good and fresh – **celery, carrots, red or green peppers, sliced raw small white mushrooms, spring onions, sprouted seeds, green beans, mange-tout or sugar snaps. Probably not all of these, just a selection.** While you can use up good leftovers, it isn't a dustbin, so avoid anything that's tired. Dress with Chinese dressing: **1 tbsp. each of sunflower oil, soy sauce, and lime or lemon juice; 1 tsp. dark sesame oil; ½ tsp. sugar**. When mixed, sprinkle one of these on the top: chopped **hard-boiled eggs, or cubes of tofu in sauce (from a tin or jar), or fresh coconut shreds**. Never the same twice; always good.

Chinese Leaves with Sharon Fruit and Walnuts.

Definitely a winter salad, using the persimmons developed into Sharon fruit in Israel. This development has got rid of a lot of the mouth-puckering tannin when they are unripe, but it's still best to leave Sharon fruit in the fruit bowl to ripen as long as you dare.
Shred **¼ head Chinese leaves**. Add **50g broken-up walnuts**, and toss with a dressing of **3 tbsp. walnut oil, juice of ½ lemon, salt** and **pepper**. Cut **2 Sharon fruit** into segments vertically, and arrange them prettily on top of the salad. When everyone has appreciated the effect, toss again, and let them serve themselves. It looks as pretty using kiwi fruit instead of Sharon fruit, but isn't quite as good to my taste.

Chinese Leaves with Pomegranate Seeds and Pumpkin Seeds.
Shred ¼ **head Chinese leaves**, and add **seeds from a pomegranate** (extracted at home or bought) and **toasted pumpkin seeds**, quantity depending on how much you like them. Dress with **2 tbsp. sunflower oil, 1 tbsp. toasted pumpkin oil if you have some (otherwise use 3 tbsp. sunflower oil), juice of 1 lemon, salt** and **pepper**. It needs no garnish, but a variation with chopped **spring onion** is also very good.

Chinese Leaves with Pineapple and Almonds.
Shred ¼ **head Chinese leaves**. Add small cubes of **pineapple, about ¼ medium** pineapple. Toast **30g flaked almonds** under the grill. Use **1 tbsp. of the pineapple juice** for the dressing, with **2 tbsp. sunflower oil, salt**, and a dash of **Tabasco**.

Chinese Leaves with Grapes and Cheese.
Shred ½ **head Chinese leaves**. Add **200g grapes**, halved. If your grapes have seeds, it makes a more refined salad to take them out, but I wouldn't bother myself. Add also **200g Red Leicester or red Cheshire cheese**. The red colour is for aesthetic reasons; if you don't have these, white Cheshire, Lancashire, Caerphilly, Wensleydale are all fine. (I've eaten this a lot, mostly for solitary lunches) Dress with **2 tbsp. mayonnaise mixed with 1½ tbsp. sunflower oil and juice of ½ lemon, ½ tsp. Dijon mustard**, and **pepper**. It doesn't need salt.

Three Fairy Salad.
Based on a recipe by Kenneth Lo, in Chinese Vegetable and Vegetarian Cooking. This is half-pickled, so start early. Cut **half a head of Chinese leaves** into 3-cm slices crosswise, then cut these slices into 3-cm. pieces. Put in a bowl with a **bunch or packet of radishes**, sliced. Sprinkle over **1 tbsp. salt**, and rub it into the vegetables. Leave for 3 hrs or more. Pour over cold water to cover, swirl round, and drain well and dry with kitchen towel. Put in serving bowl. Then gently fry **1 sliced onion** and **2 deseeded green chilis** in **3 tbsp. sunflower oil**. Lift out the veg and add to the leaves, leaving as much oil behind as you can. Add **½ tbsp. dark sesame oil** to the remaining oil in the pan, and pour the hot oil over the salad mix. Mix well. Sprinkle the top with fresh **chopped green coriander**, and serve.

Chinese Cooked Salad of Chinese Leaves.
There must be a better name, but this is at least descriptive. Cut up a **whole head of Chinese leaves** into 3-cm slices crosswise, then cut these slices into 3-cm. pieces. Blanch these for 2 mins, then drain well. Straightaway put the Chinese leaves in a lidded pan, and pour over a mix of **1 tbsp. English mustard, 2 tbsp. soy sauce, ½ tsp. salt, 1 tbsp. each wine vinegar and dark sesame oil, 1 tbsp. sherry, 2 tbsp. sunflower oil,** and **1 tsp. Chinese chili sauce**. Put on the lid, and heat the pan on high heat for just 1 min, then let the whole thing cool. Turn into a bowl. Be warned; it doesn't look attractive, but the taste is super!

The other major way of using Chinese leaves is in stir-fries. These are quick and easy to do, and difficult to give recipes for, as they need never be the same twice. The first time you do a stir-fry you need more care than in the majority of new cooking techniques, but after a few, you will find yourself simply improvising. A mixed vegetable stir-fry can be a meal in itself with rice, couscous, or other grain, or tofu or other types of protein can be added to improve its nutritional qualities. If you have never stir-fried, this is a good one to start with. The crucial thing is to have everything ready to go beforehand, peeled, chopped, mixed, in bowls, on saucers, in cups. You shouldn't have to do any preparation while the cooking is going on.

Plain Stir-Fried Chinese Leaves.
Preparation: **Cut half a head of Chinese leaves** into 3-cm slices crosswise, then cut these slices into 3-cm. pieces. Chop finely **1 small onion** with **½ a knob of ginger, 2 cloves garlic,** and **1 deseeded chili**. Mix **1½ tbsp. soy sauce** with **1 tbsp. dry sherry or white wine, 1 tsp. sugar**. Have **salt** and **dark sesame oil** out, so you don't have to look for them.
Action: Heat **2 tbsp. sunflower oil** in a wok or large frying pan over HIGH heat, and add the onion, garlic, ginger, chili mix. Toss and turn for 1 min. Add the Chinese leaves and ½ tsp. salt, and continue to turn and stir until all the pieces are coated with the oil, and wilting considerably, 2-3 mins. Add the soy sauce mix, turn down the heat to medium, and go on stirring and turning for 2-3 mins more. Sprinkle over 1 tsp. dark sesame oil, turn into a hot dish, and get people to eat it IMMEDIATELY. Don't start cooking until they are there, because stir-fried dishes lose their excellence very quickly and take on a

stewed taste. OK, we are used to this in Chinese takeaway, but it can be so much better.

Stir-Fried Chinese Leaves, a Bit Fancier.
Miss out the chili from the onion/garlic/ginger mix in the last recipe. About an hour before starting, soak **20g dried shitake, (Chinese dried mushrooms)** by pouring boiling water over them, just enough to cover. After 20-30 mins, fish them out, cut off and discard the stalk, and slice thinly. For the sauce mix, use **1 tbsp. soy sauce, 1 tbsp. sherry, ½ tbsp. hoisin sauce, 2 tbsp. stock,** and **½ tsp. sugar.** As above, stir-fry onion/garlic/ginger in **2 tbsp. oil** for 1 min, add the veg and salt, stir 2-3 mins. Add mushroom pieces and sauce mix, turn down the heat, and cook 2 mins more. You don't need sesame oil with this.

Stir-Fried Chinese Leaves and Chestnuts.
Shred **¼ head Chinese leaves.** Quarter **2 dozen chestnuts – cooked or from a vacuum pack.** Chop finely **3 cloves garlic** and **a knob of ginger**, peeled. Mix **1 tbsp. soy sauce, ½ tsp salt,** and **1 tsp dark sesame oil.** Have **½ tsp. sugar** available. Heat **3 tbsp. sunflower oil** in a wok or large frying pan, and add garlic and ginger when it is very hot. ½ minute later, add the Chinese leaves, and stir-fry for 2 mins. Add the chestnuts and the sugar, cover, and cook on moderate heat for 3 mins. Uncover, add the soy sauce mix, stir in, and serve in heated dish.

Stir-Fried Mixed Vegetables.
Chop finely **a thick slice of fresh ginger**, and mix with **1 small grated carrot.** Slice thinly **1 large onion**, peeled and halved. Sliver **a green pepper**, trimmed and deseeded, and mix with **1 stalk celery**, cut in matchsticks. Shred **¼ head of Chinese leaves.** Trim and cut into 3-cm lengths **6 spring onions**, and mix with **100g button mushrooms**, sliced. Mix **1 tbsp. soy sauce** with **3 tbsp. dry sherry.** This is a lot of bowls, etc. Action; heat **4 tbsp. sunflower** oil in a wok or large frying pan. When it's very hot, add ginger and carrots, and stir ½ min. Add the onion, stir 1 min; add green pepper and celery; 30 sec. Add Chinese leaves; 2 mins. Add everything else, 1 min, and eat straight away.

There are lots more possible things to go in a stir-fry. Chinese-y things, like water chestnuts and bamboo shoots, both from tins, or lily flowers, dried and soaked. Beans, peas, mange-tout, sugar peas. Courgettes. Asparagus. Fennel. Radishes … Not root vegetables unless you can eat them raw, like carrots. Not dried cooked pulses. Otherwise, the whole area of vegetables is open.

Chinese Leaves and Tofu Soup.
For the simplest version of this, heat **1 litre good stock**, and add ¼ **head of Chinese leaves**, shredded crosswise. Simmer 2 mins, covered, and add **500 gm cubed tofu**. Let it heat through, taste for **salt**, and serve. This may be authentic, but I find it quite bland and boring. I add **1 tbsp. soy sauce, 1 tbsp. wine vinegar**, some chopped **spring onion**, quite a lot of **pepper, ½ tsp. toasted sesame oil**, and **fresh chopped green coriander.** Taste and adjust. This turns it into a different version of hot-and-sour soup, which I love.

Fried Rice with Chinese Leaves.
The rice must be cooked in advance; allow **80g long-grain, like Patna, rice per head**, and boil in plenty of salted water for 10-11 mins, or till done. Drain well, rinse with cold water, and spread out on a baking sheet covered with a tea towel. This is to cool it as quickly as possible. Assuming this is to serve 4, slice **4 medium mushrooms** thinly, and shred thinly **one-eighth of a head of Chinese leaves (100-120 g)** Have ready **200g very fresh bean sprouts**, washed and drained. You also need an **egg**, and **a bunch of spring onions** trimmed and sliced thinly. First heat **2 tbsp. sunflower oil** in wok or large frying pan, and when hot, add the mushroom slices, and stir for about ½ min. Scoop out onto a plate. Dump the Chinese leaves into the same oil, and stir and fry 1 min. Turn onto the plate with the mushrooms. Add **another 2 tbsp. oil** to the pan, and put in the rice. Stir and turn and mix for about 2 mins, then add the bean sprouts and stir-fry for another 5 mins. It takes time and care to get all the rice hot. Add the spring onions, mushrooms and Chinese leaves, and mix in. Make a hollow in the middle of the pan, break in an egg, and stir quickly to break the egg and mix it into the hot rice. The egg must be cooked, with no soft or raw bits left. This is to the Oriental taste just as it is; every English person I've given it to has wanted **soy sauce**. So it may be as well to add 1-2 tbsp. soy sauce at the last moment, and stop your eaters pouring on too much.

This is a simple version, and I think very good. Elaborations and extras will doubtless occur, but try this first.

Tofu and Noodle Casserole.
This uses an Oriental ingredient, bean thread noodles (also known as transparent noodles, or cellophane noodles), which I much like from time to time, but many people don't. They are made from ground mung beans, not a starch at all. **100g of these noodles** are soaked in hot water for 5 mins, drained, and are then ready to absorb flavours from any liquid they are put into. They aren't eaten alone. Their texture is smooth and slippery, which is what can put people off. I'd recommend trying a dish with these noodles in a restaurant before making a family meal from them. If you are not using bean thread noodles, use **100g Chinese egg noodles** instead.   You also need **400g tofu cubes**.   Soak **25g dried Chinese mushrooms** by pouring over boiling water and letting them stand 20-30 mins. Drain, remove and throw away the stalks, and slice. Shred **¼ head Chinese leaves**. Chop finely **6 cloves garlic, a large knob of ginger**. Have ready a mix of **2 tbsp. hoisin sauce, 2 tbsp. dry sherry, 1 tbsp. soy sauce**. Also have ready **300 ml stock**, and **6-8 chopped spring onions**.
Heat **1 tbsp. oil** in a wok or large frying pan. When hot, add the ginger and garlic, and stir for ½ min. Add Chinese leaves, mushroom slices, turn 1 min, then add the hoisin sauce mix. Stir 1 min, then add the stock and the chosen noodles. Bring to a simmer, add the bean curd cubes, cover tightly, and cook for about 10 mins. Garnish with the chopped spring onions. As you can see, the cooking is less demanding than the preparation, and this gives you time to sit down and have a (quick) drink while the one-pot supper is cooking.

Pasta with Chinese Leaves and Tomato Sauce.
Much simpler than the last dish, nowhere near as exotic, but a guaranteed success for family eating. You need about **300 ml. tomato sauce**, made earlier. I would use my standard recipe, which is as follows: Put **the contents of a tin of tomatoes** in the blender. Add a **slurp of olive oil, 1-4 cloves garlic**, peeled, **salt** and **pepper**, and **dried oregano or fresh basil or fresh parsley**. Whizz. Heat this while the **pasta (say, 300g for 4)** is boiling, and sharpen the flavour with **1 tbsp. sherry or white wine vinegar**. Add **½ head Chinese leaves**, shredded, stir, cover, and simmer 5 mins or so. Taste a shred of

Chinese leaf for doneness. Drain the pasta, mix with the sauce, and serve with freshly grated **Parmesan**.

Quick Kimchee.
Kimchee is a Korean fermented-cabbage relish eaten, I believe, with practically every meal in Korea. Think of it as sauerkraut enlivened with chilis. I've never tasted the real thing, but this quick version is very pleasing without being too hot. Use it as a salad. Shred **a head of Chinese leaves**. Put in a non-metal bowl, and add **2-3 chopped chilis** – I deseed, but don't if you like hot food. Add also **2 cloves garlic**, chopped finely, **2 tbsp. soy sauce, 1 tsp. wine vinegar, 1 tbsp. salt** (not a misprint) and **1 tbsp. sugar**. Cover and let it stand at least 1 hr. Store leftovers in the fridge.

Jerusalem Artichokes

I love these knobbly little tubers with their strange almost-sweet taste and the variety of textures you can coax from them. I love the fact that they are so easy to grow – and so determined, that you get plants repeating year after year, even when you think you've dug everything up. They are too individual to be a staple food, like potatoes, but it's easy to grow them yourself and eat them often.

They do, of course, have drawbacks. They give some people – not all – dreadful wind. And they are not easy to peel -- or scrub, if that's your preference – because of their knobbles all over. Smoother and larger ones are being bred. And if you're buying and have a choice, choose the biggest and smoothest.

They were originally a North American native. They don't, to me, taste like artichokes at all. The flower bud, like sunflower buds, looks a bit like a squashed artichoke bud, and probably this is where the "artichoke" bit came from. The Jerusalem bit has all sorts of derivations, but I think the most likely is the one derived from girasol, or sunflower. Their 2m stalks in summer, and their leaves, are quite sunflower like. The French call them topinambours, which demands another strange derivation from a tribe of South American Indians. Individual, seasonal, delicious, not heavily worked on by breeders, no GM varieties anywhere – what's not to like?

I definitely prefer them peeled. Many books tell you that they can be cooked first and then peeled; I've never made this work well. Just peel them raw, cutting off very small knobs. They make your hands slightly sticky. If you're not going to use them straight away, cover them with water with the juice of ½ lemon – but it's better to peel and use.

Default.
For **500g Jerusalem artichokes**, peeled and sliced fairly thinly. Melt **30g butter**, and turn the slices in this. Add **stock** to cover, **salt** if needed, and **pepper**, and cook gently uncovered until the stock is almost gone and the vegetable is done. Squeeze in the **juice of half a lemon**, taste for seasoning, and serve.

Jerusalem Artichokes with Cream.

Just as above until the last moment, when you add **3 tbsp. cream**, some chopped **parsley**, and a **squeeze of lemon**.

Jerusalem Artichokes Provence style.

Peel and cut into chunks **500g Jerusalem artichokes**. Put them into **2 tbsp. warmed olive oil**, and cook them gently about 5 mins. Add **2 chopped cloves garlic**, and the **drained tomatoes from a tin**, broken-up. (Keep the juice for something else) **Salt** and **pepper**; **basil or oregano**, fresh or dried. Cover the pan and simmer till the artichokes are done.

Jerusalem Artichokes Braised with Leeks.

Trim and clean **250g leeks** and slice roughly. Peel **500g artichokes** and slice thinly. Melt **30g butter** in a shallow pan, add the leeks, stir into the butter, and add **6 tbsp. water.** Cook slowly till the liquid has evaporated. Add the artichoke slices and **salt**, mix well, and add **150ml. water**. Cook slowly till all the liquid is gone and the artichokes are tender, adding more water if needed. Finish with **pepper** and a **squeeze of lemon**, to taste.

Jerusalem Artichokes au Gratin.

For this, the artichokes are cooked plainly first, then finished with cheese and butter. Peel **500g artichokes**, and leave in large pieces. Boiling them is tricky, as some are done faster than others and turn to mush. I much prefer to steam them, which takes about 20 mins. When done, let cool enough to slice them thin, and then arrange in a buttered ovenproof dish. **Salt** and **pepper**, sprinkle with **25g grated Parmesan**, and dot with bits of **25g butter**. Bake at 180 till the top is browned.

Roast Jerusalem Artichokes.

They respond well to being roasted, either alone or as part of a mixed vegetable roast. For cooking them alone, peel, chunk, roll in olive oil, add a broken-up bay leaf, and roast at 180 for 20-25 mins or till tender.

Jerusalem Artichoke Chips

They make surprisingly good chips – or maybe it's just the general appeal of deep-fried food. Peel them first, and steam for just 10 mins whole. Let cool enough to halve them lengthwise, if fairly thin, or in some way make chip shapes from them. Deep-fry till golden, sprinkle with salt, and eat with a garlicky dip. I like cucumber and garlic and yoghurt, with mint if available. Dill doesn't seem to me to be a soul-mate for artichokes, splendid though it is in other contexts.

Jerusalem Artichoke Pan Fry.

Jerusalem artichokes do respond well to being crisped, though this really isn't traditional. Peel and grate **500g artichokes**, and squeeze in a towel to get rid of excess liquid. Mix with **6 spring onions**, peeled and chopped, a good sprinkle of **chili flakes**, **salt** and **pepper**, **60g plain flour**, and **4 tbsp. double cream**. Add **60g chopped hazelnuts**. Heat **2 tbsp. olive oil** in a large frying pan, dump in the mix, and spread out with a spatula. Cook slowly until browned, turn, and cook till the base is browned and the mixture is cooked through. It could easily take ½ hr. Sprinkle with a little grated **Cheddar**, and serve. This is enough for 2 as a meal.

Frittata

If you want to feed more from this amount, break up the cooked cake above before the cheese stage, and pour in **4-6 eggs** beaten with **salt** and **pepper**. Let this run among the vegetables, and then set slowly. Now it's plenty for 4-5. Again, add grated cheese to the top at the end.

Saute of Jerusalem Artichokes with Peppers.

Peel **500g Jerusalem artichokes**, and slice about 5mm thick. Heat **3 tbsp. olive oil** in a large frying pan and add the slices. Cover and cook on a low heat until they are tender and browned, turning now and then. About 20 mins. . **Salt**, and transfer to a plate. Add **1 red pepper**, seeded and diced, to the still-hot pan, and cook a couple of minutes, stirring. Add **1 chili**, seeded and chopped finely, and **1 shallot**, peeled and chopped, and cook another 2-3 mins, till the red pepper is done. Return the artichokes to the pan, turn and taste for **salt**, and add chopped **fresh green coriander** to taste. It's easy to eat a lot of this.

Mixed Vegetable Stir-Fry.

Chinese is another context in which you don't expect to see Jerusalems, but this is very good. Peel **250g Jerusalem artichokes**, and cut into small thin slices. You may need to halve large ones. Fry **1 peeled sliced onion** in **2 tbsp. sunflower oil** for 2 mins in a wok or large frying pan. Add **1 chopped clove garlic**, turn up the heat a little, and add the Jerusalem slices and **150g sliced mushrooms**. Turn often for 1 min or so, until the mushrooms start to shrink.. Then add **150g spinach** or other quick-cooking green, washed and shredded, and toss 1-2 mins more. Add a mix of **1 dsp. cornflour, 1 tbsp. soy sauce, 1 tbsp. dry sherry, ½ tsp. sugar**, and **3 tbsp. stock**, and turn till the juice has thickened. The effect of the Jerusalems here is rather like water chestnuts; try using Jerusalems as a substitute for water chestnuts in other recipes.

Salads of Jerusalem Artichokes

You sometimes see salads in which thin slices of the raw vegetable are used. My tasters and I are not keen on this, and it seems as if their special flavour develops on cooking. However, they do add a crunchy texture, which may be just what you want. I prefer to steam them lightly, after peeling, so there is still some crunch but they have more flavour. For this simplest of salads, peel and cut into chunks, and steam for 10 mins. Slice as soon as you can handle them, and dress with **extra-virgin olive oil, red wine vinegar, salt, pepper, and herbs.**

You can elaborate on this, and I think improve it, to make:

Jerusalem Artichoke and Red Pepper Salad
Jerusalem Artichoke and Broccoli Salad (either normal or purple sprouting)
Jerusalem Artichoke and Broad Bean Salad
Jerusalem Artichoke Salad with Hard-Boiled Eggs and Spring Onions
Jerusalem Artichoke and Radish Salad on Watercress (this is a favourite of mine, for the punchy flavours)

Palestine Soup.

A popular Victorian soup, which gets its name from the Palestine/Jerusalem connection. Wash, peel and slice **500g Jerusalem artichokes** and **2 medium onions**. Sweat them in **30g butter** for about 10 mins, without colouring. Add **600 ml. stock or water, salt** and **pepper**, and simmer 20 mins. Puree, either in blender or mouli-legumes. Add **300 ml. milk**. If you think it's too thin at this stage, bring to the boil, and add **1 tbsp. cornflour mixed with 2-3 tbsp. cold milk**. Stir till it thickens. Taste for **salt** and **pepper**. Finish with **30g butter swirled in, cream if you like**, and some **toasted ground hazelnuts**. A lovely ivory-coloured soup, with the full flavour of the artichokes. Hazelnuts go extremely well with artichokes, and I often add them to other artichoke dishes.

Provence-Style Soup of Jerusalem Artichokes (Puree de Topinambours a la Provencale)

Follow the directions for Palestine Soup until the soup has been pureed. Warm through with **300ml milk**. Meanwhile, fry **2 large peeled chopped tomatoes**, **a clove of garlic**, and **a chopped stick of celery** in **2 tbsp. olive oil**. After 3-4 mins, tip the whole into the soup, and garnish with torn-up **basil leaves**. A delicious reminder of warm days.

White Bean, Jerusalem Artichokes, and Tomato Stew.

This is really an assembly job. Cook **250g dried white beans – haricots, cannellini** – after soaking overnight, or use 2 tins, drained and washed. Peel **500g Jerusalems**, cut into chunks, and steam 10 mins. Make a tomato sauce; fry gently **2 chopped cloves garlic** in **2 tbsp. olive oil**, add the **tomatoes from 1 drained tin**, **salt** and **pepper**, and some **sage or oregano or marjoram**, fresh or dried. I would usually put **1 or 2 fresh chilis**, seeded and chopped, in here too. Simmer.10 mins. Then mix the 3 components, and cook very slowly covered 10 mins or so so the flavours blend. Taste, adjust, **pepper** well, eat. You will notice that this is very largely a store-cupboard dish, except for the artichokes, and thus often very useful. If you're in a real hurry, then you can use tins of baked beans instead of the beans-and-tomato sauce mix.

Jerusalem Artichoke and Leek Crumble.

Peel and slice **500g Jerusalem artichokes**; wash, trim and slice thinly **500g leeks**. Melt **30g butter** in a large saucepan, and tip in the vegetables. Sweat, covered, for 5 mins, stirring now and then, then add **100ml white wine or dry cider**. **Salt** and **pepper**. Cook 30-40 mins, till the vegetables are very tender and there is little liquid left. Turn into a shallow casserole dish. Rub **100g butter** into **200g plain flour**. Add **salt, pepper**, and **100g Sage Derby (or Cheddar-type) cheese**, grated. Spread this crumble mix over the vegetables, and bake in a hot oven, 200, until the top is crisp and brown. If you haven't got Sage Derby, try adding ½ tsp. cinnamon or garam masala to the vegetable mix – not enough to identify, enough to lift the taste.

Jerusalem Artichoke Souffle.

Peel **350g Jerusalem artichokes**, slice roughly. and cook them in **100 ml. water**, really steaming, till well-done. About 10 mins. Make a thick white sauce with **60g butter, 50g white flour,** and **200 ml. milk. Salt, pepper**; quite a lot of both, as there is a large volume of egg white to be flavoured. Put the white sauce and the artichokes and their liquid in the food processor, and whizz smooth. Add **4 oz grated Wensleydale, Caerphilly, or Cheddar** and whizz. Add **4 egg yolks,** and whizz again. Beat the **4 egg whites** (5 if you have a spare from something else) with a pinch of **salt**, till they are at the soft-peak stage. Fold in the mix from the processor, and tip all into a buttered souffle dish. Sprinkle the top with grated cheese (**25g Parmesan, grated, or 50g grated strong Cheddar**) and bake at 190 for 35 mins or so, until it is well puffed and doesn't quiver when you push the dish. Soufflés are always spectacular and well-received, and this is a good one.

Jerusalem Artichoke, Fennel and Mushroom Pie.

This is a pie with just a pastry covering, which can be either puff pastry or shortcrust. (See Basics for both of these) Puff is more spectacular; shortcrust more homely and comfortable. The stew beneath the covering is made separately, as follows; Peel and slice **500g Jerusalem artichokes**; wash, trim and slice thinly **500g leeks**. Melt **30g butter** in a large saucepan, and tip in the vegetables. Sweat, covered, for 5 mins, stirring now and then. Add the **juice of a lemon** and **150 ml. stock** – the best you have. If it has had some dried mushrooms in its making, that's all to the good. Cook for 15-20 mins. Meanwhile, cook **250g large mushrooms**, sliced, in **30g butter**, with **1 chopped clove garlic**. Fry the mushrooms until they are softened, then add **salt**, which will bring out the juices, and continue to cook until the juices have evaporated and been absorbed. Trim and cut up **a fennel bulb**. Add mushrooms and fennel to the artichoke/leek mix. Let it cool. Put all the vegetables into a pie dish, cover with your chosen pastry, and bake at 200 for 15-20 mins, till the pastry is done. This is quite a spectacular dish – Sunday dinner at the least.

Jerusalem Artichoke Tart.
In this case, the pastry is the shell on the bottom. Line a 22cm (9") tart tin with shortcrust pastry, and bake blind (Basics). Steam **200g peeled Jerusalem artichokes**, and slice. Mix with **100g-150g cooked spinach**, chopped, or similar green (cooked weight), **2 beaten eggs, 150ml double cream, chopped chives**, and generous **salt, pepper** and **nutmeg**. Pour into the pastry case and bake at 180 for 25-30 mins, till golden and set. Best warm rather than piping hot.

They also go well in a curry, with other vegetables, and leaning the spicing towards the "sweet" side – nutmeg, cardamom.

Kale and Cavolo Nero

Kales have been the least esteemed of vegetables for many years. They are just too virtuous for their own good; tough, easy to grow, stand frosts, resistant to diseases and pests, and full of desirable vitamins and minerals. As a result they have been grown by the poor, on poor land, for maximum yield, and cooked very simply – hence the low status. This is starting to change. Part of this is the River Café phenomenon, taking an Italian heritage kale, cavolo nero, and making it fashionable and expensive. Part is the whole organic/farmer's market/vegetable box movement, supplying Red Russian kale among others, reputedly the best tasting of them all. Even the supermarkets have curly kale, which may be any of several varieties, unspecified.

The idea of named varieties is alien to kale-as-it used-to-be, and the situation at the moment is messy. Red Russian kale is not the same as red kale, and pictures of either can look very different though supposedly the same. Cavolo nero is, at least, unmistakable. Incidentally, so are pretty coloured ornamental kales, which are not good to eat. Meanwhile, try whatever named varieties you can find, grow whatever your favoured seed catalogue recommends, and wait for the situation to sort itself. And meanwhile cook kale in its various forms, for taste (yes) and health and economy.

Default. Steamed and Buttered Kale.
This is not particularly good for cavolo nero, but fine for Red Russian and young tender curly kale. **500g kale,** before trimming, for 4 people. Wash very well, as the curly edges can hold on to grit and earth splashed up, which will put you and your eaters off. Remove any stalk that projects beyond the leaves. If this doesn't snap cleanly, fold the leaf so the stalk is to the right, hold with the left hand, and pull the stalk away from the leaf. (Left-handers reverse the instruction) Then either shred the leaf, or tear it into 5-cm pieces so far as possible (I prefer shredding). Steam for 3-5 mins, till tender. Then mix with **salt** and **butter** to taste, and eat. Couldn't be simpler.

Kale Cooked in Milk.
For more mature and rather tougher leaves. I found this in a Lawrence D. Hills book, "Grow Your Own Fruit and Vegetables", 1971. (Lawrence Hills founded the Henry Doubleday Research

Association, now Garden Organic, and was a pioneer of organic growing.) Heat **120 ml. milk**, add **300g or so trimmed shredded kale, salt,** and simmer covered 8 mins. Lawrence Hills points out that the milk neutralises the acidity in the vegetable, and prevents the breakdown of sulphur compounds which cause the smell of boiling greens. Cooked like this, he says, all vegetables become mild and sweet. And he's right!

Cavolo Nero with Garlic and Oil.

Remove the centre stems from **500g or so cavolo nero**, wash, and shred. Blanch in **boiling water** for 3-5 mins, till almost tender, drain well, and squeeze dry or dry in a cloth. Heat **3 tbsp. extra-virgin olive oil** in a pan with a lid, and add **2-3 cloves garlic**, peeled and sliced. When the smell rises, add the cavolo nero, **salt, pepper**, and stir round. Then cover and cook on a low heat for about 5 mins.

This can be varied by adding a suitable spice with the garlic. I like **Cavolo Nero with Cumin and Mustard Seeds**; in this case add 1 tsp. each cumin seed and black mustard seed to the oil, and add the garlic when the mustard seeds have popped. Or **Cavolo Nero with Szechwan Pepper, Cavolo Nero with Aniseed, Cavolo Nero with Rosemary and Chili,** and so on. It must be a powerful spice or herb to stand up to the strong flavour of the green.

Kale and Spinach with Pine Nuts and Currants.

Mixing the greens gives a splendid variation in texture. Clean, remove the stems from, shred into wide ribbons, and blanch **500g kale**, any kind, till nearly tender. Drain well. Clean and destem **250g spinach**, wash, and keep aside. Toast **a small palmful of pine nuts**. Soak **30g currants** in hot water to cover, and drain just before they are needed. About 10 mins before you want the dish, heat **1 tbsp. olive oil** in a large pan, and add **2 finely-chopped cloves garlic**. When the smell rises, add the kale and mix well. Cover and cook 2 mins, then mix again, add the spinach leaves, drained currants, pine nuts, **salt and pepper**. Turn down the heat, cover, and leave for 2-3 mins. As an extra grace note, while the greens have this last couple of minutes heat **50g unsalted butter** in a small pan until it starts to brown. Add the **juice of a lemon**, and pour over the greens just as you serve them. You don't have to do this last, but it's very good.

Kale Seaweed

Wash, dry and shred **curly kale** finely, and drop small amounts into hot deep-frying oil. It will sizzle and crisp very quickly. Fish it out and drain on kitchen paper. 100g kale makes a lot of seaweed. An excellent garnish which goes not only with Chinese meals but almost any hot spread. Compare this with the price on supermarket ready-made versions, which aren't even as good, and resolve never to buy it again!

Caldo Verde. This soup, from northern Portugal, is a peasant soup using the local kale/cabbage variant. Curly kale is the closest equivalent. In its basic form, it's simply potatoes boiled in water and made into a puree, with finely shredded kale added for the last two minutes and eaten with a lot of olive oil. It's actually better if elaborated a little, and I'm sure the originators did so when they could. Sweat **1 medium chopped onion** in **2 tbsp. olive oil** till soft, then add **2 or more chopped cloves garlic** and **1 chopped stem celery**. After 5 mins, add **500g boiling potatoes**, peeled and cubed, stir, and add **1 litre water (or stock if you have it). Season.** Bring to the boil, and simmer, covered, for 25-30 mins, till the potato is collapsing. Sieve or whizz or simply stir vigorously to help the potato collapse. Wash and shred very finely **300g curly kale**, add to the soup, and bring back to the boil. Cook for no more than 10 mins, till the kale reaches a state you like. This depends on the age and toughness of the kale, and it's your judgement. Taste for salt, and serve with **extra-virgin olive oil** on the table so everyone can add the amount they like. It does need some extra oil, though.

Winter Green Soup with Garlic.

This is made with a mix of winter greens; allow **400g total, half kale and half outer leaves of Batavian endive or Swiss chard leaves or – failing these – spinach.** Wash and shred the greens finely. Peel **a whole head of garlic**, and chop all the cloves. Cook **400g potatoes**, peeled and diced small, in **1 litre stock** for 20 mins. While this is cooking, cook **1 medium chopped onion** in **2 tbsp. olive oil** till soft, then add the garlic and all the greens unless you have used spinach. If there's spinach, leave it aside till the soup is nearly done. Stir to coat the greens, cover, and let sweat till the potatoes are done. When the potato is done in its pan, tip in the greens/garlic mix, and add **100 ml. white wine** and **2 tbsp. white wine vinegar.** Simmer the whole together for 10-15 mins. If there is spinach, add it 5 mins before you're ready to eat. Add **1 tsp. dried chili flakes** or more to taste, and have these on the table for people to help themselves. Have **extra-virgin olive oil** on the table, too, and good crusty bread. I prefer this soup pureed and thinned as necessary. It is really improved by a hot undertaste from the chilis.

It will be obvious from these two examples that there are many possibilities for adding kale to vegetable soups. It will enrich them and make them more nutritious. Try it in a minestrone. Add shredded kale when the soup is nearly ready, and cook till the shreds have reached your desired mix of texture and tenderness.

Pasta with Kale, Chili and Cream.

A robust dish for winter, preferably followed by a hot fruity pudding. By the conventions of entertaining you'd only give this to very good friends, but why stick with convention? Wash, shred and blanch **500g. kale** – this is a good place for Red Russian kale, if you've got it – until tender. Drain well. Heat **30g butter** – more if your conscience will let you – and add **4 chopped cloves of garlic** and **2-3 chopped fresh seeded chilis**. Stir, and before the garlic can start to brown, add the well-drained kale, and stir to mix. Add **300 ml double cream**, and ½ **tsp. salt**, stir, and let the cream reduce till you have a sauce consistency. Meanwhile, boil **300g pasta (or enough for 4 people)**, drain, and mix with the creamy kale mixture. Serve with grated **Parmesan**, or, in this particular case, another strong cheese. I like Manchego here.

Kale Colcannon.

This has two components, cooked separately and mixed together just before eating. Boil and mash **700g boiling potatoes** with **50g butter, salt** and **pepper**, and **warm milk.** Moist but not too sloppy. Meanwhile, wash, trim, shred and blanch **500g kale** until tender. Drain well. Warm through in **30g butter** with **1 bunch spring onions**, trimmed and sliced. Mix mash and kale together, and beat well. If you have any left, make green potato cakes and fry them the next day – possibly even nicer.

445

Baked Kale with Potatoes.

A different way of combining these two winter staples. Wash well **500g Red Russian or curly kale**, destem, and shred. Peel **500g potatoes**, halve lengthwise, and cut into thin slices. Cook **2 large cloves garlic**, sliced, in **2 tbsp. extra-virgin olive oil**, but don't let it colour. Tip into a bowl with the kale and potatoes, and add **1 tbsp. capers**, and **4 tbsp. white wine and the same of water**. If you eat fish, use 6-8 anchovies, chopped, instead of the capers. Mix all well, and put in an oiled oven dish. Cover, and bake at 180 for 50-60 mins, till the potato is tender. Taste for **salt**; the capers should have provided plenty. Pour over **2 more tbsp. extra-virgin olive oil**, and serve with **lemon halves**.

Kale with Crumb Crust.

It uses crumbs, but it's definitely not metaphorically crummy. Chopped cooked kale is mixed with a cheese sauce and baked with a cheese/crumb topping. Wash, stalk, chop and blanch **700g kale** in boiling salted water for 10 mins or till very tender. Drain, rinse with cold water, squeeze, and chop finely. Make the sauce from **30g butter**, melted; add **1 rounded tbsp. flour**, and blend and let cook a little. Add **300 ml. milk**, and bring to the boil, stirring, so that the sauce thickens. Season; **salt** and **pepper**, and either **nutmeg or mushroom ketchup** to taste. Take the sauce off the heat and stir in **60g grated hard cheese**, probably Cheddar, until it has melted. Mix sauce and kale, and turn into a buttered oven dish. Sprinkle with the **crumbs from 1 large slice of bread**, and then with **50g grated cheese**. Bake in a hot oven until the top is brown and bubbling. I think that either hard goat's cheese or blue cheese in the sauce (but not on top) would be good, but I haven't tried these.

Kale Pudding.

This is a good dish for using leftovers of kale and rice, but I will assume you are starting from scratch. Blanch **400g kale** as usual (wash, destem, boil till tender, drain well) Make a sauce from **30g butter**, melted, and add **1 rounded tbsp. flour**. Blend and cook a little. Add **200 ml. stock**, and thicken by bringing to the boil, stirring. Season with **salt, pepper, ½ to 1 tsp. garam masala**, and a dash of **Tabasco**. Add **100 ml. double cream**. Whizz the kale with some of this sauce in a food processor to make a puree, and mix with the rest of the sauce. To this add **100g long-grain rice, cooked (or, if leftover**

rice, 400-500 ml). Mix in **100g cubed Caerphilly or Wensleydale ---
or, of course, Cheddar**, but the softer, more acid notes of the other
cheeses go better here. Put all in a buttered baking dish, sprinkle with
50g grated cheese, the same as used in the mix, and bake at 180 till
brown and bubbly.

Stir-Fried Kale with Tofu.

This is a simple stir-fry, using just onion, kale and tofu with the usual
seasonings. But, like any other stir-fry, you can add other vegetables
which you happen to have. Do remember to note any combinations
which are particularly successful; it's very sad to do a stir-fry which
people adore and then not remember what went into it. Peppers and
mushrooms are always good bets; peas, broad or French beans,
edamame enhance most stir-fries; I always like some Szechwan
vegetable in there. First prepare the vegetables; slice thinly **1 large
onion**, and wash, trim and shred **200g kale**. If you have young tender
kale, it doesn't need blanching; if it's a bit older, blanch for 2 mins.
Cube **500g tofu**. Chop **3 garlic cloves** and a **5-cm piece of ginger**
finely, and reserve the mix on a saucer. Mix **100 ml   rice wine or
sherry or white wine** with **100 ml water** in a cup. Have **2 tbsp. soy
sauce** in another cup. Trim and chop **4-6 spring onions**, and keep
them on a saucer. Heat **2 tbsp. sunflower oil** in a wok or large frying
pan on high heat, and add the onion. Stir until it starts to soften, about
2 mins. Add the shredded kale, and continue to stir-fry until the kale is
done to your liking, probably about 5 mins. Scoop the whole lot out of
the pan, and keep warm. Add **1 tbsp. more oil** to the pan, add the
garlic and ginger, and stir briefly. Add the tofu cubes and cook,
stirring, until it starts to brown. Add the wine/water mix, and cook,
still stirring, till the liquid has lost about half its volume. Put back the
onion/kale mix, stir briefly, sprinkle with the soy sauce and mix well.
Add the chopped spring onion, and serve IMMEDIATELY.

Spicy Kale and Chickpea Stew.

For this I use my own blended chili powder, as used in chili sin carne
and elsewhere. Mix **1 tsp. allspice, 1 tsp cumin, 1-2" cinnamon
stick**, and grind, in coffee grinder or otherwise. Add **¼ tsp. cayenne
or plain chili powder**, and **½ tsp dried oregano**. Otherwise,
supermarkets sell small jars of a similar spice blend. Soak **200g chick
peas** overnight, then cook in water. No salt. Keep back 100 ml. of the
cooking water for later use. They usually take 2 hours, but it may be

447

more depending on their age. If they are still hard after 4 hours, then you have an ancient batch; discard and replace. You need to do this in advance. You can use 2 tins chickpeas, drained and rinsed, but they aren't quite as good here -- but still OK. If you want to use the tinned version, don't let it put you off trying the recipe. Cook **2 medium chopped onions, 3 stalks of celery**, chopped, and **1 green pepper**, seeded and cut into squares, in **4 tbsp. sunflower oil** quite briskly, until the onions start to brown. Add **4 chopped cloves garlic**, and stir. Add the drained chick peas, **3 tsp. of the chili spice, 2 tins of chopped tomatoes, 2 tbsp. tomato puree from a tube, 100 ml. of chick pea cooking liquid or stock, a few sprigs of thyme** and **½ tsp. dried oregano, 1 tsp. sugar, 1 tsp. salt**. Bring to the boil, stirring. Add **500g kale**, washed and shredded, and stir it in. Simmer the mixture for 30 mins. or more; it's quite flexible. Add more liquid as needed. When ready to eat, taste; it may need more salt, or more heat to your taste, which can be dried chili flakes or chopped seeded fresh chili or Tabasco sauce. I'd add the **juice of a lemon**, but this may not be your taste. Also **fresh green coriander** if I have some. Serve with boiled rice or couscous or any other grain, like quinoa. This makes a lot, for 6 people or more, but it reheats well.

Kale Tart with Goat's Cheese.
Cook **400g kale** – cavolo nero, red Russian, curly if that's what there is, by washing, stalking, shredding, blanching till tender. Drain, squeeze, and chop finely. Mix in **2 x 100g logs soft goat's cheese**, in small chunks, **3 eggs**, and **40g sultanas or raisins. Salt** and **pepper, nutmeg**. Have ready a **baked pastry shell, 23 cm (9")**, and spread the green mix in this. Sprinkle the top with **30g pine nuts, 30g grated hard goats' or sheeps' cheese, like Manchego or Ossau Iraty, or an English one if you can find it**. Cook at 180 for 10-15 mins, and eat hot or warm or cold, with a salad. You won't believe how good this is!

It seems quite easy to grow cavolo nero in the UK, and the other kales as well. But if you don't grow and can't buy, Savoy cabbage can be substituted in any of the above recipes.

Lamb's Lettuce

Lamb's lettuce has only recently become commercially available in this country, but it was foraged and grown on a small scale long before that. The wonder is that it's taken so long for supplies to be available. Growing happily through the winter, its neat little rosettes are tender, succulent, mild-flavoured. It's available in autumn, winter, and spring, but most valuable in winter when there's nothing else with these qualities. It has to be admitted that it's a relief in winter to have a salad which isn't crunchy and chewy.

There aren't a lot of recipes for lamb's lettuce. It would be a waste to cook it. All it needs – after washing, because it can be very muddy underneath – is a little light vinaigrette. One of its pleasant uses is arranged on a plate around another salad, when it doesn't even need a dressing – it picks up enough from the other dressed salad. Or just enjoy picking up the little rosettes – don't cut them up – and nibbling; or put them on top of a mixed green salad.

Lamb's Lettuce with Beetroot.
This is the classic. Cook your **beetroot** – roast, boiled, or even a packet WITHOUT VINEGAR. Peel if necessary, and cube. Dress with a vinaigrette – **extra-virgin olive oil or walnut oil or hazelnut oil** – and a **little wine vinegar or lemon juice**. **Salt** and **pepper**. Put in the middle of a serving plate and arrange the rosettes of **lamb's lettuce** round the edge. If you've used a nut oil, a few of the appropriate nuts would be good.

Salade Lorette.
Just as above, but with a healthy amount of chopped **celery** added to the **beetroot**.

Either of these can be made more of a meal by adding crumbled goat's cheese, or an acid English cheese like Caerphilly, on top.

Lamb's Lettuce with Mushrooms and Sprouted Seeds.
Make your central salad with **raw sliced mushrooms** and **sprouted alfalfa or sprouted fenugreek or whatever you have**, dressed with **vinaigrette**.

449

Once you've got into this pattern, there are all sorts of salads which can benefit from the additional presence of lamb's lettuce. Just nothing heavy, nor anything with a heavy dressing. Keep it light and fresh.

Lamb's Lettuce Soup with Nuts.

I have recently discovered this, and it comes in handy if you have overbought or over-grown lamb's lettuce. Its mildness means that few other winter veg. can substitute for it here. Sweat **1 chopped onion, 1 clove garlic** in **20g butter** for 5 mins or so. Add **400g potatoes**, peeled and cubed, and a **tiny pinch of garam masala**. Stir, then add **700 ml stock**, and simmer 20 mins. Keep a few rosettes from **200g lamb's lettuce** on one side to garnish, add the rest to the pot with **30g walnut kernels**, and just bring to the boil. Blend or otherwise make smooth. Taste for seasoning (obviously you need more salt if the stock is your own rather than Marigold). Pour into bowls and top with the reserved rosettes.

Leeks

Leeks are the delicate member of the onion family for flavour. Have you ever wept while chopping up a leek? And this comparatively soft and delicate flavour can go almost anywhere that onions go, and add refinement to all these dishes. Leeks aren't delicate in growing, though; tough as old boots as far as cold and frost are concerned. They grow well in Scotland, for example, where onions struggle.

Not everything about leeks is positive. There are a couple of drawbacks, which have to be dealt with. First is the proportion which is not usable in dishes, those hefty dark-green leaves at the top of the white cylinder. The proportion is high, and many outer leaves (traditionally called flags, like iris) can only go into stock or compost Second is the consequence of the long white usable cylinder; leeks are earthed up to produce this, and as a result dirt gets in between the layers. Different people have their favourite ways of dealing with this. I slit the leek vertically, after trimming off the top leaves. Then it can be fanned out under the tap and the dirt between the layers washed out. Other people stand trimmed leeks, with a little cut at the top, upside down in a jug of water, and leave them to soak, when most of the dirt will fall out. Any remaining can be seen as a blotch; just slit at the blotch and wash it out. If the leeks are to be sliced, life is easier; put the slices in a bowl of water, swish them around, and lift out the clean leeks. Supermarket leeks are often heavily trimmed already, but still need caution; even a bit of dirt is not nice in the mouth!

Leeks are tricky when it comes to cooking. Undercooked they can be horrid and inedible – chew chew and quietly remove! Whole overcooked leeks have a texture I really dislike, though I know people who don't. So I tend to cook whole only leeks with a diameter of less than 1 cm, little pencil-like beauties, and everything larger gets thinly sliced. Dishes involving whole leeks have been tested by friends who like whole leeks. Leeks cooked whole can be waterlogged, and are improved by pressing – a tip I picked up from Stephanie Alexander's Cook's Companion. Drain the leeks after boiling or steaming, put on a plate, cover with a clean kitchen towel, and put on top a weight sized to cover as much of the leeks as possible. Leave an hour or so. A lot of water will come out. Put this water in a stock or discard, and then proceed. Whichever way you prepare leeks, though, the flavour is lovely, either alone with support from oil or butter, or with other vegetables.

Default: Buttery Leeks.

Slice thinly **6 leeks**, wash, drain and dry in a cloth. Add to **50g melted butter** in a lidded frying pan, stir, cover, and let cook on a low heat for 10 mins. or till the leek is almost tender. Take off the lid, raise the heat, and evaporate the excess liquid, stirring quite often. **Salt, pepper, nutmeg** if you like. These leeks are quite often used in dishes, for example, leeky mash, and leek and Roquefort tart below, so it's worth making more than you need immediately and planning something else to use the extra.

Leeks Vinaigrette.

For SMALL, whole young leeks. Hover over the selection at the market and pick out the babies, less than 1 cm diameter. This is quite often fine with the stallholder, as many people want only larger ones. Clean, trim and steam or boil **12 baby leeks** until JUST tender (5 mins?) – use a knife point or skewer to test. Drain and press. Make a vinaigrette with **French mustard, wine vinegar, extra-virgin olive oil, salt** and **pepper**, pour over, and turn the leeks gently so as to keep them whole. You can serve this alone, or with chopped herbs, or with black olives, or with chopped hard-boiled egg. Or nuts, using an appropriate nut oil in the vinaigrette. Try with salted peanuts, but still olive oil.

Leeks a la Grecque.

There are lots of other possibilities for cooking veg. a la Grecque – cauli, mushrooms, courgettes, baby onions . . . For leeks, you need maybe **20 SMALL thin leeks**, cleaned and trimmed. First make the marinade: mix **300 ml water, 4 tbsp. extra-virgin olive oil, 2 tbsp. tomato paste, 30g sultanas, 1 finely chopped clove garlic, juice of a lemon, ½ tsp. coriander seeds,** cracked on a mortar with **¼ tsp. black peppercorns, 1 bay leaf, 1 sprig thyme**, and **½ tsp. salt**. Simmer this lot together 10 mins or so, add the leeks, and cook gently, covered, till the leeks are just tender – test with point of knife. Tip into a dish and let cool, and serve. It keeps overnight, but loses that first lustre – still good, just not the best. You can move it out of the Greek character by using pickled lemon instead of sultanas; I prefer this, because I'm a sucker for pickled lemon wherever I find it.

Leeks in Red Wine

This can be done with small leeks, left whole, or medium-size leeks, halved lengthwise. You need about **750g leeks** as bought. Trim and wash, and brown them in **2 tbsp. olive oil**. Start with the cut side if you are using larger leeks. Turn them over and brown the other side. If larger leeks, turn again so the cut side is down. Pour in **150 ml. red wine, 4 tbsp. stock, salt, a bay leaf**. Turn the heat down, and simmer, uncovered, until the leeks are done. Allow 10-15 mins. Test with skewer both at base and leaf end. If there is a lot of liquid left, take out the leeks and put on a warm plate, and reduce the liquid till it is syrupy. Pour over the leeks. It doesn't need garnish or anything else, just eat as it is alone, or as a vegetable dish, or, cooled, as a first-course salad.

Charcoal-Grilled Leeks.

Brings out the leek flavour, and adds the attractive grilled taste. A winner for a barbecue, even if you have meat-eaters present. If the **leeks** are large, parboil them first, about 5 mins. If they are really large, halve before parboiling. Obviously, trim and clean the leeks before parboiling. Drain well, and dry in a clean teatowel. Brush with **light olive oil** and put on the grill over the coals, turning until they are well coloured. Put on a serving plate, where you have already put **4 tbsp. extra-virgin olive oil, salt** and **pepper**, and some chopped **herbs**, turn over the leeks, and eat.

Braised Leeks with Parmesan.

Another terrific flavour to set off the leek taste. Start with **6 medium leeks, about 750g.** Trim, wash, drain, halve lengthwise, and put in a pan with a cover where they can lie flat. Ideally it would be an oval pan so they covered the bottom, but I don't have such a pan, and I don't know anyone who does. Put in **50g butter** and **150 ml. water, salt**, and bring to the boil. Cover and simmer gently until the leeks are done, testing as usual with skewer or knife-point. Start testing after about 15 mins. Turn now and then. When done, take off the lid, turn up the heat, and boil off the liquid, letting the leeks brown a little in the butter. Add **30-50g freshly grated Parmesan**. Stir, and serve straightaway.

Deep-Fried Leek Shreds.

If you have **one or two spare leeks**, and you have the deep-frier out for another reason, leeks make a delicious all-purpose garnish. Trim, shred, wash, and dry VERY WELL – otherwise the hot fat may rise up and overflow. Drop the shredded leek into **hot deep oil**, fry briefly until the shreds have changed colour, scoop out, and drain on kitchen paper or newspaper. Heap on top of almost anything savoury, where a little crispness and taste will go well.

Funges (Leeks with Mushrooms).

The recipe for this dish originated in the 14th century cookbook, The Forme of Cury. I used it a lot when I was cooking medieval feasts for moderate numbers, because it can be made beforehand and stands reheating well, and everyone always enjoyed it. Probably the originators would have used a mix of wild mushrooms, but I use the large mushrooms with visible gills easily available now. Trim and wash **8-10 small leeks**, and slice thinly. Cook them gently in **20g butter**. Meanwhile, slice **700g (or so) large mushrooms**, and fry them in **30g butter** until they are much reduced in volume, and nearly done. Add a **small knob of fresh ginger**, peeled and finely chopped, to the mushrooms, then mix leeks and mushrooms. Add **100 ml stock, salt** and **pepper, 1 tsp brown sugar**, cover, and simmer 5 mins for the flavours to blend. Thicken the juices with **1 tsp. arrowroot** mixed with **2-3 tbsp. cold stock** in a cup, and poured in. Taste for seasoning. This is improved with **1 tsp. coriander seeds**, ground, added with the ginger, but it isn't then authentic.

Leeks Baked in Tomato Sauce.

Trim, halve, wash, and drain **700g leeks**. Parboil for 2 mins, drain, and ideally press them as described above Put them in a baking dish with **2 tbsp. olive oil**. Whizz the contents of **1 tin tomatoes, 1-2 cloves garlic, ½ tsp. dried mixed herbs, salt** and **pepper**, in a blender, and pour the result over the leeks. Cover and cook at 150 till leeks are done – knifepoint or skewer test again. Hot or cold.

Leeks with Peppers.

Simple dish of mixed vegetables, to go with a pastry or soufflé or pancake dish. Trim, slice and wash **500g leeks**, Sweat them in **20g butter** with **salt** as for buttered leeks. When tender, add **4 peppers**, deseeded and cut into thin shreds. Add **1 tbsp. olive oil**, raise the heat, and cook briskly, stirring, for a couple of minutes. Lower the heat, cover, and let cook a few mins. more. Add **a handful of herbs**, chopped – a mix of parsley, marjoram, basil is good; so is parsley and tarragon; or just parsley. **Pepper**, taste for salt. This isn't good cold, because of the butter.

Leeks with Carrots.
250g each leeks and carrots. Prepare the leeks, cut into thin slices. Peel the carrots and slice very thinly. Put them together into a frying pan with **4 tbsp. hot olive oil**, add **50g currants** soaked in a little **water** and drained, and stir-fry for 3-4 mins. Taste the leek for doneness; if not cooked to your liking, go on until it is.. Add **2 tsp. grainy mustard** mixed with **2 tbsp. mild balsamic vinegar**, mix in, and eat.

Roasted Leeks with Fennel.
Clean **4 medium leeks**, and cut into 2 cm. chunks. Trim **a large fennel bulb**, and sliver into 8 wedges. Put in a roasting dish, and add **2 tbsp. olive oil, salt** and **pepper**, and **1 tsp. coriander seeds**, pounded in a mortar (or cracked in a coffee grinder). Mix with your hands. Roast at 180 for 30-40 mins. Squeeze over the **juice of a lemon**.

Leeks and Butter Beans.
Soak and cook **200g butter beans**, or use 2 tins, drained and rinsed. If cooking, add sage leaves during the cooking; if using tinned, add **3-4 sage leaves** finely shredded. Trim, slice, wash, drain **700g leeks**, and sweat in **2 tbsp. olive oil**, covered, till soft. Mix leeks and beans. If this is too dry for you, add a little **stock**, either from the cooking of the beans or elsewhere. Taste for seasoning, adding **pepper**, and **salt** if needed. Dribble with a **little extra-virgin olive oil**, and eat hot or cold. OR you can add a crumble topping to the leek-bean mix (**4 oz mixed flour and oats, 2 oz. butter rubbed in, salt, herbs**), bake, and have a more substantial dish.

Leeks and Tofu.
The plain version first, followed by variations. For the plain, trim, slice crosswise into 2-cm sections, wash and dry **500g leeks**. Cut a **packet of bean curd** into 12 or so chunks. Heat **2 tbsp. sunflower or other mild oil** in a wok or frying pan, add the leeks, and stir-fry 1 min. Add

the bean curd and stir gently, so as not to break the bean curd, 2 mins. more. Add **1 tsp salt, 2 tbsp soy sauce**, and stir another min. Eat as soon as possible.

To elaborate, **add finely chopped ginger or chili** before adding the leeks.

Or add **1 tbsp. hoisin sauce** with the soy sauce.

Or use a **black bean sauce**, home-made or commercial.

Or add other veg, such as **slivered peppers** added with the leeks. And so on.

Leeky Mash.

Boil or steam **1 kg peeled floury potatoes** (Steaming is better here, as they are less likely to fall apart in the water). Clean **500g leeks**, and slice very thinly. Melt them, without browning, in **50g butter** till soft. Drain and mash the potatoes – a mouli-legumes is the best, but seems very hard to find. Add leeks, **salt** and **pepper**, and beat, adding another **50g butter**, and gradually **double cream** to taste. At least 100 ml cream, depending on the consistency you like and the properties of the potatoes. You can eat it alone,

Or shape it into a nest on people's plates and put **a poached egg** in the nest. **Pepper** the egg, and eat.

A variation gives you modern **Anglesey Eggs**. Hard-boil **6 eggs**, shell and chop. Make a layer of half the leeky mash in a flat serving dish, and put the chopped eggs on top. Cover with the other half of the mash. Sprinkle the top generously with **grated Cheshire or Cheddar**, and brown quickly under the grill. You could have a tomato sauce, or put tomato ketchup and HP sauce on the table and let people help themselves.

Glamorgan Sausages.

This doesn't use a lot of leek, and spring onion can be used instead. However, it is a homely dish much liked by children, and deserves a place. It's easiest when made in a food processor, but not difficult without. Use **half a small leek**, trimmed, roughly sliced, washed, and chop this in a food processor with **5-6 sprigs parsley**, stalks removed.. Add to the processor **120g fresh white breadcrumbs**, whizz briefly, then add **150g grated Caerphilly, 1 level tsp. mustard powder, salt** and **pepper**. Whizz again. Add **2 egg yolks** and whizz to bind. Scoop and scrape out the mixture, making sure it holds together. (If not, add more breadcrumbs)   Divide into 12, and shape each piece into a sausage shape. Roll in **the white of an egg**, then quickly in **more breadcrumbs**. Fry in **sunflower oil** till golden brown. They go with tomato sauce and/or a leafy green vegetable.

Leek and Potato Soup.
Very simple, very basic, doesn't even need stock, and deservedly classic because it is so good. Trim, slice thinly, wash and drain **6 medium leeks**, and put them to sweat, covered, in **50g butter**. Add **1 sliced stick celery**, if you have it. Peel and cube **4 medium potatoes**, and add to the leeks. Turn round to mix with the leek juices, and leave a few mins more. Add **water to cover**, and bring to the boil. You can add a **bay leaf** and a **couple of thyme sprigs** at this point, but it isn't really necessary. Cover and simmer until the potato is done. Put the soup through a mouli, or let it cool and whizz in a blender, or use a stick blender – whichever way you have to get a smooth soup. Reheat when ready to eat, add **50-100 ml double cream, black pepper**, and a **sprinkle of chopped parsley and/or chives**.
This soup, chilled and with more cream added, becomes **Vichyssoise**, which was a very trendy soup in the 50's and 60's. I now find it too rich and bland in its original form, where you used half as much cream as soup. If you want a cold leek and potato soup, cool, and add **either yoghurt or sour cream** until it suits your taste. Garnish with chopped **chives**. I wouldn't do it myself, though.

Leek and Chickpea Soup.
This could hardly be simpler or easier, or better. I prefer it to the more complex versions using more ingredients. Trim, slice, wash and dry **1 kg. leeks**, and sweat them, covered, in **3 tbsp. olive oil** with **1 tsp salt**. Cook at least 10 mins, till nearly melted. Drain a **can of chickpeas**, rinse, and add to the leeks. Add **water or stock** to cover by about 5 cm, cover, simmer 15 mins. Blend the soup, all or some according to your choice, with a stick blender, cool and in blender, or using a mouli. When ready to eat, reheat. Add **black pepper**, probably about twice the amount you would usually use, and **50g grated Parmesan**.
I said it was simple. If you want to enrich it tastewise and nutritionally, slice **100-200g spinach** into ribbons, and add after reheating and before the pepper (reduce the amount) and Parmesan.

Leek and Egg Bruschetta.

Make buttery leeks with **500g leeks**. Hard-boil **6 eggs**, shell, and chop. Mix into the leeks with **2 tsp. grainy mustard, salt** if needed, **pepper**, and serve on toasted slices **ciabatta;** you'll need a whole loaf. Toast the bread on both sides, and rub the top with a juicy **clove of garlic.** Decorate with sprigs of **parsley.**

Alternatively, do it the English way, with **buttered slices of toast**, and grated **Cheddar** sprinkled on top.

Leek Souffle

Make buttery leeks with **500g leeks**. Make a white sauce as the souffle base: melt **30g butter**, add **30g flour** and stir in, and cook gently till the mixture honeycombs. Add **250 ml. milk**, and bring to the boil, stirring as it thickens. **Salt, pepper, nutmeg.** Then whizz the sauce and the leeks together in a food processor. Whizz in **60g. grated Cheddar.** Add **4 egg yolks**, 1 at a time, to the mixture in the processor, whizzing each in. Tip and scrape the mixture into a large bowl. In a separate bowl, beat **4 (or 5 if you have a spare) egg whites** with a **pinch of salt** added before beating. The egg whites should be very stiff. Take about a quarter of the egg whites, and beat into the leek mixture. Then tip the lightened leek mixture on top of the rest of the egg whites, Fold together lightly but thoroughly. Transfer the souffle mix to a buttered souffle dish, sprinkle with about **30g more grated cheese**, and run your finger through the mix just inside the rim. Bake at 400 for 30-35 mins, until the souffle is well risen and browned and only shakes a little when you give the dish a small sharp push in the oven. Serve STRAIGHTAWAY, to waiting eaters.

Pasta with Leeks and Mushrooms.

You could use the Funges mixture, above, but this version is nicer. Also more expensive, because of the dried porcini. Soak **20g dried porcini** in boiling water to cover for about 30 mins. Meanwhile, make buttery leeks with **500g leeks**. Start to fry **250g sliced mushrooms** – the big ones – in **30g butter**. When they start to shrink, lift the porcini from the now-cool water, cut them up if the pieces are large, and add to the frying mushrooms. Add **2 chopped cloves garlic** and leaves from **4-5 sprigs thyme** and stir in with about **½ tsp. salt.** The juices should start to run from the fresh mushrooms; continue to cook, adding the strained soaking water a bit at a time, till there is only a little juice left. Stir in the leeks. Meanwhile, have just cooked **400g pasta**; drain, and mix with the sauce. Serve with lots of grated **Parmesan**.

You could cook the leeks from scratch with the mushrooms, but this involves boiling them in the juices for some time, and I think tends to make them too soft and sticky. It does save a pan and some time, though.

Leek and Mushroom Risotto.

As with all risottos, the key is the quality of the stock you use. For this, a stock flavoured with dried mushrooms – whatever you can find cheap (or less expensive, anyhow) and tomatoes. Use a tin of tomatoes when making the stock, if good cheap fresh ones aren't available. (See Basics for basic stock) The stock needs some salt, but not a lot, as it will evaporate in the risotto and leave its salt behind. You need about **1½ litres stock**, and may not use it all. The risotto itself is nicest made with dried porcini and fresh mushrooms, but you can miss out the dried porcini if necessary. Soak **10g dried porcini** in boiling water for about ½ hr. Drain them, keeping the soaking water, and chop the porcini pieces finely. Keep these for the main risotto. Cook **250g sliced white mushrooms** separately; start to fry them in **15g butter**. When they start to change colour, add **2 chopped cloves garlic, salt** and **pepper**, and stir well. Add the soaking water from the porcini, and reduce this to a glaze, stirring. Keep aside. Start the risotto; heat **30g butter** in a large frying pan, and add **a medium leek**, trimmed, sliced, washed and dried. Stir till the leek is wilted, then add **a medium fennel**, quartered and thinly sliced, and the porcini pieces. Add **2 more chopped cloves garlic**. Stir a minute or two, then add **300g risotto rice**, and stir and turn for 2-3 mins. Add **150 ml. dry white wine**, and let this evaporate. Now start adding the hot stock, kept nearly simmering in a pan on the stove, a ladle-ful at a time. Stir, and let one addition of liquid nearly vanish before adding the next. After about 15 mins of adding liquid, add the fresh mushrooms, and continue to add liquid until the rice is cooked. Add **a small lump of butter** and **30g grated Parmesan**, stir in vigorously, and serve IMMEDIATELY. Risottos really are worth all this hassle, I promise.

Caramelised Leeks and Quinoa.

Leeks can be – though seldom are – caramelised just as onions are. Here they are cooked with the fashionable grain quinoa, but caramelised leeks can be used anywhere that caramelised onions are.

Trim **700g leeks** so just a little green is left, slice thinly, wash, drain, and dry. Put in a frying pan – or other wide pan – with a lid, and cook gently until the leeks are almost dry and starting to stick to the pan. Stir now and then. They will not be brown yet. Add **3 tbsp. olive oil** and **2 tbsp. dark brown sugar**, turn up the heat a little, and cook covered again until the leeks are brown and much shrunken. Add **200g quinoa** and **1 tsp salt**, and cook uncovered till the grains toast a little and start to pop. Add **400 ml. stock** and **2-3 sprigs thyme**, stir, cover, turn down the heat and cook till the quinoa is done (15-20 mins) Taste after 15 mins, and add a little more liquid if needed. Taste and add **salt** if needed, grind over quite a lot of **black pepper**, and eat hot or cold. Chopped herbs can be added; I like **fennel or fresh green coriander**, but not both.

Leek Strata

(you could call this Strata Florida, after the Welsh abbey of that name near Aberystwyth) Butter a baking dish suitable for bread-and-butter pudding, which is what this is. Make buttery leeks with **500g leeks**. Decrust **4 slices of bread, butter**, and cut into triangles. Layer the bread triangles, the leeks, and **a few (30-40g) currants** in the baking dish. Beat **3 eggs** with **500 ml. milk, salt** and **pepper**. Grate **200g Caerphilly or Cheddar cheese**, and mix about 2/3rds in with the eggs and milk. Pour this over the bread and leeks, and let it soak for 30-45 mins. Sprinkle the top with the remaining cheese, and bake at 150 for 40-50 mins, or till set. If it is **nasturtium** season, garnish the top with some of the flowers – it really will be Florida then! Needs a green salad or cooked green leaves.

Flamiche.

A very variable dish of Northern France, which ranges from leeks enclosed by bread dough to a rich quiche. Flamiche Beauvais-style can be made like the Leek and Roquefort tart below, substituting 100g cubed old Gouda or Gruyere for the Roquefort and leaving out the Tabasco. Add nutmeg instead. I prefer the tart, but it's worth knowing this one when a flavoured breadstuff is called for. In Italy, it would be a calzone.

Make a bread dough with **500g bread flour, 1 tsp salt, 1 pkt active dry yeast, 300 ml warm water**. (see Basics) Let it rise. While it's rising, make buttery leeks with **500g leeks**. Make them quite dry. Punch down the dough, and divide into two. On a floured surface, roll the larger half to about 25 cm diameter. Put on an oiled baking sheet. Spread the cooled leeks on this, and dot with **150g strong cheese, cubed** – Mimolette is the local version; Cheddar is fine. Roll out the other half of the dough to cover, drape it over dough and filling, and pinch the edges together, rolling the dual edge to the inside. Let the formed flamiche rise again for 30-40 mins, brush the top with **beaten egg** and slash a few slits in it, then bake at 400 for 20-25 mins. Eat warm.

Leek and Roquefort Tart.
You need a partly-baked tart shell, see Basics. For a 22 cm or 9" shell, cook **500g leeks**, trimmed, washed, and sliced about 1 cm thick, in **25g. butter**. Cover and gently cook about 10 mins. Let cool. Spread on the base of the tart. Crumble **100g Roquefort**, and distribute over the leeks. Beat **3 eggs** with **150 ml. double cream**, and add several generous dashes of **Tabasco**. I don't think salt is needed; Roquefort is quite salty. Bake at 180 for 30-40 mins, until the filling is risen and the top is a lovely brown. Let it cool 5-10 mins before eating.

There is no way this selection covers all the possibilities for leeks. Without even trying, I can think of stuffed pancakes with leeks and mushrooms, leek pie, steamed leek pudding, Persian leek kuku, frittata, proussa, which is a North African dish with potatoes, leeks and tomatoes, Middle Eastern stuffed leek leaves . . . And that's ignoring all the dishes where just one leek goes with onion, carrot, celery and garlic to form a savoury base. Leeks are not actually indispensable, like onions, but they are a flexible delight.

461

Parsnips

Parsnips have historically been popular with the English, probably because they like the sweetness. Not so with the French, who use theirs for cattle feed. But in England we have appreciated the parsnip in roasts, for making wine, and as a staple before the potato was introduced. It's nearly as flexible as carrots, and while we don't use it as much as carrots, it's a vegetable of moderate popularity and, at the moment, moderately in fashion. I'm always surprised it has no reputation as an aphrodisiac, as the shape and colour would lend themselves well.

Parsnips are definitely a winter vegetable, and seem to become sweeter after they've suffered through a frost or two. Growing good parsnips is difficult, and I'm happy to leave it to the professionals. You want them fairly small, no more than 20 cm long, and about 8 cm across at the top. Large ones produce a tough and woody core, which has to be cut out.

I think parsnips need peeling, and that this is better done before cooking. Most parsnip dishes involve a preliminary blanching of the vegetable, in boiling salted water. So cut off top and point at bottom, peel, halve or quarter depending on size, and boil for no more than 5 mins. Drain. After this, you can feel the core, and decide whether it should be removed or not. The parsnip is much more likely to become tender if cut up.

Default. Roast Parsnips.
Allow **500g parsnips** for 4 eaters. After blanching and draining, put in a roasting tin with a splash of olive oil. Roll round to coat the pieces, and roast in hot oven until they are brown and crisp. Salt and pepper just before serving.

There are many possible variations on roast parsnips, either by a garnish at the end or by adding other things to roast along with them or with additions to their roasting oil.
For example, **Roast Parsnips with Gherkins.**
Roast **500g parsnips** as above, and take them out of the roasting pan when they are done. Add to the pan **8-12 small chopped gherkins** (the

French cornichons) **or ½ a large dill pickle**, chopped. Add **2 tbsp. wine vinegar – red or white –** and stir and scrape the pan base while reducing the vinegar to a thin syrup. Pour over the parsnips.

Roast Parsnips with Toasted Hazelnuts

Roast **500g parsnips**. While they are cooking, toast **50g hazelnuts** under the grill. As they cool, wrap them in a clean teatowel, and rub to remove the skins. Put them in a small bowl of the food processor, and add **1 sliced clove garlic, ½ tsp. salt**, and **1 tbsp. hazelnut oil or extra-virgin olive oil**. Whizz to a rough paste, and toss the parsnips with this mixture.

Roast Parsnips with Harissa.

When they are done, toss with harissa to taste. Quantities depend on the heat of your harissa and how much heat you want. As a guide, though, I use **1 tbsp. rose harissa to 500g parsnips**, weighed before preparing. This responds to a yoghurt accompaniment; **seasoned yoghurt with parsley, or leftover raita** (Could be fresh, obviously, but it's a good place for leftovers)

Roast Winter Roots.

Parsnip, carrot, celeriac, potato, red onion. Don't do too much of any vegetable, Prepare and chunk the veg, cutting the onion into wedges with a little root end on each to hold it together. **A slosh of olive oil, salt** and **pepper, a few unpeeled cloves of garlic**. Turn them with your hands to mix well (the point about using your hands is that you can be gentle, and you can tell when everything is coated). Roast at 180-200 till the vegetables are tender and well browned. It needs a green salad. Leftover roast veggies can make a soup, or be used up in stock.

Roast Parsnips with Maple Syrup.

Two sweetnesses, and two distinct complementary sets of flavours. Generally adored, but you have to be careful what you serve it with. Mix **1 kg. parsnips**, blanched, with **4 tbsp. sunflower oil, 4 tbsp. maple syrup, 1 tsp. salt**. Roast in a moderate, not a hot, oven, and keep an eye on them so they brown but don't burn. You might not want pepper with them; if you do, **5-peppercorn mix** is the thing.

Parsnips with Breadcrumbs.

Roast **1 kg. parsnips**. While this is happening, make breadcrumbs from **200g decrusted bread**. Cook **2 chopped shallots** in **25g butter** till soft. Add the breadcrumbs, turn up the heat, and toss and cook till the breadcrumbs absorb the butter. Season with **salt, pepper, thyme, parsley**. Tip this mix over the parsnips when they are done, spread them out, and cook in the oven (same temperature as you've been using) till the top is brown and crunchy. You can pause between roasting and finishing; it will then take longer for the last stage.

Parsnip and Potato Mash.

Mashed parsnip on its own is too sweet for me – it's different when parsnip mash is used with other ingredients, in croquettes, for example. But for a dish of mash, I use potatoes and parsnip in roughly equal amounts. Peel and chunk **500g each parsnips and potatoes**, and boil gently till done. Drain, then mash, according to your habit; mouli is best, potato masher, fork is OK. As you mash, beat in a **lump of butter, salt** and **pepper**, and then **warm milk** till you get a puree of the consistency you like. A small dose of a single spice can set off the flavour; freshly grated **nutmeg, or cinnamon, or ground cardamom seeds**. Cardamom is used in sweet things in Scandinavian baking, so it isn't as strange as it sounds here.

Mashed Parsnips with Walnuts.

Boil **500g parsnips**, peeled and cut in small chunks. Keep **a cup of the cooking liquid** to one side before draining. Puree in the food processor with **2 sliced cloves garlic, 3 tbsp. walnut oil or extra-virgin olive oil, juice of 1 lemon, salt, pepper, parsley**. Use some of the cooking water to thin down to the right consistency. Scrape into a bowl, and mix in **50g broken-up walnuts**. Decorate the top with **whole walnuts** to serve.

Parsnip and Swede Mash.

6 parsnips, ½ a small swede. Trim, peel and chunk, and boil till done. Dip out **a cup of the cooking water** before draining. Puree in the food processor with **20g butter or more, 6-8 tbsp. cream or milk, salt, pepper**, and cooking water to give the right consistency. Try either **ground fennel seed or cinnamon** with this.

Parsnip Chips.

Just like potato chips, except that the parsnip is parboiled first. So peel **500g parsnips** and cut into chip-like shapes, blanch for 3-4 mins and drain, and then fry in **deep oil** until brown, crisp, and done. Delicious just salted, but I like a Chinese dipping sauce, with rice vinegar or white wine vinegar, soy sauce, and Szechwan peppercorns ground. (**2 tbsp. rice vinegar, 1 tbsp. soy sauce, 2 tsp. Szechwan pepper**) It sounds odd but the flavours go so well.

Parsnip Crisps.

Peel the **raw parsnip root**, then shave off thin strips with a swivel-action peeler, drop in **deep hot fat** until brown, drain and remove fat with kitchen paper. Lovely!

Salads.

I've tried parsnip salads using the raw grated vegetable, but they are not for me. The sort of worthy salad you get in wholefood cafes. Salads with cooked parsnips, on the other hand, can be very good, with the contrast of texture between soft cooked parsnip and something crunchy – celery, fennel, nuts. See also the parsnip cocktail as a first course at the end of this section.

Parsnip and Celery Salad with Walnuts.

500g parsnips, cooked till just tender. **6 sticks celery**, destringed and sliced finely crosswise. **50g walnuts**. Mix them all with a vinaigrette of **4 tbsp. walnut oil** and **1 tbsp. sherry vinegar**, with **salt** and **pepper**. A fresh chopped **mild herb**, like chives and/or parsley, to sprinkle on top.

Parsnip and Fennel Salad with Pistachios.

500g parsnips, cooked till just tender. **1 thinly sliced fennel bulb**, blanched briefly if you like (It may be crunchier than you want if left alone.) Dress with a vinaigrette of **4 tbsp. extra-virgin olive oil, 1 tbsp. white wine vinegar, 1 tbsp. plain yoghurt, salt** and **pepper**, and **a good handful of parsley**. **Mint** can go in too, if you have some. Whizz the dressing in blender or processor, and coat the mixed parsnips and fennel in this. Garnish the top with **green pistachio nuts** – not the roasted salted nuts in the shell, but the bare and beautifully coloured nuts.

465

Parsnip Soups.

The first parsnip soup I ever tried was in Jane Grigson's Good Things, which came out in 1971, and original because it used curry powder. I've made it ever since, merely substituting garam masala for her curry powder, and it's an excellent soup which was a real creation. Since then almost every writer who mentions parsnips has copied, modified a bit, and hardly ever acknowledged. Neither of the two following soups is derived from that, but I do recommend that you hunt it down, or the more elaborate version in her Vegetable Book.

Parsnip Soup with Chili and Sour Cream.

Sweat **1 large chopped onion** in **40g butter**. When it has softened, add **a small leek**, chopped, **1 chopped seeded fresh chili**, **½ tsp ground ginger or a small knob fresh ginger**, peeled and chopped, and leave 2-3 mins to sweat some more. Then add **½ tsp sugar**, **¼ tsp turmeric**, and stir. Add **500g parsnips**, trimmed, peeled and sliced, and **200g potato**, peeled and diced. Stir again, cook 5 mins, and add **1 litre stock or water**. **Salt** if needed. Bring to the boil, and simmer, covered, till the vegetables are tender. Let it cool. Whizz in a blender. When ready, reheat, and serve either the natural creamy colour, or with a sprinkle of **nutmeg** and **black pepper** on top. Have **sour cream** on the table, and add a spoon of it to each helping.

Parsnip and Butterbean Soup.

Sweat **2 large leeks** and **4 chopped celery stalks** in **40g butter**. After 5 mins or so, add **500g parsnips**, peeled and cut small, the **contents of a tin of butter beans**, drained and rinsed, and **1 litre stock**. **Salt** if the stock is not salted. Simmer covered till done. Cool and puree in a blender. Reheat, and add **100 ml. double cream**. It's fine as it is, but it looks prettier with **100g defrosted frozen peas** scattered on top.

Parsnip and Swede Gratin.

This and the two following recipes are rich, tempting, and not to be eaten too often. Any of them would make a fine centre dish for entertaining, and the one with cepes/porcini is worth a celebration in itself. For the swede/parsnip variation, slice (and keep separate) **250g each swede and parsnip**, trimmed and peeled. Chop **a small onion,** chop finely **a clove of garlic**. Layer the swede and parsnip alternately in a buttered baking dish, sprinkling each layer with onion, garlic, **salt** and **pepper**. Pour over **150 ml cream, single or double**. Cover the dish with foil and bake at 150 till the veg. are tender, about 1 hr. Take off the lid, sprinkle with **50g grated Cheddar**, and return to the oven at 180 till the top is brown.

Parsnip and Mushroom Gratin.
Trim, halve, and slice into 1-cm pieces **500g parsnips**. Boil or steam till tender, and drain. Meanwhile, cook **250g sliced mushrooms** in **30g butter** until almost dry, **salt**ing halfway through. The mushrooms can be small and white, which is prettier, or large and brown, which tastes better. Add **150 ml. double cream** to the mushrooms, and mix in the parsnips. **Pepper** and **nutmeg** (and **more salt, if needed**) to taste. Tip into a buttered dish, and flatten out the mix as far as possible. Sprinkle the top with **breadcrumbs from 1 slice decrusted bread** and **50g grated Cheddar**, and brown under the grill. You can perfectly well stop when the dish is assembled and let it cool; in this case heat and brown it in a hot oven.

Parsnip, Potato and Dried Mushroom Gratin.
Soak **10g dried porcini/cepes** by pouring boiling water over them in a small bowl, and letting soak for 30 mins. While this is happening, peel and slice thinly **500g each of parsnip and potato**, keeping them separate. Chop finely **2 cloves of garlic**, and mix with **the leaves from 3-4 sprigs thyme**. Drain the soaked porcini, KEEPING THE LIQUID, and cut into small pieces. Mix the mushroom-soaking liquid with **300 ml milk** and **150 ml double cream**. Start to layer the potatoes and parsnips in a buttered shallow baking dish, as parsnips, sprinkle fungi, potatoes, sprinkle garlic and thyme and salt and pepper, and continue till all used, with a layer of undressed potato on top. Pour over the liquid, so it comes just up to the top layer. Cover the dish with foil, and bake at 150 till a knife point slides in without resistance. (I can't tell you how long this will take, because it depends on the depth in the dish. Allow at least 1 hr.) Take off the foil, dot with about **30g butter**, and brown the top in the oven turned up to 180. It DOESN'T need cheese.

Parsnip and Potato Cakes.

Basically a soft mash, stiffened with flour, and shallow-fried as potato cakes. Homely and popular. A fried or poached egg on top makes a meal of them.

Peel and cut up **300g each parsnips and potatoes**, and boil till tender. (If boiling in the same pan, add the parsnips to the potatoes with about 10 mins to go.) Drain and mash, through a mouli, with a potato ricer, with a fork .. your preferred means. Beat into the puree **1 egg, 3 tbsp. double cream, 1 tsp. Dijon mustard, salt, pepper**, and **thyme leaves or chopped parsley** to taste. Add **flour** to make a stiff paste; start with 100g, and add more if needed. Shape pieces of the paste, about golf-ball size, into flat cakes, and fry them in batches in sunflower oil.

Parsnip and Sweetcorn Quiche.

Line, and bake blind, a 23 cm (9") flan case using **shortcrust pastry**.(Basics). Sweat **a medium chopped onion** in **25g butter**. When it has softened, add **1 tsp. ground cumin** and **2 chopped deseeded fresh chilis**. Stir and leave a few minutes, then add **300g parsnips**, peeled and grated, and **½ tsp. salt**. Cover and cook gently until the parsnips are tender. Beat well in the pan. Add **200g defrosted sweetcorn, 2 eggs**, and **100 ml. double cream**. Pour into the pastry case, and bake at 180 for 20-30 mins, till the filling has risen and browned. Let it cool a little before eating.

Parsnip, Potato and Cauliflower Korma.

Peel and dice **250g each parsnip and potato**, and break **a small cauliflower** into florets. Make the spice mix from **2 tsp. coriander seed, 1 tsp. cardamom seeds, ½ tsp fennel, ½ tsp. black peppercorns**. Grind these together, and add **¼ tsp. cayenne pepper**, or even less, and **1 tsp salt**. Fry briskly **1 large chopped onion** in **2 tbsp. sunflower oil** until it starts to brown, add **2 chopped cloves garlic** and **a small knob of fresh ginger**, peeled and finely chopped. After 2 mins, add the spices, stir, then add all the veg. and stir again to coat them. Add **200 ml plain Greek yoghurt, 200 ml. water, and 40g ground almonds**, and simmer, covered, till the vegetables are done. The sauce should have reduced and become quite thick; if it hasn't, boil hard to reduce the sauce until it is. Taste for salt. Add **100 ml. double cream**, stir in, and serve. It should be a pale rich curry with quite a lot of sauce. If you have some **kewra water** (and you may well not!) 1 tbsp. added at the last moment is the traditional finishing touch for kormas, with a beautiful aroma. It needs plain boiled rice, a tomato and onion relish, and possibly a dhal, depending on how many are eating. Vegetable kormas don't reheat well.

Parsnip and Shallot Bruschetta.

Peel and halve lengthwise **a dozen shallots**. Peel **250g parsnip** and dice. Cook both of these together in **30g butter** until they start to brown, then add **100 ml. white wine**. Cook gently till the wine has evaporated. If the parsnips are not soft by now, add **a little water** and cover the pan and cook gently till they are. Add **1 tbsp. honey, 2 tbsp. white wine vinegar, salt** and **pepper** to taste. Serve on **toasted slices of ciabatta or other bread**, with a sprig of **parsley** on top to look pretty. If you like this mix, as I think you will, you can also increase the quantity and turn into a variation of Tarte Tatin. Put the shallot/parsnip mix in a baking tin with a solid base, roll out puff pastry to cover, and cut a circle which is about 1 cm bigger all round than the tin. Put the pastry over the mix, tucking in the sides, and bake at 200 until the pastry is brown and risen. Turn out so the vegetables are on top of the pastry.

Parsnip Cocktail.

Parsnips have sometimes been called "poor man's lobster". I can't see it myself, but this cocktail does make a good starter. Peel **500g parsnips**, and cut into shapes about 3 cm long and 1 cm across. Boil or steam them till just done. Let them cool. Arrange on a bed of **shredded greens** – you can do it in a glass, but I prefer a plate – and coat them with the sauce. The sauce at its most basic is mayonnaise mixed with ketchup. I like **chipotle mayonnaise**; make mayonnaise in the blender (Basics) and just before it thickens add 1 or 2 chipotle chilis en adobo. You can go to either of these extremes, but I do recommend adding some heat to the basic sauce. Garnish with **olives – black or green – and/or capers**. Sprinkle with chopped **parsley,** if you like. Good bread, both to eat with the cocktail and to mop up any extra sauce.

Red Cabbage

At first sight, what you have is a dark red cannonball of a vegetable. But cut it in half, and you get the most beautiful abstract of purple and white. I've thought of keeping a half on display, just for looking at. You don't expect such aesthetic pleasure from a simple, useful, dependable vegetable.

Old-fashioned ways of cooking red cabbage braise it with some of apples, onions, vinegar, wine, for a long time, and produce a rich and satisfying dish. Old-fashioned here doesn't mean out of date, it means reliable and loved by many. Newer ways cook the red cabbage lightly, or use it raw in salads. These can be disconcerting, but can also be very good. It's fortunate that we don't have to choose, but can do both.

Red cabbage as bought doesn't need much preparation. Simply strip off any outside leaves that look tired, halve or quarter, and shred with a sharp knife.

Default: Braised Red Cabbage.
Sweat **2 sliced medium onions** in **30g butter** in a large casserole for about 10 mins. Add **700g red cabbage**, shredded, and stir about. Then add **1 large cooking apple**, peeled and chopped, **2 chopped cloves garlic, 1 tsp. caraway seeds, strips of orange peel from 1 orange, 2 tbsp. brown sugar**, and **100 ml. cheap red wine. Salt, pepper**, and a grating of **nutmeg.** Cover tightly, and cook in a slow oven for 2-3 hrs, checking now and then that it hasn't dried out. Taste for seasoning. If it isn't a deep rich red, add **wine vinegar or lemon juice** until it is. The glorious colour only develops if there is acid around. It reheats well, too.
This is a very variable recipe. You can use cider instead of red wine, or 4 tbsp. wine vinegar and water to make up the 100 ml. Germans do it without onion. Practically every Northern country uses chestnuts in season:
Red Cabbage with Chestnuts.
A modification of the default recipe. Leave the orange peel and the nutmeg out of the basic recipe; add **250g peeled chestnuts** and a **couple of sage leaves** with the ingredients at the beginning.

Red Cabbage and Beetroot.

Sweat **2 sliced medium onions** in **30g butter** in a large casserole for about 10 mins. Add **500g raw beetroot**, peeled and grated, and **500g shredded red cabbage**. Stir about to mix everything. Add **1 large cooking apple**, peeled and chopped, strips of **orange peel from 1 orange (or tangerine), 1 tbsp. brown sugar, salt** and **pepper**, and **4 tbsp. red wine vinegar mixed with 6 tbsp. water**. Braise covered in a low oven for 2 hrs, then stir in **4 good tbsp. cranberry sauce** from a jar. **Or 50g fresh cranberries**, stirred in. Put back in the oven another 30 mins or so. The orange here is an essential part of the flavour. If you have some, you can add **1 tsp. ground allspice berries** at the beginning – I've found preference for with and without is about equally divided.

Red Cabbage, Roast Garlic, Chili and Ginger.

Red cabbage responds to Eastern flavours, and several of my recipes use them. For this one, you need **half a head of roasted garlic**, ideally from a previous meal. If you have to start from scratch, break the cloves from about half a head, don't peel, roll in oil, and put in a small baking dish in a moderate oven till gold, about 15 mins. Shake the pan from time to time.

Meanwhile, heat **3 tbsp. sunflower oil** in a large casserole, and add **1 large onion**, chopped, **700g red cabbage**, shredded, **a knob of ginger**, peeled and chopped, and **2 fresh chilis**, seeded and chopped. Cover and sweat for 10 mins. Then add the roasted peeled garlic cloves, **2-cm. cinnamon stick, a large piece of mace, 1 tbsp. brown sugar**, and **3 tbsp. balsamic vinegar. Salt, a lot of freshly-ground pepper – up to ½ tsp**, and **100 ml. water**. Cover and cook in a low oven for 1-1½ hrs, or even longer if more convenient. Like all these long-cooked dishes, it reheats well.

Sweet-and-Sour Red Cabbage.

Shred **400g red cabbage**. Heat **2 tbsp. sunflower oil** in a large frying pan, and add **2 cloves garlic**, chopped fine, and **a knob of ginger**, also finely chopped. Stir. When the smell rises from the pan, add the red cabbage, and stir to mix. Add **4 tbsp. cider vinegar, 4 tbsp. soy sauce, 30g sultanas, 1 dsp. light brown sugar**, and **pepper**. NO salt. Simmer, covered, about 10 mins. or till the cabbage is tender but still crunchy. Thicken the juices with **1 tsp. cornflour** mixed with a little water in a cup, and stirred in. When ready to serve, sprinkle with **1 tsp.**

dark sesame oil. Add some chopped **fresh green coriander** if you have some, and aren't using it with another dish at the same time.

Red Cabbage Braised with Mustard Seeds.

Shred **700g red cabbage**. Put in a pan with **400 ml. water, 2 large onions**, sliced, **100 ml. cider vinegar, 4 tbsp. dark brown sugar, 40g butter, 2 tsp. black mustard seeds**, lightly crushed, **a bay leaf, salt** and **pepper**. Simmer, covered, for about 20 mins, then take off the lid and turn up the heat to reduce the liquid.

Stir-Fried Red Cabbage with Capers and Pine Nuts.

Toast **a handful of pine nuts** under the grill or in a frying pan with a skimming of oil. Shred **400g red cabbage**. Chop finely **2 cloves garlic**, and fry briefly in **2 tbsp. olive oil**. Add the cabbage, and stir-fry over medium heat for 5 mins or so, until the cabbage is softening – but it should still be quite crunchy. Add **2 tbsp. red wine vinegar**, the pine nuts, **1 tbsp. capers**, and **pepper** to taste, tossing meanwhile. Serve at once.

Red Cabbage and Peas, East Indian Style.

Defrost **400g frozen peas**. Shred **500g red cabbage**. Heat **2 tbsp. oil** in a large frying pan, and add **1 tsp. cumin seeds** and **a bay leaf**. When the cumin seeds start to darken, add **2 cloves garlic**, chopped finely, and **a knob of ginger**, also chopped finely. Stir for a few moments, then add cabbage and peas. **½ tsp. salt, ¼ tsp. cayenne pepper or red chili powder (not the blend, but pure)** Cook for 5 mins or a little more on fairly high heat, stirring almost continuously. Eat at once when the cabbage has softened to your taste.

Red Cabbage Soup from North-East Italy.

In its original form, this soup is loaded with preserved pork products – bacon and sausage – and is very good. Rather to my surprise, the vegetarian version is at least as good, and highly recommended.
Sweat **1 medium chopped onion** in **2 tbsp. olive oil** for about 10 mins. Add **3 chopped cloves garlic**, stir, and add **2 sticks celery**, peeled and chopped. Sweat again for 5 mins. Add **½ tin chopped tomatoes** and **500g red cabbage**, shredded, stir, and sweat 5 mins more. Add **1 litre stock, 1 tsp. salt if stock not salted**, cover, and cook on low heat for 1½ to 2 hours. Add the **contents of a tin of borlotti or cannellini beans**, drained and rinsed (or leftovers from a

previous bean cooking, or, indeed, 100g dried beans soaked and cooked) Stir, taste, thin if needed. Meanwhile, heat **2 tbsp. extra-virgin olive oil** in a small frying pan, add **2 chopped cloves of garlic** and the **leaves of a sprig of rosemary**. Let cook 30 secs. or so, then empty the entire contents of the pan into the soup. Swirl and serve quickly, while the scent of garlic and rosemary is still strong and appetising. This is a whole-meal soup, needing no more than bread, salad, wine for a real feast.

Red Cabbage Salads.

I find that a freshly prepared salad with red cabbage is just too chewy for me – I can't eat more than a few forkfuls. Some people like it like this. If you don't, you can either blanch the red cabbage in boiling water for 1 min to soften it, or make the salad ahead, and let it soften in the dressing for some hours or even overnight. I think the second way is easier but doesn't have as much softening effect.

Red Cabbage, Parsnip and Walnut Salad.

Peel and cut up **250g small parsnips**, and boil till tender. Drain. Shred **300g red cabbage**. Mix the two, and add **50g toasted walnut halves or pieces**. Dress with **6 tbsp. oil (1/2 or even all walnut, the rest neutral)** mixed with **2 tbsp. red wine vinegar, salt** and **pepper**, and leave to stand a few hours or even overnight. Any fresh chopped **green herb** you have to finish – fennel or dill is nice, but so is parsley.

Red Cabbage, Fennel, and Red Onion Salad.

Slice **a small red onion**, and (optional) soak in cold water for 10 mins, then drain. Shred **300g red cabbage**. Trim and shred **2 small or 1 large fennel bulbs**. Mix. Make a dressing with **3 tbsp. bought mayonnaise** (home-made if you have it, but you can't tell the difference here) mixed with **4-5 tbsp. plain Greek yoghurt** and **1 good tsp. mustard**. Let it stand for several hours or overnight. This responds well to some crisp fried croutons or some toasted seeds or nuts, but it is a very good salad without.

Red Cabbage and Apple Salad.

Shred **250g red cabbage**. Peel, core, and cut up **3-4 eating apples**, and mix with the cabbage. Whizz **½ tsp. black peppercorns, ½ tsp. allspice** in a grinder, and add them to **1 clove garlic** pounded and chopped with **½ tsp salt** to a paste. Add **2 tbsp. wine vinegar, 4 tbsp.**

oil, and **sour cream** to your taste. Start with 2 tbsp. You can use plain yoghurt instead of the soured cream. Add the dressing to the salad, and let is stand and soften. The acids in the dressing will stop the apple pieces browning. You might also think of putting some Feta or goat's cheese on this salad, which makes it more of a main dish.

Red Cabbage with Sesame and Vinegar.
Toast **2 tbsp. sesame seeds** under the grill, and mix with **100 ml. vinegar, 1 tbsp. dark brown sugar**, and **½ tsp. salt**. Pour this mix over **300g shredded red cabbage**. Cover the mix with a plate, and weight it to keep the cabbage submerged as much as possible. Stir now and then for 1-2 hours, and then eat.

Pickled Red Cabbage.
The last recipe is halfway to a pickle, and this one takes the next step. Pickled red cabbage is the use that most people think of, and the only way in which many people meet this vegetable. I think this is a shame. I don't like pickled red cabbage myself, so this recipe comes from friends who do. They say it is best when simple and basic, with no spices or garlic to complicate the taste.

Trim and cut up **a red cabbage** – there should be some chunks among the slivers which make up the main part. Sprinkle with **1 tbsp. salt** and mix in, and leave overnight, covered. Next day, drain, wash, and pack the cabbage into jars. Bring some **white or malt vinegar** to the boil, let it cool, and fill the jars up with vinegar. Cover with vinegar-proof lids, and leave for 1 day at least before eating. Don't make much at once, as it loses its edge and crispness in 4-5 weeks. But it's so easy that if you like it, you won't mind making it often.

There are main-dish-like things you can do with red cabbage -- layer the cooked product with chili sin carne, mix with chopped hard-boiled eggs and put in a pastry roll – but I can't recommend them Stick to exploiting its vegetable nature.

Salsify and Scorzonera

Salsify and scorzonera are always lumped together. From a cook's point of view, this is fair enough; they are long winter roots, and are treated in much the same way. From other points of view, it doesn't make sense; they are different botanical families, and they are different shapes and colours. Salsify is like an elongated carrot, with broader shoulders and a tapering hairy root, and pale yellowish-beige in colour. Scorzonera comes in long, thin, uniform black roots, and is most often (relatively speaking) seen for sale. I grew salsify once, and the experience of kneeling on a frosty January day, with my arm up to the elbow in a frozen hole, trying to get all the root, put me off. But it was easy to grow and successful. Scorzonera I haven't grown, but books tell me that it gives a bonus in the form of edible sprouting buds at winter's end. Salsify and scorzonera both add to the variety of roots available, and taste good and different. You can use either in the following recipes, but given a choice, choose salsify.

They seem to be specially Northern European vegetables; I haven't found any mentions in Italian, Californian or Australian books. In France you can buy tins of ready prepared salsify in hypermarches, and it's worth bringing back one or two as a standby.

Default. Buttered Salsify or Scorzonera.
Scrub and peel **500g roots**, and cut into lengths of 5-7 cm. Cut lengthways, too, for salsify, so the sticks are much the same thickness. Drop into boiling salted water, and cook 15-20 mins or till done. Drain. Immediately, or later, add the sticks to **40g butter** in a frying pan, and turn the sticks over low heat until golden, with some brown bits. Lovely; slightly better with some chopped **parsley**, too.

Salsify with Garlic and Parsley.
Only a little elaborated. When you have the cooked drained sticks, add them to **3 tbsp. olive oil** to which you have added **2 finely chopped cloves garlic**. Turn until lightly coloured, and add a lot of chopped **parsley**.

Parmesan Salsify.

Peel **400g salsify**, cut into chunks, and blanch with ½ **lemon** in the **salted water** for 10 mins. Drain. Mix **70g fresh breadcrumbs** with **70g Parmesan**, grated, and roll the salsify chunks in this. Bake in an oiled roasting tin for about 30 mins at 180, until the dish is golden brown. There are too many breadcrumbs and Parmesan for a coating; they toast in the roasting dish, giving lovely crusty bits to eat with the salsify.

Salsify with Seville juice.

Cook **400g salsify** as usual. Turn in a frying pan with **a knob of butter, the juice of 2 Seville oranges**, and **1 tsp. sugar**, until glazed. Add **flaked almonds** for the last minute or so.

Roast Salsify.

Alone or as part of mixed vegetable roast. Unusually, I think it's better alone, as this allows the flavour to stand out. Peel and cut **400g salsify** as usual, and mix with **olive oil, garlic,** and **thyme**. Roast about 30 mins at 160.

Salsify Fritters.

Cook **400g salsify** as usual. When drained, squeeze the **juice of a lemon** over, and leave to marinade. Make a frying batter; take **120g plain flour** with a **pinch of salt**. Stir in **3 tbsp. olive oil, 150 ml tepid water**. Beat well, and leave to stand 1-2 hrs. Just before it's needed, beat **1 egg white stiff** and fold it in. Heat **oil for deep-frying**, dip the salsify sticks in the batter, drop in a few at a time, and cook till golden. Drain on crumpled paper. Delicious, even by fritter standards, but not for every day.

Salsify Salads.

Neither salsify or scorzonera is suitable for eating raw, so any salads involve the cooked vegetable. Make a basic salad by cooking **salsify** cut into sticks, as usual, draining, and adding vinaigrette while still hot. Add **herbs, and/or hard-boiled eggs, and/or raw sliced mushrooms**, and so on. Jane Grigson's Vegetable Book has a Salad Montfermeil, where the cooked salsify is mixed with boiled potatoes and artichoke hearts. I substitute the char-grilled artichokes available in posh supermarkets, and it is indeed good. The vegetable doesn't lend itself to creamy or mayo-type dressings, and my few attempts have reinforced this idea.

Vegetable Oyster Soup

This is really a soup based on a mild joke. Salsify is vegetable oyster, and oyster mushrooms look, very vaguely, like oysters. It's rich, mild, and subtle, and I think it's an invention of some merit.

Peel and chop finely **6 shallots**, and cook gently in **25g butter**. Peel and cut into short lengths **500g salsify**, and add to the shallots. Stir. Break up **250g oyster mushrooms**, add these, and stir around. Peel and chunk **1 medium potato**, add, stir. Add **600 ml. stock or water, salt if needed**, and bring to the boil. Simmer 20-25 mins, till all the veg. are cooked. Let it cool a little, and blend smooth. Reheat just before serving, taste for salt, thin down a little if you like, and add **4 tbsp. double cream**. **Croutons** are good with it.

Salsify and Celery Stew.

Peel and cut into short lengths **500g salsify**. Cook **1 chopped onion** gently in **2 tbsp. oil**, till soft. Add **a head of celery**, broken into stalks, (keep the leaves for later), washed, destringed, and cut into slices, and the salsify, and stir well. Cook gently for 5 mins more, then add **500g potatoes**, peeled and chunked. Stir. Add **1 pt. stock, 2 bay leaves, thyme, salt** and **pepper**, and cook gently till the potatoes are cooked. Taste for seasoning, sprinkle with chopped **parsley** and the **leaves from the celery**, and serve.

Salsify and Spinach Gratin

I say spinach, but this can be made just as well using the leaves of Swiss chard, or indeed any other green. Spinach is best, though.

Cook **500g spinach** as usual, in the water than clings to the leaves; drain and squeeze. Peel and cut up **500g salsify**, and boil in salted water 10-15 mins, till done. Put the spinach in a flat ovenproof dish, buttered, and arrange the salsify on top. Pour over **300 ml cheese sauce (40g butter, 30g flour, 300 ml milk, salt, pepper, nutmeg, 60g strong Cheddar**; see Basics) and sprinkle the top with **a few breadcrumbs** and **another 30g cheese**. If the components are all still hot, brown under the grill. If not – and this is a good one to have ready in advance – put in the oven at 200 until bubbling and the top is brown and crisp.

Salsify and Stilton Tart.

Start with **a 22 cm (9") pastry case, baked blind. (or 2 x 17 cm cases)** Sweat **1 medium chopped onion** in **30 g butter**, and add **500g salsify**, peeled and cut up. Cover, and continue to cook on a very low heat until the salsify is cooked, or nearly so. Let it cool, and arrange in the bottom of the tart case. Dot with **80g mild blue Stilton**. Beat **3 eggs** with **150 ml. double cream, salt** and **pepper**, and pour into the case. Bake at 150 for 30-40 mins, or till done. Let it cool for a few minutes before eating.

Swede

What is the most grumbled-about veg in a veg. box? What causes more people to turn up their noses than any other vegetable, and say "I don't eat *that!*" Poor maligned swede, that's what. It doesn't matter that it is richly coloured and can taste splendid; it doesn't matter that it's a traditional vegetable; it doesn't even matter that many of us consume quantities of swede in the form of Branston Pickle. (In Branston, it's hidden under its American name of rutabaga, for reasons we understand quite well) No, swedes are unpopular and downmarket because they are hardy, easy-to-grow, and cheap, and often badly cooked. These are not good reasons. Use swedes more; cook them carefully; call them rutabaga if you have to, and enjoy the taste, the sensation of virtue, and the pure value.

Swedes aren't really a root, though turnips are. Swedes are a swollen stem base, like fennel and kohl-rabi. Not that this affects their cooking and eating qualities. If it looks like a root and cooks like a root, the technical, botanical differences don't really matter. It's an organ where the plant keeps its food stores over winter, to nourish itself the next year when it makes flowers and seeds, and as such it has collected vitamins and minerals and starches that the plant will need, and you can divert.

I think the default way of cooking swede should be boiled and mashed, but this will probably remind people too much of past experiences of watery mush, underseasoned and underbuttered. Get them over the hurdle with roast swede first.

Default: Roast Swede
It can be roasted alone or with other vegetables. On its own, peel **1 swede** thickly, chunk, put in a baking dish, and rub with **olive oil** and **salt. Garlic** as always in vegetable roasts. **For 500g swede, 2 tbsp. olive oil, ½ tsp. salt, and 2 cloves garlic**. Put in the oven at 180 till done, with nicely caramelised edges. About 45 mins.

Roast Mixed Roots.
Choose from **a selection of swede, parsnip, celeriac, squash, carrot, potatoes**, and prepare them as chunks. It's very easy to make too

much, and roast veg. don't reheat well. Add **at least 1 red onion, peeled and quartered, per person**, and **at least 1 clove garlic**. I'd be inclined to use half a head of garlic – just take off detachable white skins and halve crosswise. **Red peppers**, seeded and quartered, add an exotic note but aren't compulsory. Mix the lot in a baking dish, pour over some **olive oil** and **salt,** and mix together with your hands. Some **sprigs of rosemary or thyme** can be buried in the mix, for added scent and flavour. Roast at 180 for 45-60 mins, till the potatoes are cooked and all is brown on the edges. It's just lovely. A meal in itself with a salad. A selection of chutneys is also good on the table.

Swede Mash; Bashed Neeps.

As bashed neeps it's the traditional accompaniment to haggis, and there are some good vegetarian haggises about. They do need a gravy, otherwise they're too dry.

For bashed neeps, I think the swedes are better steamed or microwaved rather than boiled, to stop them getting waterlogged. Peel and cube **2 swedes**, and either steam for about an hour till very tender, or microwave in batches till done. Microwave instructions depend so much on power of the oven, and how much food you are cooking, and how it's stacked, that I shan't even try to tell you how long. Just cook it till it's done – it's going to be reheated so this aspect needn't worry you. Mash by your preferred means; the food processor is mine. You can puree swede in a food processor, as it doesn't go glue-y as potato does. The best way to reheat is in a double boiler, over boiling water; put **30g butter** in the top of the double boiler, add the mashed swede, let it sit over the boiling water till the butter is melted, and beat vigorously. Leave it to heat through, stirring from time to time. It's not going to burn. When ready to eat, add **a slurp of cream, salt to taste**, and **quite a lot (½ tsp black peppercorns, ground) of black pepper**. Sometimes, not always, I add **¼ tsp. ground ginger**, which is not identifiable but adds to the savoury flavour. This dish, by the way, illustrates nicely the difference between cooking time and time from start to finish. If you steam one night and finish the next, your time spent is a maximum of 15 mins, including washing up. If you go from start to finish on one day, you should probably start 2 hrs ahead, but you are only occupied for a little of that time.

Mashed Swede and Potatoes.

More useful than mashed swedes alone as a general accompaniment, and using swedes and potatoes half-and-half avoids the problems of a watery puree. Use **500g each of swede and potato.** Peel and chunk them both. Start boiling the swede first, and add the potatoes after 20 mins or so. This way they will be done together. Drain and mash, not with a food processor, adding **salt, pepper, butter (at least 30g for 4 people; more tastes better)**, and **warm milk** to give you the consistency you like. **Nutmeg** is a good addition if it goes with the rest of the meal. If you like, spread the puree in a flat dish, and make little holes in the top with a wooden spoon handle. Drop a little butter in each hole, which melts as it's eaten. Alternatively, chop a bunch of spring onions, peeled, and beat these into the puree.

Mashed Swede with Carrots.

500g each of swede and carrot will be plenty for 4-6, depending what else is on the table. Peel and dice the swede, and peel and cut the carrots into thick slices -- say, 6 to a medium carrot. Boil them together till the swede is well done – 40-60 mins. Drain and mash, in food processor if you like, with **60g butter, salt**, and **½ tsp. black peppercorns, ground**. Or more to taste. Fine alone, but I also like a poached egg on top of this.

Spicy Mashed Swede and Carrot.

Prepare and boil **500g each swede and carrot** as in last recipe. While they are cooking, peel and chop **1 large onion**, and fry in **30g butter** till starting to brown. Add **2 tsp. cumin seed, 3-4 chopped cloves garlic** and **1 chopped fresh chili**, and cook 1 min more. Drain swede and carrot, and put in food processor. Add the onion mix, **salt** and **pepper**, and whizz all to a puree. Taste. Add **4 tbsp. double cream if liked**, and reheat in pan on gentle heat, oven, or double boiler.

Swede and Watercress Puree.

Peel, chunk and steam **500g swede** until tender, 30-40 mins. Blanch **80g watercress** (1 supermarket packet) for 1 min. (If you have old-fashioned bunches of watercress, trim off the bottom of the bunches) Drain the watercress, cool under cold running water, and squeeze dry. Put the tender swede pieces in the food processor with the watercress, **salt** and **pepper**, and **20g butter**, and whizz smooth. Reheat over low heat, adding **4 tbsp. double cream** while stirring.

Nutty Swede.

Another puree, with texture added by ground walnuts. Steam **500g swede** as usual. While doing this, grind **50g walnut halves** in the food processor. When the swede is cooked, add to the processor, with **2 tbsp. walnut oil, salt** and **pepper**, and **thyme leaves from 2-3 sprigs**. Whizz. Reheat gently, in double boiler, low oven, or pan.

There are 5 variants of plain mashed swede above, and this by no means exhausts the possibilities. Consider chopped rocket or other herbs; mix with a thick puree of onions and rice; add chopped celery raw, so you get a crunch as you eat And leftovers, if any, can be made into cakes and fried.

Glazed Swede.

You can see this as either a braise or a variant of the reduction method. Whichever, it's a good, easy, tasty way of cooking the swede and blending in other flavours. Peel and cut fairly small **500g swede**. Cook **1 medium chopped onion** in **30g butter** until soft. Add **2 chopped cloves garlic** and the swede, and stir. After 2-3 mins, add **stock to cover, 1 tsp. sugar, salt if the stock is not salted**, and simmer covered until the swede is tender. Take off the cover, turn up the heat, and boil off the stock, stirring at the end so that the swede pieces are covered with the glaze. **Pepper** at this stage. If the flavour is not savoury enough for you, add **1 tbsp. soy sauce** and let that reduce too.

Swede Braised in Wheat Beer.

As the last recipe, except leave out the garlic, and use **200 ml. wheat beer** instead of the stock. No sugar, no soy sauce. Leave a bit more liquid in the pot. (You'll probably have to drink the rest of the bottle of beer) You can use other beers, like stout or barley wine.

Swede with Leeks, Soy and Honey.

Peel and dice (about 2 cm) **500g swede**. Grind together **2 tsp. coriander seeds, 1 tsp. black peppercorns**. Sweat the swede in **30g butter**, covered, on low heat for about 1½ HOURS. If the heat is low enough, they will not burn. Add **2 chopped cloves garlic** and the spices, and continue to sweat. When nearly done, probably another 15 mins, add **2 leeks**, washed, trimmed, and sliced crosswise in 2 cm chunks, and cook till the swede is done. Add **2 tbsp. soy sauce** and **1**

tbsp. runny honey, stir well to mix. Taste for **salt**, and serve. It takes a long time, but little effort, and it's really delicious.

Swede with Cumin and Lemon.

Peel and dice (about 1 cm) **500g swede**. Warm **2 tsp. whole cumin seeds** in **2 tbsp. sunflower oil**, and add the swede pieces after 1 min or so. Stir, turn down the heat, cover, and let the swede sweat until it is cooked (20-30 mins). Add the **juice of a lemon and its peel, shredded fine**, and stir well. When you taste, it may need more lemon; the lemon should be quite a strong taste. **Salt, a lot of pepper**, and chopped **fresh green coriander**. One of the best for use as a vegetable side-dish.

Swede with Sesame Seeds.

Peel and dice (about 2 cm) **500g swede**.. Blanch in boiling water till nearly done. Drain, and add the dice to a frying pan with **2 tbsp. sunflower oil**. Add **a small knob of ginger**, peeled and finely chopped. Cook gently till done, and add **2 tbsp. soy sauce** and **2 tbsp. toasted sesame seeds**. Mix well, and dribble over **1 tsp. dark sesame oil** just before serving.

Swedes Anna

A straight translation from the potato version. Rich, crisp, buttery, and delicious. Sniff your swedes before doing this; if they smell at all cabbagey, do something else. Peel about **700g swede**, halve, and slice very thinly. It's worth using the slicing knife on a food processor, or if you have a mandolin, use that. Swede is so hard I can't recommend using a knife. You need **60g butter**, possibly more. Butter well a fairly deep round dish, or even a cake tin, and start to arrange the swede slices in this. After every layer 2 slices thick, dot with butter, and sprinkle with a little **salt, pepper**, and **nutmeg**. Keep on till all the slices are used (or the tin is full; if you have too much swede, save for a stock or other dish) Press down to compact as much as possible. Put any remaining butter on top, cover with foil, and bake at 180 for 1 hour or till the swede is very tender, and a knife slides in very easily. If you've used a cake tin, turn out the cake; in a glass dish, turning out isn't really needed.

Swede Chips.

They are made exactly like potato chips; if you can do one you can do the other. Peel and cut up the **swede** into medium chips, about 1 cm. thick. They are best done with two fryings; for the first, fry them in **deep, moderately hot oil** until they are cooked but not crisp, 3-4 mins. Scoop them out, drain them on scrumpled newspaper or kitchen paper, and leave till just before you want them. Heat the oil till really hot, and fry the chips again in small batches. They will brown and crisp up in 1-2 mins. Scoop out, drain, **salt**, and eat straight away. When I do this I wonder why frozen food companies don't do "Oven Rutabaga Chips"; there'd be a lot of customers who'd like them.

Swede Chowder.

Sweat **1 large onion**, finely chopped, in **30g butter**. Add **2 stalks celery**, finely chopped, and cook a few mins more. Add **700g swede**, peeled and diced, and **400g potatoes,** also peeled and diced, and stir to mix them with the onion. Add **1 litre stock**, and simmer till the vegetables are tender, probably about 20 mins. You can finish the soup at this stage, or thicken it slightly. To thicken, scoop out about half the vegetables, and puree them – blender, processor, mouli – with a little of the liquid. Return to the soup pan. Add **100g corn kernels**, probably frozen and defrosted. Add **250 ml. milk or 100 ml double cream**, reheat, taste for **salt, pepper**, and sprinkle the top of the soup with freshly grated **nutmeg. A small knob of butter in each plate of soup** is a good thing; so are **croutons**.

Swede, Apple and Leek Soup.

Sweat **250g each of apples, peeled, cored and diced, and leeks, chopped**, with **150g swede**, peeled and diced, in **50g butter**, in a covered pan. Cook very gently till the veg. are softening but not browned, stirring from time to time. The apples should be a sharp variety – can be Granny Smiths, can be Bramleys. Add **500 ml. stock** and **200 ml. cider**, and simmer for 30 mins. **Salt** if your stock is not salted. Puree the mixture, in blender, food processor, or with a mouli. Reheat when needed, adding **pepper** and grated **nutmeg** to taste, and serve. An interesting, sweetish, piquant flavour.

Swede Souffle.

Make a puree from **300g swede**, peeling, chunking, and steaming or microwaving before mashing with **salt, quite a lot of black pepper,**

30g butter, and **2 tbsp. cream**. Make a white sauce from **40g butter, 30g flour, and 150 ml. stock**. When this is thickened, mix in the swede puree, and then the **yolks of 4 eggs** one by one. Beat the **whites of the 4 eggs** (or 5 if you have a spare) till stiff. Lighten the swede/sauce mix by beating in about a quarter of the egg whites, then turn this mix back on to the remainder of the egg whites and fold in carefully. Turn into a buttered souffle dish, run a fingertip round the edge of the mixture, and bake at 200 for 30-40 mins. This has no cheese at all, and I think is better for it.

Finnish Swede Pudding.

Peel and dice **1 kg swede**, and boil in salted water till soft. Drain, keeping back **100 ml. of the cooking liquid.** Mash the swede with this liquid, adding **salt, pepper, nutmeg**, and **1 tsp. dark brown sugar or black treacle**. (The black treacle is a good idea if you have some; it's not identifiable, but adds a deep caramelly note. But it isn't worth buying a whole tin for this dish alone) Add **breadcrumbs from 100g bread, decrusted, 2 eggs**, and **4 tbsp. double cream**. Beat well until all is mixed. Tip into a flattish buttered baking dish, and dot the top with **small pieces of butter**. Bake at 180 until a skewer comes out clean and dry, 30-45 mins. It should be light brown on top. This cries out for a piquant salsa; think of red peppers, or tomato (easiest) or pineapple, with spring onions, a little chili, lime or lemon juice. Or mango or tamarind chutney.

Swede and Chestnut Liberated Stuffing.

This was inspired by a recipe for turkey stuffing, but it's much nicer on its own. Crust and cube (about 1 cm) **enough wholemeal bread to make 1½ litres**. Melt **50g butter**, pour over the bread cubes, and mix to coat the cubes. Put the bread cubes on an oven sheet and bake in a moderate oven until the cubes are brown. Put in a bowl and add **200-250g prepared chestnuts** (probably vacuum-packed), broken up into smaller pieces. Melt **30g butter** in a lidded pan, and fry in it **2 medium chopped onions**. When the onion starts to brown, add **400g swede**, peeled and diced, about 1 cm. (If you are a fan of sage-and-onion, add some chopped **sage** here.) Add **250 ml stock**, cover, and simmer gently till the swede is done. Add this mix to the bread mix, and stir well. Tip the whole into a buttered baking dish, press down lightly, and add **another 250 ml. stock** to moisten. You can now leave it for several hours. An hour or so before serving, put in the oven at

180, and bake till the top is lightly browned. It needs a liquid sauce or gravy, or a vegetable in a sauce, and the flavour is lovely.

Swede and Lentil Bake

Boil **200g red lentils** as if for a dhal, with **2 dried hot chilis, a bayleaf**, and **1 tsp. salt.** While they are cooking, grate **200g swede**, peeled, and add to the lentils after about 20 mins. After 30-40 mins, when the lentils are done, beat with a wooden spoon so they turn to a puree. Take out the chilis. Sweat **1 medium chopped onion** in **2 tbsp. sunflower oil** till soft, add **3-4 chopped celery stalks**, and cook 5 mins more. Stir these into the puree. Add chopped **fresh green coriander**, probably about 30g. Turn the whole into an oiled baking dish, sprinkle **breadcrumbs from 50g bread**, decrusted, on top, and bake at 200 for 20-30 mins, till the crumbs brown. Sprinkle the top with more **fresh green coriander**, chopped, before serving. If your eaters don't like coriander, use parsley, but it's a pity. Serve with **plain Greek-style yoghurt** and **couscous**, maybe spiced. It doesn't look glamorous, but it tastes very good. If there are leftovers, you can beat it all together, adding more breadcrumbs to make a mix that holds together, and deep-fry small balls or sausage shapes.

Swede with Chickpeas and Moroccan Spices.

Soak **200g chickpeas** overnight, then cook in UNSALTED water to cover till tender, probably about 2 hrs. You re-use the cooking water, so cooking your own chickpeas is to be recommended. If you prefer to use tinned chickpeas, use 2 tins, drain and rinse, and use some vegetable stock instead of chick pea cooking water. Peel and dice (about 1 cm) **500g swede**, and blanch for 5 mins. Drain. In a casserole or saucepan, fry briskly **2 medium chopped onions** in **2 tbsp. sunflower oil** until they start to colour, then add the swede dice and fry a little more. Add **a spice mix of 5-cm. cinnamon stick, 1 tsp. cumin seeds, 1 tsp coriander seed, 1 tsp. black peppercorns, ½ tsp. blades of mace**, all ground together. Add to the spice mix **1 tsp. ground ginger, 1 tsp. paprika, 1 tsp. salt.** Then add it all to the frying mix and stir well. Stir in the drained chick peas. Add enough liquid (from cooking the chick peas, or foreign stock) to nearly cover. Add **1 dsp tomato paste** (from a tube or tin). Simmer, covered, for 15 mins. Add **1 tbsp. honey** and stir well, and then cook uncovered until the sauce has reduced and thickened. Sprinkle with chopped **fresh green coriander**, and serve over couscous.

Curried Swede.

The last two dishes have approached the spicing of swede progressively; now for a proper curry. It is a mash, with heat, spice and sour flavours incorporated, and it's delicious with non-Indian food or even as a dip.

Peel and chunk **700g swede**, and boil with a **5-cm piece of cinnamon stick, 2 large brown cardamoms, cracked in a mortar with ¼ tsp. black peppercorns**, and **1 tsp. salt.** When the swede is done, drain, and discard these spices. (If some peppercorns or spice dust is left, it will only add to the taste.) While the swede is cooking, fry **2 medium chopped onions** in **2 tbsp. sunflower oil** till starting to colour. Add a **3-cm knob fresh ginger**, peeled and chopped finely, and **2-3 seeded chopped fresh chilis**. When the swede is done, drain, and process to a puree. Add the onion mix and beat well. Taste for **salt** and add if needed. Then add the sour element, preferably as **2 tbsp. tamarind puree, otherwise the juice of a lemon**. Beat again, taste, and adjust hot/sour balance to your taste. Serve sprinkled with chopped **fresh coriander and mint in equal proportions.**

Winter Turnips – 10 cm or more in diameter – can be cooked by any of the swede recipes, but they aren't as good. I prefer to wait for small turnips in spring, and go through the winter using swede. This seems to be a general tendency, This last winter, 2010, I haven't seen any winter turnips in supermarkets, so maybe no-one was buying.

Winter Radishes

There are two major kinds of these; pungent and not-so-pungent. The not-so-pungent is mooli, and is Indian. Black Spanish Radish, and its red cousin, China Rose, are European and strong and pungent, and grow very easily -- you have to be ingenious to use up all a crop. I've grown Black Spanish many years ago, and had difficulty in persuading people to eat it, even through the outside catering I was doing at the time. So recipes for this are well-developed. I'm told you can sometimes come across black Spanish at farmers' markets, but haven't seen any. It's easy to buy in winter in northern France and Belgium. What a difference those twenty miles, from Dover to Calais, make! This year (2010) I've tried a red version, which grew well, into longish roots with rude shapes. If you grow either, it's nice to have a reliable crop which you can use through the winter.

The not-so-pungent mooli, long, white and crisp, seems to be designed for winter salads. I haven't grown this, but you can buy seeds, and it's available in many supermarkets. Mooli is also called daikon, the Japanese name. I shall treat the two types separately; they may be biologically the same species, but in the kitchen they must be treated differently.

Black Spanish Radish: Default.
Grated, with cream. Peel and grate **the radish – 1, weighing 200-300g**, will be enough for 4 – and **salt, ½ tsp**. Mix in **double cream** to taste. To my surprise, horseradish goes well in here – different pungencies set each other off. **About 1 tbsp. grated horseradish**. No pepper, no vinegar or lemon. But try omitting the horseradish and adding tomato ketchup with the cream, to taste. It looks a lot prettier, for one thing!

Winter Radish and Cheese Salad.
Grate a **Black Spanish radish –or 2—of about 300g**. Mix with **100g mild hard cheese such as Caerphilly or Wensleydale**, also grated, and dress with **150 ml. sour cream** mixed with **1 tbsp. white wine vinegar** and **2 tsp. grated horseradish**. **Salt** to taste, probably a mean ½ tsp. If not using horseradish, sprinkle with quite of a lot of 5-pepper mix, freshly ground.

Winter Radish with Red-Cooked Cabbage.

Start cooking the cabbage: cut **a large cabbage – green, white, Savoy** – into slices about 2.5 cm thick. Stir-fry **1 large chopped onion, 2 chopped cloves garlic** in **2 tbsp. oil** in a large pan which has a lid. After 3-4 mins, sprinkle with **1 tsp. Marigold stock powder, 5 tbsp. water.** Stir, cook 2 mins, add **2 slices ginger**, peeled, and the cabbage slices. Turn to coat all the cabbage with the onion mixture. Add **5 tbsp. soy sauce, 2 tbsp. wine, 2 tsp. sugar**, and **pepper**. Now add **500g Black Spanish radish**, peeled and cut up into 5-cm pieces. Clamp on the lid and cook slowly for 45-50 mins, or until the radish is tender. Stir from time to time. Fish out the ginger slices, as they aren't for eating. Authentic peasant food eaten with rice, but you can play about with it. I like some Szechwan vegetable added at the end. You can use Chinese leaves instead of the cabbage, but in this case start cooking the radish before adding the sliced vegetable. Chinese greens like bok choy, or Western greens like spinach, can also be used. Whatever you use, the strong salty flavours of soy sauce, ginger, garlic make this very appetising.

Winter Radish and Carrot Puree.

Peel and chunk **250g each of black Spanish radish and carrots**, and peel and slice a **medium onion**. Boil in a little water, or steam them until tender, and drain, keeping the liquid. Put the cooked vegetables in a food processor, add **1 tsp. grated ginger** and **1 tsp. curry paste** (or, if you have some garlic pickle, 1 tsp. of this. I find chili pickle too strong even diluted here, but you may not) Whizz smooth, adding some of the reserved liquid to thin if needed. Taste for **salt**. This goes very well under eggs, fried, poached, or even hard-boiled. Note that this is fat-free, apart from any in pickle or paste.

Curried Black Spanish Radish Soup.

This is very quick and simple, and very good too. Peel and cut up 500g black radish, **and cook in** 500ml. stock **till tender. Cool and blend with** 1 tsp (or to taste) of Thai green curry paste, or green masala paste, or even garam masala. **Reheat, adding** 150 ml. double cream, **and garnish with chopped** parsley or chives.

Winter Radish, Potatoes, and Eggs.

Peel and parboil **2 medium potatoes, 2 black Spanish radish**, for 15 mins. Drain. Fry **2 medium onions**, peeled, halved and finely sliced, in **3 tbsp. sunflower oil**; when they start to change colour, add the sliced potatoes and radishes, and sweat for 10 mins. Meanwhile, whizz in the food processor **3 seeded green chilis, a small knob of ginger, peeled, 4-6 cloves garlic, 1 large or 2 medium tomatoes, peeled (or from a tin), the leaves from a small bunch of coriander, 1 tsp. turmeric** and **1 tsp. salt**. Add this to the vegetables with **4-5 tbsp. water**, and cook another 5 mins., stirring at beginning and end. In a separate bowl, beat **4-6 eggs** – depending on number of eaters – with **salt** and **pepper**, then scramble them into the vegetable mix. Serve with chopped **spring onion** sprinkled on top. With rice or Indian breads.

Mixed Root Vegetable Pie with Miso.

Peel and cut small **200g, trimmed weight, each of black Spanish radish, carrots, swede and parsnip**. Sweat **1 small chopped onion** in **2 tbsp. olive oil**, add the veggie cubes, and sweat 5-10 mins more. Add **300 ml. stock**, and let it all simmer covered for 20-25 mins, till everything is tender and the stock has reduced a little – but not to a glaze. Meanwhile, mix **2 tbsp miso** (any sort you have) with **1 tbsp. tomato puree**, and then mix in **200 ml. stock**. (More stock, not that with the vegetables.) Add **2 tbsp. grated horseradish, a few chopped sage leaves, and a lot of chopped parsley** (from a handful of sprigs) Mix into the vegetables, and turn the whole into a large pie dish. Cover with shortcut pastry (Basics) and bake at 180 for 30 mins, or till the pastry is cooked and browned. The miso has a transforming effect on the blandness of the vegetables, making them rich and savoury. However, a WARNING; if you don't like Marmite, you won't like this.

China Rose or Black Spanish radish can be substituted for winter turnips in any recipe, and will improve the end result.

Mooli; Default.

This really isn't a recipe, it's so simple. I learnt this way of eating mooli from a Bengali friend years ago. Peel the mooli (if needed) and slice into ½-cm discs. Heap them on a plate, and nibble as an appetiser. You can have salt and lime juice if you like, but they aren't needed. Or you can dunk the discs into some kind of dip. But try the simple way first.

Mooli, Carrot and Ginger Salad

Grate **equal quantities of mooli and carrot**, and mix. Add **a small peeled knob of grated ginger, salt**, and **½ tsp. caster sugar**. Let stand for at least 30 mins, to let the flavours blend.

Lamb's Lettuce, Fennel and Mooli Salad.

This is really a lamb's lettuce salad, but it's here because of the mooli. Peel and sliver finely about **10 cm of mooli**, and sliver finely **half a small fennel bulb**. If there are leaves on the fennel, chop them finely, and save for garnish. Mix fennel and mooli with **lamb's lettuce, several handfuls washed or half a supermarket packet**. If lamb's lettuce isn't available, use a mix of baby salad leaves – but you want a mild green, not a mix with watercress or rocket. Make a dressing; **3 dsp. extra-virgin olive oil, 1 dsp. sherry vinegar or white wine vinegar, salt** and **pepper**, and **1 dsp. double cream**. Dress the salad and sprinkle the chopped **fennel leaves** over it. If you want to prepare in advance, mix fennel and mooli, add the dressing, and only add the lamb's lettuce just before serving.

Oriental Salad.

2 lettuce hearts, 2 young carrots, slivered, 10-cm mooli, slivered, and **a celery heart,** all prepared and mixed in a salad bowl. Dressing of **2 tbsp. soy sauce, 2 tbsp. white wine vinegar, 5 tbsp. sunflower oil, 1 tsp. dark sesame oil, pepper**. It probably doesn't need salt; taste and see. Pour over the salad and toss well. You can sprinkle the top with **toasted sesame seeds**. If you have pumpkin seed oil, use that instead of the sesame oil, and add toasted pumpkin seeds. If you have some smoked or marinated – or even plain – tofu, cube and put on top, when it becomes a full-meal salad.

Mooli Slaw.

Very fusion. Cut finely ¼ **white cabbage**, and add **2-3 grated carrots** and **a medium mooli, grated**. Dress with **mayonnaise** with **mushroom ketchup** added to taste, and let it sit about half an hour.

Mooli Braised with Black Beans.

The black beans here are Chinese salted dried black beans, available cheaply in large packets from Chinese stores. Take **1 tbsp. of the dried black beans**, pour boiling water over them, and leave to soak for 10 mins. Drain them, and use a pestle and mortar to pound to a rough paste (Or other means; you can use the flat of a knife blade to crush and smear on a chopping board) Chop finely together **4 trimmed spring onions, a knob of ginger, peeled, 3 peeled cloves of garlic,** and **1 green chili**, deseeded. Mix **200 ml water, 2 tbsp. soy sauce, 1 tbsp. white wine vinegar, 2 tsp. sugar, and ½ a star anise** (These come dried in flat flower shapes with 7-8 "petals"; you need 3 or 4 petals) Peel about **500g mooli**, quarter lengthwise, then slice each quarter thinly. Heat **2 tbsp. sunflower oil** in a frying pan with a lid, and add the garlic/ginger mix. Stir quickly, until the scent is released. Add the black beans and radish slices, and stir these all together for a minute or so, till well mixed. Add the stock mixture, cover, and cook slowly for 20 mins, or till the mooli is soft and tender. Boil the sauce down if necessary; the dish should not be too wet. Strong-tasting, satisfying, and therefore good on diets.

Mooli can also be used in vegetable stir-fries, as a puree, in soups . . . It can be used in any of the recipes for black Spanish radish, but the reverse isn't true. Mooli has the virtue that it's good whether raw, lightly cooked, or thoroughly cooked, so it's very flexible.

Year-Round

Potatoes
Onions
Mushrooms
Sprouted Seeds
Oddities

Potatoes

It is impossible to present a collection of recipes for a vegetable like the potato which covers even a majority of the many ways it has been used worldwide. It has been not just a staple, but the predominant part of the diet, in Peru and Ireland, and nearly as important in many other cool and/or mountainous countries. Its yields are heavy. It stores well. It can probably claim to be one of the foodstuffs with a major influence on history, along with staple grains. And because its taste is bland, it's capable of great flexibility in use. It can be – has been – eaten three times a day. And there is hardly another foodstuff with which it doesn't mix.

Potatoes can be used as main dish, side dish, salad, in soups, in breads, even in desserts. They are a mainstay of fast-food outlets and snacks. I have four books devoted to potatoes, and there is surprisingly little overlap. So what I have collected here are potato dishes that have been enjoyed by my family and friends, without aiming for completeness. I have given new potatoes their own chapter, in Spring, as there are ways to treat new potatoes that aren't applicable to the standard maincrops, or imports, available through the entire year

Potatoes come in several hundreds of varieties, and those available are constantly changing. The big division is between "floury" potatoes, for mash, frying, roasting, and "waxy" potatoes for salads. Some floury potatoes are less so than others; these are often called "all-purpose". All can be boiled. Most of my recipes use floury potatoes, because this has been the standard British product until very recently. I haven't even tried to name varieties, because those available change, and sometimes potatoes bearing a well-known name – like King Edwards – aren't what they were.

I always buy organic potatoes when possible, and whatever I grow are certainly organic. I think the taste is better. For a staple, eaten often, the absence of pesticide residues is more important than for foods eaten less often. Organic potatoes may well have more nutrients than others. And the price difference is pretty small. The thing to watch out for on organic potatoes is country of origin; I've found bags of English and Egyptian potatoes at the same price, and in the same bin.

Freshness isn't often an issue with potatoes, but sometimes in late summer and autumn you can find a locally-grown variety which has just come in, and this is worth a try whether organic or not.

POTATO DISHES, SIDES AND MAINS

Boiled/Steamed Potatoes and Variations

This is the simplest and probably most frequent way of dealing with potatoes, whether they are old, new, floury or waxy, and even here there is scope for variation. To peel or not to peel? Boil or steam? What to serve on them? This is my way with old potatoes. First I put water to boil – enough to cover the potatoes. I salt the water. (I have a book which says that salting is wasteful, because it doesn't pass the taste to the potatoes, and also people need to eat less salt so should leave it out. These can't both be right) I usually peel, especially as winter turns to spring and stored potatoes often have patches which need cutting out. If you have faith in your spuds and like the skin, just scrub well. Cut the potatoes into chunks of about the same size. My potatoes usually end up about 4-5 cm in all directions. Drop them into the warming water as they are prepared. When the water boils, turn down the heat and cover, so the boil is as gentle as possible. I reckon 15-20 mins boiling, and then prod with a thin knife blade. If this sticks so the potato piece can be lifted from the water, they are not cooked; if it slides off, it's done. If there is a mess of partly disintegrated potato in the pan, they are probably overcooked. Some cantankerous potatoes manage to stay hard in the middle and break apart on the outside; steam them next time. Drain well, in sieve or colander, and put in a HEATED dish. You can serve them as they are; sprinkle with chopped herbs; put pats of herb butter over the top. I generally have butter on the table if there isn't a gravy with the main dish, so people can add as little or as much as they like.

Steaming is much the same; it takes longer, more like 25-30 mins, but the potatoes are much less likely to break up.

I have to admit that potatoes cooked in their skins, then peeled, taste noticeably nicer. But peeling hot potatoes is a hassle; you burn your fingers and it takes time you may well not have when getting a family

495

meal to the table. If going this route, choose potatoes close to the same size, not monsters, and boil them uncut.

NEVER peel potatoes ahead and leave them to soak. It leaches out vitamins and taste.

If you want to hurry the boiling of potatoes, you can cut them into smaller cubes. At about 1 cm per side, they cook in 5-7 mins. They do lose more of their flavour this way, but it's worth knowing for an emergency, or when camping.

I haven't given quantities of potatoes in a lot of the simpler recipes. You know how many your family are likely to eat. And leftovers are not a problem. If possible, it's always worth cooking more potatoes than you expect to eat. Cold cooked potatoes have so many possibilities that they are a desirable ingredient, not a leftover. There is the whole subject of salads, see below. And various ways of frying.

Fried-Up Potatoes/Home Fries/Saute Potatoes.
These are all much the same. Slice the **cooked potatoes** into rounds, and fry in **butter, or olive oil, or vegetable oil.** Give them room to move about. Turn when the underside is browned. **Salt** when done. Marvellous with eggs, fried or poached, sausages, vegetarian or otherwise, or with fried mushrooms :and/or fried tomatoes.

Lyonnaise Potatoes.
Cook the **potatoes** as for fried potatoes. IN ANOTHER PAN, fry **a roughly equal volume of sliced onions** long and gently until golden/browned here and there. Mix the two together just before serving.

Sookhe Aloo (Spicy Indian Fried Potatoes)
Cube the **cooked potatoes , about 500g.** Heat **4 tbsp. sunflower oil**, and add a **pinch of hing (asafoetida)**, then, almost immediately, **1 tsp. each of fennel seeds, cumin seeds and black mustard seeds.** (You can mix these together ahead if you like) When the mustard seeds start to pop, add **2 dried whole chilis**, and stir. Almost immediately, add the cubed potatoes and ½ **tsp. ground turmeric.** Fry at a moderate pace until the potato cubes are partly browned. Add ½ **tsp salt**, squeeze over the **juice of ½ lemon**, and serve quickly. It's great with

any Indian meal, and also many non-Indian meals. I like it wrapped in a tortilla with yoghurt or sour cream and some shredded lettuce or other green.

Favourite Potatoes (Stovies)

Stovies is a Scottish name which can cover many dishes, from this simple potato version to one made up with potatoes, onions, vegetables and leftover meat. This basic version is truly delicious. It's best cooked in a lidded pot which can go on the stovetop and then direct to table.

Peel and slice thickly **enough old potatoes for your eaters**. I reckon about 250g per head, but teenagers eat more and small children eat less. Put the slices in the pan with **20-50g butter, enough water to cover the pan base**, and a good sprinkle of **salt**. Cover, and cook gently for 20-30 mins till the potatoes are done. If you hear sizzling before this happens, add a couple of tbsp. more water. For the best taste, they should catch just a little at the bottom. Serve in the cooking dish. Maybe a sprinkle of chopped **parsley** or other soft herb, but it's not needed.

Italian Potatoes in Milk.

This is also a favourite US way of cooking potatoes; they call it scalloped. Peel the **potatoes** and cut them into thick slices. Bring to the boil **enough milk to cover** them, add the potatoes, and simmer gently until they are done. About 20 mins. You need to hover a bit at the start to make sure the milk doesn't boil over, and stir from time to time to stop them sticking. Pour off most of the milk, which can be used for something else, leaving a few tbsp in the pan with the potatoes. There may not be much, depending on the type of potato. **Salt, pepper, nutmeg**, and some chopped **basil (nicest) or parsley**. Stir again and put in a heated serving dish. Put the pan in cold water to soak straightaway, which really helps with its washing-up.

Potato Gnocchi

Boil or steam **1 kg potatoes**, and puree them by your chosen method. Add **250g plain flour, 2 eggs, 25g butter,** and **generous salt and pepper**. Mix to a smooth paste. Using your hands, make portions of the dough into long rolls, about finger thickness. Cut these rolls into 2-cm pieces. In each of these, make a lengthwise dent, so they are curved and about the same thickness throughout. When they are all made, drop into a pan of boiling water, and simmer for 3 mins or so, till they float. Take them out of the pan, and serve them either with **butter and grated Parmesan, or with a sauce** – pesto, say, or Gorgonzola sauce.

I must admit that this is here mainly for completeness. You can buy perfectly respectable fresh potato gnocchi in every supermarket, and they aren't expensive. I used to make my own sometimes before the supermarket variety appeared, and the recipe may be useful if you live in the country, have a glut of potatoes, and can't get out for some reason. Otherwise, I'd advise buying them if available.

Pommes de terre Dauphine.

There's nothing else like this, and the brown puffy little balls are DELICIOUS. It's a mixture of cooked potato and chou paste, the sort eclairs are made from, which is then deep-fried and puffs up.

First boil or steam **600g potatoes**, and mash them well, adding **only salt and pepper**. Then make the **chou paste**. Put **150 ml water** in a pan with **50g butter**, and bring slowly to the boil, making sure the butter melts before the water boils. Turn off the heat. Tip in, all at once, **70g plain flour**, and beat well with a wooden spoon to a sticky, uniform paste. You need **2 eggs**. Break in the first egg, and mix then beat until the mixture becomes smooth, thick, and glossy. Repeat with the second egg. Then start working in the potato puree, beating hard all the time. When it all mixed in, add a little more **salt**, grated **nutmeg**, and **about 30g grated cheese**. Let it get cold.

To fry, heat a pan of **oil for deep-frying**, and drop in large teaspoonfuls of the mix, cooking about 6 at a time. They will swell. Turn over once, and when golden all over, lift out and drain on kitchen paper. Keep them hot while the rest are cooked, and serve as soon as possible in a hot dish.

This makes a lot –enough for 6-8 people – but it's hard to cut down the amounts of the chou paste and still have the mixture work. It also involves last-minute cooking, so anything else you are eating shouldn't need last-minute attention. I repeat; these are worth all the faff.

Potatoes Brayaude or a l'Echirlete.

These two French methods of producing potatoes with garlic are barely distinct; one cooks garlic with the potatoes, the other adds garlic only in the final heating in oil. As a lover of garlic, I tend to do both. Boil the **potatoes** in the usual way, adding **3-6 unpeeled cloves of garlic** to the water. Drain, keeping the garlic. Warm **2-3 chopped cloves of garlic** in **2 tbsp. olive oil** in a frying pan, then add the potatoes and heat gently, tossing the potatoes. They should not be fried, just allowed to absorb the garlic-flavoured oil. The people who get the boiled cloves can squeeze out the soft garlic within to eat with their potatoes. Chopped **parsley** at the last moment is almost essential with this.

Hash Brown Potatoes.

These are not at all like the horrid triangles you can buy frozen, or get given in Little Chefs and the like. Boil **600g baking potatoes**, whole and unpeeled, and let cool. They can wait overnight, if need be. Peel the potatoes, and grate them coarsely into a bowl. Add **150g plain flour, 1 tsp salt**, and mix together with your fingers or a large fork. You aren't trying to make a coherent mass. Heat **50g butter** with **2 tbsp. oil** in a large heavy frying pan, add all the mix, and cook at a moderate pace, turning portions often, until the spuds are crisp and brown. This takes 20-25 mins; as you can see, proper hash browns are not a spur-of-the-moment option. But they are very good indeed, and make a meal just with some coleslaw.

Mashed Potatoes

I've discussed mashed potatoes at some length in the Techniques chapter, so here I will stick to simple instructions. Boil or steam the **potatoes**, peeled or unpeeled to taste. If unpeeled, they need peeling before being mashed, and potatoes must be hot when mashed. Puree the hot, dry potatoes by your favourite method. Mine is by means of a Mouli-Legumes, but there are also potato ricers, potato mashers, which squash the pieces, or even the old-fashioned fork, which is useful when camping. The puree ends up in a warm serving dish. Now add **butter, 20-50g for 4 people, salt** and **pepper,** and beat with a fork. You should warm the milk in the potato pan, but I must admit I seldom do this, and simply add enough milk, beating in with the fork, until the mash reaches the consistency I like. 200 ml. is about right for 4, but it depends on potato variety. Now eat.

You can up the amount of butter, which is a French restaurant speciality – up to 250g butter for 500g potatoes. I have remarked before that restaurants are not trying to serve healthy, day-by-day food, and this must be a rare treat. The French also use, in different contexts, some of the potato water instead of milk, and make their mash much thinner. In this case it can be more like a solid soup than English-style mash.

Modern mash is often made with additions, such as pureed garlic, or olives, or uses extra-virgin olive oil instead of butter. I have enjoyed these when eating out, but at home I will stick to the traditional method.

Mash prepared ahead can be reheated in a double boiler, with a little extra milk beaten in. This does work, but it isn't as good as freshly-made mash.

Duchesse Potatoes.

The particular virtue of these potatoes is that they are meant to be prepared in advance, and cooked briefly at the last moment. There are times when this is just what you want.

Boil and puree the **potatoes** as for mash. In this case, however, you don't add milk, but **eggs – 2 eggs for 700g potatoes**. This makes a much stiffer puree. **Season** it well. Ideally, you would then pipe the puree into whorls, about 5 cm across, but tidy dollops of about the right size are OK. Pipe/dollop these on to a lightly oiled baking sheet, and leave till needed. Then reheat in a hot oven for 10 mins or so, till they are starting to brown on the outside. This is more impressive than it deserves.

Sometimes, there will be leftover mashed potato, or mash made deliberately to be used for something else. Croquettes and keftedes are worth trying, and you can always fry discs of mashed potato till browned on each side to go with fried egg, mushrooms, and tomato.

Potato Croquettes.

The **mash** should be fairly stiff. Chill it, to make it easier to handle. Have 2 plates, one with **a beaten egg**, and the other with **breadcrumbs**. Scoop up a couple of tbsp-worth of the mash, and use your hands to roll into a cork shape. Roll first in the beaten egg and then in the crumbs. Keep the croquettes on another plate till they are all done, then heat a pan with **oil for deep-frying**, and cook the croquettes, a few at a time, till the outside is brown and crisp. A lot depends here on the crumbs; not fresh, but quite dry and fine. Or use bought crumbs; Japanese panko at the top end or cheap orange ones at the bottom. I am happy with either; it's the crisp outside and soft inside that makes croquettes good for me. If you like – or have a bit or leftover something – you can put a small cube in the middle of the croquettes, as a surprise. A cube of cheese. A small button mushroom.

Whatever it is, it will warm through but not cook, so don't use anything that needs cooking.

Potato Kephtedes.

Again, you need a **stiff mash** for these. Add to the mash – enough for 4 people – chopped **spring onion**, chopped **parsley**, and **2 medium tomatoes**, peeled and chopped. Add **50 g flour**, and mix together well. Make small flattish rounds, about 8, and bake till browned on an oiled oven tray, in a medium oven. They are not quite substantial enough for a meal by themselves, but they go well with many things. You can also add a little chopped roast red pepper, your own make (leftover?) or from a jar, and this also improves them.

Baked Potatoes.

A busy cook's dream – scrub if needed, put them in an oven at any temperature, wait till they are done, eat. You need to have confidence in your potatoes, as it's really offputting to cut into a baked potato and find a black, rotten, stinking area. This is why potatoes sold for baking are more expensive. They are usually quite large, but provided all the potatoes you cook are about the same size, size doesn't matter. If you are using the oven simply for baked potatoes (and for 4-6 people you may well be), then a temperature of 200 is about right. A 200g spud takes about an hour, but longer won't hurt, within reason. They will cook at 150, but take much longer. To test for doneness, hold the largest of the spuds in an oven cloth, and squeeze gently. The whole inside should feel soft and giving.

I like potato skins, so I always do them in the oven, which gives a crisp skin. If none of your eaters likes the skins, then you may as well microwave the potatoes, which is a lot faster and more economical on energy. Microwaved skins don't crisp up.

I have tried the theory of putting a skewer through a baking potato to speed up the process of oven baking. It ought to work, but in my experience it makes little difference.

Eat with salt and pepper, and butter. Americans prefer soured cream with their baked potatoes.

My favourite accompaniment for baked potatoes was originally derived from Lesley Blanch, "Round the World in 80 Dishes", where it is said to come from Peru. My adapted version is now my standard, and turns baked potatoes into a meal.

Hard boil **2 eggs**, cool in cold water, shell, and take out the yolks. Mash the yolks with **250g cottage cheese, 1 chopped shallot or 4-6 spring onions, juice of 1-2 lemons, salt** and **pepper**. If too thick, thin down with milk or cream. You could chop the whites and mix them in, but in my house they are a treat for the dog. It would be more Peruvian if there was chopped chili in it, instead of pepper, but I prefer the standard. Marvellous on Bonfire Night.

Stuffed Baked Potatoes.
Most stuffings for baked potatoes can be served simply in a bowl, as a dressing, which is less effort. But sometimes you want something a little posher, which can also be ready within 20 mins. of getting in from a winter walk or cinema. In all cases, finish the stuffed potatoes in a hot oven for 10 mins if freshly made, or 20 mins if chilled.

Tex-Mex Baked Potatoes.
Bake **6 large potatoes (250-300g each)**. When done, halve the potatoes, and scoop out the pulp, leaving a shell 1-2 cm thick. Mash this potato by your preferred method. Beat in **100g cottage cheese, 100g Double Gloucester** (these make a substitute for Monterey Jack cheese), **3-4 finely chopped seeded fresh chilis, 5-6 tbsp. sour cream**, and **2 eggs. Salt** and **pepper** to taste. Beat the mixture well, then put it back in the shells, mounding it up at the top. Sprinkle with a bit **more grated cheese.** If you've made them ahead, cover lightly, and keep in the fridge if they are to wait more than a couple of hours. Finish as above, in a hot oven.

Broccoli-Stuffed Potatoes
Bake **6 large potatoes**. When done, halve them, and scoop out the pulp, leaving a shell 1-2 cm thick. Mash this potato by your preferred method. While the potato is cooking, cook **400g broccoli**, drain, and chop coarsely. Add to the potato **30g butter, about 80 ml milk, 100g grated Cheddar, salt** and **pepper**, and beat well. Add the broccoli and mix in. Stuff the shells, mounding the filling, and sprinkle with **more grated cheese**. Keep or use immediately, finishing in a hot oven as above.

With these 2 as models, you can make a whole host of different fillings. Kale or cabbage as for broccoli (think about adding some sauteed onion to this mix). Curried cauliflower. Ratatouille or other summery vegetable stews.

Potato Skins.

These have been a popular bar snack/starter for some time, but are still not often seen at home. Start by baking **potatoes** – and this is one time when it's a good thing to use the microwave. When done, halve, and scoop out most of the potato. It can be used for mash or other things using cooked potato, like potato bread (below). Cut the remaining skins, with a thin layer of potato left on, into strips about 3 cm wide. Brush or dribble with **oil, salt** and **pepper**, and bake in a hot oven till crisp, about 10-15 mins. Fill the hollow with **something savoury**; Mexican-style fillings like guacamole or chili beans are popular, but you can use almost anything which isn't too lumpy and is intensely savoury. Many dips are good here. If using an Indian filling – like small pieces of curried cauliflower – sprinkle the skins sparingly with cumin seeds before baking. Add a small dollop of yoghurt to the top. Curried chick peas would be good, too.

Roast Potatoes.

One of the joys of a traditional Sunday lunch. Peel and cut up the **potatoes**, and boil for 10 mins – no more – till partly cooked. Drain well, then put the potatoes back in the pan, put on the lid, and shake the whole assembly well. This roughens the outside and helps it to become crisp. Heat a **good splash of oil** in a roasting tin in the oven, then tip in the potatoes and stir round. Roast in a 180 oven for 30-40 mins, turning from time to time. No seasoning till the potatoes are served.

Flat Roast Potatoes.

No previous boiling needed. Peel the **potatoes**, and cut into thickish slices, about 1 cm. Put in a roasting tin in which they fit in as close to one layer as possible, but without spaces. Drizzle over **2 tbsp. oil for about 500g spuds**. Mix with your hands. Bake at 180-200 for 45 mins or so, turning once, until they are done and brown and crisp. **Salt** before serving. It doesn't need garlic cloves tucked in with the potatoes, but they are always good.

This is the simple version of a great many dishes of roast cooked vegetables, to be found under the appropriate veg.

Pommes Anna

For 4 people, allow **700g of potatoes, 80g butter**. You also need a dish with straight sides; I use a glass souffle dish, which has the advantage of being able to see the sides of the finished dish. Butter the dish well with about a quarter of the butter. Peel the potatoes and cut them in very thin slices – the thickness of a 5p piece or less, and as near uniform as you can manage. If you have a mandolin, this is ideal. You can use the slicing disc on a food processor, but to my taste this makes the slices too thin. Arrange the slices in thin layers in the dish, keeping them flat, and dotting the layers with bits of butter, **salt**, and **pepper**. Press down. Now cover the dish with foil, and bake at 180-200 until all is golden and there is no resistance to a thin knife blade. 45-60 mins, depending on the oven and the potatoes.

Fried Potatoes, many ways.

These really have far too many calories for regular use, but everyone loves them. I think the aim should be to develop discrimination, so that if you or your family are going to eat chips or other fried potatoes, you only eat REALLY good ones. As far as I'm concerned, this cuts out most chip shop chips, and those from most fast-food outlets. They are done really well in Holland and Belgium, where they are thin and crisp and golden.

Chips, or French Fries.

You need a pan for deep-frying, which can be thin and should be large. I don't think a frying basket is needed. You need **at least 5-cm depth of oil**, but it shouldn't come more than half-way up the pan, and a bit less is better I use sunflower, or groundnut, or soya oil for deep-frying; it can take a higher temperature than olive oil, and properly deep-fried food does not taste of oil. Peel **potatoes**, and cut into lengthwise slices and then into sticks. The larger your chips the less oil they absorb, but the harder it is to cook them through properly. Make sure they are dry. Heat the oil until a small piece of bread dropped in bubbles and browns in about 20 sec. Add a handful of chips – don't add too many, or the oil will bubble up and try to overflow. Move pan off heat if this overflow threatens. Keep the pan on high heat, and the chips will lose water from the outside, and the bubbles will subside. Keep moving them round with a metal skimmer, as they gradually brown. When browned to your liking, scoop them out on to newspaper. Add the next lot of chips, and while these are starting to cook, shake the chips on the newspaper round to lose as much oil as possible. Transfer them to a dish lined with kitchen paper to absorb more, and **salt** lightly. Keep these warm till you've done enough.

Potato Galette

This needs a heavy frying pan with a lid. It can be done in an ordinary frying pan covered with an enamel plate, but why make things harder for yourself? Peel **700g potatoes** and slice them thinly and evenly; wash and dry them. Melt **20g butter, 1 tbsp. sunflower oil** in the pan, add the spuds and spread them out evenly, **salt** and **pepper**. Cover the pan. Cook on a low heat for 15-20 mins; then turn them over and brown the other side. As elsewhere, I tend to turn over portions at a time rather than attempting to turn the whole thing. Press the cake together when turned. When it's done, it's easier to serve it in the pan, or divided onto plates in the kitchen.

If olive oil is used, this is the method for starting a true Spanish tortilla. See below.

Rosti

A Swiss dish, for mountaineers in winter. For the rest of us, an occasional treat. Boil **4 medium potatoes**, unpeeled, for about 10 mins. Drain. Peel when cool enough to handle, and let cool thoroughly for at least an hour. Grate them using the large holes of a box grater. Not the food processor here, alas; it spoils the texture. Sprinkle the shreds with **½ tsp. salt** and mix in gently. Heat **30g butter, 1 tbsp. sunflower oil** in a heavy frying pan, tip in the spuds, and spread them out. Fry briskly, uncovered, for about 10 mins (or less if they are browning too fast.) When the bottom is brown, turn over, adding **a little more butter** to the pan, and fry the second side until this is brown too. The edges will be crisp. Serve at once on a hot dish.

You can add some onion; fry a little chopped onion n butter till soft, and make a layer between two halves of the shredded potatoes. I prefer it without.

Gratin Dauphinois

Another dish for Alpine mountaineers, which is so delicious it has become popular – and bastardised – as a side dish in restaurants. The simplest and traditional way, from a French book on the cooking of Dauphine and the Jura:

Peel **1 kg potatoes with yellow flesh (i.e. waxy)**, wash them and dry in a teatowel. Cut into rounds as thinly as possible – quicker in a food processor. Rub the inside of a gratin dish with **a clove of garlic**. Then **butter** thickly the base and sides of this dish, using about **half of 70g butter**. Arrange the potato slices in layers, **salt**ing and **peppering** each layer. Pour over **500 ml single cream**, to cover the potatoes. Add more cream if needed, or make up the volume with milk if necessary. **Salt** and **pepper** the top, and dot with the remaining butter. Put in a low oven for a long cooking of 1½ hrs. At the end, increase the heat for 10 mins to brown the top. The point of a knife should go through the gratin without any resistance.

Note that this doesn't have any cheese AT ALL. And it's far too rich to be a side dish; make it the centre of a meal, with a green vegetable or a salad, and some fruit to finish.

Gratin Savoyard

A lighter version, from the same area. Prepare **1 kg potatoes** as above. Butter the dish with **35g butter**. Grate **150g Swiss cheese**; it should be Beaufort, but Gruyere or Emmenthal are close enough. Layer the potatoes into the dish, sprinkling each layer with **salt, pepper, grated nutmeg**, and a little of the cheese. Finish with a top layer of cheese. Pour over ¾ **litre stock** (ideally unsalted. If using Marigold, be cautious with salt between the layers, or miss out entirely) Dot with small nuts from **another 35g butter**. Bake for 1 hr. in a low oven. Test for doneness with the point of a knife.

This can be played with. Layers of onion, sliced thin, raw. Layers of cooked – but not caramelised – onion. Wild mushrooms. Each of these has a different local name.

Gratin a la Vesulienne.

This variation is more like the English versions you will find, and is really good when done as below. Use **1.5 kg potatoes, 1 litre milk, salt, pepper, nutmeg, 180g grated Swiss cheese (or English), 80g butter** and **1 clove garlic**. All the instructions are the same as for the other gratins. My book says this is for 6; unless it's the main part of the meal, this will feed more like 8-10. If cutting down, the amount of milk must be adjusted to cover the potatoes.

Tortilla Espanola, the true Spanish omelette.

All you need for this are potatoes, onions, eggs, and a quantity of olive oil. Peel **2 large potatoes – about 400g** – and cut into small dice. Roughly chop **a large onion**. Heat **10-12 tbsp. olive oil** in a medium frying pan, and add potatoes, onions, and **1 tsp. salt**. Mix, cover, and cook gently for 20 mins, till the potatoes are done. When the potatoes are cooked, drain off the oil, and keep it. Add the potato mix to **4 well-beaten eggs**. Wipe out the pan, add back about 2 tbsp. of the drained oil, and pour in the egg mix. Cook on medium heat until the bottom has set. Now turn over – authentically, by putting a plate over the pan, holding it with one hand while overturning the pan and plate with the other, allowing the tortilla to fall on to the plate. Add a little more oil to the pan, and slide the tortilla back in, scraping off any uncooked egg on the plate and adding it to the base of the pan. I think this is a highly dangerous procedure for someone who has only read about it, and would never do it. I would turn over portions of the tortilla, and press to meld them together. You can also finish the cooking of the top by putting the pan under a preheated grill. When done, and still a little damp inside, slide it out to a serving plate. It should NOT be eaten hot. Lukewarm or room temperature, in chunks as a tapa, in a roll, at a picnic, or with salad.

"English" Spanish Omelette.

Not to be despised. Use **cooked potatoes**, and fry them in **oil** with chopped **onion**. When they are starting to brown, add chopped **garlic**, and some **cooked vegetables – peas and sweetcorn, or green peppers, or green beans and chopped raw chili**. Not too many; while this is for using up leftovers, don't use all the little containers in the fridge. Add **6 beaten eggs** with **salt**, and cook slowly till the bottom is set. Turn, or finish the top under the grill.

Potato Souffle

Bake **2 large potatoes, about 250-300g each**. Peel and mash while still hot. Beat with **100 ml. sour cream, 80g strong Cheddar, salt** and **pepper**, and then beat in **4 egg yolks**. Stir in **a handful of chives**, chopped, **or 4 spring onions**, trimmed and chopped. Beat the **4 egg whites** with **a pinch of salt** till stiff. Lighten the potato mixture by beating in a quarter of the stiff whites, then fold in the rest. Turn into a buttered souffle dish, and bake at 180 for 40-45 mins. Serve AT ONCE. It still tastes as good when collapsed, but the visual impact is lost.

Pan Haggerty

A Northumberland peasant dish. Slice thinly **500g potatoes, 250g onions**. Grate **100g Wensleydale or Cheddar**. In a heavy frying pan heat **2 tbsp. oil (or 20g butter, 1 tbsp oil)**, and layer in potatoes, onions, cheese, starting and finishing with potato, and **season**ing the layers as you go. Cover, and cook gently until the potatoes are done.

The bottom should be brown; brown the top under the grill. Traditionally, beef dripping was used, not oil.

Truffade.

This is the equivalent of pan haggerty, from the Auvergne, with slight but telling differences. No onion. Cook **500g sliced potatoes** gently, in **oil** (or lard, if traditional), in a covered frying pan, with **salt** and **pepper**. They should not colour. When they are done, add **250g little cubes of Cantal cheese, or Cheddar**. Mix well with a wooden spoon. The potatoes will break up and crush, and the melting cheese sticks them together. Let the bottom brown slightly, then turn out to serve.

This is often confused with Aligot, also from the Auvergne, and also using potatoes and cheese. The cheese used makes this impossible to reproduce in the UK. It's called Tomme de Cantal, and is the very young, unpressed, unmatured version of Cantal. It doesn't keep, and it isn't a cheese you would want to eat alone. The dish starts with boiled potatoes, mashed to a puree, mixed with butter, cream, and about half the weight of tomme, and then beaten for a solid 15 mins with a wooden spoon. The result is a stringy puree. Solid, indigestible, filling, and just the thing for winter herding in the mountains. I have eaten it, and frankly I prefer the Truffade.

Potatoe Pudding

An 18th-century English recipe, tweaked. Cook and mash alone **1.5 kg potatoes**. Add **2 large carrots**, grated, **juice of 2 oranges, 50g butter, 2 eggs, 150g grated cheese, preferably Wensleydale, salt** and **pepper** to taste. Bake at 180, in a serving dish, for about 20 mins, or till browned on top.

Potato Curry, wet

Peel **4 medium potatoes** and cut into eighths. Heat **2 tbsp oil** in a pot; add a **pinch ground asafoetida (hing in Indian shops)**, then **1 tsp. cumin seeds**, then **1 dried Indian hot red pepper**, whole. Now add spuds and ½ **tsp. turmeric**, and fry for 2 mins, stirring now and then. Add **1 tin chopped tomatoes, ½ tsp salt**, and cook till done – may be as much as 1½ hours. It takes longer to cook potatoes in this dense and flavourful liquid. If they are done before you need them, it doesn't hurt to cool and reheat.

Potato Curry, dry
Peel **700g potatoes** and cut into small cubes. Chop **300g tomatoes, either fresh or the drained contents of a tin**. Heat **4 tbsp. oil**, add **2 chopped garlic cloves** and a **small knob of ginger**, peeled and chopped. Add **½ tsp. turmeric, 1 tsp ground coriander, 1 tsp. salt**, and **¼ tsp cayenne**. Cook 1 min, then add the potatoes and fry, stirring, mixing in the spices. Add the tomatoes, stir, cover, and cook over low heat till done. By this time, the curry should be nearly dry. Add **½ tsp nigella seeds**, or black cumin if you have that and not nigella, and **12 spring onions**, trimmed and chopped. Stir a couple of mins, add chopped **fresh coriander to taste**, stir again, and serve.

Potato Goulash
If you want this to taste Hungarian, you must use Hungarian paprika. It's good with Spanish, but not as good. Sweat **1 onion**, thinly sliced, in **50g butter**. Off the heat, add **2 tsp Hungarian paprika – sweet or hot**, depending on the effect you want and the one you have. Add **1 kg potatoes**, peeled and chunked, **1 tsp caraway seeds, 150 ml stock, 1 tsp salt**, and **2 bay leaves**. Simmer till the potatoes are cooked. Add **1 tbsp. cider vinegar**, or to taste; fish out the bay leaves, and stir in **4 tbsp. sour cream**. Don't boil after this. Add quite a lot of chopped **parsley**, and eat. This goes well with sausages, vegetarian or otherwise. It can also be a soup with the potatoes cut smaller and more stock.

Patatas Bravas.
This is a Spanish tapas dish, of crisp potato pieces in a spicy tomato sauce. So an ideal thing for a spread of small dishes. My version is not as they would do it in Spain, where the ingredients available are different. Start with the sauce; only you know how much heat you like, but it can easily be adjusted at the end. Fry **1 chopped medium onion and 3 chopped cloves garlic** in **2 tbsp. olive oil**. Add **1-2 chopped fresh red chilis**, then **1 tin chopped tomatoes, ½ tsp smoked Spanish pimenton, ½ tsp. salt**, and simmer 15-20 mins. Taste. If it's nowhere near hot enough, I would tend to whiz it with a little chipotle in adobo. Minor adjustments can be made with more fresh chopped red chili, or even Tabasco. If you like, finish the sauce with **1 tbsp. sherry vinegar**. I often make it with 1 chili ancho, seeded, torn into strips, soaked in boiling water, and then whizzed in the soaking water to a puree. This goes in instead of the fresh chilis and the smoked

pimenton, and gives the whole thing a warm fruity flavour. (But it's not very Spanish any more) Leave the sauce on one side, and reheat when needed. Meanwhile, peel **700g potatoes**, and cut up. You want the size to be small enough for a mouthful, and large enough to pick up with a toothpick. Say 2 cm in each direction. Heat **2 tbsp. olive oil** in a roasting tin, roll the potatoes in this, and roast in a hot oven till done and crisp. Put in a serving dish and pour over the hot sauce. You don't HAVE to use toothpicks, which will let the potatoes drip messily on to your table. In Spain, they deep-fry the potato pieces after blanching, but oven-roasting is more convenient for most of us.

Moroccan-style Potatoes

A dish for summer or autumn, when the potatoes are still first-earlies but not exactly "new" as we know them. Peel/scrape or scrub **500g potatoes,** and cut into bite-size pieces. Heat **4 tbsp. olive oil**, and add **2 red peppers**, seeded and cut into strips. Cook gently for a few mins, then add **12 chopped cloves garlic, ½ tsp. each ground cumin and coriander**, and **1 tsp. ras-el-hanout**. If you don't have this, increase cumin and coriander to 1 tsp each, or compromise the Moroccan character by using 1 tsp garam masala instead of the ras-el-hanout. Stir well for a couple of minutes, turn down the heat, then add the potatoes, the **zest and juice of 2 lemons**, and **½ tsp. salt**. Cover, and cook on a very low heat until the potatoes are done. Taste for seasoning; you may want more lemon juice, or even some chopped pickled lemon. Great with eggs, poached or fried; or with Greek yoghurt and flat breads and black olives.

Potato Stew with Butter Beans and Miso.

The butter beans: either soak overnight **200g butter beans**, and boil the next day till nearly soft; **or use 2 tins**. Peel **700g potatoes** and cut into 2-cm dice. Sweat **2 large chopped onions** in **4 tbsp. oil** until soft and transparent, even a little coloured. Take the pan off the heat and stir in **2 tbsp. miso** – whichever sort you have. Stir in **700 ml stock,** put back on the heat and add the potatoes and drained butter beans. If you have **lovage** in the garden, a small quantity – 2-3 leaflets – can be added now. Cover the pan, and simmer or ovencook (at 150) for 2 hrs, until everything is tender. Taste; you may want **salt**. I like a good sprinkle of **Worcester sauce**. Sprinkle with quite a lot of chopped **parsley** and serve. A good warming savoury winter dish.

Potato Kugel

My version is derived from the recipe in Recipes for a Small Planet, which is full of good things. Grate, ideally with a food processor, **6 medium potatoes, 2 large carrots, 1 large onion**. Tip into a sieve to drain off the liquid – there will be quite a bit – then turn into a mixing bowl. Add **1 chopped clove garlic, 2 eggs, 3 tbsp oil, 1 tsp salt, a handful of bread crumbs, ideally brown**, and **50g. milk powder**. Stir well, and turn into an oiled, flat oven dish. The dish should be pretty large, as you want the kugel reasonably thin. Best if it's suitable for serving as well. Bake at 180 for about 1 hr. The point of a knife should not feel any resistance, and should come out dry. Now sprinkle the top with **100g grated cheese**, turn off the oven, and leave the kugel there until the cheese is melted, 5-10 mins. Eat hot or cold, or even cold in a roll. Hot or cold, it needs a green vegetable and/or a salad.

French Potato Pie.

A wickedly good dish, in both senses of wicked. It will wow any non-vegetarian guests, as well as everyone else. Not for every day.

You need a deep, loose-bottomed 23 cm (9") tin for this. You need **a batch of shortcrust pastry, made with 250g flour**. (Basics). Peel **700g potatoes** and slice thinly -- by hand or in the food processor. Melt **50g butter**, and add **3 tbsp. chopped parsley, 2 tbsp. chopped chives**, and **1 tbsp. chopped tarragon**. If you have some **chervil**, add some of this, chopped, too. Now start to assemble. Roll 2/3rds of the pastry into a large circle, and drape over the mould. Use your knuckles to fit into the angle, and let the rest hang over the outside. Now layer 1/3 potatoes on the bottom, trickle over 1/3 of the herb/butter mix, sprinkle with **salt and pepper**, and repeat twice more. Fold the overhanging pastry over the potatoes. Roll the rest of the pastry into a circle 24 cm diameter (or so it fits with a little extra) Brush the folded-over overhang with water, drape the pastry over the top of the mould, and trim to fit. Use your knuckles again to push down the pastry and seal to the base pastry. Make a hole in the top of the pie using a small sharp knife, 2-3 cm across. Beat **1 egg** in a small bowl, and brush the top of the pastry. Mix the remainder with **4 tbsp. double cream**, and keep. Put the pie on a baking sheet, and bake at 180 for ½ hr. Then turn the oven down to 150, and cook until the potatoes are done when tested with a knife point. This may take another 30-60 mins. If the pastry is getting too brown, cover loosely with foil. When the potatoes are done, take the pie out of the oven. A little at a time, pour in the egg-cream mix through the hole in the top, shaking the pie so the cream flows throughout. Let it rest/finish cooking in the turned-off oven for a few mins. If all has gone well, you should be able to unmould the pie and serve it naked; if not, it will have to be served in its tin.

If there are leftovers, they are good cold. But unless you have done this for just 2 people, I doubt there will be.

Potato Pizza

Make **a batch of pizza dough with 250g bread flour**, as in Basics. Let it rise, punch down, and roll/stretch to 30-35 cm diameter on an oiled baking sheet. Peel and slice VERY thinly **300g potatoes**, and spread them over the pizza. Sprinkle with **50g or more vegetarian bacon bits, or, if non-vegetarian, with 100g chopped pancetta** gently fried to release its fat, then scooped out of the pan leaving the fat behind. Sprinkle the top with chopped **fresh rosemary leaves**, say from a 15-cm sprig, and scatter with **30g Parmesan**, grated. Bake at 250 for 10-15 mins, until the base is brown and the potatoes cooked.

POTATO SALADS

Default Potato Salad

You need salad potatoes, either new potatoes or a waxy variety, usually labelled "for salads". Boil or steam **1 kg unpeeled potatoes**, and peel while still hot. Cut them up, and pour over a vinaigrette of **120 ml extra-virgin oil** and **30 ml. white wine vinegar**, with **salt** and **pepper**. When cool, add and mix in onion flavouring. This can be **chives or spring onions or chopped shallot, or, for those you like onion, chopped white onion**. Chopped herb on top, usually **parsley**.

Many people say that a potato salad is better when the potatoes are allowed to cool in the vinaigrette, and that they absorb the flavours while they are cooling. There is definitely a difference, but 2 out of 3 people tasting both (and not knowing which was which) preferred the one with the vinaigrette added to cool potatoes. This is a relief, because this means you lose very little by making your salad with leftover boiled potatoes.

If you like mayonnaise with your potato salad, use it WITH vinaigrette, not instead of. Add the vinaigrette to the potatoes, warm or cold, first, and add mayonnaise to taste when they are cold. Personally, I prefer the lighter salad, with no mayo. But if you are using mayo, it really should be homemade here, not Hellman's or other purchased variety. You use a fair bit, and the taste is prominent.

American Default Potato Salad.
Boil **1 kg unpeeled salad potatoes**. When done, drain and cool slightly. While the spuds are cooking, stir **1 tsp salt** with **3 tbsp. cider vinegar**, until the salt is dissolved. Peel and cut up the potatoes, adding to the vinegar mix, and mixing in with a wooden spoon or rubber spatula. When they are cool, add **4-5 celery sticks**, chopped (and leaves if liked), **1 small chopped white onion, 3 chopped hard-boiled eggs**, and **mayonnaise made in the blender with 1 whole egg**. Mix together gently but thoroughly. Eat at room temperature. This is marvellous for picnics.

Potato Raita. ***
Raitas normally go with curries, but this is so good, and so much liked, that I often have it as a salad, in quantities from enough-for-me to parties for 30-40. Do try it. For small quantities I tend to use leftover boiled potatoes; for larger amounts the spuds are cooked specially. Boil about **500g potatoes** in their skins, drain, cool, peel, and cut into 1-2 cm cubes. Heat **2 tbsp. sunflower oil** in a frying pan, and add **1 tsp. black mustard seeds** and **1 tsp cumin seeds**. Let the mustard seeds pop; when this begins to die down, add **1 shallot, finely chopped, or the same amount of chopped onion**. (Amount isn't crucial). Add **1 chopped mild fresh chili**, deseeded, and stir all round. Add the potato cubes, stir, and fry. This too is variable; you can fry just enough to impregnate the cubes with the flavours, or let the cubes brown a little. Sprinkle with **½ tsp. salt**, and turn into a bowl containing **300 ml Greek yoghurt**. Stir. There should be enough yoghurt that the mixture isn't stiff, but at the same time isn't so liquid it flows on a plate. Let it cool. You can add chopped **fresh green coriander** before serving, depending on the tastes of your eaters and yourself.
If you keep this overnight, it stiffens, and you need to add more yoghurt before serving.

Mixed Potato Salads.

Almost any vegetable, cheese, or nut can go into a potato salad. Rather than a set of recipes, I'll suggest some combinations; use amounts to make a salad you like.

Artichokes
Red Pepper and Beansprouts
Green pepper and corn
Celery and Blue cheese
Red pepper and Feta
Blue cheese and walnut
Greek-style, with black olives, feta, onion
Sour Potato Salad, with onion, dill pickles, and hard-boiled egg.
Roasted vegetables
Beetroot and Blue cheese
Radish, spring onion, watercress.

This is a good place to experiment with different oils – walnut oil in the dressing for potatoes, blue cheese, walnuts, for example; or pumpkin-seed oil with potatoes, button mushrooms, pumpkin seeds. Different herbs, too.

SOUPS

Most vegetable soups use potato to give body, and as a thickener. These can be found under the appropriate vegetable. Potatoes by themselves simply don't have enough taste to make a soup; they need supporting flavours, which is usually, as a minimum, some member of the onion family. The classic soup with potato is leek-and-potato, which you'll find under Leeks What I have here is a couple of soups where the potato taste is enlivened by comparatively minor ingredients.

Sour Potato Soup

Sweat **a chopped onion** in **30g butter**. Add **500g potatoes**, peeled and cut small, and stir round. Add **700 ml stock, a bayleaf, a little salt** if needed. Cook till the potatoes are tender, then puree by your preferred method. Reheat, and add **1-2 tbsp. good vinegar** (I mean, not malt) and **quite a lot of pepper**. Sprinkle with chopped **herbs** – parsley alone if that's what you have.

Lovage Soup

Put **1 large chopped onion, 200g potatoes**, peeled and cut small, and **30g lovage leaves** in a pan with **1 litre stock**, and cook till done. Cool a little, and blend smooth. Taste for **salt** and **pepper**, reheat, and stir in **double cream to taste** just before eating. To make the soup more nourishing, you can use less stock, and thin down with milk when reheating.

Parsley and Potato Soup.

500g potatoes, peeled and diced, 4 shallots, 2 cloves garlic, chopped, **celery leaves**, chopped**, parsley stalks**, and **600 ml. stock**. Cook these all together till the potato is cooked, and blend lightly, leaving some texture. Taste for **salt** and **pepper**. Finish with **a small pot of double cream** and chopped **parsley**, lots.

These last two soups can be a pattern for a potato-and-herb soup of any kind. I'm not keen on sage, but you might be. Tarragon? Basil? Mint? Fresh green coriander? Oregano?

Breads and Rolls

Potato Bread

This makes a delicious bread with good texture, good to eat alone, and excellent toasted. The Victorians said that toasted potato bread was good because it absorbed more butter, which is hardly a recommendation nowadays, but ain't so with this one. You can't tell there is potato in it, though you can tell it's not the same as standard bread.

I wouldn't suggest this as a first breadmaking attempt. It's not difficult, though, just a bit more fiddly than usual.

Peel, cut up, and boil in UNSALTED water **300g potato**. When they are done, before draining them dip out **150 ml potato water**. Then drain the potatoes and mash very smoothly. Add **40g butter, dash of milk from 300 ml**. Scald the rest of the milk and let it cool. In your bread-making bowl, put **750g flour, 1 packet fast-acting dried yeast, 2 tsp. salt, 2 tsp. sugar**, and mix together – I just shake the bowl vigorously. Add to the bowl the cooled scalded milk, the mashed potato, and the potato water, mix to a dough, and knead for 3-5 mins.

Let it rise, punch down, and let it rise again in the bowl. The second rise is much faster than the first. Knock back again, divide in two, shape into 2 loaves and put in greased bread tins. Let these rise again, and bake at 180 till done – for me, about 35 mins. Tip out and cool on racks.

Potato Rolls

I first did these for a Harvest Supper which had to be very cheap, but filling and looking good. These rolls fit perfectly. They also taste good and are easy to make.

You need **300 ml. water in which potato has been boiled**, with **salt**. You can do this specially, or cook the potato to eat and simply use the water instead of wasting it. To this 300 ml. water add **50g butter**, warm and cut into bits, **2 tbsp. sugar, 1 tsp. salt**. Add **1 packet fast-acting dried yeast** to **500g bread flour**, mix in, then add the potato-water mix. Knead to a smooth dough. Let it rise until doubled in bulk. Punch down, divide the dough into 4, and let these pieces stand for 15 mins or so. Then roll one of the pieces into a 30-cm round, cut into 12 wedges, and roll up each wedge from the bottom. Shape into a sort-of-crescent shape, and put, seam-side down, on a baking sheet. Do the same with the other 3 pieces of dough. Let the rolls rise until they have almost doubled, and bake at 180 for 15 mins. Brush them with **melted butter**, and bake about 10 mins, till done and golden. Cool on racks. They are nicer warm, but can be reheated.

Scotch Potato Scones

Peel, steam and mash **500g floury potatoes**. **Salt** and **pepper**, and beat in **100 ml. milk**. Then mix in **100g flour**, or enough to make a rollable dough. Roll into 6-8 rounds, about the thickness of a pound coin. Cook in **a little butter** in a heavy-based frying pan, a couple of minutes on each side, so they are just starting to colour. Good with butter and jam, or with savoury mixtures.

My mother used to make something very similar for a late supper, when there was leftover mash. She added grated cheese, and they were just eaten with butter.

516

Onions and Garlic

Can't cook without them. They support almost every savoury dish, everywhere. And they have the antiquity for it; we know the builders of the pyramids had onions, garlic and leeks as part of their rations. The earliest Babylonian recipe notes include onions. But because we are so used to – habituated to – this supporting role, we don't always let them star. And they can do this. I hope I've covered the classics below, like onion soup and aioli, with a few that are standard but don't come to mind so easily.

We don't have a seasonal gap any more, when one year's onions are past it and the next year's aren't mature yet. There were various answers to this – spring onions, Welsh onions, which are perennial and grow in a cluster, with bulbs half leek, half onion – but now we rely on imports to cover the April-July gap. By March, English onions are getting soft, and trying to sprout; if buying at that time, squeeze gently, so at least they are hard when you buy them. A kitchen without onions and garlic is a sad and limited place.

ONIONS

The onions you can buy are mainly brown onions, red onions (supposed to be milder, but aren't to my palate) and Spanish onions, larger and stronger. In the US they have onions bred for eating raw, like Vidalia, which don't cook well; we hardly ever see these. There are also baby or pickling onions, which are definitely onions, not shallots, and behave like onions in the cooking. I have taken a small onion to be 50-100 g, and a medium onion 150-200g. But in most cases it doesn't matter; the end result will change if you use more onion rather than less, but both versions will be good.

What is really interesting about onions is how the flavour changes with the amount of cooking you give them. Raw onions are strongest, and the flavour is slightly muted when onions are lightly sweated to start a dish. If you cook them long and slowly, the sharpness vanishes, sweetness comes out, and caramelised onions are sweet and mellow. Roast onions, too, have this sweetness.

517

Roast Whole Onions.

4 onions, about 100g each. Red preferred, for appearance, not taste. Take a slice from the base of the onion, leaving enough to hold the rest together, and a small slice from the top. Peel. Now cut each onion downwards into wedges, stopping the knife a little short of the base. The more wedges the prettier it looks when cooked, as the onion opens up into petals. 8 – 4 knife cuts – is probably a practical number. Put the onions, base down, in an **oiled** roasting pan in which they just fit. **Salt** and **pepper**, and drizzle over **2-3 tbsp. olive oil**. Bake at 180 for about 20 mins, then take out the pan, spoon over the juices, and drizzle over **3 tbsp. balsamic vinegar** (standard, not the best). Bake another 10-15 mins. Eat them hot, alone or with other things, or warm.

Baked Glazed Onions.

Peel **4 brown onions**, about 100g each. Score the top of each about 2 cm deep, and slightly open each with your fingers. Put them in a baking dish where they fit fairly closely. Pour **4 tbsp. water** round the base. Mix **10g softened butter, 2 tbsp. honey, 2 tsp. Dijon mustard, 1 tbsp. red wine vinegar, 1 tsp. paprika or smoked pimenton, salt** and **pepper** in a small bowl, and drizzle about 2 tsp. into each onion. Bake at 180 for about 1 hr, basting and adding the rest of the sauce every 15 mins.

Onions Baked in Wine

Peel **6 medium to large onions**, all about the same size. Put in **a tbsp. olive oil** in a casserole dish which they just fit. Cook over a moderate heat; when they start to sizzle, add **150 ml. wine (red, white, pink, vermouth, what you have)**, and let it boil quickly for a minute or so. **A sprig of rosemary or thyme** added at this stage is an improvement, but only slight. Add **150 ml. water**, cover, and cook in a low oven (120-150, depending what else is there) for 1-2 hours, until the onions are cooked. Take out the onions, keep warm, and boil down the sauce until it's syrupy. **Season** it, pour over the onions, and serve. A good winter dish with little last-minute attention needed.

Creamed Onions

Peel **6 medium onions**, and slice thickly. Drop the slices in a pan of boiling salted water and cook about 1 min, then drain well. It even helps to dry them on a teatowel. Warm **300 ml single cream** with **30g butter** in a wide pan, add the onions, and cook slowly, stirring now and then, until the cream has thickened. This takes 10-15 mins. Taste, add **salt** if needed, **pepper**, and a small grating of **nutmeg**. These make a wonderful veg. to go with bean or nut burgers, or vege sausages. Mashed potato as well, ideally.

Soubise.

This is a mixture of onions and rice, cooked slowly in butter till they become a soft and homogeneous mass. Good as a vegetable, it can also be thinned with white sauce or cream to make a sauce, or thinned even more to make a soup. Small leftovers can be spread on toast to make a base for anything, or simply toasted sandwiches by itself. So it is very useful to have around.

Start by boiling **100g long-grain rice** in salted water for just 5 mins. Drain. Thinly slice **1 kg onions**, peeled, and stir into **50g butter** melted in a casserole dish. When the onions are all coated, stir in the rice, add **salt** and **pepper**. Cover, and cook in a low oven, about 130, for an hour or so, stirring now and then. The rice cooks in the onion juices; no other liquid is needed. Let it cool. When ready to serve as a vegetable, reheat on the top of the stove, and add **4 tbsp. cream, 30g grated cheese, 30g butter**. Taste for seasoning -- I like some **nutmeg**, though it's not "correct". Or you can sprinkle with **parsley**.

My Bread Sauce.

I wanted to shoehorn this in somewhere, and it fits quite well here. Most bread sauces are quite bland, with milk and bread. This is much truer to its medieval roots.

Heat **400 ml milk, ideally full-cream**, and add **1 chopped peeled onion, a bay leaf, 1 tsp. salt**, and **2-3 cloves** (the spice) Simmer a little, then put on the pan lid and leave to infuse until the milk is almost cold. Strain into a clean pan, and add **100g white breadcrumbs**, crusts removed before crumbing. Stir well, then add **at least ½ tsp black pepper, freshly ground** (for this amount a coffee grinder is best) You may well want more pepper; the whole thing should be enlivened by it. By the way, you can't reheat bread sauce; as it cools it gets more and more solid, and can only be loosened by adding more milk.

Fried Onions Done Quickly.

I got this trick from Margaret Costa's Four Seasons Cookery Book, and it's very good. Chop **onions** roughly, put in a frying pan with **a**

little butter and **water to cover**, and cook over high heat till the water is evaporated. Then they will be well-cooked, and will quickly fry in the remaining butter till golden brown. **Season**. This isn't caramelised onions, just a heap of delicious lightly-browned morsels. They go well with grilled halloumi. For meat-eaters, there's hardly a dry-cooked dish they won't enhance.

Deep-Fried Onion Rings.

I have no prejudice against frozen food when it's good, but these are much much better when homemade. Try and see. Cut **more onions than you think you will need** in thickish slices, and soak them in **milk to cover** for 20-30 mins. Fish them out when the **deep-frying oil** is hot, pushing into rings, and dip the rings in **flour**. Fry a few at a time till well-browned, drain well, eat. A heap of these as part of a starter/nibble course will be enjoyed to the point where people will eat much less main dish!

Onion Bhajjias

The commercial versions of this are just deplorable – oily, soggy, often insufficiently cooked, and much too big. The real thing explains why the idea is so popular.

Normally, bhajjias are made with sliced onion; I prefer my onions chopped. Prepare **2 medium onions**, either sliced thinly or chopped. Make the batter by whizzing in a blender or food processor **120g chick-pea flour** (besan in Indian shops), **1 tsp salt, ¼ tsp each of turmeric, ground cumin, and baking soda** (bicarbonate of soda), **2 chopped fresh green chilis**, and **120 ml. water**. Turn into a bowl, and stir in the onion. Have a pan of **oil for deep-frying** hot, and drop in fritters, in amounts of 1 heaped tbsp. Don't crowd the fritters; only fry enough at one time to give them room to move about, in one layer. Cook fairly slowly, turning now and then, until they are brown and puffy. They should take about 10 mins per batch. Drain well on kitchen paper, and continue till the mixture is used. Eat hot. They go well with fresh coriander chutney. Madhur Jaffrey says that tomato ketchup is OK, as well.

Caramelised Onions.

If you are spending time making caramelised onions, you might as well make a lot, because they have a lot of uses. I normally use **about 1½ kg onions**, and cook them in a large, heavy-based, non-stick frying pan with a lid. A heavy pan really helps in keeping the temperature constant throughout. Peel and slice the onions, and put them in the pan with **50g butter or 3 tbsp. olive oil**. Put on the lid, and cook on a low heat until the liquid has evaporated and the onions are much reduced. It takes about an hour. Stir from time to time. Then take off the lid, turn up the heat to medium, and cook till they are dark brown, soft, and tangled. Stir more often than before, to stop burning. Other cooks add things to their caramelised onions – white wine, sugar, grenadine – but I prefer mine pure and simple, with just **salt** added to taste at the end.

There are two major dishes with caramelised onions, pasta and pissaladiere (Three, if a meat-eater. Cut lamb's liver for 4 people into very thin slivers, slip into the just-cooked onions, and leave for 30 sec. Most delectable liver-and-onions ever). And then there are a lot of fortuitous uses; you wouldn't make a batch just for this, but you feel grateful when you have it.

Pasta with Onions. Use **olive oil** to cook the onions. Take out about half the above batch, after salting, and put to one side for other uses. Then turn up the heat under the remaining half, and add **a glass of white wine**. Boil it off, stirring. Add chopped **parsley** and **lots of black pepper**. Meanwhile, cook **350g pasta**. Drain when cooked, add to the onion pan, and stir and toss on medium heat for a few seconds. Grated Parmesan is the norm, but here I prefer something softer and milder, like **Fontina, Port Salut, or Caerphilly**. Cut or break the cheese into small pieces, and mix with the pasta/onions in the serving bowl. Try both, see which you prefer.

Pissaladiere. This is basically a pizza with caramelised onion, without cheese or tomato, and garnished with salty morsels, from the County of Nice in southeastern France bordering on Italy. Because it was street food, there is no fixed formula; as long as it is hot, bready, and full of onion, you can elaborate as you wish. For the basic version, have a **pizza dough made with 250g flour** ready, and roll and stretch to a 30-cm pizza, keeping the sides a little thicker than the middle. Brush with **oil**, sprinkle with **thyme leaves**, and spread over about **half the basic recipe for caramelised onions. Pepper** well. I would bake at this point and add a garnish of **black olives** at the end. Other possible decorations are sun-dried tomatoes (bake with the pizza), capers, (add at the end) and, for non-veges, anchovies (bake with) Actually, I think anchovies don't add much here, so it doesn't matter if they aren't there. Strips of roasted red pepper can be used to make a lattice for appearance' sake (add them before baking), and do actually improve the taste somewhat.

Other Uses for Caramelised Onions.
Toast, layer of onion, poached egg
In omelettes.
Make a dip – whizz with cream cheese, thin with yoghurt to dip consistency
As a vegetable, alone
Cold (when cooked with olive oil) as a garnish to salad plates
In quiche

There is a natural follow-on from pissaladiere to other onion dishes using pastry, dough, or batter.

Onion Tart from Alsace
Peel and roughly chop **700g onions**. Cook them gently in **2 oz butter and 1 tbsp. oil** in a heavy frying pan, until they are soft and pale gold. (This is a good time to use the Quickly Done Fried Onions above). **Salt, pepper, nutmeg.** Beat the **yolks of 3 eggs** with **150 ml. double cream.**, and mix into the onions as they cool. Line a 20-22 cm tart tin with **short pastry**, rolled quite thinly, and fold the edges into an upstanding rim. Pour in the filling, and cook at 180 for about 30 mins. A baking sheet under the tart tin is a good idea, as the filling has been known to leak. Eat hot.

English Cheese and Onion Pie.
My mother's Lancashire recipe, but capable of improvement in less pinched times. Basic first. Make **short pastry for a double-crust pie, 250g for a 20-cm pie**. Roll out and fit the base, and put in **2-3 chopped onions**, almost to fill. **Salt, pepper.** Cover the top with slices of **Lancashire cheese, (amount depending on pocket, but ideally 100-150g)** then the top crust. Slash the crust, and bake at 180 for 30-40 mins. As a child, I didn't like this because the onion was still very pungent. What I do now is treat the onions so they are nearly cooked before they go in – Quickly Done Fried Onions again. A little grated **nutmeg** as well as salt and pepper. Otherwise proceed as before, brushing the top with milk. But if you like the taste of raw onions, try the first way as well.

Teisen Nionod (Welsh Onion Cake)

Peel, and slice very thinly, **1 kg potatoes**. The food processor is good here. Wash the slices quickly in cold water, then drain and dry. Peel and chop **500g onions**. Using **100-150g butter**, make layers of potato and onion in a shallow ovenproof dish, putting bits of butter on each layer, and also **salt** and **pepper**. Finish with a potato layer. Cover the top with foil, and bake at 180 for 1 hr or more, until there is no resistance to a knife point stuck through the layers. Take off the foil, and leave for 10-15 mins at 200 so the top layer can brown.

Yorkshire Pudding with Onions.

This really needs a gravy to go with it, or something with a copious sauce. Peel and slice **500g onions**, and cook in **50g butter** with a sprig of **thyme** till soft but not coloured. (Quickly Done Fried Onions yet again) Make a **batter with 120g flour, salt and lots of pepper, 2 eggs, and 300 ml. milk**. You can make the batter in a food processor or blender, or beat the eggs and a little milk put in the bowl of flour, and gradually add the rest of milk beating hard. Heat a roasting tin with **1 tbsp. oil**, mix the onions into the batter, pour into the roasting tin, and bake at 200 until puffed and browned.

It occurs to me that onion lovers could have Onions in the Hole, by roasting onions first, and then surrounding with batter, and baking till the batter is risen and brown.

Flat Bread with Onions.

This is based on an Italian foccaccia, but isn't quite. It's a good simple bread, to be eaten warm. I make it with equal amounts of white and wholemeal bread flour, 250g of each making a total of 500g. You can use entirely wholemeal, entirely white, or some other mixture if that suits your supplies better.

Make a dough with **500g chosen flour, 2 tsp. salt, 1 packet active dry yeast, 3 tbsp. olive oil**, and **300 ml. warm water**. Let this rise till doubled in size. It may be slower than usual, because of the larger quantity of oil. If the rise happens more quickly than expected, so that the bread would be ready in advance of the meal, you can knock it back, knead again briefly, and let it rise again, and this will do nothing but good to the texture of the finished bread. Slice **a medium onion** very thinly, and soak in 2 changes of cold water. Drain and dry with kitchen paper or a teatowel. Roll the dough to a disc or oblong as large as your baking sheet will take, or you can make 2 thinner breads.

Spread over the onion, pressing it lightly into the dough. Pour **3 tbsp. olive oil** over the onions, and **salt** the top, with coarse sea salt if you have some. Bake at 200 until done – probably 15-20 mins, but test by thumping the bottom and listening for the hollow sound of cooked dough. Tear into chunks to eat with a spread of salads and cooked vegetables.

Sage and Onion Scones.
Mix **300g self-raising flour, brown or white**, with **½ tsp. salt**, and rub in **125g butter** (half a packet). Sweat **1 small chopped onion** in **15g butter**, till soft but not brown, and mix into the flour with **6 shredded sage leaves**. Add **150 ml. milk** to make a soft dough. Roll or pat this into a thick disc, cut out scones with a cutter, and get more scones from the reshaped trimmings. You'll probably get 9-10. Put on a baking tray, dust with **flour**, and bake at 180 till puffed and cooked. Eat warm.

Onions Stuffed with Goat's Cheese
Stuffed onions are not one of my favourite things; it's the texture I'm not keen on, not the flavour. So there's only one recipe for an enormously variable dish, where there are many many possibilities for stuffing. Chili sin carne is one appealing option, and a vegetable stew is another.

Choose **1 onion per eater, each weighing about 200g**. Peel them and boil in salted water for 15 mins. Drain. Persuade the centre shells to come out of the onion at the top, leaving 3-4 layers of shell to make a container. Put them in the baking dish at this point. Chop the removed onion, mix with **100g soft goat's cheese, 2-3 tsp capers** if you like them, the **leaves from a sprig of thyme** and some chopped **parsley**. Bind together with **an egg**. Spoon this carefully into the onion shells. Pour over each **½ tbsp. olive oil**, and bake at 180 for 30-40 mins.

Raw Onions in Salad
How you treat the onions before putting them in a salad depends on how much you like the raw onion, and the strength of the onion you are using. For the strongest effect, simply slice thinly or chop. To soften it a bit, cover the onions with cold water with salt, and let them soak 15 mins or so. Drain, dry, use. For the mildest effect, drop the sliced onions in boiling salted water and boil 1 min. Drain, plunge into cold water, drain, and dry. Choose which you prefer, and use these in any salad with raw onion.

Moroccan Onion and Orange Salad.
Peel **4 large onions**, slice into rings, and give them the boiling treatment (perhaps Moroccans have milder onions than we do, as I'm sure they don't scald them). Peel aggressively **4 oranges**, so there is no trace of white pith, and cut into thin slices. Arrange oranges and onions prettily on a flattish plate. Make a vinaigrette with **6 tbsp. walnut oil, 3 tbsp. white wine vinegar, salt** and **pepper**, and pour over the salad. Garnish the salad with **walnuts or pistachio nuts or black olives**.

Onion Salad with Sour Cream (or yoghurt)
Prepare the **onions** to your choice, in rings. Mix with **soured cream or Greek yoghurt** to taste, with **salt, lots of black pepper**, and chopped **parsley**. Pretty and quick.

Kachumber.
An Indian salad which can go with any curry. Peel **a large onion**, halve downwards through the root, and cut into thin slices. Treat to soften the taste if you like. Add **1-2 sliced tomatoes**, cut into lengthwise wedges, **1 green pepper**, halved, seeded and cut into long strips, **1 small green chili**, seeded and chopped, the **juice of 1 lime**, and **salt** to taste. Mix in chopped **fresh green coriander**, unless it's too present elsewhere in the meal.

Indian Takeaway Onion Salad.
This is the homemade version of the chopped onions given away with a takeaway Indian meal, and it's much better made freshly. Chop **an onion** finely, season with **salt, lime juice**, and **a chopped seeded chili** to taste. Chopped **herb** if liked. (If you have **lemon balm** in the garden, this is LOVELY here)

French Onion Soup.
I'm giving two versions of this. First is a translation from "La Cuisine de Madame Saint-Ange" of 1926, an immensely thick and authoritative tome. If she doesn't know what French onion soup should be, no-one does. And it's truly delectable. Second is a version of what we expect from French onion soup, dark, thin, often somewhat acrid from miscooking the onions, and served with cheesy toasts.

When it's good it can be very very good, but when it comes in tins, packets, Cup-a-Soups . . . it usually isn't.

Version 1, in very free and abridged translation. Generally, allow **25-30g onion per person.** Some find this is not enough; it can be increased to please them.. . . In general, the soup is made with water; only add milk if it suits the taste of the diners. If you have stock, it can be used with advantage; this is almost always used in good restaurants. In this case, salt will not be needed. . . . Take **2 onions, weighing about 200g together**. Peel the onions, and cut off the hard piece of the root. Slice them in 2. Cut into slices as thin as a sheet of paper, of equal thickness; two very important conditions. If the onion is cut too thickly, it will be disagreeable to find it in the soup, and the initial frying in butter will take too long. If the slices are of different thickness, the thin slices will brown and burn before the thicker parts have taken colour. On no account slice the onion while holding it in the air between the fingers. Use a solid chopping board.. . .

It should be understood that onion, butter and flour must never be darker than a golden colour. Too many people think that the onions for soup should be browned, to give colour to the soup. So treated, the onion is burnt, and the soup acquires an unacceptable bitterness, and the overheated butter also burns.

Heat **70g butter** in a heavy pan, of capacity 2¼ litres. Do not let it brown. Add the onion, and stir almost continuously with a wooden spoon, until the onion has become a uniform light gold. . . . Add **20g flour**, mix well, and continue to stir constantly on a low heat until the flour has also turned gold. . . . Add **1 litre water and 15g salt, or 1 litre stock**. Continue stirring until the soup is boiling, then simmer 8-10 mins. During this time, cut **a dozen thin (2-mm) slices from a flute**, and put them in the soup tureen. Scatter over some **pepper.** After the soup has cooked, add **250 ml boiling milk,** taste for seasoning, and pour over the bread in the tureen. If you do not wish to leave the onion in the soup, pour through a sieve.

Many people like cheese in their onion soup. For this, use good **Gruyere**, fresh and very fat, so that it will form strings in the soup. Grate **enough for 3 large tbsp. cheese**. In the tureen, put one-third of the bread slices, one-third of the cheese, and so on. Pepper each cheese layer. Pour over the soup, cover well, and let it sit at the oven mouth for a few minutes.

This soup, made as carefully as Madame St-Ange indicates, is truly superb. And very different from the conventional idea. I've never found Gruyere in England that becomes stringy in the soup, though it's easy in France. So I would use Lancashire or Wensleydale, which also don't string, but taste very good.

"French" Onion Soup.
Peel and slice **2 kg onions**. Melt **50g butter and 1 tbsp oil** in a large pan, and add the onions. Cook over medium heat 5-10 mins, stirring now and then, until the onions start to soften. Add the **leaves from 3-4 sprigs thyme**. Turn the heat to very low, cover the pan, and cook the onions 20-30 mins, until they are soft and golden yellow. Uncover the pan, turn the heat to medium, and stir in **1 tsp. caster sugar**. Cook for 5-10 mins, till the onions start to brown. Add **1 tbsp. sherry vinegar**, and continue to cook until the onions are a deep golden brown, up to 20 mins. Stir **1 heaped tbsp. flour** into the onions, cook about 2 mins, then stir in **1½ litres stock**. Add **150 ml. dry white wine, 3 tbsp. brandy, salt** and **pepper**. Simmer 10-15 mins.
Make croutes for the soup: cut **6 or 12 slices of day-old French bread, about 2 cm thick.** Bake at 150, on a greased baking sheet, till lightly browned, then rub them with **a cut clove garlic**. Spread with **French mustard, using about 1 tbsp. altogether.** Grate **120g Gruyere** and sprinkle on the croutes. Ladle the soup into 6 heatproof bowls, float the croutes on top, and put under a preheated grill until the cheese bubbles and browns. Serve immediately.
I don't have heatproof soup bowls, so I toast the croutes on their baking sheet and transfer to the soup when the cheese has browned slightly. Easier and safer – no transporting of very hot bowls from grill to eaters.
This is a much less economical soup than Madame St-Ange's, and much more like the conventional idea of French onion soup. Nonetheless, I prefer the first.

English Onion Soup.
Pale, creamy, mild, and filling. Comfort food of a very high order.
Sweat **700g peeled, chopped onion** in **50g butter** over a very low heat in a covered pan until the onions are very soft and not at all coloured. Add **600 ml stock, 300 ml milk**, and **50g fresh white breadcrumbs** (NOT from sliced loaf) **Salt** and **pepper**. Simmer 20 mins, then blend/sieve/put through mouli depending on the method

you prefer. Cool at least half-an-hour before blending. Taste the smooth soup, add a little grated **nutmeg,** and taste for salt and pepper. Reheat, and serve with a little piece of **butter** in each plate. Butter-fried croutons go well with this.

Baby Onions, or Pickling Onions.

While these would only be used for the recipes above in an emergency where you'd run out of larger onions, they have their own specific uses, and are much liked in these forms.

Glazed Baby Onions.

Peel them, allowing **3-4 baby onions per eater**. Turn them in **butter** till they are lightly browned all over; add **stock** to cover, **salt, a little sugar**, and cook at moderate speed until the stock has evaporated and a light glaze remains, turning from time to time.

Baby Onions a la Grecque.

Peel **300g baby onions**. Make the broth by mixing **250 ml. dry white wine, juice of 2 lemons, 5 tbsp. olive oil, 1 tsp. each coriander seed and black peppercorns, lightly crushed, 1 tsp. salt, 1 small dried red chili, sprig thyme and a bay leaf**. Bring this to be boil and simmer 5 mins Add the onions; they should be covered by the broth. Simmer very gently for about ½ hr. Serve cold but not chilled.

If you add 2 tbsp. tomato puree and 50g sultanas or currants to the broth, they become a la Monegasque – Monaco style. I think they are more flexible, and go with more things, in the first way, but the second has its sweet-sour virtues.

Pickled Onions.

Almost too familiar to need a description. I don't like them myself – all that malt vinegar – but almost everyone else does. This recipe starts one day, when the peeled onions are put into brine and the spiced vinegar prepared, and the two are combined on the second day. The pickle is then stored for 6 weeks before eating, so it isn't a spur of the moment preparation. And it is more expensive than the commercial versions – not that I'm trying to put you off!

Start by peeling **1 kg. baby onions**. The easiest way, when doing this in quantity, is to top and tail the onions, then cover them with boiling water and leave to stand 3-4 mins. Drain. It's then easier to complete the peeling. Put the onions in a bowl and cover with **cold water**, then drain off this water into a saucepan and dissolve **120g salt** in it (Coarse sea salt if you have it) Bring the salted water to a boil, then cool, and pour over the onions. Let them stand 24 hrs.

Put **750 ml. malt vinegar** in a pan. Add **1 tbsp. sugar, 3 dried red chilis, 1 tbsp. coriander seeds, 1 tsp allspice, 1 tsp. black peppercorns, 3 blades mace, and 3 bay leaves.** Peel and slice **a 5-cm knob fresh ginger**, and add this. Bring to the boil, simmer 5 mins, and let stand overnight so the vinegar can absorb the spice flavours.

Next day, drain the onions, rinse, and dry. Pack them into jars with vinegar-resistant lids – mayo jars do fine. The jars should be sterilised, but I rely on running them through the dishwasher. Strain the vinegar, and fill up the jars with it. You can add some of the spices if you like. Do up the jars, and store in larder or cellar for 6 weeks before eating.

Garlic

Garlic gives a vital background flavour to many many dishes; it's distinctive, but blends very well with other flavours. In many dishes, it's not so much that you can taste garlic specifically, but the dish is less balanced and rounded if it isn't there. Only over the last fifty years have the English taken enthusiastically to garlic; before that it was definitely foreign and "common". Now we often use more than, for example, cooks in Northern France, and enjoy our food more because of it.

There are a few dishes where garlic is their whole reason for being, the star, the main ingredient. Below is a selection of these.

Aioli

Don't let anyone convince you that you can make an aioli by adding garlic to made mayonnaise, even home-made. It may be perfectly pleasant, but it doesn't have the authority or texture of the real thing made from scratch. Try it once and you will see what I mean.

Allow **2-3 large cloves garlic per head, say 10 for 4 people**. (More if they are smaller) Peel the cloves, and put into a mortar with **½ tsp salt**. Pound to a puree. Add **3 egg yolks** and stir well. Now start adding drops from **500 ml extra-virgin olive oil**, not too strongly flavoured itself. French or Spanish, and not the most expensive. Stir in drops, stirring well, until the aioli begins to thicken. As it thickens, you can add the oil more quickly, until it becomes an almost solid mass. You should be able to pile it up in heaps, which don't collapse and flatten. You may not need all the oil. Add the **juice of ½ lemon**, or more to taste, when it's done.

This is the centrepiece for a meal, and should be served with potatoes boiled in their skins, carrots, hard-boiled eggs, raw pepper strips, celery, French beans, maybe chick peas. Not necessarily all of these; maybe other seasonal vegetables. And, of course, chunks of bread.

It hardly needs saying that this isn't something for 1 or 2 people, more like a lunchtime feast for a crowd. And it's good if you want to indulge non-vegetarians – add some poached fish or slices of ham, and they too will be happy.

Skordalia

A Greek version of the cold garlic/olive oil sauce, with less authority than aioli and perhaps more uses.

This is a peasant recipe, which means that there is lots of variability – no fixed formula. It can be thickened with bread, boiled potato or nuts, or any two of these or all three. The nuts can be almonds, pistachios, or pine nuts – or make an Anglicised version with hazels. I make it in a food processor, but it can be made in a mortar by pounding the solids and then letting down with the liquids.

You need **80g ground almonds**, either bought as such or, better, bought whole and ground just before using. This can be done in a coffee grinder or in the processor, so not too much hassle. Put the ground almonds in the processor, add **50g breadcrumbs from good bread, 6 large cloves garlic, peeled and sliced, 1 tsp. salt, about ½ tsp. ground black pepper (a lot)**. Whizz; add through the feeder tube **4 tbsp. red wine vinegar, 150 ml. extra virgin olive oil.** (Greek preferred here, if you have it). Taste, adjust seasoning, and assess the thickness. It should hold its shape but not too solid. Whizz in more oil if needed.

Goes with eggs, poached, boiled or fried; beetroot; fried courgettes (or even marrow cooked in the microwave); as a dip.

Garlic Butter.

Freshly made is better, and hardly any trouble if you have the butter at room temperature. For **125g butter** (half a packet), pound **2 or 3 large cloves garlic** with **½ tsp. salt** in a mortar. When a puree, pound in the butter till uniformly mixed. I like it best just like this, but you can add the **juice of half a lemon**, or some chopped **parsley**, or both, if you would like it better that way.

Garlic Bread.

Slash **a French-type stick bread** (baguette, flute) almost but not quite to the bottom, at intervals along the length. The thinner the slices, obviously, the more garlic butter and taste you can get in, and also the more calories. Insert some of the soft garlic butter between each pair of slices, trying for a bit more at the end. Wrap in foil and bake at 180 for 15 mins or so; unwrap and eat warm.

Aquapatys.

A medieval dish. The first time I made this, for 20 people, I thought 3 cloves of garlic a head would be enough. The first four people at the buffet table scoffed the lot! So allow **at least 12 cloves garlic per head**. Blanch the peeled garlic cloves for 2 mins, and drain. For 6 people, put the cloves in **200 ml. boiling water**, and add **40g butter, ¼ tsp salt, ¼ tsp. ground cinnamon**, and **a few strands of saffron**. Simmer, covered, about 10 mins, till the garlic is soft. Grate over a little **nutmeg**. Eat warm. If you want to eat them cold, use 3 tbsp. olive oil instead of the butter.

Pasta with Oil and Garlic.

Dishes don't come simpler, faster, or cheaper than this – and exceedingly tasty, too. For **400g pasta** (for 4); set a large pan of salted water to boil. Peel **3-6 large cloves garlic,** and cut in rounds. Cook VERY gently in **8 tbsp. olive oil**, until the garlic just starts to colour. Turn off the heat, and let it infuse while the pasta cooks. Drain the pasta and put in a serving dish; pour over oil and garlic, and mix well. Sprinkle on **black pepper** and chopped **parsley**. Eat. In its original form, it doesn't have Parmesan or any other cheese, but you may want to add some.

I prefer it jazzed up just a tiny bit with chili. **1 finely chopped fresh chili**, cooked with the garlic (or chili flakes added just before pouring over the pasta) adds even more punch.

Garlic Risotto

The flavour of garlic here is comparatively restrained, to match with the creamy succulence of the rice. The garlic flavour is introduced by means of a garlic stock, which is specially made for this some time in advance. So make the stock with **2 onions,** unpeeled, and cut small, **a head of garlic**, cloves separated and halved, **a bay leaf, a couple of thyme sprigs, 1 tsp. salt, and 1½ litres water**. Simmer together for 30-45 mins. Strain. Reheat when you are ready to make the risotto, and keep near simmering while you use it.

Sweat **2 chopped shallots** in **50g butter**, till softened. Add **250g risotto rice**, and stir around until the rice becomes translucent. Add **150 ml. dry white wine**, and let it evaporate/be absorbed by the rice. Stir, add a ladleful of the garlic broth, and let this too be absorbed. Keep adding ladles of broth, and stirring often, until the rice is tender, 20-25 mins. Taste for **salt**; the salt in the broth should be enough, but add more if needed. When it's ready, add a little more broth – ¼ ladle or less,-- **50g butter**, and a **handful of grated Parmesan**.   Stir vigorously to blend all these together. **Pepper** the top, and serve with **more grated Parmesan** for people to help themselves.

Garlic Soup

Another peasant dish, which comes in loads of variations depending on what this particular peasant had at the time. The basics are much the same – garlic, boiled in stock or water, with other herbs – and the finish varies, with eggs, cheese, bread all figuring in different versions. The version here is one I first tried 40 years ago, in the throes of a cold, and it cleared the sinuses and generally cheered me up, and, I think, strengthened the immune system. If you reeked of garlic after eating this soup, I'd say it kept others at a safer distance – but you don't reek, so it can't be that. Even if it doesn't cure anything, it makes you feel a lot better, rather as a tot of whisky does.

Peel the **cloves from a whole head of garlic**. Put in a pan with **1 litre water, 1 tsp salt, 2 cloves, a couple of sage leaves, chopped, leaves from a couple of sprigs of thyme, a small bay leaf,** and **3 tbsp. olive oil**. Simmer 20 mins. Meanwhile, beat **3 egg yolks** in a soup tureen till thick, and work in **2 tbsp. olive oil** by drops, as if making mayonnaise. Gradually beat a ladle of hot soup into this mix, then strain in the rest, beating. Press the solids in the sieve to extract the garlic juices. Serve with **rounds of toasted French bread** or other good bread, and some **grated cheese – Parmesan or Cheddar.**

A nice variation omits the egg yolk/oil mix, and adds a poached egg to each plate. With cheese, toast, broth, this becomes very like an Italian Zuppa Pavese, a marvellous comforting meal for one.

White Gazpacho.
I avoided trying this for years, as it doesn't sound promising. I was wrong; the taste is unexpected but delicious and really good for a warm autumn day.
Decrust **enough stale white bread to give you 200g**, tear into chunks, and soak in cold water to cover. Put **100g peeled almonds, 4 large peeled sliced cloves garlic, 1 tsp salt** in the food processor, and grind till the almonds are very fine. Squeeze the bread almost dry, and add to the processor. Whizz again. Gradually add **6 tbsp. olive oil, 3 tbsp. sherry vinegar**, through the feed tube with the motor running. Add enough of the bread-soaking water – and more plain water of needed – to make a soupy consistency. Turn into a serving dish, and add **200g GOOD white grapes**, halved, and seeded if necessary. Muscat grapes are nicest. Cover and chill thoroughly. In Spain, you'd make this in the morning before the heat of the day, and eat at lunch when it's really hot.

Roasting Garlic.
Garlic's flavour softens and sweetens after long, slow cooking, rather as onion's flavour changes. Garlic is usually roasted to bring about this change; cooking in oil, as for onions, is not practicable on a domestic basis. Roasting couldn't be simpler; take any loose skin off heads of garlic, rub oil into unpeeled heads, and cook, covered, in a low/moderate oven (130) for 30-40 mins, until the garlic offers no resistance to the point of a knife. Any leftover oil, well-flavoured with garlic, can be used again. Or add unpeeled cloves to any dish of mixed roast veg. (Better added with only 15-20 mins to go, as otherwise it can overcook) Or peel the cloves, add thyme, salt, a little oil, and wrap this in foil and cook in the oven. In all these cases the garlic becomes soft and puree-like; if it still has its peel, nick the top and squeeze out the puree, onto plate or bread or toast. There aren't many things it doesn't go with Any leftovers can be kept in the fridge, to add to, for example, mashed potatoes, or vegetables on toast, or pasta sauces, or stews. It's best done in summer or autumn, before the garlic starts to sprout – the sprout can distort the flavour of the whole assembly.

Garlic Cream Sauce.
Separate **2 heads of garlic** into cloves, and peel them. Put in cold water, bring to the boil, simmer 2-3 mins. Drain. Now put the garlic cloves in **200 ml. stock**, cook 20 mins, and add **150 ml. double cream**

Cook 10 mins more, or till garlic is soft. Blend till smooth. Reheat, salt if needed, and swirl in **25g butter**. Taste; add **juice of ½ lemon** if you think it needs it. Use with boiled root veg – potatoes, carrots – fried or poached eggs, or anything that needs a bit of liquid and more oomph.

Roast Garlic Quiche.
Have ready **a lightly baked tart shell**, either 25 cm diameter, or 2 of 18 cm. (That's 10" and 7" in old measurements) Cut **100g Gruyere or Cheshire or goat's cheese** into small cubes, and scatter these over the prebaked pastry. Squeeze the contents from **8 cloves roast garlic**, and mash to paste if needed. Add to **3 eggs** in a bowl, and beat. Add **250 ml double cream**, **salt**, and **pepper**, and pour this carefully over the cheese. Bake at 150 for 30-40 mins, till almost firm; take out, and let cool a little before serving.

Mushrooms

The mushrooms I am talking about are the various sorts of cultivated mushrooms one can buy. I've never felt the confidence to go foraging, and I'm not going to suggest anyone else does without help from someone who knows what they are doing. Anyone who DOES know what they're doing doesn't need encouragement.

The range of mushrooms available is increasing all the time. These are the ones which I have used regularly. We can buy

small closed-cup white mushrooms, not very tasty when cooked but excellent eaten raw

chestnut mushrooms, tastier

large cultivated mushrooms, and Portobello mushrooms. I always cook these; their taste and texture are excellent. The only drawback is that they tend to make everything they are cooked with grey or black, which isn't always attractive

oyster mushrooms. Again, I always cook these. They are very pretty, nice texture, but their flavour is "delicate", or not strong

fresh shiitake (Chinese) mushrooms. Very good, but they don't have the punch of the dried. Some at least of these are flown from China, though they can be grown here. (Today, Sept 2011, Tesco's were British, Sainsbury's from China)

(very occasionally) fresh cepes, (porcini). I find these at a mushroom stand at a local farmer's market. Very expensive, and worth it

(occasionally) fresh chanterelles, from the same source. Expensive and delicious

I also like to have some dried mushrooms available all the time:

Dried cepes, or porcini. Buy in the largest packet you can; the tiny packets with barely enough for one use in them are proportionately very expensive. And being dried, they keep very well.

Dried shiitake, or Chinese mushrooms. Again, buy a large packet from a Chinese shop. A very good standby, and cheaper than dried cepes. To my taste, they aren't QUITE as nice.

I don't at all approve of washing mushrooms. It's quite unnecessary with supermarket packets. Even grubby mushrooms can be wiped clean with a paper towel or damped teacloth. Likewise, you don't, EVER, need to peel commercial mushrooms. Field mushrooms, yes, I can see the point, but bought mushrooms are grown in carefully controlled conditions, and there's a lot of flavour in the peel. And while I'm on my hobby horse, not tinned mushrooms, ever. I've tried various expensive tins from France, and cheap ones in England, and none of them are worth the money. Fresh mushrooms are now so readily available that tins are just not needed.

Default: Fried Mushrooms.
This is useful for all sorts of fresh mushrooms. Given a new one, this is what I'd do to taste it. Clean the mushrooms if necessary, and slice, again if necessary. I used to break them into chunks – still do with oyster mushrooms, which tear very easily and don't cut well – but I've found with most that they taste better cut in slices. If the stems are large, twist them off, and slice crosswise into smaller pieces than those for the cap. Melt butter, or heat oil, in a frying pan, add the mushrooms, and cook until they are all heated and the surfaces have absorbed some butter/oil. Then, only then, add salt; this brings out the juices. Continue to cook until the juices have dried up, pepper, and eat. Some of the wild fungi give off a lot of juice in the second stage, with salt, and would be overcooked if these were all boiled away. In this case, fish the mushrooms out of the pan, and boil the juices down to a sticky residue. Put the mushrooms back in to heat through. These go on toast, from any sort of bread, (brioche to sourdough rye), alone as a vegetable, in bread cases, in hollowed-out rolls heated in the oven, . . . For some of these you might want a more saucy filling; in this case, add a slug of cream to the pan, let it thicken a little, and use these **Mushrooms in Cream.** Quantities: for **250g mushrooms**, use **30g butter or 2 tbsp. oil**, **½ tsp. salt**. If using **cream, about 100 ml**. A thick mix goes very well in little choux puffs, or can be used as a sauce. You can also finish the fried mushrooms with chopped garlic and parsley; for **250g mushrooms**, chop **2 peeled cloves of garlic** with **4-5 stems parsley, or half a small supermarket packet (more if you like).**

Cepes a la Bordelaise. *****
This is simply cepes fried in oil and finished with shallot and parsley, but it brings out the best taste from the best mushrooms. Try to have enough – I have tried to stretch 400g between 4, and it simply whets

the appetite without satisfying. Now I keep it for a birthday treat in autumn.

500g cepes. Clean them; take off the stalks and chop; slice the caps. Start cooking the caps in **4 tbsp. olive oil**, and add **½ tsp salt** after 5 mins. Cook another 5 mins, raising the heat to evaporate the juices if there is a lot. Stir in the stalks; cook 5 mins more. Have ready **2 shallots** chopped with **a small handful of parsley**, and put these on top of the cepes. Leave another couple of minutes so the topping is hot, but not cooked, sprinkle with the **juice of a lemon**, and slide out onto a serving dish, or (for my greedy family) portion on to **toasts**. We have this as a first course, to enjoy without distraction.

Roast Large Mushrooms

One per person is OK, 2 generous. Either large mushrooms or Portobellos. Twist out the stalks, and save for stock. Put them, stalk side up, in one layer in an oiled roasting pan that just about holds them. Drizzle **1 tsp. olive oil** over each, then distribute **bits of butter** over the top – **up to 30g per mushroom**, but probably less. **A couple of slices from a garlic clove, some thyme leaves, salt** and **pepper**, and then put in a hot, 200, oven. They take about 30 mins, and it's a good idea to baste them with their juices halfway through. They go brilliantly in a burger bun, alone or with burger garnishes, like mustard and/or bread-and-butter pickle. I don't like ketchup here, but you might.

Mixed Mushrooms on the Barbecue.

An Australian idea, from Stephanie Alexander, adapted to English conditions. Mix various sizes of **standard mushroom (closed-cup, button, open)** with **exotics (oyster, shiitake, etc)**, sliced where necessary, with **olive oil, salt** and **pepper**, maybe **a couple of cloves of garlic**, sliced, and **a sliced chili**. Put a double sheet of foil on the barbecue, turning up the edges, and spread out the mushrooms in one layer. Let cook, turning from time to time (being careful not to puncture the foil.) When done, lift mushrooms off the foil carefully, and tip onto serving dish. Chopped **parsley**? With bread as a first course.

Mushroom Kebabs

Marinate **300g small mushrooms, button or closed-cap**, in **100g plain yoghurt, 1 tbsp. olive oil, the rind and juice of a lemon, 1 finely chopped clove garlic**, and **pepper**. NO salt. Leave them for 2 hrs. or more. Pick out the mushrooms and thread them onto 4 skewers, keeping the marinade. Cook on a barbecue, or under the grill, till done. Put the rest of the marinade on a plate, and lay the skewers on it. Surround with **watercress, or rocket, or other salad leaves**. Goes well with dhal and Indian breads, as well as more Western dishes.

Duxelles.

This is an ingredient of other dishes, not a dish in itself, but it's a fridge or freezer item to make when you find some cheap white mushrooms. You can then pull it out for ease of use at a later date.

Chop **500g white mushrooms**, as large as you can find, finely, so no piece is larger than 3 mm (1/8th inch). Start cooking **2 shallots**, peeled and finely chopped, in **40g butter**. When they start to soften – about 1 min – add the chopped mushrooms and **leaves from 3-4 sprigs thyme**. Turn up the heat, and cook, stirring, until the mushrooms are cooked and the mixture is dry. **Salt** and **pepper**. If you're using some of this straightaway, add **lemon juice** to taste to the part to be used. Spread on toast under eggs; mix into mashed potato; use as part of a stuffing for pancakes or peppers or other stuffable vegetables; mix into thick white sauce to make croquettes; make a fast mushroom soup by mixing into stock, then adding cream; spread on pizza; mix with cream for an instant pasta sauce. There will be many more occasions for using this if you have some sitting there conveniently.

Portobello Mushroom Cutlets.

Allow **1 to 1½ heads per person, of the largest Portobellos you can find**. Take off the stems. Cut the heads into quarters. In a flat-bottomed bowl that will hold the largest of the pieces, beat **2 eggs** with **salt** and **pepper**, and **1 very finely chopped clove garlic**. Have a plate with **dry breadcrumbs** from good bread spread on it – probably about one-third of a standard large loaf. Dip the mushroom pieces in the egg mix, making sure they are wetted all over, then put on to crumbs and roll so the crumbs stick to each surface. You may need to pat the surfaces to make sure the crumbs are sticking. Put the breaded pieces, in one layer, on dry plates.

Heat **1-cm depth sunflower oil** in a deep frying pan, **or** heat **deep frying oil**. Fry a few pieces at a time until crusty on both sides, turning after the lower side is done. Lift out and drain, first on newspaper, then on a rack on which they can be kept warm.

Mushroom Fritters.

At the other end of the scale from the Portobello cutlets above, this uses **button mushrooms** and frying batter. Use **Frying Batter 1** (Basics) for whole buttons, or tempura batter for slices of closed-cup mushrooms. Deep-fry in small quantities, and drain well. A heap of these fritters and a sharp tomato sauce has been enjoyed by everyone I've cooked it for. Quantities – as many as you are prepared to do.

Steamed Dried Chinese Mushrooms.

This is a luxurious and expensive dish, and also can be very useful if for some reason you can't get out and have to rely on your larder. Choose **20 or more dried whole Chinese mushrooms**, close to the same size. Soak them; pour boiling water over the mushrooms in a bowl, and leave for half an hour or so. Drain. So far as I know, the Chinese don't use the soaking water, and they are so famously frugal there must be a reason. Nevertheless, I tend to use it in vegetable stock. Remove the stems and discard (Chinese; I use these in stock too). You need a heatproof bowl which can go in your largest saucepan; it can be Pyrex or one of the plastic bowls bought Christmas pudding comes in, or another heatproof bowl. Put the mushrooms in this bowl, and add **2 tbsp. soy sauce, ½ tsp salt, ½ tsp sugar, 2 slices ginger** (unpeeled; they aren't eaten) and **2 spring onions**, chopped into short lengths. If no spring onions, you can use slices from 1 shallot) Pour in **200 ml. stock**. Cover the top of the bowl with greaseproof paper tied on, or foil, or a lid if the bowl has one. Stand it in a saucepan, on spoons or some sort of support, surround with boiling water to come about halfway up the bowl, and steam for about 1 hr. Uncover the bowl, fish the ginger and onion pieces out, and steam for another 10 mins. Serve in the bowl.

Simple Mushroom Salad.

For **150g buttons or closed-cap mushrooms**. Slice thinly, put in a bowl, and dress with **3 tbsp. extra-virgin olive oil** and the **juice of a lemon**. **Salt** and **pepper**. Turn the mushrooms in the dressing, and leave to sit for at least half-an-hour. The mushrooms absorb the oil; you may need to add a little more before you serve it. It's easy to dress this up a little; **Mushroom Salad with Garlic Croutons** adds cubes of bread fried in olive oil with garlic. **Mushroom and Cheese Salad** adds a few small cubes of hard cheese to the mushrooms just before serving, and is lovely. Slices of mushroom can go into a potato salad, too; a yoghurt-y dressing is the thing for this combination.

Mushrooms a la Grecque.

Tiny button mushrooms are best here, cooked in the marinade that's used for other vegetables a la Grecque. I like them best by themselves, but they could also be mixed with baby onions, cauliflower sprigs, etc cooked in the same way.

Make the broth by mixing **250 ml. dry white wine, juice of 2 lemons, 5 tbsp. olive oil, ½ tsp. each coriander seed and black peppercorns, lightly crushed, 1 tsp. salt**, and **thyme** and **bay leaf**. Bring this to be boil and simmer 5 mins, to blend the flavours. Add **300g mushrooms**, simmer 5 mins, then let them cool together. A lovely part of a spread of small dishes.

Black Mushroom Consomme. *****

This is a thin, intense, dark-coloured broth, and most delicious. I've never made it without being asked for the recipe.

First make a dried-mushroom stock, using **2 litres water** and **30g dried cepes/porcini**. Simmer 30 mins. Then add **500-600 gm large black fresh mushrooms**, sliced fairly thinly, **1 large peeled chunked onion**, and **2 tsp. caraway seed**. Simmer, uncovered, for another hour. Let cool and stand overnight in the fridge, with the solids. Reheat, add **3 sprigs marjoram, 2 tsp. salt**, and simmer 1 hr more. The liquid should have reduced to about 2/3rds its initial volume. Now strain the soup, pressing on the mushroom residues to get the maximum of flavour out. Reheat, taste, **salt** if needed, **pepper, lemon juice?** and serve. Float **hammer-shaped slices of small white mushrooms** on top. In theory this can be served cold; I've never had enough left to try.

Cream of Mushroom Soup.

This soup is thickened with breadcrumbs rather than flour. It's derived from Elizabeth David's Potage aux Champignons a la Bressane, which uses chicken stock from the famous Bresse chickens, but adapted to a vegetarian style. Chop **400g large flat mushrooms**, and set them to cook in **50g butter**. When the juices start to run, add **2 chopped cloves garlic, some chopped parsley,** and **1 tsp. salt**. Soak about **50g crustless bread** in some **stock from 1 litre**; squeeze it and add to the soup. Add the rest of the stock and simmer 15 mins. Then puree by your favourite method – food mill, blender after cooling a bit, stick blender. Reheat, taste for salt, add **pepper** and a grating of **nutmeg**, then **100 ml. double cream**. Stir well, sprinkle more chopped **parsley** on top, and eat.

Instead of the nutmeg, a hint of fennel is very good here. Add 1 tsp. fennel seeds with the stock, and use chopped fennel leaves, not many, instead of the parsley at the end.

Mushroom Soup with Mustard.

You need **300g mushrooms**. If you use large flats, the soup will be an unattractive greyish colour, but the taste will be good. If you use closed-cup mushrooms, the soup is prettier but the taste is a lot weaker. So cut up roughly your chosen mushrooms, and cook in **50g butter** until just tender. Add **300ml. stock, 2 tbsp. dry sherry (or a little more red/white wine)**, and simmer 10 mins. Puree the soup by your preferred means. Taste for seasoning; reheat, and stir in **2 round tsp. French mustard**, followed by **100 ml. double cream**. The less the mustard is heated, the more flavour remains. So, if you've accidentally added too much mustard for your taste, you can simmer until it has weakened sufficiently, before adding the cream (which will itself soften the mustard flavour)

Mushrooms and Eggs.

The combination of mushrooms and eggs is so obvious and so flexible and so simple that it doesn't really lend itself to specific recipes. Duxelles on toast under poached, scrambled or fried eggs. Mushroom omelette, with a few fried mushrooms or mushrooms in cream. Fried mushrooms mixed into scrambled eggs. These are all good, simple, homely kitchen staples.

Pasta with Mushroom Sauce (3 versions).

Version 1. Mushrooms in cream, with grated **nutmeg**, mixed into just-cooked **pasta**, with grated **Parmesan**.

Version 2. Cultivated mushrooms are cooked with a few dried cepes/porcini, to simulate the taste of a sauce made entirely with the fresh wild mushrooms. I've never had enough fresh cepes to try these alone, but the sauce using the mixture is very good indeed.

Soak **10g dried porcini** by pouring over **200 ml boiling water**, and leaving to cool. Fish out the mushrooms and chop them finely. Filter the soaking water through a kitchen towel, or coffee filter. Chop **a small onion**, and cook briskly in **50g butter** till gold. Add the chopped porcini and the filtered soaking water, and cook till the water has evaporated completely. Chop finely **500g large flat mushrooms, or Portobellos**, and add to the pan. Add **1 tsp. salt** and **pepper**, and cook, covered for 30 mins, stirring now and then. If there is liquid left after this, boil it off. Cook **400g pasta**, drain, and mix with the sauce, **50g more butter**, some chopped **parsley**, and **50g grated Parmesan**. Serve with more Parmesan on the table.

Version 3. This is from California, using fresh and dried Chinese shiitake. It's also exceptional in using both the soaking water and the stems from dried shiitake.

Cover **30g dried Chinese shiitake** with about **300 ml boiling water**, and let them stand till cool. Lift the shiitake from the soaking water, remove the stems and keep, and slice the caps thinly. Filter the soaking water, paper towel or coffee filter. Take the stems from **250g fresh shiitake mushrooms**, and put with the stems of the dried. Slice the caps of the fresh mushrooms thinly, and put them with the slices of dried mushroom. Heat **300 ml. double cream** in a small pan, adding both sets of stems, **a chopped shallot, 5 or so sprigs of thyme,** and **a bay leaf**. When it's nearly boiling, take off the heat, cover, and let sit for 30 mins or so. Heat **2 tbsp. olive oil, 30g butter** in a frying pan, add all the mushrooms, and fry at high heat for 3 mins. Turn down the heat, **salt** and **pepper**, and add **2 finely chopped cloves garlic**. Cook another couple of mins, stirring, then add the soaking water and let it reduce to about half. Pour the cooled cream through a sieve into the pan, and boil so that the creamy mix thickens a little. Turn off the heat. Meanwhile, you have cooked **300g pasta**. When it is done, scoop out of the pan and into the sauce, and add **a little chopped marjoram** and chopped **parsley**. More **pepper** to serve. Since this is not Italian, you don't need Parmesan with it; but if you want to, why not?

Mushroom Risotto. *****

I am almost embarrassed by how many 5-star dishes come in this mushroom section. Cepes a la Bordelaise, black mushroom consomme, and now mushroom risotto. My children get to choose a favourite dish for their birthday dinner, and this is often chosen.

Pour boiling water to cover over **30g dried porcini/cepes**, and leave to cool. Fish out the porcini, chop them a little (it's nice to have identifiable pieces in the risotto), and filter the soaking water. Cook **1 finely chopped shallot** in **50g butter** in a large heavy frying pan, until translucent. Add **400g risotto rice**, and stir till it too becomes translucent. Add the soaking water and the sliced dried mushrooms, and when this has been absorbed, start adding ladlefuls from **1 litre stock** kept nearly simmering on the stove. Continue doing this, stirring often, until the rice is done. While the risotto is cooking, cook **300g large flat mushrooms**, sliced, in **25g butter** in another frying pan, **salt**ing halfway through and evaporating the juices as usual. Tip these into the risotto when it is cooked, turn off the heat, and beat in **30g grated Parmesan**. Taste for salt; add **pepper**. Eat with **more grated Parmesan**.

Mushroom Pilau.
Goes with all sorts of Indian food especially well. This is another dish where you trade appearance and taste; large flats make the rice look dark but taste better, closed-cup mushrooms look prettier but taste milder. Here, I think prettier is marginally better. Cut **300g mushrooms** in thin hammer-shaped slices, top to bottom. Soak **300g long-grain rice** in **1 litre water** for 30 mins; drain. Peel and halve **a small onion**, and cut each half into very thin slices. Fry the onions fairly quickly in **3 tbsp. oil**; when it starts to brown at the edges, add **1 finely chopped clove garlic**. Stir, add the mushrooms, cook 2 mins more. Add the drained rice, **1 small slice ginger peeled and finely chopped, 1 tsp salt, ¼ tsp. garam masala**, turn down the heat a little, and stir for about 2 mins. Add **600 ml. water**, bring to the boil, then put on the lid and cook on VERY low heat for about 15 mins, till all the water has been absorbed. Fold a teatowel, and put between the pan and the lid. Let it sit about 10 mins longer, and eat.

Mushrooms Baked with Potatoes.
If you have a few fresh cepes/porcini, this extends the flavour. But you can make it with any other sort of fresh mushroom, and it's reliably good.
Peel **500g potatoes**, and slice thinly. Slice **250-300g mushrooms**, large flats if using common mushrooms. **Butter** a shallow ovenproof dish, and distribute **1 finely-chopped clove of garlic** over the bottom. Put in half the potatoes, spread out, season, add the mushrooms in one layer, season, then the rest of the potatoes. Mix **300 ml. whipping cream** with **2 tbsp. water**, and pour over. Cover with foil or otherwise, and bake at 150 for 1 hr. Lift the lid, and assess how nearly done the potatoes are. Sprinkle the top with **50g grated mature**

Cheddar, and continue cooking until done, when there is no resistance to a knife point pushed in. Let it cool very slightly before serving.

Five-Jewel Couscous
Peel and chop **a medium onion**, and fry in **2 tbsp. olive oil** till starting to brown. Add **2 chopped cloves garlic**, cook 1 min, then add **250g couscous** and **1 chopped preserved lemon**. Add **400 ml. hot vegetable stock**, stir, then cover and cook over very low heat for about 15 mins. While this is happening, slice **100g button mushrooms**, chop **1 large tomato or 6 baby plum tomatoes**, shred **a dozen leaves of basil,** and toast **30g pine nuts**. Fold all these into the couscous when it is cooked. The raw vegetables and the cooked couscous make a lovely mixture. You can serve this with grated cheese, Parmesan or Cheddar, but that's only for cheese-lovers.

Make a **Seven-Jewel Couscous** by adding a **handful of currants** and another raw vegetable – if you have a tiny **courgette** that can be eaten raw, that's great; otherwise **radishes**, about 6.

Mushroom-Stuffed Pancakes.
These are cheese-free, invented for a vegetarian who can't eat cheese, but he hardly got any because a horde of meat-eaters fell on them.

For the filling, chop **500g Portobellos or large flats** into small pieces, about ½ cm. Cook in **25g butter, salt**ing halfway through, as usual, until dry.

Sweat **1 peeled chopped medium onion** and **1 small celery heart**, chopped, in **15g butter**, covered, about 15 min. Add **½ tsp smoked pimenton**, work in, then add **1 flat tbsp. flour**, and work in again. Add **100 ml. stock**, and stir in. Bubble to thicken this mix, then add mushrooms and work it all together. Taste; there should be enough salt from the mushrooms. Add **a slurp of double cream**, to make into a pancake-stuffing consistency. This can now rest in the fridge overnight, or you can go straight on.

Make **2 batches of pancakes** (Basics), and fill one as you cook the next. Arrange the pancake rolls in a baking dish (or 2), pour over **150ml. stock**, and heat through in a moderate oven (anywhere between 130 and 180). The pancakes absorb the stock and swell slightly. Serve with **sour cream**.

Mushroom Pie.

This is a cut-down version of a Russian kulebiaka, and much easier to make.

Boil **100g long-grain rice**, drain, and spread out to cool. Peel and chop **1 large onion**, and sweat with **3 shredded sage leaves** in **50g butter**. Destalk **200-300g large closed cap mushrooms, or small "large flats"**, and chop the stalks. Butter a large flat pie dish all over with about **20g butter**, and put in the mushroom caps, curved side down. You want just one layer; if necessary, break up some of the mushrooms to fit. Distribute the chopped stalks over the top. **Salt** and **pepper**. Now add the cooled rice, and put in this layer **3 hard-boiled eggs**, shelled and halved lengthways. Now the layer of onion, and dot this top layer with **another 20g butter**. Season again. Cover the pie dish with **half a batch of short pastry** (Basics), and bake at 180 for 30-40 mins.

Mushroom Stroganoff with Beans.

Peel and slice thinly **2 medium onions**, and cook gently in **50g. butter** till they are soft and golden. Add **250g chopped large flat mushrooms**, and cook over a slightly higher heat till the mushrooms have given up their juices and dried. Stir in **2 tbsp. flour**, then add **200 ml. stock, 4 tbsp. sherry, 1 tsp. salt**. Bring to the boil. Add a grating of **nutmeg**, quite a lot of **pepper**, and **vegetarian Worcester sauce or mushroom ketchup** to taste. It should be very thick. Stir in the contents of **1 tin cannellini or other pale beans**, then add **150 ml (1 small carton) sour cream**. Taste for salt. Serve over rice or couscous or boiled potatoes or toast – I think plain boiled rice is best here, but your choice. My husband's comment when I first made this was "It's very clever to make something so nice from such cheap things".

Three Curry Variants.
Version 1; Mushrooms with Cumin and Hing.

This is my favourite; I can eat it by itself, and it's not even fattening. Use any mushrooms – whatever's on offer the day you want them. Clean and slice roughly **700g mushrooms**. Heat **2 tbsp. sunflower oil** in a large pot, add a pinch of ground **hing**, then, immediately, **1 tsp. cumin seeds**. Almost immediately, add **2 whole dried red chilis**, stir, and add the mushrooms and **½ tsp. turmeric**. Stir all together, and add **1 tin crushed tomatoes** and **1 tsp. salt**. Cover, and simmer 15 mins. Eat straightaway, or let it stand and reheat. The second is a bit better, as the mushrooms and sauce blend their flavours, but not enough to worry about if you want it now.

Version 2: Mushrooms with Fennel and Ginger.
Make a spice mix with **¼ tsp. fennel seeds, ground, ¼ tsp. dry ground ginger, ¼ tsp. turmeric, ½ tsp. salt,** and **¼ tsp. Kashmiri chili powder or smoked pimenton..** Cut **400g mushrooms** into slices, and start to cook them in **4 tbsp. sunflower oil** on a fairly high heat. After about 2 mins, add the spice mix and **2 chopped medium tomatoes.** Cook till the mushrooms are done. Eat.

Version 3: Mushrooms and Potatoes.
Boil **300g potatoes** in their skins, peel, and cut into 3 cm cubes. Sprinkle them with a **little salt, ½ tsp turmeric,** and mix in. Cut **400g mushrooms** into pieces about the same size. Chop **a 3-cm piece of fresh ginger,** peeled, and **6 large peeled cloves of garlic** to a paste.
Fry the potato cubes in **4 tbsp. sunflower oil** in a large frying pan with a lid. Take them out and keep on a plate. Add to the remaining oil **1 tsp. whole cumin seeds** and **4 green cardamom pods,** bashed in a mortar to break them. After a few sec, add the garlic and ginger, **1 tsp. ground cumin seeds, 1 tsp. ground coriander seeds.** Stir and fry 1 min or so, then add **a tin crushed tomatoes,** potatoes, mushrooms, **1 tsp. salt,** and **a mean ¼ tsp. cayenne pepper.** Stir, bring to the boil, cover, and simmer 10-15 mins. Add **½ tsp. garam masala,** and chopped **fresh green coriander** if you have some.

Mushroom Pate.
I made this up when I'd bought 2 boxes of white, closed-cup mushrooms. I meant to eat them raw, but didn't. So I used them for this, and was astonished how many uses it has. As a sandwich filling; with toast as first course; with pasta or gnocchi; as a pizza layer; mixed with spinach for pancake filling; hotted up with chili for tortilla wraps, tacos, enchiladas; and tiny leftovers can make stuffed eggs. You may well think of more. And now I feel I never need throw away tired mushrooms again.
Melt **30g butter** in large frying pan, and slice in **600g mushrooms.** Cook gently, turning, till the juices start to run, then add **2-4 chopped cloves garlic** and **½ tsp. salt.** Stir again, and cook till all the juices have evaporated and the volume has reduced a lot. Whizz in food processor with **200g soft cheese, Philadelphia or similar -- or**

cottage cheese to make it lighter. Juice of ½ lemon; taste for **salt**. It has much more mushroom flavour than the rather bland raw small mushrooms.

Mushroom and Watercress Pate

Chop, and keep separate, **1 medium onion, 1 clove garlic, 250g large flat mushrooms**, and **75g watercress**. Cook the onion gently in **30g butter** till soft, add the mushrooms and garlic, and cook briskly for 4-5 mins. Add the watercress, and stir around for ½ min. Whizz in the food processor with **150g cream cheese, curd cheese, or cottage cheese, ½ tsp salt,** and **Tabasco** to taste. Scrape it out into a bowl and chill. Serve with toast.

Sprouted Seeds
Alfalfa, Cress, Fenugreek and Bean Sprouts

Just brilliant. Easy to do, takes no growing space, takes 30 sec. twice a day for 4-7 days, and gives you the freshest possible salad material. Squeamish people may actually worry about the fact that their food is still growing. It's cheap, and can be done even if you're housebound because of snow and ice.

I divide seed sprouts into two categories. First is (mung) bean sprouts, which are easy to buy and the hardest of the lot to produce at home. I have heard that the shop ones are soy sprouts, not mung bean, but this is not relevant. Then there are all the others; my favourite seed catalogue has 10 varieties of seeds-for-sprouting. My favourites are alfalfa, fenugreek, and peas. Cress, too, comes here, but is conventionally grown on damp paper on a plate.

You can buy "seed sprouters", but these are totally unnecessary. All you need is a large jar – the larger sizes from Hellman's mayonnaise are good – a square of cheesecloth, and an elastic band to hold it to the jar top. Put 1-2 tsp. seed in the jar, cover well with water, and leave to soak overnight. Then stretch the cheesecloth over the top, hold on with the band, and drain. Now rinse twice a day; fill the jar with water, swirl, drain. Kids love to watch the changes as little sprouts appear and grow, and the jar gradually fills up with tiny growing plants. When they are nearly ready, leave on the windowsill to green up. When ready – and this is quite a broad state – fill the jar with water and tip all out into a sieve. Eat straightaway, or keep in an enclosure (plastic bag or box, covered bowl) in the fridge for a couple of days.

Sprouted alfalfa tastes very like fresh peas. Sprouted fenugreek smells and tastes like curry. I can't get on with sprouted chick peas – too chewy and crunchy – but you may not agree. The best the catalogue can say about red clover sprouts is that they are "an excellent blood cleanser". Sprouted peas are lovely, but even nicer if you don't go the jar route, but spread on a seed tray and let them grow to 8-10 cm. These pea sprouts are extremely fashionable at the time of writing. Cress, with or without mustard, is traditional English salad stuff.

None of these really lend themselves to recipes. Put in sandwiches – hummus and sprouted fenugreek is a terrific combination. Spread on top of salads. Put in a bowl for people to pick at – which they will. Drop into a stir-fry at the last moment. Use to garnish a vegetable stew. Just heat, not cook. I like alfalfa and/or cress as a bed for stuffed eggs, with little bunches on top of each. And so on.

Sprouting seeds are incredibly nutritious, though "within the limits of the amount consumed", as Marmite jars used to say. This is a bonus, because they taste so good. And another bonus is the fact that the unsprouted seeds keep for at least 2 years. Maybe a smaller proportion sprout towards the end of this time, but most still do.

Mung beans are more difficult to sprout using the jar method, as they need to grow for a longer time to get the long white sprouts we are used to from Chinese food. They are easy to buy. But I've almost given up on buying them, because so many packets give off a stale and rotting smell when opened. If buying, look for at least 3 days until the sell-by date, and scrutinise the packet carefully. If there is any brown at the threadlike ends of the sprouts, don't buy. This will cut out at least 90% of supermarket packets, in my experience, and I've never seen them at farmer's markets. I used to know a Chinese shop where they sprouted their own, and these were reliably delicious. (The same shop used to make its own tofu, ready at 2 pm Sunday, when there were long queues, and sold out by 3 pm.) If you know a shop like this, support them!

In theory, bean sprouts are better if the threadlike end, which would become roots, is pinched off. This might even rescue a bag of dicey sprouts, if you have to. For me, the idea of going through a few hundred bean sprouts nipping off the end is a LOT too far, and I never do it.

The recipes below are for sprouted seeds like alfalfa and fenugreek, then cress (or mustard-and-) and then bean sprouts as bought. But don't restrict yourself to these. There is still a lot to be found out about the best uses for seed sprouts. And also the best ways of growing; Madhur Jaffrey, in Eastern Vegetarian, gives Indian ways of sprouting mung beans, to give tiny sprouts with still-crunchy seeds, and then uses them in various curries.

Fenugreek Sprout Slaw.
Make a dressing with **4 tbsp. mayonnaise, 50g. blue Stilton**, and the **juice of 1-2 lemons,** or more to taste. It doesn't need salt or pepper. Shred **400g white cabbage** and slice thinly **1 red or green pepper,** and mix them with **a batch of fenugreek sprouts**. Mix in the dressing, and let stand, covered, for 1-2 hrs at least.

Melon, Tomato, Ginger and Fenugreek Sprout Salad.
Peel and shred **a small knob of fresh ginger root**, and soak in **3 tbsp. light olive oil** for at least ½ hr. Pour through a small sieve, and mix the oil with the **juice of ½ lemon**, and **a little salt**. Peel, seed and cut up **half a ripe melon** into 1-cm cubes. Add **12 or so halved cherry tomatoes** and **a handful of fenugreek sprouts**. Add the dressing and mix. You can eat it straight away, but it's better – and often more convenient – to let it soak for an hour or two, to release the juices. Eat with a spoon, as a first course. If you happen to have **an avocado,** cubes of this added to the salad are lovely.

Lentil, Carrot and Alfalfa Salad.
Cook **120g Puy lentils** in water to cover, with a **couple of sprigs of thyme**, until done. Drain if necessary. Remove the thyme sprigs. **Salt**. Then add **2-3 grated carrots, 2-3 chopped spring onions**, and **a handful of alfalfa sprouts**. Dress with **3 tbsp. olive oil** mixed with the **juice of ½ lemon. Pepper** to taste.

Couscous and Sprout Salad.
Put **150g. couscous** into a bowl, cover with **200 ml. boiling water**, cover, and let stand 5 mins. Separate with a fork, and add **oil-and-lemon dressing** to taste. Then add **cress or watercress, 2-3 chopped spring onions, leaves from 4-5 sprigs of mint**, chopped, and **a handful of sprouted seeds, whatever you have**. Taste for salt, as it may well need more than the amount in the dressing. Eat straight away, or keep in the fridge, covered, overnight. It looks pretty with small tomatoes round it, but don't mix them in.

Sauteed Radishes with Sprouts.
Fenugreek is brilliant here, and bean sprouts a good second best. Very light and springlike. Slice **radishes from 3 bunches** thinly, and also **4-6 spring onions**. Heat **2 tbsp. oil** in a large frying pan, add the

radishes, and stir vigorously over medium heat for 1-2 mins. Add the spring onions and stir in, then add **1 tbsp. soy sauce**, stir in, and then **a handful of sprouts**. Stir to mix, and eat straight away.

Cannellini, Mushroom and Cress Salad.
Drain, rinse and shake dry **a tin of cannellini beans**. Thinly slice **120g small white mushrooms,** and mix with the beans. Mix **4 tbsp. extra-virgin olive oil, the juice of a lemon, salt, pepper,** and **2 tbsp. mushroom ketchup**, and mix into the beans and mushrooms. Snip over **2 boxes mustard-and-cress**, or the approximate equivalent of home-grown.

Hot Celery and Cress with Cumin.
Trim and peel the stalks from **a head of celery**, and slice thinly. Toast **1 tsp. cumin seeds** in a dry frying pan, then tip them out. Add **2 tbsp. sunflower oil** to the pan; when it's hot, add the celery, and stir it round for 2 mins. Add **1 chopped clove garlic**, and stir again for ½ min. Add **3 tbsp. dry white wine** mixed with **1 tbsp. soy sauce**, and let the sauce reduce. Add **snipped cress from 2 boxes**, and serve quickly.

Spring Greens with Mustard Seeds and Cress.
Heat **2 tbsp. oil**, and add **1 tbsp. mustard seeds**. When they pop, add **1 small chopped onion**, and cook gently till softened. Add **500g spring greens**, trimmed and shredded, and stir well. Add **4 tbsp. water**, cover the pan, and cook gently till the greens are done to your taste. Snip in **2 boxes mustard-and-cress**, and eat straight away.

Cheese and Mustard Spread, or Dip.
Chop **2 spring onions**. Mix into **150g curd cheese**, with **2 boxes mustard-and-cress** snipped. Add **2 tsp. seedy mustard**, and blend well. Taste for **salt, pepper**. Eat with toast. For a dip, thin down with **sour cream or yoghurt** to a dipping consistency. Any small amount of leftovers will make good stuffed eggs.

And don't forget **egg-and-cress sandwiches. Hard-boiled eggs** chopped, mixed with **mayonnaise**, and **1 box cress** mixed in for each 2 eggs.

Bean Sprouts (the bought kind). As well as the recipes below, and the general ideas in the first section, don't forget they can be used in stir-fries of mixed vegetables, fried rice, Chinese-style soups, fillings for egg rolls, spring rolls, and Chinese dumplings … anywhere, in fact, where an a cheap addition with crunch and freshness is desirable.

Chinese recipes always tell you to scald the bean sprouts, or boil for 30 sec., if they are to be used in a salad. This makes sense in Chinese conditions, but not in English; we can use them after a simple wash-and-drain.

Bean Sprout and Mushroom Salad.
Slice thinly **150g raw mushrooms**. Mix with **200g (more or less) bean sprouts**. Dress with a mix of **2 tbsp. sunflower oil, 1 tbsp. soy sauce, 1 tbsp. vinegar (Chinese rice, cider, white wine, in order of preference), 1 tsp. each of sugar and Chinese sesame oil.** Pour over the mix, toss, eat. Spring onions can be added if you like them; I think they are a bit too dominating for this mixture.

Korean Bean Sprout Salad.
Dressing: **3 tbsp sunflower oil, 1 tbsp. vinegar (Chinese rice, cider, white wine, in order of preference), 1 tbsp. soy sauce, 1 chopped clove garlic, 1 very finely chopped fresh chili or Tabasco to taste, 1 tsp. Chinese sesame oil**. For the salad; **200-250g bean sprouts, 1-2 red peppers**, deseeded and cut into fine slivers (to match the bean sprouts in size), and **4-6 spring onions**. Sprinkle with **toasted sesame seeds**.

Tofu, Bean Sprout, Celery and Walnut Salad.
This is a very good place to use a stronger-tasting form of tofu, marinated or smoked. If you like the very strong taste of red fermented tofu, as I do, this would be very good.
Mix **250g cubes tofu** (less for the stronger versions) with **200g bean sprouts, a shredded celery heart**, and **100g chopped walnuts**. Dressing depends on the tofu used; marinated can take **walnut oil and sherry vinegar**, the fermented version needs a **sunflower oil/lemon dressing** for the other components.

Spiced Couscous and Bean Sprout Salad.

Put **150g. couscous** into a bowl, and add **1 tsp. garam masala** and the **leaves from a sprig of thyme**. Cover with **200 ml. boiling water**, cover, and let stand 5 mins. Loosen with a fork, and add **200g. beansprouts, a handful of roast salted peanuts, 4 chopped spring onions, 2 tbsp. sunflower oil, the juice of a lemon, salt**, and **shakes of Tabasco** to taste.

Basic Stir-Fried Bean Sprouts.

For **500g beansprouts**, heat **3 tbsp. sunflower oil** in wok or large frying pan. Add **4 chopped spring onions or 2 chopped shallots**, and stir-fry ½ min. Add the bean sprouts, and stir briskly until they are all coated with fat. Sprinkle on **1 tsp. salt**. Continue to cook another minute, then add **3 tbsp. stock, 1 tsp. Chinese sesame oil**, and stir another ½-1 min. and serve and eat immediately.

This can be varied according to taste and what else is on the table; with chives, with shredded fresh chili added with the onion, with ginger and a powdered spice blend, like Chinese 5-spice or garam masala, added with the sprouts, and so on.

Stir-Fried Cucumber and Bean Sprouts.

Cut **a cucumber** in half along its length, scoop out the seeds, and slice thinly along the length. Wash and drain **300g bean sprouts**. Chop finely **2 peeled slices ginger**, and **4 spring onions**. Heat **2 tbsp. sunflower oil** in a wok or large pan, add ginger and spring onions, and stir briefly. Add the cucumber, and stir-fry for about 2 mins. Sprinkle in **1 tbsp. soy sauce**, and stir until it has evaporated and glazed the cucumber slightly. Add the bean sprouts, stir in, and cook 1 min. more. Eat straight away.

Singapore Vegetable and Fruit Salad.

Make the dressing; pound together **3 fresh chilis** (deseeded for mildness; bird's eye with seeds for incredible hotness) and **2 cloves garlic** with ½ tsp salt to a paste. Add **3 tbsp. dark brown sugar, 2 tbsp. tamarind puree**. Thin the dressing with water if you've used tamarind puree from a jar; I like it about the consistency of double cream. The salad has **half a cucumber**, cut into sticks, **100g beansprouts, a crisp pear**, peeled, cored and sliced, **a dozen or so radishes**, sliced (or use a piece of mooli), the segments of **1 or 2 fresh oranges**, depending on size, and, ideally, **something in the**

plum/peach/nectarine family. Add a **handful of salted roast peanuts** and some **coriander leaves**. Mix with a little of the dressing, and serve with the rest so people can take what they want. In increased quantities, this is a terrific buffet dish.

Bean Sprout and Mooli Soup.
Korean in origin, and used for breakfast there. Soak **12 Chinese dried mushrooms** by pouring over boiling water and leaving for 30 mins. Slice the mushrooms thinly, discarding the stems, and add the soaking water to **1 litre vegetable stock**. Bring the stock to a boil, add the mushroom slices and **400g mooli**, peeled and cubed. Cook gently, covered, until the mooli is done, about 10 mins. Add **200g bean sprouts**, cook 3-4 mins more. Season with **soy sauce** until salty enough and stir in **½ tsp. sugar**. Chopped **fresh green coriander**, and lots of **pepper**, and serve straightaway.

Bean Sprout Fritters.
Beat **2 eggs** with **1 tbsp. soy sauce**, and stir in **100g plain flour**. Add **1 chopped stalk celery, 2 chopped spring onions, half a small red or green pepper chopped finely, 50g bean sprouts**, and some chopped **fresh green coriander** if you have some. Heat **oil for deep-frying**, and drop in spoonfuls of the mix. Drain when cooked, and serve with a **dipping sauce of soy sauce and sesame oil** -- maybe with a little vinegar added, depending on your taste.

Oddities

Seakale ought to be better known and more available – a traditional English vegetable. It's forced in early spring, under large pleasing earthenware pots, to make a head of pale yellowish curving strands. If you have the luck to find some, boil and eat with melted butter, as a separate course like asparagus. I've only ever found it once, in a posh greengrocer in Abergavenny, and it deserves its reputation. Come on, growers – give us seakale!

Hamburg Parsley I have neither seen nor grown this. It is the root of a special breed of parsley, looking, from pictures, rather like a white carrot. The scattering of recipes I've seen, mostly German, treat it like any other root veg.

Laverbread This seaweed in eaten in Wales, long-cooked to a puree and then fried in small cakes dipped in oatmeal. It is also the same seaweed as the Japanese Nori, used for wrapping sushi. Nori is bought ready dried, in expensive packets. Laverbread is bought, ready-cooked, in South Wales, but hardly anywhere else. There's obviously room for developments here, because in either form it's packed with nutrients and good tastes.

Skirret. An old English vegetable, looking, in pictures I've seen, like a multi-forked carrot. The Organic Gardening catalogue has seeds.

Crosnes, or Chinese Artichokes. Obviously a great luxury at the moment; I've seen it for sale on the Net at nearly £50/kg. The part you eat is the small tubers, which sound like a refined and more delicious version of Jerusalem artichokes. Victoriana Nurseries has tubers for growing on, and they should be worth a try.

Asparagus Peas Neither a pea nor asparagus. The part you eat is little frilly pods, rather pea-like, and very pretty. They have to be eaten small, or they become fibrous and unpleasant to eat. I grew a 3m-row once; the pods were few, so I could never pick enough small ones for a vegetable even for 2. If I let them get a little bigger – say 7-8 cm – they were inedible. So my experience is pretty negative. If you have lots of room, they may be worth a try. Otherwise, we must wait for the plant breeders to make the plant more fruitful, or the fruit less fibrous.

Cardoons A relative of asparagus, it grows very well as a foliage plant around Sheffield. It is the stems that are eaten, not the thistle-like buds. And to make the stems edible, they need to be blanched; gathered together and tied in a bundle, then wrapped round with sacking or plastic to exclude light. The picture in the old Larousse Gastronomique shows a peasant in the Loire struggling to get his arms round a plant. When I tried it, my blanched head weighed about 100g, and wasn't worth the hassle of preparation. But experimental gardeners may do better than I did.

Purslane. Often seen as seed, seldom grown. Small succulent leaves, which can go in a salad or be cooked in a soup.

Dandelion. Eating dandelions should be blanched, by putting a flower pot on top. I found this attracted slugs, and got no leaves; a good way to weed. You can buy blanched dandelions in France, but so far not here, as far as I know.

Bibliography

Abel, Keith. Cooking Outside the Box. Collins, 2006
Aitken, Lynelle Scott. Vegetarian Asian. Robert Frederick, 2005
Alexander, Stephanie. The Cook's Companion. Lantern, 2004
Andrews, Colman. Catalan Cuisine. Grub Street, 1977
Atlas, Nava. Vegetariana. Comet, 1985
Bareham, Lindsay. Onions without Tears, Michael Joseph 1995;
             In Praise of the Potato, Grafton 1991;
             The Big Red Book of Tomatoes, Penguin 2000.
Barker, Alex. Potato. Lorenz 1999.
Barron, Rosemary. Flavours of Greece. Grub Street, 2000
Bastianich, Lidia Matticchio. Lidia's Italian Table. Morrow, 1998
Beck, Simone. Simca's Cuisine. Knopf, 1973
Beck, Simone, Bertholle, Louisette, and Child, Julia,. Mastering the Art of French Cookery vol. 1, Cassell 1963
             Mastering the Art of French Cookery Vol. 2, Penguin 1978
Berg, Sally and Lucian. New Food for All Palates. Gollancz, 1979
Bittman, Mark. How to Cook Everything Vegetarian. Wiley, 2007
Blanch, Lesley. Round the World in 80 Dishes. Penguin, 1962
Boxer, Arabella. Garden Cookbook. Sphere, 1977
Brown, Lynda. The Cook's Garden, Vermilion, 1992.
Burrows, Lois, and Myers, Laura. Too Many Tomatoes. Harper and Rowe, 1976
Chao, Buwei Yang. How to Cook and Eat in Chinese. Penguin, 1962
Claiborne, Craig. New York Times Cookbook. Hamlyn, 1963
Claiborne, Craig, and Lee, Virginia. Chinese Cookbook. Sphere, 1973
Costa, Margaret. Four Seasons Cookery Book. Sphere, 1972
Courtine, Robert. Hundred Glories of French Cuisine. Farrar Strauss Giroux, 1973
David, Elizabeth. A Book of Mediterranean Food, Penguin, 1955.
             French Country Cooking, Penguin, 1959.
             Italian Food, Penguin, 1963.
             French Provincial Cooking, Penguin, 1964.
             Summer Cooking, Penguin, 1965
De Groot, Roy Andries. Feasts for All Seasons. Allen and Unwin, 1973
Duff, Gail. Fresh All the Year, Pan, 1977. Vegetarian Cookbook, Pan, 1979.
Ewald, Ellen Buchman. Recipes for a Small Planet. Ballantine, 1973.
Farmer, Fanny. Boston Cooking School Cookbook. Bantam, 1961
Fearnley-Whittingstall, Hugh. River Cottage Veg Every Day. Bloomsbury, 2011.
Firth, Grace. A Natural Year. Simon and Schuster, 1972
Gayler, Paul. A Passion for Potatoes, Kyle Cathie, 2001

Glover, Brian. Onion Lover's Cookbook. Southwater, 2004

Gordon, Peter. Vegetables, the New Food Heroes. Quadrille, 2007

Gourmet Magazine, 1972-1997.

Gray, Rose, and Rogers, Ruth. River Café Cook Book Green. Ebury, 2000

Greene, Bert. Greene on Greens. Equation, 1984

Grigson, Jane. The Mushroom Feast, Penguin, 1978.
> Vegetable Book, Penguin, 1980.

Grigson, Sophie. Sophie's Table, Penguin, 1992.
> Eat Your Greens, Network Books, 1994.
> Vegetable Bible, Collins, 2009.

Hazan, Marcella. Classic Italian Cookbook, Papermac, 1980.
> Second Classic Italian Cookbook, Papermac, 1983.
> From Marcella's Kitchen, Papermac, 1987.
> Marcella Cucina, Macmillan, 1997.

Hazelton, Nika Standen. Vegetable Cookery. Penguin, 1979

Hesser, Amanda. The Cook and the Gardener. Absolute, 1999.

Hills, Lawrence D. Grow Your Own Fruit and Vegetables. Faber, 1971

Hoffmann, Susanna. The Olive and the Caper. Workman, 2004

Horley, Georgina. Good Food on a Budget. Penguin, 1969.

Jaffrey, Madhur. An Invitation to Indian Cooking, Penguin, 1978. Indian Cookery, BBC, 1982. Eastern Vegetarian Cooking, Jonathan Cape, 1983

Kafka, Barbara. Vegetable Love. Artisan, 2005.

Lambert, Eva and Tony. The Garden Grows Cookbook. Wildwood House, 1978

Lambraki, Myrsini. Cretan Cuisine for Everyone. Myrsini Editions, 2005

Larkcom, Joy. The Salad Garden, Frances Lincoln, 1984. Oriental Vegetables, Frances Lincoln, 2007

Lawson, Nigella. Forever Summer. Chatto and Windus, 2005

Lee, Nim Chee. Chinese Vegetarian Dishes. Windward, 1986

Lin, Hsiang Ju and Tsuifeng. Chinese Gastronomy. Nelson, 1969

Lo, Kenneth. Chinese Food, Penguin, 1972. Chinese Vegetable and Vegetarian Cooking, Faber, 1974. Cheap Chow, Pan, 1977

Madison, Deborah, and Brown, Edward Espe. The Greens Cook Book. Bantam, 1996

Mason, Catherine. Vegetable Heaven. Grub Street, 2006

Merchant, Ismail. Indian Vegetarian Cooking. Sainsbury, 1992.

Meyers, Perla. Art of Seasonal Cooking. Simon and Schuster, 1991.

Moon, Rosemary. Classic Vegetarian Cuisine. Tiger Books, 1995.

Olney, Richard. The French Menu Cookbook, Collins, 1975.
> Simple French Food, Jill Norman, 1981

Ottolenghi, Yotam. Plenty. Ebury, 2010

Palazzi, Antonella. Great Book of Vegetables. Simon and Schuster, 1991

Ponsonby, Julia. Gaia's Kitchen. Green Books, 2008

Radecka, Helena. Your Kitchen Garden. Mitchell Bezley, 1975

Raven, Sarah. The Garden Cookbook. Bloomsbury, 2007
Rodale's Good Food Kitchen. Vegetables. Rodale, 1982
Romauer, Irma and Becker, Marion Rombauer. Joy of Cooking. Cookery Book Club, 1969
Rowe, Silvena. Feasts. Mitchell Beazley, 2006
Rushdie, Sameen. Indian Cookery. Century, 1988
Sahni, Julia. Classic Indian Cooking. Dorling Kindersley, 1986
Saint-Ange, Madame. La Cuisine de Madame Saint-Ange. Larousse, 1958
Shulman, Martha Rose. The Vegetarian Feast. Thorsons, 1982.
    Garlic Cookery, Thorsons, 1984
Singh, Dharamjit. Indian Cookery, Penguin, 1970
Singh, Mrs. Balbir Singh. Indian Cookery. Mills and Boon, 1961
Slater, Nigel. Tender, vol. 1 Fourth Estate, 2009
Smith, Michael. Fine English Cookery, Faber, 1977.
    New English Cookery, BBC, 1985
Somerville, Annie. Fields of Greens. Bantam, 1993
Spencer, Colin. Gourmet Cooking for Vegetarians. Andre Deutsch, 1978
Spry, Constance, and Hume, Rosemary. The Constance Spry Cookery Book. Dent, 1956
Tenison, Marika Hanbury. Cooking with Vegetables. Triad/Grenada, 1982
Thomas, Anna. The Vegetarian Epicure. Penguin, 1973.
    The New Vegetarian Epicure, Penguin, 1991.
    From Anna's Kitchen, Penguin, 1996.
Time-Life, The Good Cook Series. Vegetables. Time-Life 1979
Time Life Foods of the World. The Cooking of Russia, 1969
    The Cooking of China, 1970.
    The Cooking of Germany, 1969.
    The Cooking of Vienna's Empire, 1974.
    The Cooking of India, 1978.
    The Cooking of Spain and Portugal, 1970.
Tudge, Colin. Future Cook. Mitchell Beazley 1980
Watson, Guy, and Baxter, Jane. The Riverford Farm Cook Book. Fourth Estate, 2008.
White, Merry. Cooking for Crowds. Penguin, 1976
Wolfert, Paula. Mediterranean Grains and Greens. Kyle Cathie, 1999.

566

567

577

578

583